Pitt's Employment Law

Pitt's Employment Law

By

GWYNETH PITT, LLB, MBA
Professor of Law, Kingston University

SWEET & MAXWELL

THOMSON REUTERS

Published in 2016 by
Sweet & Maxwell, 160 Blackfriars Road, London SE1 8EZ
Part of Thomson Reuters (Professional) UK Limited
(Registered in England & Wales, Company No 1679046.
Registered Office and address for service:
2nd Floor, 1 Mark Square, Leonard Street, London, EC2A 4EG)
Typeset by Servis Filmsetting Ltd, Stockport, Cheshire
Printed and bound by CPI Group (UK) Ltd, Croydon, CR0 4YY
For further information on our products and services, visit
www.sweetandmaxwell.co.uk

First edition	1992
Second edition	1995
Reprinted	1995
Third edition	1997
Fourth edition	2000
Fifth edition	2004
Sixth edition	2007
Seventh edition	2009
Eighth edition	2011
Ninth edition	2014
Tenth edition	2016

No natural forests were destroyed to make this product; only farmed timber was
used and replanted.

A CIP catalogue reference for this book is available
from the British Library

ISBN 978-0-414-05616-9

Thomson Reuters and the Thomson Reuters logo are trademarks of
Thomson Reuters. Sweet & Maxwell is a registered trademark of
Thomson Reuters (Professional) UK Limited

Gwyneth Pitt
2016

For Howard

Preface to the 10th edition

A new edition, a new Government, but no real change in the direction of policy on employment law. While the Coalition Government reduced individual employment protection in important ways, the focus of the current Conservative Administration has returned to trade unions and industrial action. The Trade Union Bill, at the Committee Stage in the House of Lords at the time of writing, will narrow the right to strike even further than was done so following the General Strike in 1926. Although the proposed changes to the check-off system may look minor, they could have a major impact on the funding of political parties and thus be of constitutional significance. In the absence of a credible opposition, it seems likely that the Trade Union Bill will be enacted in substantially its current form, and it has been dealt with in the text on that basis.

The subjugation of employment law policy to the interests of business continues unabated. It is notable that the webpage of the Department of Business, Innovation and Skills shows no minister with a portfolio flagged as involving employment, and the dedicated area for employment law matters has been removed. Should Brexit become a reality in the forthcoming EU referendum, the prospects for employment protection law are dire indeed.

Among the many interesting new cases since the last edition are several grappling with the blurring of the distinction between working life and private life in the online world: *Williams v Leeds United FC* (Ch.8) is a particularly cautionary tale. The use of social media in industrial action campaigns is exercising the Government, who fear that non-participants in industrial action could be intimidated in online hate campaigns. A new Code of Practice on Picketing is promised.

The publication of this, the tenth edition of this book, some 24 years after the first edition appeared, is something of a milestone for me. I said in the first edition that I aimed to produce a relatively short text which would cover the whole area without being superficial, and to place the legal requirements in the context of what actually happens in the workplace. Those aims remain, and although the book has grown over the years, I hope that it is not yet vying for doorstop status. It is a good time to thank all the staff at Sweet & Maxwell who have worked with me over the years for their unfailing professionalism and their patience in the face of sometimes severe provocation.

Gwyneth Pitt

Contents

Table of Abbreviations

ACoP	Approved Code of Practice
Age Regs	Employment Equality (Age) Regulations 2006
BIS	Department for Business, Innovation and Skills
CJEU	Court of Justice of the European Union
COSHH	Control of Substances Hazardous to Health Regulations 2002
DDA	Disability Discrimination Act 1995
Disability Regulations	Equality Act 2010 (Disability) Regulations 2010
DPA	Data Protection Act 1998
EC	Early conciliation
EPA 1975	Employment Protection Act 1975
EqA 2006	Equality Act 2006
EqA 2010	Equality Act 2010
EqPA	Equal Pay Act 1970
ERA	Employment Rights Act 1996
ERelA 1999	Employment Relations Act 1999
ERelA 2004	Employment Relations Act 2004
ERRA	Enterprise and Regulatory Reform Act 2013
HSWA	Health and Safety at Work, etc. Act 1974
IC	Individual conciliation
ICE	Information and Consultation of Employees Regulations 2004
KIT	Keeping in touch
LLP	Limited Liability Partnership
LLPA	Limited Liability Partnerships Act 2000
MPLR	Maternity and Parental Leave etc Regulations 1999
NMWA	National Minimum Wage Act 1998
NMWR	National Minimum Wage Regulations 1999
PCC	Pre-claim conciliation
PILON	Pay in lieu of notice

RB Regs	Employment Equality (Religion or Belief) Regulations 2003
RRA	Race Relations Act 1976
RRAA	Race Relations (Amendment) Act 2000
SDA	Sex Discrimination Act 1975
SO Regs	Employment Equality (Sexual Orientation) Regulations 2003
SPL	Shared Parental Leave
SPLIT	SPL in touch
TEU	Treaty on European Union
TFEU	Treaty on the Functioning of the European Union
TICE	Transnational Information and Consultation of Employees Regulations 1999
TULRA	Trade Union and Labour Relations Act 1974
TULRCA	Trade Union and Labour Relations (Consolidation) Act 1992
TUPE	Transfer of Undertakings (Protection of Employment) Regulations 2006
TURERA	Trade Union Reform and Employment Rights Act 1993
UCTA	Unfair Contract Terms Act 1977

Table of Cases

Table of Statutes

Table of Statutory Instruments

1. Introduction

Key Points

This chapter:
- Outlines the development of modern employment law, highlighting the importance of general principles of contract law to contracts of employment
- Comments on policy developments over the last 50 years up to and including the current Government
- Introduces the main institutions of employment law: Acas, the CAC, Certification Officer, EHRC, ILO and Low Pay Commission
- Explains employment tribunals and the EAT—their composition, jurisdiction and procedure
- Highlights the way in which EU law influences British employment law

* * *

In the mid-fourteenth century about half of the adult working population was wiped out by the Black Death. The workers who were left found that they were suddenly a scarce commodity and could command a high price for their services, much to the chagrin of the powerful landowners who employed them. The Statutes of Labourers 1349 and 1351 were soon passed, fixing wages at the pre-plague rates and making it a criminal offence for workers to leave employment without their employers' consent. In Tudor times this was transformed into a system where justices of the peace fixed wage rates for different sorts of jobs in their localities, a jurisdiction which was only abolished in the nineteenth century, although it had fallen into disuse some time earlier.

There was no free market in labour back then, and there is no free market now. Today the employment relationship is characterised by an enormous amount of statutory regulation aimed at achieving a proper balance between the interests of the parties. However, it remains the case that the central relationship between employer and worker is one of contract, on which the statutory requirements operate. Common law contract principles remain important in interpreting the statutes, although some would argue that they operate as a negative force. Contract law has always been predicated on the notion that the parties are assumed to enter freely into agreements on the basis of

1–001

roughly equal bargaining power. The role of the law is seen as facilitating the process of agreement and then supporting observance of the agreement, but not intervening to control the substance of it: the parties are free to agree pretty well what they want. Today it is generally acknowledged that equal bargaining power rarely exists, even between businesses, let alone between businesses and individuals. Hence in the post-War period we have seen legislation intervening on behalf of the weaker party to prevent undue exploitation, a trend of which the Unfair Contract Terms Act 1977 and the Consumer Rights Act 2015 are good examples.

In the employment sphere particularly, the bargaining power of the parties is inherently unequal. The employer usually holds all the trumps: but for a few exceptionally talented people, most of us are in greater need of an employer than the employer is in need of us. The would-be worker is rarely in a position to negotiate about terms. The only choice is to take it or leave it.

1–002   Yet employees can equalise the situation if they all act together. Individually they are weak, but an employer cannot ignore them if they combine and act in concert. This is the raison d'être and principal justification for trade unions. "Men who have no property except their manual skill and strength ought to be allowed to confer together, if they think fit, for the purpose of determining at what rate they will sell their property", as Sir Robert Peel put it in the debates on the Combination Acts 1824 and 1825.

The history of employment law in the nineteenth century is very much the story of trade unions' struggle to shake off criminal liability for their activities and then to achieve legal status in the eyes of the civil law. By 1906, when the Trade Disputes Act was passed, trade unions had attained a legally recognised status and were able to take industrial action in pursuit of their objectives with impunity most of the time. The attitude of the law was fairly laissez-faire; unions and employers should get on with reaching their own agreements, and if unable to do so, unions were free to take industrial action to press their demands and employers were free to dismiss workers and to try to find more amenable employees.

This historical development leads to a feature of British employment relations which is wholly unlike most of our industrialised partners: the agreements (collective bargains) made between employers and trade unions almost never have the status of binding contracts. They are informal understandings, binding in honour only. One of the problems that the law has faced is explaining how it is that these agreements have any effect as between the worker and the employer (see below, Ch.5). This is a facet of a wider issue: the law is structured on the whole to deal with disputes between two individual parties and vindicating the rights of one or the other. In practice, for many workers in the United Kingdom the work relationship is tripartite: they are represented for negotiating purposes by a trade union. The union, as the collective voice of the employees, may at times be at odds with individual members, but the traditions of the common law and the experience of judges and counsel militate against an understanding of collective interests. This tension is frequently visible in the operation of the law as it relates to trade union affairs in particular and has led some commentators to call for the replacement of common law principles by a Labour Code which would be tailored to the realities of the situation, as has happened in other countries (compare the National Labor Relations Act in the United States). The closest we have got to a Labour Code, however, during 1971–74 when the Industrial Relations Act 1971 was in force, was not a happy experience for trade unions or employers. It was ostensibly modelled on the US code, but in fact adopted many of the control measures in that legislation without the quid pro quo of union rights and safeguards; nevertheless, it dampened the enthusiasm for a code among many involved in industrial relations.

The laissez-faire, non-interventionist stance from the beginning of the twentieth century until the 1960s meant that the focus in employment relations was on the collective bargaining process. There was a consensus that this was the best way to conduct employment relations and that the role of the law should be to support the process. However, during the last 40 years of the twentieth century, the picture changed in a number of important respects. In 1963 the Contracts of Employment Act was passed, the first of what became a flood of statutes offering protection to employees, and in 1964 industrial (later called employment) tribunals were set up, with jurisdiction over statutory claims. The pace of legislation was leisurely in the 1960s but exploded in the 1970s when the action for unfair dismissal was introduced and the first anti-discrimination statutes applying to employment were passed. Far from undermining the role of trade unions, protective legislation operated for strong unions as a minimum starting point, a springboard to better terms and conditions for their members. Furthermore, trade unions had an essential part to play in helping members to enforce their rights. As legal aid is generally not available for employment tribunal claims, trade unions were needed to fill the gap.

In 1979 the Conservative administration of Margaret Thatcher was returned   **1–003**
to power with a mission, among other things, to break trade union power and to move away from collective negotiation of terms and conditions of employment. This was assisted by moves to privatise the nationalised industries, to reduce the size of the public sector and to introduce the market-driven philosophy of the private sector into the remaining public services. From the Employment Act 1980 to the Trade Union Reform and Employment Rights Act 1993 (TURERA) substantial new pieces of legislation were introduced on a biennial and sometimes annual basis. The most visible effects of these were in the field of industrial action, where it became more and more difficult to organise lawful strikes, but other important changes outlawed all manifestations of the closed shop and intervened substantially in the internal affairs of trade unions, prescribing their relationships with their members. It was during this time that the previous hostility of many trade unions to the European Union began to melt away, for it was only via EU directives and decisions of the Court of Justice of the European Union (CJEU) that there was any advance in legal protection for workers.

In 1997 the 18-year Conservative administration was replaced by a Labour Government whose watchwords were social justice and social inclusion. However, the new government was anxious to keep the goodwill of the business community and to avoid any suggestion of a return to what were perceived as the days of too much union power and too many strikes. In consequence, there was no move to reverse the Conservative changes to industrial action law, although the new Government did take the major steps of re-introducing compulsory recognition of unions by employers (see Ch.5) and improving protection for individuals taking part in industrial action (see Ch.12). Protection from unfair dismissal was strengthened, notably by raising substantially the limit on compensation, reducing the qualifying period to one year and placing more emphasis on following fair procedures (see Ch.8). Two other Government initiatives proved to be of almost equal importance in the employment law field. First, at the Treaty of Amsterdam negotiations in 1997 the United Kingdom ended its opt-out from the Social Chapter protocol, which had been agreed by all the other Member States of the European Union (EU) at the Treaty of Maastricht in 1993. That meant that a number of social policy directives, such as those on transnational consultation, part-time work and parental leave, became applicable at once and the way was opened for developments in relation to such topics as fixed-term contracts and the extension of anti-discrimination legislation. Secondly, the Human Rights Act 1998 was passed, allowing the provisions of the European Convention on Human Rights (ECHR) to be enforced in British law, which brought rights into the workplace in a wholly novel way.

Building on the requirements of EU directives, the Labour Government implemented a number of "family-friendly" policies—improved maternity rights, new rights to paternity leave and parental leave, a right to request flexible working, limits on working time and rights to paid annual leave (see Ch.6). Also in pursuance of EU policy, marginalised groups of workers such as fixed-term, part-time and agency workers gained increased rights (see Ch.3). The introduction of the National Minimum Wage can also be seen as an element of this strand of reform, although this was a purely domestic initiative (see Ch.7). In retrospect, one of the Labour administration's major achievements may be seen to be the passing of the Equality Act 2010, consolidating and extending equality law and an important step forward in the equality field (see Ch.2).

In May 2010 13 years of Labour Government came to an end. The General Election in May 2010 sent a very clear signal of dissatisfaction with the Labour administration, but a less clear message about what the public wanted instead. The main focus of the Conservative-Liberal Democrat Coalition Government was on dealing with the economic crisis. However, it is almost an article of faith for the Conservative Party that regulation of employment inhibits business growth, and so in the name of job creation and enhanced economic performance, a programme of reduction in statutory employment protection got under way. The Employment Law Review 2010–2015 was aimed in its own words at increasing labour market flexibility and reducing the burden on business. Most notable were the attacks on the right to claim unfair dismissal and the introduction of swingeing fees for all applications to employment tribunals, but there were significant reductions in equality law protection as well. It was as if civil servants had been instructed to go through the statute book and come forward with proposals to abolish or reduce any individual rights which are not guaranteed by EU law. The only consultation aimed at increasing employees' rights was *Modern Workplaces*, a consultation launched when the Coalition was still in its honeymoon period and proposing more rights to flexible working and to enhance the law on equal pay.

The General Election in 2015 resulted in a Conservative Government, the near annihilation of the Liberal Democrat representation in Parliament and subsequent changes in the Labour Party which, in the view of most objective commentators, have made it unelectable in the near future. The policies driven by what Bob Hepple memorably described as "market fundamentalism"—meaning an ideological commitment to deregulation of business regardless of actual evidence—are thus likely to be given even freer rein. The first consultations of the new administration aimed to reduce the right to take industrial action and the in/out referendum on EU membership, in 2016 could conceivably lead to the dismantling of whole swathes of legal protection for workers. **1—004**

All the new developments are dealt with at the appropriate points in later chapters. The rest of this chapter will outline some of the major institutions in British employment law. This part may be used as a reference section to be consulted when unfamiliar organisations are mentioned.

Institutions of Employment Law

Advisory, Conciliation and Arbitration Service (Acas)

The Advisory, Conciliation and Arbitration Service (Acas) was set up in 1974. Its existence as an independent statutory body with a wide remit in employment relations was established by the Employment Protection Act 1975 (EPA); the relevant law is now to be found in the Trade Union and Labour Relations (Consolidation) Act 1992 (TULRCA). Under TULRCA s.209 it is charged with the general duty of promoting improvement in industrial relations. Originally the Acas mission specifically included a duty to encourage the extension of collective bargaining, reflecting the post-War political consensus that voluntary collective bargaining was the appropriate means of regulating employment relations. However, a Government quinquennial review of Acas in 1992 recommended that this be deleted because of the decline in importance of collective bargaining (see Ch.5). Its terms of reference were altered in 1993 by TURERA, deleting the reference to collective bargaining and adding that its duty should be carried out "in particular by exercising its functions in relation to the settlement of trade disputes". This new emphasis did not make a real difference in practice to the functions of Acas, but in so far as it could be regarded as restrictive, the repeal of those words by the Employment Relations Act 1999 was welcome. **1—005**

The constitution of Acas is set out in ss.247–253 of TULRCA. It is governed by a council chaired by an appointee of the Secretary of State (who may be part-time since 1993) and has 11 other members, three of whom are specifically appointed as representing employers and three as representing trade unions. While the funding for Acas is provided by the government, its independence from government interference is specifically guaranteed by s.247(3) of TULRCA. Section 251A of TURERA granted the Secretary of State power to require Acas to charge for some services. At first Acas was reluctant to do this, as it feared that its reputation for independence and impartiality would be damaged if it were seen to be profiting from its services. However, the focus of Acas has changed in recent years to emphasise education and training and the prevention of disputes, so the number of charged services has increased.

Advice

1–006   As its name suggests, Acas has a variety of functions, which are carried out by around 900 staff, principally based at 12 regional centres across Great Britain. In practice, advice is an important function, with over 900 enquiries being dealt with by telephone helplines in 2014/15. Anyone may telephone with employment queries and receive free advice, and online facilities are also available. Advice is also given through the medium of seminars, training events (including online training) and advisory handbooks on many aspects of employment relations. These advisory handbooks must be distinguished from the Codes of Practice also issued by Acas: the latter, but not the former, have a certain legal status.

Conciliation

1–007   Conciliation may be defined as bringing disputing parties together with a view to facilitating their reaching agreement by themselves without further legal process. Traditionally, Acas's main activity has been providing individual conciliation (IC) in situations where employees are in dispute with their employer, for example where they claim to have been unfairly dismissed. This is because virtually all applications to employment tribunals had to be referred to an Acas officer for conciliation, to see if there was any possibility of settlement without going through with a tribunal hearing. Since legal aid is not available for employment tribunal hearings, it is often only when talking to an Acas officer that the claimant begins to appreciate whether or not she has a good claim; sometimes this is true of employers also.

   In April 2009 Acas began to offer a new pre-claim conciliation service with a view to helping employees and employers to settle individual disputes before they even got to the stage of a tribunal application. Cases were referred from the telephone helpline and much of the conciliation took place by this means also. This was an immediate success, with over 45,000 cases being referred in the first two years. In 2012/13 Acas noted that there was no subsequent claim to an employment tribunal in 77 per cent of the cases which went to pre-claim conciliation (PCC). So successful was this initiative that under the Enterprise and Regulatory Reform Act 2013 it became mandatory from April 2014 for all claims to be submitted to Acas for conciliation to be attempted before claimants are allowed to make an application to an employment tribunal, a scheme known as early conciliation (EC) (see below, para.1–020). The scheme has been successful, with Acas receiving 83,000 notifications under EC in 2014/15, of which only 22 per cent resulted in a tribunal claim. However, the figures may also be affected by the introduction of fees for tribunal applications (see below, para.1–018).

Acas also offers conciliation services in collective disputes. It is a voluntary process, although many collective agreements make provision for Acas conciliation in the event of deadlock on a particular issue. The idea is that an independent but knowledgeable third party acting as go-between may be able to take some of the heat out of a dispute and may sometimes be able to help the parties see a way forward. Under s.210 of TULRCA, Acas need not wait to be asked by one side before offering its services, but the parties are not bound to accept. It seems to be an effective part of the organisation's activities: in 2014/15 Acas reported 1,371 requests for collective conciliation with 87 per cent of these cases resolved without industrial action. The majority were concerned with pay and conditions; the other main issues were union recognition, changes in working practices, discipline and redundancy.

Arbitration

Acas engages in both arbitration and mediation. Arbitration involves making a decision between the parties which should become a binding settlement of the dispute. Under s.212 of TULRCA, where a trade dispute exists or appears to be imminent, Acas may offer arbitration where requested by one party to a dispute, but only as long as all parties agree. Thus the process is voluntary, and although the arbitrator's decision is not legally binding, in practice it is very likely that it will be followed. If the parties are prepared to refer the matter to arbitration, they are fairly certain to accept the result. Before setting up an arbitration, Acas should consider whether an agreement can be reached through conciliation and negotiation and should try this route first. If arbitration is inevitable, it is not provided by Acas personnel but either through the Central Arbitration Committee (CAC) or by an arbitrator selected from a panel maintained by Acas. The virtue of arbitration has traditionally been that, unlike legal proceedings, there does not have to be an outright win for one side or the other: compromises may be ordered where appropriate. Nonetheless, the binding nature of arbitration may make some parties unwilling to accept it. In 2014/15 only 19 references were made to Acas for arbitration. As a result, Acas has developed mediation services for both collective and individual disputes, which work as a half-way house between arbitration and conciliation. The parties have to reach their own agreement, but the mediator can assist by suggesting ways forward and making recommendations. In 2014/15 mediation services were used in 246 individual employment disputes.

1–008

In the 1990s the extension of arbitration to a wider range of individual employment matters was mooted, partly as a response to the ever-increasing workload of tribunals and partly in acknowledgment that tribunal proceedings are often much more legalistic than was ever intended, meaning that they are frequently not speedy, cheap or informal. The length of time that therefore elapses between the cause of the dispute and the tribunal hearing and the increasing use of legal representation means that it is, in practice, unlikely that the claimant will be re-employed at the end of any proceedings. It was therefore decided that an arbitration procedure should be set up as an alternative to tribunal proceedings. The Employment Rights (Dispute Resolution) Act 1998 inserted a new s.212A of TULRCA empowering Acas to draw up an arbitration scheme for certain individual disputes. Although it was originally intended to introduce this in 1999, it was not until May 2001 that it finally came into force.

The Acas Arbitration Scheme applies only to unfair dismissal cases where the sole question is whether or not the dismissal was unfair. If there are other issues (such as whether the worker is qualified to claim or whether there was a dismissal at all) then the case cannot be dealt with by an arbitrator but must go to a tribunal. The Scheme is voluntary and applies only where the parties agree in writing that they wish the case to be handled in this way and are prepared to waive their rights to have the case heard by a tribunal. The arbitration is carried out by an independent arbitrator appointed by Acas who is enjoined to "have regard to general principles of fairness and good conduct in employment relations" (including relevant Acas Codes of Practice) instead of applying legal tests—although he must apply any relevant EU law. This is one of the great uncertainties of the Scheme: if arbitrators do not follow legal principle, how are fairness and consistency to be ensured? Given that the arbitrator's decision cannot be appealed, there was always doubt as to whether parties would be willing to take the risk of submitting themselves to this process—a doubt borne out by the fact that in the first six years of the Scheme's operation only 55 cases were brought under the Scheme, a number which is entirely trivial when compared with the numbers of unfair dismissal claims in total. Acas initially believed that this was because of parties' ignorance of the potential benefits of arbitration, but it seems more likely that the Scheme has simply been a failure.

Codes of practice

1–009   The power of Acas to issue codes of practice "containing such practical guidance as the Service thinks fit for the purpose of promoting the improvement of industrial relations" (TULRCA s.199) is extremely important. These codes of practice are not legally binding, in that failure to follow the requirements of the code will not of itself attract liability, but they are to be taken into account whenever relevant by courts and employment tribunals (TULRCA s.207).

Any code must be produced in draft first for consultation among interested parties. It must then be approved by the Secretary of State and laid before Parliament; in the absence of positive disapprobation it will then be brought into force by statutory instrument. The first Acas Code of Practice, on Disciplinary Practices and Procedures in Employment, was issued in 1977 and had a huge influence on employers' disciplinary procedures. However, it was quite short and therefore limited in scope. A revised and extended version was rejected by the Secretary of State in 1987 but was issued instead as an advisory handbook, *Discipline at Work*. The Code of Practice was extensively revised in 2000 to take account of the new right for individuals to be accompanied during disciplinary and grievance proceedings. At the same time the opportunity was taken to expand advice on a range of matters in the light of developing case-law and theory in relation to discipline and dismissal, as well as to include two new sections on grievance procedures and the statutory right to be accompanied. Revision was again necessary in 2004 to incorporate guidance on the statutory disciplinary and grievance procedures (discussed further below, para.8–040).

Following the repeal of these procedures, a new code, the Code of Practice No.1 on Disciplinary and Grievance Procedures, was prepared which came into force in April 2009 (revised 2015). It is much shorter than the previous two incarnations, largely because failure to follow the Code may now lead to a 25 per cent uplift or decrease in compensation. Much of the detailed material which used to be in the Code is now to be found in a non-statutory Acas Guide to Discipline and Grievances at Work, which, of course, does not have the same status as the Code. Other Acas codes, dating back to the 1970s originally, cover Disclosure of Information to Trade Unions for Collective Bargaining Purposes (revised 1997), and Time Off for Trade Union Duties and Activities (revised 2010). Two new codes, on settlement agreements and flexible working, came into force in 2014 (see below, paras 8–042 and 6–023).

Acas is not the only body with the power to issue codes of practice. The Health and Safety Commission and the Equality and Human Rights Commission may also issue codes and, more controversially, since 1980 so may the Secretary of State (by virtue of s.203 of TULRCA). The Secretary of State's power was largely introduced because Acas was reluctant to risk its reputation for independence and lack of bias by publishing codes of practice on such sensitive issues as picketing and the closed shop. Those codes were drawn up by the Secretary of State, as was the code on trade union ballots. They came in for substantial criticism as attempting to legislate by the back door by introducing requirements for which there was no warrant in the legislation. It is important, therefore, to distinguish them from the Acas codes which have usually met with general approval.

Central Arbitration Committee (CAC)

The Central Arbitration Committee (CAC) was established by the Employment   **1–010** Protection Act 1975 and took over the functions of the former Industrial Arbitration Board as well as new duties under that statute. The chair, deputy chairs and members are appointed by the Secretary of State and include people with expertise in the field of employment relations as well as representatives of both sides of industry. Provisions relating to it are now to be found in ss.259–265 of TULRCA.

The EPA 1975 conferred on the CAC novel statutory powers to decide disputes where an employer refused to recognise a trade union and also where it was claimed that an employer was not affording employees terms and conditions up to the industry or local standard. Both jurisdictions were abolished by the Employment Act 1980 as one of the Conservative Government's first reforms of employment relations law, largely depriving the CAC of a meaningful role. From 1980 to 2000 the only situation where the CAC had compulsory arbitration powers was in relation to disputes over disclosure of information to recognised trade unions for the purposes of collective bargaining (discussed below, para.5–023), although it could also be called upon to act where parties voluntarily approached Acas seeking arbitration, as described above. The CAC had an average of only 21 complaints a year about disclosure of information referred to it in the 1990s, and in 1998 there were only six references about disclosure of information and no other arbitration issues at all.

The picture changed dramatically when the Employment Relations Act (ERelA) 1999 introduced a new procedure for the compulsory recognition of trade unions (below, para.5–016) and once more appointed the CAC to the duty of deciding on applications for recognition. Between June 2000, when the procedure came into force, and March 2015 trade unions made 907 applications to the CAC for recognition, resulting in recognition being awarded in 268 cases, although this seemingly low figure masks the proportion of applications which are withdrawn because the parties reach an agreement for voluntary recognition. The CAC estimates that, if this were included, it would boost the number of applications resulting in recognition to roughly half of the total. It might have been expected that there would have been a flood of applications for recognition when the legislation came into force, followed by a tailing off, but this did not occur and the level of applications stabilised at a relatively low level, with 38 applications in 2014/15. The present statutory recognition procedure has not proved to be in any sense as controversial as the 1975 version, an outcome on which the present CAC evidently prides itself.

1–011   The CAC's caseload for disclosure of information remains tiny, with just six complaints in 2014/15. It now has jurisdiction also for disputes about European Works Councils (just 16 applications in 12 years) and consultation under the European Public Limited Liability Company Regulations 2004 (SI 2004/2326). However, while the requirements for employers operating in several countries to consult across the transnational workforce may not have generated much interest, the Information and Consultation of Employees Regulations 2004, which came into force in April 2005, which now require all employers with at least 50 employees to consult with the workforce on a range of matters, has led to a slight increase in workload, with 56 complaints in 10 years. The most recent addition to the CAC's jurisdiction has come via the Companies (Cross-Border Mergers) Regulations 2007 (SI 2007/2974), which preserve employee representation rights in relation to mergers of companies from different Member States.

Certification Officer

1–012   When trade unions were first recognised as legal bodies under the Trade Union Act 1871 they had to register with the Registrar of Friendly Societies to qualify for certain advantages in relation to tax and the holding of property through trustees. While the process was not compulsory, most unions registered. Under the Industrial Relations Act 1971, however, registration took on a different complexion, and non-registration became the rallying call for trade union opposition to that Act.

The Industrial Relations Act was repealed by TULRA 1974, by which time the terms "register" and "registrar" had attracted such opprobrium that although the wish was to return substantially to the pre-1971 position, it was felt that these terms could not be used. For a while the Registrar of Friendly Societies was brought back into service, but in 1975 a new office, that of the Certification Officer, was instituted (see now TULRCA s.254).

The principal function of the Certification Officer was originally to maintain a list (not a register) of independent trade unions and to issue certificates of independence (TULRCA s.2). As will be seen (below, para.10–035), the status of independence is of some importance, and it is the Certification Officer who decides whether a trade union meets the criteria. However, from 1979 onwards the Conservative administration pursued a policy of increased intervention in the internal affairs of trade unions and the Certification Officer became a key player in its implementation.

The Certification Officer is now responsible for keeping records of the annual **1–013** financial and membership returns of trade unions, copies of union rules and the other documents which trade unions are now required to file—a list which grew considerably in the 1980s. Additionally, he has jurisdiction over complaints relating to the elections of trade union officials; ballots to set up political funds in trade unions; complaints over political expenditure; and the amalgamation of trade unions. In 1993 TURERA extended the Certification Officer's powers considerably by introducing a wide authority for him to investigate the financial affairs of trade unions on his own initiative, including a right to demand production of documents and to appoint an inspector where fraud or misfeasance is suspected (TULRCA ss.37A–E). Most recently, his jurisdiction over trade union's membership registers was extended by the Transparency of Lobbying, Non-Party Campaigning and Trade Union Administration Act 2014, and his powers to investigate and make orders are extended further again by the Trade Union Bill 2016.

The Certification Officer's functions have traditionally been a mixture of administrative and judicial duties. In relation to some matters, such as complaints about elections, the political fund rules or industrial action ballots, union members had a choice of taking their claims to the Certification Officer or to the court. The advantage of a complaint to the Certification Officer was that the procedure would be cheaper and quicker; the disadvantage was that his powers were limited to making a declaration. If the union did not comply with the declaration the member would then have to invoke court proceedings. The ERelA 1999, as part of the general policy of encouraging disputes to be settled away from courts where possible, made a number of amendments to TULRCA which basically extended the Certification Officer's powers of adjudication to some areas where he had no jurisdiction before (such as dealing with complaints of refusal of access to the union's accounts) and gave him powers to enforce his orders. Members now have to choose to complain either to the Certification Officer or to the court, but cannot do both. A right of appeal from a decision of the Certification Officer to the Employment Appeal Tribunal (EAT) on a point of law was inserted into TULRCA s.108C. The Employment Relations Act 2004 also made minor amendments to the Certification Officer's powers, including a new power to strike out complaints which are scandalous, vexatious, have no reasonable prospect of success or are otherwise misconceived (TULRCA s.256ZA(1)).

More substantial changes are being brought about by the Trade Union Bill 2016, which will give the Certification Officer new powers to set up investigations in relation to most of the matters where he currently has power to make enquiries, and also to look into possible breaches of the law of his own volition, rather than acting only when a member makes a complaint. His powers to make enforcement orders, if the union is in breach of statutory requirements, are extended and will also include a power to impose financial penalties of between £200 and £20,000, in accordance with regulations to be made under the legislation. It seems that the role of the Certification Officer in future is envisaged as being actively to police trade union compliance with legislation (including ballots for industrial action) rather than being essentially registrar-like.

1–014   The Public Bodies Act 2011 gave the Secretary of State power to merge the Certification Office with the Central Arbitration Committee as part of a general policy of reducing the number of Non-Departmental Public Bodies. This power has not been exercised to date, and it seems unlikely that it will be, in view of the larger and more proactive role in policing trade unions which the Trade Union Bill 2016 envisages. The Bill gives the Secretary of State power to make regulations imposing a levy on trade unions and employers' associations effectively to defray the expenses of running the Certification Office instead.

Employment tribunals

1–015   Employment tribunals were originally set up with a limited jurisdiction under the Industrial Training Act 1964. From these humble beginnings they have evolved to become highly important institutions, pivotal to the operation of employment law today. The process started in 1965, when they were given jurisdiction over redundancy claims by the Redundancy Payments Act, but it was the introduction of the action for unfair dismissal in 1972 which led to their workload really taking off. Apart from a dip in 2004/05, when the statutory dispute resolution procedures were introduced (see below, para.8–040) the numbers of cases increased year by year, peaking in 2009/10 when there were 236,100 claims to tribunals, a 56 per cent increase on the previous year. Cases have also become more complex, as there is a noticeable trend for an individual case to involve claims under more than one jurisdiction (e.g. discrimination and unfair dismissal). The figures over recent years show the distorting effect of some very large multiple claims (*i.e.* more than one worker suing the same employer on largely the same facts) but, even so, the increased workload is striking, and the associated costs have been an increasing concern to government. Many reforms have been introduced with a view to reducing costs, of which the most striking was the introduction of fees in July 2013 (see below, para.1–018). This has reduced the number of claims by about 70 per cent, with just 61,000 claims in the first half of 2015.

Employment tribunals were traditionally composed of three members. They are chaired by a solicitor or barrister of seven years' standing (known as an employment judge since the Tribunals, Courts and Enforcement Act 2007) and then have two lay members, from lists drawn up in consultation with bodies representing employers and workers respectively. This tripartite composition, involving representation from both sides of industry with an independent element to hold the ring, is typical of many institutions of employment law set up in the twentieth century, most of which have been dismantled since the 1980s; the same is happening in employment tribunals, as we will see. The main reason for having lay members is that they can bring their knowledge and experience of practical employment relations to bear on the issues before them, and generations of employment judges have paid tribute to the importance of their contribution. In making any decision, the lay members have an equal vote, and can thus outvote the employment judge, although most decisions are unanimous.

Because their caseload increased substantially without a corresponding increase in personnel, unacceptable delays developed in the hearing of tribunal cases. During the 1980s it got to the point where fewer than 70 per cent of cases were heard within six months of application. In an attempt to deal with this problem, TURERA 1993 introduced a power for an employment judge to sit alone on certain types of case and the categories were extended again by the Employment Rights (Dispute Resolution) Act 1998. Most of the categories where this was permissible were those involving more technical areas where it was more likely that the application of the law rather than finding or evaluating facts would be the issue: examples include disputes under the Working Time Regulations 1998 and unlawful deductions from wages, although it can include any kind of claim if the parties consent in writing to it being heard by a judge alone. At any time the employment judge may decide that a full tribunal is necessary and, before sitting alone, she should in any case consider the views of the parties if one or both is opposed, and also whether a dispute on the facts is likely so that the case would be better heard by a full tribunal.

The provision for an employment judge to sit alone drew a lot of criticism **1–016** because it was seen as undermining the basic concept of employment tribunals as "industrial juries", although in practice it appeared that employment judges were careful not to abuse their discretion. The Coalition Government, however, decided to extend the system to unfair dismissal cases, explicitly to save money through not needing to pay lay members and because it would be likely to shorten the length of hearings. Despite almost universal opposition to this proposal when it went out to consultation, the Government went ahead with it anyway, the Employment Tribunals Act 1996 (Composition) Order 2012 amending the Employment Tribunals Act 1996 s.4 with effect from April 2012. It seems extraordinary that the paradigm situation where it would be expected that lay members would have an important role—in deciding whether a dismissal was fair or unfair—should no longer be heard automatically by a full employment tribunal, and it raises the question as to whether the long-term intention is to abolish lay members entirely. Given that claims relating to those jurisdictions where a full tribunal is normally mandatory, principally discrimination claims, are relatively few in number (fewer than 15 per cent) this change means that for the vast majority of tribunal hearings, the default position will be a single employment judge.

Jurisdiction

Until 1994 the jurisdiction of employment tribunals was entirely statutory. **1–017** Although provision for the Secretary of State to extend their jurisdiction to contractual matters had existed since 1975, it was not exercised until 1994. The fact that the Secretary of State's power had not been exercised was a constant cause for criticism. When an employee is dismissed, she may well have a claim for breach of the contract of employment as well as a claim for unfair dismissal and it seemed absurd that the two claims could not both be dealt with in the same forum. The problem was highlighted when the Wages Act 1986 was passed and apparently provided an avenue for bringing contract claims in employment tribunals: the number of applications for deductions of wages rocketed, indicating the need for such a mechanism.

Following TURERA amendments, the Employment Tribunals Extension of Jurisdiction Order 1994 was made, permitting contract claims which arise or are outstanding on the termination of the employee's employment to be taken to employment tribunals, provided that the claim does not relate to: personal injuries; a term requiring the employer to provide living accommodation; intellectual property; breach of confidence; or restrictive covenants. A further limitation is that the maximum that can be claimed in a contract claim (or a number of different claims relating to the same contract) is £25,000 (an amount which has remained unchanged since 1994). It is worth noting that there is no requirement that the employee should be bringing a statutory claim at the same time. The usual limitation period for statutory claims of three months applies, so a claimant who is out of time would still have to go to the county court. The employer may counter-claim on grounds of the employee's breach of contract within six weeks of receiving the originating application. It is perhaps unfortunate that it was not decided to extend contract jurisdiction generally. For example, in *Sunderland Polytechnic v Evans* (1993), an employee disputed the amount of pay her employer had deducted after a half-day strike. It seems odd that the assembled expertise of the tribunal could still not be used in a situation like that just because there had been no termination of the contract. In deductions from wages cases, where there is no limit on the amount that can be claimed, tribunals can find themselves dealing with complex contractual claims worth thousands and sometimes millions of pounds. It seems perverse not to use their expertise more widely.

Procedure

Starting a claim

1–018   Like other tribunals, employment tribunals are meant to be cheap, speedy and informal. At one time, a tribunal claim could be started simply by writing to the tribunal with basic contact information relating to the parties, the dates of employment and a broad indication of what the claim was about. In order to save time and expense, the procedure has become steadily more formal over the years and since 2004 claims have not been accepted unless they are made on the prescribed form (Form ET1), which now runs to 10 pages (although it can be completed online). Claims must be submitted to an Employment Tribunal Office within the statutory time-limit for the claim in question, which is quite short—usually three months.

For the first 50 years of employment tribunals' existence, claims could be made for nothing, as is common with most statutory tribunals. In perhaps the most important change ever implemented, the Government exercised powers under the Tribunals, Courts and Enforcement Act 2007 to introduce fees for bringing claims from July 2013. This change has been hugely controversial, not least because the fees are substantial—£1,200 for a typical unfair dismissal claim—and are paid only by the claimant. The Government consulted only on the level of fees, not on whether they should be introduced, claiming that the reasons were to reduce public subsidy and to put tribunals on a par with the courts. There have been recent very large increases in civil court fees, although a claim for £7,000, the median award for unfair dismissal, would only cost about a third of the tribunal fee. There is a general consensus that the real motive for these swingeing fees is to deter claimants from bringing cases, and it seems that the ploy has been successful: as noted already, there were about 70 per cent fewer claims in 2014/15 than in the previous year. The union Unison challenged the fees in judicial review proceedings, claiming that they offended the principle of effective remedies in EU law and indirectly discriminated against women. The Court of Appeal did not find their evidence convincing (*R (on the application of Unison) v Lord Chancellor (No.3)* (2015)).

There are two stages of fee payment and two levels of fee. The lower level of fee is for "Type A" cases, which are considered to be more straightforward. This may be true of disputes relating to redundancy pay and written statements, but is not obviously so of claims for breach of contract and unlawful deductions, which are also Type A. Everything else, notably claims for discrimination and unfair dismissal, are categorised as Type B, with fees at a higher level. The first, "issuing fee", has to be paid on making the claim: it is £160 for Type A cases and £250 for Type B. If the claim goes forward to a tribunal hearing, a second, "hearing fee" becomes payable, which is £230 for Type A cases and £950 for Type B. Obviously, the disproportionately high second fee is to encourage claimants to settle or withdraw before having their case heard. However, it should be noted that it is quite likely that from an employer's point of view, settlements may become more expensive, as claimants will press for their fees to be included. There is the possibility of fee remission for people with very low incomes or in receipt of certain benefits, but this will not assist the majority of claimants. More significantly, claimants will usually be able to get the fees back from the employer by way of costs if they win.

A claim form will be rejected by the Tribunal Office if it is incomplete, completed incorrectly or if the correct fee has not been paid, and time continues to run against the claimant in these circumstances, so it is unwise to leave a claim until nearly the end of the limitation period.   **1–019**

As noted above (para.1–015), the sheer volume of claims dealt with frequently meant that the aim of ensuring that cases get to the tribunal quickly was not achieved. The statistics for 2012/13 showed that the average time taken to clear a tribunal case was 80 weeks—although the figure is distorted by some very long ongoing cases; even so, the median figure was 31 weeks. Over the years, there have been various attempts to expedite tribunal proceedings. Regulations in 2001 aimed to give tribunals greater powers to manage proceedings, in line with the Woolf reforms to civil procedure, which were generally designed to promote proactive case management by the courts. These rules were in turn replaced by the Employment Tribunals (Constitution and Rules of Procedure) Regulations 2004 (SI 2004/1861) which made yet more changes aimed at increasing efficiency, through strengthened case management powers, extended power to award costs and significant changes to the pre-tribunal process. These were subsequently amended on an *ad hoc* basis to take account of further changes in dismissal law. In 2011 the Coalition Government asked the then President of the EAT, Underhill J, to undertake a thorough review of tribunal procedure, to deal with a number of concerns about their efficacy, and this resulted in a new set of regulations, the Employment Tribunals (Constitution and Rules of Procedure) Regulations 2013 (SI 2013/1237), which replaced previous regulations with effect from July 2013.

The Rules of Procedure are contained in Sch.1 to the 2013 Regulations and r.2 states that the tribunal's overriding objective is to deal with cases justly, which includes ensuring the parties are on an equal footing as far as possible, dealing with the case proportionately in relation to the complexity of the issues involved, as well as expeditiously and fairly, and saving expense. While the avoidance of unnecessary formality is part of the overriding objective, anyone going to an employment tribunal expecting a cosy chat should think again. In general, tribunals follow a procedure which is akin to the procedure of ordinary civil courts, although if either party is unrepresented the employment judge often takes a more inquisitorial role. The usual procedure followed is outlined below (there are special rules for equal value claims, which are discussed below, para.7–011).

Before the hearing

1–020 As noted already, a claim form will be rejected by the tribunal staff if it is not properly filled in and accompanied by the correct fee. It will be referred to an employment judge if it appears to relate to a matter over which the tribunal has no jurisdiction, or cannot be sensibly responded to, or is an abuse of process. The employment judge can decide to reject it if so, in which case it is returned to the claimant with a brief explanation and an opportunity to request reconsideration (rr.10–13). From April 2014, a further requirement is that the claim must be submitted to Acas under its early conciliation (EC) process. EC is effectively a mandatory version of the pre-claim conciliation process which Acas piloted from 2009 with some success. The idea is that Acas can try to conciliate the dispute without the need for any claim to a tribunal. If EC is successful, the Acas officer will draw up a binding settlement agreement for the parties. If not, a certificate will be issued to the claimant by Acas confirming that she has complied with the statutory requirement to contact Acas in advance of a claim.

However, there is a world of difference between a voluntary process and a mandatory one, especially where the effect of non-compliance is that the employee cannot submit a claim to a tribunal. Thus it has been necessary for fairly complex rules to be established in the Employment Tribunals (Early Conciliation: Exemptions and Rules of Procedure) Regulations 2013 covering such matters as the format in which the claimant must ask for early conciliation; the circumstances in which the Acas officer can decide that it is not worth pursuing conciliation further; the time-limit for EC (one month); the issue of a certificate that EC has been completed; and the effect on limitation periods for making a claim (basically, that the period will be extended for the time the EC process takes). In response to the Government consultation on EC, a number of respondents expressed fears that the complexity of the process could give rise to satellite litigation, i.e. litigation about whether the procedure has been followed properly, which would undermine its main purpose of reducing disputes at the tribunal. There is a precedent for this in the short-lived statutory dispute resolution procedures (see below, para.8–040), which caused more problems than they solved; it is to be hoped that the same does not befall early conciliation.

Once accepted, a copy of the claim is sent to the respondent employer together with a Form ET3 requesting its response to the claim, and, despite the EC procedure, the matter is still referred to Acas. An Acas individual conciliation officer will again look at the claim, now particularised, and talk to the parties with a view to seeing if the matter can be settled without a hearing.

Having received the claim, the respondent must respond within 28 days, **1–021** now using the prescribed form and stating the grounds for resisting the claim. Originally the response had to be returned within 14 days, although, in striking contrast to the rigid rules on limitation periods for applications, it used to be easy for the respondent to gain extensions of that period, even after it had expired. The 2004 Rules of Procedure extended the response period, but enforced it more rigorously: importantly, an extension was only granted if the request was made before the expiry of the time-limit. This is relaxed to some extent under the Employment Tribunals (Constitution and Rules of Procedure) Regulations 2013: an application to extend may be made after the time-limit has expired and must explain why the extension is sought; if late, it must also contain a draft of the response (r.20). While failure to comply used to result in the respondent automatically being unable to take further part in the proceedings or a default judgment being issued, the employment judge is now enjoined to consider whether the claim can properly be disposed of without a hearing. If so, a judgment will be issued. If not, there will be a hearing and the judge has discretion whether or not to allow the respondent to participate.

Once the response has been received, the next stage is a "judicial sift" under r.26. Formalising a procedure initially used in the Employment Appeal Tribunal (EAT), the sift involves an employment judge considering all the documents and deciding whether the tribunal has jurisdiction over all the complaints and whether there are any parts of either the claim or the response that look so weak that they have "no reasonable prospect of success". If so, the judge can dismiss that part of the claim. The parties will be notified and have a chance to make representations by a specified date. If they do not do so, the stipulated part will be dismissed on the date specified. If they do make representations, the judge will either accept the argument and let the claim or response proceed, or will hold a hearing to decide whether it should proceed. Note that in such a case the sift will not succeed in its aims of reducing litigation and the time taken to deal with cases.

It has always been possible for parties to request further particulars and ask for disclosure and inspection of documents from the other side, with the possibility of seeking an order from the tribunal in case of non-compliance;

however, the revised Rules now permit the tribunal of its own motion to ask for further particulars, order disclosure of documents against any person (not just the parties) and also to require either party to furnish written answers to any question, if this will clarify issues or enable progress to be made.

Preliminary hearings

1–022   Due to the relative ease with which tribunal proceedings used to be able to be commenced, and especially because it was rare to order one party to pay the costs of the other, employers complained that they sometimes had to go to the expense and trouble of defending claims which were hopeless from the outset. A pre-hearing review procedure was therefore introduced, intended to filter out the hopeless cases. A pre-hearing review was ordered either on the application of one party (usually the employer) or of its own motion where it appeared that some contention (of either party, but usually the claimant) was unlikely to succeed.

Over the last decade, tribunals themselves have been encouraged to become more proactive in the management of cases, with the result that private case management discussions between the employment judge and the parties became a very common preliminary stage before a case went to tribunal. The fact that parties might have to attend and prepare for two sets of prior proceedings before the main hearing led to increased costs and time taken to dispose of cases. Thus an important innovation in the 2013 Rules of Procedure is to combine pre-hearing reviews and case management discussions into a single preliminary hearing. Under r.53, a preliminary hearing can be held in order to determine preliminary issues (such as whether the tribunal has jurisdiction, or whether an employee was dismissed); to explore the possibility of alternative dispute resolution; to decide whether the whole or any part of a claim or response should be struck out; to discuss the claim and make a case management order (the old case management discussion), and to consider whether a deposit order should be made. The intention is that there should be only one preliminary hearing, but it is possible for there to be more than one.

Where the employment judge considers that any contentions of either party have little reasonable prospect of success, she can require that party to pay a deposit of up to £1,000 as a condition of continuing the proceedings, although in making this order she must take into account the party's ability to pay (r.39). The deposit order records the contention thought to be untenable and the reasons for that view and the party is warned that persistence in the face of the order could lead to an order of costs and forfeiture of the deposit.

1–023   Preliminary hearings will usually be held in private (and may be by telephone or video-conferencing) unless they involve determination of a preliminary issue or striking out of a contention, when they should be open to the public.

The hearing

1–024   Tribunals have the right to regulate their own procedure, as long as they act within the Rules of Procedure, but in practice they usually follow something like ordinary civil court procedure. The party with the burden of proof starts:

in an unfair dismissal case, for example, this will be the employer, if dismissal is admitted, because the employer has the burden of proving the reason for the dismissal. If, however, the employer denies that the employee was dismissed, the employee has the burden of proving it, and would begin instead. Witnesses, who are invited to give evidence on oath, are examined-in-chief and then cross-examined by the other side; tribunals are usually reluctant to accept hearsay evidence or to permit leading questions in examination-in-chief even though they are not bound by the rules of evidence. Formalising recent practice, the 2013 Rules of Procedure provide that witness statements will be taken as read, in order to save time—although they should be made available for public inspection (rr.43–44).

After both sides have presented their cases and called their witnesses, they sum up and the tribunal retires to consider its decision. Where possible, tribunals try to deliver decisions orally on the day, but the decision may be reserved and written reasons sent later. Under r.62 there is no longer any requirement for tribunals to provide written reasons unless either they are requested by one of the parties orally at the hearing or in writing within 14 days of the judgment being sent out, or they are requested at any time by the EAT.

Traditionally, costs are not normally awarded against the unsuccessful party, although the new fees regime makes a difference to this, as noted above. Originally costs were only awarded against a party who had acted frivolously, vexatiously or otherwise unreasonably, but the power was extended in 1993 to include abusive or disruptive conduct of proceedings. This was extended again in 2001 to allow costs to be awarded against a claimant for his or her representative's unreasonable behaviour. The 2004 Regulations introduced wasted costs orders which could be made against parties' representatives directly, and also preparation time orders which could be made in favour of unrepresented litigants. The 2013 Regulations cure the anomaly under which an unrepresented litigant in receipt of a preparation time order could not also claim witness expenses, and also permit claimants to recover the cost of instructing a lay representative, although only to a limited extent. As claimants must now pay fees in order to start a claim, provision is made for that to be included in a costs order if they are successful. In 2014/15 tribunals made 334 costs orders against claimants and 536 against respondents. The average costs order was £3,228.

Another change brought about via the Enterprise and Regulatory Reform Act 2013 (ERRA) introduces a new s.12A into the Employment Tribunals Act 1996, according to which, if the employer has breached any of the claimant's employment rights with "aggravating features", the employer can be ordered to pay a penalty of up to half the award made to the employee, subject to a minimum of £100 and a maximum of £5,000. The money will go to the state, not to the claimant, and rather like a parking fine, the award will be reduced by 50 per cent if the employer pays within 21 days. It will be interesting to see how often this is used and what are considered to be aggravating features. The Explanatory Notes to the legislation suggest that factors such as whether the breach was deliberate, whether it was a single incident or repeated and the size of the employer will be relevant.

1–025

After the hearing

1–026   The 2013 Rules of Procedure provide a general power for tribunals to reconsider their judgments "in the interests of justice" either of their own motion or on application of a party made within 14 days of the decision being sent out (r.70). "Reconsideration" replaces the former procedure for review, and applies not only to final hearings, but any judgments made in a preliminary hearing to determine an issue also. Previously, five grounds for review of decisions were specified, of which the interests of justice was just one. It is assumed that "in the interests of justice" is wide enough to encompass the other grounds formerly specified, but it remains to be seen whether it will be interpreted any more widely than used to be the case.

Parties have a right to appeal to the EAT within six weeks of the decision being sent out, but only on a point of law. There is no appeal on questions of fact. This has led to much debate over what is a question of fact and what is a question of law, an issue taken up elsewhere in this book (see below, paras 3–016 and 8–049). Suffice it for present purposes to say that the question is really a policy issue rather than a question of legal theory. With more than 40,000 cases a year being heard by employment tribunals, if there were many appeals the EAT would be swamped. Hence there is a clear trend to limit situations in which appeal will be possible.

Employment Appeal Tribunal (EAT)

1–027   The Employment Appeal Tribunal (EAT) was set up by the Employment Protection Act (EPA) 1975 and is governed now by the Employment Tribunals Act, Pt II and regulations thereunder. It has the same tripartite structure as an employment tribunal, save that this time it is chaired by a High Court judge and the lay members are selected on the basis of having special knowledge or experience of industrial relations either as employer or worker representatives. As with employment tribunals, the role of lay members is shrinking to nearly nothing. The power for cases to be disposed of by a judge sitting alone was introduced by TURERA, but the reforms introduced in 2013 go much further: the Employment Tribunals Act s.28(2), as amended by ERRA, provides that the default position is that cases will be heard by a judge sitting alone. The rationale for this is that since the EAT only hears appeals on questions of law, there is no need for lay representation. This argument has some strength, but the fact remains that successive Presidents of the EAT have acknowledged the important contribution of the lay members. There is provision for a judge to direct that lay members should sit, but no guidance on when that is likely to be the case. As with employment tribunals, where lay members do sit, they can in theory outvote the judge: although rare, it has happened (e.g. *Nethermere v Gardiner* (1984)).

In addition to hearing appeals from employment tribunals, the EAT also has jurisdiction over appeals from some decisions of the CAC (although not in relation to the statutory trade union recognition procedure). Procedure in the EAT is governed by the Employment Appeal Tribunal Rules 1993 (SI 1993/2854) (as amended) but is generally similar to that of employment tribunals: in particular, the overriding objective of dealing with cases justly is expressed in parallel terms (r.2A). Subject to these Rules, the EAT has power to regulate its own procedure and uses that power to issue Practice Directions. The current Practice Direction was issued in 2013 and superseded all earlier versions.

The EAT is a court of record and its decisions should be followed by inferior courts, especially employment tribunals. Different divisions of the EAT are not obliged to follow their own earlier decisions and occasionally different streams of authority can appear, which makes the task of employment tribunals more difficult. In the mid-1970s, when tribunals were coping with a sharp increase in the number of unfair dismissal cases and a host of new claims under the EPA 1975, the EAT saw its duty very much as setting guidelines on the meaning and application of the law. Unfortunately the guidelines began to be treated as if they were statutory requirements, attracting the wrath of the Court of Appeal, which mounted a counter-attack stressing the importance of the words of the statute and the limited situations in which there could be an appeal from an employment tribunal (see below, para.8–050). This development was understandable, perhaps, but given the huge number of tribunal decisions being handed down each year, there is a danger of lack of uniformity if this approach is taken too literally, a danger clearly spelt out by Lord Browne-Wilkinson when he was President of the EAT. From the EAT appeals lie to the Court of Appeal—on questions of law—and thence to the Supreme Court.

Equality and Human Rights Commission (EHRC)

The first pieces of anti-discrimination legislation passed in the 1970s (the Sex Discrimination Act 1975 (SDA) and the Race Relations Act 1976 (RRA)) set up two separate Commissions, the Equal Opportunities Commission (EOC) and the Commission for Racial Equality (CRE), to promote equality and work towards the elimination of discrimination on grounds of sex and race respectively. When legislation against disability discrimination was passed in 1995, there was a strong argument for a further Commission, which was finally set up in 1999. Even before the establishment of the Disability Rights Commission (DRC) in 1999, however, there were calls for a single commission to promote equality on the grounds that this would be more effective (and economical) than three separate commissions. The argument became stronger when the European Union adopted the Framework Employment Directive (2000/78/EC) which extended protection against discrimination to discrimination on grounds of age, religion and sexual orientation. Either there would have to be a proliferation of commissions or there would have to be an amalgamation of some kind. A further consideration was the passage of the Human Rights Act 1998, for many influential commentators argued that a Human Rights Commission was needed to ensure that the Act was effective and properly understood and applied. This raised the question of whether it should subsume a proposed single equality body or whether they should be separate and distinct.

After a two-year inquiry the Joint Parliamentary Committee on Human Rights recommended that there should be a single integrated body dealing with human rights and equality. This was finally enacted in the Equality Act 2006, which set up the Commission for Equality and Human Rights and laid out its powers. The new body came into force in October 2007, replacing the former Commissions. One of its first actions was to change the name by which it is known to the Equality and Human Rights Commission (EHRC)—with an acronym easily confused with that used for the European Convention on Human Rights (ECHR).

The Coalition Government considered that the EHRC was too large, too ambitious and too expensive, and flagged its intention to change things in a 2010 consultation, *Building a Fairer Britain*. In 2012, in the Government response to that consultation, the Government's dissatisfaction with the EHRC was spelt out and plans to reform it were articulated. At the end of 2012, the Chair and existing Board were almost totally replaced, and the EHRC was required drastically to reduce its costs. This was done by shedding 130 staff, cutting its helpline and small grants programme and reducing the use of temporary staff. The Government's stated aim is to clarify and focus the EHRC's remit and to stop its involvement in non-core activities. Some amendment of its duties was made by ERRA, as discussed below.

1–029   Under Pt 1 of the Equality Act 2006 (EqA 2006) the EHRC consists of 10–15 Commissioners and has responsibility for promoting equal opportunities and human rights and awareness of good practice in relation to equality, diversity and human rights. In addition to taking over the duties and powers of the existing Commissions, the EHRC also covers equal opportunities in relation to sexual orientation, religion or belief and age. It has a duty to monitor the effectiveness of the equality and human rights legislation (EqA 2006 s.11) and to report on a quinquennial basis to the government on progress towards a society congruent with its duties to promote equality and human rights (EqA 2006 s.12, as amended by ERRA). Like its predecessor Commissions, the EHRC has general duties to work towards the elimination of discrimination, to promote equality of opportunity and to keep under review the working of the legislation (equality law is discussed generally in Ch.2, below). The wider functions with which it was initially invested have been stripped away under the Coalition Government's reforms. Its "mission statement" in s.3 of EqA 2006, which enjoins the EHRC to exercise its functions with a view to developing a society which respects the dignity and worth of individuals and groups and which understands and values diversity, equality and human rights, was considered for abolition, but survives for the time being. Not so the novel duty under EqA 2006 s.10, which required the EHRC to promote good relations and good practice between groups and to work to eliminate group discrimination. "Groups" are defined in s.10 not merely as comprising a class of people sharing a characteristic, but also as including smaller groups sharing more than one protected characteristic. This provision for the first time showed some recognition of the problems of multiple discrimination—that is, the greatly increased difficulties faced by people who fall into more than one of the protected categories. While the definition of "groups" remains in EqA 2006 s.10, the duties on the EHRC to promote good relations, etc, were abolished by ERRA.

In order to carry out its duties, the EHRC has powers to undertake research and educational activities, and, like Acas, may issue codes of practice which must be taken into account by tribunals and courts in any cases where it is relevant (EqA 2006 s.15(4)). With the coming into force of the Equality Act 2010 (EqA 2010), consolidating and extending all existing equality legislation, the EHRC published a new Code of Practice, together with extensive guidance designed for different groups of users. It should be borne in mind, however, that it is only the Code which has to be taken into account in legal proceedings. The EHRC may give assistance with proceedings brought under the anti-discrimination legislation, usually where there is a question of principle, and it has expressly been given capacity to institute or intervene in judicial review proceedings (EqA 2006 s.30).

Investigations and inquiries

The EOC and CRE had power to conduct formal investigations either where   **1–030** they thought it fit to do so, or if asked to do so by the Secretary of State. These could be general investigations, for example looking at a particular sector of industry, or named-person investigations. The situations where named-person investigations could be conducted were cut down by the restrictive interpretation of the House of Lords in *R v CRE, ex p Prestige Group plc* (1984), where it was held that the CRE could not embark on a formal investigation into a named person or company unless it had at least some grounds for suspecting that unlawful acts were taking place—which would be difficult to come by without some investigation. This was dealt with in EqA 2006 by giving the EHRC power to conduct inquiries and investigations. Inquiries, under s.16, can be thematic (such as looking at the causes of unequal outcomes), sectoral (such as looking at employment patterns in particular industries) or may relate to one or more named parties. However, if any named party is suspected of committing an unlawful act, the inquiry must avoid any reference to this and an investigation under EqA 2006 s.20 should start instead. It will still be necessary for the EHRC to have a belief that a named person or organisation has committed an unlawful act before embarking on an investigation. Where the EHRC concludes, following an investigation, that an unlawful act has taken place, it can issue the relevant person with an unlawful act notice in accordance with EqA 2006 s.21. This is broadly equivalent to the former power of the previous Commissions to issue non-discrimination notices. However, the EqA 2006 goes further, in that it allows the EHRC to put a requirement to develop an action plan in an unlawful act notice (ss.21(4) and 22) as well as giving it power to enter binding agreements not to take legal action provided that the discriminator agrees to refrain from further discrimination and to take such other actions as may be specified.

Public sector equality duty

The Race Relations (Amendment) Act 2000 (RRAA), passed as a result of the   **1–031** Stephen Lawrence Inquiry, introduced a wide general duty for public authorities not only to eliminate unlawful discrimination but also to promote equality of opportunity and good relations between different racial groups, along with specific duties for identified public authorities. EqA 2006 extended this public sector duty to the additional grounds of sex and disability, but not to sexual orientation, religion or belief or age. EqA 2010, as part of the harmonisation of all strands of equality legislation, provides for a single public sector equality duty, applicable to all the protected characteristics (except for marriage and civil partnership—see below, para.2–017), which replaced the previous duties from April 2011. The EHRC has an important role in the enforcement of the public sector equality duty, in that it has powers to assess whether a public authority is carrying out its duty properly and can issue a compliance notice, requiring specific action, if it forms the opinion that a public authority is not performing its duty (EqA 2006 ss.31–32). Apart from the EHRC's powers, the only other way that the public sector duty can be enforced is by judicial review proceedings, either brought by the EHRC or by any section of the public which can demonstrate a sufficient interest to have legal standing for this purpose.

The general public sector equality duty, set out in s.149 of the EqA 2010, requires public authorities (listed in Sch.19 to that Act) to have due regard, in the performance of their functions, to the need to eliminate unlawful discrimination, harassment and victimisation; to advance equality of opportunity; and to foster good relations between different groups. This applies to any function carried out by the public authority or by private sector bodies acting on its behalf. "Having due regard" to something does not necessarily indicate that action will result, but the fact that the Act now refers to advancing equality, rather than just promoting it, is thought to make the duty stronger. Under EqA 2010 s.153 ministers are given powers to impose specific duties on particular public authorities by regulation.

In 2012 the Coalition Government appointed an independent steering group to review whether or not the public sector equality duty was operating as it was intended to do. As the duty had only been in force for little more than a year, this review might be regarded as premature. The steering group's report in 2013 noted that there was a tendency on the part of public sector organisations to carry out little more than a tick-box exercise, and that there was a need for clearer guidance on what actions were necessary and in order to reduce unnecessary bureaucracy. A full review of the duty is scheduled for 2016, once it has been in force for five years.

Socio-economic duty

1–032 There is plenty of evidence that social status and levels of family income have a major impact on people's life chances and contribute greatly to social inequality. It has become recognised increasingly that socio-economic disadvantage coupled with membership of a group disadvantaged through, for example, ethnicity, gender or disability leads to more than double disadvantage—rather, each is likely to compound the effects of the other. For this reason, a major change in the EqA 2010 was the introduction of a positive duty for public authorities (listed in EqA 2010 s.1(3) and (4)) which would apply when they are making decisions of a strategic nature about how to exercise their functions. Section 1 states that, when making such decisions, public authorities should "have due regard to the desirability of exercising them in a way that is designed to reduce the inequalities of outcome which result from socio-economic disadvantage" (EqA 2010 s.1(1)).

It will be noted that, as with the public sector duty, this would only require authorities to "have due regard"—not actually to do anything; also, that they would only have to contemplate the desirability of addressing socio-economic disadvantage. Nonetheless, the socio-economic duty was potentially a significant departure from previous law in its recognition that achievement of equality does not take place in a vacuum devoid of economic and social pressures. Its inclusion in the Act was, however, highly controversial and the Coalition Government decided against implementing it, and considered repealing it. For the time being, however, it remains on the statute book, but it is not in force. Should it ever be implemented, it would be up to the EHRC to enforce it, as for the public sector duty described above.

Human rights

Under s.9 of EqA 2006 the EHRC has duties to promote awareness, understanding and protection of human rights, their importance, and good practice in relation to human rights. The human rights referred to are the Convention rights—those rights under the European Convention on Human Rights (ECHR) which are enforceable in the United Kingdom by virtue of the Human Rights Act 1998 (HRA). These are reproduced in HRA Sch.1: those which are most relevant in the field of employment law are the right to a fair trial (ECHR art.6—see para.8–039), the right to privacy (art.8: see para.4–024), freedom of thought, conscience and religion (art.9: see para.2–052); freedom of expression (art.10); freedom of association (art.11: see Ch.10) and the general prohibition on discrimination (art.14: see para.2–002).

1–033

The ECHR is a treaty emanating from the Council of Europe, a society of 47 European democracies. This Council of Europe is not to be confused with the European Council, which is the main policy-making body of the European Union. Until the HRA 1998 the ECHR was enforceable in the United Kingdom only by taking individual action in the European Court of Human Rights, which was an expensive and long-drawn-out process. The HRA 1998 provides for the enforcement of Convention rights in two ways. First, s.3 articulates a general duty to interpret all legislation consistently with the Convention so far as possible. If an interpretation consistent with the Convention is not possible, the court has no power to set aside legislation, but when the case reaches the level of the High Court, Court of Appeal or Supreme Court a declaration of incompatibility can be made, which leads to a fast-track procedure for government review of the law. Secondly, s.6 imposes a duty on public authorities to ensure that their actions are compatible with Convention rights.

Section 6 means that employees of public authorities can enforce Convention rights directly against their employers, but this does not apply to anyone employed by a private sector employer. There is some parallel here with the concepts of vertical and horizontal direct effect in EU law, where a worker employed by an emanation of the state may be able to rely on the terms of a directive while a private sector worker cannot. It is likely that if a public worker succeeded in a claim that some facet of employment law was inconsistent with Convention rights there would be political pressure to reform the law generally. However, the position for employees in the private sector may not be so different in practice. Since courts and tribunals have a duty to interpret the law in accordance with Convention rights, private sector workers may gain the indirect protection of Convention rights provided that they can frame a claim based on a separate cause of action (*X v Y* (2004)).

1–034   The Conservative administration elected in 2015 has some so far inchoate proposals to repeal the Human Rights Act and to replace it with a "British Bill of Rights". It is as yet unclear what is proposed, or indeed, whether the Government fully understands the issues involved.

European Union (EU)

1–035   The United Kingdom joined the then European Economic Community (EEC) on 1 January 1973 by accession to the Treaty of Rome, the fundamental treaty underpinning the organisation. This was given effect in British law by the European Communities Act 1972. British membership has transformed the employment law scene as will be apparent throughout this book. While the initial treaties constituting the EEC were aimed at economic goals, it was always the intention of the founders that the ultimate objective should be a closer political union between the Member States with aspirations to more than economic cooperation. A major step towards this was taken by the Single European Act agreed by the Member States in 1986 and implemented in the United Kingdom by the European Communities (Amendment) Act 1986. This extended the areas in which the EEC could legislate to social policy (including employment) and also increased the use of qualified majority voting by allowing the process to be used for measures designed to harmonise the functioning of the internal market. In employment law this was particularly important because, while unanimity was still required for general employment law matters, majority voting could be used for health and safety measures. In the face of a Conservative administration in the United Kingdom during the 1980s and up to 1997 which opposed almost every improvement to working life proposed by the European Commission, it was only by an extended interpretation of what amounted to health and safety legislation (e.g. the Pregnant Workers Directive 1992, below, para.6–006 and the Working Time Directive 1993, below, para.6–043) that any progress was possible.

The next stage was the Treaty on European Union (the Treaty of Maastricht) in 1992, under which the EEC became the European Community (EC) and the European Union (EU) was set up. From the point of view of employment law the main importance of the negotiations leading to the Treaty on European Union was the promulgation of an annexed Protocol containing the Agreement on Social Policy. In 1989 all Member States, with the notable exception of the United Kingdom, agreed upon a Community Charter of the Fundamental Social Rights of Workers. The Social Charter, as it became known, had no legal status as such, but was a very clear indication of the way that most Member States wanted to see social policy developing and a potential source for directives and other EC instruments. At the Maastricht negotiations, proposals to include the Charter within the Treaty of Rome were blocked by the veto of the United Kingdom, with the result that the other members added the Protocol to the Treaty on European

Union stating their intention to implement it if necessary by directives applying only to those signatories (this happened with the European Works Councils Directive, below, para.5–026).

The Treaty on European Union made provision for a further Inter-Governmental Conference to take place to consider amendments to the Treaty of Rome. By the time of the final negotiations in the summer of 1997, the Conservative administration had been replaced by the new Labour Government which had committed itself to accepting the Social Charter. So the Treaty of Amsterdam in 1997 revoked the United Kingdom opt-out and included the terms of the Agreement on Social Policy in the Treaty of Rome. In 2001 the Treaty on European Union and the Treaty of Rome were merged by the Treaty of Nice, which came into force in February 2003. Shortly after this, proposals were made for an EU Constitution, which proved highly controversial because of the infringement of state sovereignty implied. However, some reforms were essential, especially with the rapid enlargement of the EU to 28 Member States. Many of the reforms were contained in the Treaty of Lisbon, agreed in 2007 but not in force until 2009 when ratification by Member States was completed. As a result, the EU has legal personality and all references to the European Community are dropped. The amended Treaty of Rome became known as the Treaty on the Functioning of the European Union (TFEU) and the Maastricht Treaty became the Treaty on European Union (TEU).

In 2000 the EU adopted a Charter of Fundamental Rights which restated its commitment to human rights as laid out in the ECHR and also contained a chapter (arts 20–26) on equality. With the ratification of the Lisbon Treaty in 2009, the Charter was put on a legal footing: TEU art.6(1) states that the Charter has the same legal status as the treaties, but cannot be taken to extend the competence of the EU. Because of concerns that this might nonetheless lead to an impact on domestic law, the United Kingdom and Poland insisted on an opt-out, to the effect that nothing in the Charter should allow the CJEU or a domestic court to find that any UK laws or administrative practices are inconsistent with the fundamental rights and freedoms in the Charter. Nevertheless, the Court of Appeal has since held that primary legislation which is in conflict with Charter Rights should be disapplied (*Benkharbouche v Embassy of Sudan* (2015)). **1–036**

Membership of the EU carries with it obligations to implement in British law the requirements of the Treaties and directives and to submit to the jurisdiction of the Court of Justice of the European Union (CJEU) as final arbiter on the interpretation of EU law. Member States cannot always be relied upon to implement directives promptly or properly, and so quite early on the CJEU developed the doctrine of direct effect, meaning that Community legislation can in some circumstances have immediate effect in Member States even if implementing legislation has not been passed or is incorrect. In *Van Gend en Loos* (1963) the CJEU held that Treaty Articles would have direct effect provided that they were clear, unconditional and did not require further implementation. Most importantly for sex discrimination law, in *Defrenne v Sabena* (1976) it was held that what is now TFEU art.157(1) stipulating equal pay for men and women for equal work had direct effect (see below, Ch.2). The first cases on direct effect involved what is called vertical direct effect, meaning that Treaty Articles could be relied upon in actions involving the state, since it would be wrong to allow the state to benefit from its own failure to implement EU law. However, in *Defrenne v Sabena* it was held that TFEU art.157(1) also had horizontal direct effect, meaning that a claimant could rely on it as against another private citizen.

In *Van Duyn v Home Office* (1974) the CJEU extended the doctrine of direct effect to directives, again subject to their being sufficiently precise and unconditional and not requiring further implementation: this can be relied on by individuals once the deadline for implementing the directive has passed. Although *Marshall v Southampton and South West Hampshire AHA* (1986) (another sex discrimination case) made it clear that this was limited to vertical, not horizontal, direct effect it also indicated that the concept of "the state" should be construed widely for the purposes of vertical direct effect, to include the state as employer as well as governing authority, and extended to embrace "emanations of the state". Thus, in that case, a health authority responsible for managing hospitals and employing hospital staff was held to be an emanation of the state and the claimant was able to rely directly on the Equal Treatment Directive (76/207/EEC) against it. In *Foster v British Gas* (1990) (also concerned with sex discrimination) the CJEU defined an emanation of the state as including:

> "a body, whatever its legal form, which has been made responsible, pursuant to a measure adopted by the state, for providing a public service under the control of the state and has for that purpose special powers beyond those which result from the normal rules applicable in relations between individuals."

On that basis the House of Lords held that British Gas was an emanation of the state (*Foster v British Gas* (1991)).

1–037   What happens if there is a conflict between British law and EU law and the claimant cannot rely on direct effect of the EU law? Since EU law is supreme, in *Von Colson v Land Nordrhein Westfalen* (1984) the CJEU set out the duty of national courts to take EU law into account in interpreting national laws and to interpret them in accordance with EU law so far as possible. In *Marleasing SA v La Comercial Internacional de Alimentación* (1990) it was made clear that this applied to national laws which preceded the relevant EU measure as well as those made after it (which could be assumed to have been intended to implement it). In *Inter-Environnement Wallonie ASBL v Region Wallonie* (1997) the CJEU held that during the transposition period for a directive a Member State should not take any measures liable seriously to compromise the result prescribed by the directive. This principle was extended with stunning effect in *Mangold v Helm* (2006) where the CJEU held that Germany should set aside a statutory provision conflicting with the Framework Employment Directive (2000/78/EC) on age discrimination even though the period for transposition of that part of the Directive had not expired. In these ways EU legislation can have indirect effects even if it cannot be used directly.

The possibility of British legislation being subject to judicial review to check its compliance with EU law was accepted in *R v Secretary of State for Employment, ex p EOC* (1995) where the House of Lords granted a declaration that a statutory provision excluding part-time workers from employment protection rights contravened art.141, the Equal Pay Directive (75/117/EEC) and the Equal Treatment Directive (76/207/EEC). Where there is doubt as to whether or not EU law is applicable to a case arising in British courts, or there is doubt as to the meaning of EU law, the court or tribunal hearing the case can refer it to the CJEU. This can be done at any level, from employment tribunal to the Supreme Court. The CJEU will answer the questions put by the national court and the case then returns to the original forum for decision in the light of the CJEU's advice.

Where British law is clearly not in accordance with directly effective EU law and it is not possible for the British court to interpret its way out of the difficulty, then the British law must be set aside, even if it was passed by Parliament after the Community law was made (*R v Secretary of State for Transport, ex p Factortame* (1990)). If a directive cannot be relied on by the claimant because it would involve giving it horizontal effect against a private party, then an individual may have an action against the state for any losses caused (*Francovich v Italian Republic* (1992)) provided that the directive was intended to confer rights on individuals. The first and greatest impact of EU law in employment was in the field of sex discrimination and equal pay, but it has subsequently pervaded nearly every aspect of the employment relationship. Since the Treaty of European Union there has been a procedure whereby directives in the employment field can be adopted on the joint recommendation of representatives of workers and employers ("the social partners") and, as has been seen, alterations to the Treaty of Rome have greatly extended the areas in which the EU is competent to legislate. It is therefore to be expected that EU law will continue to be an important source of new developments for British employment law in years to come—provided that the United Kingdom remains a member. The referendum on this will be held in June 2016.

International Labour Organisation (ILO)

The International Labour Organisation (ILO) was established in 1919 by the Treaty of Versailles as an organ of the League of Nations. However, to indicate its independence from the League of Nations, that part of the treaty was detached and reformed as the separate Constitution of the ILO. Since the Second World War it has been a separate agency with a special relationship with the United Nations. It has a tripartite structure with representatives of employers, workers and governments. The mission of the ILO is to promote fair working conditions in all countries. Its main method of doing this is by the adoption of Conventions and Recommendations. ILO Conventions are treaties on particular issues (such as freedom of association, non-discrimination, minimum wage protection) which, once agreed by the ILO, are opened for signature by Member States. Once a state has ratified a treaty, it has the usual obligations under international law to abide by the treaty—which may mean that it has a duty to change municipal law to give effect to it.

While there is no body comparable to the CJEU to enforce compliance, states have obligations to report regularly on their compliance with the Conventions

1–038

which they have ratified. The reports are considered by the ILO's Committee of Experts, which may, in case of non-compliance, specifically draw attention to this in its report by means of a "special paragraph", which should be severely embarrassing, especially to a country such as the United Kingdom which would consider itself as a leader in setting global standards, and should therefore result in action to remedy the defect. After all, since states are under no legal compulsion to accede to treaties in the first place, they should be expected to abide by the obligations which they voluntarily undertake. As will be seen, however, in later chapters, this has not always been the case for the United Kingdom, especially in relation to trade union internal affairs and industrial action.

In the rare event of a state wishing to renege from standards which it has previously agreed, it must withdraw from (denounce) the treaty, usually after giving a stipulated period of notice. Generally a change in the political complexion of the government in the United Kingdom has not led to a change in policy on these international obligations. However, in the 1980s legislation of the Conservative Government was held by the ILO to be in breach of accepted conventions on more than one occasion and a number of conventions were denounced.

Low Pay Commission

1–039 The Labour Government originally set up the Low Pay Commission in 1997 to assist it in implementing its manifesto commitment to legislating for a national minimum wage. At that stage it had no legal status, but under the National Minimum Wage Act 1998 (ss.5–8 and Sch.1) it was put on a statutory footing. The Low Pay Commission consists of a chair and eight members appointed by the Secretary of State and having an appropriate balance of members with trade union and employer association experience as well as independent members. The Government largely followed the Commission's advice in setting the initial national minimum wage in April 1999 (see below, para.7–053) and has continued on the whole to do so since.

 # Further Reading

Virtually all of the public bodies discussed in this chapter issue Annual Reports, which are an invaluable source of information about their work and their perceptions of it. These are available from their websites, along with other useful data:

Acas	http://www.acas.org.uk
CAC	http://www.gov.uk/government/organisations/central-arbitration-committee
Certification Officer	http://www.gov.uk/government/organisations/certification-officer
Equality and Human Rights Commission	http://www.equalityhumanrights.com
European Union	http://europa.eu
ILO	http://www.ilo.org

Low Pay Commission   *http://www.gov.uk/government/organisations/*
                                   low-pay-commission

❏ L. Dickens and A.C. Neal (2006), *The Changing Institutional Face of British Employment Relations*, Kluwer Law International
❏ L. Dickens (2012), *Making Employment Rights Effective*, Hart Publishing
❏ P. Davies and M. Freedland (2007), *Towards a Flexible Labour Market*, OUP
❏ B. Towers and W. Brown (2000), *Employee Relations in Britain: 25 Years of ACAS*, Blackwell
❏ Sir Michael Burton (2005), "The Employment Appeal Tribunal October 2002– July 2005", 34 ILJ 273
❏ N. Busby and M. McDermont (2012), "Workers, Marginalised Voices and the Employment Tribunal System: Some Preliminary Findings", 41(2) ILJ 166
❏ T. Choudhury (2006), "The Commission for Equality and Human Rights: Designing the Big Tent", 13 *Maastricht Journal* 351
❏ C. O'Cinneide (2007), "The Commission for Equality and Human Rights: a New Institution for New and Uncertain Times", 36 ILJ 141
❏ B. Hepple, (2013), "Back to the Future: Employment Law under the Coalition Government", 42(3) ILJ 203
❏ C. La Hovary (2013), "Showdown at the ILO? A Historical Perspective on the Employers' Group's 2012 Challenge to the Right to Strike", 42(4) ILJ 338
❏ J.K. MacMillan (1999), "Employment Tribunals: Philosophies and Practicalities", 28 ILJ 33
❏ *Modernising labour law to meet the challenges of the 21ˢᵗ century*, (2006) EU Commission, (COM(2006) 708 final)
❏ *Resolving Workplace Disputes*, BIS Consultation Paper (January 2011) and Government response November 2011

2. Equality Law

Key Points

This chapter:
- Explains the EU and human rights law background to equality law
- Highlights that anyone with a contract for personal service is protected from discrimination—not just employees
- Looks in detail at the "protected characteristics" of age, gender reassignment, marriage and civil partnership, pregnancy and maternity, race, religion or belief, sex and sexual orientation
- Examines the concept of direct discrimination
- Explains the conditions for indirect discrimination
- Explains the concept of harassment
- Explains the concept of victimisation
- Examines disability discrimination, noting how it differs from other protected grounds
- Looks at when an employer will be vicariously liable for discriminatory actions by employees and others
- Outlines the remedies for discrimination

***

Introduction

The principle of freedom of contract generally means that you are free to enter contracts with whoever you like on whatever terms you agree. In fact, much of employment law is about regulating the terms which can be agreed between the parties to a contract of employment, mainly in order to protect employees, as we will see in later chapters. Equality law represents a major inroad on both elements of the principle of freedom of contract, since it means that employers may not refuse to enter an employment relationship because the worker has one of a number of protected characteristics, and also that there must be no unlawful discrimination in the terms and conditions of the contract.

2–001

There are two reasons for looking at equality law at this stage. The first is that it applies even before the employment relationship has been formed. Employers must be careful not to discriminate unlawfully during the whole recruitment process, from advertisement to appointment. Secondly, while most employment law focuses on employers and employees, equality law applies to a wider range of employment relationships than just contracts of employment.

Equality is accepted as a fundamental human right, recognised in all the major international treaties and conventions on human rights. Thus the Universal Declaration of Human Rights 1948 art.2, states:

"Everyone is entitled to all the rights and freedoms set forth in this Declaration without distinction of any kind, such as race, colour, sex, language, religion, political or other opinion, national or social origin, property, birth or other status."

2–002   This is echoed by art.14 of the European Convention on Human Rights 1950, which is in similar terms but also includes the ground of "association with a national minority". In 2000 the European Union adopted a Charter of Fundamental Rights which includes a chapter on Equality. Article 21(1) states:

"Any discrimination based on any ground such as sex, race, colour, ethnic or social origin, genetic features, language, religion or belief, political or any other opinion, membership of a national minority, property, birth, disability, age or sexual orientation shall be prohibited."

When the Lisbon Treaty was ratified in 2009 the Charter was given equivalent legal standing to the TEU and TFEU; however, it does not create any new legal rights and its importance is generally seen as increasing the visibility of fundamental rights, especially for citizens of the European Union, as showing the direction in which EU policy will develop, and most of all, in its use as an aid to interpretation by the CJEU.

That all people should have equal human rights is easy enough to understand, but what does the principle of equality mean in relation to employment? Originally the law attempted only to prohibit discrimination on some (but not all) of the grounds listed in the treaties. The idea was to remove the barriers to participation by preventing factors such as sex or race being taken into account in employment decisions. If this were done, it should ensure that workers had an equal chance to compete for the best job opportunities on the basis of merit. "Equality" in this sense meant equal opportunity, and equal opportunity was to be established by eliminating consideration of irrelevant factors from the decision-making process.

2–003   The prohibition on discrimination could be supported by purely economic considerations as well as by an appeal to moral values, in that removing the influence of irrelevant factors should ensure greater economic efficiency and better functioning of the labour market. Indeed, the reason for including the original version of TFEU art.157(1) in the Treaty of Rome, which stipulates that women must receive equal terms and conditions with men, was economic rather than being prompted by high-minded principle. Only some of the six founding Member States had laws providing for equal pay for men and women. Those that did feared that they would be uncompetitive compared with those which allowed women to be used as cheap labour—hence the requirement that Member States should ensure that men and women should have equal terms for work of equal value (see further, Ch.7).

However, since then the European Union has moved on to espouse a more ambitious concept of EU citizenship, reflected in the shared values set out in the Charter of Fundamental Rights and aiming at an ideal of inclusiveness which would celebrate diversity and enable all EU residents to participate equally in society. At the same time, the debate around equality has shifted as the realisation has grown that preventing discrimination on grounds of irrelevant characteristics is not enough to ensure equal participation in the labour market. For example, when the Equal Pay Act 1970 came into force in 1975, the gap between the average pay of full-time women and full-time men was 25 per cent. Forty years on, the gap has only narrowed to 15 per cent and if the hourly pay of all employees, including part-timers, is considered the gap is still nearly 19 per cent. Unemployment rates of minority ethnic groups remain stubbornly higher than among the white majority and members of minorities remain largely invisible in senior positions in the public sector and even more so in the private sector. People with disabilities are far more likely to be unemployed than non-disabled people and are paid less when they do get work. Prejudice continues to limit employment opportunities for gay people and those who belong to identifiable religious minorities.

These facts help to explain why there has come to be a greater emphasis on the principle of equality as entailing equality of outcome, or substantive equality, meaning that there must also be a focus on the results of employment decisions. Equality in this sense is seen as only being achieved if all groups are getting a proportionate or fair share of the opportunities available. The underpinning justification for this kind of approach to equality is essentially the idea of equal participation, and this means that it is possible to sidestep some of the difficult arguments about merit, which focus on whether or not the process for awarding the opportunity has been fair and transparent but which tend to overlook the problematic nature of the concept of "merit" itself. It is also an approach which justifies a requirement to make adjustments to meet the needs of particular groups in order to enable them to participate on an equal footing. The best example of this is in relation to workers with disabilities. There are situations where a worker's disability will impede her capacity to perform some aspects of her work, even though it does not prevent her doing the job well overall and perhaps excelling in other aspects. However, without a law compelling the employer to consider whether she could be the best candidate for the post, provided some adjustments were made for her disability, she might be unlikely to be appointed. In these circumstances, the overriding social interest in assisting people with disabilities to participate as full members of society, including contributing in the workplace, justifies the law requiring employers to make reasonable adjustments to enable this to happen.

This shift in emphasis from formal equality of opportunity to substantive **2–004** equality of outcome is also evidenced in the positive duties to promote equality in the Equality Act 2006 (EqA 2006), and it provides the reason why this area of law is now better characterised as "equality law" rather than just as "discrimination law"—and it is notable that this language is also now adopted by the legislation.

Influence of EU law

2–005 Membership of the European Union has been without doubt the most important and dynamic influence on British equality law. Originally this was only in the field of sex discrimination and it resulted from the original art.119 of the Treaty of Rome, which provided that Member States must maintain "the principle that men and women should receive equal pay for equal work" (now TFEU art.157(1)). This article may seem to be mainly relevant with regard to achieving parity in terms and conditions once people are actually employed, but it acted as the springboard for the Equal Treatment Directive of 1976 (76/207/EEC) which required implementation of the principle of equal treatment for men and women not only in relation to terms and conditions of employment but also recruitment, training, promotion and dismissal. Article 119/TFEU art.157(1) was held to have direct horizontal and vertical effect in *Defrenne v Sabena* (1976), meaning that litigants can rely on it to found claims in any British court or tribunal even if it has not been fully implemented by national legislation (see above, para.1–036). The importance of directly effective EU law is dramatically illustrated by *Marshall v Southampton & SW Hants AHA* (1986), where a female dietician claimed that the health authority's policy of requiring women to retire at 60 while men retired at 65 was in breach of the Equal Treatment Directive (76/207/EEC). Under British legislation this difference was permissible and it was thought to be consistent with EU law, which allowed exceptions in relation to death or retirement. However, the CJEU held that a contractual term about retirement ages was a term about dismissal, which meant that it was subject to the requirement of equal treatment in the Equal Treatment Directive. While the CJEU held that the Equal Treatment Directive had only vertical, not horizontal, direct effect, this was enough for the claimant, as her employer was considered to be an "emanation of the state". The result was that the Government had to act swiftly to equalise retirement ages for women and men through the Sex Discrimination Act 1986.

While British membership of the European Union had an immediate and dramatic impact in combating sex discrimination, it had no direct impact on other kinds of discrimination until more recently. This was because there was no legislative base in the Treaty of Rome to allow the European Union to act on other forms of discrimination. However, in 1997 the Treaty of Amsterdam amended the Treaty of Rome by introducing what is now TFEU art.19, empowering the European Union to take action against discrimination "based on sex, racial or ethnic origin, religion or belief, disability, age or sexual orientation". This was swiftly followed by two directives based on the article. The Framework Employment Directive (2000/78/EC) required Member States to legislate against discrimination in employment on grounds of religion or belief, disability, age or sexual orientation. Member States were given until the end of 2006 to implement the provisions relating to disability and age discrimination, but the rest had to be in place by December 2003. The Employment Equality (Religion or Belief) Regulations 2003 and the Employment Equality (Sexual Orientation) Regulations 2003 implemented the Directive in relation to those grounds and the disability provisions were dealt with by the Disability Discrimination Act 1995 (Amendment) Regulations 2003. The Government took full advantage of the extra time given to implement the age discrimination provisions, with the Employment Equality (Age) Regulations 2006 coming into force only on 1 October 2006. The Race Directive (2000/43/EC) covers all discrimination on grounds of racial or ethnic origin, including not only employment but also discrimination in spheres such as social security, education and the supply of goods and services. It was implemented by the Race Relations Act 1976 (Amendment) Regulations 2003. In 2010, in the final days of the Labour administration, all the different equality enactments were finally brought together in a single Equality Act 2010 (EqA 2010), to which reference will be made hereafter.

Since the two landmark directives in 2000 there have been further amendments to sex equality law. The Equal Treatment Amendment Directive (2002/73/EC) amended the Equal Treatment Directive (76/207/EEC) to align it with the Framework Employment Directive and the Race Directive, and the Goods and Services Directive (2004/113/EC) extended the principle of sex equality to the provision of goods and services, although further discussion of this is beyond the scope of this book. Finally, in 2009 the Recast Equal Treatment Directive (2006/54/EC) came into force, replacing, inter alia, the 1976 Equal Treatment Directive and the 2002 Equal Treatment Amendment Directive. In what follows, the replacement articles are referred to in preference to the former provisions, although it should be noted that the language is not identical in all cases. This is because the Recast Equal Treatment Directive not only consolidates the relevant EU legislation, but also incorporates established principles from the case-law of the CJEU.

Influence of the ECHR

As noted already, art.14 of the European Convention on Human Rights (ECHR) also prohibits discrimination, and over a wider range of protected grounds than EU law. What is its legal effect? Unfortunately, so far as equality law is concerned, art.14 promises more than it delivers, because it is not a freestanding Convention right but only prohibits discrimination in relation to the enjoyment of the other rights and freedoms in the ECHR. Protocol 12 to the Convention, in force from 2005 for those states which have ratified it, would make the prohibition on art.14 discrimination into a free-standing right—but to date the United Kingdom has not even signed Protocol 12, much less ratified it. **2–006**

As a result of the HRA s.6 (see above, para.1–033) the jurisprudence of the European Court of Human Rights is influential in the interpretation wherever claims involving Convention rights are being considered. In relation to equality law, ECHR art.8 is relevant in relation to sexual orientation and art.9 in relation to religion or belief, as discussed below.

The Equality Act 2010, most of which came into force in October 2010, brings together all existing legislation on discrimination in employment, meaning that it no longer makes sense to look at, for example, sex discrimination and race discrimination on their own. The rest of this chapter will first look at the scope of the legislation—who and what is covered, and then at the "protected characteristics"—the grounds on which it is unlawful to discriminate. The various forms of unlawful discrimination are then considered, before looking at forms of liability and remedies. Disability discrimination is dealt with separately from the other grounds, as it has a number of specific differences from the general scheme. Similarly, as equal pay for men and women is still dealt with separately from other forms of discrimination in the Equality Act 2010, this is held over to Ch.7.

2–007   There is room for argument as to how far existing case-law on the previous enactments remains relevant in relation to the Equality Act 2010. Much of the Act consolidates the previous statutes and statutory regulations, but there are important differences and the wording of some existing provisions has changed in small but possibly significant ways. The preamble to the Act states that it makes provision, inter alia, "to reform and harmonise equality law and restate the greater part of the enactments relating to discrimination and harassment . . ."—which is not much of an aid to interpretation, although it may be possible to take account of what was said in Parliament when the Act was being debated in accordance with the principles in *Pepper v Hart* (1993). In addition, the EHRC has published a Code of Practice on Employment, which must be taken into account by any court or tribunal in proceedings where it is relevant (EqA 2006 s.15(4)). In what follows, existing case-law is referred to where it is considered that the law remains the same and any differences or possible differences are discussed where appropriate.

Scope of equality law

Who is covered?

2–008   The EqA 2010 provides protection for those in "employment", defined in s.83 of the Act to cover not only employees (i.e. those working under a contract of service: see below, Ch.3) and apprentices, but also anyone who is employed under, or applies to be employed under, "a contract personally to do work". This formulation differs very slightly from the former legislative definitions, but there is no alteration in meaning. In *Mirror Group v Gunning* (1986) the Court of Appeal held that the test for a contract personally to do any work was whether the dominant purpose of the contract involved a personal obligation to perform work. In that case the respondent had applied for the distributorship of the appellant's newspapers which had become vacant on the retirement of her father. She claimed that she had been rejected on grounds of sex. The Court of Appeal held that the dominant purpose of the distributorship contract was the efficient distribution of newspapers rather than a requirement to perform work, and that even if the contract required work, it was largely irrelevant who did it, and so it could not be said to require a personal obligation to work. The Court of Appeal also held that the reference to "any work" referred to the type of work rather than the quantity so that a personal obligation to perform a very small amount of work would not be enough to bring a contract within this category. The "dominant purpose" test received some criticism in *Mingeley v Pennock and Ivory* (2004) but was said by the Court of Appeal to be well established and therefore to be followed. The claimant in that case, a private hire cab driver, failed to get his race discrimination case off the ground because his contract with the taxi firm allowed him complete freedom to choose when to work or, indeed, whether to work at all. In these circumstances the Court of Appeal held that he had no obligation to perform work and thus could not bring himself within the definition of employment—although they expressed doubts as to whether Parliament would have intended to exclude this kind of situation.

Although mutuality of obligation (to provide work and to do work) is increasingly important in identifying a contract of employment (see para.3–007), the EAT held in *Windle v Secretary of State for Justice* (2014) that it is not essential to identifying a contract personally to do work. Thus a series of discrete contracts could all be contracts personally to do work even if not linked under an overall global or "umbrella" contract.

A more significant flaw with the "dominant purpose" test was revealed in *Jivraj v Hashwani* (2011), where an arbitration clause in a contract stipulated that the arbitrator should be a member of the Ismaili community. One party later argued that the clause was invalid because it discriminated on grounds of religion. The Supreme Court held that an arbitrator was not employed under a contract personally to do work. While the dominant purpose test was, in their view, one way of identifying a contract personally to do work, it did not address whether the person was "employed under" such a contract. Drawing on the CJEU's discussion of the employment relationship in *Allonby v Accrington & Rossendale College* (2004) the Supreme Court held that "employment under" a contract entailed some element of subordination, so that the worker could be said to be under the direction of the employer. Although appointed by the parties, an arbitrator is expected to exercise independent judgment, and thus the contract lacked that element of subordination (see also *Halawi v WDFG UK Ltd* (2015)).

Agency workers are rarely considered to be in any kind of contractual relationship with the agency's client or end-user of their services (*James v Greenwich BC* (2008): see para.3–018) and thus may not usually claim to be "in employment" for the purposes of bringing a discrimination claim against the end-user with whom they have been placed (*Muschett v HM Prison Service* (2010)). However, under EqA 2010 s.41, a principal may not discriminate against a contract worker in the same way as an employer may not discriminate against someone in employment. This is apt to protect some agency workers, although the contract worker must be employed by the agency in order get protection, by virtue of s.41(5)(a) (carried over from the previous law). In *Burton v Higham* (2003) temporary agency workers were held by the EAT to have contracts personally to perform work for the agency and this was sufficient for the purposes of the section.

2–009

Where the EqA 2010 s.41 is applicable, it may be expected that it will be interpreted liberally: in *Harrods Ltd v Remick* (1997) it was held that the store could be liable for race discrimination in refusing store accreditation for certain employees of firms operating franchises inside Harrods. The store's argument that they did not "work for" Harrods but for the franchisees was rejected, on the grounds that they were actually selling Harrods' goods, wore the Harrods uniform and were subject to the store's code of conduct. However, not every situation where a principal benefits from work done by another party's employee will fall within this protection. In *Jones v Friends Provident Life Office* (2004) the Northern Ireland Court of Appeal noted that this is a question of fact and degree, meaning that the decision of the original tribunal should usually stand; also, as the provision covering agency workers was to ensure that employers did not avoid discrimination legislation by bringing in sub-contractors, it was appropriate for it to be widely construed. Another example is *Leeds City Council v Woodhouse* (2010) where once again the Court of Appeal placed as much emphasis on the fact that in practice there was a very close relationship between the council and its wholly owned subsidiary as on the contractual arrangements in finding that the claimant, an employee of the subsidiary, came within the definition of contract worker.

In *BP Chemicals Ltd v Gillick* (1995) an agency worker was able to sue the principal for sex discrimination when she was not allowed to return to work for them following maternity leave (see also *Patefield v Belfast City Council* (2000)).

2–010   There is special provision to prohibit employment agencies from discriminating unlawfully, both in relation to who they take on to their books and the terms which they offer (EqA 2010 s.55).

It should be noted that in *Allonby v Accrington & Rossendale College* (2004) the CJEU held, in construing TFEU art.157(1), that the term "worker" has an EU law meaning and applies to people who supply their services for and under the direction of another, for which they receive remuneration, provided that they are not self-employed, in the sense of not being in a relationship of subordination with the person who receives their services. Where such a worker was in an "employment relationship" of this kind with an employer, the CJEU held that they were entitled to rely on art.157(1) even if they had no direct contract with the employer. There has been surprisingly little successful reliance on *Allonby v Accrington & Rossendale College* since. However, it suggests a possible argument for a wider conception of the employment relationships which should, in EU terms, be covered by equality law. In *X v Mid-Sussex CAB* (2013) the Supreme Court held that volunteers who do not have an enforceable obligation to work are not protected from discrimination by either UK or EU law, declining to refer the question to the CJEU.

Apart from those "in employment" in the sense discussed above, the EqA 2010 contains particular provisions prohibiting discrimination in relation to partnerships, barristers, office-holders, qualifications bodies and trade unions (EqA 2010 ss.44–57).

What is covered?

One of the reasons for dealing with equality law at this stage is that it applies   **2–011** to recruitment and selection for employment as well as the employment relationship once it has been entered into. EqA 2010 s.39 prohibits discrimination in: arrangements as to who should be offered employment (e.g. advertising, interviewing and appointment procedures); the terms on which employment is offered; access to training, benefits and promotion; and in relation to dismissal or any other detriment. However, in relation to sex discrimination only, any disparity in the actual terms and conditions of the contract of employment fall under EqA Pt 5 Ch.3 rather than Pt 5 Ch.1 (which deals with all other forms of employment discrimination). This is dealt with in Ch.7 of this book. Thus to offer a female applicant a lower salary than would be offered to a male applicant contravenes EqA 2010 s.39; to pay a female employee less than a male employee is actionable under EqA 2010 s.66.

Originally there was doubt as to whether equality law prohibited discrimination taking place after dismissal. In *Adekeye v Post Office (No.2)* (1997) the Court of Appeal held that the protection against race discrimination ceased once employment had terminated. In *Coote v Granada Hospitality* (1999) the EAT accepted that it was bound to adopt the same interpretation in relation to sex discrimination, but referred to the CJEU the question of whether this was compatible with what are now arts 17 and 18 of the Recast Equal Treatment Directive (2006/54/EC), which require that there must be effective remedies for breach of the Directive. The CJEU held that the principle requiring effective remedies would be infringed if employers could take retaliatory steps affecting the employee after the employment had ended (as the employer had done here, by refusing to give Ms Coote a reference for a new job) and that someone in the applicant's position should be protected by the law. The House of Lords considered the whole question of discrimination arising after employment had terminated in *Relaxion Group plc v Rhys-Harper* (2003) and *D'Souza v Lambeth LBC* (2003) and held that the sex and race legislation could be interpreted as covering post-employment discrimination. The point has been put beyond doubt in subsequent legislation (EqA 2010 s.108).

Protected Characteristics

The nine "protected characteristics"—those grounds on which discrimination   **2–012** must not take place—are now listed alphabetically in EqA 2010 s.4: age, disability, gender reassignment, marriage and civil partnership, pregnancy and childbirth, race, religion or belief, sex and sexual orientation. However, this deracination may hinder an understanding of their development, so they are dealt with here roughly in the chronological order in which they evolved, except for disability, which is in a separate section (see below, para.2–067).

Race

2–013   The first Race Relations Act was passed in 1965, but it made no attempt to outlaw discrimination in the employment field. It did set up the Race Relations Board with powers of investigation and conciliation and this was quite important as it was the precursor of the EOC, CRE and ultimately, the EHRC. The 1968 Race Relations Act prohibited racial discrimination in employment, but was not very effective. It was felt that conciliation, education and persuasion would be more likely to produce results than a series of legal proceedings. Thus complaints of discrimination had to be made to the Race Relations Board, which alone could bring proceedings, and would do so only if all else failed. In the end, this screening process was a serious deterrent to claims and came to be seen as a major defect of the Act.

Building on this, and on American experience, the Sex Discrimination Act was passed in 1975. In 1976 a new Race Relations Act was passed with parallel provisions, modified as necessary. Initially sex and race discrimination law proceeded on parallel paths, but as a result of EU law developments, sex discrimination law advanced considerably in the last two decades of the twentieth century while race discrimination law did not always keep pace. Following the adoption of TFEU art.19 and the Race Directive (2000/43/EC) it could be argued that race equality law had advanced further than sex equality law, raising the much-discussed issue of whether there is or should be a hierarchy of protected grounds.

"Race" is defined in EqA 2010 s.9 as including colour, nationality and ethnic or national origins. The previous law defined "racial grounds" exhaustively as colour, race, nationality or ethnic or national origins. "Race" has been dropped because the concept that there are biological differences between groups of humans is now discredited, but this does not reduce the coverage of the protection. The new definition, by use of the word "including", seems to allow at least the possibility of defining race more widely than colour, nationality and ethnic or national origins. None of these terms is defined by the Act. In *BBC v Souster* (2001) an English journalist who had presented Rugby Special for BBC Scotland claimed that the BBC replaced him with a Scotswoman because he was English. The Court of Session held that this was capable of constituting discrimination on grounds of "national origin" and also that "nationality" need not be defined exclusively in terms of citizenship. Therefore, although the English, Scots and Welsh have common nationality as citizens of the United Kingdom, they can be regarded as having different national origins (see also *Northern Joint Police Board v Power* (1997)).

2–014   The inclusion of "ethnic origin" was clearly to cover groups such as Jews who do not constitute a separate race or nationality, yet whose group identity is based on more than just religious adherence. In the leading case, *Mandla v Dowell Lee* (1983), the House of Lords had to consider whether Sikhs constituted an ethnic group. The claimant was an orthodox Sikh boy, required by the custom of his religion to grow his hair. He was refused admission to a private school unless he would give up wearing his turban and have his hair cut to the regulation length. Lord Fraser defined ethnic groups in these terms:

"For a group to constitute an ethnic group . . . it must, in my opinion, regard itself, and be regarded by others, as a distinct community by virtue of certain characteristics. Some of these characteristics are essential; others are not essential but one or more of them will commonly be found and will help to distinguish the group from the surrounding community. The conditions which appear to me to be essential are these: (1) a long shared history, of which the group is conscious as distinguishing it from other groups, and the memory of which it keeps alive; (2) a cultural tradition of its own, including family and social customs and manners, often but not necessarily associated with religious observance. In addition to those two essential characteristics the following characteristics are, in my opinion, relevant; (3) either a common geographical origin, or descent from a small number of common ancestors; (4) a common language, not necessarily peculiar to the group; (5) a common literature peculiar to the group; (6) a common religion different from that of neighbouring groups or from the general community surrounding it; (7) being a minority or being an oppressed or a dominant group within a larger community, for example a conquered people (say, the inhabitants of England shortly after the Norman conquest) and their conquerors might both be ethnic groups."

That this remains the leading authority on the issue is confirmed by the EHRC Code of Practice on Employment. On this basis, Sikhs, Jews (*Seide v Gillette Industries* (1980)) and gypsies (*CRE v Dutton* (1989)) have naturally been held to constitute ethnic groups, although Rastafarians have not (*Dawkins v Department of the Environment* (1993)). In *Walker v Hussain* (1996) it was assumed that Muslims did not constitute a distinct ethnic group although the point was not argued. The reason would seem to be that Islam, like Christianity, is so widespread that it is not possible to identify any common characteristic among its adherents beyond their religious faith. This is far less important now, since discrimination on grounds of religion or belief has been independently unlawful since 2003 (see below, para.2–024).

Since "race" is defined according to different criteria, an individual may belong to a number of different racial groups—for example, a black British person of Afro-Caribbean descent. A racial group may comprise a number of different racial groups: for example, in *R (E) v Governing Body of JFS* (2010) it was held that a school's admission policy discriminated against everyone who was not of Jewish descent.

In the public consultation before the Equality Act 2010 was passed there was **2–015** some lobbying for caste to be included as an aspect of race, especially since a report of the Dalit Solidarity Network in 2006 arguing that this is a live problem in the United Kingdom, a finding reinforced by research for the Government in 2010. The result was that EqA 2010 s.9(5) gave the Secretary of State power to make regulations to add caste should the need arise. This was amended by the Enterprise and Regulatory Reform Act 2013 (ERRA) to require this to happen, but the power remains unexercised (and will expire under a sunset clause after five years). At the time of the ERRA amendment, the Government indicated that it proposed to consult on making caste discrimination unlawful in 2014 and to bring in changes from 2015, but this was abandoned in the run-up to the 2015 General Election and has not been revived since. In *Chandhok v Tirkey* (2015) the EAT held that the concept of ethnic origin was wide enough to encompass a claim of caste discrimination, even while accepting that there was no settled definition of the meaning of "caste".

Sex

2–016   The first legislative attempt to address the question of sex discrimination was the Sex Disqualification (Removal) Act 1919. This limited measure merely removed existing bars on women entering certain professions. It did not prohibit discrimination in training or selection for these professions. Thus, after 1919 a woman could become a solicitor, for example, but a university did not have to treat her application to read law equally with one from a man, and employers could refuse to employ her just because she was a woman. That remained the position until the passage of the Sex Discrimination Act 1975 (SDA). In a nod towards recognition of the real problem that the statute was meant to address, the SDA was framed in terms of making discrimination against women unlawful, even though it was always the case that discrimination against men was just as unlawful as discrimination against women. This is lost in harmonisation, with EqA 2010 s.11 saying simply that sex means a man or a woman.

Marriage and civil partnership

2–017   At one time it was not unusual for women to have to give up work on getting married and this was the reason for making discrimination against married people unlawful under the SDA. Following the Civil Partnership Act 2004, the protection was extended to civil partners as part of the general policy of equating the legal status of marriage and civil partnerships, even though there is no particular evidence of discrimination in employment on grounds of civil partnership status per se as opposed to homosexuality. EqA 2010 s.8 now states that the status of being married or a civil partner is a protected characteristic. Since the Marriage (Same Sex Couples) Act 2013, marriage also includes same-sex marriage, of course.

It appears that discrimination against single or divorced people on grounds of their marital status remains lawful. While art.2(1) of the Equal Treatment Directive (76/207/EEC) referred to discrimination on grounds of "marital or family status", this was in the context of sex discrimination, so would apply only if this could be proved as well. There is no mention of marital or family status in art.14 of the Recast Equal Treatment Directive (2006/54/EC) which replaces art.2 of the 1976 Directive.

In *Hawkins v Atex Group Ltd* (2012) the company's chief executive had handed director appointments to his wife and daughter despite instructions to the contrary. His wife's claim that it was direct marriage discrimination when she was dismissed by the company was rejected by the EAT. The company's objection was not on grounds of her marriage, but who she was married to.

Pregnancy and maternity

Pregnancy is something which only happens to women and so it might seem obvious that discrimination on grounds of pregnancy would be regarded as a form of sex discrimination. Thus, soon after the SDA came into force, women attempted to use it to argue that pregnancy discrimination was sex discrimination. The problem they encountered was that the Act outlawed *less* favourable treatment on grounds of sex, not *un*favourable treatment, meaning that there had to be a comparison with someone of the opposite sex with relevantly similar characteristics. The necessity for comparison caused particular problems in pregnancy discrimination cases. If a woman is dismissed because she is pregnant then under the Employment Rights Act 1996 (ERA) s.99 the dismissal is automatically unfair. However, to rely on this an employee used to have to have been employed for two years. In *Turley v Allders* (1980) the claimant did not have the requisite period of continuous employment and so she claimed under the SDA instead, since it had no minimum qualifying period of employment. The action failed, because the EAT held that there was no male equivalent to a pregnant woman. In *Hayes v Malleable WMC* (1985) the EAT held that a comparison could be made between a pregnant woman and a man with a long-term health problem; it would thus be sex discrimination if a woman was dismissed on grounds of pregnancy if a man would not be dismissed for needing the same amount of absence because of illness. This analogy, it is submitted, was misplaced: pregnancy is not an illness and is usually planned; it is not really comparable to an unexpected absence caused by illness or accident. However, in a later decision, with a five-member tribunal especially assembled to deal with the point, the EAT reiterated the *Hayes* approach and it was confirmed by the Court of Appeal (*Webb v EMO (UK) Ltd Cargo Air* (1990), (1992)).

2–018

Meanwhile, the CJEU decided in *Dekker v VJV Centrum* (1991) that a woman who was not appointed to a post for which she had been adjudged the best candidate because she was pregnant at the time of the interview had been the victim of direct sex discrimination. However, at the same time the CJEU also held, in *Hertz v Aldi Marked* (1991), that dismissal for sickness absence resulting from a difficult pregnancy did not involve unlawful discrimination where the employee had had her full maternity leave and a man needing a similar amount of sickness absence would also have been dismissed. In the view of the House of Lords, this left some doubt as to how far, if at all, comparison with a sick man could be relied on and *Webb v EMO* was referred to the CJEU, which made its decision in 1994.

Webb v EMO concerned a small air freight company with 16 employees. One of the import clerks, S, discovered that she was pregnant in June 1987, so she would need maternity leave early in the following year. W was taken on in July to be trained by S to take over her job during S's maternity leave; importantly, however, the firm expected to keep W on after S returned to work. Two weeks later, W discovered that she was pregnant as well and would need maternity leave around the same time as S. Because she would not be able to cover for the critical period, W was dismissed. The CJEU held that dismissal in these circumstances constituted direct sex discrimination. The court considered that the fact that the employer would have dismissed a man who was similarly absent, for illness or other reason, at the critical time was nothing to do with the issue: the dismissal was on grounds of pregnancy, which affects only women, and comparison with sickness was inappropriate. It is notable, however, that both the Advocate-General's opinion in the case and the judgment of the CJEU laid emphasis on the fact that this was a contract for an indefinite period—thus her unavailability applied only to a relatively small portion of her expected employment, even though an important time from the employer's point of view. This was seized on by the House of Lords when the case returned to them for consideration (*Webb v EMO (No.2)* (1995)). However, in *Tele Danmark v Brandt-Nielsen* (2001) the CJEU held that it was unlawful sex discrimination and contrary to the Pregnant Workers Directive to dismiss an employee who disclosed that she was pregnant one month after she commenced a six-month fixed-term contract. The baby was due in the fifth month of the contract and she had known that she was pregnant when she got the job but did not tell the employer. The CJEU held that these facts made no difference (see also *Jimenez Melgar v Ayuntamiento de Los Barrios* (2001)).

2–019   Most of the heat went out of the issue in relation to pregnancy and discrimination following the implementation of the Pregnant Workers Directive (92/85/EEC), which rendered all dismissals on grounds of pregnancy or childbirth automatically unfair regardless of length of service or whether the contract was indefinite or for a fixed term (ERA s.99; see below, para.6–018). Having first applauded the apparent demise of the "sick man" comparison as a result of the CJEU's decision in *Webb v EMO* (1994), some commentators began to have second thoughts. Did this mean that "benign" use of the sick man comparison, in favour of a pregnant woman, was also ruled out? For example, if employees on sick leave are entitled under their contracts to full pay for the first six months, does this mean that a woman absent because of pregnancy or childbirth should get full pay for six months? If so, this would be more generous than their statutory entitlements (see below, para.6–006).

A number of cases were referred to the CJEU in the wake of *Webb v EMO* to test the position. The final resolution may be regarded as strong on pragmatism but short on logic. The general approach of the CJEU has been to treat pregnancy as a "special case": gender-based, so that unfavourable treatment for this reason will constitute sex discrimination, but a unique situation, so that different treatment of maternity rights and sickness rights will not necessarily do so. Thus dismissing a woman following a disciplinary hearing which she was unable to attend because of her pregnancy was sex discrimination (*Abbey National v Formoso* (1999)), as was the failure to allow a woman the opportunity to have an annual performance review (and thus a chance of a pay increase) because her maternity leave meant that she had not been at work for sufficient time during the relevant year (*Caisse Nationale v Thibault* (1998)). But in *Gillespie v Northern Health and Social Services Board* (1996) the CJEU held that women were not entitled to full pay during maternity leave even though men and women on sick leave would get full pay. The court held that women on maternity leave were in a special situation which could not be compared with men or women on sick leave. On the same principle, it held in *Boyle v EOC* (1998) that a condition that women return to work for a certain period after maternity leave to qualify for enhanced pay was not sex discrimination even though employees on sick leave did not have to comply with this condition to qualify for full sick pay.

The CJEU has not abandoned its decision in *Hertz v Aldi Marked* (1991) that sickness absence arising from pregnancy or childbirth can be compared with other kinds of sickness absence (thus not treating pregnancy and maternity leave as a special case in these circumstances). Its final position as laid out in *Brown v Rentokil* (1998) is that it will be sex discrimination to dismiss a woman for any reason related to pregnancy or childbirth during a "protected period" comprising pregnancy and such period of maternity leave as is provided for under national law. This includes dismissal for an illness related to pregnancy and childbirth. However, after the period of maternity leave has ended, if a woman is still absent through illness, she can be dismissed if a man would have been dismissed for a similar amount of absence, even if her illness is related to pregnancy or childbirth. But in making this comparison, the absence during the protected period of pregnancy and maternity leave must not be taken into account.

The Equal Treatment Amendment Directive (2002/73/EC) stated expressly   **2–020** that any less favourable treatment of women related to pregnancy or maternity leave should be treated as sex discrimination (see art.2(2)(c) of the Recast Equal Treatment Directive (2006/54/EC)) with the result that this was added to the SDA in 2005.

Under EqA 2010 s.4, "pregnancy and maternity" is promoted to being a protected characteristic in its own right. It differs from the other protected characteristics in that there is a wider definition of what constitutes direct discrimination (EqA s.18), but no protection from indirect discrimination on this ground (EqA s.19(3)). As protection from discrimination for pregnancy and maternity lasts only during the "protected period", defined by EqA s.18(6) in accordance with EU law as being from the beginning of pregnancy to the end of maternity leave, the possibility of a sex discrimination claim remains relevant for less favourable treatment related to pregnancy or maternity outside this period.

Gender reassignment

Discrimination on grounds of gender reassignment has been unlawful since   **2–021** 1999. This was not originally a protected ground in the legislation and it was thought that discrimination against transsexuals would only be unlawful sex discrimination if an employer treated male-to-female transsexuals differently from female-to-male transsexuals. This position, however, required radical review following the CJEU's decision in *P v S and Cornwall CC* (1996). The claimant in this case was dismissed from his post because he proposed to undergo gender reassignment surgery and to live thereafter as a woman. He claimed that this was sex discrimination. The employment tribunal considered that the claim was not sustainable within the terms of the SDA, but referred to the CJEU the question of whether this was inconsistent with the Equal Treatment Directive. Could this be said to be discrimination on grounds of his sex? The United Kingdom argued that it could not, as the employer would clearly have treated a female-to-male transsexual in the same (unfavourable) way.

The CJEU held that this was unlawful sex discrimination, for two main reasons. First, the court described the Equal Treatment Directive (76/207/EEC) as giving expression to the fundamental principle of equality in EU law. Secondly, the fact that the person concerned would be treated less favourably by comparison with persons of his or her former sex showed that the discrimination was on grounds of sex. This entailed a change in the law which was carried out by the Sex Discrimination (Gender Reassignment) Regulations 1999, making less favourable treatment of a person unlawful if it was on the ground that she or he "intends to undergo, is undergoing, or has undergone gender reassignment". Gender reassignment was defined as a process undertaken with medical supervision, presumably in order to ensure that that there could be some precision in deciding whether a particular person was in that situation or not.

Under the EqA 2010, gender reassignment is also promoted to being a protected characteristic in its own right, rather than being an appendage to sex discrimination. The definition, in EqA 2010 s.7(1), is also wider than before:

"A person has the protected characteristic of gender reassignment if the person is proposing to undergo, is undergoing or has undergone a process (or part of a process) for the purpose of reassigning the person's sex by changing physiological or other attributes of sex."

2–022 This retains the idea that no medical intervention need be involved, and the reference to "proposing to undergo" could be satisfied perhaps with something less certain than an intention. It is also clear that protection extends to someone who starts the process but discontinues it. The main change, however, is that there is now no requirement for any kind of medical supervision. It remains the case that transvestitism, or cross-dressing, is not protected by the law.

In establishing transsexual discrimination, EqA 2010 s.16 specifically provides that less favourable treatment of someone who is absent from work because they are undergoing gender reassignment compared with treatment of someone absent for sickness or injury constitutes discrimination, as does less favourable treatment compared with treatment of someone absent for a different reason, unless this is reasonable in the circumstances.

Under the Gender Recognition Act 2004, transsexuals who have lived in the acquired gender for at least two years can apply for a gender recognition certificate which enables them to receive a new birth certificate in their new identity and which then entitles them to be treated from that point onwards as if they had originally been born of that sex for most purposes. Even without such a certificate, the House of Lords held in *A v Chief Constable of West Yorkshire Police* (2004) that a transsexual person must be treated in all respects as belonging to the acquired gender and that the equality legislation could properly be so interpreted.

Sexual orientation

It was thought by many that the reasoning in *P v S and Cornwall CC* (1996) would mean that discrimination against homosexuals on grounds of their sexuality would also constitute sex discrimination. However, this turned out not to be the case. In *Grant v South West Trains* (1998) the employing company gave travel concessions to the spouses or live-in partners of their employees but refused to extend the concession to Ms Grant's lesbian partner. *Grant v South West Trains* was referred to the CJEU and the Advocate-General duly opined that the case was indistinguishable from *P v S and Cornwall CC*. Not so the CJEU, which accepted the argument of the UK government that if the employer would have treated a male homosexual in the same (unfair) way as it treated female homosexuals, there was no sex discrimination. This, of course, was precisely the comparison which it had rejected in *P v S and Cornwall CC*. References to the fundamental principle of equality in EU law, so vaunted in that case, were conspicuous by their absence in *Grant v South West Trains*. It would, of course, constitute sex discrimination if female homosexuals were treated differently from male homosexuals (*Pearce v Governing Body of Mayfield School* (2003)). **2–023**

Sexual orientation was included in the Framework Employment Directive (2000/78/EC) as one of the grounds on which employment discrimination should be made unlawful and as a result the Employment Equality (Sexual Orientation) Regulations 2003 were passed, which came into force in December 2003. These are now replaced by EqA 2010 s.12 which defines the protected characteristic as "a sexual orientation towards—(a) persons of the same sex, (b) persons of the opposite sex, or (c) persons of either sex". Thus discrimination against homosexuals, heterosexuals and bisexual people is covered. It may seem surprising that heterosexuals are included, but at least in America there has been a case of a heterosexual working in a theatre alleging that the predominantly gay management discriminated against her because of her sexual orientation.

Religion or belief

Discrimination on grounds of religious belief or political opinion has been unlawful in Northern Ireland since 1976 (currently under the Fair Employment and Treatment (Northern Ireland) Order 1998) but it was not perceived as a problem in the rest of the United Kingdom and was not originally included in the anti-discrimination legislation. As noted above (para.2–014), some religious groups such as Sikhs and Jews gained protection under race discrimination law because they met the tests of being an ethnic group (*Mandla v Dowell Lee* (1983); *Singh v Rowntree Mackintosh* (1979); *Seide v Gillette Industries* (1980)). The way that the term "ethnic group" has been interpreted has given rise to criticism, partly on the ground that it embodies values based on a Judaeo-Christian concept of religion (e.g. the emphasis on long shared history, which precluded Rastafarians being held to be an ethnic group in *CRE v Dutton* (1989)) and partly because of the perceived unfairness of not extending protection to the biggest ethnic minority likely to suffer discrimination in the United Kingdom, namely the Muslim community. (Although discrimination against Muslims is almost bound to be indirect **2–024** discrimination on grounds of race, in that most Muslims in Britain are of Asian heritage, it has been generally assumed, although not authoritatively decided, that they do not constitute an ethnic group within the meaning of the EqA 2010 s.9.)

The Framework Employment Directive (2000/78/EC) required Member States to legislate against discrimination on grounds of religion or belief in the employment field and so the Employment Equality (Religion and Belief) Regulations 2003 were passed. While the Directive contains no definition of the terms "religion or belief" the 2003 Regulations originally defined them as, "any religion, religious belief, or similar philosophical belief". This was criticised because it said that "other beliefs" had to be "similar" to religion, yet there was no such limitation in the Directive. The argument was accepted by the Government, which substituted a new definition in EqA 2006. This definition has been carried across unchanged in EqA 2010 s.10, which states that a reference to religion means any religion and also includes lack of a religion, and a reference to belief means any religious or philosophical belief, and also includes a lack of belief.

Freedom of thought, conscience and religion, including the right to manifest one's religion through worship, teaching, practice and observance, is guaranteed by art.9 of the ECHR, although manifestation may be limited, inter alia, in order to protect the rights and freedoms of others. As we have seen already (para.1–033), Convention rights are enforceable in the United Kingdom and Convention jurisprudence is therefore relevant in construing equality law in relation to religion or belief.

2–025   So far as religion is concerned, the EHRC Code of Practice on Employment states categorically that the Baha'i faith, Buddhism, Christianity, Hinduism, Islam, Jainism, Judaism, Rastafarianism, Sikhism and Zoroastrianism all count as religions under the Act. Convention jurisprudence has taken an inclusive approach to what constitutes a religion, recognising almost without question the Church of Scientology (*X and Church of Scientology v Sweden* (1978)); the Moon Sect (*X v Austria* (1981)); the Divine Light Zentrum (*Omkarananda and the Divine Light Zentrum v United Kingdom* (1981)); and Druidism (*Chappell v United Kingdom* (1987)). The EHRC Code of Practice, however, states that a religion must have "a clear structure and belief system". This seems an unwarranted limitation on the concept of religion, as opposed to the concept of a "religious organisation" (relevant to exceptions, below para.2–040), and also at odds with the current willingness of tribunals to judge whether someone has a religious belief in a subjective way, as shown in *Eweida v British Airways* (2010), where it was held that it was not necessary for the claimant to show that anyone else held the same view of what her religion required, an approach taken also by the European Court in *Eweida v United Kingdom* (2013).

In *Campbell and Cosans v United Kingdom* (1982) the European Court held that beliefs to be protected under ECHR should have a certain level of cogency, seriousness, cohesion and importance; be worthy of respect in a democratic society and not incompatible with human dignity. In *McClintock v DCA* (2008) a magistrate on the family panel who considered that children should not be placed in the care of same-sex couples was held not to have suffered disadvantage because of his belief, as his view was founded not so much on his Christian beliefs as his opinion that this was not a good environment for children to be brought up in. The EAT held that only beliefs, not opinions based on accurate or inaccurate facts, were covered. In *Grainger plc v Nicholson* (2010) the question was whether a belief in climate change which informed many aspects of the claimant's lifestyle was protected under the legislation. Holding that it was, and drawing on the earlier cases, the EAT laid down five conditions for a belief to be protected:

(i)   that the belief must be genuinely held;
(ii)   that it must be a belief, and not, as in *McClintock v DCA*, an opinion or viewpoint;
(iii)   that it must relate to a weighty and substantial aspect of human life and behaviour;
(iv)   that it must attain a certain level of cogency, seriousness, cohesion and importance; and
(v)   that it must be worthy of respect in a democratic society, must not be incompatible with human dignity and must not conflict with the fundamental rights of others.

This formulation has been adopted in the EHRC Code of Practice on Employment.

One of the biggest issues in Great Britain in relation to belief is likely to be the extent to which political beliefs are covered (they are already protected in Northern Ireland). The Explanatory Notes to the 2003 Regulations stated categorically that political beliefs were not covered, but case-law on the ECHR has recognised pacifism (*Arrowsmith v United Kingdom* (1980)); Nazism (*X v Austria* (1963)); fascism (*X v Italy* (1976)); and Communism (*Hazar, Hazar and Amik v Turkey* (1991)) as protected beliefs, suggesting that this is open to question. It is notable that the EHRC Code of Practice and the Explanatory Notes to the EqA 2010 stop short of saying that political beliefs are not covered. In *Grainger v Nicholson plc* Burton J expressed the obiter view that "belief in the political philosophies of Socialism, Marxism, Communism or free-market Capitalism might qualify", and in *GMB v Henderson* (2015) an employment tribunal's finding that belief in "left-wing democratic socialism" was protected was not challenged on appeal.

Age

Age is distinct from other protected characteristics in a number of ways. Probably   **2–026**
no characteristic is completely immutable, but age is the most changeable of all. It is also unusual in that people may suffer discrimination in employment for being too young as well as for being too old. In addition, age discrimination has long been entrenched in social institutions including the workplace. Thus, people used to be required to retire on reaching a particular age, but many employment benefits are associated with seniority and thus put older workers at an advantage; pay rates are often reduced for younger workers, redundancy payments are greater for workers with longer service, and so on. Finally, stereotypes

abound in relation to age: older workers may be seen as out of touch, slow to learn new skills, reluctant to change, unable to cope with new technology. Younger workers may be regarded as immature, unreliable, lacking commitment and unwilling to work hard.

The result of such stereotyped views was a situation at the turn of the century where prejudice against younger workers led to institutionalisation of the practice of paying them less than other workers through the differential levels set for the National Minimum Wage, introduced in 1998 (para.7–053 below). For older workers, a Cabinet Office report in 2000 (*Winning the Generation Game*) found that the number of people over 50 not working in paid employment had doubled in the previous 20 years to nearly 3 million—one-third of the age group. It estimated that about 2 million of these were not voluntarily unemployed: they were the victims of restructuring and the move to "leaner" business organisations, hampered in their attempts to find new jobs by the negative perceptions of employers and society more generally. The same report calculated the loss to the national gross domestic product of these unemployed over-50s' work at £16 billion per year and the cost of additional benefits and lost taxes at £3.5 billion per year.

National and EU policy on older workers has undergone a major shift in more recent years, driven mainly by recognition that the ageing, retired population is growing at a much faster rate than the population of working age. As people live longer, greater pension provision is required, but economic recession has led to occupational pension schemes becoming less generous and the age of state pension entitlement being progressively raised from 65 at present to 67 by 2026–2028. Instead of encouraging people to take early retirement to make way for younger workers, the policy now is geared to lengthening working lives to reduce the economic burden of the non-productive older population.

2–027   As the above indicates, the impetus for preventing age discrimination has more to do with economic considerations than respect for human rights. Thus it may not be surprising that until art.13 of the Treaty of Rome (now TFEU art.19) and the Framework Employment Directive (2000/78/EC), age discrimination was not mentioned in most international instruments, such as the ECHR or the ILO Convention No.111 on Discrimination in Employment. To a limited extent age discrimination could amount to sex discrimination, as in *Price v Civil Service Commission* (1978) (see below, para.2–050) or even race discrimination. In *Perera v Civil Service Commission (No.2)* (1982) the EAT held that an age limit could constitute indirect discrimination on grounds of race, in that non-British nationals working in the United Kingdom might be older than a British citizen by the time they gained comparable qualifications.

The Framework Employment Directive (2000/78/EC) included age as a protected characteristic for the first time, but gave Member States an extra three years to legislate against age discrimination in employment, recognising that it raised some particularly difficult issues. The United Kingdom took full advantage of this dispensation: the Directive was not implemented until the Employment Equality (Age) Regulations 2006, in force from 1 October 2006.

Now, EqA 2010 makes discrimination unlawful where it is based on the claimant's age group (defined as "a group of persons defined by reference to age, whether by reference to a particular age or a range of ages": EqA 2010 s.5). As will be seen, however, there are numerous exceptions to the prohibition of age discrimination, most notably that even direct discrimination can be justified, which means it is less protected than the other prohibited grounds (see below, para.2–056).

Dual discrimination

There has been increased awareness over recent years that discrimination may occur not because of one protected characteristic, but because of the interplay of a number of characteristics. So a female employee may be bullied, for example, not just because she is a woman, but because she is very young and from an ethnic minority. Or a man may be passed over for promotion because he is over 50 and has a disability. One characteristic on its own might not have caused less favourable treatment: it arises from the coincidence of more than one attribute. In *Bahl v Law Society* (2004) the claimant brought sex and race discrimination claims against the Law Society, but the essence of her claim was that she had been treated less favourably because she was a black woman. The claim was lost on the facts, but the Court of Appeal also held that the tribunal had erred in failing to distinguish between racial elements and sexual elements in her treatment: the claims of race discrimination and sex discrimination had to be considered separately.

2–028

Against this backdrop, the novel provision in EqA 2010 s.14, which would allow a claim for direct discrimination because of a combination of two characteristics, would be an important step forward in protection. However, it has been strongly attacked from opposite viewpoints. From the point of view of employers, the argument is that this would create more complexity than ever in discrimination proceedings, making them even longer and more expensive than they presently are. There is something in this: if a claimant made a claim on the basis of s.14, say for combined sex and age discrimination, she would be bound to run separate claims for sex discrimination and age discrimination alongside it, in case the combined claim failed, so there would inevitably be additional difficulty and time involved in dealing with the case. The attack from the other side is obvious: why limit this to two characteristics, not more, and why limit it to direct discrimination? In the first example given above, for instance, the obvious claim would be harassment rather than direct discrimination, and three characteristics are in play.

The Coalition Government decided not to bring this provision into force, so these issues will not be tested in the foreseeable future. However, it may be that existing law can ameliorate the situation to some extent. In *Ministry of Defence v Debique* (2010) the claimant, a national of St Vincent, was forced out of the army because, as a single mother, she was not available for duty 24 hours a day, seven days a week. UK army personnel were allowed to have a family member live with them to provide childcare, but the claimant could not bring her sister over from

St Vincent to do this because of immigration rules. The EAT upheld her claim for indirect sex and race discrimination. One of the Ministry of Defence's grounds of appeal was that the employment tribunal had erred in looking at the combined effects of the requirements in finding that they resulted in indirect sex and race discrimination instead of keeping the two claims distinct. The EAT rejected this, holding that claims could not always be compartmentalised and that the tribunal's decision recognised the reality of the double disadvantage suffered by the claimant.

Concept of Discrimination

2–029   What is actually meant by "discrimination"? In British law there are essentially four types of prohibited conduct which are unlawful across all, or nearly all, of the protected characteristics. They are direct discrimination, indirect discrimination, harassment and victimisation; the term "discrimination" is sometimes used in this book in a general sense to refer to all four of these. EU law has a slightly different way of defining discrimination, expressly identifying instructions to discriminate as a form of discrimination, but referring to victimisation more as a kind of remedy (Race Directive (2000/43/EC) arts 2(4), 9; and Framework Employment Directive (2000/78/EC) arts 2(4) and 11).

The central concepts in practice are direct and indirect discrimination. Direct discrimination embodies the concept of adverse treatment because of one of the protected characteristics, including, but by no means limited to, intentional and overt discrimination. Indirect discrimination embodies the notion of adverse impact, where an apparently neutral condition has a greater effect on one group rather than another. A major difference between them is that it is possible to defend indirect discrimination as justified in the circumstances. No such defence is available for direct discrimination (except in the case of age discrimination). Victimisation attempts to protect those who suffer adverse treatment as a result of their involvement in other discrimination proceedings. Harassment used to be regarded only as a form of direct discrimination but has become an independent ground as a result of EU directives. Discrimination on grounds of disability has additional elements in its definition, which is why disability discrimination is dealt with separately from the other grounds (see below, para.2–067). In what follows, each of the four main concepts will be considered in turn.

Direct discrimination

2–030   Direct discrimination is now defined in EqA 2010 s.13(1) as treating a person less favourably than others are or would be treated "because of" a protected characteristic. Under the previous law, there was a difference between the characteristics of sex, disability and age on the one hand and race, religion or belief on the other. In the case of sex, disability and age, the adverse treatment had to be on the grounds of the *complainant's own* sex, disability or age, respectively. For race, religion or belief and sexual orientation, it was enough if the discrimination was on grounds of race, religion or belief, or sexual orientation.

The importance of the difference is shown by *Showboat v Owens* (1984), where a white man employed as manager of an amusement arcade was dismissed for refusing to obey an instruction not to admit young blacks to the arcade. It was held that this was direct race discrimination: he had been treated less favourably (by being dismissed) on racial grounds—it did not matter that his own race was not the reason (see also *Weathersfield v Sargent* (1998)). Had the claimant in the case been dismissed for refusing to obey an instruction not to admit women, he would not have been able to claim direct sex discrimination, because his complaint would not have been grounded on his own sex.

Now that the formulation has changed to "because of a protected characteristic", it follows that the wider test applies to all the protected characteristics, with the exceptions of marriage and civil partnership, where EqA 2010 s.13(4) still provides that the less favourable treatment must be because the claimant is married or in a civil partnership; and pregnancy, where s.18(2) stipulates that only unfavourable treatment because of the claimant's own pregnancy is unlawful. While in general the wider formulation is to be welcomed as increasing protection, there is a danger that, in some circumstances, it could be too wide. In *Redfearn v Serco Ltd* (2006), under the previous race discrimination law, the company, which had a contract to provide a bus service for mainly Asian elderly and disabled people in Bradford, sacked a driver when he was elected as a local councillor for the BNP, a political party associated with racist policies. The EAT held that this was a dismissal on racial grounds because racial considerations had played a part in the employer's decision. If correct, this would have led to the absurd result that if an employer dismissed an employee for racially harassing another employee, the harasser would have a good claim for race discrimination! The Court of Appeal avoided this result by holding that the legislation had to be construed purposively in the light of its overall aim of eliminating discrimination. The fact that racial considerations had entered into the company's decision to dismiss the driver did not mean that the decision could be characterised as having been taken on racial grounds and thus there was no direct discrimination on grounds of race. However, the distinction between racial considerations and racial grounds may be thought to be slight, and it sits uneasily with the established principle (repeated in the EHRC Code of Practice on Employment para.3.11) that it is enough if the protected characteristic is part of the cause of the less favourable treatment: it need not be the main or only cause (cf. *Nagarajan v London Regional Transport* (2000)). It may be noted that Redfearn pursued his case to the European Court, which held that his right to freedom of association had been infringed by his dismissal (*Redfearn v United Kingdom* (2013) discussed below, para.8–083). The Labour Government resisted calls to put a purpose clause into the EqA 2010 which would have supported the approach taken by the Court of Appeal in *Redfearn*.

A common way in which employers can fall foul of direct discrimination is by acting on stereotyped assumptions about the capacities or predilections of particular protected groups. Thus in *Skyrail Oceanic Ltd v Coleman* (1981), acting on the assumption that the husband's job must be more important than the wife's was held to constitute direct sex discrimination and so, similarly, was the assumption in *Horsey v Dyfed CC* (1982) that the wife would be bound to move to follow her husband's work. This is also very likely to crop up in relation to disability discrimination. It is very common for employers and others to make stereotypical assumptions about the capabilities of people with particular kinds of disability (e.g. *Aylott v Stockton-on-Tees BC* (2010)); for example, judging that a particular job cannot be done by a wheelchair user, without actually investigating properly whether that is the case.

Discrimination through perception

2–031 The Age Regulations used to state expressly that discrimination on grounds of age included one's *apparent* age, since people are often perceived as being older or younger than they actually are. However, even without such express provision, in *English v Thomas Sanderson Blinds Ltd* (2009) the Court of Appeal upheld a claim for harassment on grounds of sexual orientation in circumstances where the claimant was known by his colleagues to be heterosexual but was nonetheless subjected to homophobic abuse (because he had been to public school and lived in Brighton!). Discrimination could be on grounds of a protected characteristic where the claimant was *perceived* to possess it, whether or not the perception was correct, and where the claimant was treated as possessing it, even if he did not. The EHRC Code of Practice on Employment and the Explanatory Notes to the Equality Act 2010 both say categorically that discrimination through perception now applies to all the protected characteristics (except marriage and civil partnership and pregnancy) as "because of" has the same meaning as "on grounds of" under the previous law.

Discrimination by association

2–032 In a similar way, discrimination by association, where the claimant is less favourably treated because of her association with someone in a protected group, may be said to be less favourable treatment "because of" the protected characteristic even though the claimant does not possess it herself. This is certainly the view taken by the EHRC Code of Practice on Employment and the Explanatory Notes to the Equality Act 2010. As noted already, marriage and civil partnership are an exception, because EqA 2010 s.13(4) states that in this situation the less favourable treatment must be because the claimant himself is married or a civil partner. The position in relation to pregnancy is problematic: under EqA 2010 s.18(2) it is direct discrimination to treat a woman unfavourably because of her own pregnancy, which appears to rule out the possibility of discrimination by association on this ground. The EHRC Code suggests that someone treated less favourably because of their association with a pregnant woman might have a claim for sex discrimination, but in *Kulikaoskas v MacDuff Shellfish* (2011), decided before EqA 2010 came into force, the EAT in Scotland held that a claim of less favourable treatment based on association with a pregnant woman was not actionable as sex discrimination, holding that this was not required by either the Pregnant Workers Directive (92/85/EC) or the Recast Equal Treatment Directive (2006/54/EC). The Court of Session referred the question to the CJEU in 2012 but the case was settled before any hearing.

Under prior disability discrimination legislation, claimants were protected only from less favourable treatment because of their own disability, but in *Coleman v Attridge Law* (2008) where the claimant argued that she had been less favourably treated because she was the main carer for her disabled son, the CJEU held that discrimination through association with a disabled person was covered by the Framework Employment Directive. The CJEU's view was that this situation was clearly within the purpose of the Directive. It remains to be seen whether it would take a similar view in relation to discrimination by association with pregnancy.

Causative link

To constitute direct discrimination, the less favourable treatment must be "because of" the protected characteristic. As noted above, the legislative intention here was merely to simplify the language but not to change the meaning from the earlier "on grounds of" formulation. Unfortunately, that concept itself was not free from difficulty, as is shown by the fact that several cases have gone to the highest court on the issue of what level of causative link is needed between the less favourable treatment and the protected characteristic. It is established that the motivation of the employer is not a decisive factor. In one of the leading cases, *James v Eastleigh BC* (1990), which concerned sex discrimination, Mr and Mrs James were both aged 61. She was allowed free admission to the municipal swimming pool, but he was not, because free admission was only allowed to those who had reached state pension age—which at that time was 60 for women but 65 for men. The council clearly had no intention to discriminate on grounds of sex: it was following the common policy of giving concessions to pensioners. The House of Lords held, first, that the test of whether an action is done on the ground of sex is objective not subjective. That means, if the action causes less favourable treatment of one sex, or the less favourable treatment would not have occurred but for the complainant's sex, it is direct discrimination. Intention, motive or purpose of the discriminator are irrelevant to the issue of liability. Secondly, they held that to use a criterion which was itself discriminatory on grounds of sex (like state pension age) must inevitably involve direct discrimination. Thus, the Council was liable for direct discrimination.

The "but-for" test adopted here (and also in the earlier House of Lords' decision in *R. v Birmingham CC ex p EOC* (1989)) came to be regarded as too crude a test in victimisation cases (below, para.2–063), leaving the law in some confusion. This was clarified in the restatement of the Supreme Court in *R (E) v Governing Body of JFS* (2010). In this case, Lord Phillips stated that, in direct discrimination cases, the first task is for the court or tribunal to identify the alleged discriminator's reason for the treatment in question, meaning the factual criteria applied in reaching the decision. If a protected characteristic featured as (one of) the facts applied in reaching the discriminator's decision, there is direct discrimination. Secondly, he said that the "but-for" test is just one way of identifying the factual criterion used—but not the only way. It may not be clear whether the protected characteristic figured in the alleged discriminator's thinking or not. If there is doubt on this point, then *to that extent only* it may be necessary to investigate his or her thought processes—but only to see whether the protected characteristic

2–033

was influential or not. Finally, the Supreme Court reaffirmed that the motive of the alleged discriminator is not relevant. The facts of *R (E) v Governing Body of JFS* were that the school only admitted those children recognised as Jewish by the Office of the Chief Rabbi, which meant that their mothers had to be Jewish by descent or by conversion. The Supreme Court held by a majority that a test of descent discriminated on grounds of ethnic origin and that this constituted direct race discrimination. The fact that the school's motive was to comply with religious law as explained by the Chief Rabbi—a benign rather than a malign motive—was of no consequence.

Comparators

2–034   Direct discrimination requires that the employer treat the claimant *less* favourably than she or he treats or would treat others. This means that there has to be a comparison between the claimant and either a real or a hypothetical comparator. According to EqA 2010 s.23, in making a comparison, "there must be no material difference between the circumstances relating to each case". This is essentially no different from the previous law; it does not mean that the situation of the claimant has to be exactly the same as the real or hypothetical comparator, but that they must be relevantly similar. It should be noted that this gives courts and tribunals discretion to exercise value judgments as to what they regard as relevant circumstances and this has been particularly notable in relation to sex discrimination. The difficulty in identifying a comparator for a pregnant woman has been discussed already (above, para.2–018). Because art.2(2)(c) of the Recast Equal Treatment Directive (2006/54/EC) states that any less favourable treatment of a woman "related to pregnancy or maternity leave" is unlawful discrimination, the EOC was able successfully to argue that the comparison element should be removed in relation to pregnancy and maternity (*EOC v Secretary of State for Trade and Industry* (2007)). As a result of this, EqA 2010 s.18(2) provides that *un*favourable treatment of a woman because of pregnancy or an illness arising out of pregnancy constitutes direct discrimination if it occurs during pregnancy or maternity leave: there is no need for the comparison element. Conversely, if an employer treats a woman who is pregnant or on maternity leave more favourably than other employees, this will not constitute sex discrimination against men (EqA 2010 s.13(6)(b)), although in *Eversheds Legal Services Ltd v De Belin* (2011) the EAT held that this is subject to a proportionality requirement. In that case, the EAT held that, in scoring two employees against a number of criteria in a redundancy exercise, a firm went beyond what was proportionate in giving a woman absent on maternity leave the maximum possible score for an activity where no real score was possible because of her absence. As a result, she had a slightly higher overall mark than her male colleague, who successfully sued for direct sex discrimination.

Note that outside the protected period, which begins with pregnancy and ends at the end of maternity leave, any claim for discrimination related to pregnancy would have to be brought as a sex discrimination—which would mean that the woman would have to show *less* favourable treatment by comparison with a real or hypothetical comparator.

A striking example of the discretion tribunals and courts have through their selection of what are relevantly similar circumstances is the approach taken to dress codes. A dress code can apply to both men and women; however, as conventions relating to male and female dress are different, the rules as to dress may be different for each sex. In *Schmidt v Austicks Bookshops Ltd* (1978) it was held that it was not direct discrimination to forbid women to wear trousers where men had to wear jackets and ties. The decision was approved by the Court of Appeal in *Smith v Safeway plc* (1996), who stated the principle as follows:

> "Rules concerning appearance will not be discriminatory because their content is different for men and women if they enforce a common principle of smartness or conventionality, and taken as a whole and not garment by garment or item by item, neither gender is treated less favourably in enforcing that principle."

In *Smith v Safeway plc* (1996) a male delicatessen assistant who wore his **2–035** long hair in a ponytail had been dismissed for refusing to have it cut short. Female assistants were permitted to have long hair, provided it was tied back, but men were not. On this basis, the EAT held that there was a direct comparison between the treatment of a man and a woman and the man had clearly been treated less favourably. However, the Court of Appeal held that this was not the appropriate comparison, preferring to consider whether or not there were rules applying to men and women in general. The rejection of a straight comparison and the choice to frame the comparison of dress code rules in terms of their overall impact rather than considering whether some elements were equally applicable to men and women is a clear exercise of discretion based on value judgments which has nothing to do with the principle of equality (see also *DWP v Thompson* (2004)). Compare *McConomy v Croft Inns* (1992), where the Northern Ireland High Court considered that it was no longer unconventional for a man to wear earrings, and a dress code which forbade this to men but not to women resulted in men being treated less favourably.

Segregation

In the United States it was at one time held that "separate but equal" provision **2–036** for blacks and whites was not racially discriminatory. Leaving aside the fact that such provision is rarely equal, segregation on racial grounds seems inherently wrong, and EqA 2010 s.13(5) puts the point beyond argument by declaring that it constitutes less favourable treatment. This does not apply to other protected characteristics, presumably because it was not thought to be a problem except for race. Segregation is an issue which an employer must approach with some sensitivity, since it is possible that members of minority racial groups, particularly if their first language is not English, may manifest an associational preference for others of the same group. If the employer, hoping to achieve a proper racial mix, moves people about, it would be likely to amount to less favourable treatment on racial grounds. But if departments or shifts are staffed entirely by members of one racial group, then there is the possibility of running foul of the segregation provision. This very problem arose in *FTATU v Modgill* (1980) where a particular shift in a furniture factory was staffed entirely by workers of Asian origin. Their shift worked 42½ hours per week as against the 40 worked by other shifts. They claimed that the segregation provision had been contravened. It was found that the all-Asian shift had arisen from the preferences of the workers rather than being imposed by the employer; also that the extra time worked was because it was that particular shift rather than because of their racial origin. In the circumstances the EAT found that there had been no direct discrimination.

Exceptions

2–037   The reason why direct discrimination is such a powerful concept is that, generally speaking, once it is shown, the claimant has won. There is no defence that the treatment was justified in the circumstances. For example, in *Ministry of Defence v Jeremiah* (1979) only men were required to work in the shop producing colour-bursting shells. The work was dirty and workers had to shower at the end of the day, and as Lord Denning explained,

> "A woman's hair is her crowning glory, so it is said. She does not like it disturbed: especially when she has just had a 'hair-do'. The women at an ordnance factory in Wales are no exception. They do not want to work in part of the factory—called a 'shop'—which ruins their hair-do."

The men were paid extra "obnoxious" pay for this work, but nonetheless claimed that they were being discriminated against on grounds of sex. This was direct sex discrimination, not excused by the benign or even chivalrous motive of the employer (see also *R (E) v Governing Body of JFS* (2010) above, para.2–033).

Age discrimination is the sole exception to this rule. The Framework Employment Directive (2000/78/EC) art.6 states that different treatment, i.e. direct discrimination, on grounds of age may be objectively and reasonably justified by a legitimate aim, such as government employment policy, labour market or vocational training objectives, provided that the means of achieving them are appropriate and necessary. Thus EqA 2010 s.13(2) gives an exemption for less favourable treatment on grounds of age if it is a proportionate means of achieving a legitimate aim. In *R (Age Concern England) v Secretary of State for BERR* the CJEU stated that there were no significant differences between the test of justification for direct age discrimination and the general test of justification for indirect discrimination (discussed below, para.2–054). However, in *Seldon v Clarkson, Wright & Jakes* (2012) the Supreme Court noted that the cases so far considered by the CJEU had all been challenges to the laws of Member States. So far as individual employers and employees are concerned, the Supreme Court held that direct age discrimination could *only* be justified if the reasons were consistent with the social policy objectives articulated in art.6, namely government employment policy, labour market or vocational training objectives, as opposed to reasons relating to the individual employer. These policy objectives are usually variants on the theme of inter-generational fairness and personal dignity—the latter meaning that it may be preferable to retire an older worker than to dismiss him or her for declining levels of performance.

Apart from on grounds of age, direct discrimination cannot be justified. There **2–038** are, however, certain exceptional circumstances where it is possible to stipulate that a worker either must have, or must not have, a particular protected characteristic. As these are exceptions to the general rule, they should be interpreted strictly.

Occupational requirements

The Race Directive (2000/43/EC) art.4, the Framework Employment Directive **2–039** (2000/78/EC) art.4 and the Recast Equal Treatment Directive (2006/54/EC) art.14(2) all permit (but do not mandate) Member States to make an exception where, by reason of the nature or context of the work, a protected characteristic is a "genuine and determining occupational requirement", provided that the requirement has a legitimate objective and it is proportionate to apply it. The previous law made provision for "genuine occupational requirements" and, in the case of sex and race, there were also lists of "genuine occupational qualifications". Under the EqA 2010, the lists of genuine occupational qualifications have gone and there is just a general exception, tucked away in Sch.9, for "occupational requirements" which are applied as a proportionate means of achieving a legitimate aim. To arguments that omission of the words "genuine and determining" watered down the requirements of the Directive, the government's answer was that any such requirement would obviously have to be genuine, and if it were not determining, it would not be a requirement. It will be seen in due course whether this is the case: it is notable that the EHRC Code of Practice on Employment para.13.7 says only that there must be a link between the requirement and the job. On the other hand, the Act will have to be interpreted in accordance with EU law, and in relation to occupational requirements the CJEU has held, until recently, that exceptions to the principle of equality must be interpreted strictly (see, e.g. *Johnston v Chief Constable of the RUC* (1986), *Sirdar v Army Board and Secretary of State for Defence* (1999)). The CJEU has also held that such exceptions should be transparent and kept under review, to see whether they are still needed (*Commission v France* (1986)). It may be noted also that under the previous UK law there was a clear tendency to construe these exceptions strictly (see, e.g. *Lambeth v CRE* (1990) and *Tottenham Green Under Fives', Centre v Marshall (No.2)* (1991)). However, in the first case to reach the CJEU on this exception in the Framework Employment Directive, *Wolf v Stadt Frankfurt am Main* (2010), the CJEU appeared to adopt a lower standard of scrutiny than previously in holding that an age-limit of 30 on recruitment of firefighters was a genuine occupational requirement.

Exceptions for religion

There are two special exceptions relating to religion, derived from the previous **2–040** law and now contained in EqA 2010 Sch.9. One essentially permits religious organisations to discriminate *against* people because of their sex or sexual orientation; the other permits them to discriminate *in favour of* co-religionists.

Under Sch.9 para.2, where the employment is "for the purposes of organised religion", it is permissible directly to discriminate because of sex, sexual orientation, transgender status, and marriage or civil partnership, provided that either the "compliance principle" or the "non-conflict principle" is engaged. The compliance principle is engaged where the discrimination takes place in order to comply with the doctrines of the religion: the obvious example would be a ban on women being ministers of religion for religious groupings which hold that only men can be priests. The non-conflict principle is engaged where the requirement is applied to avoid conflicting with the strongly held religious convictions of a significant number of the religion's followers. The EHRC Code gives this example:

"An evangelical church could require its ministers to be married or hetero-sexual if this enables the church to avoid a conflict with the strongly held religious convictions of its congregation."

It is notable that the non-conflict principle allows direct discrimination just to avoid giving offence to people for non-doctrinal reasons; however, it is fair also to point out that this particular compromise between competing rights has existed since the SDA 1975, although it was limited under that Act to ministers of religion. Much depends on what is regarded as employment "for the purposes of an organised religion": attempts by the government to define it as applying to posts which involve leading or assisting in religious services or promoting or explaining the doctrines of the religion were defeated in the House of Lords during the passage of the legislation, so it is for courts and tribunals to decide. When this exemption was introduced in relation to sexual orientation discrimination in 2003, it was challenged by a number of trade unions by way of judicial review in *R (Amicus) v Secretary of State for Trade and Industry* (2004) on the basis that there was no warrant for this derogation in the Framework Employment Directive. The challenge was rejected by the High Court, which stressed the narrowness of the similar statutory wording and indicated that it should be interpreted strictly. In particular, Richards J doubted whether teachers in faith schools could be regarded as employed for the purposes of an organised religion.

2–041   The second exception, under Sch.9 para.3, allows an employer who "has an ethos based on religion or belief" to apply a requirement that a worker should be of a particular religion or belief if, having regard to the employer's ethos, the nature of the employment and the test of proportionality, this is an occupational requirement. Note that this does not say in so many words that the requirement must be to be of the same religion or belief as the employer, but that is the situation which is envisaged. In *R (Amicus) v Secretary of State for Trade and Industry* (2004) Richards J expressed the obiter view that faith schools could be regarded as organisations with an ethos based on religion, which would give them the possibility of making use of this exception. In the first case to reach the EAT on the issue, *Glasgow City Council v McNab* (2007), two interesting points emerged. The claimant was an atheist who had therefore not been considered for the post of principal pastoral care teacher in a Roman Catholic school. The EAT held that being of a particular religious faith was not a determining characteristic of the post, since giving religious guidance was not a major part of the job and could be provided by another teacher where necessary. Furthermore, the EAT pointed out that the employer was the City Council—not the school—and the council certainly could not be regarded as having a religious ethos. As most faith schools are under the aegis of local edu-cation authorities, this suggests that the religious ethos exception will rarely be invoked in relation to teachers.

In *Jivraj v Hashwani* (2011) the issue for the Supreme Court was whether an arbitration clause in a contract between two Ismaili businessmen, which stipulated that the arbitrator should be Ismaili, was valid. As noted above (para.2–007) the Supreme Court held that the arbitrator's appointment was not subject to equality law, but they held obiter that, if it were, it would have come within the exception for employers with an ethos based on religion or belief. It is not, however, obvious that a preference for a co-religionist to deal with disputes indicates that the employer's business is underpinned by a religious ethos and it is submitted that it would be unfortunate if this obiter dictum were to be regarded as the last word on the matter.

Positive action and positive discrimination

British equality law broadly adopts a symmetrical model, so that, for example, **2–042** although the problem that sex equality law aims at is discrimination against women, discrimination against men is also prohibited. This means that positive discrimination is usually unlawful, since discrimination in favour of one protected group would simply be discrimination against other groups who are entitled to equal protection under the legislation. The one major exception to this is in relation to disability, where the protection is asymmetrical. Only less favourable treatment of someone with a disability is prohibited, not less favourable treat-ment of someone without a disability by comparison with a disabled worker. This means that it is lawful for an employer to engage in positive discrimination in favour of disabled workers. Unfortunately, this does not apply to one of the only groups of employers which would have been likely to make use of this facility, namely local authorities, because of the provision in s.7 of the Local Government and Housing Act 1989, that all appointments to local government service must be made on merit.

Prior to the enactment of the EqA 2010, the only limited situation in which positive or reverse discrimination—that is, allowing preferential treatment of one group at the expense of another—was permitted was in relation to train-ing. Employers or training bodies could offer training to members of an under-represented protected group only in order to equip them for a job—although they would then have to compete for the job on the same footing as other candidates.

EU law actually permits a much higher degree of positive discrimination. The Equal Treatment Directive 1976 originally stated that measures designed to remove existing inequalities which affected women's opportunities was per-mitted, but it was held in *Kalanke v Bremen* (1995) that this did not cover a situation where a state law provided for a female candidate automatically to be preferred over an equally qualified male candidate whenever women were under-represented (i.e. there were fewer than 50 per cent) in the particular employment grade. This decision caused a political uproar as other Member States had similar laws and the European Commission itself operated a similar policy! In consequence, when faced with almost the same issue in *Marschall v Land Nordrhein-Westfalen* (1998) the CJEU managed to distinguish *Kalanke*. In *Marschall*, the law preferring women was the same as in *Kalanke* except that it contained a proviso that the preference would not apply "if reasons specific to another candidate predominate". This allowed some flexibility to appoint a better male candidate even where he and the female candidate had equal qualifications. In 1997 the Treaty of Amsterdam amended the Treaty of Rome to add a new subparagraph art.141(4) (now TFEU art.157(4)), stating that:

> "With a view to ensuring full equality in practice between men and women in working life, the principle of equal treatment shall not prevent any Member State from maintaining or adopting measures providing for specific advantages in order to make it easier for the under-represented sex to pursue a vocational activity or to prevent or compensate for disadvantages in professional careers."

2–043   This has not led to any substantial difference in practice in EU law. In *Abrahamsson v Fogelqvist* (2000) the CJEU held that automatic preference of the under-represented sex over a better-qualified candidate of the opposite sex contravened the Equal Treatment Directive, although in *Lommers v Minister van Landbouw, Natuurbeheer en Visserij* (2002) it stated that provision of childcare facilities to women and men on an unequal footing was not necessarily unlawful as long as men were not excluded altogether. The key test is whether the positive discrimination provision is proportionate in the circumstances.

The Equal Treatment Directive (76/207/EEC) was amended in 2002 in line with the wording of TFEU art.157(4), and the present wording, now found in art.3 of the Recast Equal Treatment Directive (2006/54/EC), permits Member States to maintain or adopt measures compatible with that provision "with a view to ensuring full equality in practice between men and women". Comparable provisions are found in the Race Directive (2000/43/EC) art.5 and the Framework Employment Directive (2000/78/EC) art.7 for the other protected characteristics.

EqA 2010 s.158 now provides for positive action in terms which are wider than the former "training for under-represented groups" provisions. If any person (an employer, usually, for our purposes) reasonably thinks (a) that people with a particular protected characteristic suffer a disadvantage connected to it; or (b) have different needs from people without that characteristic; or (c) have a disproportionately low participation rate in a particular activity, then it is not unlawful to take proportionate action (a) to enable or encourage them to overcome the disadvantage, (b) to meet their needs or (c) to enable or encourage them to participate in the activity. While this would clearly cover training for a particular job dedicated to one protected group only, it is capable of wider application. As before, this is permissive rather than mandatory, so it is perhaps unlikely that many employers will make use of it, although public sector organisations may be more interested because of their public sector equality duty (see above, para.1–031).

2–044   Earlier editions of this book insisted on a bright line distinction between positive discrimination and positive action, while recognising that these are not terms of art. The essence of the distinction argued for was that, whereas positive discrimination postulates taking a less well-qualified candidate in order to choose someone from one of the protected groups, positive action does not preclude taking the best candidate available. Positive action is designed to get more members of the under-represented groups into a position where they will be the best candidates. Thus the placing of advertisements in publications which are more likely to reach minorities, and statements that applications from them are particularly welcome may improve the application rate and thus the chances of minority candidates being appointed. In the case of women, allowing flexitime working, job-sharing and the provision of child-care facilities increase the chances of many to work. Special career counselling for members of under-represented groups may assist them to achieve promotion, and so on. Such activities have never been contrary to the law, because they are aimed at increasing the pool of applicants for recruitment or promotion, but final appointments would still be on merit.

However, EqA 2010 s.159 provides for the possibility of using a protected characteristic as a decisive factor in recruitment or promotion, a form of what this book would call positive discrimination, but which appears in the Act under the title of positive action—perhaps to increase its acceptability. It permits an employer to use the protected characteristic in a "tie-break" situation for recruitment or promotion when faced with two candidates who are otherwise equally qualified. This is dependent on a number of conditions. First, the employer must reasonably think that people with the protected characteristic in question are either at a disadvantage because of it, or have a disproportionately low representation in the post in question. Secondly, it can only be done on a case-by-case basis: the employer may not have a policy of preferring people with the protected characteristic (this is to keep in line with the EU case-law, above). Thirdly, it must be a proportionate means of achieving the aim of minimising disadvantage connected with the characteristic or encouraging greater participation by the protected group.

One of the crucial questions with this provision is, how similarly situated do candidates have to be before a court would consider them to be as qualified as each other? It will also be important to know how much evidence will be required for a reasonable belief in disadvantage or disproportionately low participation.

Age exceptions

Recital 14 of the Framework Employment Directive (2000/78/EC) states that it is without prejudice to national provisions laying down retirement ages, and art.6 provides that even direct age discrimination may be justified. The most controversial exception based on this in British law was the provision, in force from 2006–2011, which permitted employers to impose compulsory retirement on people over 65 (or the employer's normal retirement age, if that was higher) provided a statutory consultation procedure was followed. **2–045**

The lawfulness of compulsory retirement ages in national legislation was the subject of two references to the CJEU: *Palacios de la Villa v Cortefiel*

Servicios SA (2007) and *R (Age Concern England) v Secretary of State for BERR* (2009). In both cases, the CJEU held that the Directive was capable of applying to this situation, despite Recital 14. This meant that any such rules had to be objectively and reasonably justified by being shown to pursue a legitimate aim of social policy and to be a proportionate means of achieving such an aim. The CJEU warned that mere generalisations as to the benefits of a retirement policy on the labour market (e.g. in freeing-up posts for younger workers) should not be regarded without more as providing sufficient evidence of this. When the case returned for decision in the light of this guidance, in *R (Age UK) v Secretary of State for BIS* (2009), the Administrative Court held that the government had a legitimate aim in setting a mandatory retirement age, namely, maintaining confidence in the labour market by giving employers some certainty as to their responsibilities to older workers and a degree of flexibility in dealing with them. The Court also held that setting the age at 65 was a proportionate means of achieving that aim—at least, it was in 2006, when the Regulations were passed, which was the point at which the decision had to be judged. However, the judge indicated that if the matter was being considered for the first time in 2009, he would have regarded a default retirement age of 65 as too low.

The government had already committed itself to reviewing the 65 age-limit in 2011. As a result of this case, the review was brought forward to 2010, leading to the Employment Equality (Repeal of Retirement Age Provisions) Regulations 2011, repealing the default retirement age of 65 from October 2011. Thus, to compel someone to retire because they have reached a specific age is now unlawful age discrimination unless it can be justified.

2–046   The EqA 2010 Sch.9, para.11 provides that it is not age discrimination to continue to have different rates for the National Minimum Wage (see further, para.7–053) and para.10 preserves the system whereby redundancy payments for older workers are higher than for younger workers (see further, para.9–020). It is also still possible for employers to use length of service as a reason for giving greater benefits to longer-serving employees. Where the length of service criterion is five years or less, it is exempt from the Regulations. If it is more than five years the employer must demonstrate a reasonable belief that it fulfils a business need. In *Rolls Royce plc v Unite the Union* (2009) the Court of Appeal held that using length of service as one criterion among a number of others in a redundancy selection procedure would be justified as a proportionate means of achieving a legitimate aim—namely, rewarding loyalty and promoting a stable workforce. Finally, although pension schemes are subject to the general non-discrimination principle, most age-related rules and practices in relation to pension schemes are expressly exempted.

Burden of proof

2–047   One of the biggest problems in direct discrimination cases is proving that discrimination has taken place. This is particularly so when it is alleged at the recruitment stage. Frequently a job applicant knows only that he or she has been rejected; not why, nor who was appointed instead. Even if you know the identity of the successful candidate, you may well not know whether his or her qualifications for the job were superior to your own. Even if you know that your qualifications were better, in many jobs other skills, personality and experience matter a great deal too. The question, "who was the best candidate?" may not have an obvious answer. For the same reasons, discrimination may be occurring unconsciously. It is a fact that we all tend to prefer people like ourselves. If a board of interviewers composed predominantly of white males is thinking about who will "fit in" best with the organisation, they are apt to think it will be a white male.

The difficulties of proving discrimination when the relevant information is peculiarly within the knowledge of the employer led many to argue that the burden of proof should be on the employer to disprove discrimination, even though this would be contrary to the general principle of law which requires claimants to establish their claims. The Burden of Proof Directive (97/80/EC) required Member States to legislate for the burden of proof to shift to the employer in sex discrimination cases where the claimant established "facts from which it may be presumed that there has been direct or indirect discrimination" (see now art.19 of the Recast Equal Treatment Directive (2006/54/EC)). Similar provisions were included in the Race Directive (2000/43/EC) art.8 and the Framework Employment Directive (2000/78/EC) art.10. Thus EqA 2010 s.136 provides that if there are facts from which a court could decide, in the absence of any other explanation, that a person has contravened the Act, the court must hold that the contravention occurred unless that person can show that he or she did not contravene it. This replicates the previous law on the subject.

This effectively involves a two-stage process: first, the claimant proves the facts from which an inference could be drawn; if that is done, then secondly, the employer must disprove discrimination. Guidance on how tribunals and courts should now approach the issue of the burden of proof in direct discrimination cases was given by the EAT in *Barton v Investec Henderson Crosthwaite Securities* (2003) and refined by the Court of Appeal in *Igen Ltd v Wong* (2005) into a series of propositions, as follows:

1. The claimant must prove, on the balance of probabilities, facts from which a tribunal could conclude, in the absence of adequate explanation, that the employer has committed an act of unlawful discrimination.
2. If the claimant cannot prove such facts, she fails.
3. In deciding this question, the tribunal must bear in mind that it is unusual to find direct evidence of direct discrimination.
4. This means that the outcome at this stage will depend on how far the tribunal is prepared to draw inferences from the facts it has found.
5. The tribunal does not have to be convinced, at this stage, that they would definitely draw an inference of unlawful discrimination—only that they "could" draw such an inference from the facts which have been proved.
6. At this stage, in deciding what inferences could be drawn the tribunal should assume that there will be no adequate explanation.
7. Inferences can include any that it is just and equitable to draw from an equivocal or evasive reply to a statutory questionnaire.

8. Tribunals must also take account of relevant codes of practice and may draw inferences from an employer's failure to comply with such a code.
9. If the claimant does prove facts as described in (1), above, then the burden of proof shifts to the respondent.
10. The respondent must then prove that he did not commit the discriminatory act.
11. To do this, the respondent must prove, on the balance of probabilities, that the treatment complained of was in no sense whatsoever on the prohibited ground.
12. Thus the tribunal must consider not only whether the respondent has an explanation, but also whether that explanation is sufficient to discharge the burden of proof that the prohibited ground was not a ground for the treatment in question.
13. Since relevant facts are normally in the possession of the respondent, cogent evidence will normally be expected in order to discharge the burden of proof. Tribunals should examine carefully explanations given for a respondent's failure to deal properly with the questionnaire procedure or the recommendations of a code of practice.

While, as always, there should be no gloss on the words of the statute, nonetheless this guidance is regularly referred to. In *Hewage v Grampian Health Board* (2012) the Supreme Court noted that tribunals might not always distinguish the two stages clearly in their decisions, but this would not be an error provided that it was clear that the claimant had been required to prove the facts relied on in establishing a prima facie case. And in *Brown v Croydon LBC* (2007) the Court of Appeal clarified that it is not an error for the tribunal to move directly to the stage of considering whether or not the employer has an adequate non-discriminatory explanation, since in this case it would be impliedly accepting that the claimant had a prima facie case.

2–048 It is to be hoped that these guidelines will encourage tribunals to be more prepared to draw uncomfortable inferences. In the past many employers have been able to get away with the "lousy employer" defence, as explained by the House of Lords in *Zafar v Glasgow City Council* (1998). In this case an employee who had been dismissed for sexual harassment claimed that he had been the victim of race discrimination. The tribunal found that the Council's conduct of the disciplinary and dismissal proceedings fell far below the standards of a reasonable employer: there was unreasonable delay in dealing with the matter and some allegations were not properly investigated. The House of Lords held that the fact that the employer had acted unreasonably in relation to this employee did not mean that he had been treated less favourably than anyone else would have been: the employer might have acted just as unreasonably towards other employees.

The statutory questionnaire procedure referred to in propositions 7 and 13 requires further comment. The procedure was introduced in the SDA and the Race Relations Act 1976. The claimant filled in a questionnaire stating the occasion on which she thought the discrimination occurred, and the reasons for thinking there was discrimination. The employer was asked whether or not it did discriminate. If the employer denied discrimination, then further information by way of reply to the claimant's questions had to be supplied. This long-standing procedure was in due course extended to the other protected grounds and included in the EqA 2010. As the *Igen Ltd v Wong* guidance shows, the procedure was capable of having some probative value as well as eliciting useful information for the claimant. However, it is not required by EU law, and so it became a candidate for repeal in the Coalition Government's crusade against regulation. Despite 83 per cent of respondents to consultation opposing any change, the procedure was repealed by ERRA from April 2014. This means that claimants are now only able to use the general methods of disclosure and inspection to obtain information.

How far is it possible to discover whether or not you were better qualified than the other candidates? Relevant information is usually sought by way of an order for the disclosure and inspection of documents. But much of the information which is relevant may be confidential—e.g. references. Guidelines on this problem were given by the House of Lords in *Nassé v Science Research Council* (1979). Confidentiality of documents is not per se a reason to refuse disclosure. The test is whether the proceedings can be fairly disposed of without this information. In order to make this decision, it may well be appropriate for the employment judge to look at the documents first. In exercising its discretion over disclosure the court must take into account the interests of third parties. Thus disclosure may be ordered subject to certain conditions; e.g. excising information that would allow individuals to be identified, or covering up confidential parts. Thus it is possible, though difficult, to get this information. Usually other evidence giving rise to at least some question about the appointment will have to be available first. The court will not order disclosure for a "fishing expedition".

Is it relevant to proof of discrimination to point out that the employer has a **2–049** workforce composed almost entirely of men, or of white people? Possibly not: it could be that they are the only ones qualified for the job in question. However, if the workforce is composed mostly of workers drawn from the local area, which has a 20 per cent ethnic minority population, but the business employs only 5 per cent of workers from ethnic minorities, this would seem to raise a question to be answered.

In an early case the EAT took the view that evidence of this kind was not relevant, for even if it disclosed past discrimination, that would not prove that discrimination had taken place on this particular occasion. The Court of Appeal took a more realistic view in *West Midlands PTE v Singh* (1988). Singh, of Indian origin, was employed as an inspector on the buses and sought promotion to chief inspector. To support his claim that he had been discriminated against in being refused promotion he wanted statistics going back four or five years relating to the ethnic origins of those applying for promotion both for the post of chief inspector and posts of a similar grade, and the ethnic origins of those who were successful. The Court of Appeal ruled that this evidence was relevant. Balcombe LJ pointed out that ethnic monitoring was recommended by the CRE Code of Practice, presumably for this sort of purpose, and that employers frequently point to the presence of women or ethnic minorities in their workforce in order to disprove discrimination. Thus statistics can cut both ways: they can be used to support or to rebut a claim of discrimination.

Indirect discrimination

2–050   In the White Paper preceding the SDA, the government envisaged that only intentional discrimination should be unlawful. Motive would be what mattered, not impact. However, the then Home Secretary, Roy Jenkins, was persuaded by a visit to the United States during the summer recess that of far more importance in achieving equality of opportunity was preventing the effect of apparently neutral practices and policies which in fact excluded women or ethnic minorities. The US Supreme Court decision in *Griggs v Duke Power Co* (1971) laid the foundation for the concept of indirect discrimination in the British statutes. In *Griggs* the company administered an aptitude test to all job applicants. It was shown that significantly fewer blacks than whites passed the test, and that the skills examined by the test were not particularly relevant to the jobs applied for. In these circumstances, it was held that the test was discriminatory.

This concept of "adverse impact discrimination" was given statutory form in the United Kingdom as indirect discrimination. Its potential to catch apparently innocuous requirements and thus to begin to address systemic discrimination was demonstrated at an early stage. For example, in *Price v Civil Service Commission* (1978) applicants for the post of Executive Officer had to be aged between 17½ and 28. The claimant, aged 32, successfully argued that this was indirect discrimination against women, since between these ages many women are likely to be out of the labour market bringing up small children.

The original definition of indirect discrimination required claimants to identify a "requirement or condition" which had the effect of screening out people with their protected characteristic. This was interpreted as meaning that a discriminatory criterion was only unlawful if it constituted an absolute bar to appointment if one did not meet it. Unfortunately, this could drive a coach and horses through the legislation, in that it allowed discriminatory preferences free rein, as long as they were not expressed as absolute requirements.

2–051   As a result of changes in EU law from 1997 onwards a new definition of indirect discrimination was introduced across the whole of equality law. This is now to be found in EqA 2010 s.19. Indirect discrimination exists if a "provision, criterion or practice" is applied to a person which is discriminatory in relation to a protected characteristic which she or he possesses. A provision, criterion or practice will be discriminatory if four conditions are fulfilled: first, that the employer applies it, or would apply it, equally to people who do not have the protected characteristic; secondly, that it puts, or would put, people with the protected characteristic at a particular disadvantage when compared with these others; thirdly, that it puts this particular claimant at that disadvantage; and finally, that the employer cannot show it to be a proportionate means of achieving a legitimate aim.

The reference to a "provision, criterion or practice" rather than a "requirement or condition" deals with the problem of discriminatory second-order preferences which do not amount an absolute bar to appointment but which could nonetheless be taken into account by a recruitment panel. Indeed, in the first case on the new law to reach the EAT a very liberal definition was adopted. *British Airways v Starmer* (2005) concerned a female Airbus pilot who sought to reduce her hours to 50 per cent after she had had a baby. The company refused to allow this, on grounds that it would be difficult to reorganise schedules and costly to train replacements. After she sued for indirect sex discrimination (because in practice it is harder for women with family responsibilities than men to work full-time) the company introduced a policy that pilots could only reduce to 75 per cent of full-time hours, citing safety reasons for the new rule. The EAT held that the decision not to allow her to go part-time could be described as a "provision, criterion or practice" even though the company argued that it was a one-off decision and not a standing policy at the time when she asked. This risks blurring the difference between indirect discrimination and the duty to make reasonable accommodation for individual employees, which currently exists only for disability discrimination.

The condition that the provision, criterion or practice should disadvantage a group identified by sharing a protected characteristic is obviously essential in order to show its discriminatory impact. If a rule adversely affects some employees and not others, but there is no common thread between those affected, then there may be a problem, but it is not a problem of discrimination. However, this raises two questions: first, how do you define a group; and secondly, how much adverse impact do you have to show as between the protected group and the comparator group for indirect discrimination to be established?

The first question was raised quite starkly in *Eweida v British Airways plc* (2010). **2–052** The claimant wished to wear a cross symbolic of her Christian belief over her uniform, in contravention of the employer's dress code. Wearing a cross was a manifestation of her religious belief, but no one suggested that it was a requirement for Christians. In these circumstances, the Court of Appeal held that since she could not show others of the same belief who would also be disadvantaged by the provision, criterion or practice, she had failed to establish indirect discrimination. In contrast, in *Mba v Mayor and Burgesses of Merton* (2014), the claimant was a Sabbatarian, a minority Christian group who consider that working on Sunday is wrong. She worked in a care home and claimed indirect discrimination on grounds of religion or belief when she was rostered for Sunday duties. Since there was evidence of at least some Christians holding this view, the Court of Appeal accepted that there was group disadvantage without any discussion of how big a group needed to be. If at the time of her original claim Eweida had been aware of the nurse dismissed for wearing a cross on a chain, whose case was later joined with hers in proceedings before the European Court, would the two of them have been considered as a sufficiently large group for the purposes of this condition?

Eweida took her case to the European Court arguing an interference with her right to freedom of religion under ECHR art.9, joined with three other cases (including that of the nurse, Chaplin). In *Eweida v United Kingdom* (2013) the

European Court applied a proportionality test in deciding whether the interference with her right to manifest her religion was justified, and held that it was not: while the employer had a legitimate aim in wishing to project a consistent corporate image, the refusal to allow any deviation from this was disproportionate (although Chaplin's claim was not upheld, because the employer's objection in her case was based on health and safety). This suggests that in the case of religion or belief only, it will no longer be necessary to show adverse impact on other people sharing the claimant's belief, and EqA 2010 s.19 will have to be interpreted accordingly. However, this still falls short of requiring employers to make reasonable accommodation for employees' religion or beliefs.

The other problematic aspect of group disadvantage concerns the comparison element. The original formulation of this for the anti-discrimination statutes of the 1970s stated that there would be adverse impact if the proportion of women, or married people, or members of a particular racial group who could comply with the provision under attack was "considerably smaller" than the proportion of the comparator group who could comply. This frequently involved difficult discussions of statistical evidence and some confusion on the part of tribunals as to what conclusions they should draw from it. The new formulation simply refers to putting the claimant's group at a particular disadvantage compared with the comparator group. One way of showing this could still be through the use of statistical evidence. However, it could be shown in other ways, such as evidence of experts or other witnesses.

2–053   In direct discrimination cases, the comparison is with a real or hypothetical individual (sometimes more than one); in indirect discrimination, the group disadvantage requirement means that the comparison must be with a group or pool of people who do not have the protected characteristic, but as EqA 2010 s.23 puts it, "there must be no material difference between the circumstances relating to each case". It is not always obvious how the pool for comparison should be drawn, and in *Grundy v British Airways plc* (2008) the Court of Appeal stated that there was not necessarily a single correct answer to the question, yet how the pool is composed may effectively decide the case. A good recent example is *Naeem v Secretary of State for Justice* (2014) where Muslim chaplains employed in the prison service complained that they were disproportionately found at the lower end of the pay scale compared with Christian chaplains. This was true if all chaplains employed were considered, but the reason for the discrepancy was that progression through the pay scale depended on length of service. Until 2002 there had been no Muslim chaplains employed, so none of them could have comparable service to the Christian chaplains employed before this date. The EAT held that the pool for comparison should not be all chaplains, but only those employed since 2002: there was a material difference in the circumstances between Muslim chaplains and Christian chaplains employed before 2002. If the pool for comparison was all chaplains employed since 2002, there was no evidence of the Muslim chaplains being lower scales comparatively. (The Court of Appeal upheld the decision on different grounds: *Naeem v Secretary of State for Justice* (2016).)

The next condition is that the individual claimant must actually be put at a disadvantage by the provision, criterion or practice, or would be put at disadvantage if it were applied. It will continue to be the case that this will be judged according to whether in practice the claimant is at a disadvantage, not whether theoretically this is the case. In *Mandla v Dowell Lee* (1983) it was theoretically possible for the Sikh claimant to comply with the school rule to have a short haircut, but the House of Lords held that it would not be reasonable in practice to expect him to do so.

In *Essop v Home Office* (2015), it was claimed that a test for promotion disproportionately screened out black and ethnic minority employees over the age of 35, thus constituting indirect race and age discrimination. A test case brought on behalf of a number of claimants went to the Court of Appeal on the question of whether they had to show not only this adverse impact, but also that each one of them had failed the test because of belonging to that group (and not, for example, because they had not bothered to prepare for it). The Court of Appeal held that this was indeed the case, and that it was not enough for them to prove (a) the fact of group disadvantage, and (b) their membership of the group. This is a very surprising result, which seems to fly in the face of established principle—readers will have noted the similarity between the facts of this case and those of the American case, *Griggs v Duke Power Co*, which is the foundation of the concept of indirect discrimination and where proof of adverse impact was enough. The reasons for a group being disadvantaged by a provision, criterion or practice may be many and various, and notoriously difficult to establish. The strength of the concept of indirect discrimination is that it sidesteps such sterile debates and focuses on substantive outcomes, and if they are unequal, the criterion causing that inequality becomes suspect and cannot be used unless the need for it is justified. The decision in *Essop v Home Office* is under appeal; in the meantime, we turn to the question of justification.

Justification

Even if a provision, criterion or practice does tend to rule out members of a protected group, in indirect discrimination claims the employer has the chance to claim that it is justified. In *Bilka-Kaufhaus v Weber von Hartz* (1986) the CJEU, construing what is now TFEU art.157, held that an employer would have to show "objectively justified" grounds to make out the defence. This involves three elements—the employer's objective for the rule having an adverse impact must: (a) correspond to a real need on the part of the undertaking; (b) be appropriate to that end; and (c) be necessary to that end.   **2–054**

This standard is broadly codified in the Directives, which state that the provision, criterion or practice must be "objectively justified by a legitimate aim, and the means of achieving that aim are appropriate and necessary" (Recast Equal Treatment Directive (2006/54/EC) art.2(1)(b); Race Directive (2000/43/EC) art.2(2)(b); Framework Employment Directive (2000/78/EC) art.2(2)(b)). In EqA 2010, this has been translated as a requirement that the provision, criterion or practice is "a proportionate means of achieving a legitimate aim". The Government denied that this was weaker than the formulation in the Directive.

It should be reasonably easy in most cases for an employer to show that its aim for a particular policy was legitimate. For example, in *London Borough* of *Islington v Ladele* (2010) the Court of Appeal held that the council's aim of providing its services on a non-discriminatory basis was legitimate and justified it in refusing to permit a Christian registrar not to conduct civil partnerships because this conflicted with her religious beliefs, even though some other councils had accommodated employees with religious objections to civil partnerships by excusing them from such duties. Similarly, in *Allen v GMB* (2008) the Court of Appeal held that it was legitimate for a union to achieve the best possible deal for its members in general, although this meant that some groups would lose out overall.

2–055   A particular issue which has arisen is whether saving costs can on its own be a legitimate aim; some commentators argue that this is not sufficiently important to amount to a justification on its own and that this is also the position taken by the CJEU (see *Fuchs and Kohler v Land Hessen* (2011)). In *Cross v British Airways plc* (2005) the EAT thought that saving money was a legitimate factor when combined with other reasons for the employer wanting to change terms and conditions of employment. The legitimacy of the "cost plus" argument was endorsed by the Court of Appeal in *Woodcock v Cumbria Primary Care Trust* (2012), although the "plus" element in that case was very small. The claimant had been a chief executive, whose post disappeared in a restructuring. He was told that he was at risk of redundancy, but was not actually given notice of dismissal, continuing to be employed on temporary projects while he looked unsuccessfully for another NHS post. His contract entitled him to a 12-month notice period. Some nine months after his post disappeared, the Trust decided that he should be given notice of redundancy. At this point, they realised that he was almost 49, and if he was given notice to expire after his 50th birthday, he would become eligible for very generous NHS redundancy terms, which would cost the Trust an extra £500,000. The redundancy consultation period was therefore cut short and he was given notice of dismissal for redundancy to expire a few weeks before his 50th birthday. As there was a genuine redundancy, which had only been hurried up because of the cost implications and to avoid the claimant getting an unexpected windfall, the Court of Appeal held that this was a cost plus situation and the age discrimination was justified (cf. also *HM Land Registry v Benson* (2012)).

The main area of contention in most cases is whether or not the employer's use of the provision, criterion or practice is proportionate. In *R (Elias) v Ministry of Defence* (2006) (a race discrimination case not involving employment) the Court of Appeal adopted a three-stage approach to proportionality: first, whether the objective is sufficiently important to justify limiting a fundamental right; secondly, whether the measure is rationally connected to the objective, and finally, whether the means chosen are no more than necessary for achieving the objective. In *Homer v Chief Constable of West Yorkshire Police* (2012), another age discrimination case, the Supreme Court stated that in applying the proportionality test it is important that the measure being scrutinised should be *both* appropriate as a means of achieving the aim and reasonably necessary, in the sense of not going further than it needed to.

The employer will be in a stronger position where it has actually engaged in the balancing process before imposing the provision, criterion or practice: see, for example, *Azmi v Kirklees BC* (2007), where, before imposing a condition that the claimant, a Muslim woman classroom assistant, should not wear a veil covering her face while teaching, the school had investigated whether this actually impeded her performance, and found that it did, and had looked into possible alternative ways of dealing with the situation. However, in judging proportionality it is also clear that the tribunal may properly take a different view from the employer as to where the balance lies. In *Hardy & Hansons plc v Lax* (2005) the employers refused to allow a woman to change from full-time to part-time work on her return from maternity leave, citing operational reasons to justify this. The tribunal thought that the employers had exaggerated the difficulties and held that the decision (which indirectly discriminated on grounds of sex) was not justified. The employers appealed, arguing that they should be allowed some leeway if their decision was reasonable, a bit like the "reasonable responses" test for unfair dismissal (see below, para.8–047). This was rejected by the Court of Appeal.

As noted above (para.2–037), age discrimination is different from all the other   **2–056** protected characteristics in that it is possible to have a defence of justification even for direct age discrimination. In *Seldon v Clarkson, Wright & Jakes* (2012) the Supreme Court held that direct age discrimination (in that case, compulsory retirement) could only be justified by reference to government employment policy, labour market or vocational training objectives, as opposed to reasons relating to the individual employer (see above, para.2–037). In *Seldon*, the Supreme Court accepted the firm's aims as fitting within the social policy objectives of inter-generational fairness—sharing job opportunities between older and younger workers and workforce planning, and dignity—avoiding the need to apply performance management to older (and probably senior) workers whose performance might be declining. The case was remitted to the employment tribunal on the issue of whether they had been applied proportionately and it held that the retirement age of 65 was proportionate; an appeal to the EAT was dismissed (*Seldon v Clarkson, Wright & Jakes (No.2)* (2014)).

The Supreme Court handed down its judgment in *Homer v Chief Constable of West Yorkshire Police* (2012) on the same day as its judgment in *Seldon*. *Homer* was a case of indirect age discrimination and the Court made it clear that for indirect age discrimination, acceptable reasons for justification are wider—in particular, taking account of the needs of the particular business.

Part-time workers and indirect sex discrimination

Since the vast majority of part-time workers are women, it was recognised early   **2–057** on that less favourable treatment of part-time workers was usually prima facie indirect discrimination on grounds of sex. The landmark case in EU law recognising this was actually an equal pay case from the United Kingdom, *Jenkins v Kingsgate* (1981), where part-time workers were paid a lower rate than full-time workers on the grounds that they were less productive for the company and there was a higher administrative cost associated with their employment. The CJEU confirmed that this was would be indirect discrimination on grounds of sex and thus unlawful unless it could be justified—the case was ultimately remitted to an employment tribunal on this point. As a result of the Part-time Workers Regulations 2000, less favourable treatment of part-timers may be actionable even without proving adverse impact on grounds of sex (see below, para.3–022). However, these Regulations only apply if part-timers are treated less favourably than full-timers and would not cover the situation where an employee—usually a woman—asks to change from full-time to part-time work, perhaps because of family commitments. In *Home Office v Holmes* (1984) the EAT (in an unreserved decision) held that a refusal to permit a woman who had previously been full-time to return to part-time work after was indirect sex discrimination and not justified on the facts. The EAT was at pains to say that the case was limited to its own facts and should not be regarded as establishing a general right to go part-time after maternity leave, but predictably, this was exactly what a number of female employees sought to argue.

In *Clymo v Wandsworth LBC* (1989) the claimant was a branch librarian who wanted to job-share with her husband, who was also a librarian employed by the council, but in a lower grade. The council rejected this on the grounds that the post was a managerial position for which they were entitled to stipulate a full-time worker. The EAT enthusiastically accepted this, stating that some jobs by their nature would require full-time commitment (a managing director was the example they gave) although others (cleaners, in their example) would not be in that category. No prizes for guessing which sexes predominate in these exemplars! This is now quite an old authority, however, and in recent times it has become less easy for employers to justify requirements for full-time working (see, e.g. *British Airways plc v Starmer* (2005) and *Hardy & Hansons v Lax* (2005)). It would certainly be very unwise for an employer to refuse a woman's request to work part-time without giving it very serious consideration.

Harassment

2–058   The concept of harassment did not appear in the original anti-discrimination legislation. Once again American jurisprudence and legal theory were influential. The American Equal Employment Opportunities Commission originally defined sexual harassment as being of two main kinds: first, unwelcome sexual advances and other verbal or physical conduct of a sexual nature where submission to or rejection of the conduct would affect the recipient's employment; and secondly, conduct having either the purpose or effect of creating an intimidating, hostile or offensive working environment. In British law, this concept of harassment became accepted as a form of direct sex or race discrimination, on the basis that it amounted to treating someone less favourably on grounds of sex or race (*Porcelli v Strathclyde Regional Council* (1984); *De Souza v AA* (1986)).

British law was in turn influential when the European Union turned its attention to harassment and the two-pronged definition of harassment was largely adopted for all forms of harassment—in the Race Directive (2000/43/EC) for race discrimination, in the Recast Equal Treatment Directive (2006/54/EC) for sex discrimination and in the Framework Employment Directive (2000/78/EC) for discrimination on other grounds. These directives define harassment as unwanted conduct related to the protected reason which has the purpose or effect of violating the dignity of a person *and* of creating an intimidating, hostile, degrading, humiliating or offensive environment (my emphasis). However, British case-law had already accepted that harassment could occur *either* where the conduct violated dignity *or* where it created a poisoned atmosphere and this wider formulation has been retained in the new statutory definition of harassment, now to be found in EqA 2010 s.26.

Harassment is defined in s.26(1) as "unwanted conduct related to a relevant protected characteristic" which has the purpose or effect of either violating the dignity of the claimant, or creating an intimidating, hostile, degrading, humiliating or offensive environment for the claimant. The characteristics of pregnancy and maternity and marriage or civil partnership are not relevant characteristics for this purpose, so harassment on these grounds would be actionable only insofar as it would constitute harassment related to sex or sexual orientation.

The main change from the previous law is that, to be actionable, harassment need only be "related to" a relevant characteristic, not "on grounds" of it. This suggests that a wider range of conduct than previously will come within its purview, a conclusion reinforced by the EHRC Code of Practice, which uses a number of examples recognisable from earlier case-law on harassment, which it states would clearly be capable of being found to be harassment under the present law, although in the past, the cases may have been lost. For example, the facts of *Brumfitt v Ministry of Defence* (2005), where a training officer used offensive and obscene language directed at both men and women in his audience, which the claimant found offensive to her as a woman, appear in the Code. The case was lost at the time because (in a direct sex discrimination claim) the woman was treated in the same way as men. The view expressed in the Code is that this would be related to her sex and thus actionable as harassment today, even though the remarks were not directed at her and men and women were not treated differently.

Similarly, harassment because of association with someone who has a pro-   **2–059**
tected characteristic, or because the claimant is perceived as having a protected characteristic, would be covered (cf. paras 2–031 and 2–032, above). The previous law had already reached this position for some protected grounds: for example, in *Saini v All Saints Haque Centre* (2009) the Hindu manager of an advice centre was removed from his post because of his religious beliefs and the claimant, a senior advice worker, was subjected to bullying and intimidatory interviews in an attempt to obtain evidence against the manager. This was held to be harassment of the claimant on grounds of religious belief, even though it was the manager's belief, not his, which was at issue. Also, as seen already, in *English v Thomas Sanderson Blinds Ltd* (2009) the Court of Appeal allowed a claim of harassment because of homophobic abuse by co-workers even though the claimant was known to be heterosexual. If the approach in the Code is followed, such situations will clearly constitute harassment related to a protected characteristic.

There is no need for the claimant to show that there have been detrimental consequences for him or her as a result of the harassment—something which often used to be a sticking point when harassment was only actionable as a form of direct discrimination. Thus the central question for the tribunal will be whether or not there is a violation of the claimant's dignity and/or a poisoned atmosphere. In judging this, EqA 2010 s.26(4) provides that the recipient's perception is to be taken into account, along with the other circumstances of the case, but this subjective element is qualified by an objective test as well: "whether it is reasonable for the conduct to have that effect". This is to guard against an over-sensitive—or over-zealous—claimant arguing harassment in circumstances where it is highly unlikely that others similarly situated would have been offended.

As well as harassment in a general sense, s.26(2) also makes unlawful sexual harassment, defined as "unwanted conduct of a sexual nature" which has the purpose or effect of either violating the claimant's dignity or creating a poisoned atmosphere. This is included separately because there are two forms of harassment included in the Recast Equal Treatment Directive (2006/54/EC)). Article 1 of that Directive defines "harassment", which is unwanted conduct related to sex with the purpose or effect of violating dignity and creating a hostile environment, and "sexual harassment", which is unwanted verbal, non-verbal or physical conduct of a sexual nature with the same purposes and effects. It is difficult to imagine what would fall under the second form, sexual harassment, which would not already be encompassed in the general definition of harassment, especially since the harassment need only be related to the protected characteristic. Thus it seems that the definition of sexual harassment should be seen as having been included *ex abundante cautela* and to demonstrate express compliance with the Recast Equal Treatment Directive.

2–060   EqA 2010 s.26(3) defines a third form of harassment, applicable only to sex and gender reassignment, where the claimant is treated less favourably because of her submission to, or rejection of, the unwanted conduct related either to sex or gender reassignment. This is called "quid pro quo" harassment in the United States. It means not only that someone who rejects such conduct could claim, but also that an employer would be liable for unlawful harassment of a woman, for example, who receives some benefit from submitting to unwanted sexual conduct. Presumably this is included for sex and gender reassignment only because it is not seen as a problem in relation to the other protected grounds.

The effect of making harassment a freestanding head of discrimination is that it is no longer necessary to get involved in speculative comparisons with how the perpetrator might have behaved towards someone without the protected characteristic. At the same time, the definition of "detriment" in EqA 2010 s.212 has been changed so as to exclude conduct which amounts to harassment, with the effect that harassment is no longer actionable as direct discrimination.

Harassment may also be actionable in other ways. In *Waters v Commissioner of Police of the Metropolis* (2000) the House of Lords held that an employer could be liable in negligence if it could foresee that bullying or harassment was likely to take place and did nothing to stop it. The Protection from Harassment Act 1997, which was really aimed at protecting people from stalkers, has also been used in workplace bullying situations and in *Majrowski v Guy's and St Thomas's NHS Trust* (2006) the House of Lords held that employers could be vicariously liable for acts of employees contrary to that Act.

Harassment by third parties

In *Burton v De Vere Hotels* (1996) the EAT held that an employer could be directly **2–061** liable for discrimination consisting of the acts of third parties: not only employees, but also customers, clients and others. The action was brought against a hotel which had been booked for a club dinner, attended by 400 men. They had invited as after-dinner speaker a comedian notorious for sexually explicit and racial jokes. Two young Afro-Caribbean waitresses clearing tables at the end of the dinner attracted his attention and in the course of a speech containing many offensive words and jokes he made insulting comments directed at them too. The EAT held that although the hotel could not be vicariously liable for the actions of third parties, it was directly responsible for discrimination in these circumstances because, as employers, they had control of the situation in which the harassment took place. Members of the hotel management were present to supervise the event. They could at least have minimised the effects of the harassment by withdrawing the waitresses as soon as the comedian became offensive. Failure to do so meant that the employer had directly subjected them to a detriment, namely the racial harassment.

Burton v De Vere Hotels was relied on in numerous cases over the next six or seven years, but was then disapproved by the House of Lords in *Pearce v Governing Body of Mayfield School* (2003). This case involved a lesbian teacher forced out of her job by homophobic abuse by pupils at the school and the central issue was whether gender-specific abuse (e.g. calling her a "dyke") was sex discrimination even though it was clear that a male homosexual teacher would have been subjected to similar abuse. The House of Lords held that this did not constitute direct sex discrimination because a male homosexual would have been treated just as badly as the female homosexual claimant had been. However, even though it was not essential to their decision, the Law Lords went on to hold that even if it had been discrimination, the school would not have been liable for the actions of the pupils. The school's liability was argued to reside in its failure to protect her. Only if it could be shown that this was itself an omission to act on grounds of her sex would the school be liable. Although the House of Lords' comments were strictly obiter, *Burton v De Vere Hotels* could no longer be regarded as good law in the light of this and so, unfortunately, an important spur for employers to ensure a harassment-free workplace was removed.

The compatibility of this position with EU law was canvassed in *EOC v Secretary of State for Trade and Industry* (2007). Although the Equal Treatment Amendment Directive (2002/73/EC) did not expressly require employers to be liable for the actions of third parties, the court noted that the Government's own factsheet suggested that under the Directive employers could be liable when they were aware of harassment by third parties, such as customers or suppliers, and did nothing to try and remedy the situation. It was suggested that the law should reflect this, and as a result the Government of the day introduced a change—but for sex discrimination only.

2–062 The EqA 2010 extended the liability of employers for acts of third parties in certain limited circumstances to all the protected characteristics. The limitations were that it applied only to harassment: not to other forms of discrimination, and it was subject to two conditions: first, the employer must know of the harassment, and secondly, there must have been such harassment on two other occasions (a "three strikes and you're out" rule)—although the harasser did not have to be the same person each time. This provision did not survive the Coalition Government's search and destroy policy for anything which might go further than absolutely required by EU law and was repealed by the ERRA.

It remains arguable, however, that the view once espoused by the Government, that employers can be liable for third party harassment in situations where they know about it and do nothing, may yet be vindicated. In *Sheffield City Council v Norouzi* (2011) the EAT upheld a tribunal's decision that the claimant could rely directly on the Race Directive (2000/43/EC), since the council was an emanation of the state, and thus be liable for failing to do enough to protect the claimant from harassment by a third party (an inmate of a council home for troubled children) when it had clearly been put on notice of the problem. It seems, however, that this would not assist employees of private sector employers (*Conteh v Parking Partners Ltd* (2011)).

Victimisation

2–063 Victimisation is defined by EqA 2010 s.27 as subjecting someone to a detriment because she or he has done a protected act. The protected acts are laid out in s.27(2); they are: bringing proceedings under the EqA 2010; giving evidence or information in connection with such proceedings; doing anything else in connection with the Equality Act; and making an allegation that the Act has been contravened. In addition, subjecting someone to a detriment for making a pay disclosure will also count as victimisation (EqA 2010 s.77: see below, para.7–020).

The object of the prohibition on victimisation is to prevent people from being discouraged from making complaints because of fear of repercussions at work. Indeed, it could be argued that there is a need for such anti-victimisation provisions on a wider scale, for example in unfair dismissal cases. However, while the purpose of the provisions is straightforward, their interpretation has caused problems. One difficulty has been removed: it was previously necessary to show that the claimant had been treated *less favourably* than others because of her protected act, raising the usual difficult questions about the attributes of a real or hypothetical comparator. Under EqA 2010 s.27 it is only necessary to show that the claimant was subjected to a detriment because of her act.

What amounts to a detriment? EqA 2010 s.212 says only that it is not conduct which amounts to harassment under s.26, so recourse must be had to earlier case-law. The question frequently arose in harassment cases where the complaint was essentially that the harassment itself constituted the detriment. Is being offended or upset or humiliated by insulting behaviour enough to found an action? The leading authority is the decision of the House of Lords in *Shamoon v Chief Constable of the Royal Ulster Constabulary* (2003), where the issue was whether a police inspector suffered a detriment by having the duty of conducting annual appraisals of junior officers taken away from her following complaints about her manner. The House of Lords stated that the test was whether or not a reasonable worker would take the view that he or she had been put at a disadvantage, whether or not there were any adverse physical or economic consequences. While an "unjustified sense of grievance" would be insufficient, Lord Scott indicated that detriment should be considered from the victim's point of view, and detriment was found in the case, as a reasonable worker might well find it demeaning to have duties removed from her.

The remaining area of difficulty is the degree of causative link necessary **2–064** between the protected act and the detrimental treatment. In *Aziz v Trinity Street Taxis* (1988) the protected act was making secret recordings of conversations with colleagues in the taxi association which the claimant planned to use in race discrimination proceedings against the taxi association. The Court of Appeal accepted the association's argument that it would have expelled anyone guilty of such a breach of trust, so although the claimant had done a protected act, and had been detrimentally treated in consequence, they held that it was not by reason of the race discrimination legislation but by reason of his underhand conduct. This comes perilously close to treating the motive of the employer as determinative of cause.

The House of Lords considered the issue in *Nagarajan v London Regional Transport* (1999). In this case, a tribunal found that members of an interview panel that rejected the claimant were at least subconsciously influenced by the fact that he had made several claims of race discrimination against the company in the past (protected acts for the purposes of the victimisation claim). The House of Lords held that if the protected act was a "substantial reason" or an "important factor" leading to the less favourable treatment (even subconsciously), a claim for victimisation would succeed; the protected act need not be the only or even the main reason.

Unfortunately, almost at once the House of Lords had second thoughts. In *Chief Constable of West Yorks Police v Khan* (2001) a police sergeant of Indian origin sued for race discrimination when he failed on several occasions to gain promotion. While these proceedings were ongoing he applied for an inspector's post in a different force. The West Yorkshire Police refused to give him a reference in case it prejudiced the case. The sergeant therefore added a claim for victimisation. The Court of Appeal held that if he had not brought the discrimination proceedings he would have been given a reference and that his victimisation claim therefore succeeded. In adopting this "but-for" test the Court of Appeal was following its understanding of the House of Lords' decision in *Nagarajan v London Regional Transport*. The House of Lords reversed, holding that the treatment complained of had to be "by reason of" the protected act and that this required more than causation (but for the protected act the less favourable treatment would not have occurred): it also required some level of mental connection between the two facts by the employer. Also, in a display of semantic nicety, they also held that it was the existence of the other proceedings, rather than the fact that the claimant had brought them, which was the relevant reason here. The claimant's victimisation claim was therefore rejected. It is frankly hard to square this with *Nagarajan*.

2–065   The fact that the EqA 2010 uses the word "because" for the causal connection suggests that it is intended that the test of causal link should be the same as for direct discrimination, discussed above, para.2–030. The difference is that, in victimisation cases, the link must be between the detrimental treatment and the protected act rather than between the less favourable treatment and a protected characteristic.

A different aspect of victimisation surfaced in *Derbyshire v St Helens MBC* (2007) which arose out of a multiple equal pay claim brought by 500 women employed as catering staff in the council's school meals service. The council offered a settlement which was accepted by all but 39 of the women. The council then wrote to all the catering staff warning that if those women's claims succeeded, it was likely that there would be job losses and the school meals service might close altogether. This was reinforced in a similar letter sent only to the 39 claimants. The House of Lords upheld their claims for victimisation. It was perfectly all right for an employer to attempt to settle claims out of court and to provide information to employees—but these letters overstepped the mark and amounted to illegitimate pressure on the employees to abandon their claims. The House of Lords held that the test for this was what the effect of the pressure would be on a reasonable employee, not whether the employer was acting in good faith.

Post-employment victimisation

2–066   Under the pre-2010 legislation, there was originally doubt as to whether victimisation taking place after dismissal was actionable. In *Adekeye v Post Office (No.2)* (1997) the Court of Appeal held that there was no protection from race discrimination once employment had terminated. In *Coote v Granada Hospitality* (1999) the EAT accepted that it was bound to adopt the same interpretation in relation to sex discrimination, but it referred to the CJEU the question of whether this was compatible with the Equal Treatment Directive (76/207/EEC), which requires that there must be effective remedies for breach of the Directive (see arts 17 and 18 of the Recast Equal Treatment Directive). The CJEU held that the principle requiring effective remedies would be infringed if employers could take retaliatory steps affecting the employee after the employment had ended (as the employer had done here, by refusing to give her a reference for a new job) and that someone in the claimant's position should be protected by the law.

The House of Lords considered the whole question of discrimination arising after employment had terminated in *Relaxion Group plc v Rhys-Harper* (2003) and *D'Souza v Lambeth LBC* (2003). It held that the legislation could be interpreted as covering post-employment discrimination, provided that the connection between the post-employment discriminatory act and the employment could be proved; at the same time the legislation was amended to make clear that post-employment victimisation was covered.

A problem arose with the drafting of the EqA 2010, in that s.108(7) appeared to exclude this liability. Conflicting authority in the EAT was resolved by the Court of Appeal in *Rowstock Ltd v Jessemey* (2014), holding that words should be read into the Act to make it clear that post-employment victimisation continues to be unlawful, in order to remain in line with EU law.

Disability Discrimination

There are some differences between disability discrimination and discrimination relating to the other protected characteristics, the main one being that there are additional forms of unlawful discrimination which apply only to disability. For that reason, it probably makes sense to deal with it separately. The scope of the protected ground will be considered first, then the forms of disability discrimination.

2–067

Background

Laws to prevent discrimination against people with disabilities were originally introduced in many countries, including the United Kingdom, to provide some protection in employment for soldiers returning from war. The original British legislation, the Disabled Persons (Employment) Act, was passed in 1944 and imposed a quota requirement related to the proportion of disabled people thought to be in the workforce. At least 3 per cent of the workforce of employers with 20 or more employees were meant to be people registered as disabled. This legislation was widely recognised to be ineffective, but there was little impetus for reform until campaigning began in 1993, inspired by the American experience. The comprehensive and ambitious Americans with Disabilities Act 1992 was predicated on the philosophy that a society which excludes people with disabilities from social institutions, including the workplace, is denying them their civil rights. This provided both a powerful argument for reform and a single banner under which groups representing people with different disabilities could unite. The Civil Rights (Disabled Persons) Bill, heavily influenced by the American Act, was introduced as a private member's Bill and almost became law in 1994. It was defeated by the filibustering of a few Conservative MPs, in circumstances which caused a public outcry. This led the Conservative Government to bring forward its own proposals, finally passed as the Disability Discrimination Act 1995 (DDA). In fact, the Act was not brought into force until December 1996, when supporting regulations, guidance and a code of practice had been prepared. While weaker than the reformers had proposed and wished for, the DDA was nonetheless a great improvement on the former position.

2–068

In 1999 the Labour Government set up a non-statutory body, the Disability Rights Task Force, to advise it on the legislation. The Task Force, together with the Disability Rights Commission (from 2000), was active in pressing for improvements to the DDA. In addition, the inclusion of disability in the Framework Employment Directive (2000/78/EC) made some reform to the DDA essential. The reforms required to comply with the Directive were carried out by the Disability Discrimination Act 1995 (Amendment) Regulations 2003 and reforms based on the recommendations of the Task Force and the DRC were contained in the DDA. All, of course, are now repealed and replaced by the provisions of the EqA 2010.

Definition of disability

2–069   Unlike some of the other protected characteristics, in relation to disability, the question of whether a particular claimant satisfies the definition of having this protected characteristic is frequently a major contested issue, and therefore often heard as a preliminary point before the main proceedings on whether discrimination has taken place. The burden of proof is on the claimant to show that she or he comes within the definition of a disabled person (*Morgan v Staffordshire University* (2002)) so employers often defend a claim by denying that the claimant is a disabled person in the first place.

The basic definition of disability is found in EqA 2010 s.6. It is expanded in Sch.1 to the Act, the Equality Act 2010 (Disability) Regulations 2010 (the Disability Regulations) and the Equality Act 2010 Guidance on the Definition of Disability issued in accordance with EqA 2010 s.6(5). It is also dealt with in Appendix A of the EHRC Code of Practice, although there is far more detail in the Statutory Guidance on the Definition. It is a pity that, having consolidated everything else into one statute, there is still a separate set of regulations on the definition of disability, meaning that recourse is necessary to at least three different instruments on the single issue of who is a disabled person.

EqA 2010 s.6 states that a person has a disability if she or he has a physical or mental impairment which has a substantial and long-term adverse effect on his ability to carry out normal day-to-day activities. Mental impairment covers mental illness as well as learning disabilities. This could include depression, if the effects are severe enough (*Kapadia v Lambeth LBC* (2000)). The Disability Regulations provide that psychopathic or anti-social disorders such as kleptomania or paedophilia are excluded. Addiction to alcohol, tobacco or drugs does not count as a disability, although physical manifestations of such dependency (such as liver or heart disease) are capable of doing so (e.g. *Power v Panasonic* (2003)). As the Statutory Guidance makes clear, the cause of a disability is not at issue: what matters is the effects on the claimant. Nonetheless, surprise was expressed in the media when the CJEU decided in *Kaltoft v Municipality of Billund* (2015) that, while obesity is not per se a disability, it is capable of being one if it is severe enough substantially to impair a person's normal abilities. The claimant was a childminder in Denmark who claimed that he had been selected for redundancy on grounds of his obesity, and that this amounted to disability discrimination.

2–070   There is a distinction between sickness and disability, although they may sometimes overlap. An illness may cause a disability, or an illness may be sufficiently incapacitating and long term to amount to a disability, but disabilities may also be congenital or result from an accident. The Framework Employment Directive (2000/78/EC) does not define disability, but the CJEU held in *Chacón Navas v Eurest Colectividades SA* (2006) that dismissal for sickness alone would not be covered. The court elaborated on this in *HK Danmark (acting on behalf of Ring) v Dansk almennyttigt Boligselskab* (2013), where it placed emphasis on the UN Convention on the Rights of Persons with Disabilities to which the European Union had recently acceded. In this case, involving two workers with long-term illnesses which prevented them from working full-time, the court held that disability included illnesses resulting in long-term limitations in a worker's ability to participate in professional life, and that this included situations where the impairment did not prevent them working completely, but did limit the amount of work which they could undertake. The UN Convention definition was also expressly adopted in *Kaltoft v Municipality of Billund* (2015).

Until amendment in 2005, mental illness was only covered if it was "clinically well-recognised", an indication that the law originally adopted a "medical model" of disability. This means that the question of who is disabled is one which is essentially to be answered by medical experts. This was presumably thought to have the advantage that the test would depend on objective facts and that a fair degree of precision could be obtained. In practice, it has turned out to have the disadvantage that in any case where the issue of disability is contested it is virtually essential for both parties to call expert medical evidence, adding substantially to the cost of the proceedings. In *Kapadia v Lambeth LBC* (2000) the employer argued that the employee was not disabled by his depression, given that he had successfully applied for promotion while receiving treatment. But since the employer had not produced any medical evidence, preference had to be given to the uncontradicted evidence of the employee's psychologist and doctor to the effect that he was. More fundamentally, however, disability rights activists argue that the biggest problem facing people with disabilities is the blinkered attitude of the rest of the community, who frequently perceive them as having greater limitations than is in fact the case or who exhibit irrational prejudices. They therefore argue that a "social model" of disability would be more appropriate, which would treat people as disabled if they are liable to be perceived as disabled or to suffer from prejudice against people with disabilities. There are some elements of disability discrimination law which do adopt the social model, so that certain conditions which are perceived as disabilities are included, even though they would not in reality affect someone's performance (such as severe disfigurement or past disability: see EqA 2010 Sch.1, paras 3 and 9).

In a change from the previous position, which dealt with the matter only in codes of practice, EqA 2010 s.212 now defines "substantial" as meaning "more than minor or trivial". Factors such as the time taken to do something, or the manner of doing it are among the things to be taken into account in deciding how substantial an effect is. When the law against disability discrimination was first introduced, tribunals were inclined to interpret "substantial" as meaning "very large". In *Goodwin v Patent Office* (1999) the employee suffered from paranoid schizophrenia. At a time when he was not on proper medication his behaviour towards his colleagues was bizarre, leading to complaints and his eventual dismissal. Despite this, an employment tribunal held that the effects of his mental illness were not substantial, since he was able to live alone and look after himself and carry out his work to a satisfactory standard. The EAT held that the tribunal had misdirected itself on the meaning of "substantial" and substituted a finding that he was disabled, reminding tribunals that people with disabilities usually develop effective coping strategies to enable them to function in an often hostile environment and warning that this should not be allowed to obscure the actual degree of impairment. Due to evidence that blind and partially sighted people were failing to convince tribunals that they were disabled, so effective were their coping strategies, special provision had to be made to state in terms that anyone who is certified as blind or partially sighted by a registered ophthalmologist must count as a disabled person (see now the Disability Regulations 2010 reg.7).

In the case of progressive illnesses (such as muscular dystrophy or rheumatoid arthritis), the effects may not at first be substantial, or there may be periods of remission. People with such disabilities will nevertheless receive the protection of the Act as soon as the illness manifests itself in any adverse effect on their normal day-to-day activities (EqA 2010 Sch.1, para.8). The Disability Rights Commission pressed for people with progressive conditions to be covered from the point of diagnosis, since it is from this point that they may suffer discrimination and but this has been implemented only in relation to cancer, multiple sclerosis or HIV infection (EqA 2010 Sch.1, para.6).

2–071   An impairment which would be likely to have a substantial effect if it were not being treated or corrected is to be treated as if it actually has that effect (EqA 2010 Sch.1, para.5). This makes sense, since an employer may be unwilling to believe in the effectiveness of the treatment and might discriminate against someone with a disability even though it causes no adverse effect in practice: epilepsy controlled by medication might be an example. In *Goodwin v Patent Office* (1999) the EAT described this situation as "deduced effects" of the disability. This important point was overlooked by the employment tribunal in *Kapadia v Lambeth LBC* (2000) which decided that the effects of the claimant's depression were not substantial. This finding could not stand in the face of medical evidence to the effect that without regular counselling sessions from his psychologist he would have had a complete mental breakdown. A sight impairment which would be substantial but is corrected by wearing spectacles or contact lenses is not to be treated as substantial (EqA 2010 Sch.1, para.5(3)).

A long-term effect is defined in EqA 2010 Sch.1, para.2 as one which is capable of lasting for a year or more, or the rest of the claimant's life, although its severity may vary over time. An impairment which ceases, but which is likely to recur is treated as continuing, and if it is likely to recur more than 12 months after its first occurrence, it will be taken to have a long-term effect (although hay fever is specifically excluded by regulation). In *SCA Packaging Ltd v Boyle* (2009) the House of Lords held that a condition was "likely to recur" if it "could well happen", taking the view that, in this context, Parliament did not intend to require a more than 50 per cent chance of recurrence but, rather, whether there was a risk which should be guarded against. Lord Rodger went so far as to comment that if a course of treatment is undertaken on medical advice, an employer can assume that if treatment is stopped, the impairment is always "likely to recur".

Whether an impairment is likely to recur is to be judged at the time of the action alleged to constitute discrimination. In *Richmond Adult Community College v McDougall* (2008) the college made a job offer to the claimant, but withdrew it when they got an occupational health report on her which disclosed that she had a history of mental illness, including a short period when she had been sectioned. The mental illness had only lasted for a relatively short period and, at the time the college took its action, there was no real likelihood of it recurring. The college argued, therefore, that she was not a disabled person within the meaning of the EqA 2010, because the disability was not "long-term". Shortly after the college withdrew the job offer, the claimant became seriously ill once more and she was sectioned again. If this information was taken into account, it was clear that her illness would be regarded as long-term for the purposes of EqA 2010. The Court of Appeal held that facts occurring after the employer's decision but before tribunal proceedings should not be taken into account. EqA 2010 focuses on whether the employer's action is lawful or not, which should be judged in the light of what was known at the time of that action.

If a claimant has two separate impairments, each of which lasts less than 12 **2–072** months, they cannot be aggregated to make a "long-term" effect. However, if one impairment either develops into something else, or causes a different impairment, they can be taken together, and in *Patel v Oldham BC* (2010) the EAT warned tribunals against finding fine distinctions between medical conditions.

The final condition is that the disability must affect the worker's capacity to undertake "normal day-to-day activities". These used to be exhaustively defined in the legislation, but the government consultation paper preceding EqA 2010 expressed the view that the statutory list of capacities was of little assistance in deciding whether someone was disabled and could actually work as an extra barrier to a disability claim as claimants strove to show which capacities were impaired. In the absence of a definition, the main issue which arises here is whether work activities which are not also normal day-to-day activities are covered by this definition. In *Chacón Navas v Eurest Colectivades SA* (2006) the CJEU stated that the concept of disability involved impairments which "hinder the participation of the person concerned in professional life", and this formulation was repeated in *HK Danmark (acting on behalf of Ring) v Dansk almennyttigt Boligselskab* (2013). It should be noted, however, that in neither case was the CJEU directly considering the question of whether an impairment which only affected working activity would be within the definition of disability. In the light of the CJEU's decision in *Chacón Navas*, the EAT held that taking examinations or assessments should be regarded as normal day-to-day activities in *Paterson v Commissioner of Police of the Metropolis* (2007). No doubt with these cases in mind, the EHRC Code of Practice on Employment says:

> "Day-to-day activities . . . include—but are not limited to—activities such as walking, driving, using public transport, cooking, eating, lifting and carrying everyday objects, typing, writing (and taking exams), going to the toilet,

talking, listening to conversations or music, reading, taking part in normal social interaction or forming social relationships, nourishing and caring for one's self. Normal day-to-day activities also encompass the activities which are relevant to working life" (App.I para.15).

As the EAT pointed out in *Aderemi v London & South Eastern Railway Ltd* (2013), the test is probably whether the activity in question is the sort of thing which is common in lots of jobs, which can therefore be regarded as a normal day-to-day activity, or whether it is something relatively rare, such as the high degree of motor skills needed for a consultant surgeon or the ability to with-stand contact with chemicals not used in everyday life. An example of the kind of impairment which does not affect normal day-to-day activities is provided by *Chief Constable of Lothian and Borders Police v Cumming* (2010) where the claimant's application to become a police constable was rejected because her sight in her left eye was below the vision standard set by the police force even though this caused her no significant problems in her day-to-day life. It was held that she was not a disabled person.

In addition to people with current disabilities, EqA 2010 Sch.1, para.9 also treats as disabled someone who has had a disability in the past, even though it may now no longer have any effect. This again is in recognition that an employer might not be prepared to accept that there is no risk of recurrence and could still discriminate because of a past condition. This may especially be the case with mental illness. In *Greenwood v British Airways* (1999) an employee was refused promotion because he was regarded as unreliable by reason of his previous absence record caused by depression. The employment tribunal held that he was not disabled because he was not suffering from depression when he applied for promotion. The EAT held that he had established that the depression consti-tuted a past disability and so he should have been treated as a disabled person for the purposes of the law: it was not necessary to show that he continued to suffer from the effects of depression.

Forms of disability discrimination

2–073   When the DDA was passed in 1995, two forms of discrimination were defined: less favourable treatment related to a disability—which was, however, subject to a defence of justification—and failure to make reasonable adjustments. Victimisation was also unlawful, but harassment was only covered if it came within less favourable treatment. A concept of direct discrimination on grounds of disability was introduced in 2003 in order to comply with the Framework Employment Directive (2000/78/EC), but no change was made on indirect dis-crimination. However, as part of the programme of harmonising protection across all the protected characteristics, protection against indirect discrimina-tion on grounds of disability was introduced in the EqA 2010. It may be doubted if this will add significantly to the protection of disabled workers, since two spe-cific forms of disability discrimination are still provided for in the Act and these are likely to give greater protection in practice. They have evolved considerably from their original format.

Discrimination arising from a disability

EqA 2010 s.15 establishes a new ground of discrimination for disability only: **2–074** unfavourable treatment "because of something arising in consequence" of the claimant's disability, which cannot be justified as a proportionate means of achieving a legitimate aim.

This replaces the former protection from less favourable treatment for a reason related to disability, which was emasculated by the House of Lords' decision in *Mayor and Burgesses of Lewisham v Malcolm* (2008). In that case, which was actually a case about provision of services rather than employment, the claimant, who suffered from schizophrenia, sub-let his council flat at a time when he was not taking his medication. Sub-letting was a breach of the terms of his tenancy and the council moved to evict him. He claimed that this was disability-related discrimination, because it was as a result of his untreated schizophrenia that he let his life get out of control and sub-let the flat. Because he had to show that he had been *less* favourably treated for a disability-related reason, it was necessary to consider the attributes of an appropriate hypothetical comparator. The Court of Appeal, following established authority, held that the comparison should be with someone without schizophrenia, who would therefore not have sub-let the flat. The majority of the House of Lords, however, considered that this made it too easy to establish disability-related discrimination. In their view, the appropriate comparison here should be with someone who did not have the claimant's disability but who had sub-let his flat. As the council would obviously have evicted such a person too, the claimant had not established disability-related discrimination. This effectively equated disability-related discrimination to direct discrimination because of disability, meaning that the protection was nugatory.

Hence the new concept of discrimination arising from disability. As EqA 2010 s.15 refers to *unfavourable* treatment rather than *less favourable* treatment, the comparison issue is avoided: the essential question is one of causation. The wording also makes it clear that it applies where the employer's reason for action is not the disability itself (which would be direct discrimination) but something which arises in consequence of the disability: examples might be absence from work caused by a need for medical treatment, challenging behaviour which is a manifestation of a mental impairment, or under-performance because of a physical impairment. If an employer were to discipline or dismiss a worker for one of these reasons, it would be disability discrimination unless the employer could show that it was a proportionate response in the circumstances.

There is an important qualification to be noted: under s.15(2) an employer **2–075** will not be liable for discrimination arising from disability if he can show that he did not know, and could not reasonably be expected to know, of the claimant's disability. This is likely to be a highly contested issue: a crucial factor will be how much convincing tribunals will need before accepting that an employer could not reasonably be expected to know of the disability (and note that the burden of proof for this is on the employer). The EHRC Code of Practice on Employment, paras 5.13–5.19, states categorically that an employer will be taken to know if information is gathered on its behalf, whether by it human resources department or another agency, even if that has not been passed on to those dealing directly with an employee, and recommends, therefore, that employers should make appropriate arrangements for sharing information while having regard to privacy and confidentiality. Even if an employee has not disclosed a disability, the Code states that the employer should consider whether this is a possibility, suggesting that employers may need explicitly to have regard to this before making any decision to discipline or dismiss an employee for lack of capability or even misconduct.

Pre-employment medical checks

2–076   For people with disabilities, the question of when, to whom and how far to disclose the nature of their impairment can be fraught with difficulty. If they do not disclose it, they may be unable to complain that they have been treated unfavourably because of its consequences. They will also be unable to rely on the employer's duty to make reasonable adjustments (below, para.2–077). On the other hand, if they disclose it too early or to too many people, they risk either not getting a job at all, or being held back by managers' conscious or unconscious assumptions about what they can or cannot do.

For many years, campaigners for disability rights have argued that employers should not be able to ask for information about health or disability status at the recruitment stage, because it makes it too easy to screen out people with disabilities ostensibly for other reasons. This has now been enacted by EqA 2010 s.60, which prohibits employers from making enquiries about health before making a person an offer of employment, except in limited circumstances. First, it is allowable to ask whether a potential recruit can take part in activities which will be part of the recruitment assessment process, and/or whether she will need any adjustments to take part. Secondly, job applicants can be asked whether they are able to perform an intrinsic function of the work (asking would-be scaffolders about their ability to climb ladders to a significant height is the example given in the EHRC Code of Practice). Thirdly, it is allowable to ask questions for the purpose of monitoring equality and diversity. Fourthly, where what is proposed is positive action in accordance with EqA 2010 s.158 (above, para.2–042). Finally, where having a particular disability is an occupational requirement for the post (e.g. where the post involves services to a particular disabled group and it is important for the postholder to share that disability).

The success of this provision will depend on how strictly tribunals interpret the exceptions, especially that which allows questions about ability to carry out intrinsic functions of the work. If an employer asks health-related questions in breach of s.60, it is open to the EHRC to make an application to the court for an injunction to prevent the practice, even if there is no identifiable victim. However, if an individual is asked such a question and afterwards brings a disability discrimination claim, the burden of proof will shift to the employer to disprove discrimination (s.60(4), (5)).

Disability: failure to make reasonable adjustments

The duty on employers to make reasonable adjustments for people with dis-   **2–077**
abilities is hugely important in practice in terms of making it possible for disabled
people to compete on a more level playing field in the world of work. The duty,
now to be found in EqA 2010 s.20, is essentially unchanged from the previous
law, although it is now broken down into three requirements. First, where a provision, criterion or practice applied by the employer places a disabled employee
or job applicant at a substantial disadvantage compared with someone who is
not disabled, then the requirement is for the employer to take such steps as
are reasonable in the circumstances to prevent it from having that effect. To
use an example from the EHRC Code of Practice, if the employer has a policy of
reserving car parking spaces for senior managers only, this would disadvantage
an employee with a mobility impairment who is not a senior manager. A reasonable adjustment would be to reserve a parking space for the disabled worker.
Secondly, where any physical feature of premises occupied by the employer
puts a disabled worker at a substantial disadvantage compared with others, the
requirement is to remove or alter the obstacle, or provide a means of avoiding
it: an obvious example would be widening doorways or putting in ramps to
make premises accessible to wheelchair users. Thirdly, where a disabled person
would be put at a substantial disadvantage by the absence of some auxiliary aid
or service, the reasonable adjustment would be to provide it. Examples might
be provision of voice recognition software for someone who cannot use a conventional keyboard, or employing a part-time reader to assist an employee who
is blind. While this third requirement is new, it was already implicit in the DDA.

EqA 2010 s.21 goes on to provide that failure to comply with the duty to make
reasonable adjustments constitutes discrimination. It should be noted that this
is not an anticipatory duty: an employer need not make adjustments to the rules
or the workplace to try to avoid disadvantage to disabled people in general—
that would be impossible, given the infinite variety of kinds and degrees of
disability. The duty is individual in nature, and is owed to existing employees,
applicants for posts and anyone who has notified the employer that she may be
an applicant for employment (EqA 2010 Sch.8, para.5). In *Hainsworth v Ministry
of Defence* (2014) the Court of Appeal held that it could not be extended to
making an adjustment to enable a non-disabled employee to care for a disabled
family member.

While the list of examples of reasonable adjustments which used to be given in
the legislation has now been dropped from the statute, it appears unchanged in
the Code of Practice, with some additions. Suggested reasonable adjustments
include: making adjustments to premises (e.g. wheelchair ramps); allocating
some of the disabled person's duties to another person (e.g. occasional driving
duties could be reassigned where a disability prevents a worker from driving);
transferring him to fill an existing vacancy; altering his hours of working or training (e.g. allowing flexitime or even part-time working: failure to consider allowing an employee recovering from ME to work at home was a breach of the
duty in *Hillingdon LBC v Morgan* (1999)); assigning him to a different place of
work or training; allowing him to be absent during working or training hours

for rehabilitation, assessment or treatment; giving, or arranging for, training or mentoring (whether for the disabled person or any other person); acquiring or modifying equipment (e.g. a talking computer for someone with a visual impairment, or a modified telephone for someone with a hearing deficiency); modifying instructions or reference manuals; modifying procedures for testing or assessment; providing a reader or interpreter, and providing supervision or other support. This last does not extend to a duty to provide personal assistance to an employee to enable him to work (*Kenny v Hampshire Constabulary* (1999)). In *Archibald v Fife Council* (2004) the House of Lords held that the duty to make reasonable adjustments could include redeploying a worker who had become disabled to a higher grade post following retraining, without making her go through a competitive interview: as Baroness Hale put it, "to the extent that the duty to make reasonable adjustments requires it, the employer is not only permitted but obliged to treat a disabled person more favourably than others". The one reasonable adjustment now mentioned in the statute is providing information in an accessible format (s.20(6)).

2–078   In assessing what is reasonable, the previous legislation listed various factors to be taken into account. Again, while the list has been dropped from the statute, it appears in the Code of Practice. The factors are: the likely efficacy of the adjustment; its practicability for the employer; the cost to the employer; how disruptive it would be; the employer's financial and other resources; the availability of financial or other assistance from other sources (e.g. government grants through the Access to Work scheme); and the type and size of the employer. So far as cost is concerned, the Code of Practice suggests as one rule of thumb that it would be reasonable to expect an employer to spend at least as much as it would cost to recruit and train a replacement for the job. It should be noted that s.20(7) states that it is not reasonable to expect the disabled person to pay any of the costs of compliance.

It is specifically provided, in EqA 2010 Sch.8 para.20, that the duty to make reasonable adjustments does not arise if the employer does not know of, and cannot reasonably be expected to know of, the disability. Thus in the case of job applicants who could be disadvantaged by the employer's usual recruitment practices, the onus will be on them to make known the existence of their disability and their needs in order for the employer to have a duty to accommodate them (*Ridout v TC Group* (1998)). As noted already, this may put the disabled person in a dilemma, for she may fear that premature disclosure of her disability may lead to her application being screened out at an early stage, ostensibly for other reasons. However, if special arrangements are going to be needed, then it is inevitable that this disclosure will have to be made. In the case of existing employees, if their disability is not apparent, it will require their being prepared to disclose it appropriately, or else the employer will have no obligation to make a reasonable adjustment.

Before returning to the remaining issues, which apply to all protected characteristics in the same way, it is worth pausing to consider the relationship between different forms of disability discrimination by looking at an example. Suppose that a disabled employee takes six months' sick leave because of her disability and is dismissed in consequence. If the employer would not have dismissed another employee requiring six months' sick leave for some good reason other than disability, this will be direct discrimination (which cannot be justified). If, on the other hand, the employer would dismiss any employee who cannot work for six months, for whatever reason, this will not be direct discrimination against the disabled employee. However, it may well constitute discrimination arising from disability as it is unfavourable treatment because of her absence, which is something which arises from her disability. It may also be discrimination through failure to make a reasonable adjustment, for example by modifying the automatic dismissal rule. This example illustrates an interesting feature of disability discrimination which makes it more complicated than some of the other protected characteristics: the same set of facts can constitute more than one kind of discrimination. In relation to the other protected characteristics, it may sometimes be difficult to identify which kind of discrimination a particular set of facts gives rise to, but usually it can only give rise to one kind.

Employers' Liability

Discriminatory acts can well be carried out not by the employer directly but by an employee, or even by the employer's customers or clients: harassment is a good example of this. What is the employer's responsibility for the discriminatory acts of other people? The liability of employers for harassment by third parties has been considered already (para.2–061). In relation to discriminatory acts by employees, EqA 2010 s.109 provides that an employer is liable for the acts of employees done in the course of their employment, whether or not done with the employer's knowledge or approval. The employer will have a defence if it took such steps as were reasonably practicable to prevent employees from committing unlawful discrimination. This provision is the same as the previous law.   **2–079**

Whether or not employees' actions were "in the course of their employment" was originally interpreted as being the same as the common law test for vicarious liability in tort. However, in *Jones v Tower Boot Co Ltd* (1997) the Court of Appeal held that there were important differences between the statutory formulation and the common law test (e.g. the defence available under the statute has no common law counterpart) so that it was not appropriate to treat them as identical. In *Jones v Tower Boot* a 16-year-old apprentice of mixed race had been subjected by two fellow employees not only to verbal racial abuse but also to serious physical attacks. The EAT took the view that this was so far removed from what they were employed to do that it could not possibly be said to be in the course of employment for the purposes of vicarious liability. The Court of Appeal, recognising that it would be anomalous if the employer was more likely to escape liability the more serious the harassment was, and taking account of the purpose of the legislation, held that the words "in the course of employment" in the statute should be given their normal meaning, not the technical meaning used in relation to vicarious liability. On this basis the boy's attackers could be said to have been acting in the course of employment and the employer was liable.

In *Chief Constable of Lincolnshire Police v Stubbs* (1999) the EAT held that the employer could be liable for harassment taking place outside working hours where it took place during social events which could be regarded as extensions of work (a leaving party and the regular team drink after work). However, in *Sidhu v Aerospace Composite Technology Ltd* (2000) racial harassment happening during a day's outing to a theme park organised by the employer for workers and their families was held by a tribunal to be outside the course of employment, and this was upheld by the Court of Appeal, even though the employer had used its disciplinary procedure in relation to those involved, which seemed to indicate that the employer at least considered it as an extension of employment! The case illustrates the difficulty of attacking tribunal decisions, as long as the tribunal has applied the correct legal test.

2–080   An employer has a defence to a claim of direct discrimination if it has taken reasonably practicable steps to prevent discriminatory acts. In *Balgobin v Tower Hamlets LBC* (1987) two cleaners employed by the council at a hostel complained of sexual harassment by a chef working in the same place. The council relied on the fact that it had a clear equal opportunities policy promulgated to employees, and that there was proper and adequate supervision of employees at work. In these circumstances the EAT held that the employer had established the defence, rejecting the claimants' argument that all reasonably practicable steps had not been taken because sexual harassment was not a specific disciplinary offence and because the chef was not moved from his post after a disciplinary hearing (see also *Canniffe v East Riding of Yorkshire Council* (2000)). Note that even if the employer has a defence under the statute, the actual perpetrator may still be held liable and so could be ordered to pay compensation.

Remedies

2–081   If finding a complaint of discrimination proved, a tribunal has power under EqA 2010 s.124: (a) to make an order declaring the rights of the parties; (b) to require the employer to pay compensation; and (c) to make a recommendation.

Declaration

2–082   A declaration is "an order declaring the rights of the parties in relation to the complaint": i.e. it is a statement that there has been discrimination, and is always given where a complaint is upheld. It may be thought a rather redundant remedy, but at one time compensation was not available for indirect discrimination so successful claimants might have been left without any remedy if not for the declaration. However, in practice, a claimant is going to be more interested in one or both of the other two remedies.

Compensation

2–083   Discrimination is a statutory tort and, in principle, damages should be assessed as for any other tort with the aim of compensating the claimant so that she is in the position in which she would have been but for the unlawful conduct (*Ministry of Defence v Wheeler* (1998)). Unusually, however, it is expressly provided that claimants can be compensated for injury to feelings (EqA 2010 s.119(4)). This can be particularly important in harassment cases where the victim may not suffer any quantifiable financial loss. In *Essa v Laing Ltd* (2004) the Court of Appeal held that all loss flowing directly from the discriminatory act was recoverable, even if it was not foreseeable, and in *Chagger v Abbey National plc* (2010) they further held that this could include "stigma loss"—to reflect the claimant's reduced chances of gaining new employment in the same field because of the stigma associated with having brought the proceedings (see below, para.8–009).

The position in relation to compensation for discrimination was transformed as a result of *Marshall v Southampton & SW Hants AHA (No.2)* (1994). In 1989, following her successful discrimination claim (see above, para.2–005) an employment tribunal awarded Ms Marshall a sum nearly double the maximum then allowed under English law (including a sum for interest on the award) on the basis that EU legislation requires remedies to be adequate. The case was referred to the CJEU, which held in 1993 that the statutory limits on compensation were in breach of art.6 of the Equal Treatment Directive (76/207/EEC) (art.18 of the Recast Equal Treatment Directive (2006/54/EC)), as was the ban on allowing interest. As a result the ceiling on compensation in sex discrimination cases was removed and provision was made for the payment of interest; this was later extended to all the protected characteristics.

One group who benefited greatly from the removal of the limit on compensation were women dismissed from the armed forces on grounds of pregnancy, which the Ministry of Defence conceded in 1991 was a breach of the Equal Treatment Directive, although it had been permitted under the SDA. In *Ministry of Defence v Cannock* (1994) the EAT held that the correct approach to future loss of earnings was to ask what the chances were of the woman staying in the employment. In the case of the armed forces, women and men usually sign up and stay for fixed terms of many years and so the figures awarded under this heading were often high.

Employees who are dismissed because of disability discrimination are another **2–084** group who may receive high awards of compensation, because of the extra difficulties they face in finding comparable employment. In one of the first cases on compensation, *British Sugar v Kirker* (1998), an award of £103,146 to a visually impaired chemist aged 40 was upheld. The major element in the award was for loss of earnings because the tribunal considered it very likely that he would never obtain a comparable job. Given very high levels of unemployment among people with disabilities, it is possible that this could be a regular feature of awards for discriminatory dismissals on grounds of disability (see also *HM Prison Service v Beart (No.2)* (2005)).

Vento v Chief Constable of West Yorkshire Police (No.2) (2003) contains useful guidance on the award of compensation for injury to feelings. The Court of Appeal reiterated the guidance given in *Alexander v Home Office* (1988) and *Armitage v Johnson* (1997). First, the objective of the award is restitution. It should not be minimal, for this trivialises and diminishes respect for the public policy behind the Act; but excessive awards could have the same effect. Secondly, awards should bear "some broad, general similarity" to awards in personal injury cases—but the overall value in everyday life of the award contemplated should also be borne in mind. The Court of Appeal ruled that compensation for injury to feelings should fall into three broad categories according to their seriousness and indicated the financial boundaries of each one. In *Da'Bell v NSPCC* (2010) the EAT recommended that these figures should be uprated for inflation, and they now stand as follows. For the most serious cases, such as a lengthy period of sustained sexual or racial harassment, as in *Armitage*, compensation should normally be between £18,000–£30,000. The middle band, for serious cases not falling in the top band, should be £6,000–£18,000; and for "less serious" cases—such as an isolated incident without major consequences–the award should be up to £6,000. The Court of Appeal thought that awards below £500 should be avoided as tending to trivialise the gravity of injury to feelings.

Finally, it should be noted that compensation for discrimination is not confined to pecuniary loss, and sometimes aggravated damages may be appropriate.

Recommendations

2–085   Tribunals have power to make recommendations under EqA 2010 s.124(3) that the respondent take within a specified period action appearing to the tribunal to be practicable for the purpose of obviating or reducing the adverse effect on the complainant of any matter to which the proceedings relate. If an employer fails to comply with a recommendation, any award of compensation can be increased.

The original formulation in EqA 2010 s.124 was wider than this, in that the recommendation could be aimed at reducing adverse effects not only on the complainant, but also on any other person. This addressed serious limitations in the previous law in two respects: first, because it was not limited to the individual claimant, and secondly, because it did not need to be limited to the specific act of discrimination which gave rise to the proceedings. This meant that a tribunal had power to make general recommendations that, for example, the employer should draw up an harassment procedure, or revise its recruitment practices. In pursuance of the "no gold-plating" policy, the tribunal's power has been cut back by the Deregulation Act 2015 to recommendations affecting the complainant only. The recommendation may still relate to "any matter" to which the proceedings relate, but the scope is much reduced by the requirement that it must be limited to effects on the claimant.

It remains the case that there appears to be little scope to use the recommendation power to put things right for the claimant in the most obvious way possible—by recommending that she or he be given a job/promotion, etc. In *North West Thames RHA v Noone* (1988) the Court of Appeal held that a health authority found to have discriminated directly against the claimant on grounds of race could not be ordered to offer the next available vacancy to the claimant because statutory procedures require such posts to be advertised. However, it did say that if she applied again, a future interview board should be apprised of the previous history. In *British Gas v Sharma* (1991) the EAT relied on this decision to hold that a tribunal did not have the power to recommend that the claimant should be promoted to the next available vacancy in a particular clerical grade. This seems to go further than warranted by the Court of Appeal's decision. The EAT held also that this would be tantamount to positive discrimination, and that it also failed because no time-limit was specified. Only the last ground seems supportable. To give the victim of discrimination the next post is not to discriminate in her favour but merely to ensure that she has the most appropriate form of compensation for the wrong done to her. Indeed, if this remedy is to be seen as at all effective, it is essential that such orders should be able to be made.

Further Reading

- ☐ M. Bell (2002), *Anti-Discrimination Law and the European Union*, OUP
- ☐ M. Connolly (2011), *Discrimination Law*, 2nd edn, Sweet & Maxwell
- ☐ B. Doyle (2008), *Disability Discrimination: Law and Practice*, Jordan Publishing, 6th edn
- ☐ E. Ellis and P. Watson (2013), *EU Anti-Discrimination Law*, 2nd edn, OUP
- ☐ S. Fredman (2011), *Discrimination Law*, 2nd edn, OUP
- ☐ B. Hepple (2014), *Equality: the Legal Framework*, 2nd edn, Hart Publishing
- ☐ H. Meenan (ed.) (2007), *Equality Law for an Enlarged Europe*, CUP
- ☐ L. Vickers (2008), *Religious Freedom, Religious Discrimination and the Workplace*, Hart Publishing
- ☐ R. Allen and G. Moon (2006), "Dignity Discourse in Discrimination Law: a Better Route to Equality", 6 EHRLR 610
- ☐ M. Bell (2015), "Mental Health at Work and the Duty to Make Reasonable Adjustments", 44(2) ILJ 194
- ☐ L. Clarke (2006), "Harassment, Sexual Harassment, and the Employment Equality (Sex Discrimination) Regulations 2005", 35 ILJ 161
- ☐ G. Clayton and G. Pitt (1997), "Dress Codes and Freedom of Expression", 1 EHRLR 52
- ☐ H. Collins (2003), "Discrimination, Equality and Social Inclusion", 66 MLR 16
- ☐ M. Connolly (2009), "Rethinking Victimisation", 38 ILJ 149
- ☐ E. Dewhirst (2015), "Are Older Workers Past Their Sell-by Date? A View from UK Age Discrimination Law", 78(2) MLR 189
- ☐ S. Fredman (1997), "Reversing Discrimination", 113 LQR 575
- ☐ S. Fredman (2001), "Equality: a New Generation?", 30 ILJ 145
- ☐ M. Freedland and N. Kountouris (2012), "Employment Equality and Personal Work Relations—a Critique of *Jivraj v Hashwani*", 41 ILJ 56
- ☐ S. Hannett, (2003), "Equality at the Intersections: the Legislative and Judicial Failure to Tackle Multiple Discrimination", 23 OJLS 303
- ☐ A. Lawson (2011), "Disability and Employment in the Equality Act 2010: Opportunities Seized, Lost and Generated", 40 ILJ 359
- ☐ C. McCrudden (1998), "Merit Principles", 18 OJLS 543
- ☐ C. McCrudden (2012), "Two Views of Subordination: the Personal Scope of Employment Discrimination Law in *Jivraj v Hashwani*", 41 ILJ 30

❑ H. Oliver (2004), "Sexual Orientation Discrimination Perceptions, Definitions and Genuine Occupational Requirements", 33 ILJ 1
❑ G. Pitt (2007), "Religion or Belief: Aiming at the Right Target?" in H. Meenan (ed.), *Equality Law for an Enlarged Europe*, CUP
❑ G. Pitt (2011), "Are Occupational Requirements Genuinely Necessary?", 11(1) *Contemporary Issues in Law* 1
❑ G. Pitt (2011), "Keeping the Faith: Trends and Tensions in Religion or Belief Discrimination", 40 ILJ 384
❑ G. Pitt (2013), "Taking Religion Seriously", 42 ILJ 398
❑ D. Schiek (2002), "A New Framework on Equal Treatment of Persons in EC Law", *European Law Journal* 290

3. Employment Status

***

The relationship between an employer and a worker is governed principally by contract. It is true that for many workers—especially those classified as employees—the contract is overlaid by a mass of statutory regulation of great importance. However, much of the legislation (e.g. the law of unfair dismissal and redundancy) is predicated on the background of contractual principles and thus requires an understanding of the contractual position before it can be applied. This is a two-way process: interpretation of the legislation has had an effect on the development of contract law applied to the contract of employment. Of course, for much of the time the relationship between the employer and worker will carry on without reference to the contract, and it may also be affected by informal understandings and arrangements that are without contractual effect. While everything goes smoothly, law is forgotten. However, when the chips are down, if there is a problem, it will ultimately be resolved by reference to the

3–001

contractual arrangements. The contract of employment is therefore central to the relationship of the employer and the worker.

We saw in Ch.2 that the Equality Act (EqA) 2010 applies in the employment field to all those with a contract personally to execute any work or labour. It is now necessary to divide up that category more precisely: we must distinguish between those personally providing work under a contract of employment; those personally providing work on a self-employed basis who count as "workers" for statutory purposes; other self-employed workers; and the few personally providing work but not falling into any of these categories. There are five reasons for making these distinctions. First, the statutory employment protection rights already referred to are usually only available to those having a contract of employment, not to the self-employed. Secondly, at common law, certain terms are implied into every contract of employment, but not into other kinds of relationship. Thirdly, liability for tax and National Insurance contributions varies according to the status of being an employee or self-employed. Fourthly and relatedly, entitlement to some social security benefits is reserved to employees. Finally, an employer's duty of care towards, and responsibility for the acts of, employees is much greater than the duty to, and responsibility for, self-employed workers. In this and the following chapters, it is the position of employees which will be the central concern.

Employees and Independent Contractors

3–002 The worker who has a contract of employment is called an employee. In times past this area of the law was known as the law of master and servant and it is not wholly unknown for these terms to be used even today, though they are rather archaic. Yet the contract of employment is very commonly referred to as a contract of service, as a convenient way of distinguishing it from a contract for services, which is the kind of contract under which the self-employed person works. In law, the self-employed worker is most likely to be referred to as an independent contractor. The term highlights the fact that the worker supplies work under a contract, but is not in the same state of dependence on the employer for work as the employee is. The intermediate category of "worker", used for certain statutory purposes, is examined later (see below, para.3–010).

Who is an employee?

3–003 How is an employee to be distinguished from an independent contractor? The definition in s.230(1) of the Employment Rights Act 1996 (ERA) is not very helpful, as it defines an employee as someone with a contract of employment, itself defined as a contract of service or a contract of apprenticeship. So the answer has to be found in the common law.

In the nineteenth century (when the issue usually arose in the context of establishing the employer's responsibility for acts of, or towards, its employees) the test was said to be one of control. "A servant is a person subject to the command of his master as to the manner in which he shall do his work" (Bramwell LJ, *Yewens v Noakes* (1880)). It was soon realised that control over the manner of working might be exercised by the employer of domestic servants or unskilled manual workers, but was hardly appropriate where the worker was taken on precisely as the possessor of a needed skill, or where she would be expected to exercise a degree of discretion in performance of the work. Not only brain surgeons but even football players are not really subject to the control of their employer as to the manner in which they do their work—a fact apparently regretted by football managers at least. So, in a case concerning an injured football player claiming for an industrial injury (*Walker v Crystal Palace FC* (1910)), the Court of Appeal gave the test a different slant by focusing instead on whether the employer had the right to control the background arrangements for the work—when and where it was done, holiday entitlements and so on. Given that the football club's control here extended even to requiring that the player should not reside in a public house, the court had no difficulty in deciding that the contract was a contract of employment. (For a recent example, see *White v Troutbeck SA* (2013).)

This emphasis on the context of the work was developed into the so-called "organisation" or "integration" test, classically propounded by Lord Denning in *Stevenson Jordan and Harrison v MacDonald & Evans* (1952):

> ". . . under a contract of service, a man is employed as part of the business and his work is done as an integral part of the business; whereas under a contract for services, his work, although done for the business, is not integrated into it but is only accessory to it."

However, while this test may have been useful in establishing the employee 3–004 status of hospital consultants and other highly skilled professionals, it is increasingly inappropriate to the modern labour market, with its emphasis on flexible employment and the need to match supply and demand ever more closely. More and more, businesses have stripped down to a core of permanent, full-time workers, usually with indispensable professional skills, who receive the security elements traditionally associated with employment: pension and sickness schemes, structured career advancement and severance payments. These are supplemented by supply workers, taken on for particular tasks but having no permanent relationship with the organisation, and "flexible workers", who are generally available because in the locality in which they live they have no other outlet to work under the conditions they need (e.g. to work part-time or at home), and who can thus be safely called on only when needed, for whatever hours suit the firm, and, of course, need only be paid for those hours.

One might describe this situation as referring to different classes of worker rather than neutrally to different kinds. However, the point to make for the present discussion is that the workers in the two last categories may or may not be employees of the firm. Often it is part of their attraction to the employer that they are not employees, because it reduces the administrative and other overheads and the employer's responsibility for them. But it is clear that the work they do is an integral part of the work of the business. Thus it is suggested that the integration test is less and less likely to be useful in the future. Take, for example, the task of cleaning a hospital. In the past, hospitals employed cleaners to do the work and supervisors to see that they did it properly. The work is clearly essential to the successful running of the organisation. Since the 1980s it has become common for hospitals to outsource their cleaning needs: that is, they buy in the services of cleaners under a contract entered into with another organisation, or indeed with representatives of the former employees as a group. It is clear in this case that the cleaners are no longer employees of the hospital; yet it is equally obvious that the task of cleaning remains as integral as ever it was to the running of the hospital. In relation to agency workers, the inadequacy of the integration test has been pointed out in *Tilson v Alstom Transport Ltd* (2011) and *Smith v Carillion (JM) Ltd* (2015).

The inadequacies of these tests have led courts and tribunals to adopt a multi-factor approach: they take into account all the possible relevant factors and weigh them against each other to reach their decision. A most useful survey of the authorities is to be found in the judgment of Cooke J in *Market Investigations v Minister of Social Security* (1969). He distilled the following factors: whether or not the worker provides personal service; control, which "will no doubt always have to be considered, although it can no longer be regarded as the sole determining factor"; whether the employer or the worker provides the tools and equipment; whether the worker hires his own helpers; what degree of financial risk the worker takes, if any; what responsibility for investment and management the worker has, if any; and how far the worker profits directly from good work. Cooke J summarised the position in this test: "Is the person who has engaged himself to perform these services performing them in business on his own account?"

3–005   Cooke J's test concentrates on whether the worker can really be regarded as an individual entrepreneur and has the advantage of emphasising the economic realities of the situation. Another case using the multi-factor approach provides a different emphasis. In *Ready Mixed Concrete v Minister of Pensions and National Insurance* (1968) the company instituted a scheme whereby delivery of its concrete to customers would be carried out by a team of "owner-drivers". The issue was whether the owner-drivers were employees of the company: if so, the company was liable to pay National Insurance contributions in respect of them. It was the company's position that they were self-employed—and so they were described in their extensive written contracts. The case highlights the difficulties of the multi-factor approach, as almost every factor was equivocal.

First, the drivers were the owners of the lorries and had to keep them maintained at their own expense. However, they were buying the lorries on hire-purchase from a subsidiary of the company; they had to paint them in the company colours, and the company could instruct them to carry out repair work and specify where it should be done. Furthermore, they could not use the lorries for work for anyone but Ready Mixed Concrete. Secondly, as regards personal service, the drivers could delegate the work to another competent driver—but the company had the right to insist on the driver himself performing. Thirdly, control: the drivers had no fixed hours of work and could choose their own routes. Yet they had to be available when required and to obey reasonable orders "as if . . . an employee". What about the risk of profit and loss? Essentially they were paid by results: typical of the self-employed worker, but also common among employees, such as the piece-worker or the sales representative remunerated by commission calculated as a percentage of sales. In any case, they received a guaranteed annual minimum wage.

MacKenna J held that there were three conditions for a contract of service: first, that the employee undertakes to provide his or her own work or skill to the employer in return for a wage or other payment; secondly, that the employee agrees to be subject to the employer's control to a sufficient degree "to make that other the master" (a somewhat circular test!); and thirdly, that the other provisions of the contract are consistent with its being a contract of service. In the end the judge found that there was nothing here inconsistent with the contention that the drivers were independently running their own small businesses, as the company had argued. However, as many have pointed out, if the judge had framed the question in the opposite way, asking if there was anything inconsistent with its being a contract of service, he would probably have found nothing inconsistent with that either. True, the driver could delegate, and so the fundamental requirement of personal service might seem to be missing, but in reality the terms of the drivers' contracts were in some respects internally inconsistent. The right to delegate was to a large extent theoretical, given that the company had the right to demand personal service.

The decisions in *Market Investigations v Minister of Social Security* (1969) and **3–006** *Ready Mixed Concrete v MPNI* (1968), although only High Court decisions, have both been frequently cited over the years as indicating the correct approach to the distinction between employees and independent contractors. However, it is arguable that they actually pull in different directions and are not entirely consistent with each other, as *Express & Echo v Tanton* (1999) shows. The claimant in this case had been employed as a delivery driver for the newspaper company until being made redundant in 1995. Thereafter, he was taken on by the company again as a delivery driver, but on a self-employed basis. It was the clear intention of the parties that he should not be an employee of the company, although it is not clear how much choice he had in the matter. His job was exactly as it had been before: he drove the company's van on the route laid down by the company, conformed in all respects to instructions given to him and was paid a fixed fee decided on by the company. However, the contract also contained a "substitution clause" to the effect that if the claimant was unwilling or unable to drive, he should find another driver at his own expense. This clause had been invoked for a lengthy period when the claimant was ill. Despite this the EAT upheld the employment tribunal's decision that this was in substance a contract of employment. The Court of Appeal reversed: relying on the decision in *Ready Mixed Concrete* they held that personal service was essential for a contract of employment and that this factor was lacking because of the substitution clause. However, had the court applied the "in business on his own account" test from *Market Investigations* it seems highly unlikely that they could have held that the claimant was an independent contractor.

In a different context, Elias J suggested that the "in business on his own account" test was sufficient only to identify one category of self-employed worker, in that someone might be properly categorised as self-employed, but not in their own business undertaking (*James v Redcats* (2007), below, para.3–010). It is also true that today tribunals almost invariably start by considering the test as stated in *Ready Mixed Concrete*. But it is arguable that the focus on the formal obligation to give personal service inherent in this test means that workers who actually have no independence at all will not be recognised as employees.

The danger of the decision in *Express & Echo v Tanton* (1999) is that it hands unscrupulous employers an easy way of avoiding the responsibilities inherent in the relationship of employer-employee, with the added advantage of passing some of the risks to the worker! This is shown by *Staffordshire Sentinel Newspapers Ltd v Potter* (2004), where the claimant was a home delivery agent responsible for the distribution of the company's newspapers, under an agreement which expressly stated that it was not a contract of employment. The year after *Express & Echo v Tanton* was decided, the company varied the contract by introducing a substitution clause. In the face of this express clause, with no evidence that it was a sham (although hardly ever relied upon), the EAT held that the claimant could not possibly be an employee because there was no requirement of personal service. There has been some mitigation of this position since. In *MacFarlane v Glasgow City Council* (2001), gym instructors employed by the Council had to organise their own replacement if they were ill or otherwise unable to take a class. As the substitutes had to be from the Council's own list and were paid by the Council, and also because this was a practice which had grown up, rather than there being an express substitution clause in the contract, the EAT held that this was distinguishable from *Express & Echo v Tanton* and that the instructors were employees. In *James v Redcats (Brands) Ltd* (2007) the EAT held that a substitution clause did not defeat the obligation of personal service where it applied only if the worker was unable to work (as opposed to simply being unwilling to do so).

3–007   Related to the requirement for personal service is the further requirement that the parties must have undertaken mutual obligations under the contract—on the part of the employer, to offer work, and on the part of the employee, to accept and to be ready and willing to carry out work. In the same way that employee status can be negated by a substitution clause, it appears that a clause in the contract negating mutual obligations may be effective in denying employment status no matter how far other factors point in the direction of an employer-employee relationship. In *Quashie v Stringfellows Ltd* (2013) lap dancers were taken on by a nightclub under a written contract which specified that they were self-employed and that the contractual terms applied only on occasions when they were at work. The club exercised a high degree of control over their activities, deciding which shifts they were to work, making stipulations about their costumes, requiring adherence to a strict disciplinary code, fining them for infractions and reserving the right to terminate immediately for any breach. The dancers clearly had to give personal service: they were appointed after auditions and there was no provision for substitutes. Crucially, however, the dancers received only the fees they earned from customers, which the customers paid to the club and which the club then paid to the dancers with deductions for its commission, a "house fee", and any fines. In these circumstances, the Court of Appeal upheld a tribunal decision that a dancer who wished to claim unfair dismissal was not an employee. The club had undertaken no obligation to pay her for any work: she got only what the customers paid, less deductions—and she could even be out of pocket at the end of a night's work. Thus, despite the presence of a very high degree of control exercised under a one-sided contract which clearly demanded personal service, the payment arrangements, also designed to favour the club, were held sufficient to negate mutual obligation.

It is hardly surprising that the use of substitution clauses and clauses negating mutual obligation are increasingly being placed in contracts, particularly where the pattern of work is in any sense atypical, in order for employers to try to avoid the legal consequences of employee status. This may raise the argument that the substitution clause or denial of mutual obligation clause is a sham, put in by the employer simply as a means of avoiding the obligations which would be incurred towards an employee. This argument was considered by the Court of Appeal in *Consistent Group Ltd v Kalwak* (2008). The case concerned a group of Polish workers recruited by an agency, Consistent, in Poland to come and work in hotels and food processing plants in the United Kingdom. The agency provided them with accommodation, translation and interpretation services and organised their transport to and from work. They worked continuously for a third party client until unhappiness over wage levels led to some of them making enquiries about joining a trade union, following which their contracts were abruptly terminated. There were express terms in their contracts which stated, first, that the agency had no obligation to provide them with work and they had no obligation to accept work which was offered; secondly, that if they accepted an assignment, they had to find a substitute if they could not work, and thirdly, that the written agreement included all the terms agreed (an "entire agreement" clause). The EAT upheld the tribunal's finding that in practice the workers were constrained to accept all assignments, in contradiction of the clause negating mutual obligations, which was characterised as a sham. It held that they were actually employees of the agency. The Court of Appeal reversed, principally on the ground that a contract could only be categorised as a sham if both parties intended it to paint a false picture of their respective obligations. This caused alarm, as it seemed to show a relatively easy way in which an employer could avoid a contract of employment arising, since it is generally the employer, not both parties, who wishes to avoid the workers gaining the status of employees. However, shortly afterwards the point was reconsidered in *Protectacoat Firthglow Ltd v Szilagyi* (2009), where a differently constituted Court of Appeal showed an understanding of this danger and restated the previously understood position, that if the evidence shows that the true relationship of the parties is different from what is described in the contractual document, then the tribunal or court must give effect to the substantive relationship rather than what is stated in the document. The point finally reached the Supreme Court in *Autoclenz Ltd v Belcher* (2011), which preferred the approach to sham terms of *Protectacoat Firthglow Ltd v Szilagyi* to that of *Consistent Group Ltd v Kalwak*. Thus a contractual obligation can be found to be a sham not only where both parties have a common intention to deceive other people, but also where the facts indicate that the substance of the contract is different from what has been formally stated.

Express & Echo v Tanton (1999) and *Ready Mixed Concrete v MPNI* (1968) also indicate the relevance of another factor as yet unmentioned: the name given to the relationship by the parties. MacKenna J framed his question in the way he did in *Ready Mixed Concrete* because the parties themselves alleged that it was a contract of employment. In some ways it may seem strange that the parties' opinions should matter since courts frequently say, in this and other contexts, that they will decide according to the substance of the contract, not according to the label given to it by the parties. Thus in *Ferguson v John Dawson* (1976) the claimant was injured when he fell off a roof at the defendants' construction site. Contrary to regulations, there was no guard rail on the roof. If the claimant had been an independent contractor, he would have been responsible for his own safety and unable to sue the company. As was not uncommon in the construction industry, he was working on "the lump"—where workers contracted as a gang for the job and were paid without deductions for tax and National Insurance, on the basis that they were self-employed and responsible for their own deductions. However, the claimant was employed as an unskilled labourer, and was clearly subject to the control of the site agent. Where tools were required, the company provided them. He was paid an hourly wage. In the circumstances the Court of Appeal held that, despite the label apparently given by the parties to the relationship, the substance was a contract of employment.

3–008 It seems, however, that the label given by the parties can be a relevant factor, but only if other factors do not dictate a different answer and if the label is the product of genuine agreement between the parties. Here Ferguson had no choice but to be employed on these terms, and probably little appreciation of any other than the fiscal consequences of the difference. This was not the case in *Massey v Crown Life Insurance* (1978). Massey, the branch manager of one of the insurance company's offices, asked to change his status from employee to independent contractor because it would be economically advantageous to do so. The company agreed and repaid his pension contributions. He registered himself as "John Massey and Associates", and that organisation (Massey under another name) was appointed manager of the branch. His duties were effectively unchanged. Then he was dismissed on one month's notice and sought to claim unfair dismissal.

The Court of Appeal held that the new agreement represented a genuine change in status, rather than an attempt to deprive the Inland Revenue of tax (which would have been illegal), and was consequently binding on both parties. While reaffirming the general principle that a different label could not alter the substance of the relationship, the court held that if the contract were capable of being either a contract of service or one for services, then the explicit agreement of the parties was relevant in resolving the ambiguity. They distinguished *Ferguson* on the basis that no such explicit agreement existed in that case.

It may be felt, looking at the last two cases in particular, that the decisions of courts are sometimes swayed by what is at stake, and that they are more likely to hold that the claimant is an employee where health and safety are at issue. Indeed, this is explicitly recognised in the Court of Appeal's decision in *Lane v Shire Roofing Ltd* (1995). The claimant here had been in business on his own as a builder, but as work was scarce, he hired himself out to the defendant company. The company was anxious not to incur liability to employees and recruited workers for particular jobs, paying them a daily rate. Lane was offered an all-in fee to re-tile the porch at a house and was injured when he fell from his ladder while doing the job. He argued that the company was negligent in not providing scaffolding to give him a safe place from which to work. The company argued that he was not an employee. Giving the main judgment in the Court of Appeal, Henry LJ drew attention to the differences in the employment background in the mid-1990s from what pertained in the 1960s: more temporary and casual jobs, more self-employment and more flexible working arrangements, making it more difficult to apply the traditional tests. He also remarked that "when it comes to the question of safety at work, there is a real public interest in recognising the employer/employee relationship when it exists . . .". This set the tone for the court's decision. Although Lane had his own business, was paying tax on a self-employed basis, worked without supervision and had been taken on for the particular job only, it was held that he was not an independent contractor. These factors, in the court's view, could as well apply where someone was working under a short-term contract of employment. The question asked by the court was, whose business was being carried out on this occasion? The answer was that it was the company's, and it therefore owed Lane a duty of care as an employee. The realistic approach of the court (and the implicit use of the "in business on his own account" test) is to be welcomed and could assist in bolstering the position of casual workers, to be considered below (para.3–011). However, one can take issue with the implication that recognition of the reality of the situation is more important in health and safety cases than anywhere else. It may be that the factor of control rightly has more weight where this is the question, but it is submitted that it is equally important to ensure that employees are recognised as such for all employment protection purposes, and that it would be undesirable if different tests were to develop for identifying contracts of employment according to what was at stake.

Employee shareholders

From 1 September 2013 employers have had a novel and lawful way of avoiding   **3–009**
some employment protection legislation, by inviting employees to take on the status of "employee shareholders". This new employment status was established by ERA s.205A, introduced by the Growth and Infrastructure Act 2013. It effectively allows an employer to buy out an employee's statutory rights in return for giving the employee shares in the employer company. The scheme is thus confined to companies limited by shares, but these are the main vehicles of business in the United Kingdom. The company has to offer the employee fully paid-up shares to the value of at least £2,000. The employee does not have to accept and will have an action for detriment or automatic unfair dismissal if subjected to disadvantage or termination of contract for not agreeing (ERA

ss.47G, 105G). If, however, shares are accepted in return for taking on employee shareholder status, the employee will have no rights thereafter to claim unfair dismissal (except automatic unfair dismissal—see below, para.8–079) or a statutory redundancy payment, and certain other protection rights are reduced or eliminated.

It seems extraordinarily crass to implement a measure allowing employment protection rights to be bought out in this way, and entirely contrary to the whole thrust of protective legislation in the past which has always contained strong anti-avoidance measures. The price is insultingly low (and the share value will, of course, fluctuate and could go down substantially) and the employee shareholders may find themselves a disadvantaged class compared with other shareholders. They need not be given rights to vote, to receive dividends, nor even to participate in any surplus if the company is wound up: these points must be covered in a written statement given to employees before agreement. It seems unlikely that many employees will be tempted by such a deal. It may not be of much advantage to employers either, since one piece of protection added when the measure was going through Parliament was that no agreement would be binding on employees unless they had received independent advice, at the employer's expense, and then had a seven-day cooling-off period to consider the matter.

"Workers"

3–010   In Ch.2 we saw that the EqA 2010 applies not only to employees but to anyone with a contract personally to execute any work or labour (discussed above, para.2–008). This is similar to the definition of "worker" contained in ERA s.230(3), as being someone employed under a contract of employment or any other contract "whereby the individual undertakes to do or perform personally any work or services for another party" except where the other party is a professional client or customer of a business undertaking carried on by the individual. The essential difference is the proviso in ERA s.230(3), explained by the EAT in *Cotswold Developments Construction Ltd v Williams* (2006) as drawing a distinction between someone who actively markets his services as an independent person to the world in general (who would come within the proviso) and someone who is recruited by the principal to work for the principal as an integral part of the business operation (who would count as a "worker") (see *Hospital Medical Group Ltd v Westwood* (2012) as an example of the latter). In *James v Redcats (Brands) Ltd* (2007) a different EAT considered that even someone who did not market their services generally could be regarded as having a "worker's contract", the business being created by the contract, as in that case, where the claimant worked as a self-employed courier for the company.

The category of "worker" was once important in relation to employers' liability for health and safety and the payment of wages without deductions. It had virtually ceased to have much practical importance until the Labour Government indicated in its White Paper, *Fairness at Work*, (Cmnd.3968, 1998) that it wanted to encourage the flexible labour market, but not at the expense of fair minimum standards of protection for those employed on non-standard work contracts. The first steps with this policy were taken with the Public Interest Disclosure Act 1998 (now ERA 1996 ss.43A–43L), the Working Time Regulations 1998 and the National Minimum Wage Act 1998, all of which were made applicable to "workers" (defined in exactly similar terms to ERA s.230(3); cf. also the Trade Union and Labour Relations (Consolidation) Act 1992 (TULRCA) s.296(1)), rather than just to employees. The Employment Relations Act (ERelA) 1999 s.23 went further, giving the Secretary of State power to extend all employment protection rights to individuals other than employees. Should this power be exercised, one option would be to extend rights generally to "workers". A consultation exercise on this was carried out in 2002, but no further proposals ever came forward. Thus workers cannot make claims for unfair dismissal or redundancy payments, for example.

More recent extensions of employment protection have been mixed. The statutory right to be accompanied in disciplinary and grievance proceedings (ERelA 1999 s.10) and the Part-time Workers (Prevention of Less Favourable Treatment) Regulations 2000 apply to workers, but protection for those on fixed-term contracts and rights to leave for family reasons are limited to employees. It is worth noting that extending employment protection rights to workers would not help someone like the claimant in *Express & Echo v Tanton* (1999) because the definition of "worker" also emphasises the need for personal service, although a limited power of delegation is not inconsistent with this (*James v Redcats (Brands) Ltd* (2007)).

Casual workers

With the advent of the flexible workforce, tribunals and courts have faced new problems in deciding the nature of the relationship between parties where the worker regularly performs certain tasks for the employer but does not conform to the standard, full-time, permanent, employee paradigm. In the case of some categories of worker, such as casual workers and agency workers, this has led courts and tribunals to place great emphasis on particular aspects of the usual tests for identifying a contract of employment. In the case of casual workers, such as seasonal workers, many homeworkers and some catering workers, the factor most emphasised is the necessity for mutual obligations between the parties: "There must in my judgment be an irreducible minimum of obligation on each side to create a contract of service", as Stephenson LJ put it in *Nethermere v Gardiner* (1984). The difficulty for casual workers is that while the work may be done regularly, and there may be an expectation that it will continue to be offered to and performed by the same people in the future, there is no binding legal obligation either on the employer to offer it or on the workers to perform it in the future. A more recent variant, the so-called "zero hours contract" has recently been subject to legislative regulation, and is dealt with separately below. Other casual work arrangements may be described as "on call" or "stand by" contracts. The question with all of them is what level of mutuality of obligation is a necessary factor for the existence of a contract of employment.

3–011

This was the main issue in *O'Kelly v Trusthouse Forte* (1984). At one of its hotels in London the company dealt with a lot of functions. This meant it had a fluctuating need for staff, and it relied heavily on casual workers. Of these, some were used a great deal and were given priority when work was available. They were termed, accurately if paradoxically, "regular casuals". In addition to about 100 regular casuals, there were another 200–300 "casual casuals". In practice there was enough work for the regular casuals to be employed full time and they had no other jobs. Further, there were special grievance and disciplinary procedures applicable to them and they received a kind of holiday pay. The company provided their uniforms; while on duty they were subject to the control of the function supervisors; they were paid according to the hours actually worked; tax was deducted and social security contributions made as if they were employees. What of mutual obligation?

Work was assigned by the employer preparing a roster showing who was needed to work the following week. A worker could decline any particular shift— but to do so jeopardised future offers and could lead to someone being removed from the list of regulars. In these circumstances the employment tribunal held that there was no legal mutual obligation, although the economic power of the employer and corresponding weakness of the workers meant that in practice the workers were obliged to accept work when it was offered. The EAT reversed, holding that the tribunal had failed to distinguish between two separate questions: first, what was the relationship of the workers and the company when they were actually carrying out work having accepted an offer for a specific engagement; and secondly, what was the nature of the overall relationship (or "general engagement")? In the view of the EAT, when they had accepted a specific engagement, the casual workers were under a legal obligation to work and the employer had a legal obligation to allow them to work, so they were employed on a contract of employment. On the facts of the case, there was no need to consider the general engagement.

3–012   The EAT's decision was in turn reversed by the Court of Appeal, essentially because it considered that this was a question of mixed fact and law on which the EAT should not have interfered with the decision of the employment tribunal. Nonetheless, the EAT's identification of two separate issues in relation to the specific engagement and the general engagement has been widely accepted since. Thus in *Clark v Oxfordshire HA* (1998) the claimant had been employed as a "bank nurse", meaning that she was on call to be offered employment as and when the health authority needed her. Except that her contract specifically stated that there was no guarantee of work being available, her terms and conditions were the same as for other nurses. The Court of Appeal held that in the absence of mutual legal obligation there could be no overall or "umbrella" contract of employment in relation to the general engagement, but as the employment tribunal had not considered the separate question of the nature of the specific engagement the case was remitted on that point. In *Cornwall CC v Prater* (2006) the Court of Appeal finally took the further step and held that a home tutor, engaged by the council on numerous separate contracts over a 10-year period to teach children unable to attend school, should be regarded as an employee for each of those individual engagements.

As very many employment protection rights are dependent on accumulating a certain period of continuous employment, finding that a specific engagement is a contract of employment will not assist many casual workers: for example, they cannot claim unfair dismissal unless they have two years' continuous employment. In *Cornwall CC v Prater* the claimant was able to string her separate engagements together into a period of continuous employment by invoking the "temporary cessation of work" provisions (see below, para.3–031), but this will not always be possible. However, there are many employment protection issues where continuity is not required, such as common law implied terms of the contract and payment of tax and National Insurance (remember that *Market Investigations v Minister of Social Security* (1969) was itself a case about a casual worker, yet the issue of mutual obligation posed no problems there). Furthermore, there are now several grounds on which dismissal will be automatically unfair, and for these a finding of a specific engagement will be sufficient. The employer's duty of care to employees, which is one of the most important incidents of a contract of employment, does not depend on continuity and, as noted above, following *Lane v Shire Roofing* (1995) it seems inconceivable that a court would find that a casual worker was not an employee for this purpose except in very special circumstances. This is borne out also by the Privy Council decision in *Lee v Chung* (1990).

Are there any circumstances in which the general, as opposed to the specific, engagement between a casual worker and an employer can be regarded as a contract of employment? One possibility is where the arrangement has gone on for some time, so that what started out as a casual relationship can be said to have hardened into a situation where there is a legal obligation to provide work and to accept work. This occurred in *Nethermere v Gardiner* (1984). The claimants were homeworkers who worked as machinists, putting pockets in trousers. They had no fixed hours of work, and were paid according to the number of garments processed. The claimant usually worked between five and six hours a day. She got daily deliveries of work and the sewing machines were provided by the employer. There was, however, no obligation on the employer to provide work, nor on the claimant and the other homeworkers to accept it. The arrangement continued for about four years until terminated by the employer. The Court of Appeal held that on the facts the employment tribunal was entitled to find that the necessary "irreducible minimum of obligation" did exist in this case. Stephenson LJ commented, "I cannot see why well founded expectations of continuing homework should not be hardened or refined into enforceable contracts by regular giving and taking of work over periods of a year or more" (see also, *Airfix Footwear v Cope* (1978)).

While these cases may be seen as an attempt to take account of the realities of the situation, there has been a return to a harder line in recent cases, which may yet require *Nethermere v Gardiner* and *Airfix v Cope* to be reconsidered. In *Carmichael v National Power plc* (2000) the Court of Appeal held that a letter of appointment which required tour guides at a nuclear installation to work "on a casual as required basis" could be construed as importing sufficient mutual obligation to amount to an overall contract of employment: on the part of the employer, to offer them a reasonable share of such work as it had to offer, and

3–013

on the part of the workers, to accept a reasonable amount of such work as was offered. However, this was reversed by the House of Lords, which reverted to the traditional interpretation that there was no mutual obligation between the parties in these circumstances. The letter of appointment simply set up a framework within which a series of ad hoc, specific contracts (which might or might not be contracts of employment) took place. This is not to say that there cannot be mutual obligations in a situation where the amount of work fluctuates and even dwindles to nothing in certain periods: a relief manager whose workload (and pay) depended entirely on whether the employer needed him to stand in for other managers in the area, was held to be an employee by the EAT in *Wilson v Circular Distributors Ltd* (2006). The difference between this case and *Carmichael v National Power plc* was that the claimant in *Wilson* was under an obligation to accept work when offered (from which the EAT deduced an obligation on the part of the employer to offer work when it was available). In *Carmichael*, the tour guides had a choice as to whether or not they accepted work when offered and the evidence was that they had refused work on various occasions.

The application of these principles in *Stevedoring & Haulage Services Ltd v Fuller* (2001) raises concern about whether the argument that mutual obligation can develop over time will remain tenable. The case concerned dockers with permanent contracts of employment who were made redundant and then re-employed at once as casual workers. They were required to sign a letter which expressly stated that they were not employees, that they did not have to accept work when offered and that the company was not under any obligation to offer them work. It also spelt out that they had no sick pay, holiday entitlement, etc and that although they would be taxed as employees, this was for administrative convenience. They then worked on a regular basis for the company for a further three years. The employment tribunal held that the original agreement in the letter was subject to an implied term that they would be offered a reasonable amount of work and that they must accept a reasonable amount—rather like the Court of Appeal's analysis in *Carmichael*. This was roundly rejected by the Court of Appeal: if the express terms of the agreement stated that there was no mutual obligation, it was not possible to imply a term saying exactly the opposite. The case was not argued on the basis that there was a variation of the agreement over time, as in *Airfix* or *Nethermere*, but if it had been, the answer might well have been that there had been no alteration in conduct during the three years and so no variation could be identified.

Another issue raised by these cases is whether it is possible to argue that the written agreement does not represent the true picture and that a contract which appears to be for casual work in fact involves continuing obligations. We saw in *Ferguson v John Dawson* (1976) (above, para.3–007) that the "label" given by the parties to their relationship is not treated as conclusive: the courts consider the substance of the relationship, not the form. As with substitution clauses, it is possible for a worker to argue that a clause denying mutual obligations to provide or undertake work is a sham. If the evidence shows that the true relationship of the parties is different from what it says in the contract, the court may hold that a term is a sham even if both parties did not have an intention to deceive the outside world (*Autoclenz Ltd v Belcher* (2011)).

Zero hours contracts

Zero hours contracts are a particular variety of casual work arrangements which **3–014** have become prevalent in recent years. Usually, they take the form of a written framework agreement stipulating the rights and duties of the parties if and when work is undertaken—but there is no guarantee that any work will be offered at all. Sometimes they imply that the worker is under an obligation to accept work when offered, even though there is no reciprocal obligation on the employer to offer work. Although it is highly unlikely that such a legal obligation would exist, its expression in a written agreement may be enough to mislead workers, especially where the agreement also contains an exclusivity clause, prohibiting the worker from working for anyone else.

From the point of view of employers, zero hours contracts offer the ultimate in flexibility, freeing them from any obligation to pay workers except when they are actually required, and absolving them of the need to plan carefully, since they can call on their zero hours workforce at short notice. If the precarious nature of the arrangement also means that the workers do not count as employees and so do not qualify for employment protection rights, then so much the better. It is claimed that the flexibility inherent in these arrangements also suits some workers, such as students or retired people who only want to work occasionally, but it is hard to credit that total uncertainty as to one's timetable or income is seriously sought after by many people. In addition, as with most casual work, if you turn down work when it is offered, you are less likely to be offered work in future. The number of people working on zero hours contracts is not clear, but is estimated to have increased rapidly in the last few years to more than a million; it seems unlikely that more than a minority of these would choose to work under these conditions.

In December 2013 the Government issued a consultation document on the use and abuse of zero hours contracts. It identified only two problems with their use: first, exclusivity clauses, which might mean a worker got no work from their "zero hours employer" and could not work for anyone else, and secondly, a "lack of transparency" meaning that workers did not always appreciate that they had a zero hours contract, or what it entailed. It decided to ban exclusivity clauses to deal with the first issue and to encourage the development of codes of practice to deal with the second. Thus the Small Business, Enterprise and Employment Act 2015 amended ERA to introduce new ss.27A and 27B. Under ERA s.27A(1), a zero hours contract is defined as a contract of employment or worker's contract under which the worker's undertaking to perform work is conditional on the employer making work available, but where there is no certainty that any work will be offered. ERA s.27A(3) states that any clause prohibiting the worker from working for someone else, or requiring that she gets the employer's permission to do so, will be unenforceable.

As numbers of respondents to the Government's consultation pointed out, **3–015** ERA s.27A could easily be avoided by employer's guaranteeing workers very small numbers of hours, thus taking the contract out of the zero hours definition. In consequence, ERA s.27B gives the Secretary of State wide-ranging powers to make regulations to deal with avoidance. Additionally, the Exclusivity Terms in Zero Hours Contracts (Redress) Regulations 2015 provide workers with the right to make an employment tribunal claim if they suffer a detriment or dismissal for working for another employer in defiance of an exclusivity clause. In October 2015 BIS issued guidance on the use of zero hours contracts, but no codes of practice are yet forthcoming.

Numerous problems remain. First, and most importantly, the amendments to the law only deal with exclusivity clauses, which are a problem, but not the major problem with zero hours contracts. Secondly, proving detriment is likely to be difficult and the amount of compensation could be small, so it seems unlikely that many workers would take the expensive route of suing the employer. Thirdly, ERA s.27A only applies if the zero hours contract is either a contract of employment or a worker's contract as defined by ERA s.230. If this is not the case, for example, where the agreement clearly rules out mutual obligations to offer and accept work, then it appears even that limited protection will not apply.

Law and fact

3–016   The history of *O'Kelly v Trusthouse Forte* (1984) (above, para.3–011) illustrates another important point. So far as statutory jurisdiction is concerned, appeals lie from employment tribunals to the EAT (and above) only on questions of law, not on questions of fact. This means that provided that the tribunal directs itself correctly on the law, that there is evidence on which it could have reached its decision, and that its decision is not perverse on the evidence, it cannot be disturbed by a higher court on the ground that the higher court would have reached a different decision from the tribunal.

There are good reasons for this rule: after all, it is the tribunal which hears the witnesses, and thus has the best opportunity for judging their truthfulness and accuracy. It would make no sense to allow another court to study a transcript of evidence (even if one existed, which in a tribunal would not be the case) and to make different findings of fact. But the difficulty is that the issues which have been held to be questions of fact are rather wider than what one would usually understand to be factual. You might think that a question of fact is one which is capable of objective verification—that is, you can say whether the answer is true or false. That is not what it means in this context. There is little doubt that the Court of Appeal has extended the category of issues which count as questions of fact as a matter of policy, in order to cut down the number of appeals to higher courts.

Now, it may be the case that reasonable people, fully instructed in the relevant law, could still disagree as to whether a particular dismissal was fair or unfair, which is why the tribunal's decision is to be treated as a question of fact and not disturbed on appeal. But it seems surprising that a question about the correct categorisation of a contract should be treated as one of fact. It seems to be a question of law *par excellence*, requiring as it does a detailed knowledge of contract law to answer it. Nevertheless, in *O'Kelly v Trusthouse Forte* the Court of Appeal held that the question of whether or not someone was an employee was a mixed question of fact and law, and therefore the employment tribunal's decision should not be disturbed unless there was a misdirection on the law. This decision has been criticised, but received the approval of the Privy Council in *Lee v Chung* (1990). The Privy Council emphasised that the determination has to depend on an investigation and evaluation of the factual circumstances in which the work is performed: and this should be regarded as a question of fact (although it is worth noting that in that case the Privy Council held that the decision of the original court was perverse and substituted its own view!). The only, limited exception to this comes as a result of the House of Lords' decision in *Davies v Presbyterian Church of Wales* (1986) (concerning the status of a minister of the church, which has often given rise to problems as to the identity of the employer), where it was held that if the contract were wholly in writing, its construction would be a matter of law.

Agency workers

The number of workers employed on temporary work through an employment agency has increased substantially in recent years and temporary employees are now reckoned to constitute some 7 per cent of the entire workforce. Temporary workers sign on with an agency which undertakes to try to place them in suitable employment for temporary periods. They are in some respects like casual workers in that the agency does not have an obligation to find work for them, and they do not have an obligation to accept work when it is offered. However, as argued above, mutuality of obligation should not be regarded as decisive in determining their status. They may or may not be fixed-term workers: sometimes the contract period will be clearly defined at the outset and sometimes it is indefinite. However, agency workers are expressly excluded from the ambit of the Fixed-term Employees (Prevention of Less Favourable Treatment) Regulations 2002 (see below, para.3–027). Statutory regulations made under the Employment Agencies Act 1973 (the Conduct of Employment Agencies and Employment Businesses Regulations 2003, as amended) require agencies to give temporary workers written statements of the terms and conditions of employment, to deduct tax and National Insurance contributions from their pay as for employees and to state whether they are employees of the agency or self-employed. This might be thought to go some way towards resolving their ambiguous status, but was held not so in *Wickens v Champion Employment* (1984), where despite the fact that the written statement described the temporary workers as having a contract of service with the agency, the EAT held that they were not the agency's employees. The factors which the EAT focused on in deciding that the contract could not be one of employment were the lack of control over their work, the lack of mutual obligation, the fact that each engagement was treated as a separate contract and that the temporary workers were stated to be responsible for their own safety. Yet if not employees, temporary workers do not look much like self-employed workers in business on their own account either. In *Ironmonger v Movefield Ltd* (1988) the EAT held that an employment tribunal had fallen into error precisely because it reasoned that since the agency worker was not self-employed, he must be an employee, and if he was not the employee of the client firm then he must be the employee of

3–017

the agency. The EAT held that there were other possibilities besides the division of employee or self-employed—although unfortunately declining to enlighten us further on the nature of such a contract, other than saying it was sui generis!

There was a tendency for a while to assume that *Wickens v Champion Employment* had settled the status of temporary workers, but this was denied by the Court of Appeal in *McMeechan v Secretary of State* (1995). In this case, an employment agency became insolvent while owing wages to the claimant. In these circumstances, an employee can claim unpaid wages from the Secretary of State instead, and this is what the claimant did. The employment tribunal thought that it was bound by *Wickens* to hold that he was not an employee. The Court of Appeal held that there was no rule to this effect and cases would depend on their own facts. As in the casual work cases, the court drew a distinction between the "general" and the "specific" engagements, and held that in this case the claimant could be regarded as an employee of the agency when actually working on his last specific engagement (for which the wages were owed). The court did not consider the nature of the overall relationship, because it was not necessary for their decision.

One issue not addressed in *McMeechan* was the fact that in the tripartite situation, it is the client or end-user, not the agency, who has control over the worker's day-to-day work. This was a central issue for a later Court of Appeal in *Montgomery v Johnson Underwood Ltd* (2001). The claimant in this case had been placed by the agency with a client for whom she had worked for well over two years. When the arrangement was suddenly terminated, she sued the agency for unfair dismissal. Although this, too, was a specific engagement, the Court of Appeal on this occasion rejected the argument that the agency could be her employer, because of their lack of control over her day-to-day work (see also *Bunce v Postworth Ltd* (2005)). This line of argument, together with the fact that most standard contracts between agencies and temporary workers now expressly state that they are not contracts of employment, generally closes off the opportunity for agency workers to claim that they are employees of the employment agency. *Consistent Group Ltd v Kalwak* (2008) (above, para.3–007) is an example of an unusual case where the agency exercised such a high degree of control over the surrounding circumstances of the workers' employment that the employment tribunal held that it could be regarded as their employer. However, this will rarely be the case and, as we saw, the claim was lost on other grounds.

3–018   What about the client, or end-user, of the agency worker's services? The stumbling block here is that the agency worker has no direct contractual relationship with the client. The client contracts with the agency for a worker to be supplied. However, in *Franks v Reuters Ltd* (2003) the Court of Appeal reached the surprising decision that an employment tribunal had erred in not considering whether or not there was an implied contract of service between the agency worker and the client. This was followed soon after by *Dacas v Brook Street Bureau* (2004), the unfair dismissal claim of a cleaner who was supplied by BSB to Wandsworth Council, where she worked for four years before being sacked. She originally claimed unfair dismissal against BSB and Wandsworth Council, but her claim against Wandsworth had been dropped by the time the case reached the Court of Appeal. The court confirmed that she could not claim to be the agency's employee, but also said that she could well have had a claim against Wandsworth through an implied contract of service.

Neither of these cases was actually authority for saying that agency workers were employees of the end-user—the case was remitted in *Franks* and the remarks in *Dacas* were obiter. However, in *Cable & Wireless plc v Muscat* (2006) the Court of Appeal took the final step and upheld an employment tribunal's decision that an agency worker was the employee of the end-user through an implied contract of employment. Essentially, they held that the tribunal had properly considered all the evidence, including the conduct of the parties as well as the express agreements, and had made no error of law. Importantly, the Court of Appeal felt that provided the end-user was actually paying the worker's wages, it made no difference that the payment was made indirectly (through the agency) rather than directly to the worker.

As frequently happens when there is a ground-breaking common law development, the next stage is to backtrack. In *James v Greenwich LBC* (2007) the EAT faithfully considered the question of whether an agency worker might have an implied contract of employment with the end-user, as required by *Dacas*, but found that there was no necessity to imply such a contract, given that the claimant's relationship was fully dealt with by express agreements between her and the agency and the agency and the end-user. In reaching this conclusion, the EAT stressed that a contract could only be implied when it was necessary to do so and signalled that this would be a high hurdle to jump. This decision was upheld enthusiastically by the Court of Appeal (*James v Greenwich LBC* (2008)), where the leading judgment was given by Mummery LJ, who had also given the leading judgment in *Dacas v Brook Street Bureau*! Subsequent decisions have reinforced the position that it will indeed be rare for an implied contract of employment to arise between the agency worker and the end-user (e.g. *Tilson v Alstom Transport* (2011), *Smith v Carillion (JM) Ltd* (2015)).

This case-law shows clearly that the law relating to the legal status of agency **3–019** workers is not very satisfactory. In some cases agency workers may genuinely be skilled entrepreneurs hiring out their services on an independent basis, so that it is acceptable to treat them as self-employed, but it is contrary to reality to regard the large numbers of temporary secretarial and clerical staff in that light. At present the chances are usually against them being able to establish their status as employees and so to access employment protection rights. Regulation 36 of the Working Time Regulations 1998, and the National Minimum Wage Act 1998 s.36, both make special provision for agency workers by stating that they are to be treated as if they have a worker's contract with either the agency or the principal, according to which has the responsibility for paying the agency worker. This is an approach which could usefully be adopted more widely, although it has not been adopted in the latest piece of legislation, the Agency Workers Regulations 2010 (SI 2010/93).

The Agency Workers Regulations 2010, which came into force in October 2011, were passed in order to implement the Temporary Agency Work Directive

(2008/104/EC). This Directive was a long time coming. The issue of working conditions for temporary workers was referred to the social partners by the EU Commission as long ago as 1996, along with the issue of fixed-term workers. However, the social partners were unable to agree and so temporary workers were left out of the agreement which became the Fixed-term Work Directive (99/70/EC). The EU Commission therefore produced its own draft Directive in 2002 but it was strenuously opposed by business leaders and therefore by some governments (including the UK). Agreement was finally reached in 2008 and the Temporary Agency Work Directive (2008/104/EC) was passed in November 2008, with a due implementation date of 5 December 2011.

As with the Directive, the main thrust of the Agency Workers Regulations 2010 is to give agency workers the right to equal treatment with the permanent workforce of the end-user. The Regulations do not, therefore, deal with the very important problem of employment status and the fact that long-term agency workers usually do not accrue rights to claim unfair dismissal and redundancy in the same way as employees. Even more oddly, reg.3 defines an agency worker as an individual who has either a contract of employment with the agency (which, as seen above, is rarely the case) or who has any other contract to perform work and services personally for the agency. It could well be argued that an agency worker does not work "for" the agency in any sense: they work for the client or end-user on behalf of the agency. Thus it may take some creative purposive interpretation to ensure that the Regulations are not deprived of any effect at all.

3–020   Under the Agency Workers Regulations 2010 reg.5 agency workers have a right to the same basic working and employment conditions as if recruited by the end-user (called "the hirer" in the Regulations) directly to do the same job. This is subject to a 12-week qualifying period, which must be in the same role with the same hirer. Such a derogation was permitted by the Directive and this qualifying period was agreed by the TUC and CBI in 2008. To prevent hirers getting around the Regulations by artificially breaking the assignment for a week or so, reg.7 provides that continuity will not be broken unless the break is at least six weeks. Furthermore, if the break is for reasons such as sickness, pregnancy, parental leave, industrial action and other things listed in reg.7(8), continuity will not be broken if the break is not more than 28 weeks. Other provisions are designed to stop hirers making cosmetic changes to the agency worker's role in order to argue that she has not been performing the same role for 12 weeks. The danger, remains, however, that agency workers may simply end up being employed for shorter assignments where end-users wish to avoid the equal treatment provisions.

The relevant employment conditions which should be equalised under the Agency Workers Regulations are those relating to pay, working time and annual leave (reg.6). "Pay" is defined quite broadly to include not only basic salary, but also fees, commissions, and some bonuses and other payments connected with employment. A major issue here will be how to decide what terms the agency worker would have got if recruited directly by the hirer. At one end of the spectrum, reg.5(3) provides that if there is an existing comparable employee, doing the same or broadly similar work on terms and conditions which are not abnormal in any sense, then equal treatment is satisfied if the agency worker gets the same terms. At the opposite end, if the agency worker is taken on for a unique role, or if the hirer negotiates terms individually with each worker so that there are no standard terms and conditions, the equal treatment provision will presumably not apply. In the area in between, it remains to be seen what evidence will be deemed relevant in deciding whether the agency worker is being treated "as if" directly employed.

There is evidence that agency workers do receive less favourable terms and conditions than permanent workers, so to that extent the Agency Workers Regulations 2010 are to be welcomed. But the significant problem posed by their lack of job security, even when they have worked for the same person for a long time, is arguably a more pressing issue and it is unfortunate that it has not been addressed.

Apprentices and trainees

We saw at the outset that the definition of "employee" in ERA s.230(1) includes **3–021** someone with a contract of apprenticeship. Apprenticeship once involved an indenture of seven years, with the apprentice living with and learning from his master under the auspices of the craft guilds. This system had broken down by the nineteenth century, but the salient characteristics of apprenticeship, that its main purpose is training the apprentice and that it is for a fixed term, during which period the right of the employer to dismiss is restricted, remained. Today, traditional apprenticeships have declined to trivial numbers, but there has been a huge rise in government-funded schemes which involve training for young people to gain qualifications while they work. Are these to be regarded as apprenticeships? If not, those engaged on them might find themselves without employment protection rights, for it was held in *Wiltshire Police Authority v Wynn* (1980) that "Where the primary object of the contract is teaching or learning, then there is no contract of service" (per Dunn LJ).

In *Flett v Matheson* (2006) the Court of Appeal held that a 16-year-old engaged on an advanced modern apprenticeship should be regarded as an apprentice even though the training and education was not provided solely (or even primarily) by the employer, but through a third-party government-funded training provider at a college. The agreement described him as an apprentice, had training as its main purpose, envisaged a lengthy period of training and restricted the employer's powers to dismiss. It is likely that a similar approach would be taken to comparable apprenticeship schemes.

In *Daley v Allied Suppliers* (1983) the EAT held that the Race Relations Act did not protect a young trainee taking part in work experience under the Youth Opportunities Programme because her attendance for work was voluntary. In these circumstances the EAT held that there was no contract in existence at all. The legislation was subsequently amended to prohibit training bodies from discriminating unlawfully (see now, EqA 2010 s.55). Specific provision is also made in other employment protection statutes such as the Working Time Regulations

1998 (see below, para.6–044) and the National Minimum Wage Regulations 1999 (see below, para.7–054).

Part-time workers

3–022   Until the historic decision of the House of Lords in *R v Secretary of State ex p EOC* (1994), a week only counted for the purposes of computing continuity of employment if it involved 16 hours of employment. Part-timers who worked between eight and 16 hours per week could count those weeks as part of a qualifying period of continuous employment, but only if they had worked for five years or more. What this meant in practice was that part-timers who worked for fewer than eight hours a week never qualified for things like unfair dismissal protection and redundancy pay, and part-timers working between eight and 16 hours a week had to work five years to qualify as against two years for other workers.

As we saw in Ch.2, less favourable treatment of part-time workers is unlawful sex discrimination unless it can be justified objectively. This appeared to be limited to provisions in contracts of employment until the CJEU decided in *Rinner-Kühn v FWW Spezial-Gebäudereinigung Gmbh* (1989) that German legislation excluding part-time workers from the right to receive sick pay required objective justification. The EOC therefore commenced proceedings for judicial review in 1990, seeking a declaration that the statutory threshold provisions which made it more difficult for part-timers to establish sufficient continuous employment were in breach of what is now TFEU art.157(1), the Equal Pay Directive 1975 and the Equal Treatment Directive 1976 in relation to the right not to be unfairly dismissed, to receive compensation for unfair dismissal and to receive redundancy pay.

Given that the discriminatory effect of the hours requirement was established, the main issue in the House of Lords was whether or not it could be objectively justified. The then Conservative government's argument was that the rules meant that there were more part-time jobs available than there would be if employers were exposed to these liabilities. Whereas naked assertion of this "fact" had sufficed for that government in the political arena, the House of Lords required some proof. This was not forthcoming; indeed, the evidence was that in other EU countries where part-timers received the same protection as other workers, the number of part-time jobs had actually increased. The EOC was therefore granted its declaration that the hours requirement for redundancy pay was a breach of TFEU art.157(1) and the Equal Pay Directive, and the conditions for unfair dismissal claims were at least a breach of the Equal Treatment Directive, if not also of TFEU art.157(1). The House of Lords did not pronounce on whether unfair dismissal compensation could be regarded as "pay" for the purposes of TFEU art.157(1) and it was not until the CJEU's decision in *R v Secretary of State ex p Seymour-Smith* (2000) that it was definitively settled that it was. However, the Government responded to the House of Lords' decision in *R v Secretary of State ex p EOC* by promulgating the Employment Protection (Part-time Employees) Regulations 1995. The regulations abolished all hours requirements so that there is no longer a minimum threshold for protection and periods of qualifying service are equalised (see now, ERA s.212).

Meanwhile, the position of part-time workers was being addressed at EU level in accordance with the Social Charter aspiration of improving employment conditions for various forms of "atypical" work relationships, including part-time work. The subject was referred to the "social partners" (i.e. UNICE, CEEP and ETUC as representatives of management and labour) in accordance with TFEU art.155, and they agreed a Framework Agreement in 1997. This was implemented by the Directive on Part-time Work (97/81/EC), and in the United Kingdom by the Part-time Workers (Prevention of Less Favourable Treatment) Regulations 2000.   **3–023**

The Regulations apply to "workers" defined in reg.1(2) in almost the same way as for ERA s.230(3) (see above, para.3–010). Under reg.5 a part-time worker has a right not to be less favourably treated on grounds of working part-time than a comparable full-time worker, unless that treatment can be objectively justified. In judging whether or not there is less favourable treatment the pro rata principle is to be used, meaning that the part-timer's treatment should be proportionately the same as the full-timer's unless there are objectively justified grounds for any difference. Workers who were full time and then change to part-time work, whether or not after a period of absence such as maternity leave, have a right not to be treated less favourably than they were before going part-time. Under reg.6 a part-time worker who believes that she has been treated less favourably may request a written statement of the reasons for this, which must be provided within 21 days. Part-time workers may make a complaint to an employment tribunal which can make a declaration, award compensation and recommend that the employer takes action to remedy the adverse effects on the complainant of the less favourable treatment. They also receive protection from detriment for exercising their rights under the Regulations and dismissal on this ground is automatically unfair (reg.7).

One crucial issue in assessing the effectiveness of the Regulations relates to the condition that less favourable treatment can only be established by comparison with an actual full-time comparator (cf. *Carl v University of Sheffield* (2009); under EqA 2010 hypothetical comparisons with how someone without the protected characteristic would be treated is allowed). This means that a part-timer will have no claim under the Regulations unless there is a "comparable full-time worker", defined as someone employed by the same employer under the same type of contract and engaged on broadly similar work (and, where relevant, having a similar level of qualification, skills and experience) (reg.2(4)). As a result of the Fixed-term Employees (Prevention of Less Favourable Treatment) Regulations 2002, the fact that the contract of either the part-timer or the full-timer is for a fixed term will not prevent them from being regarded as comparable.

The first case to reach the House of Lords on this issue resulted in a liberal approach to the issue of comparison. *Matthews v Kent and Medway Towns Fire Authority* (2006) was a test case on behalf of more than 12,000 retained (i.e. part-time) firefighters, who wanted to gain access to the same occupational pension scheme and other benefits as full-time firefighters. The two issues in the case were first, whether the retained firefighters had the same kind of   **3–024** contract as the full-time firefighters, and secondly, whether they could be said to be engaged on the same or broadly similar work. The House of Lords dealt with the first point summarily: both had contracts of employment and that meant that they had the same type of contract. As to whether their work was broadly similar, the employer argued that the retained firefighters were mainly called on just to fight fires in emergency situations, while the full-timers had significant other responsibilities: educative, preventive and administrative (such as issuing fire certificates). The House of Lords did not accept this, noting that it was almost inevitable that if one group was full-time and one group was part-time, the full-timers would do additional things. However, if both groups spent a lot of time carrying out the core activity of the enterprise, their work was likely to be broadly similar. Finally, the House of Lords said that differences in levels of qualifications, skills and experience were only relevant if they had a genuine impact on the work that the part-timers were actually carrying out (see, e.g. *Carl v University of Sheffield* (2009)). In *Moultrie v Ministry of Justice* (2015), however, the EAT upheld a tribunal finding that part-timers and full-timers were not employed on broadly similar work, even where 85 per cent of their work was the same, in circumstances where the work which was not the same was actually a very important part of the full-timers' role.

Another question which has arisen in relation to the construction of reg.5 is whether the less favourable treatment has to be *solely* on the grounds of the worker being part-time—an apparent restriction which appears in art.4(1) of the Part-time Work Directive (97/81/EC), but not in reg.5. In *Sharma v Manchester City Council* (2008) one out of four categories of part-time lecturers employed by the council argued that they were less favourably treated than full-time lecturers, because their hours could be changed from year to year. An employment tribunal found against them, on the grounds that this was not solely because they worked part-time—as shown by the fact that the other categories of part-time lecturers were not subjected to this treatment. This was reversed by the EAT, who considered that such a restrictive interpretation could not have been intended by the Directive, and even if it were, this was a situation where the UK Regulations offered greater protection than EU law. The Court of Session in Scotland had taken a different view in *McMenemy v Capita Business Services Ltd* (2007), but the EAT declined to follow it. In *Carl v University of Sheffield* (2009) a later EAT followed *Sharma v Manchester City Council* in preference to *McMenemy v Capita Business Services Ltd*.

Less favourable treatment can be "justified on objective grounds" under reg.5(2)(b). In *O'Brien v Ministry of Justice* (2012) the CJEU expressed the test in the terms familiar from equality law: the less favourable treatment must be in response to a genuine need on the part of the employer, be appropriate for achieving the objective, and necessary for that purpose (cf. para.2–054, above). The case concerned fee-paid part-time judges, who did not receive pro rata pension rights (unlike part-time judges working on fractional contracts). When the case returned to the Supreme Court, the Ministry of Justice essentially argued that its budget would not permit it to pay pensions for fee-paid judges, who were usually undertaking these duties as an adjunct to well-paid practice as solicitors or barristers. The Supreme Court held that this was an argument based on cost alone, and that this could not be an acceptable justification (*O'Brien v Ministry of Justice* (2013)).

The Part-time Work Directive sought to encourage enhanced opportunities **3–025** for part-time work, but this is not expressed as a binding obligation and it is not addressed in the Part-time Workers (Prevention of Less Favourable Treatment) Regulations 2000. The Secretary of State also deliberately chose not to promulgate a code of practice on part-time work and instead guidance on compliance was issued. The guidance does make reference to increasing part-time opportunities, but as it has no legal status employers are free to ignore it.

Fixed-term contracts

While no one really expects that a contract of employment will go on forever, it **3–026** is nonetheless usual to enter them on a permanent basis. The vast majority of contracts of employment are therefore of indefinite duration, although they may be terminated by either party giving notice (see below, para.8–004). However, sometimes an employer may have a genuinely short-term need for workers and in these circumstances will wish to employ the worker for that specific period only. Examples might be catering staff to work during Wimbledon fortnight, fruit pickers to bring in the harvest, someone to cover another employee's maternity leave or a builder to work on a construction project.

It can be seen that some of these sorts of employment have something in common with casual work. It obviously makes sense for employers to be able to make use of fixed-term contracts when there is a genuine short-term need. However, the form is capable of abuse, for example where the employee has a succession of fixed-term contracts, with all the attendant insecurity, but the employers will not make the position permanent because they want to avoid incurring the responsibilities which they would have to a permanent employee. At common law, expiry of a fixed-term contract would not constitute a termination by the employer, which would also raise the possibility of such employees not being able to claim unfair dismissal if their contracts were not renewed. For this reason, the definition of dismissal for both unfair dismissal and redundancy always included expiry of a fixed-term contract without renewal (see further below, para.8–026), although this was not a total answer, because employers could—and frequently did—require employees to sign waivers giving up their rights to claim unfair dismissal or redundancy payments.

The Employment Relations Act 1999 abolished unfair dismissal waiver clauses, but did not touch the redundancy waiver. At about the same time, however, changes occurred at EU level as part of the programme to improve employment protection for atypical workers. As with the Part-time Work Directive (97/81/EC), the matter was referred to the social partners, whose agreement became the Fixed-term Work Directive (99/70/EC), mainly implemented in the United Kingdom by the Fixed-term Employees (Prevention of Less Favourable Treatment) Regulations 2002. One of its reforms was to repeal the redundancy waiver.

3–027   The Fixed-term Work Directive had two main aims: to prevent discrimination against workers on fixed-term contracts by comparison with those on permanent contracts, and to limit the abuse inherent in allowing employers to keep people on a series of successive fixed-term contracts. The Directive also made it necessary to introduce a new, wider definition of what would count as a fixed-term contract. In *Wiltshire CC v NATFHE and Guy* (1980), the Court of Appeal had held that a fixed-term contract meant one with a defined beginning and end: in effect, that the start and end date should be known at the outset. Thus in *Ryan v Shipboard Maintenance* (1980), where a skilled ship repair worker was taken on by the company for the duration of specific projects, and carried out 31 different jobs over five years, it was held that these were not fixed-term contracts. This was because it was not known in advance precisely when each job would end. This had the unfortunate result that employees on "task" or "purpose" contracts had no unfair dismissal or redundancy rights because the expiry of their contracts did not amount to a dismissal in law. Regulation 1(2) of the Fixed-term Employees (Prevention of Less Favourable Treatment) Regulations 2002 now defines a fixed-term contract as including not only one which terminates on expiry of a specific term, but also one which terminates on completion of a specific task or on the happening of a specific event. This means that in a case like *Ryan v Shipboard Maintenance* the only question now would be whether or not continuity was preserved between the successive contracts (see below, para.3–029).

Under reg.3, fixed-term employees have the right not to be treated less favourably than comparable permanent employees, unless the treatment can be objectively justified. Following the model of the Part-time Workers (Prevention of Less Favourable Treatment) Regulations 2000 (and the EqA 2010 on equal pay, see below, para.7–013) comparison has to be made with an actual comparator and the pro rata principle applies. In one of the first cases under the Regulations the Court of Appeal held that allowing a fixed-term contract to expire without renewing it (in circumstances where the employee was just short of one year's continuous employment) could not itself constitute less favourable treatment (*Webley v Department for Work and Pensions* (2005)). Unlike the EqA 2010 provisions on equal pay, it is possible for an employer to argue justification on the basis that the job package for the fixed-term employee is as favourable as that of the permanent employee, taken as a whole, rather than on a term-by-term basis.

The issue of successive contracts is more difficult to deal with. The idea of setting an upper ceiling, whether in number or length of time, sounds sensible— but not if it results in the employer replacing the fixed-term employee with another fixed-term employee when she approaches the limit, rather than making her permanent. That would result in the employee's rights being reduced rather than enhanced. Regulation 8 deals with this by instituting an upper limit for successive fixed-term contracts of four years, but allowing the possibility of this being modified by a collective agreement or workforce agreement. Where this limit is exceeded, the contractual term relating to the duration has no effect and the employee is treated thereafter as a permanent employee.

There are exceptions to this position. First, an initial fixed-term contract can **3–028** be for any period: it is only if there is a renewal which takes the whole period beyond four years that reg.8 kicks in. Secondly, the four-year period can be exceeded if the employer can show objective justification for continuing it as a fixed-term contract. This was construed strictly by the EAT in *Secretary of State for Children, Schools and Families v Fletcher* (2009), where regulations made under an EU treaty limited the period of employment for teachers in schools in Europe for the children of EU officials to nine years. There was no such limit in the treaty itself: the regulations were made by the international board of governors of the schools. The EAT held that the Secretary of State could not rely simply on the existence of the regulations as justifying the fixed term: it had to be independently justified. In the absence of such justification, the claimant teacher was entitled to a declaration that his employment was permanent. Thirdly, there are exclusions for people employed on Government training schemes, apprentices, agency workers and members of the armed forces (Fixed-term Employees Regulations 2002, regs 14, 18–20). In *Hudson v Department for Work and Pensions* (2013) the Court of Appeal held that these contracts are totally excluded from the Regulations, so that an employee who had been employed on fixed-term training contracts for three years and six months, and who then got a further fixed-term contract which was not under a training scheme, could not count the earlier service to get her over the four-year qualification period.

In the past, fixed-term contracts were regularly used by employers in order to avoid employees gaining employment protection rights. Now that it has become impossible for employers to insist that fixed-term employees should waive their rights to claim unfair dismissal and redundancy, the distinction between permanent and fixed-term employees has become of much less importance for most practical purposes. As with the Part-time Workers (Prevention of Less Favourable Treatment) Regulations 2000, fixed-term employees can ask for written statements, apply to a tribunal and receive protection from detriment or dismissal in connection with their rights. There is one major difference, however. As the title indicates, the Fixed-term Employees (Prevention of Less Favourable Treatment) Regulations 2002 apply only to "employees" not to "workers". This is an unfortunate departure from the more inclusive trend of recent legislation.

Continuity of Employment

As has been seen already, casual workers may face problems in establishing that **3–029** they count as employees, because the employer has no definite legal obligation to offer them work, and they have no legal obligation to accept it. Thus there would seem to be three possibilities for casual workers: (i) they are not employees; (ii) they are employees, but they work under a series of separate contracts of employment; and (iii) they have ceased to be casual, because it has come to pass that their series of contracts takes place in the context of a "global" or "umbrella" contract (as discussed above, para.3–012).

Even if they have been classified as employees, both casual and other temporary workers will face another hurdle in terms of legal protection. This is that many employment protection rights require a certain period of continuous employment before the employee qualifies for the right in question. For example, it is necessary to have been employed for two years in order to be able to claim for unfair dismissal or for redundancy payments.

Continuity has two aspects. First, continuity must not be broken. Secondly, certain periods of continuity must be built up for the different employment protection rights. If continuity is broken in any week, the counting must start afresh. Usually any week in which continuity is not broken also counts towards the overall period. There is one notable exception in relation to industrial action, where ERA s.216 provides that any week in which the employee is taking part in a strike or is locked out does not count towards the period of continuous employment, but also that it does not break continuity. Subject to these points, a week in which the employee has no contract breaks continuity. Note, however, that it is only necessary for a contract to be in existence during the week for that week to count: it does not matter whether the employee actually does any work under the contract (*Welton v Deluxe Retail Ltd* (2013)). However, ERA s.212(3) provides for three exceptional cases where weeks in which no contract is in existence will not only not break continuity but will also count towards the period of continuous employment. The three cases are:

- absence through sickness or injury;
- temporary cessation of work; and
- absence by arrangement or custom.

Absence through sickness or injury

3–030   Generally the contract of employment continues to exist while an employee is off work because of sickness or injury—nor does this depend on whether or not sick pay is payable. In such a situation there is no problem about continuity because the employee continues to be employed under a contract of employment. This exception goes further, however, and provides that even if the contract has been terminated because of the employee's sickness, the employee can still be continuously employed, and count in the weeks of absence, provided that the employee recommences work with the employer within 26 weeks of the termination.

This makes sense. In general, sickness arrangements are more generous for higher status jobs than for those of lower status. One employer might keep someone employed and continue to pay them throughout a long illness; another employer might keep the contract alive, but not pay salary, or at least not after a certain length of time; a third might terminate the contract altogether. Where sick pay is not payable, it may be almost a matter of chance whether the employer keeps the contract alive or terminates it formally. If the latter, it seems reasonable that the worker's continuity should be preserved if he recovers sufficiently to return. If that return is within six months, it is likely to be referable to the previous period of employment.

Temporary cessation of work

Some difficulty has arisen in interpreting the exception which preserves continuity where the employee is absent through a temporary cessation of work, an exception frequently relied on by casual workers trying to link together a series of contracts. There is no upper time-limit on the length of the cessation. In *Ford v Warwickshire CC* (1983) the House of Lords held that the temporariness or otherwise of an absence should be judged with hindsight, looking back over the whole duration of the relationship to decide whether the absence was temporary in relation to the whole time worked. On the facts of the case they were thus able to hold that where a teacher had worked on eight fixed-term contracts from September to July each year, the absences between contracts were temporary, and she had continuous employment (see also, *Cornwall CC v Prater* (2006), above, para.3–012). In *Hussain v Acorn Independent College* (2011) the EAT considered the summer vacation as a temporary cessation of work when the claimant had only worked from April to July to cover another teacher's absence, and then taken up a further contract for less than a year from the following September. **3–031**

Absence by arrangement or custom

The third exception is a situation where, although absent, the employee is to be regarded as still employed "by arrangement or custom for all or any purposes". As the wording suggests, this is capable of covering ad hoc personal arrangements (e.g. unpaid leave to tend a dying relative) as well as generally recognised occurrences. In *Lloyds Bank v Secretary of State for Employment* (1979) it was held to cover a bank clerk who worked a one-week-on, one-week-off arrangement, although there was no contract for the week off. This might seem a surprising analysis, though the justice of the result is unquestionable. **3–032**

Unfortunately, a much stricter approach was taken in *Curr v Marks & Spencer plc* (2003) where a female manager with 17 years' service was encouraged to take advantage of a new child break scheme at the end of her maternity leave. The scheme allowed her to return to an equivalent level post after four years, but spelt out that she would have to resign at the end of her maternity leave. During the absence, the arrangement required her to work for the company for at least two weeks a year. In fact, she worked for five separate periods amounting to over one year in total. Five years after she returned to work full-time she was made redundant and the company argued that the four-year child break had broken her continuity of employment. The Court of Appeal reluctantly rejected her argument that this was an absence by arrangement during which she was regarded by both parties as continuing in employment, essentially because it was so clear that it was a resignation followed by a re-engagement. However, the decision does rather beg the question of how an employee can be regarded as continuing in employment by reference to a contract of employment when by definition ERA s.212(3) only applies in situations where there is no contract of employment!

A similarly unfortunate result was reached in *Booth v United States* (1999), where the employer deliberately introduced two-week breaks between fixed-term contracts for maintenance workers, apparently with the aim of preventing them building up sufficient continuous employment to entitle them to statutory protections. The EAT held that the device was effective: since the employer clearly did not wish the contract to continue during the break, it could not be said to be one where there was any arrangement or custom for it to continue. It may be doubted whether this should still be followed in the light of the CJEU's decision in *Adeneler v Ellenikos Organismos Galaktos* (2006) to the effect that permitting unlimited fixed-term contracts as long as they were separated by at least 20 days was incompatible with the Directive, because it allowed employers easily to evade the law.

Special Types of Work Relationship

Company directors and partners

3–033 Most commercial operations in the United Kingdom are carried out through the medium of companies limited by shares, which can range from massive global corporations to small enterprises essentially involving a single owner. The big advantage of carrying on business through a limited company is that it is sepa-rate from its owners and so, if it fails, they only lose their shares, not their entire personal property. Partnerships traditionally do not have the benefit of limited liability—each partner is potentially liable to the full extent of his or her personal property for partnership debts. For those professions such as solicitors, account-ants and doctors, prohibited by law from forming limited companies, this could be a substantial risk. In 2000 the Limited Liability Partnerships Act introduced a hybrid form of partnership which, like a company, would have separate legal personality from the partners, and under which the partners could enjoy limited liability. Such partnerships are designated by LLP after their name. Most firms of solicitors and accountants have now switched from being regular partnerships to becoming LLPs. The question which arises in relation to both companies and LLPs is whether or not directors or partners can be regarded as employees (or workers), given that they also have responsibility for running the enterprise.

So far as companies are concerned, in business although not in law there is a well-recognised distinction between executive directors, who are involved in the day-to-day running of the company, and non-executive directors, who are expected to attend board meetings but whose main duty is to advise on broad policy issues (or sometimes to lend their title or fame to the company).

Non-executive directors are most unlikely to be employees of the company. So far as executive directors are concerned, the position is not clear-cut. It depends entirely on the nature of the contract which they have with the company. In *Parsons v Albert J Parsons & Sons Ltd* (1979), although the director worked full-time in the family business, he had no express service contract, and directors were paid such sums as were voted to them at the general meeting each year as "directors' emoluments". It was held that he was not an employee. Contrast *Morley v CT Morley* (1985) where the family butcher's business had been incorporated by a father and his two sons who worked full time for it. They all claimed redundancy payments when the business folded and were treated without discussion as employees by the EAT. It is likely that in this case they drew salaries from the company as employees, and in practice it seems that the method of payment may be important (cf. *Eaton v Robert Eaton Ltd* (1988)).

In *Buchan v Secretary of State* (1997) the EAT suggested a general principle **3–034** that a director who was the controlling shareholder of a company, in effect a self-employed businessman carrying on his business through the medium of a company, should not be regarded as an employee for the purposes of employment protection legislation, whatever the contractual arrangements, on the grounds that it would be undesirable if the person able to decide whether or not the company went into liquidation were able to claim from the Secretary of State for unpaid wages. However, in *Secretary of State for Trade and Industry v Bottrill* (1999) the Court of Appeal held that there could be no such general rule, commenting acidly that it was difficult to see how the possession of a controlling shareholding could turn a contract of employment into something different (see also, *Connolly v Sellars Arenascene Ltd* (2001)). At the request of the Secretary of State, the court in *Secretary of State for Trade and Industry v Bottrill* went on to give guidance as to how tribunals should approach such cases: having emphasised that it is always a question of fact for the tribunal, the court said that the first question would be whether the contract of employment of such a director is genuine or not (if entered into just when the company got into trouble, it might not be). Secondly, the tribunal should consider the nature of the contract according to the usual tests, including the degree of control exercised by the company over the director.

The second part of this guidance gave rise to some confusion, because on one reading, it seemed to suggest that the existence of a controlling shareholding, which would mean in practice that the director was incapable of dismissal, was a factor to weigh in the balance in judging the nature of the director's contract with the company—and would militate against a finding that she or he was an employee. As Underhill J put it in *Nesbitt v Secretary of State for Trade and Industry* (2007), the guidance in *Bottrill* seemed inconsistent with the actual decision in the case. Thus the Court of Appeal was again asked for guidance in *Secretary of State for Business, Enterprise and Regulatory Reform v Neufeld* (2009). The court once more stated that there was no reason why a shareholder and director of a company could not be an employee, even if he had total control over the company—this had been established law since the Privy Council decision in *Lee v Lee's Air Farming* (1961). It essentially reiterated the guidance in *Bottrill* that the issue is a question of fact and the tribunal should consider whether the contract is genuine or a sham (cf. para.3–007, above). It is in relation to that question that the amount of control exercised by the director claiming to be an employee is mainly relevant. Once that issue is out of the way, the tribunal should consider whether the contract is a contract of employment taking into account the usual factors and the actual performance of the contract—but not whether or not the claimant is a sole director or has a controlling shareholding.

Where directors do have an express contract of service the Companies Act 2006 s.188 provides that it may not be for more than two years without the agreement of a general meeting, and copies must be open to inspection by the shareholders. This is intended to reduce the amount of compensation that the company might have to pay if it removes a director from office, and to ensure that members have the information on which to make an accurate assessment of the costs.

3–035   As a traditional partnership in England and Wales has no separate legal personality, the assumption has been that partners cannot also be employees, because it is a logical impossibility for a person to employ himself. The Limited Liability Partnerships Act 2000 (LLPA) s.4(4) expressly states that a partner in an LLP is not to be regarded as employed unless he or she would be so regarded if the partnership was a traditional partnership. Hence in *Tiffin v Lester Aldridge LLP* (2012) the Court of Appeal held that a fixed share partner was not an employee for the purposes of being able to claim unfair dismissal and redundancy. Although he was not a full equity partner (he contributed only a small amount of capital and received a correspondingly small share of profits) he did have some share in management and would be regarded as a partner if it were an unlimited traditional partnership under the Partnership Act 1890. The Supreme Court approached the interpretation of LLPA s.4(4) in a similar fashion in *Clyde & Co LLP v Bates van Winkelhof* (2014), although the issue in that case was whether the claimant, an equity partner, could be regarded as employed on a contract personally to provide work or services (cf. para.3–010 above) for the purposes of a whistleblowing claim. The Supreme Court held that LLPA s.4(4) did not apply in this situation, since it must be interpreted as referring to employment under a contract of employment only, not to a contract personally to provide work or services. It went on to hold that she was employed under such a contract, so her whistleblowing claim could go ahead.

It seems, therefore, that even full partners may be regarded as "workers" in some circumstances, and it may be that the last word has not been said on whether they may at least sometimes also be regarded as employees.

Office holders

3–036   Office holders have traditionally been regarded as a separate kind of worker from employees and independent contractors. The distinguishing factor about an office holder is that the office has some sort of public status and exists independently of the person holding it for the time being. An example might be the Archbishop of Canterbury. Historically the relevance in employment law of finding that someone was an office holder was that he or she was entitled to public law remedies: i.e. the rules of natural justice had to be observed before any disciplinary or dismissal decision and such a decision was subject to judicial review (see below, para.8–019). Essentially this meant that such workers had employment protection before the statutory rules were developed.

Today, ironically, the question is most likely to arise where someone is claiming statutory protection available only to employees (such as unfair dismissal) and it is alleged that she is not qualified through being an office holder rather than an employee. In *102 Social Club v Bickerton* (1977) it was pointed out that, for the purposes of the legislation, some office holders may be held to be employees as well as office holders, although some may not. In *Johnson v Ryan* (2000) the EAT identified three kinds of office holders: those whose rights and duties are defined by the office they hold; those who have the title of office holder but who are in reality employees with a contract of service; and those who are both office holders and employees. Company directors may fall into this final category, although not all company directors are employees (see above, para.3–034).

It seems clear that office holders in the last two categories will be able to claim the employment protection rights available to employees. It is less clear what the position is for the "true" office holder. In *Lincolnshire CC v Hopper* (2003) it was argued that a registrar of births, deaths and marriages, who was clearly an office holder, could also be regarded as having a contract of employment with the local authority which was responsible for appointing her, paying her and to whose disciplinary procedure she was subject. This was rejected, however, by the EAT on the grounds that only the Registrar General had power to remove her from office. The EAT held that it was an essential characteristic of a contract of employment that the employer should have the power to dismiss. This left the unfortunate registrar in the position of being subject to the local authority's disciplinary procedure but having no reciprocal right to take action against the authority! This seems anomalous and it would make more sense for all office holders to be clearly equated to employees. Discrimination law was amended to make it clear that it would apply to office holders, because of these doubts (see EqA 2010 ss.49–50).

Another group of office holders who have usually been denied employment protection rights are ministers of religion. While priests in the Church of England may be regarded as office holders because of the church's established status, this is not automatically the case in relation to ministers of other denominations or religions. In *President of the Methodist Conference v Parfitt* (1983) and *Davies v Presbyterian Church of Wales* (1986) the Court of Appeal and the House of Lords respectively held that ministers did not have a contract of employment, either because of the spiritual nature of the work or because of a lack of intention to create legal relations, but held back from deciding whether or not they were office holders. In *Percy v Church of Scotland* (2006) the House of Lords held that whether or not an associate minister of the Church was an office holder was not determinative of whether she had a contract for personal service. They held that she fell within the EqA 2010 definition of a person in employment and thus had standing to bring a claim of sex discrimination against the Church. It was argued for the claimant in *New Testament Church of God v Stewart* (2008) that *Percy v Church of Scotland* had brought about a sea change in the status of ministers of religion. The Court of Appeal did not go so far,

3–037

but did say that *Percy* meant there was no longer a presumption of a lack of intention to create legal relations. Upholding an employment judge's decision that the claimant minister was an employee, the court referred to art.9 of the European Convention on Human Rights and made the important point that, in such cases, tribunals should also take into account the doctrines of the religion insofar as they may have a bearing on whether a legally enforceable relationship was intended. Both of these points were confirmed by the Supreme Court in *President of the Methodist Conference v Preston* (2013) where, however, it was held that the arrangements between a Methodist minister and her church were not contractual. So far as the Church of England is concerned, holders of ecclesiastical offices have been put into broadly the same position as employees in relation to statutory employment protection rights by virtue of the Ecclesiastical Offices (Terms of Service) Regulations 2009 (SI 2009/2108). For other Christian denominations and other religions, it will depend on the particular arrangements between the minister and the church.

Crown servants

3–038   Crown servants hold office at the pleasure of the Crown at common law, and thus in theory would enjoy no security of tenure. However, most employment protection legislation is specifically extended to them, although with some exceptions (ERA s.191). It remains debatable whether or not Crown servants, or some of them, can be regarded as having contracts of employment. For this reason the Employment Act 1988 provided that if their terms did not amount to a contract of employment, they would nonetheless be treated as doing so for the purposes of the law of industrial action (now TULRCA s.245). What this means is that anyone organising a strike among civil servants is at the same risk of liability for interference with contracts as any other union organiser.

Police

3–039   All police officers are office holders (*Ridge v Baldwin* (1964)). Thus they qualify for public law remedies, but not for most employment protection rights. Under ERA s.200 they are excluded from all rights except to receive a written statement of terms, a minimum period of notice and redundancy payments. Under the Police Act 1964 s.17, the Chief Constable or police authority is treated as their employer for the purposes of vicarious liability.

Volunteers and interns

3–040   It might be expected that volunteers who work for charitable and similar organisations would not be interested in trying to establish employee status, although volunteering has become increasingly professionalised, with volunteers often being required to undertake training and expected to commit a defined amount of time for a minimum period. There are also some aspects of employment protection law, such as anti-discrimination legislation, which it could well be argued ought to apply to them. The same could be said of unfair dismissal protection.

However, the traditional view is that a volunteer does not have a contract and therefore cannot possibly count as an employee or a worker.

In *Murray v Newham CAB* (2001) the EAT seemed to open the door to them at least by a crack. The claimant claimed for disability discrimination after being rejected as a CAB volunteer. His application for training for the CAB required him to sign a document agreeing to a number of things: his role; a minimum hours commitment of two days a week; a minimum of one year's service; and notification of absences, holidays or resignation. In return, he would be provided with training and support. He would not be paid, but he would be able to claim expenses. An employment tribunal held that this was not an application for "employment" because there was no sanction for non-performance and, crucially in their view, no pay. The EAT held that the tribunal had erred in finding that there were no mutual obligations and apparently considered that the agreement which he had signed was legally binding. However, it remitted the question of whether it was a contract of service or a contract personally to undertake work to the tribunal and the point was not taken up in subsequent proceedings. The point came before the Supreme Court in *X v Mid-Sussex CAB* (2011), where a volunteer who wished to claim for disability discrimination argued that the Framework Employment Directive (2000/78/EC) reference to the prohibition of discrimination on grounds, inter alia, of "occupation" meant that English law should be interpreted to allow her claim. The argument was rejected by the Supreme Court, which considered that the Directive was not intended to cover voluntary activity and it was not necessary to refer the question to the CJEU.

Employment law in the UK was unfamiliar with the expression "intern" until the events leading to an attempt to impeach the US President in the 1990s. Despite this inauspicious start, the term has become increasingly used for various kinds of work experience programmes whose main feature is that the person doing the work, often a recent graduate or a student working during a vacation, is frequently working for nothing. If this is the case, it would seem that the intern is in effect a volunteer, and would thus be unlikely to qualify for any employment protection rights.

If the intern receives payment, then the likelihood is that there would be a 3–041 contract, but it might be a training contract rather than a contract of employment (above, para.3–021). Insofar as they have a contract to provide personal service, interns may be able to bring themselves within the definition of "worker" (above, para.3–010), which would given them some protection—in particular, the right to claim the national minimum wage.

Further Reading

❑ L. Dickens (1992), *Whose Flexibility? Discrimination and Equality Issues in Atypical Work,* Institute of Employment Rights
❑ M. Freedland (2003), *The Personal Employment Contract*, OUP
❑ M. Freedland and N. Kountouris (2011), *The Legal Construction of Personal Work Relations*, OUP

- E. Szyszczak (1990), *Partial Unemployment: the Regulation of Short-Time Working in Britain,* Mansell
- M. Bell (2011), "Achieving the Objectives of the Part-time Work Directive? Revisiting the Part-time Workers Regulations", 40 ILJ 254
- A. Bogg (2012), "Sham Self-Employment in the Supreme Court", 41 ILJ 328
- H. Collins (1990), "Independent Contractors and the Challenge of Vertical Disintegration to Employment Protection Law", 10 OJLS 353
- A. Davies (2007), "The Contract for Intermittent Employment", 36 ILJ 102
- S. Deakin (2007), "Does the 'Personal Employment Contract' Provide a Basis for the Reunification of Employment Law?", 36 ILJ 68
- G. Davidov (2005), "Who is a Worker?", 34 ILJ 57
- M. Freedland (2005), "From the Contract of Employment to the Personal Work Contract", 35 ILJ 1
- J. Kenner (1999), "Statement or Contract? Some Reflections on the EC Employee Information (Contract or Employment Relationship) Directive after *Kampelmann*", 28 ILJ 205
- P. Leighton and M. Wynn (2011), "Classifying Employment Relationships: More Sliding Doors or a Better Regulatory Framework?", 40 ILJ 5
- G. Pitt (1985), "Law, Fact and Casual Workers", 101 LQR 217
- J. Prassl (2013), "Employee Shareholder 'Status': Dismantling the Contract of Employment", 42 ILJ 307

4. The Contract of Employment

Key Points

This chapter:
- Discusses formation of employment contracts and the requirements for a statutory written statement of particulars
- Considers how contracts can be varied
- Looks at the contractual status of handbooks, policies and other documents
- Explains when terms can be implied into employment contracts
- Looks at the duties of employers and employees implied by law into all employment contracts
- Specifically considers the duties to provide work, to respect privacy, to maintain mutual trust and confidence, to obey lawful orders and to cooperate
- Explains the duty of fidelity and the exception for whistleblowing
- Outlines the law relating to restrictive covenants

***

Chapter 3 dealt with the definition of the contract of employment. In this chapter we will examine how contracts of employment come into being and their content. In practice, parties will usually enter a contract after the stages of advertisement, interview, offer and acceptance. The offer may be made and accepted at the interview, or may be made later by a letter of appointment. While a limited amount of negotiation may be possible, perhaps over the starting date or the starting salary, most prospective employees need the position more than the employer needs their particular individual qualities, and so the contract tends to be entered on the employer's terms. This does not mean, however, that it will be totally one-sided. Very many employers, especially large organisations, recognise trade unions and bargain with one or more trade unions about the principal terms and conditions of different groups of workers; a new employee

4–001

will be taken on within the framework of the collectively agreed terms. Further, at common law, judges have developed the concept of terms which are to be regarded as implied into every contract of employment simply by virtue of the employment relationship; these implied terms are sometimes expressed as the common law duties of employer and employee. Finally, the inherent inequality in the bargaining relationship (particularly where there is no recognised trade union) has been recognised with the result that certain protective measures for employees have been introduced by statute. Most of these statutory protection rights are not incorporated into the contract of employment; rather, they exist alongside and supplement contractual rights, although they will override any less favourable inconsistent contractual term. Some, such as the equality clause derived from the Equality Act (EqA) 2010 s.66, are implied into the contract of employment.

The result is that where there is a question about the respective rights and liabilities of the employer and worker, the answer may require a fairly complex analysis of a variety of different sources, to establish first what the parties actually agreed, and secondly, whether there are other constraints affecting the position.

Formation

4–002   In general no special formalities are required for entry into a contract of employment: as with other contracts, the agreement may be purely oral. There are some exceptions, of which the most notable are the contracts of merchant seafarers and contracts of apprenticeship, which have to be in writing.

References

4–003   Employers have no general obligation to provide references in respect of employees seeking alternative employment, although most are willing to do so. To have any value, a reference must be entirely frank, and so employers have traditionally been unwilling to provide them except on a confidential basis. Under the Data Protection Act 1998, employees do not have a right to see a reference which their employer sends to a prospective employer. Although this is "personal data" within the meaning of DPA s.1, there is a specific exception covering it in DPA Sch.7, para.1. However, it is open to an employee to ask their new employer for a copy of a reference supplied by a previous employer and the Information Commissioner's Employment Practices Code recommends that this should be made available. Under DPA s.7(4), access should not be given to information which identifies a third party unless the third party consents or it is reasonable to go ahead without their consent. It is quite difficult to strike a balance here between the referee's right to privacy and the employee's right to know what information is held about him or her. Some employers now deal with this by seeking the referee's consent to disclosure, but if the referee refuses, it may be difficult in practice to edit the reference in such a way as to protect the referee's identity and so an employer would probably be justified in refusing disclosure.

Note, however, that since the request for disclosure can only be made to your own employer, not to the employer who provided the reference, unsuccessful job applicants are unlikely to get to know what their references said, although they may draw inferences from a continuing failure to get other work. But can anything be done about an unfavourable reference (short of changing your referee)?

If the reference contains defamatory matter, it is protected by qualified privilege, which means that the referee will not be liable unless she acted maliciously. In *Lawton v BOC Transhield* (1987), Tudor Evans J was prepared to accept that an employer owed a duty of care to an employee in preparing a reference, although finding that there had been no breach on the facts of that case. The decision was subsequently criticised as inconsistent with the law of defamation. It was argued that to allow an employee a right of action where the employer had prepared a reference negligently was to permit the defence of qualified privilege to be defeated by carelessness rather than only by malice.

The issue came before the House of Lords in *Spring v Guardian Assurance*   **4–004**
(1994). The claimant had worked for an insurance firm as an authorised representative selling Guardian Assurance policies. He left to set up his own business selling policies for a different insurance company. As required by the rules of the relevant regulatory authority, the second insurance company approached Guardian Assurance for a reference regarding him. The reference impugned the claimant's honesty as well as his competence and was aptly described as "the kiss of death" to his career in the insurance industry. It was found that the referee had acted honestly but negligently in drawing it up.

By a majority, the House of Lords held that an employer owed a duty to the subject of a reference to take reasonable care in drawing it up. This did not mean that the employer would be taken to warrant that facts relied on or stated were true, but only that the employer had taken reasonable care in assembling the facts and verifying them. The main policy reason against imposing a duty of care in these circumstances was said to be that employers might be deterred from giving frank references. This did not seem a very real or serious risk to the majority, especially when balanced against the serious consequences for the employee. As they pointed out, liability for negligently prepared references has existed since *Hedley Byrne v Heller* (1964), the only difference being that the duty in that case was owed to the recipient rather than the subject. In *Hedley Byrne* the referee had included a disclaimer of liability, which is one way an employer could protect itself, although it should be remembered that this would have to pass the reasonableness test imposed by the Unfair Contract Terms Act 1977 s.2.

Two other points of interest arise from *Spring v Guardian Assurance*. First, it was not finally decided whether the claimant's contract was one of employment or for services; however, in the view of the House of Lords, the employer's duty was the same in either case. Secondly, while holding the claim to be made out in tort, the majority also considered that a comparable implied duty could exist in some circumstances in contract. Lord Woolf thought that, in a case like this, where employment would be impossible without a reference from the former employer, there would be a duty on the employer to provide a reference.

4–005   It is possible that *Spring v Guardian Assurance* deterred some employers from giving references; others reacted by confining themselves to purely factual statements. However, such a policy will not necessarily absolve them from liability. In *Bartholomew v Hackney LBC* (1999) a reference stated truthfully that disciplinary proceedings for gross misconduct had been commenced against the claimant at the time when he took voluntary severance from the council, but did not state that he had strenuously denied wrongdoing and had claimed race discrimination against the council. By analogy with the law of defamation the Court of Appeal held that accurate statements could give an unfair impression and accepted that the employer had a duty not to give an unfair or misleading impression overall, even if each individual statement in the reference was correct. However, the employer was not under a duty to give a full and comprehensive reference either, and overall the reference in this case could not be said to be unfair.

An example of a truthful reference being held to be unfair is *TSB Bank plc v Harris* (2000), where the employer was entirely accurate in telling the prospective employer of the claimant that she had had 17 complaints made against her by customers, of which four had been upheld and eight were still outstanding. The trouble was, the bank had not told her about 15 of these, so this information came as a shock to her as well as to the prospective employer (who withdrew the job offer). She had never had the chance to offer any comments or explanation in relation to them. In these circumstances the EAT held that the bank had committed a fundamental breach of the implied contractual duty to maintain mutual trust and confidence. In *Jackson v Liverpool City Council* (2011) the Court of Appeal pointed out that the employer's duty to give a fair reference means that the substance should be fair, not necessarily that it is procedurally fair. In that case, the employer's reference included comments about alleged performance failures which had come to light after the employee left, but also pointed out that he had not had the opportunity to reply to the allegations. The manager giving the reference had explained the circumstances more fully in a telephone call to the prospective employer. Although the claimant had not had the chance to respond to the charges, the court considered that the employer had given the factual information fairly (taking account of the telephone call as well as the written reference) and could not be said to have breached its duty of care.

Under the Rehabilitation of Offenders Act 1974 s.4(2), where a reference is sought in relation to someone who has a "spent" conviction, the referee has a duty not to mention the conviction or the ancillary circumstances. In such a case, the referee is protected from any legal liability. However, there are by regulation various exceptional situations where this does not apply.

Conditional offers

4–006   Some employers require employees to pass a medical examination before taking up employment. In that case, the offer of employment will be conditional on a satisfactory report. Today it is not uncommon to find employers who only take up references once they have decided to offer someone a job. This seems odd, since the whole point of the reference is to help assess the candidate's suitability, and it should thus be taken into account as part of the selection process. In *Wishart v NACAB* (1990), the claimant was offered a job "subject to receipt of satisfactory written references". The references indicated that he had had quite a lot of sick leave, and the employer therefore decided to withdraw the offer. The claimant claimed that the references would have been regarded as satisfactory by a reasonable employer, and that an objective standard was the appropriate test to use. The Court of Appeal thought this was just about arguable, but tended to the view that the correct test is whether or not the references are seen as satisfactory by the employer in question. It is submitted that this is the better view, and that the test here must be subjective.

In the unusual case of *Cheltenham BC v Laird* (2009) the question arose as to whether the employer could sue the employee on the basis of untrue statements in a pre-employment health questionnaire. The job offer was expressly made conditional on the employee receiving medical clearance and stated that termination could follow if material facts were withheld. The High Court considered it was possible for an employer to sue a former employee for damages for fraudulent and negligent misrepresentation on this basis, although finding on the facts that the employee had given truthful answers and was not liable. It should be noted that the use of pre-employment medical questionnaires is now subject to some limitation under EqA 2010 s.60: see above, para.2–076.

If an offer is unconditional and has been accepted then, of course, neither party has the right to vary or withdraw from it. In *Sarker v South Tees Acute Hospitals NHS Trust* (1997) the EAT held that withdrawal of an accepted offer before the date on which the employment was due to start was a termination of employment in breach of contract, giving the claimant a cause of action in an employment tribunal.

Written Particulars of Terms

The variety of sources from which the terms of the contract may be drawn can result in confusion as to what has been agreed, and therefore to unnecessary disputes. Thus the very first provision of all the protective legislation was the requirement, introduced by the Contracts of Employment Act 1963, that employees should receive a statement in writing of the principal terms and conditions of the contract. This now appears, in amplified form, in the Employment Rights Act 1996 (ERA) Pt I. Substantial changes were effected by the Trade Union Reform and Employment Rights Act 1993 (TURERA) in order to comply with the 1991 EU Directive on Proof of the Employment Relationship (91/533/EEC), and further amendments were made by the Employment Act 2002.

4–007

Under ERA ss.1 and 198, employees with one month's service are entitled to a written statement of their main terms and conditions, although the employer has two months in which to provide it. Employees whose employment is for less than a month and certain seafarers and share fishermen are excluded from this right. The particulars may be provided in a written statement especially for that purpose, or they can be provided instead in a letter of engagement or written contract of employment, provided that it covers the same ground. The particulars may be provided in instalments, provided that one of them ("the principal instalment") includes all of the following: the identity of the parties; the date of commencement; whether any previous period of employment counts as part of the employee's continuous employment; any terms about holidays; job title or job description; and place of work or mobility clause.

The other matters to be included are: pay, or the method of calculating it; intervals at which wages are paid; hours of work, including any rules on overtime; sick pay and pension arrangements, if any; the length of notice to be given on either side; and details of any collective agreements affecting the contract. If the employment is not expected to be permanent, the particulars should state the period for which it is expected to continue, or the finishing date in the case of a fixed-term contract. If there are no terms on any of these matters, this must be expressly stated. Job title can be important: a "till operator" probably cannot be transferred to duties in the store room; however, an "unskilled worker Grade 1" can be asked to do any type of unskilled work, and would have no legitimate complaint if taken off what she has come to regard as "her" job. From an employer's point of view, there are obvious advantages in flexibility and it may seem like a good policy not to use job descriptions and to draw job titles widely so that staff can be used in whatever way seems best at the time. However, that policy backfired in *Nelson v BBC* (1977) where the employee was a Grade 3 producer who had always worked in the Caribbean Service. When that service was closed down, he successfully resisted the employer's argument that he was redundant, because his contract merely described him as an employee in that particular grade, and this was backed up by an express mobility clause elsewhere in the contract. On the other hand, in *Land Securities Trillium v Thornley* (2005), where the employee's contract contained the common flexibility clause stating that she could be required to undertake "any other duties which may reasonably be required of you", the EAT held that the term could not be construed in such a way as to allow her to be moved from her job as a practising architect to an essentially managerial role.

4–008   The requirement to stipulate the place of work, or alternatively that the employee may be required to work at different places, was introduced by TURERA and should have reduced the number of disputes over whether an employee can be moved to a different location without her agreement (which often arises in relation to redundancy: see below, Ch.9).

ERA s.3 further requires that the written statement should either include or refer the employee to another reasonably accessible document containing details of any disciplinary rules applicable to the employee, to whom she can apply if dissatisfied with a disciplinary decision and any consequent further steps. At one time, employers with fewer than 20 employees were exempt from this requirement, in the interests of reducing the regulatory burden on small businesses. However, in its 2001 Consultation Paper on dispute resolution (*Routes to Resolution*, DTI 2001) the Government expressed the view that lack of knowledge of disciplinary rules and procedures was a major cause of employment disputes going to employment tribunals. The Employment Act 2002 therefore removed the exemption for small employers and also amended ERA s.3 so that the written statement (or other document) should also specify the disciplinary and dismissal procedures as well as the rules. It is also mandatory for the statement to say to whom the employee should complain if he has a grievance. In *Goold (Pearmak) Ltd v McConnell* (1995) failure to provide a grievance procedure was held to be a fundamental breach of contract by the employer.

Under ERA s.4 the employer has a further obligation to inform employees of any changes in their terms and conditions within a month of the change. This is to ensure that the statement is kept up to date. It must be noted, however, that this does not confer on the employer any right to make such changes: any variation must be agreed between the parties, as with any other contract (see below, para.4–013).

Status of the written statement

The written statement is not the same thing as a written contract of employ-   4–009
ment. A contract creates the rights and duties of the parties; the written statement merely declares what they are after they have been agreed, and it follows that it is therefore capable of being inaccurate. This distinction may be easy enough for a lawyer to grasp, but may not be so obvious to ordinary employers and employees, especially given the special veneration that lay people reserve for things in writing. It is an important distinction, for if a document is held to be a written contract, it will be presumed that it accurately records the terms agreed by the parties and it will be very difficult to persuade a court that the terms are otherwise. If it is a statement, then it has no special legal status and could be a mistaken record of what was agreed. Indeed, as was pointed out in *System Floors v Daniel* (1981), a written statement supplied to meet the employer's statutory obligation is not an agreed document: it represents only the employer's unilateral view of the agreement. In addition, it is relevant to look at the conduct of the parties to discover the meaning of written particulars, while that would not usually be permissible in relation to a written contract (*Glendale Managed Services v Graham* (2003)).

That said, it remains the case that the written statement will usually be the best evidence, and sometimes the only evidence, of the agreement; also that it seems unlikely in many cases that the decision to give a written contract rather than a written statement is made consciously. In *System Floors v Daniel* the document was headed "Written statement" and the employee's signature was merely to indicate receipt; in *Gascol Conversions v Mercer* (1974) the employee signed a document headed "Non-staff employees' contract of employment": this was held to be a written contract. One may perhaps doubt whether the parties realised that the difference in wording would have the result that the former employee, but not the latter, would be able to claim his terms were different.

Enforcing the obligation

What happens if an employer fails to provide the written statement? When the   4–010
requirement was originally introduced, failure to comply was a criminal offence!

This was overkill perhaps, but the present "sanction", that the employee may apply to an employment tribunal for a declaration of what should have been included (ERA s.11), is not entirely satisfactory either: it is hardly a way to endear oneself to one's employer, and it is thus unlikely that the employee will take such action unless some more serious problem has arisen. Previous editions of this book suggested that a more effective sanction would be to require an employer to pay two weeks' pay to an employee if it failed to provide a written statement, by analogy with the sanction under ERA s.93, where an employer fails to provide a written statement of reasons for dismissal. It is encouraging to see a move in this direction. Under the Employment Act 2002 s.38, tribunals must award an employee who successfully brings proceedings under some other jurisdiction (such as unfair dismissal or discrimination) an extra two to four weeks' pay if it transpires that the employer was in breach of its duty to provide a written statement. Unfortunately, this claim is not freestanding and no award will be made if the employee is unsuccessful. It is difficult to see the rationale for these restrictions, since the wrong to the employee is the same in all cases and should be independent of any other claim.

Another problem arising under ERA s.11 concerns the jurisdiction of the tribunal, and comes about because of the continuing rule that tribunals do not have complete jurisdiction over purely contractual issues. If the statement is not given, is incomplete, or is said to be inaccurate, does it not mean that the tribunal will have to find out what the terms of the contract are, in order to make a declaration of what particulars the employee should have been given? But if so, does this not mean that the tribunal is exercising jurisdiction over contractual matters while the contract is still ongoing? The issue received detailed consideration from the Court of Appeal in *Mears v Safecar Security* (1982). The court concluded that the tribunal clearly had the right and the duty to correct a statement which was incorrect as well as to state the terms where no statement had been given. In doing so, it should investigate what the actual agreement of the parties was. So far, so good; however, Stephenson LJ went even further than this and held that where there was no evidence of what the parties had agreed on a matter which should have been contained in the written statement, then the tribunal should nonetheless determine what they should have agreed, in effect inventing the term which would best fit in the circumstances. This was doubted by another Court of Appeal in *Eagland v British Telecom* (1992). Pointing out that Stephenson LJ's remarks were obiter, Parker LJ drew a distinction between mandatory terms (necessary incidents for the contract of employment to exist) and non-mandatory terms (e.g. terms about pensions, sickness or holidays). If non-mandatory terms were not reflected in the written statement then tribunals should not invent them. In the case of mandatory terms, tribunals would have power to declare an agreement if one were discoverable, but if not, he doubted the tribunal's power to impose terms which had not been agreed. As the Court of Appeal in *Eagland* recognised, this guidance was also obiter; however, as it is the product of further reflection on the matter and accords better with general principle, it is undoubtedly to be preferred. Finally, it remains the case that the tribunal has no power to interpret the contract and make a declaration as to its meaning (*Construction Industry Training Board v Leighton* (1978); *Southern Cross Healthcare v Perkins* (2011)).

Other Documents

Employers may use all sorts of papers to communicate with their employees. **4–011**
Lots of employers have staff handbooks, or works rules books; the noticeboard
is an important means of communication in many work-places, large employers often have an in-house journal and today there is usually also a company
intranet. Many registered companies now give their employees a version of the
annual report that they must give to their shareholders and this is recognised as
good practice. The purpose of these documents varies; some are designed to be
acted on by the workers; others are merely for information; and others still are
a public relations exercise designed to build a corporate image and to develop
a positive feeling among the workforce towards their employer. Not only does
the function vary from company to company, but it may well be that the same
document carries out more than one function. For example, a staff handbook
may well contain general information about the history and structure of an
organisation as well as details of holiday entitlements, disciplinary and grievance
procedures, and so on.

Whether or not other documents have any contractual status will depend on
the intention of the parties and whether or not they have been incorporated
into the contract of employment. As this will be a question of fact in each case,
it is not possible to make generalisations about particular classes of document.
Express incorporation of a document, where a letter of appointment, the contract or even the written statement expressly refers to it, is unlikely to cause
too many problems, unless the document fulfils more than one function, where
it may be difficult to know whether a particular section is intended to have
contractual effect. In *Bateman v Asda Stores Ltd* the employer avoided this
problem by stating clearly which parts of the staff handbook were intended to
be contractual. This is discussed in more detail in relation to collective agreements (see below, para.5–009). It is worth noting that in *Harlow v Artemis
International Corporation Ltd* (2008) the High Court dismissed an employer's
argument that express incorporation of the staff handbook—which referred to a
physical document at the time the contract was made—could not be interpreted
as incorporating a folder entitled "HR Policies and Procedures" which appeared
only in virtual form on the staff intranet.

Implied incorporation will usually depend on whether the parties have acted
in the past as if this kind of document is part of the contract, as well as a consideration of whether the kind of thing it covers is appropriately viewed as a
contract term. In *Trusthouse Forte v Adonis* (1984) a notice was posted saying,
"Last warning. Anyone smoking in non-smoking areas will be dismissed for gross
misconduct". Two days later the employers issued an updated written statement
to employees which included smoking in prohibited places under the category
of ordinary misconduct for which a final warning would be given. Six months
later the employee was dismissed for smoking in a non-smoking area. The EAT
clearly treated the notice as capable of having contractual effect, although on
the facts it was negated by the inconsistent written statement, which had been
issued later. Had the sequence of events been reversed, the dismissal would
probably have been fair. In *Taylor v Secretary of State for Scotland* (2000) it was

held that an equal opportunities policy which had been notified to prison officers by circular was incorporated into their contracts of employment in the light
of evidence that other changes to contracts had been implemented in the same
manner. However, in *Grant v South West Trains* (1998) the High Court declined
to find that an equal opportunities policy was incorporated on the strength of
a contractual statement that employees should act in the spirit of it. The policy
was in "very general, even idealistic" terms and the manner of its agreement
indicated that the parties did not intend it to be binding.

4–012   Mixed messages were a problem in *Crédit Suisse Asset Management v Armstrong*
(1996), where the company sought to rely on a restrictive covenant contained in a
staff handbook. The handbook had been issued in 1994 with a covering memorandum which described it as "largely an update of existing terms" but urged staff to
"try to find time to read it". The memorandum also said that the new handbook
superseded previous documentation and that it contained "important contractual
rights and obligations". The employees argued that they were not bound by this
because the memorandum had misrepresented the contents, by describing it as
"largely an update . . .", and if it was meant to be contractual, it was strange that
the memorandum only said, "try and find time to read it". However, the Court of
Appeal pointed out that the index at the front of the handbook had a footnote
stating that the provisions of the handbook were contractual; furthermore, the
employees were highly paid investment fund managers: "men of experience and
sophistication", in the court's estimation, who were used to dealing with complex
documents. In these circumstances, the handbook could be taken to be incorporated. It is possible that this could be regarded as a gloss on the principle laid
down in *Jones v Associated Tunnelling* (1981) (below, para.4–014), which therefore
might not apply if the employee had a sufficient degree of knowledge and experience to realise the significance of a variation introduced in this way.

One of the most important reasons for knowing whether or not a particular
document has contractual effect is to know whether it is binding on the employer
as well as the employee. The point is famously illustrated by *Secretary of State v
ASLEF (No.2)* (1972). In the course of an industrial dispute, the rail workers instituted a work-to-rule. This involved their zealous adherence to all the instructions
in their enormous rule-book, and had the desired effect of causing havoc on the
railways. The beauty of the tactic, as they saw it, was that they were not acting
in breach of their contracts of employment; they were carrying out its terms to
the letter! The argument, not surprisingly, did not commend itself to the Court
of Appeal, which found against them on a number of points. One reason was
that the court denied that the rule-book was a part of the contract. Rather, it
contained the employer's standing instructions on how the work was to be done.
The implication of this finding was that the rule-book provisions were within the
unilateral discretion of the employer and could thus be changed without the
prior agreement of the workers. Thus by insisting on following the rules when
the employer wanted them to be disregarded, the employees were in breach of
contract.

Another example of the discretion which this kind of interpretation vests in
the employer is *Dryden v Greater Glasgow Health Board* (1992). Dryden was an

auxiliary nurse, who smoked 30 cigarettes a day. Until 1991 the Health Board provided smoking areas within the hospital, but then it decided that it should implement a complete no-smoking policy. Consultation took place from 1990; staff were given plenty of warning and offers of help to give up. A few days after the policy was finally implemented, Dryden resigned because she could not cope with the ban. She claimed unfair dismissal, so the tribunal had to decide whether introducing the ban on smoking was a breach of contract by the employer. The Scottish EAT held that it was not. This concerned the employer's rules governing behaviour in the workplace, and they were not contractual terms. In the view of the EAT, making rules for the conduct of employees was within the employer's discretion as part of the right to give reasonable orders. If the employer is entitled to make rules, it is also entitled to change them.

Variation of the Contract

Since contracts of employment typically last for some time, there is bound to be a need to change things from time to time. How can this be done? Essentially, as with any other contract, a change to its terms can only be effected by both parties agreeing to the variation. This is normally done as part of the general round of pay negotiations. If the employer wants changes, it can make any pay increase conditional on employees agreeing. If negotiations are carried out with one or more trade unions via collective bargaining, then agreement by the unions will suffice (see below, para.5–009). **4–013**

If employees will not agree to the change, then the employer may try to insist on introducing it unilaterally, but this will be a breach of contract, usually a fundamental breach. In practice, however, the employee may not be able to insist on her right to continue on the old terms; if the employer pushes the issue to the point of dismissing those who will not consent to a change, it does not follow that the dismissal will be unfair, even though there is a breach of contract (see below, para.8–074). Many employees in any case would rather keep their job than win unfair dismissal compensation, which is rarely sufficient in the long term.

If the employer introduces a unilateral variation and the employee does not treat this as grounds to terminate the contract, the employer is likely to argue that she has affirmed the contract as varied. Can it be said that working under new terms without protest shows that the employee has accepted the variation? In *Solectron Scotland Ltd v Roper* (2004) the EAT held that the question to be answered was whether the employee's conduct in continuing to work was only referable to his having accepted the new contract. Thus if the terms of the new contract affected him immediately and he nonetheless worked without protest, this would be evidence of acceptance. But if the change had no effect on him, then his conduct in continuing to work could be referable to the old contact, and would not indicate acceptance.

In *Jones v Associated Tunnelling* (1981) the employee was issued with a new written statement which included a mobility clause. He made no protest until some four years later when the employer tried to move him from the place **4–014** where he had been employed. The EAT held that agreement could not be implied solely from his failure to protest at a time when the variation had no immediate practical effect on him, for he might well have no wish to precipitate a confrontation with the employer. Similarly, in *Aparau v Iceland Frozen Foods* (1996) the claimant had been employed as a cashier by Bejams, which was taken over by Iceland. Following the takeover, Iceland issued all staff with new written terms and conditions of employment, which included a mobility clause. Iceland relied on the employee's failure to object to this term to show that it was now part of the contract. As the term had no effect on the employment relationship until the day when they asked the cashier to move, the EAT held that mere continuance of employment without objection could not be taken to indicate acceptance. (See also *Harlow v Artemis International Corporation Ltd* (2008)—failure to complain about changes to enhanced redundancy payments not taken to indicate acceptance of the variation.)

On the other hand, in *Farnsworth v Lacy* (2013), an employee was promoted to a senior management grade, but not sent a new contract until some six months later. It contained a restrictive covenant which had not been included in his original contract. Under this contract, he also gained rights to some new benefits, such as medical insurance cover for himself and his family. The High Court held that by applying for these benefits, he had indicated acceptance of the new terms (and was therefore bound by the restrictive covenant).

What happens if the employee continues to work but expressly states that she does not accept the change? In *Burdett-Coutts v Herts CC* (1984) the Council wrote to employees purportedly changing their conditions in a way which resulted in an overall reduction in pay. They continued to work under protest, and then brought an action claiming arrears of pay. They were successful, as the variation had not been agreed. However, this cannot go on indefinitely. In *Henry v London General Transport Services Ltd* (2002) the Court of Appeal held that employees who had worked a new rota system for two years, albeit having made their opposition clear, had to be taken to have agreed the revised terms. In *Robinson v Tescom Corporation* (2008) the claimant objected to the employer unilaterally making a substantial increase in the geographical area in which he would have to travel and stated that he would work under protest. However, instead of doing this, he refused to work according to the new terms. The EAT held that he had been fairly dismissed for misconduct: having said that he would work to the new terms, albeit under protest, he was failing to obey the reasonable instructions of his employer by not doing so.

4–015   It is possible for the employer to reserve a right under the contract to vary its terms without getting the employees' agreement (either individually, or via collective bargaining). In *Wandsworth v D'Silva* (1998) the Court of Appeal thought that clear language would be needed to reserve such a power, which they described as "unusual", and stated also that courts would seek a construction which would avoid an unreasonable infringement of employees' rights. It may perhaps be less unusual for employers to reserve a power to vary the contract unilaterally than the Court of Appeal thought, given a number of recent cases on the issue, in which case employees may be in a vulnerable position. In *Bateman v*

Asda Stores Ltd (2010) the employer was held to be entitled to change such a fundamental term as the payment system without the agreement of employees, because the staff handbook had expressly reserved the right to change terms and conditions. One argument put forward for the employees was that if the employer had an unfettered right to change any term, the contract would be too uncertain to stand. The EAT held that there was no uncertainty: the employer had an unambiguous right to change anything!

The need for clear and unambiguous language is illustrated by *Norman v National Audit Office* (2015) where a statement in the employee's appointment letter that terms were subject to amendment was held by the EAT to be merely stating the obvious rather than reserving a right for the employer to alter them unilaterally. In *Sparks v Department of Transport* (2015) the staff handbook stated, "your contract cannot be changed detrimentally without your agreement". This was interpreted by the High Court as giving the employer a right unilaterally to introduce improvements or neutral changes, but not to introduce detrimental changes such as the stricter attendance management system which was proposed.

If the employer does have an unambiguous unilateral right to change the contract, it may be limited by the implied term not to act in such a way as to undermine mutual trust and confidence in the employment relationship (see below, para.4–026). In *Birmingham City Council v Wetherill* (2007) the Court of Appeal held that the employer's power unilaterally to vary car user allowances was subject to an implied term that the power would not be exercised capriciously or arbitrarily and that employees would be given reasonable notice of any change, in order to give effect to the reasonable expectations of the parties, and this was referred to also in *Bateman v Asda Stores Ltd* (2010). In *Birmingham City Council v Wetherill* the court also considered that a variation under ERA s.4 could be validly notified by a general circular brought to the employees' attention, rather than individual notification to each employee being required (see also *Attrill v Dresdner Kleinwort* (2013)).

Custom and Practice

The phrase "custom and practice" is widely used in industrial relations, but its   **4–016**
meaning in law is opaque. As Davies and Freedland point out, it is necessary to consider whose custom and practice we are talking about: is it a cloak for managerial prerogative, so that if the workforce acquiesces for long enough, they will be bound by it? Or does it mean that where the workers do things "their way" without objection, then they have a right to do it that way? Or does it refer to some sort of joint regulation? There is no clear answer to these questions, although it is true to say that on the whole the courts lean towards the managerial prerogative. In the Part-time Workers (Prevention of Less Favourable Treatment) Regulations 2000 there is a very unusual legislative reference to custom and practice as the test for determining whether a worker is full-time or part-time. It seems likely that it is managerial practice which will be decisive here.

For a custom to be regarded as part of the contract, it must pass similar tests to customary law: i.e. that it is reasonable, notorious (meaning very well-known in this context) and has existed for a very long time. In *Sagar v Ridehalgh* (1931) the employer claimed the customary right to make deductions from a weaver's wages for bad work, either on the basis that this had been the practice in their factory for more than 30 years or on the basis that it was customary in the whole Lancashire cotton weaving trade. The Court of Appeal found both grounds established, and held that it was immaterial if the weaver did not know of the practice.

Now that written statements must be given, the scope for there to be customary terms in the contract is likely to be limited. In times of rapid technological change, to claim a customary right to work in the way to which one has been accustomed is unlikely to be received with judicial sympathy. In *Cresswell v Board of Inland Revenue* (1984) employees feared that computerisation of all tax records would ultimately lead to job losses. Failing to get the assurances they sought on the subject, they refused to cooperate in using the computers and claimed a customary right to do the work manually as before. This latter-day Luddism received short shrift from Walton J, who held that the employer could properly require them to do what was the same job albeit done by different methods.

4–017 Does this indicate that while it may be difficult for employees to argue for contractual rights based on custom, it may be easier for the employer? This potential one-sidedness was recognised by the EAT in *Duke v Reliance Systems* (1982) where Browne-Wilkinson J said that for a unilateral management policy to become a term of employees' contracts on the basis of custom and practice, there were at least two conditions: first, that it had been drawn to the attention of employees, and secondly, that it had been acted on without exception over a substantial period of time.

This was applied, although not to the advantage of the employees in question, in *Quinn v Calder* (1996). In the mid-1980s the management of the company had decided, as a matter of policy, to give enhanced redundancy payments to smooth the path of compulsory redundancies. The arrangements were contained in a management policy document and had not been the subject of negotiation with the recognised trade unions, although they were generally known to the union and the workforce, and had been applied on all four occasions when there had been redundancies between 1986 and 1994. However, in summer 1994 the claimants were made redundant and were not given the enhanced payments. They claimed that it was an implied term of their contracts that they should receive the enhanced payments. Using the test in *Duke v Reliance Systems*, the EAT held that they were not entitled to the payments. This was a unilateral management policy (not a collectively agreed term) and, although it was known to employees, it had not been brought to their attention in any official or systematic way. The conditions were not therefore fulfilled.

There have been a number of other cases where employees have argued that they are entitled to enhanced redundancy payments, based on custom and practice (e.g. *Albion Automotive Ltd v Walker* (2002) and *Solectron Scotland Ltd v*

Roper (2004)). In *Park Cakes Ltd v Shumba* (2013) the Court of Appeal stated that in such cases relevant issues to consider would be the number of times, and length of period over which such payments had been made; whether they were always calculated in the same way; the extent to which they had been publicised to employees, and how they had been described: if the evidence was consistent with the payments being discretionary, the employees would be unlikely to discharge the burden of proving a contractual entitlement based on custom and practice. An example of custom and practice being recognised as a source of contractual terms can be found in *Henry v London General Transport* (2002) (below, para.5–011).

Implied Terms

Contracts of employment differ from many other kinds of contract in that they are usually intended to be indefinite. It would be impossible, in making the contract at the outset, to cover absolutely every eventuality. It follows that there will frequently be situations where the parties just have not reached agreement on a particular point. In these circumstances, it may be appropriate to fill the gaps by implying terms into the contract.

4–018

Terms may certainly be implied according to the usual contract law tests: i.e. when it is necessary to give "business efficacy" to the contract (*The Moorcock* (1889)) or according to the "officious bystander" test (*Southern Foundries v Shirlaw* (1940)): where something is so obvious that it goes without saying, and if there had been someone standing by listening to the parties make the agreement who had suggested that they express the term, they would have silenced him with a testy "Of course!" In *Liverpool CC v Irwin* (1977) the House of Lords continued with the orthodox view that courts cannot imply terms into contracts just because the term would be a reasonable one for the parties to have agreed. However, they suggested that terms could be implied when the nature of the contract indicated that there was a need for such a term, as in the situation where there was an ongoing contractual relationship such as employer and employee and the contract as agreed was incomplete in some crucial respect.

An example of this could be *Courtaulds Northern Spinning Ltd v Sibson* (1988). The employee, an HGV driver, had left his trade union after a dispute, causing bad feeling among the other employees who were all members. To avoid trouble, the employer proposed to move him to a different depot a mile away. He argued that this was a breach of contract as there was no express mobility clause in his contract. The Court of Appeal held that there must be some term about place in his contract: he had to work somewhere. Thus if there was no express term, one would have to be implied, because of the nature of the relationship, to complete the contract. But not every contract of employment would have the same term on place implied into it, unlike, for example, an implied term such as mutual trust and confidence, which is the same for all contracts of employment. In the event, as he was a driver and therefore did not work always in the same place anyway, they held that it would be reasonable to expect him to work from a depot a mile away and held that it was an implied term of the contract that he could be so moved.

4–019   This is subject to the caveat that the term may not be essential in this sense and the gap may have been left deliberately. In *Ali v Christian Salvesen* (1997) the employee was employed under an annualised hours contract which meant that he only became entitled to overtime after having worked 1,824 hours in a year. This had been agreed through collective bargaining. Ali was made redundant after five months during which time he had regularly worked more than 40 hours a week, but had not received any overtime. He argued for an implied term that he should be entitled to pro rata overtime in these circumstances; the employer argued for a literal interpretation of the contract. The Court of Appeal considered that this was not an example of an incomplete contract: the terms had been settled through free collective bargaining and, in the circumstances, an omission of a term on this point was more likely to have been deliberate. In consequence, no term as to overtime should be implied.

It has been argued that while the courts are reluctant to imply terms into the contract when it amounts almost to inventing them for the parties, they are more prepared to imply terms to control the employer's express powers under the contract. Thus in *United Bank v Akhtar* (1989) the bank included an express mobility clause giving it the right to move employees to any branch in the United Kingdom and a discretion as to whether or not it would give relocation allowances. The claimant, a bank clerk in the lowest grade, was given less than a week's notice to move permanently from the Leeds branch where he worked to the Birmingham branch. His request for three months' notice to sort out a move (he had a house to sell and his wife was ill) was rejected, the bank relying on the mobility clause. The EAT held that although an implied term could not contradict an express term, it could control its exercise. In this case, they implied a term that the bank should give reasonable notice of exercise of the mobility clause, so as not to make it impossible for him to comply with his contractual obligation to move (cf. *Birmingham City Council v Wetherill* (2007), para.4–015 above). Similarly, in *Johnstone v Bloomsbury HA* (1991) a junior hospital doctor worked under a contract which provided for a basic 40-hour week, but also for unlimited overtime (although it should not average out at more than an extra 48 hours per week!). He argued that to be required to work an average 88 hours per week and sometimes to work over 100 hours per week would damage his health. By a majority, the Court of Appeal agreed that the express term which allowed this extraordinary amount of overtime was subject to the control of an implied term, although one judge held that it was subject to an implied term that the power to demand overtime would be exercised reasonably, and the other held that it was subject to the implied term that an employer must take reasonable care to ensure the health and safety of employees.

In *Horkulak v Cantor Fitzgerald International* (2004) the Court of Appeal held that where an employer had discretionary power under the contract, its exercise was subject to an implied term that the discretion would be exercised in good faith and not in a perverse or irrational fashion. The court suggested that this was in accordance with the implied duty on both parties to maintain mutual trust and confidence in the employment relationship, a view reiterated in *Attrill v Dresdener Kleinwort* (2013). This could provide a mechanism for considerable control over the managerial prerogative, although not if there is an express term which provides no room for its exercise (such as an express power to dismiss without good cause, as in *Reda v Flag Ltd* (2002)).

These cases lead us to a consideration of another kind of implied term in employment contracts. Certain types of contract are so prevalent that they receive repeated judicial scrutiny, and in the end develop their own special rules. Contracts of employment are in such a category. There are certain terms which are held to be implied by law into every contract of employment just because it is a contract of employment. These implied terms are frequently expressed as being duties of the employer and employee respectively. **4–020**

Two major duties of the employer are the subject of separate chapters. The duty to pay wages is the most fundamental duty of the employer, furnishing as it does the basic consideration for the contract. It is now subject to considerable legislative control and is dealt with below in Ch.7. The employer's duty of care to its employees is a large subject and greatly amplified by statutes on health and safety at work; these matters are dealt with in Ch.14. There remain three other duties of an employer which must be considered: the duty to provide work for the employee; the duty to respect the employee's privacy; and the duty to maintain mutual trust and confidence, an implied duty of more recent vintage.

Duty to provide work?

Does the employer have a duty simply to pay wages, or is there also a duty to supply the employee with work? It may seem odd that the question ever arises, but in fact there are situations where an employee may not be content to remain at home with pay but without work, not least because this is hardly going to be a permanent situation. **4–021**

The classic view is that there is no duty to provide work: "Provided I pay my cook her wages regularly, she cannot complain if I choose to take any or all of my meals out" (per Asquith J in *Collier v Sunday Referee* (1940)). However, there have always been two well-recognised exceptions to this. Where wages depend on commission for the work actually done, or the worker is paid by the piece, it is recognised that an employer has a duty to provide work to give the employee a chance to earn his wages. Thus in *Devonald v Rosser* (1906) a rollerman at a tinplate factory was given six weeks' notice. He argued that the employer had a duty to provide him with work for those six weeks. The court held it was a necessary implication from the terms of the contract (which provided for payment by the piece) that the employer would find him a reasonable amount of work to do and his damages were assessed by reference to his average earnings over the previous six weeks. Similarly, in *Turner v Goldsmith* (1891) it was held to be an implied term in the contract of a salesman paid by commission that he would be sent a reasonable supply of samples to sell.

Secondly, where the refusal of work denies the employee a chance of enhancing her reputation, there is a duty to provide work. In *Clayton & Waller v Oliver* (1930) Oliver was to be employed in one of the three leading roles in a musical called *Hit the Deck*. The employer then reneged. Oliver was entitled to damages for the loss of the opportunity to enhance his reputation. In addition to performers, this exception could extend also to writers such as journalists.

4–022   Beyond these two exceptions, it is generally thought that there is no right to work at common law. In a few cases (e.g. *Nagle v Feilden* (1966); *Edwards v SOGAT* (1971)) Lord Denning attempted to establish such a right. One of the notable examples of this was *Langston v AUEW* (1974) where he quoted several of his own judgments as well as Longfellow's "Village Blacksmith" in support of this contention. This line of authority ceased on Lord Denning's retirement.

As long ago as *Turner v Sawdon* (1901), the Court of Appeal rejected the argument that a failure to provide work would mean that the employee's skills would deteriorate, denying that the employer had a duty to keep the employee in service in such a manner as to enable him to become *au fait* with his work. However, that argument has been treated more sympathetically in recent cases dealing with "garden leave". It has become common for firms to insist on lengthy periods of notice for their senior executives, and, if they resign, to refuse either to have them at work or to release them to a new employer before the notice period is up. The employee may spend months with nothing to do but the garden. The reason for this phenomenon is that companies are worried about their confidential information reaching a competitor—and this seems a safer method of dealing with the problem than a restrictive covenant. By the time the executive moves to her new employer, her information will be out of date.

In *Provident Financial v Hayward* (1989), the fact that the skills of an accountant would not atrophy in the period under consideration was treated as a relevant consideration by the Court of Appeal (see also, *Breach v Epsylon Industries* (1976)), but *William Hill v Tucker* (1998) went a good deal further in using the right to work argument in this context. The employee was a senior dealer who had been specifically charged with developing spread betting, a risky form of betting which was then relatively novel. When his employer tried to hold him to a six-month garden leave period he claimed that it was a breach of his right to work. The Court of Appeal agreed, mainly because of their construction of this particular contract. The employee held a unique position and maintenance of his skills in this developing area did require frequent practice. Furthermore, references in the contract to the employee having to work such hours as were necessary for the proper performance of his duties, to the employer's commitment to developing employees' skills and to an express right to suspend in disciplinary cases were held to be inconsistent with the notion that the contract allowed for the employee to be remunerated without the opportunity to work.

4–023   While the first ground for the decision would limit it to special classes of employment, the terms in the contract itself that were relied on as indicating a right to work are very common and would therefore suggest that very many employees could argue that they had a right to work even if they could not show any risk of their skills atrophying. The EAT in *Christie v Johnston Carmichael* (2010) distinguished *William Hill v Tucker* in relation to a chartered tax accountant who was put on garden leave for his three-month notice period on the grounds that his post was by no means unique and he would be unlikely to become deskilled in such a period, which perhaps suggests that the concept will not be pressed into general service. Also, insofar as this is an implied term of the contract, it is open to an employer to negate it by express provision allowing for garden leave, and this is commonly done in relation to senior executives.

No express provision for garden leave was made in relation to three senior employees in *SG & R Valuation Service Co LLC v Boudrais* (2008), but the company suspended them on full pay on discovering that they were intending to leave to work for a competitor, taking with them confidential information belonging to their employer and soliciting other employees to join them. The employees argued that this infringed their right to work and was a fundamental breach of contract entitling them to leave immediately (which would allow them to join the competitor without serving a notice period). Applying *William Hill v Tucker* (1998), the High Court agreed that their right to work had been infringed. They worked as international consultants specialising in the hotel sector and their skills included underwriting property valuations and attracting new clients and this depended heavily on up-to-date knowledge of the sector and maintaining current contacts. These skills would quickly go stale. The fact that their remuneration was significantly dependent on performance bonuses was also relevant to the judge's decision. However, the court further held that an employee could not invoke the right to work unless she or he was ready and willing to work—which further encompassed the notion that there should be no reason why the employer should not provide work for them. In view of their serious misconduct, the employees had not shown that they were ready and willing to work in accordance with their contracts and so were not entitled to claim for a breach of the right to work (cf. also *RDF Media Group v Clements* (2008) and *Standard Life Healthcare Ltd v Gorman* (2010)).

Duty to respect the employee's privacy

Privacy issues are increasingly dealt with by legislation and the whole area is affected by art.8 of the ECHR, which guarantees individuals' rights to respect for their private life (subject to the provisos in art.8(2)). It seems that an implied obligation on the employer to respect the employee's privacy should be recognised as providing a coherent conceptual framework for these developments and as enabling courts and tribunals to fill any gaps. There are three main aspects to privacy in employment. The first aspect concerns the employee's right to know what information is held about her: this has been considered above in relation to references (see para.4–003). The second aspect concerns the privacy of information about the employee; and the third is about non-intrusion into the employee's private life. An obligation not to disclose information about an employee was recognised in *Dalgleish v Lothian and Borders Police Board* (1991), where the local council wanted to discover which council employees had not paid their poll tax (community charge) and asked the Police Board to disclose this information. By analogy with the cases establishing the employee's duty to the employer in relation to confidential information, the court granted an injunction

4–024

to prevent this on the grounds that it would be in breach of the employer's duty of confidentiality. This is now reinforced by statute. Under the Data Protection Act 1998 employers have a duty to ensure that personal data is only obtained for specified, lawful purposes and is used only for those purposes. The information kept must be accurate, up-to-date, relevant and not excessive—suggesting that personnel records should be regularly culled of old and irrelevant information. The Act contains strict limitations on the processing of such information, which includes its disclosure, and further guidance is given by the Information Commissioner's Employment Practices Code (2005).

Surveillance and monitoring of employees' activities and communications has become particularly sensitive with the advent of increasingly sophisticated and relatively inexpensive technology enabling it to happen. There is a divergence of view between those who feel that employees should not leave their human rights behind at the office door and those who think that an employer is entitled to know what goes on in its time and on its premises. The vulnerability of an employer if employees misuse the firm's e-mail, for example, also provides a good reason for employers to wish to monitor. In *Halford v United Kingdom* (1997) the claimant, who was Assistant Chief Constable of the Merseyside police force, claimed that there was an invasion of privacy contrary to art.8 of the ECHR where her office telephone had been tapped to get information about sex discrimination proceedings which she had instituted against the force. The European Court of Human Rights rejected the Government's argument that employees should have no general expectation of privacy for their telephone calls at work and that an employer should be able to monitor calls without the employee's knowledge, and held that there was a breach of art.8. However, the case was unusual in that she had been provided with a phone specifically for her private use. Furthermore, the court seemed to accept the argument that the proper test was "reasonable expectation", suggesting that an employer could avoid liability provided employees were informed that they would be subject to monitoring (*Copland v United Kingdom* (2007), *Atkinson v Community Gateway Association* (2014)).

While art.8 and the Human Rights Act 1998 may offer limited protection, EU developments may be of more use. The Regulation of Investigatory Powers Act 2000, passed to implement the Telecommunications Data Protection Directive (97/66/EC) and to take account of the Human Rights Act, creates a civil wrong of intercepting communications on private as well as public systems, which is actionable by either the sender or the recipient (s.1(3)). Unfortunately, the thrust of the Act was watered down considerably by the Telecommunications (Lawful Business Practice) (Interception of Communications) Regulations 2000 which allow exceptions for legitimate business purposes. These include ensuring compliance with internal regulatory procedures, monitoring quality and investigating unauthorised use—which appears to give employers pretty much *carte blanche* to monitor widely, provided they take reasonable steps to bring this to employees' attention. However, employers have to comply with the Data Protection Act 1998 (itself passed to implement the EU Directive on Data Protection (95/46/EC)) and any monitoring which involves the collection of information (e.g. recording the results of observation) must comply with that Act. Where communications are intercepted, employers must comply with both the Data Protection Act 1998 and the Lawful Business Practice Regulations 2000. The approach of the Information Commissioner's Employment Practices Code, Pt 3 on Monitoring at Work (revised 2011) is far more worker-orientated than the Lawful Business Practice Regulations and firmly discourages routine surveillance and monitoring. It emphasises the need to balance the adverse impact on employees with the benefits to the employer and tends to take a stronger view of what constitutes adverse impact. Nonetheless, it recognises that employers may need to engage even in covert surveillance of workers in situations where criminal activity or equivalent malpractice is suspected (e.g. in *McGowan v Scottish Water* (2005)).

Another form of invasion of privacy which was held to be a breach of art.8 by the European Court of Human Rights was the intrusive questioning of members of the armed forces about their sexuality and relationships in *Smith and Grady v United Kingdom* (1999) and *Lustig-Prean and Beckett v United Kingdom* (2000). While employees of public authorities may now rely on art.8 directly by virtue of the Human Rights Act 1998, other employees can only do so indirectly, for example in the context of a constructive dismissal claim. In *Pay v Lancashire Probation Service* (2004) the EAT stated that a dismissal in violation of an employee's Convention rights could not be regarded as fair, although on the facts it was held that it was no infringement of the employee's right to privacy when he was dismissed because of his involvement in (lawful) sadomasochistic activities which were publicised on the internet. This was not an activity in the private domain (see also, *X v Y* (2004)). Pay pursued the claim to the European Court of Human Rights, but lost there too. The court held that even if art.8 was engaged (in that only like-minded people would be likely to know of his activities)—which they did not finally decide—the Government could rely on the qualification in art.8 permitting restriction in order to protect the rights and freedoms of others—in this case, to preserve the reputation of his employer (*Pay v United Kingdom* (2009)). **4–025**

Duty to maintain mutual trust and confidence

Since the late 1970s a new implied term of the contract of employment has become established: the implied term that neither side should act in such a way as to damage the mutual trust and confidence which ought to subsist between them in order for the contract to be carried out properly. This developed at first in the context of unfair dismissal, where in order to establish constructive dismissal the employee would have to show that the employer had committed a fundamental breach of contract. There might be situations where the employer had acted very badly but the abusive behaviour could not be pinned to a specific contract term, and in such cases, it began to be argued that the employer's behaviour undermined the employment relationship so severely that it should be regarded as a fundamental breach of contract. For example, in *Robinson v Crompton Parkinson* (1978) an employee of many years' standing and good character was accused of theft. He was acquitted and asked for an apology. It was refused and he left, claiming unfair dismissal. The EAT stated that there was a duty of mutual trust and confidence which could be breached in these sorts of circumstances, although **4–026** not in this particular case. However, it held that there was a breach in *Courtaulds v Andrew* (1979) where a manager had a row with a foreman of 18 years' service which ended with the manager saying, "You can't do the bloody job anyway". In *Gardner v Beresford* (1978) it was held that an arbitrary or capricious refusal to give a wage rise to one employee when everyone else got one could be a breach of this term, although it was not on the facts of the case; and in *Post Office v Roberts* (1980), where without adequate grounds a senior officer described an employee as wholly unsuitable for promotion, such a breach was found.

These were all EAT cases, and there are many others to like effect. The duty to maintain mutual trust and confidence was accepted as an implied term in employment contracts by the Court of Appeal in *Woods v WM Car Services* (1982) and *Lewis v Motorworld* (1985). In 1997 it was recognised by the House of Lords in *Malik v BCCI* and its parameters were explored. In that case, which arose out of the collapse of the Bank of Credit and Commerce International after years of fraudulent dealing came to light (see below, para.8–009), the House of Lords stated the duty (in so far as it related to an employer) in the following terms:

". . . the employer shall not, without reasonable and proper cause, conduct itself in a manner calculated or likely to destroy or seriously damage the relationship of confidence and trust between employer and employee"

(per Lord Steyn).

The Law Lords held that whether or not the term had been breached was to be judged objectively, meaning that it was not necessary to show that the employee had actually lost confidence in his employer (although that could be relevant to the question of remedies) but whether the employer's conduct was likely to bring about such a result, regardless of the employer actual intention. It followed that it was not necessary to show that the employer's breach was aimed directly at the employee, nor that the employee knew of the breach before his employment terminated. The Court of Appeal has since held that the objective test of whether the term has been breached means that it is not appropriate to apply the "range of reasonable responses" test, used in unfair dismissal law, to decide whether there was a breach (*Buckland v Bournemouth University HEC* (2010): see below, para.8–029).

Malik v BCCI was a landmark because not only was it the House of Lords' endorsement of the implied duty to maintain mutual trust and confidence but it also sanctioned the possibility of a claim for damages for the loss caused (although the claim by BCCI employees subsequently failed: *BCCI v Ali (No.2)* (2002)). Predictably, this led to a flood of damages claims and, equally predictably, this led to some retreat by the courts. The most important manifestation of this is the House of Lords' decision in *Johnson v Unisys Ltd* (2001) to the effect that the term does not apply to a decision to dismiss the employee (see further below, para.8–010). While most claims for damages for breach of the implied term have been unsuccessful, it is worth mentioning two which did succeed. In *French v Barclays Bank* (1998) the Court of Appeal held it was a breach of the implied term of mutual trust and confidence when the employer changed to the employee's detriment the terms of a bridging loan which they had granted to assist him in moving house when they relocated him. In *Gogay v Herts CC* (2000) the employer was found to be in breach by suspending the employee without reasonable grounds to do so and the Court of Appeal upheld an award of £26,000 damages for psychiatric injury caused by the breach.

There is no limit to the kind of behaviour which might constitute a breach of the duty to maintain mutual trust and confidence; however, an interesting recent trend shows employees using it to attack employers' handling of contractual disciplinary procedures (e.g. *Leeds Dental Team v Rose* (2014); *Yapp v Foreign and Commonwealth Office* (2015); *Stevens v University of Birmingham* (2015)). **4–027**

It is to be noted that the duty to maintain mutual trust and confidence applies to both employers and employees although, as was pointed out in *Malik v BCCI*, it has more impact on employers in that employees have always been subject to fairly stringent duties of good faith under the contract. It clearly has considerable potential for control of the managerial prerogative, if tribunals and courts wish to use it in that fashion, since all sorts of conduct may be held to fall within the scope of the duty: Lord Nicholls described it as a "portmanteau, general obligation" in *Malik v BCCI*. Indeed, some commentators suggest that it may in time subsume all the other specific duties, in that it may be conceptualised as their underlying rationale. However, there are some advantages in breaking down the implied terms into more specific obligations, as discussed here.

Duty to obey reasonable and lawful orders

The most fundamental duty of the employee is to obey the employer's orders: working as instructed is the employee's basic consideration under the contract, as providing remuneration is the basic consideration of the employer. Breach of this duty is invariably regarded as a fundamental breach of contract which at common law entitles the employer to dismiss the employee without notice. It is for this reason that a strike is certain to be a breach of contract at common law, for the employees are not prepared to accept instructions to work. The classic modern statement of the duty is found in the judgment of Lord Evershed MR in *Laws v London Chronicle* (1959): **4–028**

> "wilful disobedience of a lawful and reasonable order shows a disregard—a complete disregard—of a condition essential to the contract of service, namely the condition that the servant must obey the proper orders of the master, and that unless he does so the relationship is, so to speak, struck at fundamentally."

A modern example of its use is *Dunn v AAH Ltd* (2010), where senior executives were held to have to have been lawfully summarily dismissed for their failure to obey clear instructions about risk reporting to their employer.

The duty as stated does not require unquestioning obedience to every instruction—although the employee who justifiably refuses may find that she is dismissed just the same. In *Morrish v Henlys* (1973), the employee, a van driver, used to take fuel from the company's pump and fill in the amounts in a book. He noticed that the amounts were being altered; when he protested to the manager he was told not to worry, it was just to make the figures balance. He was unwilling to go along with this, and was eventually dismissed for refusing to leave the entry in its changed condition. He successfully claimed that the dismissal was unfair. Even if it was common practice, as the employer alleged, it could not be a reasonable order "to connive at the falsification of one of his employer's records", as the NIRC put it.

While an order to do something unlawful clearly need not be obeyed, it is more difficult to decide what is an unreasonable order. Many disputes arise over whether a duty is within the employee's job description. Presumably, a "machine operator" cannot reasonably be instructed to clean the factory floor instead—but what if it is just a temporary expedient so that she has something to do while her machine is being mended? The answer is not clear-cut. No doubt it will depend on the circumstances: whether a similar level of skill is required, the status of the different work, how temporary it is, and perhaps on the state of the job market altogether. Subject to the rules on redundancy (see below, Ch.9) an employment tribunal might well be persuaded that an employee was unreasonable in not accepting instructions to do work outside the strict confines of the contract, particularly if the business was under pressure. This shades into the next issue to be examined: does the employee have a duty to cooperate with the employer?

Duty to cooperate

4–029   There is now considerable judicial support for the idea that the employee owes an implied duty to perform the contract in a cooperative manner. The starting point is *Secretary of State v ASLEF (No.2)* (1972), considered above in relation to whether the rule-book was a contractual document (para.4–012). The Court of Appeal held that the work-to-rule was a breach of an implied term, expressed by Lord Denning as a duty not to wilfully obstruct the employer's business, or by Roskill LJ as a duty not to obey instructions in a wholly unreasonable way which has the effect of disrupting the business. Buckley LJ expressed the term as an aspect of the duty of fidelity, a duty to promote the employer's commercial interests, an idea which was developed further in *Ticehurst v British Telecom* (1992) (discussed below, para.12–006). In general, while accepting that no one has an obligation to do more than she has contracted to do, the court seemed to suggest that employees had a duty to be cooperative.

This conclusion has been criticised as inconsistent. It is clear that employees have a duty to obey reasonable orders and to observe the terms of the contract— and equally clear that they cannot be expected to do more. Therefore, it is argued, there is no scope for this implied duty: if the employee ignores contractual requirements or refuses to obey reasonable orders, he is in breach of contract; in any other case he is acting perfectly legitimately. While this seems a powerful argument, it cannot be denied that the notion of an implied duty of cooperation is becoming established—and that it may be used to require employees to do more than the contract requires. For example, in *Sim v Rotherham BC* (1986), involving industrial action by teachers, the council deducted from a teacher's wages a sum representing a 35-minute period during which she refused to cover for an absent colleague. She sued for her full wages, claiming that it was no part of her contract to cover. Scott J held that as members of a profession the contractual obligations of teachers were more likely to be defined by the nature of their profession than detailed specifically. These professional obligations included a duty to cooperate in the running of schools in accordance with the reasonable instructions of the head teacher. The decision in *Cresswell v Board of Inland Revenue* (1984) that employees could not refuse to take part in the computerisation of their work may be seen as an aspect of the same trend.

Perhaps the correct conclusion is that for professional workers, who enjoy a high degree of discretion and self-direction in the arrangement of their work, it may be necessary to read in a limitation in terms of a duty of overall cooperation with the employer's undertaking; this seems to be the message from *Ticehurst v British Telecom* (1992). However, for other workers it is submitted that the combination of contractual undertakings and the duty to obey reasonable orders is the beginning and end of their contractual obligations, and that there is no room for further demands to be made on the employee via this alleged implied duty.

Duty of fidelity

It has long been recognised that the employment relationship is one of those involving duties of good faith, sometimes expressed as a duty of fidelity, or a duty to give good and faithful service. The duties are extrapolated to a large extent from the law of agency, and may be subdivided into a number of more specific duties.   4–030

Secret profits

An employee is under an obligation not to make a secret profit from the employment relationship, for example by taking bribes from a supplier to ensure that orders are placed with that supplier rather than another. It is clear that this is a fundamental breach of contract (*Boston Deep Sea Fishing v Ansell* (1888); *Devis v Atkins* (1977); *Neary v Dean of Westminster* (1999); *Tesco Stores Ltd v Pook* (2004)).   4–031

Disclosure of misconduct

In *Bell v Lever Bros* (1932) the House of Lords held that an employee is not under a duty to disclose her own wrongdoing to the employer: the contract of employment imposes a duty of good faith, but it is not a contract of the utmost good faith (*uberrimae fidei*). This position was narrowed by *Sybron v Rochem* (1983), where the employee was manager of the European operations of the company. Shortly after he took a generously compensated early retirement, it was found that in conspiracy with several other employees he had been systematically defrauding the company for years by diverting business opportunities to a rival company which he had set up. The Court of Appeal held that he was in breach of a duty to disclose the wrongdoing of his subordinates even though that would inevitably have led to his own misconduct being revealed. *Bell v Lever Bros* was   4–032 distinguished on the grounds that the employees in that case were innocent of fraud, which was not the case here, and that the issue in that case had been whether there was a duty to disclose one's own wrongdoing, not that of another.

The duty to disclose the misconduct of others was not said to be an implied term of every employment contract, but existed here because of the employee's position in the hierarchy: he was a senior executive, the manager of the European operation. However, a number of questions remain: does a senior executive have a duty to report the misconduct of her peers and superiors as well as inferiors, and does anyone in a position of superiority have a duty to report her subordinates' misconduct, even if she is not very senior?

In *Neary v Dean of Westminster* (1999), Lord Jauncey, acting as a special commissioner appointed by the Queen as Visitor to Westminster Abbey, had to decide whether the Abbey organist-choirmaster had been guilty of gross misconduct over fees which he had received for performances by the choir outside the Abbey. The judge was critical of the petitioner's failure to disclose information about this to the Abbey authorities, but rather than finding that this constituted a breach of contract in its own right, he held, first, that it undermined mutual trust and confidence so that there was a breach of that implied term, and secondly, that the petitioner's profits were therefore secret profits, so that he was in breach of that aspect of the good faith duty. In *Nottingham University v Fishel* (2000) a senior embryologist employed by the university who used other university staff to assist his private work abroad was held to have committed a breach of contract because he had not obtained his employer's consent for either his work or theirs. However, it was held that he had no duty to disclose his own misconduct, nor that of the staff who assisted him, since on the facts, unlike *Sybron v Rochem*, he did not appreciate that their actions were in breach of contract.

4–033   The crucial issue appears to be whether or not the employee can be said to have a fiduciary duty towards the employer beyond the general duty of fidelity under the contract of employment. In the case of company directors, this is straightforward, as it is well established that they have a fiduciary duty to act in good faith in the best interests of the company. In *Item Software (UK) Ltd v Fassihi* (2004) the Court of Appeal held that this extended to requiring a director to disclose his own wrongdoing and that he could be liable in damages for breach of this duty (cf. also *Brandeaux Advisers (UK) Ltd v Chadwick* (2011)). Other employees, particularly senior employees, may be taken to have a fiduciary duty where the circumstances point this way (e.g. *Tesco Stores Ltd v Pook* (2004)), but it seems that, for the time being at any rate, employees do not have a general duty to disclose their own misconduct or to blow the whistle on their colleagues (cf. *Helmet Integrated Systems Ltd v Tunnard* (2007), *Ranson v Customer Systems plc* (2012)).

Competition

4–034   In *Sybron v Rochem* (1983) the misconduct consisted in setting up a competing company and expropriating business which should have gone to the employer. However, so far as directors of companies are concerned, it is only the latter activity which is a breach of the implied duty of good faith. In the absence of express agreement, competition per se is not objectionable, provided that the director can keep on the right side of the nearly invisible barrier between that and a conflict of interests.

If the law is relaxed so far as senior executives such as directors are concerned, one would expect it to be at least as relaxed as regards ordinary employees. However, in *Hivac v Park Royal Scientic Instruments* (1946), the employer of employees engaged in very specialised work making parts for hearing aids was granted an injunction to prevent a rival company from employing them on the same work in their spare time. While it is accepted that what the employee does in his own time is his own business, it seems that this is subject to a limitation if it can be shown to damage the employer's business. In *Nottingham University v Fishel* (2000) it was held that the work which the embryologist did for clinics abroad was not in competition with his employer, although using other employees of the university in this work did raise a conflict of interest and duty which was a breach of his fiduciary duty to the employer.

The mere fact that the employee is intending to leave and set up in competition involves no breach of the good faith duty, even though many employers may regard it as disloyal. In *Laughton v Bapp Supplies* (1986) two young men working in the supplies department in a fairly junior capacity wrote to suppliers of their employer outlining their intention to set up on their own and asking for details of products and prices. When their employer heard of it, he immediately dismissed them. It was held to be unfair: they were not in breach of the duty of good faith by intending to compete. It would have been otherwise if they had been accumulating confidential information or trying to steal the employer's customers, but that was not the case. By way of contrast, in *Lancashire Fires v SA Lyons* (1997) a senior employee of the claimant company (in fact, the founder's brother) used his spare time to acquire and renovate business premises and equipment with a view to setting up his own competing business, making use of contacts acquired during his employment as well as his thorough knowledge of the company's processes. It was held that this was a clear breach of his duty of fidelity, and the Court of Appeal suggested that, "any employee with technical knowledge and experience can expect to have his spare time activities in the field in which his employers operate carefully scrutinised in this context". In *Helmet Integrated Systems Ltd v Tunnard* (2007) the employee, who was employed as a salesman, had an idea for a new safety helmet which would compete with one of his employer's main products. He sought funding to develop the idea and had designs produced before resigning his employment. The employer argued that since he had an express duty to report on competitor activity, he should have reported his own activity and was in breach of his fiduciary duty in not doing so. The Court of Appeal held that, as a middle-ranking salesman, the employee was not in the position of a fiduciary. Although he would have had a duty to report this activity if it were done by a third party, so far as his own activities were concerned, this was trumped by the consideration that the right to compete on leaving implies a right to prepare to compete while still employed. On the facts, the employee had not breached any other aspect of the duty of fidelity in the preparations he had made while still employed.

4–035 Once the employee has left employment, there is of course no implied term that she may not compete. However, employers frequently try to limit possible competition from former employees by inserting restraint of trade clauses into contracts of employment. The validity of these is considered below.

Confidential information

4–036 While competition in the employee's own time may be all right in itself, such activity carries a high risk that confidential information belonging to the employer will be used, and this will most certainly be a breach of the duty of good faith. Misuse of confidential information is a major concern for employers not only in relation to existing employees but also those who have left. The leading authority on how far the employer can protect information is *Faccenda Chicken v Fowler* (1986), where the Court of Appeal held that there were two types of confidential information. The first kind consists of trade secrets or information of such a highly confidential nature that it should be treated as if it were a trade secret: the employee can be restrained from using this even after leaving employment. The second is information which is confidential, in that it would be a breach of the duty of good faith for the employee to use it for her own purposes, or to disclose it to someone else while employed, but which she would be entitled to use after leaving. Both kinds are to be distinguished from the employee's ordinary skill and knowledge, albeit gained from the employment, which the employee must be free to use subsequently.

The difficulty arises in trying to classify different types of information as being one kind or the other. Clearly secret formulae or processes will be trade secrets, but what about policies and strategies? The attitude of the employer towards the information, for example, whether its availability was restricted, and whether its confidentiality was impressed on the employee, may be relevant, although the employer cannot turn non-confidential matter into confidential information by treating it as secret. In *Faccenda* the ex-employee had used a package of sales information: the list of customers, the delivery routes, the customers' usual requirements, the times of deliveries, and pricing policy. The Court of Appeal held that this package fell into the second category: it would no doubt have been a breach of duty for the employee to disclose this information while still employed, but after employment he was free to use it, in the absence of any valid restraint of trade clause. This must be read subject to the caveat that had the employee deliberately memorised the information (or worse, copied out the information) while employed with a view to using it later, there would be a breach of the duty of good faith (*Robb v Green* (1895)). In *Lancashire Fires v SA Lyons* the employee argued that a particular process unique to the company was not subject to a duty of confidence because it had never been stressed to him that it was a secret, and it had become part of his skill and knowledge. The Court of Appeal did not accept that the employer must point out to an employee the precise limits of what is to be regarded as confidential and held that, on the facts, the employee must have known that he was using confidential information. An injunction was granted to prevent a further breach of the obligation of confidence.

Some extension of the protection for employers may be discerned in *Crowson Fabrics Ltd v Rider* (2008) where senior employees who had gone into competition with their former employer argued that information which they had taken in the form of documents or computer files was either in the public domain or part of their own knowledge built up over many years. The High Court accepted that the information was not confidential in the sense discussed above—but that by taking the information in the form they had, the employees had greatly reduced the time it would have taken them to reassemble or reconstruct it after leaving, thus providing their new business with a springboard which would enable it to be highly competitive from the word go. The former employer was therefore entitled to an injunction ("springboard relief") on the grounds that their copying of the information was a breach of their duty of fidelity, regardless of whether the information therein was confidential (cf. also *PennWell Publishing (UK) Ltd v Ornstien* (2007)).

Whistleblowing

The general duty that confidential information must not be disclosed has always been subject to an important common law exception, that disclosure may be justified where it is in the public interest. Thus in *Initial Services v Putterill* (1968) a former employee revealed to the *Daily Mail* that the company was involved with others in a price-fixing scheme contrary to the Restrictive Practices Act, and in *Lion Laboratories v Evans* (1985) another ex-employee blew the whistle on a breathalyser machine widely used by police forces but whose accuracy was in doubt. In both cases injunctions to prevent disclosure were refused to the former employers on the grounds that what was revealed was in the public interest. 4–037

A number of highly publicised cases either of whistleblowers being victimised for their actions or, worse, of disasters occurring from failure to heed their warnings, created the climate for the passage of the Public Interest Disclosure Act 1998, which attempts to clarify the parameters of public interest disclosures and to create a framework where employees can blow the whistle responsibly and remain in their jobs without fear of reprisal. The Act works by introducing ss.43A–43L into the Employment Rights Act 1996, making it automatically unfair to dismiss workers or subject them to any detriment where they have made a protected disclosure. Note that it is not only employees who are protected: in fact ERA s.43K defines workers even more widely than ERA s.230(3) (see above, para.3–010) and explicitly includes agency workers, homeworkers and trainees, among others. The provisions were amended in important respects by the Enterprise and Regulatory Reform Act (ERRA) in 2013.

Disclosure of information was originally protected where the worker honestly believed on reasonable grounds that it tended to show one of the following: commission of a criminal offence; failure to comply with a legal obligation; miscarriage of justice; danger to health or safety; damage to the environment; or the deliberate concealment of any of these (ERA s.43B). In *Parkins v Sodexho Ltd* (2002) the EAT held that failure to comply with a legal obligation could cover a situation where an employee claimed that he had been dismissed for complaining to the employer that the employer was in breach of contract.

This meant that there was a huge overlap between s.43B of ERA and other claims, extending automatic unfair dismissal protection when the dispute was essentially a private contract matter. As a result, ERRA amended ERA s.43B so that to be a qualifying disclosure, the person making it must additionally have a reasonable belief that the disclosure is made in the public interest, as well as showing one of the breaches listed above. No definition of public interest is given, so it is likely that this will give rise to further litigation. In one of the first cases to reach the EAT, *Chesterton Global Ltd v Nurmohamed* (2015), it was held that a disclosure alleging that the employment contracts of 100 senior managers were being breached by the employer involved a sufficient section of the public to be covered, even though the claimant was particularly motivated by the fact that he was one of the senior managers affected and even though the employer argued that this was essentially a private employment dispute of the *Parkins v Sodexho* kind.

4–038 The wrongdoing in question need not be wrongdoing on the part of the employer: ERA s.43B refers to actions by "any person" (*Hibbins v Hester Way Neighbourhood Project* (2009)). It is also clear that the question is whether the whistleblower honestly believes on reasonable grounds that the allegations are true: not whether they are true in fact (*Darnton v University of Surrey* (2003)). Similarly, where the disclosure is of information tending to show that a criminal offence has been committed, it is enough if the employee honestly believes that the conduct would constitute a criminal offence, not whether that is a correct view of the law (*Babula v Waltham Forest College* (2007)).

The protection was originally qualified by the requirements that the worker must be acting in good faith, making no personal gain from the disclosure and acting reasonably in the circumstances (ERA s.43G(1)). In *Street v Derbyshire Unemployed Workers' Centre* (2004) the Court of Appeal held that an employee was not protected where she honestly believed in the allegations she was making against a colleague, but made them because she held a grudge against him. This was problematic, since people often act from mixed motives (even the most public spirited among us is unlikely to be wholly above a little *schadenfreude*), and in any case, this could inhibit the disclosure of misconduct which ought to be brought to light. ERRA therefore amended ERA s.43G to remove the good faith requirement, although the other limitations remain. It may be taken into account in considering remedies, however: a tribunal may reduce compensation by up to 25 per cent if the claimant did not act in good faith.

A further requirement is that the worker must make the disclosure to a proper person (ERA s.43C). Disclosure is protected if it is made to the employer or to the third party who is actually responsible for the problem; to a legal adviser; where the employer is a public body, to the relevant Minister; or to a person prescribed by regulations (ERA ss.43C–43F). Under the Public Interest Disclosure (Prescribed Persons) Order 1999 regulatory bodies such as the Audit Commission, Information Commissioner, Health and Safety Executive and many more are so prescribed.

4–039 Under ERA s.43G, disclosure to anyone else can be protected, but only if the worker has reasonable grounds to believe that she will be victimised or that evidence will be destroyed or concealed if she goes to the employer and there is no prescribed regulator to go to instead. In deciding whether the worker acted reasonably, tribunals are expressly told to consider the identity of the recipient of the information, the seriousness of the failure and the likelihood of recurrence and whether or not the worker has complied with the employer's own procedure. It is thus unlikely that disclosure to the media will be regarded as reasonable except in the most extreme cases.

Workers have a right not to be subjected to a detriment for making a protected disclosure (ERA s.47B) and dismissal or selection for redundancy on these grounds is automatically unfair (ERA ss.103A, 105). As with other automatic unfair dismissal situations, there is no qualifying period of employment for this, and it is also provided that there will be no limit on the compensatory award in these cases. One anomaly is that detriment has to be "on the ground that" the employee has made a protected disclosure, while dismissal is protected only if the sole or principal reason is the disclosure. In *Feccitt v NHS Manchester* (2012) the Court of Appeal declined to use a but-for test in deciding whether detriment had been on the grounds of the claimants' protected disclosure, asking instead whether the disclosure was "a material factor" in the employer's decision.

In *Virgo Fidelis Senior School v Boyle* (2004) the EAT stated that awards for injury to feelings could be made in protected disclosure cases, in line with the guidance for discrimination cases in *Vento v Chief Constable of West Yorkshire Police (No.2)* (2003) (see above, para.2–084) and in another analogy with discrimination cases, the Court of Appeal held that protection against detriment continues after termination of the contract in *Woodward v Abbey National* (2006).

Restrictive covenants

As Lord Denning pointed out in *Littlewoods v Harris* (1978), there may be situations where the identification of the confidential information which the employee may not use even after termination of her employment is so difficult that the employer may seek to resolve the problem by getting the employee to agree not to work for a rival firm after leaving, or not to set up in competition on her own account.

4–040

Such a contract is in restraint of trade, in that it inhibits the employee's right to earn a living by any legal means, which is bad for her and not in the public interest either. Originally all covenants in restraint of trade were regarded as void for these reasons. However, towards the end of the nineteenth century, the House of Lords developed the law to its present position which is, essentially, that a covenant in restraint of trade is prima facie void, but may be upheld if it complies with two conditions: first, that it is reasonable as between the parties, and secondly, that it is reasonable having regard to the public interest (*Nordenfelt v Maxim Nordenfelt Guns and Ammunition* (1894)).

In the case of employees, the courts are aware that the parties are unlikely to be in an equal bargaining position and that restrictive covenants should therefore be scrutinised more strictly than, for example, restrictive covenants entered into by the seller of a business who promises not to compete with her successor. Thus in *Herbert Morris v Saxelby* (1916) the House of Lords held that a restraint would be void unless it was protecting some genuine proprietary interest on the part of the employer, "whether in the nature of trade connection or in the nature of trade secrets" (per Lord Parker); it would be void if it was only directed at avoiding competition or prevented the employee using the personal skill and knowledge acquired during employment.

4–041   Thus the restrictive covenant must not be too wide in its subject-matter and it must also not be too wide in terms of the geographical and temporal limits placed on the employee's activities. This will be a question of fact: in *Nordenfelt v Maxim Nordenfelt Guns and Ammunition* (1894) a worldwide restraint lasting 25 years was upheld on an inventor of weapons, but in view of his key position, the large payment he received to agree to it, the worldwide nature of the trade and, it would seem, the fact that this restraint kept the business in England (public interest having a parochial nature), it was reasonable. But in *Mason v Provident Clothing* (1913) a restriction on trading within 25 miles of London for three years after termination was held to be void in relation to a sales representative who had worked entirely in Islington.

Where a clause is too wide, the court may sever the unreasonable part and enforce the rest, but only if this can be done by leaving something intelligible after striking out the offending part (the "blue pencil rule"). The court will not rewrite the contract for the parties. Furthermore, severance will only be carried out of a separate, unenforceable promise; if the court construes the covenant as being one indivisible promise, it will stand or fall as a whole even though it might have been upheld if some words had not been present. Thus in *Attwood v Lamont* (1920) the employee had been the manager of the tailoring department of a store carrying on business as a general outfitter, draper, tailor and haberdasher. The covenant which the employer sought to enforce prohibited him from carrying on the trades of tailor, dressmaker, general draper, milliner, hatter, haberdasher or outfitter. Only a restriction on the first activity would have been legitimate, but although it would be possible to strike out the other words, the Court of Appeal refused to do so on the grounds that this was a single, indivisible agreement and the doctrine of severance permitted only separate promises to be removed.

In *General Billposting v Atkinson* (1909) the House of Lords laid down the important principle that a restrictive covenant would not apply if a contract of employment was wrongfully terminated by the employer. In *Briggs v Oates* (1990) this principle was applied where a five-year fixed-term contract was terminated one year before its expiry by the dissolution of a partnership. Although the restrictive covenant in the employee's contract expressly said that it applied to termination "for whatever reason", Scott J held that it could not apply where the termination was caused by the employer's repudiatory breach. He went on to hold that, if the covenant could be interpreted as meaning exactly what it said and thus survive a wrongful termination, it would be an unreasonable restraint of trade, and unenforceable on that ground. This led to a number of cases where covenants which purported to apply regardless of how the contract was terminated (even, in one case, where it expressly stated "whether lawfully or unlawfully") were attacked on the grounds that they were unreasonable restraints and thus void ab initio. If correct, this meant that the employee could escape from the restrictive covenant even if the contract had in fact been terminated lawfully. A conflict of authorities was resolved by the Court of Appeal in *Rock Refrigeration v Jones* (1996). Pointing out that prior to *Briggs v Oates* such clauses had frequently been construed by the higher courts without any attack on this particular ground, the court held that the argument was founded on an assumption which was erroneous, namely that a restrictive covenant could survive a wrongful termination of the contract by the employer. It could not, because of the principle in *General Billposting v Atkinson*. It did not follow that the clause was void from the start. Thus, if the contract were terminated unlawfully by the employer, the covenant would not apply; if it were terminated lawfully, it would depend on its terms whether or not it was an unreasonable restraint of trade according to the usual tests. The court did not accept that there were any stronger arguments here for striking down the clause on the grounds that employees might be inhibited through thinking that it gave the employer greater protection than applies generally to clauses which are ultimately found to be too wide.

In *Kores v Kolok* (1959) the Court of Appeal refused to enforce a contract **4–042** between two competing employers that neither would employ the former employees of the other for a period of five years after termination. It is clear that, had a restriction of that kind against working for a competitor been included in the employees' contracts, it would not have been enforceable, and it would be strange if this could be circumvented by such an agreement between employers. However, this leaves open the question of whether a restrictive covenant aiming to stop an employee poaching other employees can be valid. In *Dawnay, Day & Co v De Braconier d'Alphen* (1997) the Court of Appeal, following its earlier unreported decision in *Ingham v ABC Contract Services* (1993), held that an employer has a legitimate interest in maintaining a stable, trained workforce which could be protected by use of a reasonable non-solicitation clause.

If the employer is prepared to pay a salary, it may be possible to achieve the same effect as a restrictive covenant through a garden leave provision. Instead of obtaining a promise that the employee will not work for a rival for a certain time after leaving, the contract contains a provision for a long period of notice to be given. If the employee tries to leave, the employer insists that the employee is held to the notice period, but not required to work (thus allowing the employee's contacts and knowledge of the inside workings of the business to go stale and out of date). This is clearly more beneficial to the employee, as at least he will be paid; thus an injunction to stop an employee working for a competitor during a year-long notice period was granted in *Evening Standard v Henderson* (1987). However, garden leave provisions are also capable of abuse and have restrictive tendencies. Thus in *Provident Group v Hayward* (1989) the Court of Appeal suggested that these terms also would be subject to scrutiny and not enforced if wider than necessary, and in *William Hill v Tucker* (1998) it went so far as to say that they should be judged by the same standards as restrictive covenants. In *GFI Group Inc v Eaglestone* (1994) the notice period of a highly-paid options broker was reduced from 20 weeks to 13, which the court thought was all that was necessary to protect the employer's business. However, it should be noted that cases tend to turn very much on their own specific facts, so generalisation is difficult.

Further Reading

❏ J. Craig (1999), *Privacy and Employment Law*, Hart Publishing
❏ Y. Cripps (1995), *The Legal Implications of Disclosure in the Public Interest*, 2nd edn, ESC Publishing
❏ M. Freedland (2003), *The Personal Employment Contract*, OUP
❏ L. Vickers (2002), *Freedom of Speech and Employment*, OUP
❏ J. Ashton (2015), "15 Years of Whistleblowing Protection under PIDA: Are We Still Shooting the Messenger?", 44(1) ILJ 29
❏ L. Barmes (2004), "The Continuing Conceptual Crisis in the Common Law of the Contract of Employment", 67 MLR 435
❏ D. Brodie (1998), "Beyond Exchange: The New Contract of Employment", 27 ILJ 79
❏ D. Brodie (2001), "Legal Coherence and the Employment Revolution", 117 LQR 604
❏ D. Brodie (2008), "Mutual Trust and Confidence: Catalysts, Constraints and Commonality", 37 ILJ 329
❏ M. Ford (2002), "Two Conceptions of Worker Privacy", 31 ILJ 135
❏ B. Hepple (1981), "A Right to Work?", 10 ILJ 65
❏ D. Lewis (2005), "Providing Rights for Whistleblowers", 34 ILJ 239
❏ D. Lewis (2013), "Resolving Whistleblowing Disputes in the Public Interest: Is Tribunal Adjudication the Best that Can be Offered?", 42 ILJ 35
❏ J. Lindsay (2001), "The Implied Term of Trust and Confidence", 30 ILJ 1
❏ H. Oliver (2002), "Email and Internet Monitoring in the Workplace: Information Privacy and Contracting-out", 31 ILJ 321
❏ G. Pitt (1995), "Rights and Employee Rights: The Case of Free Speech" in *Understanding Human Rights*, ed. C. Gearty and A. Tomkins, Mansell

5. Collective Bargaining

Key Points

This chapter:
- Explains the concept of collective bargaining
- Discusses how collective agreements can be enforced
- Considers the incorporation of collective agreements into contracts
- Explains what is meant by recognition of trade unions
- Outlines the statutory recognition procedure
- Examines other mechanisms which mandate provision of information to workers and their rights to be consulted

***

Collective Bargaining

Collective agreements between trade unions and employers were traditionally   5–001
the major source of terms and conditions of employment for the majority of
workers in this country. In entering a contract of employment the bargaining
power of the potential employee is much less than that of the employer: the
worker needs the job more than the employer needs the particular individual.
The main purpose of trade unions is to redress this balance by harnessing the
collective power of all the employees. The employer may be able to resist the
demands of one individual, but will have to pay attention to a body representing
the whole workforce.

Unfortunately in real life this redress of the balance through trade unions does
not mean that a perfect equilibrium is obtained. Some employers will always
have the upper hand, perhaps because work in their industries is so desirable
that it is easy to find replacements for a recalcitrant workforce, perhaps because
of high unemployment. Employers also have the upper hand where unions are

weak, as in industries where there is a high turnover of staff, or where the workers are in small groups and therefore have difficulty in invoking the power of numbers. The hotel and catering industry is a prime example of both factors. Better publicised are those situations where the union has had the upper hand, such as transport or traditional heavy industries, where there are long traditions of high union membership and of loyalty to union instructions.

Nonetheless, in the period from the end of the Second World War to the end of the 1970s, the prevailing orthodoxy was that voluntary collective bargaining was the appropriate method of regulating employment relations. This policy manifested itself in a number of ways. Under the Fair Wages Resolution of 1946 government contractors were required to implement terms and conditions no less favourable than those resulting from collective bargaining in their industry in their region. This scheme was taken further under Sch.11 to the Employment Protection Act 1975 which allowed unions or employers' associations to refer a case to Acas where a particular employer was alleged to be providing terms and conditions less good than those recognised within the trade or industry or than the general level prevailing in the trade or industry. These provisions pre-vented employers who did engage in collective bargaining from being undercut by those who did not and gave an incentive for the latter to engage in collective bargaining, since if they could have collectively agreed terms imposed on them willy-nilly, they might as well have a say in them.

5–002   Other examples of the law's support for collective bargaining were found in the fact that Acas was originally set up with the purpose, among other things, of promoting collective bargaining; in the provision of a legal mechanism to force employers to recognise trade unions under the Employment Protection Act 1975 and to disclose information to them; and the wages councils system, which was designed to foster the development of collective bargaining in poorly paid indus-tries with weak unionisation.

From 1980 to 1997 there was a very clear shift away from this position, fuelled at least in part by the Conservative Government's general antipathy towards trade unions. The Employment Act 1980 abolished the Sch.11 procedure and stat-utory recognition for unions; the Wages Act 1986 drastically curtailed the powers of wages councils and the Trade Union Reform and Employment Rights Act 1993 (TURERA) finally abolished them altogether, along with Acas's duty to promote collective bargaining. In the view of that government, as expressed in its Green Paper *Industrial Relations in the 1990s* (Cmnd.1602) and White Paper *People, Jobs and Opportunity* (Cmnd.1810), collective bargaining hampered flexibility—presumably because changes could only be made after negotiation—and was also in opposition to concepts of individualised contracts and merit-related pay, which it believed should be encouraged. As an employer itself, the Conservative Government showed a clear preference for bargaining to be carried out at local level rather than at national level. This may partly have been because industrial action—the union's traditional final sanction if collective bargaining is not suc-cessful—is easier to deal with if it affects only one workplace rather than the whole country, as well as making less of a splash in the media. It will be seen when the law relating to industrial action is examined (see below, Chs 12 and 13) that the trend of reform there was to reduce lawful industrial action to bite-sized chunks which offered more chance of successful resistance. This trend was not reversed by the Labour administration in power from 1997 to 2010 and the current Conservative Government is presently considering even greater limits on rights to take industrial action.

While the policy of the British Government from 1979 to 1997 was away from collective bargaining, the thrust at European level was in the opposite direction. The "social dialogue" between representatives of management and labour began at an informal level in the 1980s but was given formal status through the addition of what is now TFEU art.154 by the Single European Act in 1986. This instructs the EU Commission to endeavour to develop the social dialogue, and makes an interesting parallel with the former duty of Acas to promote collective bargaining, abolished in 1993. The Protocol on Social Policy, finally acceded to by the United Kingdom in 1997, also encourages collective negotiation as a central means of dealing with employment issues and its provisions now are included in the TFEU. Article 154(2) instructs the Commission to consult management and labour before submitting proposals on social policy for Community action and art.155 enables the implementation of directives via agreements between management and labour. This procedure was used for the Part-time Work Directive (97/81/EC) (see above, para.3–022) and the Parental Leave Directive (97/75/EC) (see below, para.6–020). Another facet of EU policy supporting the social dialogue is the requirement for businesses to provide information to and consult with the workforce (see below, para.5–022).

The advent of the Labour administration of 1997 signalled a new approach to collective bargaining. Central to the Employment Relations Act 1999, the single piece of legislation that it was prepared to pass during its first term, was the implementation of its longstanding commitment to reintroduce a statutory recognition procedure where this was the wish of the majority of the relevant workers. Obviously, this had the potential for re-invigorating collective bargaining and enabling its extension. The new statutory recognition procedure was brought into force in June 2000. So far, its potential has arguably not been realised. It is true that in the run-up to its introduction a large number of new voluntary agreements for recognition were agreed, but in the first 10 years of its operation the Central Arbitration Committee (CAC) reported that it had ordered recognition for collective bargaining in respect of some 32,500 workers: significant for them, no doubt, but a very small percentage of the working population. What is not known, however, is how many collective agreements were entered "voluntarily" by employers in the knowledge that the union could make an application under the statutory procedure if they did not agree. The number of applications for recognition have varied between 28 and 118 a year, but from the all-time low in 2010–2011, numbers have picked up again, with 38 applications in 2014–2015. In 2012, just over 29.2 per cent of all employees were covered by collective agreements: 16 per cent of employees in the private sector and 63 per cent in the public sector. The overall trend is that coverage is gradually declining.

5–003

Collective bargaining is carried on at a variety of levels in this country, and the picture can therefore be confusing. It may be industry-wide, at national level, or it may be at company level, or plant level or a combination of these. It may be that some matters are settled at national level and others at local level (as has traditionally been the case in most kinds of public employment) or it may be that national agreements provide a baseline on which local agreements are built (as in *Gascol v Mercer* (1974)). The preference for local bargaining evinced by the Conservative Government has been mentioned already. An additional advantage, in their view, was that it allowed account to be taken of local circumstances. However, it should be remembered that collective bargaining takes time and, to be effective, it requires the participation of people of sufficient seniority to be able to give undertakings for one side or the other. Where bargaining is devolved to plant level, it is necessary to consider whether the benefits of flexibility, if any, are worth the extra costs in terms of staff time and the additional pressure on local employment relations. Furthermore, to take local circumstances into account risks producing even greater regional stratification of the job market than presently exists, reducing opportunities for movement and thus reducing one kind of flexibility.

Where collective bargaining does take place, the workforce is usually treated in a number of separate groupings, or bargaining units, reflecting different kinds of terms and conditions. Sometimes different unions represent the different groups, sometimes one union represents them all, and sometimes different unions represent the same group—which tends to make the process very fragmented. Even though some employees may not be members of the union, where the union is recognised for their grade, it will bargain on their behalf as well, as an employer would be reluctant to have the administrative chaos that would result from treating non-members separately from members.

5–004   Collective agreements depend on the union being recognised by the employer for the purposes of collective bargaining. If the employer does recognise the union, then there will be procedural agreements to regulate their relationship. These are agreements which lay down what topics may be the subject of negotiation, how often the two sides meet, who chairs the meeting, how many representatives they have and so on. The procedure agreement may also make provision for industrial action, perhaps stipulating that conciliation must be tried first, or that a certain period of notice must be given. Procedural collective agreements, then, provide the framework within which bargaining about substantive issues such as pay and other terms and conditions of employment takes place. The resulting agreements on these matters may be termed substantive agreements. How is either kind to be enforced?

Legal enforceability of collective agreements

Union and employer

5–005   There are two major problems to be overcome before collective agreements can be legally enforced. One is the legal doctrine of privity of contract, under which the only people who can enforce a contract are those who are party to it. Therefore, even if the contract is made for the benefit of a third party (such as the union member/employee), that third party has no standing to enforce it. Under the Contracts (Rights of Third Parties) Act 1999 this position is modified if the contract expressly provides for enforcement by the third party or if it confers a benefit on him or her and does not otherwise indicate an intention that the third party should not be able to enforce it. However, that brings us to the other, most important reason why collective agreements cannot legally be enforced, which is that almost invariably collective agreements are not contracts between employers and unions at all. This is a feature of British employment relations which is almost unique in the industrialised world and certainly among our EU partners. As a result there are sometimes problems in fitting EU directives into British law.

The original reasons for the non-enforceability of collective agreements as between the employer and the union are historical. Collective bargaining was an important force before trade unions were recognised as being bodies able to enter contracts at all; also, until 1971, if the agreement was between a union and an employers' association as opposed to an individual employer, it was probably unenforceable by virtue of the Trade Union Act 1871 which prohibited the legal enforcement of contracts between trade unions: by a curious quirk, employers' associations used to fall within the definition of trade unions.

By the 1960s this position had become entrenched, with neither management nor unions expecting or seeking legal recognition of their agreements. By that time Otto Kahn-Freund had provided a satisfactory theoretical underpinning for this position: collective agreements, he said, were not contracts because neither side had the requisite intention to create legal relations. This explanation of the legal position was accepted by the Donovan Commission, of which Kahn-Freund was a member, and in the only case where the matter was considered, *Ford v AUEFW* (1969). The position was essentially satisfactory to both sides of industry. If a union or employer did not deliver on their promises, they would have no credibility for the future. This was a more effective sanction than suing for breach of contract. It was also recognised that if agreements were to be legally enforceable, they would need to be couched in language that would withstand judicial scrutiny—which would no doubt involve considerable legal expense coupled with a decrease in comprehensibility.

The Industrial Relations Act 1971 attempted to reverse the position by introducing a presumption that all written collective agreements were legally enforceable contracts, in the hope that this would facilitate greater control over employment relations. The attempt failed, as it was bound to, because you cannot force parties to enter contracts if they do not want to do so. The Act had to allow employers and unions who did not want to enter legally binding contracts to insert a clause to that effect. In practice virtually all agreements after the Act included this exemption clause, known by the acronym TINA LEA (This Is Not A Legally Enforceable Agreement).

5–006

When the Industrial Relations Act 1971 was repealed by the Trade Union and Labour Relations Act (TULRA) in 1974, it was thought necessary to put the previous understanding on a statutory footing. Thus it provided that a collective agreement is conclusively presumed not to be legally binding unless it is in writing and contains a specific provision, however worded, that it is intended to be legally enforceable (see now Trade Union and Labour Relations (Consolidation) Act 1992 (TULRCA) s.179). The Conservative Government in power from 1979 again wanted to change this position, largely in the hope of making unions liable should they break agreements about procedures to be followed before taking industrial action. Change was mooted in the 1981 Green Paper, *Trade Union Immunities* (Cmnd.8128), which noted the prevalence of enforceable agreements among Britain's industrial competitors; however, the idea was rejected reluctantly, recognising that change depended on employers and unions being willing to change. After all, as TULRCA s.179 makes clear, it has always been open to employers and unions to enter binding agreements if they want to. It is now clear that where the legal enforceability of a collective agreement is at issue, then the only question is whether or not there is a s.179 statement: other questions about the intentions of the parties are irrelevant (*Monterosso v ITF* (1982)). There are possible ambiguities, however, in the reference in that section to a ". . . provision (however expressed) . . .". The *National Coal Board* v *NUM* (1986) case arose out of the attempt by the NUM to prevent the NCB from entering negotiations with the newly formed Union of Democratic Miners as well as themselves. Under the 1946 Agreement between the NCB and the NUM, made shortly after the nationalisation of the coal industry, the NUM had exclusive negotiating rights for miners. The NCB purported to terminate that agreement preparatory to entering a new arrangement with both unions. The NUM argued that the agreement was legally binding and that it would be a breach of contract for the NCB to terminate it, because of the use of the terms "binding" and "being bound" in the agreement. This argument was rejected by Scott J, who regarded the terms as equivocal. In the circumstances, he did not believe that they were meant to mean "legally bound". In the context, this judgment was no doubt correct; however, the case indicates a potential source of difficulty.

Single union deals

5–007   Since employees can belong to whatever union they want, and since in the United Kingdom there is no tradition of one union per industry, it is possible for employers to discover that a whole range of unions represent different groups among their employees. The report of *Ford v AUEFW* (1969) reveals that Ford workers at that time belonged to at least 19 different unions, and in 1985 Austin Rover was negotiating with eight unions in respect of its workforce (cf. *Austin Rover v AUEW (TASS)* (1985)). While an employer may not be obliged to recognise all, or indeed any, of these unions, in practice if employers recognise one union they frequently accept all those which have a significant representation in the workforce. However, getting agreement from a number of different unions with different policies can be time-consuming and difficult. Thus during the 1980s it became common for companies setting up new plants to seek to control this proliferation by offering exclusive negotiating rights to just one union, representing everyone from unskilled manual workers to senior management. This was a particular trend with foreign investors, who were used to dealing with single unions and having binding collective agreements. The company would require a quid pro quo in return for promising exclusive recognition: usually this meant that the union had to agree to employees being totally flexible about their duties (no demarcation disputes) and to binding arbitration in the event of a dispute. Sometimes the employer would wish to go as far as a no-strike deal.

So far as the law is concerned, employees cannot be restricted to joining only one union, for it would be a breach of their right to freedom of association (see below, Ch.10). However, if the employer will only recognise one union, that provides a powerful incentive for the workforce to join that union in preference to any other. As between the employer and the union, the undertaking to recognise the union exclusively is not enforceable unless the parties intend the collective agreement to be binding between them, and comply with TULRCA s.179 to make it so. Many of the single union deals which were concluded in the early 1990s were binding contracts.

Union as agent

If a collective agreement has no legal effect as between the employer and the union, how can it have any effect on the relationship between the employer and the individual worker? A superficially attractive idea, to a lawyer at least, is an explanation in terms of agency. This would seem to accord with reality: the union is after all negotiating on behalf of its members. It also has the advantage of being a relationship familiar to lawyers: where an agent negotiates on behalf of a principal with a third party, the result is an enforceable contract between the principal and the third party with the agent dropping out of the picture. If this analysis is adopted, then an individual employee could enforce the terms of the collective agreement with the employer and vice versa. (The agreement would not fall foul of TULRCA s.179, because that refers to agreements made between unions and employers.) Yet the difficulties of the agency approach are quickly obvious. First, an agent must act for defined principals. So how could such an agreement apply to employees taken on after the agreement had been made? How would it apply to non-members? The agency of the union would have to be derived from the fact of membership, so it could not possibly be regarded as the agent of non-members; yet collective agreements invariably apply to all the workers in the relevant bargaining unit, not just the union members. Secondly, it would mean that if the member who did not like a particular agreement left the union, or otherwise withdrew her authority for the union to act, she would not be bound by the collective agreements, which would be highly inconvenient to say the least. Finally, trade union members would probably be rather surprised to learn that simply by joining a union they had invested it with authority to make all sorts of decisions on their behalf.

It is submitted that the position in relation to agency is correctly stated in the EAT decision in *Burton Group v Smith* (1977) where Arnold J said:

> "There is no reason at all why, in a particular case, union representatives should not be the agents of an employee to make a contract, or to receive a notice, or otherwise effect a binding transaction on his behalf. But that agency so to do does not stem from the mere fact that they are union representatives and that he is a member; it must be supported in the particular

5–008

case by the creation of some specific agency, and that can arise only if the evidence supports the conclusion that there was such an agency."

This test was applied in *Harris v Richard Lawson Autologistics Ltd* (2002) where the workforce had repeatedly re-elected the shop steward who had previously negotiated on their behalf. The Court of Appeal considered that the steward had therefore been held out as having authority to make a binding agreement on holiday pay on behalf of the employees, even if he had not followed the required procedure of putting this to the membership first. The employers had no reason to think that the proper procedure had not been followed. Similarly, in *Edwards v Skyways* (1964), where the union negotiated ex gratia payments for a group of pilots who were being made redundant, it was held that the pilot could enforce the agreement when the company tried to renege. However, where membership alone is relied on to establish the relationship of principal and agent, it has usually been rejected (cf. *Holland v London Society of Compositors* (1924), and *NUGSAT v Albury Bros* (1979) on the effect of membership of an employers' association).

The agency approach could also lead to strange results in the field of industrial action. If the union instigated strike action in breach of the law, would individual members become liable as principals? The idea may seem improbable, yet in *Chappell v Times Newspapers* (1975) newspaper proprietors responded to the union's statement of its intention to continue industrial action by stating that they regarded all union members as having repudiated their contracts of employment. Two union members sought an injunction to stop their employer from treating them as dismissed: they had not said or done anything. Lord Denning said that they must be taken to have authorised what the union had done on their behalf! The statement was obiter, but it indicates dangers inherent in the agency approach (see also, *Boxfoldia v NGA* (*1982*) (1988), below, para.12–004).

Incorporation into individual contracts

5–009 If the agency argument is rejected, as authority and reason suggest it should be, then the question remains: how are collective agreements to have effect at the individual level? The answer is, they have effect if and in so far as they become incorporated into the individual's own contract of employment. If a term of a collective agreement is imported into the individual employee's contract then it may be enforced by the individual in the same way as any other term of the contract. Note that this means it is being enforced because it is a term of the contract of employment, not because it is a term of the collective agreement.

Express incorporation

5–010 How does incorporation take place? The most straightforward situation is where the contract of employment expressly refers to the collective agreement and incorporates its terms, as in *National Coal Board v Galley* (1958) and *Marley v Forward Trust* (1986). Yet even with express incorporation there can be confusion if it is not clear exactly what is incorporated. In *Gascol v Mercer* (1974) the national collective agreement for gas fitters specified a 40-hour basic working week. The local collective agreement specified a 54-hour week, and this is what Mercer had in fact been working. When he was made redundant, he claimed a payment based on his earnings over a 54-hour week. Since he had signed a written contract which referred to the national agreement, it was held that this was binding on him, regardless of what had happened in practice. A further source of uncertainty is the fact that even with express incorporation, a court will still examine whether or not an individual term is apt for incorporation (*Kaur v MG Rover Group Ltd* (2005); see below, para.5–012).

Where the collective agreement is not a binding contract between the employer and the union, either side can withdraw at any time without penalty. What effect does that have if the agreement has been incorporated in an individual's contract? In *Robertson v British Gas* (1983), the claimant's contract as a meter reader was to be found in part from his 1970 letter of appointment which said, "bonus conditions will apply". The bonus scheme had been laid down in a collective agreement, subsequently updated. However, in 1981 British Gas terminated the agreement, and argued that since there was no agreement, there was no bonus scheme. The Court of Appeal disagreed. The letter of appointment expressly incorporated the collectively agreed bonus scheme and the claimant was therefore entitled to a bonus under his contract. The demise of the collective agreement could not affect this entitlement. He could therefore claim a bonus on the basis of the last existing agreement.

This case illustrates how important the precise form of the incorporation can be. From an employer's point of view, there is a lot to be said for a contract which incorporates "the collective agreement in force for the time being", since it avoids the need constantly to update individual contracts or written statements. It may also mean that if the employer withdraws from the agreement, the employee loses any benefits previously incorporated. This would not apply in a case like *Robertson v British Gas* because there a contractual document (the letter of appointment) categorically stated that bonus conditions would apply, and so a scheme had to be found from somewhere. But if the letter had simply said that workers were employed according to the terms of the collective agreement in force for the time being, it would seem that withdrawal from the agreement would mean that there were no longer any terms in the employee's contract on the matters previously covered by the agreement. Support for this view is found in *Cadoux v Central Regional Council* (1986) where rules drawn up by the employer were held to be expressly incorporated into the contract of employment; yet because as employer's rules they were subject to unilateral change, the Court of Session further held that benefits under the rules could be removed by the employer's unilateral act (see also, *Airlie v City of Edinburgh DC* (1996)). The case starkly illustrates the potential disadvantages for employees in agreeing to be bound by "the agreement in force for the time being". In effect they sign a blank cheque and may find themselves bound in the future by rules not at all to their taste.

Implied incorporation

Where express incorporation of a collective agreement has not taken place it **5–011** may yet be found that the agreement has been impliedly incorporated into individual contracts. If the facts indicate that both employer and employee intended that the agreement should be part of the contract then the way will be clear for holding that it has been impliedly incorporated. The clearest evidence of such an intention will usually be that the parties have consistently acted as if the agreement were part of the contract: e.g. if wage rates, holidays, overtime, etc have always been fixed by reference to the collective agreement. In *Alexander v Standard Telephones and Cables (No.2)* (1991) the claimants argued that a redundancy selection procedure was impliedly incorporated into their contracts. Hobhouse J distinguished between matters of day-to-day relevance such as pay and hours of work where it would be fairly clear from the course of conduct what the parties' intentions were, and matters which arose only occasionally such as the need to make redundancies. The evidence here was that although the collective agreement had been in existence for some time it had never actually been used in a redundancy situation because in the past there had always been enough volunteers, and it had not been necessary to declare compulsory redundancies. In these circumstances, the judge held that there was insufficient evidence from the conduct of the parties to support the argument that they intended impliedly to incorporate the collective agreement on redundancy selection into individual contracts of employment.

In *Henry v London General Transport Services Ltd* (2002) it was accepted that a collective agreement could be impliedly incorporated on the basis of custom and practice. The claimants, who argued that they were not bound by a collective agreement, conceded that it was custom and practice in the trade for all relevant employees to be bound by collective agreements made between their union, the TGWU, and the employer, but only if the agreement had been approved by a majority in a ballot first. They contended that this had not taken place. The Court of Appeal remitted the case to the tribunal on the question of whether employees were bound by the collective agreement even though there had been no ballot. The case raises interesting questions about unions' authority to act on behalf of their members in collective bargaining, which is rarely dealt with expressly in union rules (see below, Ch.11 and *Allen v GMB* (2008)).

Which terms are incorporated?

5–012   It is fairly clear that not all parts of all collective agreements are appropriate for incorporation into the bargain between the individual employee and the employer. Earlier the distinction between procedural and substantive collective agreements was mentioned. Procedural matters are hardly likely to be regarded as apt for incorporation. Thus in *National Coal Board v NUM* (1986), where the NUM was attempting to enforce the old collective agreement and stop the recognition of the UDM, the NUM also argued that the entire 1947 Agreement was incorporated into the contracts of the individual miners. The argument was rejected on the grounds that the procedural agreement was inappropriate for incorporation into individual contracts.

However, the distinction between what is procedural and what is substantive is not always clear-cut. What about a redundancy selection procedure? In one sense, this is procedural, because it will cover such things as timetables for consultation, and the criteria for selection; but, on the other hand, it is an aspect of the collective agreement which is of the first importance to individuals, and more likely to affect them than many matters which may be clearly incorporated. In *Young v Canadian Northern Railway* (1931), the Privy Council held that a collective agreement providing for "last in, first out" in a redundancy situation was not apt for incorporation into individual contracts and an employee dismissed in contravention of the policy had no claim. However, the opinion seems to take an overstrict view of the process of incorporation. In *Marley v Forward Trust* (1986), the Court of Appeal held that a collective agreement which provided for a six-month trial period for workers redeployed in a redundancy situation could be relied on by an employee, although *Young* was not cited to the court and this particular point was not discussed. In *Alexander v Standard Telephones and Cables (No.2)* (1991) Hobhouse J reviewed the authorities and held that the selection procedure (last in, first out) was not apt for incorporation, although other parts of the agreement dealing with redundancy (such as enhanced rates of pay for redeployed workers) were. Similarly, in *Lee v GEC Plessey* (1993) Connell J held that the terms of a collective agreement providing for enhanced severance payments were appropriate for incorporation in individual contracts, and the Court of Appeal took the same view in *Keeley v Fosroc International Ltd* (2006). It seems unreasonable to distinguish between different elements of a redundancy procedure, holding that while some parts are enforceable, the selection procedure itself is not. In *Airlie v City of Edinburgh DC* (1996) the EAT held that express incorporation of a collective agreement meant exactly what it said: incorporation of the whole collective agreement. Thus the employees were bound by a term as to the right of the employer and the union to give each other notice of termination of an incentive bonus scheme. If such a term was considered suitable for incorporation, it is difficult to see why a redundancy selection procedure should not be. The process whereby courts decide whether or not terms are appropriate for incorporation is opaque and in practice gives judges quite a high degree of discretion. *Kaur v MG Rover Group Ltd* (2005) is a good example of this, where the Court of Appeal's minute examination of the language used in two expressly incorporated collective agreements would have been more appropriate for a taxation statute (cf. also *Anderson v London Fire and Emergency Planning Authority* (2013)). Their ultimate conclusion in *Kaur* was that a commitment contained in the collective agreement stating (in capital letters) that there would be no compulsory redundancies was not intended to express more than the employer's hope that this would be the case. Perhaps part of the sub-text is a desire not to fetter the ability of management to respond to difficult circumstances: this is apparent in the Court of Appeal's decision in *Malone v British Airways plc* (2010), which held that individual cabin crew staff could not treat a clause in a collective agreement about staffing levels on flights as an enforceable term of their contracts of employment, because if it were, the consequences for the employer could be disastrous.

No-strike clauses

While employees may find themselves bound by the terms of changing collective agreements over which they have only limited control, they are provided with one important protection by TULRCA s.180. This states that any collectively agreed term which has the effect of restricting or prohibiting the right of workers **5–013** to take industrial action will not become part of the individual's contract of employment unless the collective agreement is made by an independent trade union; is in writing; expressly states that such terms may be incorporated into contracts of employment; and is reasonably accessible for workers to consult during working hours. It is also required, of course, that the worker's contract should actually incorporate the term, either expressly or impliedly.

By implication, it would appear that a term requiring notice to be given of strike action would be regarded as something binding on an individual rather than as a matter of procedure (cf. *Alexander v Standard Telephones and Cables (No.2)* (1991)).

Recognition of Trade Unions

5–014 It is of the first importance for a trade union to be recognised by an employer as the bargaining agent for its employees. There is little point in workers belonging to a trade union unless that union has power to negotiate on their behalf. Collective bargaining is the basic reason for the existence of the trade union, but it can only take place if the employer will recognise the union for this purpose.

When collective bargaining was seen as the best way of running employment relations—which includes the whole of the period from the Second World War up to the advent of the Conservative Government in 1979—the law supported and encouraged the extension of collective bargaining in various ways. In 1975 the Employment Protection Act introduced a scheme whereby an independent trade union could refer a recognition dispute to Acas for investigation. Acas could recommend recognition, and failure by an employer to comply could lead ultimately to the sanction of the employer being compelled to accept an unbargained betterment to the employees' terms and conditions of employment. The 1975 procedure foundered on two rocks: first, Acas was not given the requisite powers to carry out investigations. This was dramatically illustrated in the bitter Grunwick dispute shortly after the legislation came into force, where the employer was able to undermine completely an Acas investigation into the wishes of the workforce by the simple expedient of refusing Acas access to the workplace, as he was quite entitled to do (see *Grunwick v ACAS* (1978)). Secondly, there was no consensus, even among trade unionists, as to what level of support there should be before recognition should be granted. While Acas decisions were ultimately upheld by the House of Lords, by then the damage had been done and there was a general lack of confidence in the scheme. Its abolition by the Employment Act 1980 was not seriously opposed. This left a situation, persisting for 20 years, where recognition was at the discretion of the employer, meaning also that the employer could derecognise a union at any time without being required to follow any procedure for consulting the workforce first. If the trade union was recognised by the employer, it was entitled to certain rights: to disclosure of information for collective bargaining purposes (see below, para.5–023); to consultation over redundancies, transfers of undertakings and health and safety (see below, paras 9–041 and 14–040) and to time off for trade union duties and activities for its members and officials (see below, para.6–033).

But if the employer did not wish to disclose information or give time off, it could simply cease to recognise the union.

In 2009 the European Court of Human Rights held that the right to freedom of association guaranteed by art.11 of the European Convention on Human Rights (ECHR) entailed a right to engage in collective bargaining (*Demir and Baykara v Turkey* (2009): see para.10–003 below). However, it seems that this does not require a particular employer to recognise a particular trade union (*R (Boots Management Services Ltd) v CAC* (2014)).

This position was changed dramatically as a result of the new statutory rec-   **5–015**
ognition scheme introduced by the Labour Government, fulfilling its election pledge in 1997. The Employment Relations Act 1999 introduced a new Sch.A1 into TULRCA, setting out the statutory recognition procedure. In accordance with a commitment given at the time of the Employment Relations Act 1999, a review of the working of the Act was carried out in 2003. It concluded that the recognition procedure was generally working well, but some improvements could be made. These were carried out by the Employment Relations Act 2004 (ERelA 2004), amending TULRCA Sch.A1.

The statutory recognition procedure

In striking contrast to the scheme in the Employment Protection Act 1975, the   **5–016**
current statutory recognition scheme is extremely detailed, running to over 200 paragraphs. The general thrust is aimed at giving the parties the opportunity to agree at each stage, with reference to the CAC for decision where that is not possible. The statutory scheme applies only to employers who have at least 21 workers. This does not include professionals (*R v CAC ex p BBC* (2003)), but by virtue of the Agency Workers Regulations 2010, agency workers are treated as employed by the employment agency for this purpose. The right to apply for recognition is afforded only to independent trade unions (see below, para.10–035). The process is triggered by the union (or unions) making a written request for recognition to the employer which identifies the group of workers (the "bargaining unit") in respect of whom recognition is sought. To avoid undue procrastination, the employer is required to respond within 10 working days, although it can request time to negotiate in which case the period for response is extended by 20 days.

Under TULRCA s.178(1), collective bargaining is defined as negotiations connected with a long list of matters: terms and conditions of employment; recruitment and dismissal; allocation of work; discipline; trade union membership or non-membership; facilities for union officials; and machinery for negotiation about any of these, including issues around recognition. However, where recognition results from the statutory recognition procedure, the range of matters on which the employer will have to negotiate is much more limited: it is confined to pay, hours and holidays, unless the parties agree to extend it further.

Amendments by ERelA 2004 make it clear that pensions are not part of pay for this purpose, although the Secretary of State has power to add this to the three core topics at a later stage.

Compulsory recognition

5–017 If the employer is not willing to grant recognition, the union may apply to the CAC, whose first step is to decide whether the application meets the general validity criteria. The most important hurdle at this stage is that the union must show a sufficient degree of prior support: under TULRCA Sch.A1, para.36 this is defined by two conditions: 10 per cent of the members of the bargaining unit must be union members, and a majority of workers must be in favour of recognition. Where this is disputed, evidence (such as lists of union members or a petition signed by those who want union representation) can be presented to the CAC case manager in confidence, to assuage workers' fears of retaliatory action from the employer if they are seen to support the union. No application will be accepted if any of the workers in the proposed bargaining unit are already covered by a recognition agreement, even if it is with a non-independent union (see below, para.10–035). This provides an opportunity for employers to head off recognition of an independent union by recognising a "sweetheart" union, as illustrated by *R (NUJ) v CAC* (2006). In this case, the NUJ was negotiating with Mirror Group Newspapers for recognition in respect of journalists in its sports division, where it had a significant number of members. While the negotiations were ongoing, the company suddenly recognised the British Association of Journalists, which had only one member in the sports division, in respect of these workers instead. The Court of Appeal held that this prevented the NUJ's application (see also *R (Boots Management Services Ltd) v CAC* (2014)).

It is also clear that this stratagem is effective where the employer recognises the competitor union after the original union's application has been lodged. In similar vein, if another union submits a competing application for recognition (and it competes if there is an overlap of even one worker in the proposed bargaining units) neither application will be accepted by the CAC. There is nothing to stop more than one union submitting a joint application in respect of the same workers, as long as they can show that they will cooperate with each other. In order to prevent constant fights over recognition, if an unsuccessful application has already been made, there is a moratorium of three years before another application can be made in relation to substantially the same group of workers.

The second step is to decide whether the bargaining unit is appropriate. Once an application has been accepted the parties are again invited to try and reach their own agreement on this, but in the absence of that, the CAC panel must decide, and is instructed above all to consider whether the unit is compatible with effective management. As far as possible it should also take into account existing national and local bargaining arrangements, the desirability of avoiding small, fragmented units and the characteristics and location of the workers as well as the views of the employer and union (para.18). In *R v CAC ex p Kwik-Fit (GB) Ltd* (2002) the Court of Appeal held that the CAC acted correctly in first considering the bargaining unit proposed by the union. Any counter-proposal made by the employer should be considered only if the union's proposal is inappropriate, but it is not the role of the CAC to decide whether the bargaining unit suggested by the employer is better than that proposed by the union.

This was clarified by the EReIA 2004. *Ex p Kwik-Fit* also made it clear that the court will be reluctant to overturn a CAC decision, since it is an expert body. In *R (Cable & Wireless UK Ltd) v CAC* (2008) the High Court reiterated this, upholding the CAC's decision that 370 workers defined by occupation in a workforce of 4,600 constituted an effective bargaining unit, despite the employer's argument that this was too fragmented, as the 370 workers were scattered across the whole country. Decisions will be overturned only if they are illegal or irrational, meaning that they have been made without reference to a relevant matter, or have taken something irrelevant into account, or have failed to construe a statutory provision correctly.

Having identified the bargaining unit, there are two possible routes to recog- **5–018** nition. Automatic recognition may be awarded where the majority of workers in the bargaining unit are already members of the relevant union or unions (para.22). According to the Government's original proposal, recognition would have followed automatically in all cases where the union already had a majority. However, this was a topic on which the CBI lobbied intensively and ultimately successfully, in that this is now subject to the qualification that the CAC should order a ballot even in these circumstances if any one of three conditions is ful-filled. These are: (i) that it would be in the interests of good industrial relations to hold a ballot; (ii) that a "significant number" of members within the unit tell the CAC that they do not wish the union to represent them (one wonders why they would belong in these circumstances); or (iii) that other evidence is produced (presumably by the employer) which leads the CAC to that conclusion. Concerns that this would lead to a situation where balloting would become the norm are not borne out by the statistics. Up to the end of March 2015, 126 applications for recognition without a ballot had been allowed and there had been 223 ballots, although it is not clear how many of these might have qualified for automatic recognition.

The CAC may order a workplace or postal ballot (in contrast to other secret ballots, which have to be fully postal) but does not conduct the ballot itself: a "qualified independent person" is appointed by the CAC to carry it out. To deal with the problem which arose in *Grunwick v ACAS* (1978), para.26 stipulates that an employer has a duty to cooperate generally with the ballot and specific duties to provide the CAC with names and addresses of workers in the bargain-ing unit and to allow the union reasonable access to the workforce to enable it to put across its case for recognition. Guidance is given in the Secretary of State's Code of Practice on Access and Unfair Practices during Recognition Ballots (2005). Should the employer fail in any of these duties, the CAC may order recognition without a ballot. Costs of the ballot are borne equally by the employer and the union. Unlike other ballots, gaining a majority in its favour will not necessarily be enough for the union to gain recognition: it is further neces-sary that the union must be supported by at least 40 per cent of the workers in the bargaining unit. This means that a high level of participation in the ballot will be necessary and that any abstention in effect counts as a vote against. This may account for the fact that, in 223 ballots, unions have not succeeded in 81, although participation rates have been high. Although TULRCA Sch.A1 makes no express provision for the CAC to have general supervisory authority over the ballot, including power to order a re-run if appropriate, the Court of Appeal held that this was contemplated by the statutory procedure and allowable in *R (Ultraframe (UK) Ltd) v CAC* (2005). If the requisite majority is achieved the CAC will make a declaration that the union should be recognised. A declaration in favour of recognition will usually last for three years, in that an employer may not apply to derecognise the union within three years of a CAC declaration (para.97).

At this point the union will become entitled to the rights of recognised unions outlined above (para.5–014). However, the declaration would not on its own mean that collective bargaining would actually take place. Thus following a declaration in favour of recognition the parties have 30 days in which to agree a "method of collective bargaining"—in effect, a procedural collective agreement dealing with the scope of negotiations, how meetings will take place and what is to happen if agreement cannot be reached. Again, the structure of the Schedule gives the parties every opportunity to reach their own agreement on this, but in the end, if they cannot agree, the CAC will impose a method. In doing this, the CAC must take account of the Trade Union Recognition (Method of Collective Bargaining) Order 2000, which provides among other things that the imposed method will be legally binding on the parties. The method set out in the Method of Collective Bargaining Order is extremely prescriptive, which may help to explain why, up to the end of March 2015, the parties reached their own agreement in 234 cases and the CAC only had to make an order in 24 cases.

5–019   TULRCA Sch.A1 stops short of imposing a requirement on an employer to bargain in good faith (as is required in the United States) or stipulating for arbitration to follow if agreement fails. The Government's reasoning for this was that there are no such requirements for voluntary collective bargaining and that this procedure is intended to put unions for whom recognition has been ordered in the same position as unions engaging in voluntary collective bargaining, not in a stronger position. This rather overlooks the important difference that the employer who is involved in voluntary collective bargaining is already prepared to engage in negotiation, which will not be the case with an employer who has been forced to recognise a union. There are limited sanctions for an employer who fails to comply with the method of collective bargaining imposed by the CAC (as it is a legally enforceable contract the union may apply for specific performance of it), but if the employer is prepared to go through with the charade without giving any ground, it is difficult to see what can be done about it.

Voluntary recognition

5–020   In keeping with the general policy of encouraging the parties to reach their own agreements in so far as possible, TULRCA Sch.A1 makes provision for "agreements for recognition" in Pt II which is headed, perhaps misleadingly, "Voluntary recognition". An agreement for recognition arises where the union has made a formal request for recognition under Pt I of Sch.A1 but then exits from the procedure for one of a variety of reasons laid out in para.52 in circumstances where the employer has agreed to recognise the union. Such an agreement will also last for three years. However, this situation should be distinguished from genuine voluntary recognition, which was the kind of recognition which preceded the statutory procedure: for this reason, the CAC calls it "semi-voluntary recognition" in its Guide to the procedure. Where unions and employers are prepared to engage in genuinely voluntary collective bargaining the statutory procedure will have no effect. However, if an employer engaged in this kind of voluntary collective bargaining should derecognise the union, the union will have the option of making an application under the statutory procedure.

Derecognition

Employers who wish to end collective bargaining arrangements no longer have   5–021
the option of instant derecognition, at least where the union is recognised in accordance with the statutory procedures. First of all, the employer can always apply for this if the number of workers employed falls below 21. Otherwise, the CAC will not entertain applications for a union to be derecognised for three years after a declaration of recognition has been granted. Thereafter, the procedure mirrors the recognition procedure. The employer must first make a written request to the union to end recognition arrangements, making an application to the CAC if the union does not agree. If the original declaration resulted from a ballot, the CAC must then apply the 10 per cent rule in reverse, deciding whether 10 per cent of the workers definitely favour ending bargaining arrangements and whether the majority would be likely to do so. Even if the employer makes no application, it is possible for the workers themselves to seek derecognition by the same route. The CAC then orders another ballot, with the same requirements as for recognition. If the original declaration was automatic, the employer's application must state that fewer than half of the workers in the bargaining unit now belong to the union. If this is so, derecognition is not ordered automatically; rather, if the CAC decides that this is the case, it will order a ballot.

Finally, Pt VI of Sch.A1 makes special provision for workers to apply for the derecognition of a non-independent trade union. This may be done at any time by application to the CAC, which will apply the usual admissibility tests. If the application is admissible, a ballot will be ordered.

Information and Consultation

Having accurate and up-to-date information about the employer's business is   5–022
obviously critical for successful bargaining by trade unions. However, the need for information goes beyond this. People like to know what is going on and if they are kept in the dark they often feel insecure, anxious and resentful. This is as true in the workplace as outside it. There is a view that workers are entitled to more than just information about what is going on: a view that their voice should be heard in the policy-making process and that they should be represented in important decisions affecting the business. This philosophy finds expression in countries such as Germany with the system of employee representation through works councils and worker-directors who sit on the boards of companies. This was briefly considered in the United Kingdom with the Bullock Committee's Report on Industrial Democracy 1977 (Cmnd.6706) but was never

close to becoming reality, given that there was a fair degree of scepticism on the part of trade unions as well as employers. The United Kingdom remains firmly wedded to the notion that the purpose of business is to enhance value for shareholders. Although lip service is frequently paid to stakeholder theory, which would certainly identify the workforce as key players, this tends to manifest itself as an expression of the need to keep the workforce on board with whatever the business wants to do rather than as a reason for genuinely taking workers' interests into account. Thus many companies now give employees an annual report which contains the same sort of information that they give to their shareholders—which is after all in the public domain. The Employment Act 1982 introduced amendments to the Companies Act 1985 so that the directors' report in companies employing more than 250 people had to include a statement describing what action had been taken to introduce, maintain or develop the systematic dissemination of relevant information to employees; consultation with employees on matters likely to affect them; encouraging their involvement with the company through employee share schemes and similar arrangements; and achieving employee awareness of the financial and economic factors affecting its performance. This was repealed by the Companies Act 2006; power to make similar regulations exists under that Act, but has not yet been exercised. Similarly, s.172 of the Companies Act 2006 requires companies to have regard to the interests of their employees as well as their shareholders—but as employees have no standing to enforce it, it is pretty much a dead letter.

The divergence between the philosophies of the "social model" of business and the "enterprise model" creates tensions at EU level. As early as the 1970s there were proposals for directives which would require employee participation in decision-making in the enterprise, notably the so-called "Vredeling directive" and the draft fifth directive on harmonisation of company law. Both were controversial and failed to progress because of the need for unanimous agreement. In 1994, however, the European Works Council Directive (94/45/EC) was agreed as a tangible result of the Protocol on Social Policy. Its passage was no doubt aided by the fact that the United Kingdom at that time had opted out of the Protocol and was thus in no position to oppose it. The EU Commission realised that this could be the way to break the log-jam of stalled social policy measures. History showed that measures giving workers consultation and information rights were fairly uncontroversial, but that there was no consensus on measures designed to involve them in decision-making. Thus there had been no great problems in introducing the duties to inform and consult the workforce on particular issues (redundancies, transfers of undertakings and health and safety, below, paras 9–041 and 14–040) which were introduced in the 1970s and 1980s. Hence the Commission decided that the best way forward was to produce a single new directive requiring businesses at national level to inform and consult their workforces, complementing the European Works Councils Directive on transnational information and consultation. Despite opposition from a few countries (led by the United Kingdom, which had by now signed up to the Protocol on Social Policy), the Information and Consultation Directive (2002/14/EC) was agreed in March 2002.

In British law, employers who recognise trade unions have had a duty to disclose relevant information to them since as long ago as 1975. While recognition was genuinely voluntary, this was neither controversial nor onerous and it fell well short of requiring employers to involve workers in decision-making. The duties to consult over redundancies, transfers of undertakings and health and safety have been implemented in the United Kingdom by requiring employers to consult through trade unions where there is a recognised trade union, or through elected employee representatives where no union is recognised. As a result of the European Works Council Directive and the Information and Consultation Directive, there are now two further situations in which employers are required to give information to and consult with the workforce, regardless of whether a trade union is recognised. Controversially, these do not give primacy to the trade union channel. Each of these three main information obligations will be examined in turn, and brief mention will be made of more recent specific consultation obligations introduced to comply with later directives.

Disclosure of information under TULRCA

Unions which are recognised (whether voluntarily or under the statutory procedure) are entitled to disclosure of information according to TULRCA ss.181–185 (introduced in 1975). Section 181 imposes a duty on employers who recognise unions to disclose to the union all information which the union requests, which is both information without which the union representatives would be impeded to a material extent in carrying out collective bargaining, and information which it is in accordance with good industrial relations practice to disclose. By virtue of the Agency Workers Regulations 2010, this must also include information relating to the use of agency workers in the undertaking. **5–023**

The major limitation on the right is that it only applies in relation to those matters for which the union is recognised for collective bargaining. Thus in *R v CAC ex p BTP Oxide Ltd* (1982) the company negotiated with the union on some matters, such as salaries, but had carried out a job evaluation scheme without involving the union. It did give the union the right to represent workers dissatisfied with their new gradings. The union sought disclosure of information about the job evaluation scheme. It was held that it was not entitled to the information since it did not have negotiating rights on this topic. This limitation is particularly relevant to recognition under the statutory procedure since it only obliges the employer to bargain about pay, hours and holidays.

Even if the union is recognised for collective bargaining, the right to disclosure is limited to the topics listed within the statutory definition of collective bargaining, i.e. negotiation about the matters listed in TULRCA s.178. Thus even if the employer recognised the union for the purpose of bargaining about its investment strategy, for example, it is unlikely that the union would have a right to seek information about it, because it would be outside the statutory definition of collective bargaining.

The Acas Code of Practice on Disclosure of Information to Trade Unions for Collective Bargaining Purposes (Acas Code No.2, 1977, updated 1997) aims to give guidance on the kind of information which it is good industrial relations practice to disclose. Its examples of the kind of information which could be **5–024** relevant to collective bargaining are: pay and benefits, including job evaluation schemes, breakdown of earnings by grade, sex, etc; conditions of service, including policies on recruitment, redundancy, promotion, health and safety; analysis of staff make-up, including staffing plans and investment plans; data on performance, such as productivity, efficiency, the state of the order book; and financial information, including cost structures, gross and net profits, assets and liabilities (para.11).

This list, which the Code stresses is not exhaustive, is wide-ranging. However, there are further restrictions on the right to disclosure in TULRCA s.182, which lists a number of exceptions. Disclosure is not required if it would be against the interests of national security; if it would be a contravention of statute; if the information has been communicated in confidence; if it relates specifically to an individual, unless he has consented to its disclosure; if it would cause substantial damage to the employer's undertaking; and if it was obtained for the purpose of legal proceedings. It is clear that any forward-looking planning information could be useful to the employer's competitors, and so might come within the exception where there is a risk of substantial damage to the undertaking. As the Code points out, cost information on individual products, detailed analysis of proposed investment, marketing or pricing policies and the make-up of tender prices could be used by a competitor to the serious detriment of the undertaking. Unfortunately, this is just the information likely to be useful to a trade union.

A less defensible restriction is found in TULRCA s.182(2), which provides that the employer need not produce originals of the information for the union, but may draw up a document especially for the purpose of disclosure. This means that there can be an editing, filtering process, which may affect the way the material is understood, given the importance of presentation in these matters. Furthermore, the employer is not required to assemble any information if its compilation would involve an amount of work or expenditure out of reasonable proportion to its collective bargaining value. Presumably the union could circumvent this if it were prepared to bear the cost.

5–025 The Acas Code recommends that employers and unions should agree a procedure for requests for disclosure of information (covering such matters as length of time for a response) and that where possible, they should agree those items of information that the union should be supplied with on a regular basis, (e.g. an annual analysis of the workforce by gender and ethnic background). Where an employer refuses to disclose information which has been requested, the union's remedy is to complain to the CAC. If the CAC thinks it is capable of being settled by conciliation, it will refer the question to Acas. If this is not the case, or if conciliation fails, then the CAC will conduct a hearing and make a declaration specifying the information which should have been disclosed (if any) and a timetable within which it should be made available (TULRCA s.183). If the employer still fails to comply, the union must again complain to the CAC and this time may present a claim for improved terms and conditions for employees. The CAC's ultimate sanction, therefore, is not to order the employer to disclose the information, but to make an award of terms and conditions to employees. It does not seem a particularly appropriate remedy for the kind of breach involved. In practice, the disclosure of information provisions appear to work satisfactorily, in that there are very few applications to the CAC under this jurisdiction (just six in 2014–15, for example).

European Works Councils

The European Works Council Directive (94/45/EC) was an initiative resulting from the Protocol on Social Policy and was adopted by all Member States except the United Kingdom in September 1994. It came into force in September 1996. Following the United Kingdom's agreement to the Protocol, it was extended to the United Kingdom with effect from December 1999 and was implemented by the Transnational Information and Consultation of Employees Regulations 1999 (TICE). Even before this it was reckoned that 100–300 British companies carrying on business in other Member States were already affected by the Directive.

5–026

The purpose of the Directive is to encourage consultation with employees and the sharing of information among all the employees of multinationals at EU level through the creation of a European Works Council (EWC) or an equivalent transnational information and consultation procedure. It applies to businesses with at least 1,000 employees in the European Union which have at least 150 employees in two different Member States. Such businesses must set up an EWC if requested by at least 100 employees or their representatives from at least two different establishments in at least two Member States. Once a valid request has been made, management has six months in which to set up negotiations on the form of the EWC with a "special negotiating body" consisting of between three and 17 members elected or appointed from the workforce. It is up to this body to decide on the appropriate mechanism for carrying out the obligation to inform and consult employees, and they may decide in writing that this should be done by establishing an information and consultation procedure instead of an EWC. If so, the procedure must include provision for the information and consultation representatives to be able to hold meetings to discuss the information and make their views known. This should ensure some element of collective consideration takes place, although it may depend on the representatives being proactive in this regard.

If the special negotiating body cannot reach agreement on how the EWC should be set up, or fails to do so within three years, the fall-back arrangements set out in the Schedule to TICE will come into play. These state that the EWC will be composed of between three and 30 members elected or appointed by the employees' representatives or, if there are no such representatives, elected by the workforce. There must be at least one member from each Member State where the business operates, and additional members should be in proportion to the numbers of employees in each state. It should receive information about and be consulted on matters affecting the business at the European level, or affecting plants in at least two different states and should meet at least once a year. It may invoke expert assistance, and all costs are to be borne by the business. Agreements set up in accordance with the fall-back arrangements are known as "Article 6 Agreements".

5–027   During the period between the Directive being passed and coming into force, the derogation in art.13 assumed great importance: provided multinational enterprises had an information and consultation agreement in place, covering the whole workforce, before the deadline for implementation of the Directive, it would not apply to them. This led to tremendous activity between 1994 and 1996 as affected companies hurriedly put together such arrangements in the hope of avoiding the more stringent measures in the Directive. Agreements made in this way are known as "Article 13 Agreements". The art.13 derogation was a major reason for British multinationals adopting works councils, because although the Directive did not apply to them when it came into force, there was a good chance that it would at some time in the near future, as indeed proved to be the case. Yet as that would be after the September 1996 deadline, companies would be stuck with the procedures laid down in art.6 of the Directive. Rather than risk this, a number of large British companies decided instead to set up information and consultation agreements before September 1996.

Under TICE reg.2, the representatives of employees for the purposes of the EWC or information and consultation procedure are trade union representatives (where there is a recognised trade union) *and* any other employee representatives who are elected or appointed by employees to positions where they are expected to receive relevant information on behalf of employees (but excluding employees who represent the workforce only on specific issues such as health and safety or redundancies). The most likely example of the latter category would be members of an employees' council or works council set up by the employer as an information conduit or consultative body. This means that even where there is a recognised trade union, its representatives may not be the only channel of representation.

In practice the European Works Councils Directive has not had a huge effect. A study by the European Trade Union Confederation (ETUC) estimated that only one-third of companies affected by the legislation had been prompted to set up an EWC and, in 15 years, only 13 applications have ever been made to the CAC under this jurisdiction. One reason for this may be that the Directive (and TICE) only mandate consultation over transnational issues. This may exclude many issues of interest to the workforce. It is also the case that employees of a company may see its plants in other European countries as competitors rather than as colleagues with similar interests.

National consultation

5–028   Building on the European Works Council Directive and the longstanding EU requirements to consult workers over redundancies and transfers of undertakings (see below, para.9–040) the EU Commission first proposed a general information and consultation directive in 1998. The basic idea was to promote social dialogue between management and workers in accordance with TFEU art.154. Even though the business case for improved communication was emphasised, the directive was opposed by representatives of employers and was blocked for some years by a coalition of four Member States led by the United Kingdom. In

2001 the other three countries dropped their objections and the United Kingdom reluctantly followed suit. The Information and Consultation Directive (2002/14/EC) was agreed in March 2002 for implementation by March 2005. The final version, however, dropped the most controversial provision which would have rendered void any decision taken by management in the absence of consultation complying with the directive. It was implemented in the United Kingdom by the Information and Consultation of Employees Regulations 2004 (ICE). From April 2005 the Regulations applied only to undertakings with at least 150 employees (counting all employees in the United Kingdom for this purpose) but they were progressively extended and since April 2008 have applied to undertakings with 50 or more employees.

The structure of ICE has quite a lot in common with the TICE Regulations, with a dash of the statutory recognition procedure thrown in. It is intended that the statutory system should not impede voluntary arrangements for information and consultation and this is reflected in the provisions relating to pre-existing agreements. If there is no pre-existing agreement relating to information and consultation, the statutory scheme will be triggered by a request in writing from 10 per cent of the workforce (subject to a minimum of at least 15 employees and a maximum of 2,500 (reg.7)). However, if there is a valid pre-existing agreement, it requires 40 per cent of the employees to make the request, or else the employer can choose to ballot employees as to whether they want a new arrangement. If a ballot is held, there must be a majority in favour, who comprise at least 40 per cent or more of all employees, in order for the employer to be obliged to negotiate a new agreement (reg.8). This is a very high percentage: as with the statutory recognition procedure, an abstention counts as a vote against.

There is a clear incentive for employers wishing to avoid the statutory scheme for information and consultation to make a valid pre-existing agreement. To be valid, the agreement must have been entered into before a valid employee request was received; be in writing; cover all the employees of the undertaking; have been approved by the employees; and set out how the employer is to give information to the employees or their representatives and seek their views on it (reg.8). There may be more than one agreement, provided that together they cover all employees. In *Stewart v Moray Council* (2006) an employee of the council who had presented a request on behalf of over 500 employees (but fewer than 40 per cent) complained to the CAC that the council's claimed pre-existing agreement did not meet the requirements of ICE reg.8. The council relied on three agreements, covering the whole workforce, which had been approved by the representatives of recognised trade unions. The CAC decided that the agreements clearly covered all employees even though they had been entered into only with the recognised union: as noted already, collective agreements cover all employees in the bargaining unit, not just the union members. More controversially, the CAC decided that approval by the trade union representatives could be taken to be approval by all employees, where the union was recognised in respect of all the employees and the majority of the workforce belonged to it. However, one of the three agreements did not adequately fulfil the final requirement of specifying how employees would be informed and consulted. In these circumstances, the employee's complaint was upheld, compelling the employer to begin negotiations for a new agreement.

5–029   Where a new agreement is needed, the employer has six months in which to negotiate it with employee representatives. These representatives must be elected by all the employees, even if there is a recognised trade union. It is only if no agreement can be reached that the fall-back procedure (termed the "Standard Information and Consultation Provisions" in the Regulations) set out in ICE regs 18–20 comes into play. The standard provisions require the employer to arrange a ballot to elect members of an information and consultation committee, which should consist of one representative per 50 employees, subject to a minimum of two and a maximum of 25.

Where a pre-existing or negotiated agreement is reached, the parties can decide on the scope of the information to be provided and the extent of consultation. If not, the standard provisions state that information must be provided on three areas: the development of the undertaking's activities and its economic situation; the state of employment in the undertaking and measures anticipated if there is a threat to employment; and any decisions likely to lead to substantial changes in work organisation (including redundancies and transfers) (reg.20). The employer must also consult about these three areas—and in the case of the last (decisions affecting work organisation), the consultation must be with a view to reaching agreement. It is this aspect which makes employers particularly nervous because they fear that it will draw them into collective bargaining even where they have not recognised a trade union.

If an employer fails to comply with obligations under ICE, the representatives can apply to the CAC for a declaration to that effect. The CAC can also make an order specifying what the employer needs to do to comply with the procedure. In these circumstances, the complainant may then apply to the EAT within three months for a penalty notice to be issued under ICE reg.22, which gives the EAT power to order a penalty of up to £75,000. This power was invoked in *Amicus v Macmillan Publishers Ltd* (2007), where the employer effectively ignored employees' requests for a procedure and failed to cooperate with the CAC. The EAT awarded a penalty of £55,000, to reflect the seriousness of the default and also to act as a deterrent to other employers who might be tempted to act similarly. At the other end of the spectrum, £10,000 was awarded in *Darnton v Bournemouth University* (2009) where the employer's initial delay in responding was because of a mistake, but the delay caused thereby was substantial.

Other information and consultation obligations

5–030   As a result of EU directives, two further obligations to provide information to and consult with employees have been introduced in recent years. The European Public Limited-Liability Company Regulations 2004 (SI 2004/2326) were passed to implement the EU Statute for a European Company ("Societas Europaea" or SE)—a new form of registered company. The relevant directive mandates employee involvement, which could be via information and consultation arrangements, but could even involve employee representation on the board of the company. The Regulations make arrangements for this which are similar to those for EWCs. As the establishment of SEs is entirely voluntary, it appears that little use has been made of this option to date in the United Kingdom. They are paralleled by the European Co-operative Society Regulations 2006 (SI 2006/2078), implementing the EU Statute for a European Co-operative Society (SCE). Finally, the Company (Cross-Border Mergers) Regulations 2007 (SI 2007/2974) implement the Cross-Border Mergers Directive (2005/56/EC) and aim, among other things, to protect existing employee participation rights when companies from different Member States merge. Readers are referred to company law books for further information about these provisions. The CAC has jurisdiction in relation to complaints under them, but none have been made to date.

Further Reading

- [ ] A. Bogg (2009), *The Democratic Aspects of Trade Union Recognition*, Hart Publishing
- [ ] P. Davies and M. Freedland (1983), *Kahn-Freund's Labour and the Law*, 3rd edn, Chs 3, 5 and 6, Stevens
- [ ] B. Bercusson (1994), "Collective Bargaining and the Protection of Social Rights in Europe", in K. Ewing, C. Gearty and B. Hepple (eds), *Human Rights and Labour Law*, Mansell
- [ ] B. Bercusson (2002), "The European Social Model Comes to Britain", 31 ILJ 20
- [ ] A. Bogg (2006), "Politics, Community, Democracy: Appraising CAC Decision-Making in the First Five Years", 35 ILJ 245
- [ ] M. Carley and M. Hall (2000), "The Implementation of the European Work Councils Directive", 29 ILJ 103
- [ ] M. Doherty (2013), "When You Ain't Got Nothin' You Got Nothin' to Lose . . . Union Recognition Laws, Voluntarism and the Anglo Model", 42(4) ILJ 369
- [ ] R. Dukes (2008), "The Statutory Recognition Procedure 1999: No Bias in Favour of Recognition", 37 ILJ 236
- [ ] G. Gall (2012), "Union Recognition in Britain: The End of Legally Induced Voluntarism?", 41 ILJ 407
- [ ] H. Gospel and G. Lockwood (1999), "Disclosure of Information for Collective Bargaining: The CAC Approach Revisited", 28 ILJ 233
- [ ] M. Hall (1996), "Beyond Recognition? Employee Representation and EU Law", 25 ILJ 15
- [ ] B. Simpson (2000), "Trade Union Recognition and the Law, a New Approach", 29 ILJ 193
- [ ] B. Simpson (2007), "Judicial Control of the CAC", 36 ILJ 287
- [ ] Lord Wedderburn (2000), "Collective Bargaining or Legal Enactment: The 1999 Act and Union Recognition", 29 ILJ 1
- [ ] Lord Wedderburn (1997), "Consultation and Collective Bargaining in Europe: Success or Ideology?", 26 ILJ 1
- [ ] A. Wilson (1984), "Contract and Prerogative: A Reconsideration of the Legal Enforcement of Collective Agreements", 13 ILJ 1

6. Statutory Employment Protection Rights

Key Points

This chapter:
- Looks at legislation which aims to make it easier to combine work and family life: maternity rights, paternity rights and rights to parental leave
- Considers the extended right to seek flexible working
- Explains when workers may receive guaranteed pay and pay if suspended on medical grounds
- Discusses employees' rights to time off—for trade union duties and activities, duties as employee representatives, public duties and for study and training
- Considers rights under the Working Time Regulations to limits on working time, rest breaks and paid annual leave
- Outlines the law on Sunday working

***

In the mid-1970s the Labour Government and trade unions entered an informal "Social Contract" which was essentially to the effect that unions would show restraint in wage claims in return for favourable legislation. The Government kept its side of the bargain by passing the Employment Protection Act 1975 which introduced a range of new rights for trade unions and workers. The trade

6–001

union rights, such as the right to be recognised, to disclosure of information for collective bargaining purposes and to protection for their members from discrimination are discussed elsewhere (see paras 5–014, 5–023 and 10–005). The positive rights for individual employees have since been greatly extended, partly as a result of EU directives and partly as a result of the commitment to "family-friendly" policies of the Labour administration of 1997–2010 and the Coalition and Conservative Governments succeeding it. These positive rights are the subject of this chapter.

Until the Employment Protection Act 1975 statutory protection for employees had mainly been negative, in the sense that it merely gave some protection from dismissal, or more probably a right to compensation for certain kinds of dismissal. This Act addressed the ongoing relationship between employer and employee rather than its termination and gave employees maternity rights, rights to time off for specified activities and certain kinds of pay protection. Some trade unionists regarded this development with a degree of suspicion because these kinds of matters had traditionally been the subject of collective bargaining. If they were dealt with by statute, it could undermine the position of trade unions: why bother to belong to a union if it is not negotiating for you? However, others regarded the statutory advances as providing a minimum benchmark and measured their success according to how far they could per-suade employers to offer terms which were better than the statutory minimum, accepting that for weak or non-unionised workers there was a need for a statu-tory safety net.

The positive rights given by the Employment Protection Act are now to be found in the Employment Rights Act 1996 and associated sets of regulations. Strictly they are not a source of contract terms, for (unlike the equality clause under the Equality Act (EqA) 2010 s.66, for example) they do not operate by way of implication into the contract of employment but rather exist alongside it and override inconsistent contractual provisions.

Family Rights

6–002　There is much talk today of the "work-life balance". In the country with the longest working hours in Europe, how far can the law intervene to ensure that workers are able to allocate sufficient time to family life? In its second and third terms, between 2001 and 2010, the Labour Government placed a lot of empha-sis on measures to assist those in the workplace with family responsibilities, building on the maternity rights introduced in 1975 and the requirements of EU directives in the 1990s. These mainly took the form of increased entitlements to paid and unpaid leave to allow parents more time to care for their children, but it would be fair to say that they transformed the basic legal entitlements of working parents. This is one area where the main political parties are broadly in accord: the *Modern Workplaces* consultation paper, published under the Coalition Government in 2011, proposed greater flexibility in parental rights and extending flexible working to all employees, and the final elements of this have been implemented under the present Conservative administration.

Maternity rights

Women are accorded four basic rights in connection with pregnancy and child- **6–003** birth: a right to time off for ante-natal care; a right to maternity pay; a right to maternity leave, which may now encompass shared parental leave; and a right not to suffer detriment or dismissal on grounds of pregnancy and childbirth.

Time off for ante-natal care

The right to time off for ante-natal care set out in ERA s.55 was actually intro- **6–004** duced by the Employment Act 1980 as a response to figures showing that the United Kingdom had one of the worst records for perinatal deaths among industrialised countries. There is no qualifying period of service for this right. The Children and Families Act 2014 introduced new ss.57ZA–57ZS into ERA, extending time off rights in three main ways: first, by introducing a new right for time off to accompany a pregnant woman to an appointment, secondly, by introducing a right to time off for adoption appointments, and thirdly, by extending the rights to agency workers as well as employees.

A woman has a right to paid time off in order to attend an ante-natal appointment advised by her doctor, midwife or health visitor. The employer is entitled to ask for written proof of the appointment—a letter or appointment card—and indeed, of the pregnancy. It is not an absolute right: the employer's duty is not to refuse the time off unreasonably. Thus an employer would presumably be entitled to ask that the woman should go in her own time so far as possible. However, the employer is not entitled to ask her to make the time up on another occasion: that is not time off.

Where time off is unreasonably refused, the woman may apply to an employment tribunal for a declaration to that effect. The tribunal can also award her a sum equal to what she should have been paid for the time off. If the employer subjects an employee to a detriment or dismisses her for exercising her right to paid ante-natal leave she will have a remedy for detriment or dismissal connected with pregnancy or childbirth, which is discussed further below, para.6–018. It will also constitute discrimination on grounds of pregnancy or maternity under EqA 2010.

The right to unpaid time off to accompany a woman to an ante-natal appoint- **6–005** ment was introduced by the Children and Families Act 2014. It is available to someone who is in a "qualifying relationship" with the mother—her spouse or civil partner, the child's father, intended surrogate parents, or a non-relative who lives with the woman in an "enduring family relationship". The right is to attend up to two appointments, with the overall absence lasting a maximum of six-and-a-half hours each time. The employer can ask the employee to sign a written declaration of his or her entitlement to this right. Although it is a right to unpaid time off, if it is unreasonably refused, the remedy is for the tribunal to award the employee twice their regular hourly rate for the amount of time refused.

In the case of adoptive parents, the right is for time off to attend adoption appointments intended to help them bond with the child prior to the adoption.

One parent (if there are two) is entitled to paid time off for up to five appointments; the other is entitled to unpaid time off for up to two.

It is worth noting that in addition to permitting time off for ante-natal care, once notified of pregnancy, an employer has an obligation under the Management of Health and Safety at Work Regulations 1999 (SI 1999/3242) to carry out a risk assessment of the work in relation to that particular employee. If the assessment reveals any risk to the woman or her unborn child, the employer's duty is to take reasonable steps to avoid the risk, for example by altering her working conditions or hours of work. If no other means of avoiding the risk is possible, the employer will be obliged to suspend her on full pay.

Maternity pay

6–006   Until 1987 women were entitled to a state maternity allowance (provided that they met National Insurance contribution requirements), and after 1975, to six weeks' maternity pay from their employer (provided that they met the service qualification). The Social Security Act 1986 changed this position in so far as it placed the duty to provide state maternity pay on the employer, largely to avoid the overlap inherent in the employer and the state both administering a maternity pay system. The reform followed the philosophy which had already been implemented in relation to sick pay (discussed below, para.7–050).

The picture was radically changed by the Pregnant Workers Directive (92/85/EEC). The health and safety argument underpinning the Directive was that women could endanger their own health and that of the child through continuing to work because of anxiety over keeping their jobs if they did not have rights to maternity leave. Hence the Directive introduced a right to maternity leave and also to maternity pay, on the basis that a leave right would be of little use if a woman could not afford to use it. Member States were therefore required to establish a right to maternity pay for at least 14 weeks but could stipulate a qualifying period of service for this of not more than one year. The Directive did not, however, require that pay should be at the usual level, but only that it should be an "adequate allowance"; furthermore, that an amount equivalent to sick pay would be deemed to be adequate (art.11). In *Gillespie v Northern Health and Social Services Board* (1996) the CJEU was asked whether it was contrary to EU law not to grant full pay during maternity leave. The argument was that maternity pay should be regarded as "pay" within the meaning of what is now TFEU art.157. Therefore, since discrimination on grounds of pregnancy is sex discrimination in EU law (*Dekker v VJV Centrum* (1991) and *Webb v EMO* (1994), above, para.2–018), and since maternity pay is a consequence of pregnancy, it was unlawful discrimination if full pay was not given during maternity leave. If this argument had been successful, it would have gone much further than what was required by the Pregnant Workers Directive.

While agreeing that maternity pay was covered by TFEU art.157, the CJEU managed to avoid the decision that full pay should therefore be given by holding that the situation of women on maternity leave was unique and could not be compared with the position of either men or women who were at work. Thus they were not entitled to full pay, but they were entitled to have any backdated pay increase taken into account in assessing the income-related component of their maternity pay. This part of the decision was implemented by the Statutory Maternity Pay (General) Amendment Regulations 1996. In *Alabaster v Woolwich plc* (2004) the same reasoning was applied where a pay increase was awarded before the maternity pay period started but after the reference period used by statute to calculate the salary-related element of her maternity pay. The CJEU held that the claimant should have received the benefit of the pay increase and this was implemented by the Statutory Maternity Pay (General) (Amendment) Regulations 2005.

The CJEU's reasoning in *Gillespie* is hardly convincing, relying as it does on the **6–007** manipulation of the concept of comparing like with like. If women on maternity leave are not to be compared with men and women at work, why was it a breach of EU law not to give them the benefit of any backdated pay increase? However, the uneasy position, whereby the sick man comparison is valid in some situations but not others, is now entrenched. So where a statutory scheme provided full pay for workers off sick but excluded from this women absent because of a pregnancy-related illness (before their maternity leave started), this was held by the CJEU to be unlawful sex discrimination (*Høj Pedersen v Kvickly Skive* (1999)). The converse is also true: if workers who are on long-term sick leave receive reduced pay, it is not unlawful to reduce similarly the pay of a woman on long-term sick leave for a pregnancy-related illness before her maternity leave has started (*North Western Health Board v McKenna* (2005)). *Gillespie* left open the question of whether a woman on maternity leave could claim full pay if a man taking a comparable amount of sick leave would get full pay: in *Todd v Eastern Health and Social Services Board* (1997) the Northern Ireland Court of Appeal held that such an arrangement was not a breach of EU law. The point did not arise directly in *Boyle v EOC* (1998), for the civil service maternity pay scheme provided that women should get full pay during maternity leave, as they would for sick leave. However, in the case of maternity leave, the entitlement to full pay was dependent on the women returning to work after maternity leave for at least one month. No such condition applied to sick pay entitlement. Nonetheless, the CJEU held that there was no breach of the equal pay principle: following *Gillespie*, it held that pay during maternity leave and pay during sick leave were not comparable.

In 2010 the EU Commission proposed amending the Pregnant Workers Directive to increase maternity leave to 18 weeks, of which the first six should be on full pay. The European Parliament voted to extend this to 20 weeks on full pay—but this was defeated in the Council of Ministers. Apart from any contractual entitlement to maternity pay, most working women are entitled either to Statutory Maternity Pay or to maternity allowance.

Statutory Maternity Pay (SMP)

Women who have 26 weeks of continuous employment by the fifteenth week **6–008** before the expected week of childbirth and whose average earnings are at or above the lower earnings limit for the payment of National Insurance are entitled to SMP from their employer for a period of 39 weeks (extended from 26 weeks since April 2007). It is paid at the rate of 90 per cent of their usual pay for the first six weeks ("the higher rate") and then at a rate equivalent to Statutory Sick Pay (SSP) for the remaining 33 weeks ("the lower rate"; £139.58 in 2015). The Work and Families Act 2006 provided for the period of maternity pay to be increased to 52 weeks and this was originally planned to be implemented in 2009–10, but the proposal has since been dropped.

Employers are entitled to a rebate on their SMP payments, which they may set off against the National Insurance contributions which they transmit to the Inland Revenue in respect of the workforce. However, whereas the rebate used to be set at 104 per cent of the cost (the extra amount reflecting the additional administrative burden for the employer) it was reduced in 1994 to 92 per cent, except for small employers (those paying less than £45,000 in National Insurance contributions annually, who currently get a 103 per cent rebate).

The right to SMP is independent of the question of whether the employee has a statutory right to maternity leave and SMP is payable even if she has no intention of returning to work. However, the position is complicated in that many employers are prepared to pay more than the statutory requirement (e.g. 100 per cent of earnings, and for a longer period than six weeks) but only on condition that the employee returns to work for a certain time. As a matter of contract there is nothing to prevent this, and the employer would be entitled to claim back the extra if the employee did not in fact return.

6–009   An employee is not entitled to SMP in any week in which she works for the employer. However, the Work and Families Act 2006 modifies this position so that a woman may undertake up to 10 days work with her employer ("keeping in touch" days) during her maternity leave without either bringing that period to an end or jeopardising her right to maternity pay. To qualify for SMP a woman must give her employer 28 days' notice (in writing, if so requested) of the day it should start, but this can be combined with notice of maternity leave.

Maternity allowance (MA)

6–010   Women who do not qualify for maternity pay from their employer may yet qualify for maternity allowance as a state contributory benefit. They have to have worked and made National Insurance contributions for 26 weeks out of the 66 weeks before the expected week of childbirth. Maternity allowance is equivalent to SMP at the lower rate and to SSP (£139.58 in 2015) and is paid for 39 weeks. Note that for this benefit the woman need not have been employed by the same employer, or even have been an employee at all: she could have made contributions as a self-employed person.

Maternity leave

6–011   The Employment Protection Act 1975 introduced the original right for an employee to return to work up to six months after the birth of her child, in effect providing for a period of statutory maternity leave. However, this was only available to women with two years' continuous service. The Pregnant Workers Directive required that all women workers should have at least 14 weeks' leave, and should be compelled to take at least two weeks at the time of childbirth. The right to 14 weeks' leave regardless of length of service was implemented in

1994. This meant that there came to be two kinds of maternity leave: the basic maternity leave, available to all women ("ordinary maternity leave"), and the additional right to return after extended leave, available to those who had completed the qualifying period of service ("additional maternity leave").

In pursuance of its "family-friendly" work policies the last Labour Government made substantial improvements to these entitlements, which are now contained in the Maternity and Parental Leave, etc Regulations 1999 (MPLR), as amended. The service qualification for additional maternity leave was removed by amendments in 2006 for women whose babies were born on or after 1 April 2007 with the result that all women who qualify for ordinary maternity leave also qualify for additional maternity leave. While there are still separate rights to ordinary and additional maternity leave under ERA ss.71 and 73 respectively, there is now very little difference between them in practice. Together, they are termed "statutory maternity leave".

Ordinary maternity leave lasts for 26 weeks (ERA s.71) and is followed by additional maternity leave, which also lasts 26 weeks, meaning that altogether a woman can take a whole year off (and may also exercise other parental leave rights as well). The notice provisions for qualifying for maternity leave used to be horrendously complicated and the penalty for a false step was loss of entitlement. The position is now much improved. Although a woman will still lose her right to maternity leave if she fails to give the proper notice, the notice requirements have been reduced and simplified. By a deadline of the 15th week before the expected week of childbirth the woman must inform her employer (a) that she is pregnant; (b) what the expected date of birth is (by medical certificate, if requested); and (c) when she expects her maternity leave to start.

She need only put this in writing if requested by the employer and she can **6–012** change her mind about the start date—as long as she still has time to give at least 28 days' notice of the new date. A request for SMP may be incorporated in this notice. On receipt of the notice the employer must then give the woman notice of the date on which her maternity leave will end, which will be at the end of the additional maternity leave period. There are considerable advantages in this: it is the employer, not the woman herself, who must now do the calculation and both parties will know at the outset what the date is. This should reduce the number of cases where women lose their rights because of some miscalculation. If the employer fails to notify her of this date then she is protected from detriment or dismissal if she does not return on that date. Furthermore, she has the right to return before that date without giving notice.

In two situations the start of maternity leave is automatically brought forward. The first is if the birth occurs before the notified date. In this case, maternity leave will start at the date of birth and the employee must give notice to the employer as soon as is reasonably practicable thereafter. The second is if the employee is absent for a pregnancy-related reason at any time after the fourth week before birth is due. Again, this triggers the maternity leave period automatically. This is to stop employees taking sick leave rather than maternity leave at this stage, which they might wish to do if the employer pays for sick leave at the normal contractual rate. The rule has been criticised as inflexible, however, because a woman who intended to work until closer to the birth could lose her right to do so just for one day's absence, even if she were fit to return the following day.

Additional maternity leave begins the day after ordinary maternity leave ends. At one time, the employee had to give notice of her intention to take this additional period of leave, but now the presumption is that she will and no notice is required. The employer no longer has the right to require her to reaffirm her intention to return while she is taking additional maternity leave, but the 2006 amendments to MPLR clarify that reasonable contact between the employer and the woman on maternity leave will not bring the leave period to an end and, specifically, that the woman may attend work for up to 10 "keeping in touch" days during her whole period of statutory maternity leave without ending it.

6–013   A curiously paternalistic provision in the Pregnant Workers Directive requires that employed women should have a compulsory period of at least two weeks' leave before and/or after birth: under ERA s.72 and reg.8, this is a two-week period starting with the date of birth. The employee may not work for the employer during those two weeks and it is a criminal offence on the part of the employer to contravene this.

Section 71 of ERA provides expressly that the contract of employment continues during ordinary maternity leave by stating that all terms and conditions of employment apply as if she were not absent, with the important exception of any terms and conditions about "remuneration". The reason for the exception is that pay is dealt with by the maternity pay provisions, above. The word "pay" was not used because of the very wide meaning it has been given in EU case-law on the scope of TFEU art.157 (see below, para.7–042). However, there was confusion also about the scope of "remuneration". In consequence, reg.9 now states that "only sums payable to an employee by way of wages or salary are to be treated as remuneration". This means that employees remain entitled to other benefits (such as use of a company car or private medical insurance) during maternity leave and that annual leave entitlement continues to accrue. By virtue of the Social Security Act 1989 Sch.5, maternity leave is treated as pensionable employment and the employer is liable to continue to pay full contributions on the employee's behalf (see also, *Boyle v EOC* (1998)). Continuation of the contract also means that the employee remains bound by its terms, in particular by the obligation of good faith and the duty to maintain mutual trust and confidence.

The fact that the contract continued in this way during ordinary maternity leave but not during additional maternity leave used to be the main difference between the two entitlements. However, EU case-law made no distinction between different kinds of maternity leave and the Government therefore decided that they should be aligned. In consequence, MPLR reg.9 was amended from October 2008 so that employees are entitled to the benefit of all terms and conditions of employment during additional as well as ordinary maternity leave.

6–014   At the end of additional maternity leave the employee is entitled to return to work without giving further notice. If she wishes to return before the end of that period she must give eight weeks' notice of her return date to the employer. Only if she gives less than the required notice is the employer entitled to postpone her return, and then only so far as is necessary to comply with the statutory notice requirement (reg.11). There is still a difference between ordinary and additional maternity leave in terms of the right to return to work. MPLR reg.18 provides that at the end of ordinary maternity leave the employee is entitled to return to the job in which she was employed before her absence. At the end of additional maternity leave, she has a prima facie right to return to her original job, but if it is not reasonably practicable for her to do so, the employer can assign her to a suitable alternative position. Obviously, this is much less advantageous for the employee. The success of the right to return provisions is dependent on how far they actually guarantee the employee a return to her former position as if she had never been away. If the employer is allowed to slot her in anywhere then she is disadvantaged through taking the leave and equality of opportunity is denied.

The right to return from both kinds of leave is subject to an exception where the employee becomes redundant while on ordinary or additional maternity leave. In this situation she is entitled to be offered a suitable alternative vacancy if one exists (reg.10). This means that she may actually be better off than other employees in a similar situation, who should be considered for alternative posts or else their dismissals may be unfair, but who do not have any entitlement as such, and who will therefore be considered after any employee on maternity leave.

Failure to allow the employee to return after maternity leave will otherwise constitute automatically unfair dismissal (reg.20), unless the employer can show that it was not reasonably practicable on grounds other than redundancy to allow her to return to a suitable and appropriate job and she has unreasonably refused an offer of such a job with an associated employer. In these circumstances the dismissal will not be automatically unfair, but the employee could claim unfair dismissal on general principles if she had two years' employment, or possibly for discrimination on grounds of pregnancy and maternity. Where an employee has a contractual right to maternity leave as well as her statutory right, she can exercise the rights together as a composite right, taking advantage of whichever has the most favourable terms in any respect (reg.21). If the employee is ill and unable to return to work at the end of maternity leave she is entitled to be treated like any other sick employee and has the corresponding obligation to comply with the usual contractual arrangements for notifying sickness absence. In deciding whether or not to dismiss her on grounds of incapability the employer must ignore all absence during pregnancy or maternity leave: it will be unlawful sex discrimination if this is taken into account (*Brown v Rentokil* (1998) above, para.2–019).

Where the employer takes on a temporary replacement for an employee on maternity leave, s.106 of ERA provides that if the replacement employee is given notice in writing at the outset that his employment is only temporary because it is as a replacement for an employee on maternity leave, and if the ultimate dismissal is to make room for the returner, the dismissal of the replacement will count as being for "some other substantial reason". This means that it can be justified as a fair dismissal, although it does not follow that it will be.

6–015

Shared parental leave

6–016   The discussion of maternity rights above must now be read in tandem with the new right to shared parental leave, introduced by the Children and Families Act 2014. In essence, this is a right for a mother to pass part of her maternity leave (and pay, where applicable) to the other parent: the idea is to involve both parents more equally in caring for their child during its first year of life. It is separate and distinct from the right to unpaid parental leave (see below, para.6–020).

Shared parental leave has to be instigated by the mother. She must be entitled either to maternity leave, or to SMP or maternity allowance, and the other parent must be an employee who expects to share primary responsibility for the care of the child at the time of its birth or placement for adoption. In the normal case, both parents will be employees, although probably with different employers, and the scheme will involve the mother giving up part of her maternity leave and it being taken by the father. However, the mother could be a self-employed woman with an employed partner: if she is entitled to maternity allowance, her partner may qualify to take shared parental leave even though she has no entitlement to leave herself. She qualifies as long as she has worked for 26 weeks in the 66-week period up to the expected week of childbirth, earning above the National Insurance limit (£30 per week in 2015) in at least 13 of those weeks. The other parent must have worked for the same employer for 26 weeks by the fifteenth week before the expected week of childbirth, and must still be working for that employer when taking any period of shared parental leave.

Shared parental leave must be taken in blocks of at least one week—but can be taken in discontinuous blocks. So it may not be a case of the mother taking the first six months and the father taking the next six months, but it could mean the mother taking three months, passing to her partner for two months, coming back for two months, and passing to her partner for the remainder—or even both parents taking some leave at the same time.

6–017   It will be clear that the arrangements could be potentially complex. For that reason, there are some detailed notice requirements. The basic rule is that eight weeks' notice must be given before any period of shared parental leave can start. The trigger is for the mother to give eight weeks' notice that she intends to bring her maternity leave to an end and to institute shared parental leave. This notice, once given, is irrevocable—unless she gives it before birth, in which case she will have up to six weeks after the birth to change her mind and withdraw the notice. The other parent must provide his employer with a notice of his eligibility for shared parental leave. At this initial stage, the parents are required to provide each employer with a non-binding indication of their expected pattern of leave, in order to assist planning, but this can be varied by notice.

The possibilities for stopping and starting are not infinite. Each parent can give up to three notices for periods of shared parental leave. If the notice is for a period of continuous leave, then it must be accepted by the employer. If it is for a discontinuous period of leave, then it is subject to the employer's agreement. There is a discussion period of 14 days from the date of the request for the employer to consider it. If the employer refuses a request for discontinuous leave, the employee must take the total period requested as a continuous block, or else withdraw the request and submit a new one. Finally, each parent may work for 20 "in touch" days (called SPLIT days—shared parental leave in touch days) without bringing their period of shared parental leave to an end.

The system of shared parental leave came into force on 5 April 2015, for the parents of babies expected after that date. It remains to be seen how it will work in practice and how far it will be taken up by parents.

No detriment or dismissal on grounds of pregnancy

The Employment Protection Act 1975 made it automatically unfair to dismiss a woman for pregnancy, but this applied only to women with two years of continuous service. It was also subject to two major exceptions: if the employee was incapable of doing her work or it became unlawful to employ her as a result of her pregnancy, she could be fairly dismissed if there was no other suitable alternative work available. This no doubt appeared to strike a fair balance between the interests of employers and employees at that time. However, it fell a long way short of giving women real job protection in case of pregnancy, which is essential if they are to be equal in the workplace.

6–018

As pregnancy is a condition related only to one sex, it was inevitable that pregnant workers would seek assistance under the Sex Discrimination Act, a campaign which was ultimately successful (see *Webb v EMO* (1994), above, para.2–018). But greater assistance was forthcoming from Europe, not only in the form of the CJEU but by directive. The Pregnant Workers Directive (92/85/EEC) was adopted in October 1992. It was opposed by the UK Government, but because it had been proposed as a health and safety measure, it could be approved by the qualified majority voting procedure and the United Kingdom had no right of veto. Implementation was required by October 1994 and was carried out in the United Kingdom principally by the Trade Union Reform and Employment Rights Act 1993 (TURERA). Further amendment followed in the Employment Relations Act 1999. By virtue of ERA s.99, as amended, dismissal is automatically unfair if the reason or principal reason for it is connected with: pregnancy; childbirth; suspension on maternity grounds in accordance with ERA s.66 and taking or seeking to take maternity leave, adoption leave, paternity leave, parental leave or time off for ante-natal care. In *Mayr v Bäckerei und Konditorei Gerhard Flöckner OHG* (2008) the CJEU held that a woman undergoing IVF treatment was not protected from dismissal under the Pregnant Workers Directive until the fertilised embryo was actually implanted (which happened three days after she was dismissed). However, they held that to dismiss a woman on grounds that she might become pregnant (by undergoing IVF treatment) was direct sex discrimination contrary to the Equal Treatment Directive (76/207/EEC) (see now the Recast Equal Treatment Directive (2006/54/EC) art.14).

If it would be contrary to any enactment or Code of Practice for the employee to continue in her employment while pregnant, dismissal will be automatically unfair; she has a right instead to be offered any suitable alternative employment or to be suspended on maternity grounds (ERA s.66). The suspension will be on full pay unless she has unreasonably refused alternative work, in which case she need not be paid. To complete the dismissal protection, selection for redundancy on any of these grounds is also automatically unfair. Further assistance is provided by ERA s.92(4), which stipulates that an employer who dismisses an employee while she is pregnant or on maternity leave must give her a written statement of the reasons for her dismissal regardless of her length of service or whether she actually asks for one. It is important to notice that there is no longer any continuity or hours requirement for this protection: every woman worker has it from day one.

6–019   Until 1999, only dismissal for reasons connected with pregnancy and childbirth was expressly dealt with by statute. If an employee suffered detriment short of dismissal on these grounds she would have had to bring a claim of sex discrimination. That remains possible, but in the Employment Relations Act 1999 the opportunity was taken to rationalise remedies for leave for family reasons, among other things by extending the right not to suffer detriment to detriment on grounds of pregnancy or childbirth. This is now contained in ERA s.47C, and the Maternity and Parental Leave etc Regulations 1999 reg.19: the specific situations protected mirror exactly the provisions for automatic unfair dismissal.

Thus the protection for women workers is now much more extensive. If *Webb v EMO* (1994) were to arise today, there is no doubt but that the dismissal would be unfair, even if the new employee had been taken on just to cover the maternity leave period. Presumably, however, it will still be necessary to establish a causal link between the pregnancy-related reason and the dismissal. Thus an employer who dismisses a woman for an unacceptable rate of absence without knowing that she is pregnant could perhaps be taken to have acted fairly even though her pregnancy could account for some of it: this puts a premium on a woman giving early notice to her employer (cf. *Del Monte Foods Ltd v Mundon* (1980)).

In *Berrisford v Woodard Schools* (1991), a case brought under the SDA, an unmarried matron at a church boarding school for girls was dismissed when she announced her pregnancy and that she had no intention of getting married. The EAT held that this was a dismissal on grounds of morality rather than pregnancy and that no discrimination had occurred because there was evidence that a male teacher who lived with a woman had been instructed to marry her or leave, so both sexes were treated the same in comparable circumstances. The reasoning would not work now, because in these circumstances, the matron would have been dismissed for a reason connected with her pregnancy, and it would be automatically unfair (see also, *O'Neill v Governors of St Thomas More School* (1996)).

Parental rights

Unpaid parental leave

6–020   While there are good reasons for making special provision for women in relation to childbirth it is not as clear that any extended period of leave should be limited to mothers, for this simply reinforces stereotyped views on who should carry out family responsibilities. At the same time, strong arguments can be put forward for allowing a period of paternity leave at the time of birth.

The majority of EU countries have had some kind of provision for paid or unpaid parental leave for some time and the EU Commission was pushing for a directive on parental leave from as long ago as 1983, but proposals were always blocked by the United Kingdom. It is ironic that, 20 years on, the United Kingdom is now quite advanced, especially with the new right to shared parental leave (see above, para.6–016). In 1994 it was decided to deal with the issue under the procedure stipulated in the Protocol on Social Policy annexed to the Treaty of European Union, the agreement whereby the other Member States could take forward social policy matters without the United Kingdom. Under that procedure there had to be consultation with representatives of management and labour ("the social partners") before proposals on social policy could be put forward (see now, TFEU art.154). Under TFEU art.155, representatives of management and labour can themselves reach agreement on these issues and ask the Council to implement their agreement. This is what happened in relation to the Parental Leave Directive. Agreement on a framework directive on parental leave was reached in December 1995 and then implemented by the Council in June 1996 (96/34/EC). Following the Labour Government's acceptance of the Agreement on Social Policy, the Parental Leave Directive was extended to the United Kingdom (97/75/EC), and implementation was carried out by the Maternity and Parental Leave, etc Regulations 1999. The original provision for 13 weeks' leave was increased to 18 weeks in 2013 by the Parental Leave (EU Directive) Regulations 2013, to comply with the revised Parental Leave Directive (2010/18/EU).

Essentially parental leave is an entitlement to up to 18 weeks of unpaid leave per child, to be taken between birth and the child reaching the age of 18. Both parents are entitled to such leave and it cannot be transferred from one to the other. This is an attempt to counteract social stereotyping which tends to place responsibility on the mother alone to take time off to look after children. However, the fact that the leave is unpaid means that very many employees, especially men, will be unwilling or unable to take advantage of it. Employees do not qualify for parental leave until they have one year's continuous employment. If an employee changes jobs he will have to serve one year with the new employer before being entitled to take any leave remaining to him. Parents of a child who is adopted also have this right.

6–021 MPLR reg.17 provides that the contract of employment continues during parental leave, but with most obligations suspended. The employee remains bound by terms as to notice, confidential information, acceptance of gifts or other benefits, competition and the implied term of good faith. The employer is bound by the implied term of mutual trust and confidence and any terms relating to notice, disciplinary and grievance procedures and compensation for redundancy. If the employee takes parental leave of four weeks or less, either independently or adding it on to ordinary maternity leave, she has the right to return to the job she was doing before the absence. However, if the employee takes parental leave of more than four weeks (or adds any parental leave on at the end of additional maternity leave) the employer may instead reassign her to a different job, if it is not reasonably practicable to allow her to return to her former job and provided that the alternative is suitable and appropriate (reg.18).

Within these parameters the Maternity and Parental Leave, etc Regulations 1999 leave it to employers and employees to make their own arrangements on how to implement parental leave, by individual, collective or workforce agreement. If no such agreement is reached, however, the default scheme set out in Sch.2 to the Regulations will apply. The default scheme states that leave has to be taken in minimum periods of one week and that the employee can only take a maximum of four weeks in any one year. This has been criticised because a parent who wished to take one day's leave in order to take a child to a dental appointment, for example, would lose a whole week's leave. A fine example of the rigidity of the scheme is afforded by *Rodway v South Central Trains Ltd* (2005), where an employee's request for a day's annual leave to care for his child when other arrangements fell through was denied and so he took the time as parental leave instead. His employer disciplined him for this and he claimed that he had been subjected to a detriment for exercising his parental leave rights. But since he had only taken one day, as opposed to a week (which would presumably have inconvenienced his employer much more), the Court of Appeal held that this could not be regarded as an exercise of his parental leave right.

The answer to situations like this is to make an individual agreement to override the default scheme. The default scheme requires the employee to give at least 21 days' notice of leave. A father wishing to take leave at the time a child is born must give 21 days' notice of the expected week of childbirth and adoptive parents should give 21 days' notice of the date of placement. In these two situations the employer must allow the leave, but in other circumstances the default scheme allows the employer to postpone it for up to six months if "the employer considers that the operation of his business would be unduly disrupted" by the proposed leave. The employee has a right to complain to an employment tribunal within three months that the postponement is unreasonable, in which case the tribunal can award such compensation as it considers to be just and equitable (ERA s.80). Regulations 19 and 20 extend the protection of ERA ss.47C and 99 (protection against detriment and dismissal) to an employee who is dismissed or subjected to a detriment for taking or seeking to take parental leave.

6–022   Symbolically at any rate, the parental leave provisions are an important step forward in assisting employees to achieve an appropriate balance between work and family responsibilities, and, indeed, in recognising that men have families too. However, evidence to date suggests that take-up of the right is fairly low, presumably because the leave is unpaid.

Flexible working

6–023   At a relatively late stage of the passage of the Employment Act 2002 through the House of Commons, a new and controversial provision was added allowing the Secretary of State to make regulations to permit parents to seek changes to their contracts of employment to facilitate their childcare responsibilities. The right to request flexible working patterns is contained in ERA Pt 8A as amended by the Children and Families Act 2014. Originally, it applied to employees with children aged under six, or disabled children aged under 18, but in 2007 it was extended to carers for adult dependants, and from April 2009 the age limit for children was raised to 16.

Under the Children and Families Act 2014, the right was extended to all employees from June 2014. It was felt that this would assist employees in achieving an appropriate work-life balance and thus keep in the labour market people who might otherwise have left. The extension to all employees was also said to help to remove any stigma which might be felt by parents or carers in asking for flexible working. It should be noted, however, that this is a right to *request* flexible working: it by no means follows that the request must be granted. A new Acas Code of Practice (No.5) on Handling Requests for Flexible Working and Acas Guidance on handling such requests were published in 2014.

There is a 26-week qualifying period for the right. An application for flexible working must be made in writing and on receipt the employer must either agree or hold a meeting to discuss the proposal as soon as possible. The strict time-limits which used to apply to all stages of the procedure have been abolished. Instead, the employer is enjoined to deal with the request in a reasonable manner, and within an overall three-month time period. The employee no longer has an entitlement to be accompanied by a co-worker at any meeting to discuss the application, although this is recommended as good practice. It is also good practice to allow the employee to appeal if the application is rejected, but this too is no longer an entitlement. It remains the case that the employer can only reject a request for flexible working on the nine "business grounds" specified in ERA s.80G—such as additional costs, detrimental effect on company performance, etc.

The most severe limitation on the right to flexible working is that the employee can only bring a claim in a tribunal if the employer has failed to follow procedure or has reached a decision on incorrect facts. That seems to limit the tribunal's opportunities to review the substance of an employer's decision, leading many commentators to express concern that employers would get away with merely "going through the motions". However, in *Commotion Ltd v Rutty* (2006) the EAT pointed out that a tribunal would have to make some sort of inquiry into the realities of the situation in order to decide whether or not the employer's decision was based on incorrect facts and therefore the tribunal in the case had not misdirected itself by investigating whether or not there was any evidence for the employer's assertion that allowing flexible working would be detrimental to the performance of the business (and concluding that there was not).

6–024

The remedy for breach of this right is somewhat limited—even if a claim is successful, the maximum a tribunal can award is eight weeks' pay (i.e. £3,800 in 2015).

Paternity rights

6–025   While parental leave was introduced in part in the hope of encouraging fathers as well as mothers to take their share in combining childcare with work, originally there were no specific provisions for fathers. Many firms had introduced a scheme for paternity leave which permitted fathers two weeks off at the time of a child's birth and this pattern found its way into the legislation. The Secretary of State was given power to make regulations for paternity leave and pay by the Employment Act 2002 and the Paternity and Adoption Leave Regulations 2002 came into force in December 2002. Paternity leave is available to the father of the child or the mother's partner (who could be a same-sex partner or a close relative) provided that he or she is likely to take major responsibility for bringing up the child. They must have been employed for 26 weeks by the fifteenth week before the expected week of childbirth. Paternity leave lasts for a maximum of two weeks and must be taken within eight weeks of the child's birth. It is paid at the rate of lower rate SMP and SSP, which was £139.58 per week in 2015, or 90 per cent of actual earnings if lower.

Fathers taking paternity leave are protected from detriment and dismissal on that account, as with the other family leave rights. The issue of whether dismissal was "connected with" paternity leave was raised by *Atkins v Coyle Personnel plc* (2008). The employee took one week's paternity leave but agreed to remain contactable by telephone and email while he was away. His line manager rang and insisted on speaking to him although he was told the employee was sleeping after a wakeful night with the baby. A heated conversation ensued, after which the employee was dismissed. The EAT felt that this was too indirectly related to his paternity leave to be regarded as connected with it, and dismissed his claim. In hindsight, he would thus have been better off declining to be in contact while he was on leave!

Adoption rights

6–026   There was a degree of doubt about whether maternity rights could be claimed by mothers who were adopting children. When the Employment Act 2002 introduced a range of other family-friendly rights the opportunity was taken to regularise the position. Effectively the Paternity and Adoption Leave Regulations 2002 give adoptive parents equivalent rights to natural parents: one parent may take ordinary and additional adoption leave, mirroring maternity leave, and partners can take the equivalent of paternity leave. They are also entitled to parental leave. The parents of adopted children can also claim adoption pay which is comparable to maternity pay and paternity pay and now have rights to time off for adoption appointments.

Leave for dependants' care

6–027   The Parental Leave Directive (96/34/EC) also required Member States to give workers the right to take time off for urgent family reasons such as sickness or accident. In the original draft of the Employment Relations Act (ERelA) 1999, this was going to be time off for domestic incidents, raising interesting questions as to whether malfunction of a washing machine or sickness of the family pet would be regarded as sufficiently disruptive to count as a justification for time off. However, the Government stepped back from the brink and the final version of this new right was framed as being for the care of (human) dependants. Section 57A of the ERA gives employees a right to "reasonable" time off (not necessarily paid) to take action that is necessary in the following circumstances: to assist when a dependant is ill, giving birth or has been injured or assaulted; to arrange care for an ill or injured dependant; because of the death of a dependant; because of unexpected disruption to care arrangements for a dependant; or to deal with an unexpected incident concerning the employee's child during school hours.

"Dependant" is defined in ERA s.57A(3)–(5) to mean the spouse, child or parent of the employee, or someone who lives in the same household who is not an employee, lodger, tenant or boarder. This is apt to include unmarried partners, including same-sex couples, and more remote relatives or friends, provided that they live in the employee's household. In relation to situations where a dependant is ill, injured or assaulted the definition of dependant is extended to include "any person who reasonably relies on the employee" for assistance in these circumstances. This could include relatives or friends who do not live with the employee, or a neighbour.

Time off for dependant care is intended to cover unforeseen occurrences: if the employee wants time off to deal with a situation which she knows is coming up, such as moving house or taking a child to a new school, she should arrange to take annual leave or parental leave, if appropriate. Thus in *Qua v John Ford Morrison* (2003) the EAT held that the right did not extend to looking after a sick child during a period of illness, except insofar as that was necessary to deal with the immediate crisis and to make arrangements for his ongoing care. The employee should have used annual leave or parental leave if she needed to care for him herself. Similarly, in *Forster v Cartwright Black* (2004) the EAT held that leave for the death of a dependant was for such things as making funeral arrangements and dealing with official notification, but not for coming to terms emotionally with the situation.

Although it is therefore in the nature of things unlikely that the employee will seek permission in advance to take the time off, if she does, and it is unreasonably refused, she has a right to complain to a tribunal within three months. The tribunal will make a declaration and can award such compensation as it considers to be just and equitable having regard to the seriousness of the employer's fault and any loss to the employee (ERA s.57B). By the same token, the employee will frequently be unable to give notice prior to taking the time off. Section 57A(2) of the ERA therefore stipulates that the employee should notify the employer as soon as reasonably practicable of the reason for his absence and how long it is likely to last. The Act envisages that the employee may sometimes only be able to notify the employer after he has returned to work. This means that an employer faced with an employee who is absent without explanation may need to review disciplinary procedures for dealing with unauthorised absences. Absence from

6–028

work without permission would normally be a fundamental breach of contract justifying summary dismissal (see *Hanley v Pease* (1915)). An employer who made no inquiries and did not give an employee an opportunity to explain the situation before dismissing him would no doubt be liable for unfair dismissal on general principles (see below, para.8–050) but this would not apply to anyone with less than two years' service. However, if the employee was entitled to take the time off by virtue of s.57A, any such dismissal will be automatically unfair under ERA s.99. As with rights to maternity and parental leave, there is no continuous service requirement for the right to time off for dependant care. In addition, employees may bring an action under ERA s.47C if they are subjected to a detriment for exercising their time off rights. Again, as with other time off rights, the employer is not entitled to ask the employee to make up the time later and any insistence that the employee should do so would amount to a detriment under ERA s.47C.

Guarantee Payments

6–029   The object of the provisions on guarantee payments in ERA ss.28–35 is to provide employees with a minimum payment where they are laid off work through no fault of their own. Two points should be noted at the outset. First, no employer has the right to lay workers off without pay unless that right is embodied in the contract of employment. If there is no contractual right, the employer would be committing a fundamental breach which would entitle the employee to leave and claim that she had been constructively dismissed (see below, para.8–028). Secondly, if the lay-off lasts for four weeks or more the employee may be entitled to leave and claim a redundancy payment (see below, para.9–019).

The qualifying period of service for this right is only one month (ERA s.29). The employee is entitled to guarantee pay if laid off for one of two reasons: a diminution in the requirements of the employer's business for work of the kind that the employee is employed to do (ERA s.28(1); compare the definition of redundancy, below, para.9–005); or because of any other occurrence affecting the normal working of the business in relation to work of the kind that the employee is employed to do.

The employer has a defence if she offers the employee suitable alternative work for the day which he unreasonably refuses—a defence which is again modelled on the redundancy provisions (ERA s.29(4)). Rather more significantly, the employee is not entitled to payment if the reason for the lay-off is a strike, lock-out or other industrial action involving the employer or any other company in the same group (ERA s.29(3)). So if supplies dry up because there is a strike in a different part of the enterprise, the employees will not get guarantee payments even if they are not involved in any industrial action themselves. This may seem harsh, but can be justified on the ground that such an exclusion was found in most of the collective agreements which made provision for guarantee payments before the Act was passed, and it has a parallel also in that social security benefits are not normally payable in those circumstances. Incidentally, if there is a collective agreement covering these matters, the parties can opt out of the statutory scheme provided that the contractual scheme is at least as advantageous, and there are a number of opted-out agreements. Even if an agreement is not opted out, any contractual right to pay during a lay-off would reduce the employer's liability under ERA ss.28–35.

It may perhaps be doubted whether the right is worth this amount of legislative effort. Broadly, the amount payable is the employee's gross daily rate of pay subject to a maximum which has always been ridiculously low. In 2015 it stood at only £26 per day. Further, guarantee pay can only be claimed for a maximum of five days in any three-month period. Not only are the sums involved very small, but the overall effect of this is simply to stave off by a few days the payment of other benefits. Apart from the guarantee payment, a worker would normally be entitled to jobseeker's allowance after three workless days. Therefore, the worker who receives a guarantee payment (worth roughly the same as jobseeker's allowance) gets paid for the first three days, and the employer has to pay for the next two instead of the state. If the worker is still laid off after that, she will have to wait for three days, and will then qualify for jobseeker's allowance. **6–030**

If an employer refuses to pay guarantee pay, then the employee has a right of recourse to the employment tribunal.

Suspension on Medical Grounds

Under health and safety regulations a business may sometimes be required to shut down its operations. In such a situation, employees remain entitled to their regular pay even if they cannot work, unless the employer has a contractual right to suspend them. If the employer has a right to suspend them in these circumstances and the shut-down was required under regulations listed in ERA s.64 (Control of Lead at Work Regulations 2002; Ionising Radiations Regulations 1999; COSHH Regulations 2002), then ERA s.64(1) provides that the employees are entitled to a week's pay for every week of shut-down up to a maximum of 26 weeks. **6–031**

An employee need only be employed for one month in order to receive this protection (ERA s.65(1)) and if the employee is dismissed because of the shutdown in these circumstances, the qualifying period for unfair dismissal is also reduced to one month (ERA s.108(2)). However, the employer has a defence where the employee unreasonably refuses suitable alternative employment during the suspension period (ERA s.65(4)) and the employee has no entitlement if she is unfit to work through illness during that time. As usual, the employee's remedy is to apply to an employment tribunal, which can order the employer to pay the requisite amount.

Time Off Rights

The Employment Protection Act 1975 introduced a range of rights to time off work in certain circumstances, which are now found in the ERA and TULRCA. **6–032**

Since 1975 further time off rights have been introduced: the right to paid time off for ante-natal care and the right to time off for dependant care, discussed above (paras 6–004 and 6–027) and rights to time off for employee representatives. The rights to time off for trade union duties and activities; for employee representatives; and for public duties are discussed here; time off to look for work in a redundancy situation is discussed in Ch.9 (see below, para.9–022) and time off for safety representatives in Ch.14 (see below, para.14–041).

Time off for trade union duties and activities

6–033   Lay trade union officials—that is, workers who are members of a trade union and hold office in the trade union rather than being employed by it, have an important role in representing the union in the workplace. Where the union is recognised, they will represent it in local negotiations with the employer and are also likely to be the representatives of choice for the matters on which it is mandatory by statute for the employer to consult with representatives of the workforce (on which, see para.5–014 above). Usually they will also advise and represent members involved in disciplinary or grievance proceedings with the employer; even in workplaces where the union is not recognised, the employer is normally content for union officials carry out this role. In practice, lay union officials will end up doing quite a lot of this work on a voluntary basis in their own free time; however, it is obvious that they will also need time during working hours to communicate, meet with and represent members if they are to do the job properly (and, indeed, if anyone is going to be prepared to take on such a demanding role). Before 1975, any time off had to be negotiated with the employer, but two very important rights to time off for trade unionists were introduced by the Employment Protection Act 1975 and are now contained in TULRCA ss.168–170. Guidance on their application is contained in the Acas Code of Practice on Time Off for Trade Union Duties and Activities, revised in 2010, and amplified in the Acas Guide to Trade Union Representation in the Workplace, issued at the same time. While there is no service qualification for the exercise of these rights, they are limited to the officials and members of recognised trade unions (see above, para.5–014).

Paid time off

6–034   Officials of recognised trade unions are entitled to paid time off for two purposes: to carry out their duties, and to receive relevant training. Two kinds of duty qualify for paid time off under TULRCA s.168(1): negotiations with the employer or performing functions on behalf of employees. However, not all such duties qualify. The right to paid time off is limited to duties which fulfil the conditions of being related to matters listed in TULRCA s.178 (issues which can be the subject of collective bargaining), and, in the case of negotiations, matters on which the employer recognises the union for bargaining purposes. In the case of other functions on behalf of employees, the employer must have agreed to their performance by the union.

The formulation of duties for which paid time off is allowed was narrowed by the Employment Act 1989 effectively to reverse a Court of Appeal holding that an official's duties could relate to matters other than those on which the employer was prepared to negotiate with them (*Beal v Beecham Group* (1982)). In *Adlington v British Bakeries* (1989) the Court of Appeal held that preparatory work was included within the definition of duties. Thus officials of the Bakers' Union were entitled to paid time off to attend a one-day workshop on the implications of the repeal of the statute regulating hours of work in the industry. The question to be asked is whether any particular preparation or advisory meeting is sufficiently proximate to the negotiations with the employer—a question of fact where a tribunal's decision should not normally be overturned. The decision remains valid after the amendment, although it must now be read as applying to a more restricted range of duties (cf. *London Ambulance Service v Charlton* (1992)), and the Code of Practice indicates that preparation for meetings and reporting back to members are included (para.14). Meetings with other union officials and interviews with constituents who have grievances are still included within an official's duties, provided that they relate to matters for which there is recognition; and if an official can represent a member in disciplinary proceedings, she should also have paid time off to represent the member against the employer in an employment tribunal, even though this is not spelt out in the Code.

Paid time off for training is now limited in the same way to duties relating to matters in respect of which the union is recognised by the employer; additionally it must be approved by the employee's own union or by the TUC (TULRCA s.168(2)). There may need to be agreements over how many officials can be away at any one time.

Paragraph 19 of the Code of Practice draws attention to the fact that the statute does not require payment for time when the official would not otherwise be at work, but goes on to say that if the official works flexible hours, such as a night shift worker, and has to perform representative duties during normal hours, this should be paid. As a matter of good practice, this is undoubtedly true, but it is possible that the Code here goes beyond what the law strictly requires. In *Hairsine v Hull CC* (1991), where the employee worked an evening shift and took time off from that in lieu of time he had spent at a training course during the day, it was held that he was not entitled to be paid for it. Had he asked simply for pay to represent the time spent on daytime duties, it is likely that that would have been refused. On the other hand, in *Ryford Ltd v Drinkwater* (1996) the EAT seemed to accept that leaving a night shift early in order to get some sleep before a morning negotiating meeting was time off to which the official was entitled, although the issue in the case was different and this point was not argued. **6–035**

Similar issues arise in relation to part-time workers. If part-time workers go on a full-time training course for trade union duties, for example, should they get their normal pay, or should it be grossed up to full-time pay? In *Arbeiterwohlfahrt der Stadt Berlin v Bötel* (1992) the CJEU held that it would be indirect sex discrimination contrary to TFEU art.157 to pay a part-time worker receiving full-time training to be a staff council representative in Germany less than full-timers on the same course. This case was distinguished by the EAT in *Manor Bakeries v Nazir* (1996), where a part-timer had claimed equal pay for full-time attendance at a union conference, on the basis that conference attendance was not "work"—something that could only be said by someone who had never done it. Subsequently, in *Kuratorium für Dialyse v Lewark* (1996), on facts similar to *Bötel*, the CJEU reiterated that "pay" in the context of art.157 includes anything received by the employee from the employer which is referable to the contract of employment, even if only indirectly. This reinforced the view that *Manor Bakeries v Nazir* was wrongly decided, and that was the conclusion of another EAT in *Davies v Neath Port Talbot County BC* (1999), holding that a part-time worker who was elected as a union safety representative was entitled to pay at the full-time rate for her attendance at a full-time training course. In so far as TULRCA s.169 was inconsistent with this, the EAT held it should be set aside. However, since the claim proceeds on the basis of indirect discrimination, there is the possibility of the employer being able to justify paying less to the part-timer. In *Lewark* the CJEU indicated that it thought the justification put forward for the inequality (that the independence of the staff council might be jeopardised if councillors got more for being members than they would from their ordinary work) might be sufficient, although this should be balanced against the fact that part-timers might be reluctant to take on such posts if they had to do much more of the work in their own time than full-timers did. It is relevant to note that the Code of Practice on Time Off states categorically that staff who work part time will be entitled to be paid if staff who work full time would be entitled to be paid (para.19).

Two other rights to paid time off should be mentioned. First, a lay union official who accompanies a worker to a disciplinary, dismissal or grievance hearing in accordance with ERelA 1999 s.10 is entitled to paid time off for this purpose (see further, below, para.8–038). Secondly, the Employment Act 2002 put the role of the Union Learning Representatives on a statutory footing and gave them an entitlement to reasonable paid time off. Union Learning Representatives are union officials whose role is to promote learning in the workplace among their co-workers. They may not necessarily have any other official union capacity. Union Learning Representatives are entitled to a reasonable amount of paid time off to carry out their functions, which include identifying learning needs, arranging for needs to be met, providing advice to workers and consulting with the employer about these matters. Some practical advice is given in the Acas Guide to Trade Union Representation in the Workplace.

6–036   Where a complaint that paid time off was wrongfully refused is upheld, the tribunal must make a declaration to that effect and may award compensation. This should be such amount as the tribunal considers to be just and equitable given the employer's default and any loss to the employee (TULRCA s.172). In *Skiggs v South West Trains Ltd* (2005) the EAT held that a tribunal was wrong to make no award of compensation just because the employee had not lost any pay, pointing out that this would normally be the case where the employer refused to allow the employee time off. Section 172 of TULRCA expressly states that the employer's default is a factor to be taken into account, and a reasonable and proportionate award by way of reparation to the employee for the wrong done to him ought to have been made. However, it was held in *Ryford Ltd v Drinkwater* (1996) that there is no liability for refusing to agree to a request for time off where the employer is not aware of the request. This reinforces the advice given in the Code of Practice that employers and unions should agree effective procedures for making and processing requests.

In 2012 the Government launched a consultation about the cost of paid time off for union officials in the Civil Service. One of its concerns was that there were some officials spending 100 per cent of their time on union duties for indefinite periods of time. In its response to the consultation, the Government indicated its intention to reduce the amount of paid time off for civil servants for union duties and activities, in particular by limiting the amount of time any individual could spend on union duties to 50 per cent of their overall time. This idea has been taken up in the Trade Union Bill 2016, which inserts a new TULRCA s.172A enabling a Minister of the Crown to make regulations requiring public authorities (to be widely defined) to publish information about how many union representatives it has (including health and safety and union learning representatives), what proportion of their time is spent on union activities (called "facility time" in the Bill), and what proportion of the employer's pay bill this represents. New TULRCA s.172B then gives the Minister a reserve power to make regulations to set caps on these, in the light of the information disclosed.

Unpaid time off

As well as paid time off for officials, members of recognised trade unions are enti-   6–037
tled to unpaid time off during working hours for trade union activities (TULRCA s.170). Acting as a representative of the union is stated to be an activity, and would cover things like being a member of the national executive of the union, or a representative at branch, area or regional meetings or at the annual conference of the TUC. Taking part in industrial action is specifically stated not to be a trade union activity, which is hardly surprising; however, the Code of Practice, para.62 suggests that an official representing members who are on strike could be carrying out her duties and thus entitled to paid time off under TULRCA s.168. Further examples of trade union activities given by the Code are taking part in union elections and attending meetings to discuss or vote on the outcome of negotiations. In practice, in some situations where paid time off is not available to officials under s.168, they may be entitled to unpaid time off under TULRCA s.170.

In *Luce v Bexley LBC* (1990) the NUT sought permission from local authorities for teachers who were union officials to have time off in 1988 to attend a lobby of Parliament over the Education Reform Bill (later Act). The lobby involved all teaching unions and had been organised by the TUC. Considering that it was essentially an expression of political and ideological objection to the legislation, an employment tribunal held that the employer was entitled to refuse time off on the ground that this was not a trade union activity. The EAT upheld the decision, but warned that it would be too sweeping to turn down all lobbying. Lobbying, said the EAT,

> "is the presentation of arguments intended to persuade a member of Parliament to vote in a particular way on a particular issue. It is to be contrasted with an approach which is in essence based upon mere protest."

Thus if it could be shown that the lobbying was of the persuasive kind rather than the protest kind, and that the issue was relevant to the employment of the members, it could count as a trade union activity. This might have been possible on the facts here, but the claimant did not help himself by failing to give evidence or call any witnesses!

Where unpaid time off is wrongly refused, the tribunal again makes a declaration and can award just and equitable compensation, taking account of the degree of blame attaching to the employer and the loss to the employee (TULRCA s.172).

How much time off?

6–038   The Act does not stipulate how much paid and unpaid time off officials and members should get: it is such amount as is reasonable. The consultation and research exercise which took place before the Code of Practice on Time Off was revised in 2010 showed that, even as statute has increased the potential role of trade union representatives, so there has been a "thinning out" on the ground, with fewer union representatives representing more members on a wider range of issues. This led to some unions to call for minimum amounts of time off to be specified, although others opposed it on the grounds that employers might interpret minimum specifications as maximum limits. The Code of Practice is not very specific, recommending that the parties should try to reach advance agreement taking into account the size of the organisation and the number of workers; the production process; the need to maintain a service to the public; and the need for safety and security. At least there is now recognition (in para.43) of the difficulties unions face in ensuring effective representation for certain groups of members, not just shift workers, part-time workers and homeworkers, but also workers without fixed locations and those with particular domestic commitments or special needs, including language requirements.

Particular problems identified by union officials were the reluctance of line managers actually to permit officials to take time off and the inadequacy of "cover" arrangements. If union representatives are still expected to complete all their normal work as well as carrying out their trade union duties, then any apparent permission to take time off is illusory. The Code now addresses this by stating specifically that employers should ensure that work cover and/ or workload reductions are provided when time off is required (para.45), and emphasising the importance of line managers understanding the law on time off and planning provision of cover or workload reduction for representatives (para.54).

In practice, a certain amount of flexibility is almost certain to be necessary in the interests of both sides, but the right to time off is not unlimited. In *Wignall v British Gas* (1984) a NALGO official employed as a meter reader by British Gas had for many years been an active trade unionist and was vice-chair of his district committee and a member of 22 committees. As a result he was getting 12 weeks' leave a year from the employer, some paid and some unpaid. He asked for a further 10 days' unpaid leave in order to edit a magazine for members; it was held that the employers acted reasonably in refusing this.

To date, the provisions for time off for trade union duties and activities have **6–039** not caused great dispute between employers and workers, no doubt because they have been limited to members of recognised trade unions and recognition used to be a voluntary process. An employer who did not wish to allow employees time off for these matters could simply refuse to recognise a union. However, there is no evidence that this has become more contentious now that compulsory trade union recognition has been introduced.

Time off for employee representatives

In *EC Commission v United Kingdom* (1994) the CJEU held that UK law on con- **6–040** sultation with the workforce over redundancies and transfers of undertakings did not properly implement the relevant EU directives because it only provided for consultation with recognised trade unions. This meant that non-unionised workforces, or those where the employer refused to recognise a union, had no rights to be consulted. As a result the law had to be changed in order to allow for consultation with employee representatives (see further, below, para.9–041). It was further necessary to make provision for employee representatives in other areas where EU law provided for consultation or negotiation, such as health and safety, working time, members of European Works Councils and information and consultation representatives. In general, such employee representatives receive the same protection as trade union representatives while they are carrying out their duties, but their rights to time off are not always the same. Under ERA s.61 employees who are representatives for the purposes of redundancy and transfers consultation are entitled to reasonable paid time off for their duties and for training for their duties (although the training provision was only introduced in 1999). Employee health and safety representatives are also entitled to paid time off for their duties and training (see below, para.14–041) as are employee trustees of occupational pension schemes (ERA s.58). Employees who are representatives for the purposes of transnational and national information and consultation have a right to paid time off to perform their functions, but do not expressly have a right to paid time off for training (TICE regs 25–26; ICE regs 27–28). Curiously, however, employee representatives for purposes of making workforce agreements (mainly under the Working Time Regulations 1998, but also in other areas) have no express statutory rights to time off at all. There are also no codes of practice covering time off for employee representatives, even though it might be felt that this is an area where guidance is especially needed. In the consultation before the revised Acas Code of Practice on Time Off for Trade Union Duties and Activities was issued in 2010, the extension of the code to non-union employee representatives was considered, but it was decided that it would not be appropriate. However, in parallel to the new Code and the Guide to Trade Union Representation in the Workplace, in 2010 Acas also issued a Guide to Non-Union Representation in the Workplace, outlining the rights of employee representatives, advising agreements on time off and encouraging employers to allow such representatives to have access to facilities and training, even in situations where they might not be entitled to them by statute.

Time off for public duties

6–041 Many public institutions, most notably the criminal courts, are heavily depend-ent on the work of volunteers. It is important that lay magistrates, school gover-nors and so on should represent a wide cross-section of society and not become the preserve of the middle classes or the retired. Hence the formalisation in ERA s.50 of what already was the practice of many employers, a right to time off for certain kinds of public duties. There is no service qualification for this. An employee is entitled to time off under ERA s.50 if she is: a magistrate; a member of a local authority, health service body or education body; a member of a prison visiting committee; a member of a statutory tribunal; or a member of the Environment Agency. Activities for which time off should be allowed include attendance at meetings and sub-committee meetings and other things approved by the body (e.g. visits or inspections). There is no provision in the Act for pay, and employers vary as to their practice on this.

The allowance once again is for reasonable time off, as to which ERA s.50(4) states that regard should be had to: how much time off is needed to carry out the duties (e.g. magistrates are required to be available for a certain number of sittings and training sessions); how much time the employee has already had for other public duties or for trade union duties and activities; and the circum-stances of the employer's business and the role of the employee in the business. Clearly it will be more difficult for a key employee to take much time off.

A tribunal which upholds a complaint must make a declaration that time off should have been allowed and may order compensation (ERA s.51). It does not have power to stipulate how much time off should be given, or that it should be paid: however, it may make recommendations on the amount of time off, which may be expected to carry weight with the employer (*Corner v Bucks CC* (1978)).

Time off for study and training

6–042 The Apprenticeship, Skills, Children and Learning Act 2009 amended the Employment Rights Act 1996 by introducing a right for employees to request time off for study or training (ERA ss.63D–K). So far it applies only to organisa-tions with at least 250 employees. Employees who have 26 weeks of continuous employment may request unpaid time off for some sort of formal course of study or training—although it need not require attendance at a specific place of study (it could involve e-learning, for example) and it need not lead to a qualification. The crucial requirement is that it should improve the employee's effectiveness in the employer's organisation and thus enhance the performance of the employer's business. Like the right to request flexible working (see above, para.6–023), the right is to make a request and have it considered—it does not follow that it will necessarily be granted.

The employee's request must give details of the proposed training, the time commitment involved, the name of the body giving the course, any qualification which might result from it, and how the organisation would benefit from the employee undertaking it. Only one request can be made per 12 months. The procedure for dealing with such requests is laid down in the Employee Study and Training (Procedural Requirements) Regulations 2010. On receipt of an application, the employer may either agree to it, or hold a meeting with the employee within 28 days to discuss it. The employee has a right to be accompanied at this meeting. Following the meeting, the employer must inform the employee of their decision within 14 days. The employer may only turn down a request on one of the 10 grounds specified in ERA s.63F(7)—which are mainly concerned with inconvenience to the business—and the employee must be given a right of appeal. The employee has a right or recourse to an employment tribunal if a request is refused, but the tribunal can only intervene if the employer has either failed to follow the procedure or has proceeded on an incorrect factual basis.

Limits on Working Time

Traditionally in the United Kingdom there has been little statutory control over working hours, largely because it was thought to be adequately dealt with by voluntary collective bargaining. In the nineteenth century the Factories Acts introduced limits on the working hours of women and young workers, but they did not apply to men or to employment outside their scope. Despite being instrumental in the framing of ILO Convention No.1 on Hours of Work (1919), which provided for a maximum eight-hour day and 48-hour working week, the United Kingdom declined to ratify it. Thus it was not until the Working Time Regulations 1998 came into force on 1 October 1998 that there was any general regulation of working hours in this country.   6–043

The Regulations were passed in order to implement the 1993 Working Time Directive (93/104/EC). The Directive, which should have been brought into force by 23 November 1996, was passed as a health and safety measure under what is now TFEU art.153, which meant that it did not require unanimous agreement. The legal basis of the Directive was challenged by the United Kingdom, which claimed that it was really an employment measure, requiring unanimity. However, in *United Kingdom v Council of the European Union* (1997) the CJEU held that it was primarily a health and safety measure and properly passed under art.153. Implementation finally took place in 1998, nearly two years late. The Working Time Regulations have subsequently been amended many times, partly in response to revisions in the Directive. In 2003 the original Directive was repealed and replaced by the consolidated Working Time Directive (2003/88/EC) which came into force in August 2004. Despite its title, it is its provision for paid holidays which has been the most important effect of the Directive.

Scope of the Working Time Regulations

In line with the general policy of extending the scope of employment protection rights, the Working Time Regulations cover "workers", defined as including employees and those working under contracts to perform personally any work or services (reg.2). It is clear that this can include some self-employed workers (*Redrow Homes (Yorkshire) Ltd v Wright* (2004)). Trainees and agency workers   6–044 are expressly included and there is no qualifying period of employment. In *Union Syndicale Solidaires Isère v Premier Ministre* (2011) the CJEU held that casual and seasonal workers were included and stressed that any exceptions to the coverage of the Directive should be construed restrictively.

The Working Time Directive (93/104/EC) originally allowed the exclusion of workers in all forms of the transport industry, because of the difficulties caused by their unusual working patterns. Another important group excluded, at the behest of the United Kingdom, were doctors in training. However, it was never intended that these exclusions should be permanent and in May 1999 agreement with the EU social partners was reached on the Horizontal Amending Directive (2000/34/EC) (HAD) to extend the Directive generally, and specific directives were passed to deal with mobile workers in the following industries: seafarers, road transport and aviation.

The HAD was implemented in the United Kingdom by the Working Time (Amendment) Regulations 2003. The result is that the Working Time Regulations now apply in full to all non-mobile workers in these industries and to mobile and non-mobile workers in the rail industry. The position for road transport is more complicated, because the Road Transport Directive (2002/15/EC) only applies to those workers who are covered by the EC Drivers' Hours Regulation—broadly, long-distance lorry drivers. Other mobile road transport workers (such as taxi drivers or motorcycle couriers) are covered by the amended Working Time Regulations, but do not have the usual entitlements to rest breaks. Junior hospital doctors are now covered by the Regulations—but only since 1 August 2004. Their position was exceptional, in that their maximum working hours were permitted to average 58 hours per week until July 2007, and then 56 per week from 1 August 2007 to 31 July 2009. Many in the medical profession (including junior doctors themselves) argue that bringing them within the 48-hour rule means that the adequacy of their training is being compromised.

6–045   Another contentious exclusion in the Regulations was the "unmeasured working time" category. Article 17 of the Directive allowed Member States a derogation:

> "when, on account of the specific characteristics of the activity concerned, the duration of the working time is not measured and/or predetermined or can be determined by the workers themselves . . ."

This wording was reproduced almost exactly in the Regulations (reg.20) along with the non-exhaustive list of examples, which includes "managing executives or other persons with autonomous decision-taking powers". On one view this would take out almost all professional workers who have a large amount of autonomy as to how they organise their time and whose work time tends to be defined in terms of the tasks to be performed rather than in terms of set hours. However, given that the Directive is a health and safety measure, it seems hardly likely that such a large group should be excluded and the better view is that very few workers would actually fall into this category. This alarmed the business community which balked at the prospect of having to get written agreements from their professional workers to work beyond the limit and having to keep records of how much work was being done. Their lobbying proved so successful that even before the Regulations had been in force for a year the Government proposed an amendment which was carried through at the end of 1999. This stated that workers whose work was partly predetermined and partly unmeasured could choose voluntarily to work beyond the limit on hours and that the Regulations would not apply to this voluntary extra time. The danger of this, of course, was that for large numbers of workers "voluntary" extra time would become compulsory in practice. More to the point, this allowed an exception not provided for in the Working Time Directive. For this reason, the trade union Amicus complained to the European Commission in 2000 and the Commission later began infraction proceedings against the UK. Two days before the hearing, in January 2006, the Government laid amending regulations before Parliament providing for the repeal of the voluntary extra time provision, effectively conceding the argument. This means that unless workers come within the unmeasured time exception, the employer must take steps to ensure that they keep to the average 48-hour week, unless they have agreed to an opt-out (see below, para.6–047).

The 48-hour week

The basic rule in reg.4 is that average working time for each seven-day period should not exceed 48 hours, including overtime. However, this is a limit on *average* working hours, taken over a standard reference period of 17 weeks (or longer, in certain circumstances). In practice, this should mean that workers can do well above 48 hours for quite sustained periods without going over the limit and should give sufficient flexibility to meet most employers' surges in demand or unforeseen shortages of staff. "Working time" is defined as any time when the worker is working, at the employer's disposal and carrying out his duties. In *Landeshauptstadt Kiel v Jaeger* (2004) the CJEU held that all three elements of the definition had to be fulfilled for time to be considered as working time. However, at the same time the CJEU held that while on call at the workplace the worker (a hospital doctor) did meet all three requirements, even though he usually only had to work during half of his on-call time and was provided with a room and a bed to rest when he was not actually needed. Similarly, in *SIMAP v Conselliera de Sanidad y Consumo de la Generalidad Valenciana* (2000) the CJEU held that time when employees were on call and at the employer's premises would count as working time, but not if they were on call at home. The crucial element therefore seems to be whether the employee is on call at the workplace or not (see also *Dellas v Premier Ministre* (2006)). The European Commission proposed to amend the Working Time Directive to introduce a concept of on-call time, and specifically, a concept of "inactive on-call time" which would not count as part of working time subject to contrary agreement. However, the proposal to amend the Directive failed in 2009, mainly because of the Council of Ministers' failure to agree on the future of the opt-out (considered next) and so it looks as if there will be no change on this in the immediate future. It is worth noting that in *Vorel v Nemocnice Český Krumlov* (2007) the CJEU held that paying doctors only 20 per cent of their usual rate for on-call time, unless they were actually called on to work, did not breach the Directive.

6–046

Using the three-part test the CJEU has also held that where workers travelled directly from their homes to different clients each day, according to instructions given by their employer, all their travelling time should be regarded as working time, including the travel from home to the first client and from the last client to their homes (*Federación de Servicios Privados del sindicato Comisiones Obreras v Tyco Integrated Security SL* (2015)). This could have implications for many peripatetic workers in the United Kingdom, such as care workers providing home care, not only in relation to pay, but also in relation to rest breaks and overall working time. The EAT further held in *Edwards v Encirc Ltd* (2015) that time spent on trade union activities by employees who were officials of a recognised trade union also constituted working time.

The opt-out

6–047 Individual workers can opt out of the 48-hour limit (reg.5). This derogation was controversially included in the Directive at the behest of the then UK Conservative Government, but only for seven years in the first instance. Those who argued against the opt-out were concerned that financial or other pressures could mean that workers effectively had to opt out of the protection and that the limit would become a dead letter. Furthermore, if the justification for the limit in the first place is health and safety, it can be argued that it cannot be justified to allow workers to choose to put themselves at risk. However, the opt-out is still supported by the current Government and the result is that there is a deadlock over the issue in the EU Council of Ministers. European Commission proposals to phase it out over a period of years were rejected by the Council of Ministers in June 2006. The European Parliament attempted to insist that the opt-out should be phased out, but no agreement was reached, with the result that the revised version of the Working Time Directive failed completely in 2009.

A worker who opts out can change his mind on giving seven days' notice, unless he has agreed to a longer period (which cannot be more than three months). Regulation 5 originally required that any opt-out agreement should be in writing and that employers should keep records of its terms plus the actual number of hours worked by the opted-out worker. Again, pressure from business led the Government to water down this requirement in an amendment to the Working Time Regulations in 1999. It is no longer necessary for the agreement to be in writing and the employer need only keep a general record. This is bad news for workers, as the potential for argument about what was agreed and whether the agreement is being adhered to is greatly increased. In *Pfeiffer v Deutches Rotes Kreuz* (2005) the CJEU stressed that not only did the opt-out have to be the individual choice of the worker, but that consent must be expressly and freely given. This could constitute an indirect encouragement for employers to keep adequate records.

Subject to the exceptions noted, the limit on working time is mandatory and an employer who fails to take all reasonable steps to ensure compliance is guilty of a criminal offence. Workers who are penalised or dismissed for insisting on their rights under the Regulations are protected from detriment and dismissal under

ERA ss.45A and 101A. In *Fuss v Stadt Halle* (2010) a firefighter was transferred from frontline duties, which involved 54 hours a week, to an office post when he sought to enforce the 48-hour limit in art.6 of the Working Time Directive (2003/88/EC). The German court referred to the CJEU the question of whether it was sufficient if the worker subjectively considered that he had suffered a detriment (by being transferred to other work), or whether this had to be established objectively. As the state had made no provision for an opt-out at the time, the CJEU held that the question of detriment was not relevant. However, they indicated that transferring the worker in these circumstances deprived him of his right to enforce the 48-hour week in his existing post and thus contravened the Directive; this further suggests that it would almost certainly be considered as detrimental if the opt-out were in force. The CJEU also held in that case that art.6 was sufficiently precise and unconditional to be directly effective. An additional means of enforcement can be seen in *Barber v RJB Mining* (1999), where the High Court held that the 48-hour limit was contractual and workers were entitled to a declaration that they were not contractually bound to work until their average hours dropped below the limit.

There are further restrictions for night workers, defined as workers who as **6–048** a normal course work at least three hours of their daily working time during the night. In *R. v Attorney General (Northern Ireland) ex p Burns* (1999) the High Court in Northern Ireland confirmed that someone who worked nights one week in every three was a "night worker": the test was whether she regularly worked nights, not whether the majority of her working time was at night. Under reg.6, the normal working hours of night workers should not exceed eight in any 24-hour period, averaged over 17 weeks. As with the 48-hour limit, this is mandatory and enforcement is similar.

Rest breaks

The Working Time Regulations also make provision for daily rest, weekly rest and **6–049** rest breaks during the working day. Under reg.10, adult workers are entitled to 11 hours' rest and young workers to 12 hours' rest in each 24-hour period. In the case of shift workers changing shift, this does not apply, although they should get an "equivalent period of compensatory rest". There is an exception also for workers whose working day is split (e.g. cleaners). Adult workers are entitled to a 24-hour rest period in every seven days (although this can be averaged as 48 hours in every 14 days (reg.11)). Young workers should get 24 hours a week. This is in addition to daily rest. As the Working Time Regulations treat rest periods as "entitlements" the DTI (now BIS) Guidance originally stated that, "employers must make sure that workers can take their rest, but are not required to make sure that they do take their rest". In *Commission of the EC v United Kingdom* (2006) the CJEU upheld a complaint that the wording in this Guidance was an encouragement to non-compliance, in that the negative way that it was put could make it less likely that workers were actually able to benefit from the minimum rest periods. However, the CJEU did not go so far as to say that employers must force workers to take breaks or even that employers should take active steps to promote employees' exercise of their right to rest breaks, and in the end all that happened was that the DTI removed the second clause from the Guidance quoted above.

So far as rest breaks during the working day are concerned, it may be surprising to find that break entitlement only arises when the working day is longer than six hours (reg.12). The conditions for this (length, location, etc) can be laid down in a collective or workforce agreement, but in the absence of agreement, the worker's entitlement is only to a 20-minute break, spent away from the workstation. In *Gallagher v Alpha Catering Services Ltd* (2005), involving catering workers whose job was to load and unload food and drink on to aeroplanes, the Court of Appeal held that "downtime" between flights, when the workers had to remain in radio contact and be at the employer's disposal, could not be counted as rest breaks.

In *Corps of Commissionaires Management Ltd v Hughes* (2009) the EAT held that the 20-minute fall-back entitlement for a working day of more than six hours applied however long in excess of six hours the worker worked—i.e. a worker is not entitled to 20 minutes every six hours. This starkly illustrates the point that, while there may be some advantages in having specific provision about rest breaks, the minimum entitlements under the Regulations are really very limited and probably much less than most workers are currently entitled to under their contracts.

Annual leave

6–050   In practical terms, probably the most important provision in the Working Time Regulations is reg.13 which introduced the entitlement to paid annual leave. Under the Working Time Directive (2003/88/EC) art.7, this is a right to four weeks' paid leave a year. Following amendment by the Work and Families Act 2006, the entitlement was increased by 0.8 weeks, meaning that workers working a standard five-day week became entitled to a further eight days holiday a year. This was meant to give workers the equivalent of bank holidays on top of their annual leave entitlement.

One of the problems for employers in relation to annual leave is whether they can stop workers taking paid leave before they have "earned" it: many employers treated leave as accruing proportionately during the year and refused to let employees take more paid leave than was accrued. In part concession to employers' fears on this score, the Working Time Regulations originally stipulated a 13-week qualifying period for the right to annual leave, but this was successfully challenged by BECTU as contrary to the Directive (*R v Secretary of State ex p BECTU* (2001)). The Regulations were amended to remove this requirement in October 2001. The fact that an employer can reach agreement with an employee to claw back pay if the employee leaves before the end of a leave year having used up more than her proportionate entitlement suggests that the employer should not be able to insist upon accrual.

Another major issue has been to decide whether it is acceptable for the employer to designate part of the worker's regular pay as "holiday pay" so as to avoid having to pay the worker when they actually take leave. This kind of "rolled-up" payment is used in particular by employers of casual or temporary workers. After a number of conflicting decisions in national courts, the CJEU settled the matter in *Robinson-Steele v RD Retail Services Ltd* (2006), holding that the payment for leave should be clearly separate from normal pay so that an employer could not simply designate part of the usual pay as a holiday pay element. While the Working Time Directive does not specify when holiday pay should be paid, the CJEU considered that it implied that the payment for leave should be made when the leave was actually taken. Otherwise there would be a danger of making payments to workers in lieu of them actually taking leave, which would be contrary to art.7(2) of the Directive (*Federatie Nederlandse Vakbeweging v Staat der Nederlanden* (2006)).

The most recent controversy in relation to annual leave has been the question of how annual leave intersects with sick leave. Can a worker on long-term sick leave (which may be unpaid, or paid at a lower rate than normal pay) claim their entitlement to (paid) annual leave and does annual leave continue to accrue while an employee is on sick leave (which may be long-term)? In the joined cases *Stringer v HM Revenue and Customs* and *Schultz-Hoff v Deutsche Rentenversicherung Bund* (2009) the CJEU answered both questions in the affirmative, despite the argument of the United Kingdom that Working Time Directive was aimed at safeguarding the health of people who were actually *working*. For good measure, the CJEU also held that where the employment is terminated while the worker is on sick leave, she is entitled to payment for any annual leave which has accrued but which she has not been able to take because she is on sick leave. *Pereda v Madrid Movilidad SA* (2009) involved the converse situation: could an employer insist on the employee taking annual leave entitlement while on sick leave? Again, the CJEU construed the Directive in favour of employees by holding that it had to be the employee's choice. **6–051**

These decisions raised associated questions about how far into the future accrued annual leave could be carried and whether this applied to all annual leave, or only the four weeks guaranteed by the Working Time Directive. In *Neidel v Stadt Frankfurt am Main* (2012) the CJEU held that the Directive applies only to the minimum amount and it is up to Member States to decide whether they wish to extend it to all annual leave. In relation to the length of the carry-over, the CJEU accepted that some limitation is permissible in *KHS AC v Schulte* (2012). In that case it upheld a 15-month restriction, but in *Neidel v Stadt Frankfurt am Main* (2012) it held that nine months was too short, since the leave related to a 12-month reference period.

A final issue is about the level of pay during annual leave. In *British Airways plc v Williams* (2012) 2,750 pilots successfully challenged the company's policy of paying them only basic pay while they are on annual leave. While working, in addition to basic pay, they would receive various allowances for flying time and time away from base. In the light of the CJEU's advice that they should receive normal pay, but not necessarily payments to cover expenses which they would not incur while on leave, the Supreme Court remitted their claims to the employment tribunal to assess their precise entitlement. Since then, the EAT has held that where employers require employees to do overtime, these payments are to be taken into account in assessing "normal pay" for the purposes of the Directive-required four weeks' paid leave, even if the overtime is not guaranteed (*Bear Scotland Ltd v Fulton* (2015)). In response to this decision, the Deduction from Wages (Limitation) Regulations 2014 introduced a two-year time limit on how far back the worker can claim. The Northern Ireland Court of Appeal went further in *Patterson v Castlereagh BC* (2015), holding that even voluntary overtime could be taken into account, if it is part of a worker's normal pattern of work—a question of fact to be decided by the employment tribunal.

Sunday working

6–052   After several years of false starts at reform, the Sunday Trading Act 1994 came into force at the end of August 1994, permitting shops to do what many of them had already been doing for some time. In the debate over whether Sunday trading should be permitted, a major consideration was the position of shop workers and a concern to protect them from being compelled to work on Sundays.

Protection for shop workers is now provided by Pt IV of the Employment Rights Act 1996 and it is important to notice that it applies to all shop workers except for those employed to work only on Sundays. "Shop worker" is defined as anyone who is or may be required under their contract of employment to do shop work, which is work in or about a shop at a time when it is open to customers. It is as yet untested as to whether work "about a shop" is construed as including making deliveries to it.

Shop workers who were already employed on 25 August 1994 (when the Sunday Trading Act came into force) have the status of "protected shop workers". This means that they cannot be required to work on Sundays, that dismissal or selection for redundancy for such refusal is automatically unfair and they must not be subjected to any detriment short of dismissal either. Similar protection is afforded to "opted-out shop workers", who are any other shop workers except those employed exclusively for Sundays. To gain the protection, however, these workers must serve the employer with written notice of their wish to opt out of Sunday working, which only becomes effective three months later. While receiving protection from dismissal or other retaliatory action on grounds of having given the notice during that time, such an employee can be required to work on Sundays until the three months are up.

6–053   These provisions override anything in the contract of employment and protection is not dependent on any qualifying period of continuous employment. In other words, while there is nothing to stop an employer discriminating in recruitment and only taking those who express willingness to work on a Sunday, once in the job an employee will be entitled to change her mind. The employer must give new employees a statement of their rights to opt out within two months of their starting work. Both protected shop workers and opted-out shop workers will lose their protection if they opt in to Sunday working, by giving written notice to this effect and then agreeing with the employer actually to work on Sunday, although there is nothing to stop them opting out again at a later stage.

There is no requirement that workers should receive premium rates for Sunday working, although this was included in the Code of Practice agreed between USDAW and the Shopping Hours Reform Council (SHRC), representing major retailers. Equally, financial inducements to workers to persuade them to work Sundays do not constitute a detriment to those who do not. Nor is it an actionable detriment if the employer does not give additional weekday hours to an employee who opts out to make up for hours formerly worked on Sunday.

While the protection for shop workers looks complete, concerns have been expressed that individuals can actually find it quite difficult in practice to stand on their rights, especially as payment systems can be manipulated to render Sunday working an economic, if not a legal, necessity. Historically shop workers have been a low paid and fairly vulnerable group of workers and the protection given against compulsion to work on Sundays must be seen in the context of other developments which reduce their protection. These are first, the abolition of the wages council applicable to the industry in 1993, which used to set minimum hourly rates; and secondly the Deregulation and Contracting Out Act 1994, which removed all restrictions on weekday opening hours for shops.

Further Reading

- ❑ N. Busby and G. James (2011), *Families, Care-giving and Paid Work*, Edward Elgar Publishing
- ❑ E. Caracciolo di Torella and P. Foubert (2015), "Surrogacy, Pregnancy and Maternity Rights: A Missed Opportunity for a More Coherent Regime", 40(1) ELRev 52
- ❑ G. James (2008), *The Legal Regulation of Pregnancy and Parenting in the Labour Market*, Routledge-Cavendish
- ❑ G. Pitt and J. Fairhurst (1998), *Blackstones Guide to Working Time*, OUP
- ❑ S. Evans and R. Lewis (1987), "Anti-Union Discrimination: Practice, Law and Policy", 16 ILJ 88
- ❑ A. McColgan (2000), "Family Friendly Frolics? The Maternity and Parental Leave etc Regulations 1999", 29 ILJ 125
- ❑ DTI (2000), *Work and Parents: Competitiveness and Choice*, Cm 5005
- ❑ BIS (2013), *Modern Workplaces: Shared Parental Leave and Pay: Government Response*, BIS/13/1167

7. Pay

***

While the duty to pay remuneration is far from being the employer's only duty under the contract of employment, it is certainly the central element of the consideration given by the employer. In this chapter the most important statutory measures on the protection of wages will be considered: the right of men and women to equal pay; wages during sickness; deductions from wages; and protection for the lowest-paid workers.   **7–001**

Equal Pay

At one time the idea of a woman's rate for the job which was less than the man's   **7–002**
rate for exactly the same job was considered perfectly acceptable. No doubt this was to a large extent bound up with the stereotypical assumption that men work as breadwinners for the family, whereas the woman's wage was merely "pin-money"—a top-up for the extras rather than an essential component in the family budget. Today vestiges of such outdated ideas remain, although no one would seriously deny that anyone doing a job ought to have a right to the rate for that job regardless of personal characteristics irrelevant to its performance.

The right to equal pay—which actually means equal terms and conditions of employment, not just pay—was originally enacted by the Equal Pay Act 1970 (in force 29 December 1975). Relevant to its passage was not only ILO Convention No.100 (1951), which requires equal remuneration for work of equal value, but also that it was necessary for British entry to the European Union. Article 157 of the TFEU stipulates adherence to the principle of "equal pay for male and female workers for equal work". This was inserted in the original Treaty of Rome in 1957 not so much because of philosophical notions about the equality and dignity of human beings but because some of the original six EU members had equality laws and others did not. It was felt by those who did that businesses in their countries would be at a competitive disadvantage with those who could get away with using women as a cheap source of labour. Since then, however, the institutions of the European Union have shown a genuine commitment to furthering the cause of equality for women by imaginative extrapolation from the bare statement of the principle of equal pay for equal work.

One reason that it took over five years to bring the Equal Pay Act into force is that on its own it would have probably had a bad effect on women's job prospects. In the absence of any law prohibiting discrimination at the point of job entry, a law which required terms offered to be the same for men and women could simply have made it more difficult for women to get jobs. Thus the Equal Pay Act had to wait for the Sex Discrimination Act 1975 and both were brought into force together. It was always intended that there should be a lengthy period before the Equal Pay Act was brought into force so that employers would have plenty of notice of what was expected of them and would have time to clean up their act without the need for wholesale disruption of established pay and grading systems. Today both of these statutes have been repealed and the whole law on equality is to be found in the Equality Act (EqA) 2010 Pt 5, Ch.3 of which deals with equality of terms.

7–003   At the time that the Equal Pay Act came into force, the difference between the average hourly pay of men and the average hourly pay of women was 30 per cent. It is an indictment of the legislation that, 40 years later, the gap is still 19 per cent. The EqA 2010 mainly consolidates existing law on equal pay, but it does contain some novel provisions which aim to alleviate this problem.

Since equal pay for men and women is an aspect of sex discrimination it follows that this is an area where EU law has an enormous impact. As noted already, TFEU art.157 requires that "Each Member State shall ensure that the principle of equal pay for male and female workers for equal work or work of equal value is applied". This was amplified by the Equal Pay Directive 1975 (75/117/EEC), now subsumed within the Recast Equal Treatment Directive (2006/54/EC). As noted already, TFEU art.157 has been held to have direct effect (see above, para.2–005) and in *Jenkins v Kingsgate* (1981) the CJEU held that art.1 of the Equal Pay Directive (art.4 of the Recast Equal Treatment Directive) does not go further than art.157, but only deals with its application. Thus, in any action based on art.157 in a domestic court or tribunal it is possible to rely on the Directive to assist in interpreting the Treaty article.

Under the previous law there was a clear dichotomy between cases falling under the Sex Discrimination Act 1975 and those falling under the Equal Pay Act 1970. The Equal Pay Act dealt with sex discrimination in relation to terms of the contract only. Discrimination in relation to other employment matters, such as recruitment, promotion opportunities, dismissal and non-contractual benefits could only be brought under the Sex Discrimination Act. The 2007 consultation before the EqA 2010 proposed that this distinction between contractual and non-contractual matters should be preserved, reasoning that any apparent advantages in simplification of the law by bringing terms of the contract within general sex equality law would be outweighed by the uncertainty caused by abandoning well-established case-law and the need to develop new principles through lengthy litigation. In addition, there would be difficult issues about enforcement and remedies. The Government subsequently reported that 70 per cent of respondents supported this approach and the contractual/non-contractual distinction is preserved in EqA 2010. Thus, while non-contractual sex discrimination is dealt with in Pt 5 Ch.1 of the Act, alongside all the other protected characteristics, sex discrimination about terms is dealt with separately in Pt 5 Ch.3. The structure remains basically the same as under the Equal Pay Act, so existing case law continues to be relevant to its interpretation. Also relevant is the EHRC's Code of Practice on Equal Pay, published in 2011.

Under EqA 2010, women and men can make a claim when they are employed **7–004** on work that is equal to that of a comparator of the opposite sex (s.64(1)). Section 65 provides that work is equal in three situations: when it is like work to that of the comparator; when it is work rated as equivalent to that of the comparator; and when it is work of equal value to his. This is exactly the same as the old law on the point. However, EU case-law has established that unfavourable treatment on grounds of pregnancy and maternity must be treated as unlawful discrimination without the necessity of showing that a comparator has been treated more favourably. As a result, the EqA 2010 makes special provision for "maternity equality". We will first consider the equal work situations where comparison is needed under EqA 2010 s.65.

Like work

Work is defined as "like work" by the EqA s.65(2) if (a) "it is the same or broadly **7–005** similar" to that of the comparator, and (b) "such differences as there are between their work are not of practical importance in relation to the terms of their work". In comparing the two jobs, the frequency, nature and extent of any differences are to be considered (s.65(3)). This replicates the previous definition of like work in updated language. On the whole a fairly liberal approach has been taken to what is like work, the keynote being established in the first case to reach the EAT on its interpretation, *Capper Pass v Lawton* (1977). In that case, a woman who worked as the sole cook in the directors' dining room, preparing lunch for 10 to 20 people a day, claimed that she should get the same hourly rate as two male assistant chefs who worked under the head chef preparing 350 meals a day in six sittings, two for breakfast, lunch and tea in the works canteen. Although there were obvious differences between what they did, the EAT held that they were not of practical importance, and that this was like work.

Where it is alleged that there are differences between what the woman and the man do, the tribunal must consider whether in practice this is the case. In *Shields v E Coomes (Holdings) Ltd* (1978) male counter staff in a betting shop got a higher hourly rate than female counter staff. When challenged, the employer claimed that these shops were at risk of robbery and that a man was employed at each for security reasons. There had been no incidents at the claimant's shop in the three years that she had worked there, and the men received no training for their security role. The Court of Appeal held that the existence of the claimed difference consisting in the men's security role could not be established. It was based purely on stereotypical assumptions about sex rather than on any extra duties which the men had to perform in practice. In this case Bridge LJ recommended a two-stage approach to the question, deciding first whether the jobs are broadly similar, and if so, then moving on to consider whether any differences which do exist are of practical importance.

It is possible that the Court of Appeal's approach in *Shields v Coomes* (1978) is more stringent than the position in EU law. In *Angestelltenbetriebsrat der Wiener Gebietskrankenkasse v Wiener Gebietskrankenkasse* (1999) graduate psychologists and medical doctors were all engaged in providing psychotherapy services as employees of the Vienna Area Health Fund. The graduate psychologists, predominantly women, earned substantially less than the doctors and claimed that as they were doing the same work they should receive the same pay. The employer argued that this was not the same work because the psychologists and doctors had entirely different training and skills, and although ostensibly both groups were providing the same services, inevitably they drew on different knowledge and expertise derived from their separate disciplines. Furthermore, the doctors could be called on to perform other medical duties for which the psychologists would not be qualified (although there was no evidence as to whether this happened in practice or, if so, how often). The CJEU held that in these circumstances the two groups were not engaged in the same work, mainly because of their different training and qualifications, but the court also adverted to the fact that the doctors could be called on to do different things. The result in this specific case may seem supportable, although if it were true that psychotherapeutic services as performed by the two groups were qualitatively different it might be expected that there would be evidence of different kinds of patients being referred to each, or at least some assessment of which kind of practitioner would be most appropriate for each patient. If any such system was in place, no evidence of it appeared in the decision of the CJEU.

7–006   It is possible for different qualifications and skills to result in unequal terms for employees engaged on like work, but this is normally done by accepting that the work is the same but that there are other factors specific to the employees justifying the difference (cf. *Glasgow City Council v Marshall* (2000), see below, para.7–024). The fact that that approach was not taken in this case seems to allow some weakening of the equal pay principle. There is no reason why British equal pay law should not be more demanding than EU law and it is to be hoped that British courts will stand by the principle in *Shields v Coomes* that the possibility of extra duties for the man which he is not called upon to perform in practice does not prevent his work being like work with that of the woman.

In *Dugdale v Kraft Foods* (1977) the EAT held that differences in the time at which work was done did not justify a difference in basic rates of pay. Where employees work unsocial hours, the appropriate recompense is a premium for those shifts rather than a difference in basic terms. This should not be used as a device to pay men more: in *NCB v Sherwin* (1978) the EAT held that the employer had no defence to a like work claim where the premium paid was well above usual uplift for night work (which they said was about 20 per cent). It might be justifiable to pay a different basic rate for night work if the fact of doing it at night makes it different in nature, because there is no supervision and there are frequently emergencies to cope with (see *Thomas v NCB* (1987)).

As well as differences in the actual tasks performed, it was held by the EAT in *Eaton v Nuttall* (1977) that differences in responsibility could constitute differences of practical importance. In that case, both the man and the woman were employed as production schedulers, but she was dealing with much less valuable items, so a mistake on her part would have nothing like as serious consequences as a mistake by him. His higher pay was therefore justifiable.

Work rated as equivalent

On its own, the provision for equal pay when men and women are employed   **7–007** on like work would have little effect, for despite more than 40 years of anti-discrimination legislation there is still de facto segregation in a lot of the job market. Some work is still done predominantly by women and some by men. There are still very few male secretaries and female mechanics; in textiles men tend to have the (skilled) tailoring work and women the (less skilled) machinists' jobs. In manual work in particular it is not at all uncommon to have a plant which is all male or all female (although in the latter case, there will often be male managers).

Hence the need for a mechanism which permits a comparison to be made between totally different jobs. This is provided under EqA 2010 s.65(1)(b), which provides that jobs are to be considered equal work if they have been rated as equivalent. Section 65(4) explains that this means the jobs of the woman and the man should have been rated under a job evaluation study as being of equal value in terms of the demands made on the workers.

What is a job evaluation study? It is now defined in EqA 2010 s.80(5) as:

> "a study undertaken with a view to evaluating, in terms of the demands made on a person by reference to factors such as effort, skill and decision-making, the jobs to be done . . . by some or all of the workers in an undertaking or group of undertakings."

The idea is that common factors can be identified between entirely different jobs and their relative worth can be assessed by scoring each post against each of the chosen criteria. Note that this involves a comparison of what jobs demand: it is not an assessment of the performance of the people actually doing the jobs. Thus, it is first necessary to have an accurate description of what each job involves. Then criteria must be selected against which the demands of the job can be measured and scored. Job evaluation is not an exact science: there is room for value judgments at the point of deciding which factors should be taken into account (e.g. if physical environment is taken into account, people who work outside in all weathers will score more highly than those who work in comfortable offices), and in choosing how different criteria should be weighed against each other (e.g. should responsibility for decision-making be treated as more or less important than physical effort?) as well as in the actual scoring process. For these reasons, it is good practice for employers to consult with trade unions or other employee representatives over the design and implementation of any job evaluation study, although this is not a legal requirement.

In *Bromley v Quick* (1988) the Court of Appeal held that only analytical job evaluation studies of the kind described above would be acceptable for the purposes of equality law. The comparison must be done on an objective basis. While an employer has discretion as to which factors are rated, it is important that the criteria be objectively justifiable. In *Rummler v Dato-Druck* (1987) the CJEU held that this does not mean that factors which tend to favour one sex (such as strength) may not be taken into account: what is important is that the study should not give undue weight to such criteria, since that would amount to unjustifiable indirect sex discrimination.

7–008 In practice, a job evaluation study is a tool whereby an employer can demonstrate that differential pay between different jobs or grades is justified and it is thus mainly used by employers as a defence mechanism, because if a valid job evaluation study is in force, employees covered by it cannot bring equal value claims unless they can show that the job evaluation study was discriminatory or otherwise unreliable (EqA 2010 s.131(6)); equal value claims are discussed below, para.7–009).

If a job evaluation study has been carried out, but the employer does not accept the results, it cannot be used to found a claim for equal pay (*Arnold v Beecham Group Ltd* (1982)). However, if the job evaluation has been accepted, but not implemented (e.g. because it would be too expensive to do so), then it is possible for a woman to claim equal pay on the basis of it (*O'Brien v Sim-Chem Ltd* (1980)). In *Redcar and Cleveland BC v Bainbridge (No.1)* (2008) the Court of Appeal held that women who had been placed by a job evaluation study in a grade *higher* than men who actually earned more than them could nonetheless claim equal pay with them. This followed the CJEU's ruling to similar effect in relation to equal value claims in *Murphy v Bord Telecom Eireann* (1988): the Court of Appeal rejected the council's argument that that decision was confined to equal value claims only and thus avoided reaching what would have been a manifestly absurd and unjust decision. Later in the same litigation (*Redcar and Cleveland BC v Bainbridge (No.2)* (2008)) the question arose as to whether a woman rated equally with a man could claim equal pay retrospectively, on the basis that the jobs had not changed and if they were now rated equally, they should have been treated equally in the past. This argument was rejected by the Court of Appeal.

A woman who believes that the job evaluation itself is discriminatory may attack its validity, but a tribunal has no power to substitute its own judgment of relative worth and it cannot compel an employer to carry out a new study (*England v Bromley LBC* (1978)). This is the greatest limitation of s.65(1)(b), in that it is entirely dependent on the employer being willing to institute a job evaluation study. Thus it was not surprising to find that, in the lead up to the 1983 reforms, only a minority of employers ever did so, and that very few equal pay claims were brought under this head.

Work of equal value

In 1982 the EC Commission sued the United Kingdom before the CJEU on the grounds that it had not implemented the Equal Pay Directive 1975 properly. The essence of the complaint, which was upheld, was that there was no means by which an employee could initiate a claim where her work was dissimilar to a man's but where she thought it was as valuable (*Commission of the EC v United Kingdom* (1982)). Hence in 1983 the Equal Pay Act was amended to introduce a third situation where equal pay could be awarded: where a woman's work is held to be of equal value to that of a man.

7–009

This is now found in EqA 2010 s.65(1)(c), which provides that a woman is entitled to equal pay where her work is of equal value. Section 65(6) states that work is of equal value where it is equal in terms of the demands that it makes on her by reference to factors such as effort, skill and decision-making. In effect, this requires a mini-job evaluation study of the comparative value of the woman's job with that of the man or men who she has chosen to be compared with, usually undertaken by an independent expert (drawn from an Acas panel of suitably qualified people) appointed by the employment tribunal. However, there is an important qualification to the right to claim for work of equal value: a claim may only be brought under this heading if it is *not* "like work" within the meaning of s.65(2) nor work which has been rated equivalent to the comparator's within the meaning of s.65(4) (EqA 2010 s.65(6)(a)).

In *Pickstone v Freemans* (1987) female warehouse operatives got the same rate of pay as a male warehouse operative, but claimed that their work was of equal value to that of a male warehouse checker. The employer argued that as there was a man employed on the same work as them who got the same pay as them, this was a situation to which the "like work" paragraph applied and they could not avoid it by choosing to compare themselves with a different man. If this argument were correct, it would blow a huge hole in the equal value protection because it would mean that provided an employer always employed a "token man" on the same work as the women, they would never be able to claim under the equal value heading. However, on a literal reading of the section, this is what it seemed to mean.

The House of Lords declined to interpret the Equal Pay Act in a way which would be so subversive of what was intended when the equal value claim was introduced, stressing the importance of interpreting national law in accordance with EU law whenever possible. Thus they held that a woman would only be unable to claim equal value if it were held that the actual comparator she had chosen was employed on like work, or was employed on work rated as equivalent to hers. This is now reflected in the wording of EqA 2010 s.65(6)(a).

7–010

The prohibition on an equal value claim if the woman's job and the man's job have already been compared under a valid job evaluation scheme and rated differently was taken a step further in *Dibro Ltd v Hore* (1990). In that case the job evaluation study was only instituted after the equal value claims had been lodged, yet it was held that this barred the equal value claims. In other words, an employer can instigate a job evaluation study as a way of heading off an equal value claim. Another way of looking at it is to say that a woman (or her union) can persuade an employer to carry out a job evaluation study by a few strategic equal value applications.

Procedure for bringing an equal value claim

7–011 The procedure for bringing an equal value claim is complex. It is contained in EqA 2010 s.131 together with the Employment Tribunals (Equal Value) Rules of Procedure in Sch.3 to the Employment Tribunal (Constitution and Rules of Procedure) Regulations 2013 (SI 2013/1237) (the Equal Value Rules), supplementing the usual tribunal procedure rules contained in Sch.1 to those Regulations. These make provision for a two-stage or three-stage procedure.

As with other tribunal claims, the claimant's ET1 form is sent to Acas, who can try to help the parties reach a conciliated settlement. Assuming this does not happen, a Stage 1 hearing takes place. At this point, the tribunal has the options of determining the claim or appointing an independent expert to investigate and report on it. The Stage 1 hearing is something like a preliminary hearing in other tribunal proceedings (see above, para.1–022), and is essentially designed to establish whether there is any reason for the claim not to progress. One situation where the tribunal can conclude that it should be stopped at this point is where the jobs have already been rated differently under a valid job evaluation scheme (EqA 2010 s.131(6)). The employer may also at this initial stage raise the material factor defence: i.e. that there is a genuine material factor, other than a difference of sex, between the man and the woman which justifies any inequality in terms (discussed below, para.7–024). This may raise a dilemma for the employer because the material factor defence may only be used once. It used to be the case that the employer had two opportunities to raise the material factor defence: at this initial stage and, if failing there, by way of defence if the jobs were found to be prima facie of equal value. However, in an attempt to expedite these cases, the rules were changed in 1994 so as to remove the second opportunity. Thus the employer has only one chance to use this argument.

Originally, where an independent expert was appointed, the report was meant to be submitted within six weeks, but in practice this deadline was rarely met. This was the greatest contributory factor to the inordinate delays in equal value cases. Reforms were made in 1994 and 1996 in an attempt to speed things up by giving tribunals the power to be more proactive in managing the process. The 1996 reforms allowed the tribunal to determine the merits of an equal value claim without getting an independent expert's report, but the complexity of the issues in such cases means that this would hardly ever be appropriate. The limited success of the earlier reforms led to more changes in 2004, when the Equal Value Rules were introduced, which aim so far as possible to clarify the issues in writing before the substantive hearing and to ensure that strict time-limits apply to each stage. At the Stage 1 hearing the tribunal should now normally make orders requiring the parties to exchange details of the job descriptions of the claimant and her comparators, with a view to supplying the tribunal with a joint written statement 28 days before the next hearing indicating the matters on which they agree, the issues on which they disagree and a summary of their reasons for disagreement. The tribunal should also fix the date of the next hearing, taking account of the indicative timetable annexed to the Equal Value Rules (which aims to have the claim dealt with in 25 weeks if no independent expert is appointed and in 37 weeks if there is an independent expert).

Where an independent expert is appointed, the next hearing is a Stage 2   **7–012** hearing which, according to the indicative timetable, should take place within 10 weeks of the Stage 1 hearing. At the Stage 2 hearing, the tribunal's task is to make a decision on the factual matters which are still in dispute between the parties. The independent expert may be asked to assist in the fact-finding, but the tenor of the Regulations is to make it clear that determination of the facts is the role of the tribunal. The independent expert must then prepare her report on the basis of the facts as found or agreed—and no others (Equal Value Rules r.8(1)(b)). At the Stage 2 hearing the tribunal should also fix a date for the report to be submitted and for the substantive hearing.

The final stage is the substantive hearing, where the independent expert's report must be admitted in evidence unless the tribunal considers that it is not based on the facts established at the Stage 2 hearing. Formerly, it could also be excluded if it reached a perverse conclusion or was unsatisfactory for some other reason, giving the parties extensive opportunities to attack it. However, it is still possible for the parties to argue that the independent expert's conclusions should not be accepted. Parties frequently employ their own experts to this end, again increasing the cost, length and complexity of equal value proceedings. Thus the Equal Value Rules now restrict the use of other experts by stating that the permission of the tribunal will be necessary and that the tribunal may limit their evidence to particular issues (Equal Value Rules r.11). The independent expert's report will usually include a conclusion as to whether the jobs compared are of equal value, but it is clear from the decision of the Northern Ireland Court of Appeal in *Tennants Textile Colours v Todd* (1989) that accepting the expert's report into evidence does not imply acceptance of that conclusion. The tribunal could reach a different conclusion—although this is probably an unlikely contingency. Once all the evidence has been heard, the tribunal makes its decision in the usual way.

Clearly the former procedure for equal value claims was defective. It was enormously cumbersome and long-winded. The first case under the provisions, where the EOC gave assistance, took over four years from start to finish (*Hayward v Cammell Laird* (1988)). In 1993 the EOC requested the EU Commission to consider infringement proceedings on the grounds that the statutory procedure was so defective that it constituted a breach of art.2 of the Equal Treatment Directive. This was backed up by further evidence in 1994, but the EU Commission declined to take action. Before the EqA 2010 was passed the EHRC called for reforms to tribunal procedure, but these were not taken up in the legislation.

Conditions of claim

7–013   The EqA 2010 retains nearly the same conditions for claiming equality of contractual terms as existed under the Equal Pay Act 1970. Thus, the claimant must be employed, she can usually only compare herself with a real comparator, the comparator must be employed by the same employer, or an associated employer, and they must either be employed at the same establishment, or at establishments to which common terms and conditions apply. Each of these conditions needs to be considered in the light, not only of English law, but also of CJEU judgments on their scope.

Employment status

7–014   EqA 2010 s.80 states that equal contractual terms can be claimed by people employed under a contract of employment or apprenticeship or any other contract to do work personally, as well as by holders of personal or public offices. These concepts have been discussed already (see above, paras 2–008 and 3–036). However, in *Allonby v Accrington & Rossendale College* (2004) the CJEU held that TFEU art.157 applies more widely to "workers"—a term which they held had a specific meaning for this purpose. A worker is "a person who, for a certain period of time, performs services for and under the direction of another person, for which he receives remuneration", but does not include "independent providers of services who are not in a relationship of subordination with the person who receives the services". The claimant in the case was a part-time lecturer who had been directly employed by the college on a series of fixed-term contracts. To avoid the costs of having to give such part-timers comparable terms to full-timers, the college refused from 1996 to employ part-time staff directly, but instead acquired their services through an employment agency set up for that purpose, with which the part-timers had to register as self-employed workers. Among other things, this meant that they could no longer be members of the teachers' pension scheme because they were not employed by the college. The CJEU held that provided that a worker is in an "employment relationship" with the employer in the sense they had stipulated, the precise nature of their legal relationship did not matter. The clear implication of the decision is that an employment relationship could exist even though there was no contractual nexus between the parties at the particular time, as in this case. As claimants can rely on TFEU art.157 directly in national courts and tribunals, it is open to women to claim that they have an employment relationship in this sense for the purposes of an equal pay claim, even if they do not fall precisely within the terms of EqA 2010 s.80.

The comparator

7–015   An important difference between a claim for equality in contractual terms and a claim for discrimination in non-contractual pay matters is that for equal pay claims it has always been the case that an actual comparator has had to be identified by the claimant. It was not enough for a woman to adduce evidence that if a man were employed, he would enjoy better terms and conditions than her. This was criticised as inconsistent, because for all other discrimination claims, comparison with how a hypothetical relevantly similar comparator would be treated is allowed. If, for example, a claimant argued that he was paid less because of his race, he could compare himself with how a hypothetical person from a different racial group would be treated: so why should the position be different for discrimination on grounds of sex? Nonetheless, in *Macarthys v Smith* (1980) the CJEU held that this approach was in accordance with what is now TFEU art.157, and in the consultation before EqA 2010 the Government indicated that it had no intention of changing this, arguing among other things that the practical difficulties of making a hypothetical comparison would mean that it would have little benefit in practice.

In the event, EqA 2010 retains the requirement for a real comparator in most cases, but introduces one exception where a hypothetical comparison can be used. Under EqA 2010 s.71 if a claimant can establish that there is direct discrimination in relation to pay, but there is no comparator of the opposite sex, then a claim of sex discrimination will lie. The rather unrealistic scenario given as an example in the Explanatory Notes to the Act is where "An employer tells a female employee 'I would pay you more if you were a man'".

The wording of the equal pay legislation seems to suggest that the woman and the man must be employed at the same time. This was the issue in *Macarthys Ltd v Smith* (1980), where a woman taken on as the stockroom manager discovered that she was being paid considerably less than her male predecessor. The CJEU held that TFEU art. 157 did not require speculative comparisons with what a hypothetical male might have got for the same work, but also that the principle of equal pay should not be limited by a requirement of contemporaneity. Thus in the absence of any good reason for the difference, she was entitled to equal pay.

In *Diocese of Hallam v Connaughton* (1996) the EAT held that comparison **7–016** with a successor was also possible, but in *Walton Centre for Neurology and Neuro Surgery NHS Trust v Bewley* (2008) a later EAT held that *Connaughton* was decided *per incuriam* because the EAT relied on what it thought was part of the judgment of the CJEU in *Macarthys Ltd v Smith* whereas it was actually an argument put forward by the European Commission which was rejected by the Court. The Commission had argued that a claimant should be able to rely on how a hypothetical comparator would be treated, but the CJEU held that there had to be an actual comparator and a "concrete appraisal" of her work compared with his. In *Walton Centre v Bewley* the EAT went so far as to say that comparisons with a successor should not be allowed because that would be too speculative to constitute the requisite concrete appraisal. However, it is submitted that this is too sweeping and that it should be possible to compare with a successor in some circumstances. Alternatively, this could be one of the situations in which s.71 should permit a hypothetical comparison.

EqA 2010 s.79 retains the further requirement that the comparator be employed by the same employer as the claimant, or by an associated employer of her employer, and must be so employed either at the same establishment, or at a different establishment which shares common terms and conditions with hers. "Associated employers" are defined in the usual way as meaning companies within the same group. In *Glasgow City Council v Unison Claimants* (2014) the Court of Session adopted a purposive approach in deciding that limited liability partnerships to which the council had transferred some employees were capable of being an associated employer, even though they were not companies in the sense used in the Companies Acts.

It is clear that by limiting comparisons to people employed by the same employer (or associated employers) the EqA 2010 is more restrictive than TFEU art.157. In *Defrenne v Sabena* (1976) the CJEU said that the principle of equal pay could be relied on when unequal pay is received for equal work "which is carried out in the same establishment or service, whether private or public". This suggested that workers should be able to compare themselves with employees of another employer in the same establishment (e.g. where sub-contractors have workers on the same site as employees of the main contractor) or with employees of another employer in a different place, provided that they are engaged in the same service (e.g. teachers working for different education authorities at different schools).

7–017   The question was referred to the CJEU by the Court of Appeal in *Lawrence v Regent Office Care Ltd* (2002). The claimants were women employed in catering and cleaning by contractors who provided these services for North Yorkshire County Council. Most had previously done exactly the same work as direct employees of the council, but as a result of compulsory competitive tendering contracts for much of the catering and cleaning function were won by outside contractors to whom the employees were transferred by virtue of TUPE (see below, para.9–023). The council had rated their jobs as having equal value to those of male manual workers, but the contractors paid them at a lower rate. Thus, although the private contractors were separate legal entities and independent of the council, they argued that they were still employed in the same undertaking and should be allowed to compare themselves with the council's male manual workers. In its decision the CJEU expressly stated that comparisons under TFEU art.157 are not limited to men and women working for the same employer. However, it held that differences in terms had to be attributable to a single source—such as a collective agreement or a legislative provision. In this case, following the TUPE transfer, the women and their former colleagues were employed by two different employers with different arrangements for negotiating terms and conditions. Comparisons in this situation were not permissible.

The decision suggests that the Court of Session in Scotland must have been right in holding (in a decision made after the Advocate-General's opinion in *Lawrence v Regent Office Care*) that teachers employed by one education authority could compare with those employed by other education authorities (*South Ayrshire Council v Morton* (2002)). Since a single collective agreement applied to all the teachers, the Court of Session considered that comparisons could be made across the boundaries of the education authorities implementing it.

Unfortunately, while the decision of the CJEU in *Lawrence v Regent Office Care* (2002) established the principle of cross-employer comparisons, the result in the case itself pointed to a way for employers to avoid its effects. The claimant in *Allonby v Accrington & Rossendale College* (2004) wanted to compare herself with a former male colleague employed directly by the college. She was continuing to work there, but as a self-employed worker supplied by an employment agency and on considerably worse terms and conditions than before. The CJEU held that since her terms and conditions and those of the male teacher were not attributable to a single source, TFEU art.157 could not apply. Her terms were now negotiated with the agency, while his were negotiated with the college. The fact that the level of pay she received was influenced by the amount which the college paid the agency was not considered by the CJEU as sufficient to hold that there was a single source responsible for them both. Thus by the simple act of interposing the agency between the college and the part-time lecturers, the effects of the equal pay principle could be avoided.

The CJEU test has also been used in the opposite situation, to hold that the **7–018** fact that parties are employed by the same employer does not necessarily mean that there is a single source of terms and conditions so as to allow cross-establishment or cross-departmental comparisons. *Robertson v Department for the Environment, Food and Rural Affairs* (2005) involved male civil servants working for DEFRA seeking parity with female civil servants employed in the Department of Environment, Transport and the Regions. All were employed by the Crown and, until the 1990s, all had common terms and conditions. Between 1992 and 1995 powers to negotiate terms and conditions were progressively devolved to individual departments and government agencies. In these circumstances the Court of Appeal held that although legally there was a single source employer, the decisions in *Lawrence* and *Allonby* meant that the court should look for the location of the body responsible in practice for negotiating their terms and conditions—and that was at the level of the individual Departments. Similarly, in *Armstrong v Newcastle-upon-Tyne NHS Hospital Trust* (2006) the Court of Appeal held that there could be no comparison across the four different hospitals belonging to the Trust where some elements of terms and conditions had been harmonised but others were decided at the level of each hospital. In neither of these cases did the Court of Appeal consider that there was sufficient doubt to refer any questions to the CJEU.

Where there is a single employer, employees can compare themselves with any other employee at the same establishment, but cross-establishment comparison can take place only if there are "common terms and conditions" in the different establishments (EqA 2010 s.79(4)). The term "establishment" has never been defined in the legislation, nor significantly tested in the courts. In *City of Edinburgh Council v Wilkinson* (2010) the EAT held that a purposive construction of the term should be adopted and that it should not be limited to a single geographical location. Thus, for employees in council employment but working in different places, the starting point should be that all council workers were employed at a single establishment unless facts could be found to suggest that there were subsets which should be regarded as separate establishments. This view is now reflected in the EHRC Code of Practice on Equal Pay, para.53.

A liberal view of what constitutes common terms and conditions across different establishments was taken by the House of Lords in *Leverton v Clwyd CC* (1989). A nursery nurse claimed parity with clerical staff employed by the council at a different establishment. The council, which had hundreds of staff, had concluded a comprehensive collective agreement with NALGO covering all staff and recorded in "the Purple Book", containing six separate pay scales. The House of Lords construed this as a situation where there were common terms and conditions for all the employees covered, rejecting the argument that common terms and conditions had to be in some sense similar. In *British Coal v Smith* (1996), 1,286 women employed as canteen workers and cleaners by British Coal at 47 different establishments claimed equal pay with 150 male surface mineworkers and clerical staff employed at 14 different establishments. The employer argued that "common terms and conditions" did not apply across the establishments because, while national bargaining dealt with most matters, some terms and conditions were negotiated at area or even plant level. In particular, entitlement to concessionary coal was dealt with at area level, and incentive bonuses at plant level, meaning that surface mineworkers and clerical staff at different pits did not have exactly the same terms and conditions. Despite these differences the House of Lords held that there were common terms and conditions for the purposes of equal pay legislation. It was enough if their terms and conditions were broadly similar: they did not have to be exactly the same.

7–019   This liberal approach was continued by the Supreme Court in the most recent case on the subject, *Dumfries and Galloway Council v North* (2013), where female classroom assistants and nursery nurses working in schools sought to compare themselves with men employed in a variety of manual jobs such as road workers and refuse collectors working in very different locations. Different collective agreements applied to the two groups. The Supreme Court held nonetheless that they could be regarded as employed on common terms and conditions if the men would be likely to be employed on broadly comparable terms if they worked at the same establishment as the women—however unlikely such a contingency might be in practice.

Subject to the conditions discussed above, the claimant may choose whoever she wants to be compared with and may choose more than one comparator. However, she must be realistic. In *Leverton v Clwyd CC* the claimant identified 11 male comparators doing clerical work, some of whom were on Scale 3 and some on Scale 4. Could she really be claiming that her work was of equal value with both of these when it was accepted that they were not of equal value with each other? The House of Lords warned that in such circumstances the employee risks having her claim, or at least part of it, not treated seriously.

Another limitation on the right to choose a comparator is that the claimant cannot try to enhance the chances of showing that a payment system has an adverse impact on women by limiting her choice of comparator artificially, a point made by the Court of Appeal in *Cheshire & Wirral Partnership NHS Trust v Abbott* (2006). This was an equal value claim by female domestic staff employed in the Trust's hospitals, because domestic staff (predominantly female) were excluded from a bonus scheme which was available to hospital porters, an exclusively male group. They argued that the bonus scheme therefore had an adverse impact on women which the employer could not justify. The Court of Appeal accepted the employer's argument that the comparator group should be extended to include catering workers as well as porters, since the catering workers also did work of equal value and also had access to the bonus scheme. The claimants did not want the catering workers in the comparison because they were also a predominantly female group, but the Court of Appeal considered that it was for the court to decide on the composition of the comparator group in an indirect discrimination claim and the group could not be arbitrarily limited by the claimants' choice.

Pay secrecy

A final problem that a woman may encounter in identifying a suitable compara- **7–020** tor is that if her male colleagues do not choose to reveal details of their terms and conditions, she has no right to obtain such information. Secrecy about pay is quite common and a surprising number of employers actually prohibit employees from disclosing their details of their own pay to their colleagues. Banning such secrecy clauses was one of the key reforms which the EHRC called for in the run-up to the EqA 2010. However, the actual reform contained in EqA 2010 s.77 does not go quite so far. Instead, it provides that a contract term purporting to prevent a worker from disclosing information about her contract terms, or seeking such information from a colleague, is unenforceable, in so far as the disclosure is made or sought as a "relevant pay disclosure". A relevant pay disclosure is defined as a disclosure made or sought for the purpose of finding out whether there is a connection between pay and having or not having a particular protected characteristic. An employee who makes or seeks a relevant pay disclosure will receive protection from victimisation on that account.

There are a number of problems with this. First, the fact that secrecy terms are unenforceable rather than unlawful means that employers can still put them in contracts and rely on the chilling effect that they are likely to have on employees' communications, and even the fact that workers may well not realise that they are unenforceable. Secondly, it would appear from the terms of s.77 that general discussions about pay are not protected, if they are not for the specific purpose of seeing whether there is unlawful discrimination, a view reinforced by the example given in the EHRC Code of Practice at para.107. Thirdly, it is unclear whether discussions about discretionary payments, such as bonuses or performance payments which are not contractual, would be protected.

It seems, therefore, that voluntary disclosure of pay information may not change significantly despite the new provision. Another new provision, EqA 2010 s.78, would have enabled regulations to be made requiring employers to publish relevant information about the gender pay gap in their workforce, but the Coalition Government decided against bringing this into force.

Apart from this, a trade union may help in getting general information about **7–021** terms, although not about specific individuals (see above, para.5–023). Of course, once a claim has been lodged with a tribunal it is possible to request further and better particulars and disclosure of documents, but at that stage it would be a bit late for a claimant to discover that she had selected the wrong man. In 2003 an equal pay questionnaire procedure was introduced, along the same lines as those which had been in use for sex and race discrimination claims since the 1970s. This fell victim to the Coalition Government's policy of removing employment protection not mandated by EU law, and the questionnaire procedure was abolished by the Enterprise and Regulatory Reform Act 2013.

Less favourable terms

7–022   Having established that her work is the same as or of equal value to that of an appropriate comparator of the opposite sex, a claimant is in a position to invoke the sex equality clause. This is explained in EqA 2010 s.66(2) as being a provision which has the effect of modifying the contract so that any less favourable term is made equal and any term in the man's contract which is missing from the woman's is inserted.

The reference to "less favourable" terms again brings in a notion of comparison which provides an opportunity for value judgments with the potential to limit the ambit of the equality principle (see above, para.2–035). In *Stadt Lengerich v Helmig* (1995) overtime rates for all workers were only paid on completion of the normal hours for full-time workers. Part-time workers claimed that this was less favourable treatment because, unlike full-time staff, they were not paid overtime for hours in excess of their contracted hours. However, the CJEU held that there was no difference in the treatment of full-time and part-time workers here, as both groups had to work the same number of hours in order to get overtime rates.

Discrimination has been defined by the CJEU on a number of occasions as treating like cases differently or in treating unlike cases in the same way (e.g. *Gillespie v Northern Health and Social Services Board* (1996)). In effect, in this case the claimants were arguing that they were the same in relevant respects to the full-timers, but treated in a different manner. The CJEU, however, denied that this was different treatment by choosing to treat as relevant only the fact that they received the same pay for the same number of hours as full-timers and choosing to treat contracted hours as not relevant. Another way of looking at the facts would have been to say that these were unlike cases (part-timers and full-timers) being treated the same, in that all had to work more than 38 hours a week to get overtime rates.

7–023   If prima facie discrimination had been established in *Stadt Lengerich v Helmig* (1995) it would have been indirect sex discrimination rather than direct, on the grounds that most part-timers are women. Thus it would have been open to the employer to make out the defence of justification, which would probably have succeeded on these facts. The significance of the CJEU's holding that the part-timers' terms were not less favourable is that this line of inquiry is closed off. The same approach was taken by the House of Lords in *Barry v Midland Bank* (1999), another striking example of the scope for judicial choice inherent in the concept of comparison. The claimant had worked full-time for the bank for 11 years but returned to work part-time after maternity leave, taking voluntary redundancy two years after that. The bank's severance pay scheme was based purely on final salary and number of years' service, so her severance payment thus took no account of the fact that she had been full-time during most of her time with the bank. She claimed that the scheme had an adverse impact on part-timers who had previously worked full-time—nearly all of whom were women.

The claimant's complaint in this case was that the employer was treating different groups (full-timers and part-timers) in the same way although they were relevantly different. The majority of the House of Lords held that the purposes of the scheme had to be taken into account in deciding whether or not the part-timers were in a relevantly different situation from the full-timers. These were twofold: compensating employees for loss of income and rewarding past service. The House of Lords held that the part-timers and full-timers were the same in these respects: their severance payments were based on actual income, which is what they were losing, and their past years of service. Since the claimant had not got over the first hurdle of showing prima facie discrimination, the question of justification did not arise. Once again, the appropriate field of inquiry was closed off.

It is hard to square these two cases with *Elsner-Lakeburg v Land Nordrhein Westfalen* (2005). Under German law, teachers had to work overtime if required, but only got paid for it if they worked at least three additional hours in a month. Note that, unlike *Stadt Lengerich v Helmig*, both part-time and full-time teachers were treated as doing overtime as soon as they had completed their contractual hours. Nevertheless, a part-time teacher complained that the three-hour threshold was more onerous for her than for a full-time teacher because it was equivalent to 5 per cent more than her usual hours, while it was only 3 per cent more of a full-timer's hours: and the CJEU agreed! So, in this case, the CJEU accepted that paying overtime under the same conditions to full-time and part-time workers was actually differential treatment of the two groups. If this affected considerably more women than men (i.e. if more women than men worked part-time) then it was contrary to TFEU art.157 unless objectively justified.

In effect, these cases demonstrate that decisions about what constitutes the same or different treatment are far from being wholly neutral and objective.

The "material factor" defence

The employer will have a defence if it can show that the difference between the terms of the claimant and her comparator is due to a material factor which does not itself discriminate directly or indirectly on grounds of sex (EqA 2010 s.69). This largely reproduces the effect of the previous law, but with clearer wording. The defence used to be known as the "genuine material factor" defence, but "genuine" was dropped on the basis that it was unnecessary: if the factor was not genuine, it would not be taken into account in any case.

What sorts of factors will justify differences of pay for work which is the same or of equal value? The central situation which this is aimed at is a difference in the

7–024

personal equation. Thus differences in length of service, levels of performance, merit and qualifications are capable of being material factors which will justify differences in terms and conditions. In *Clay Cross v Fletcher* (1978) the Court of Appeal indicated that only matters relevant to the personal characteristics of the workers being compared could count as a material difference, ruling out external factors such as skills shortages which might result in higher pay being offered. However, the House of Lords disagreed and made it clear in *Rainey v Greater Glasgow Health Board* (1987) that material factors are not confined to personal differences but could involve external factors. While some of the more common factors are discussed below, it should be noted that no exhaustive list can be given. It must, of course, still be genuine (in the sense of not being "a sham or a pretence" as the House of Lords put it in *Strathclyde Regional Council v Wallace* (1998)), it must be material, and it must not discriminate directly or indirectly on grounds of sex.

The requirement of materiality has led to debate as to whether or not the reason has to be objectively justified in all cases. In *Jenkins v Kingsgate* (1981) the CJEU held that a factor other than sex which predominantly affected women (in that case, part-time working) would be contrary to TFEU art.157 unless its use could be justified. This was strengthened in *Bilka-Kaufhaus v Weber von Hartz* (1986) (another case involving part-timers) where the CJEU held that the employer would have to show that any factors having a disparate impact on men and women "correspond to a real need on the part of the undertaking, are appropriate with a view to achieving the objectives pursued and are necessary to that end". The issue was whether this requirement of objective justification applied whenever the material factor defence was raised, or only where the factor was tainted with sex discrimination, in that it had a disproportionate effect on women. For example, in *Yorkshire Blood Transfusion Service v Plaskitt* (1994) the factor relied on by the employer was that it had made a mistake in putting the man on a higher grade. In terms of the *Bilka* test, this would clearly not constitute objective justification. However, it was a genuine reason, and it was not related to sex. In those circumstances, the EAT held that the employer had established the defence, pointing out that the equal pay legislation is not about achieving fair wages but about eliminating sex discrimination (see also *Tyldesley v TML Plastics* (1996)). This approach was endorsed by the House of Lords in *Strathclyde Regional Council v Wallace* (1998) and *Glasgow City Council v Marshall* (2000). Provided that the employer's reason is genuine, and material in the sense of being "significant and relevant" (per Lord Keith in *Rainey v Greater Glasgow Health Board* (1987)), the employer will not have to prove further that it is a good reason, from the point of view of a reasonable observer, unless it is a factor which affects women disproportionately.

7–025   Some commentators have argued that these decisions of the House of Lords were superseded by the CJEU's decision in *Brunnhofer v Bank der Österreichischen Postparkasse AG* (2001), which they read as indicating a need for objective justification of all material factors, regardless of whether they have an adverse impact on one sex. This argument succeeded in the EAT in *Sharp v Caledonia Group Services Ltd* (2006), but subsequently, in *Armstrong v Newcastle-upon-Tyne NHS Hospital Trust* (2006), the Court of Appeal reiterated the orthodox view as laid down in *Glasgow City Council v Marshall* (2000). The orthodox position is impliedly supported by the EHRC Code of Practice on Equal Pay.

There is a danger in requiring only that the employer's reason is genuine without also requiring that it should be objectively justified, in that it could permit prejudice to creep in by the back door. For example, in *Tyldesley v TML Plastics* (1996) the employer was paying a newly appointed man one-third more than a woman doing the same job, because he was perceived to have more knowledge and experience of total quality management systems. The tribunal considered that there was no objective evidence supporting this perception. Is it unduly sceptical to fear that unfounded but genuine perceptions about relative worth of employees will usually work to the benefit of men?

Market forces

The CJEU formulation in *Bilka* was adopted by the House of Lords in considering   7–026
whether market forces could count as a material factor justifying a difference in pay in *Rainey v Greater Glasgow Health Board* (1987). In the earlier case, *Clay Cross v Fletcher* (1978), a male clerk was taken on at a higher salary than the two female clerks because he was already earning that much in his present job. The fact that he would not come for less was rejected by the Court of Appeal as a material difference. The court accepted the argument that market forces tend to undervalue work done by women—this was a prime reason for unequal pay.

This approach was overruled by the House of Lords in *Rainey*. In that case female prosthetists working in the National Health Service claimed equal pay with male prosthetists who had been recruited from the private sector at a higher rate of pay, which reflected the fact that they already earned rather more than Health Service rates. There was no plan to phase out these differential rates over time. Rejecting the *Clay Cross* dictum that only the personal equation rather than extrinsic forces could constitute a material factor, the House of Lords held that their different routes of entry to the employment were attributable to sound, objectively justified reasons and that the difference in pay was therefore justified.

The extent of the market forces defence received welcome clarification in the important decision of the CJEU in *Enderby v Frenchay HA* (1993). In that case, senior speech therapists employed by the health authority claimed that their work was of equal value with that of male principal pharmacists and male clinical psychologists, whose salaries exceeded theirs by up to 60 per cent. The employees pointed out that speech therapists were predominantly female whereas the comparator professions were predominantly male. This, they alleged, was the real reason that speech therapists were paid less. One of the employer's justifications for the difference in pay with the pharmacists was that an overall shortage of applicants for those jobs meant that higher starting salaries had to be offered. It was accepted, however, that this would not account for the whole of the difference. While accepting that market forces could constitute a material factor, the CJEU indicated that the defence would only hold good for such part of the difference as could be attributed to that reason. Thus, if a proportion of the difference could not be accounted for in this way, there would be no objective justification in respect of it.

7–027   Both *Rainey* and *Enderby* proceeded on the basis that the condition for higher pay (route of entry to the profession in *Rainey*, *de facto* sex segregation in *Enderby*) had an adverse impact on women and therefore indirectly discriminated on grounds of sex. Thus the factor put forward as a defence had to be objectively justifiable. However, in *Ratcliffe v North Yorkshire CC* (1995) the House of Lords went a step further and upheld an employment tribunal's finding that, in that case, market forces were directly discriminatory. The work of the claimant catering assistants, all women, had been rated as equivalent to that of male manual workers employed by the Council in 1987, so they got equal pay. But when compulsory competitive tendering for certain services was introduced, the Council's own direct service organisation lost one of its contracts because it was undercut by a private company which paid its all-female workforce less than they did. To be sure of getting the remaining contracts, the Council made the women redundant and then took them back on lower rates of pay. The employment tribunal held that the women's pay had been reduced because of market forces, which was a material factor; however, they considered that it was a material factor based on sex. Crucially, the tribunal found as a fact that catering work was low-paid precisely because it was done almost exclusively by women, and the lack of available part-time work where they lived meant that women would accept work on poor terms. This was ultimately upheld by the House of Lords.

Financial constraints

7–028   Market forces can work in the opposite direction to depress pay: limited budgets may lead to employers paying less than the recognised rate for the job. In *Strathclyde Regional Council v Wallace* (1998) the claimants were women teachers who were "acting up" as principal teachers, but not being promoted or paid at the principal's rate. They claimed parity with male principal teachers, who were admittedly doing like work. The tribunal found that the reason for the difference was financial constraints on the council, coupled with its particular promotion rules. The House of Lords held that this was a material factor and, as it was not based on sex, they were not entitled to equal pay. The difference between this and cases like *Rainey* or *Enderby* is that here there was no evidence of the factor affecting women more than men. In fact, of 134 unpromoted teachers who claimed to be acting as principals, 81 were men and 53 were women. A gloss is put on this by *Benveniste v University of Southampton* (1989), where it was found that financial constraints which had led to a woman lecturer being taken on at a lower rate than normal in 1981 had eased a year later (surely the only university in the country where this was the case!). It was held that the university could no longer use the financial situation as a defence to her claim for equal pay.

If financial or budgetary constraints lead to the implementation of employment policies which have a disproportionate impact on one sex, however, it is clear that they will infringe the equal pay principle unless they can be objectively justified (*Steinicke v Bundesanstalt fur Arbeit* (2003); *Schönheit v Stadt Frankfurt am Main* (2004)).

Collective bargaining

In *Enderby v Frenchay HA* (1993), the main argument for the employer was that, **7–029** as the pay structures in each case resulted from free collective bargaining which was not affected by sex discrimination, this constituted sufficient justification (a material factor) for the difference. The CJEU held that this was not an acceptable reason on its own for unequal pay where the result of the process adversely affected one sex. Separate collective bargaining could explain the differences, but would not on its own justify them. Thus in *British Coal Corporation v Smith* (1996) separate bargaining had led to jobs done by male ancillary workers (such as gardeners) being assimilated to the better-paid "surface mineworker" grade, whereas this had not happened with ancillary work done by women (such as catering). Such an adverse impact required further justification beyond simply pointing to separate bargaining structures, and in the absence of any explanation the House of Lords held that the women were entitled to equal pay (cf. also *British Airways plc v Grundy (No.2)* (2008)).

It is because of separate collective bargaining giving rise to systemic sex discrimination in pay structures that the recent major public sector pay litigation has arisen, as *Redcar and Cleveland BC v Bainbridge (No.2)* (2008) illustrates. In local government, prior to 1997, three national collective agreements covered different groups of workers. The White Book covered manual workers, the Purple Book covered administrative, professional, technical and clerical (APT&C) staff and the Red Book covered skilled craft workers. In each case, the national agreement was supplemented by collectively bargained local agreements. One of the issues in the case was whether women manual workers (mainly catering workers and care workers) covered by the White Book could claim equal pay with male manual workers (street sweepers and gardeners) in the same or a lower grade where they received the same basic pay, but the male workers got productivity bonuses or various allowances (attendance allowances, wet weather allowances) which the female workers did not get. It was held that these bonuses and allowances did not serve any real purpose and were a disguised way of paying these categories of workers (mainly men) more—and the fact that it had come about through collective bargaining did not prevent it being indirect sex discrimination.

In 1997, the relevant trade unions and local government employers entered a new "single status" collective agreement, known as the Green Book, which was to be applicable to all local government employees. This entailed carrying out local job evaluation schemes so that all existing employees (about 1.4 million nationally) could be assimilated into the single pay structure—a massive undertaking, fraught with difficulty because inevitably different groups of workers would be winners and losers. Negotiating the job evaluation schemes and applying them took several years: in 2003 a deadline of 2007 was imposed for full implementation—ten years after the original agreement on the Green Book, it will be noted—and even then the majority of local councils missed the deadline. Frustrated at the lack of progress, many women instituted equal pay claims and this was greatly encouraged by various firms of "no-win, no-fee" solicitors, who took on hundreds of cases against local councils, initially in the North East of England. This led to the numbers of equal pay cases lodged with tribunals increasing at a staggering rate: whereas there were 4,400 equal pay claims in 2003/04, this doubled to more than 8,000 in 2004/05, doubled again to over 17,000 in 2005/06 and shot up to over 44,000 in 2006/07 and nearly 63,000 in 2007/08! While the figures have reduced in subsequent years, with 23,600 in 2012/13, this is still an enormous number of cases. The increase is almost entirely accounted for by multiple claims in the public sector—not just local government, but also the Health Service, where a similar move to a single pay structure (a project called "Agenda for Change") has been ongoing since 2004.

7–030   *British Coal Corporation v Smith* (1996) and *Redcar and Cleveland BC v Bainbridge (No.2)* (2008), like *Enderby*, involved disadvantaged groups composed almost exclusively of women; however, in *British Road Services v Loughran* (1997) the Northern Ireland Court of Appeal held that this was not an essential requirement. The relevance of the proportion of women in the lower-paid work is that it identifies it as work being done predominantly by women and therefore at risk of being rated lower on that account. Thus the number of women in the bargaining unit is certainly pertinent, in that it indicates whether or not there is adverse impact which requires objective justification. The Court of Appeal went further in *Bailey v Home Office* (2005), holding that objective justification was required where the advantaged group was predominantly male and the disadvantaged group contained a significant number of women, even if they did not constitute a majority. That case concerned claims by 2,000 administrative staff in the Prison Service for parity with prison officers where their posts had been rated equivalent under the Prison Service Job Evaluation Scheme. The Court of Appeal also expressly stated that it is not necessary to identify a condition or practice which causes the adverse impact on one sex if the statistical evidence indicates that there is a sufficient pay disparity.

Where separate collective bargaining structures, untainted by discrimination, result in unequal pay for different groups of workers but do not indicate an adverse impact on women, the material factor defence can be relied on (*Glasgow City Council v Marshall* (2000)).

Performance-related pay and productivity bonuses

7–031   Giving additional "merit" payments for some staff over and above what others receive for the same job because of particularly good performance has long been a standard management practice. In the 1980s its newer incarnation, performance-related pay, was seen by some management gurus, and especially by the then government, as the prime way of producing keen, highly motivated workers. In general, the idea is that targets are set for employees and their final salary in any particular year will contain a retrospective element reflecting how far they do or do not meet their targets. It would be cynical to suggest that for those in the lower echelons of management this policy worked to depress basic

salary levels while for higher management, especially in newly privatised industries, it was a green light for massive hikes in pay levels.

The danger with any kind of merit payment or performance-related pay is
that the judgments about who is deserving may be very subjective; if subjective,
there is every chance that prejudice and discrimination may seep in, even unconsciously. The point was well taken by the CJEU in the *Danfoss* case (*Handels-og
Kontorfunktionaerernes Forbund i Danmark v Dansk Arbejdsgiverforening (acting
for Danfoss)* (1991)), where minimum rates of pay were set for each grade, but
differentials were permitted according to merit. It was alleged that the system
resulted in women generally being at the bottom of each grade and earning less
on average than the men. The CJEU held that, given the resulting disparity in
pay and given that the criteria on which decisions were made were "lacking in
transparency" (in that the employees did not know what the criteria were and
how they were implemented) there was a potential breach of the Equal Pay
Directive. The burden was therefore on the employer to prove that the differences in pay were not discriminatory. Specifically considering criteria which have
a discriminatory impact, the CJEU held that reference to length of service was
acceptable (although see below, para.7–033), but that reference to flexibility (in
hours and place of work) or training must be justified by the employer showing
their importance in relation to the work to be done, because they would tend
to screen out women. This emphasis on openness requires employers operating
merit payment schemes to ensure that clear criteria are adopted and applied
objectively; to consider whether any criteria have a discriminatory impact, and
if so, whether they are justifiable on objective grounds, and to monitor the outcomes in relation to performance-related pay and other discretionary or merit
pay systems.

The same considerations apply in relation to piecework. In *Specialarbejder-
forbundet i Danmark v Dansk Industri acting for Royal Copenhagen* (the *Royal
Copenhagen* case) the CJEU held that TFEU art.157 applied to piecework systems
so that if a particular system had the consequence that the average piecework earnings of women (here employed as blue pattern painters on Royal
Copenhagen china) were lower than the average earnings of men (employed as
automatic machine operators) doing work of equal value, the difference would
require justification by the employer. One difficulty here is that on a piecework
system, differences in pay may well result purely from different work rates: this
is, of course, the difference which the payment system is trying to take account
of. However, provided that there are sufficiently large groups of workers to
compare (so as to iron out any fortuitous or short-term differences) and all are
included in establishing the average rate, the CJEU considered that appropriate
comparisons could be made.

It goes without saying that additional payments based on performance must **7–032**
be genuine. This was one of the issues in *Redcar and Cleveland BC v Bainbridge
(No.1)* (2008): the female local government manual workers complained that
refuse collectors (mainly male) got productivity bonuses, while there was no
productivity bonus scheme applicable to their jobs. The EAT held that having
a productivity bonus scheme for a predominantly male job while there was no

equivalent scheme for a predominantly female job was not a breach of the equal pay provisions, as long as the evidence showed that the reason for this was the nature of the job and whether or not it lent itself to such a scheme. However, the evidence showed that, while it might have done in the past, the productivity bonus scheme for refuse collectors had long since ceased to have the purpose or result of improving productivity, and had just become an addition to pay. It could not therefore be relied upon as a material factor (cf. also *Hartlepool BC v Dolphin* (2009) and *Sunderland City Council v Brennan* (2012)).

Length of service

7–033   In *Danfoss* (1989) the CJEU specifically stated that length of service was an acceptable criterion for different pay, even if it had an adverse impact on women. The issue was raised again for a more detailed exploration in the light of developing CJEU jurisprudence in *Cadman v Health and Safety Executive* (2006). The claimant was an inspector of five years' standing who claimed equal pay with four male colleagues in the same grade who earned between £4,000 and £9,000 a year more than her. This was because of their longer service (some of it acquired in more junior posts) which led to them being placed on higher points on an incremental pay scale. The CJEU reaffirmed that length of service was a valid criterion for unequal pay, on the grounds that it served the legitimate objective of rewarding experience which enabled the worker to perform his duties better. They thus opened the door a chink by accepting that the employer would have to justify use of this criterion if the worker provided evidence raising serious doubts as to whether length of service did indeed serve this objective in relation to a particular post.

Cadman was remitted to an employment tribunal in the light of this guidance, but was then stayed while another case against the Health and Safety Executive dealing with the same point was heard by the Court of Appeal. The issue in *Wilson v HSE* (2010) was very similar: a female Grade 3 inspector sought equal pay with three male Grade 3 inspectors who were higher on the 10-year seniority ladder than her. Evidence was accepted by the employment tribunal that five years was the period needed for inspectors to reach their optimum level. In these circumstances, applying *Cadman* the Court of Appeal held that the claimant had adduced sufficient evidence to show that the 10-year incremental period was longer than could be justified and to that extent could not be relied on as a material factor justifying unequal pay.

In this connection, it is worth remembering that EqA 2010 Sch.9, para.10 exempts incremental scales of not more than five years from scrutiny on grounds of age discrimination, and allows even longer periods of service to constitute a valid criterion for unequal terms provided that the employer can show that this "fulfils a business need" (see above, para.2–046).

Red-circling and pay protection

7–034   One of the first kinds of material factor to be accepted as valid was the practice of red-circling, where an employee who was once on a higher-rated job is moved to a lower-rated job, often because of ill health, or because the job has been regraded, but continues to have his pay protected at the higher rate. Workers of the opposite sex in the lower-rated job cannot claim equal pay: the fact that he (as it usually is) has been red-circled on the payroll for special protection can constitute a material factor making a difference between their cases.

This is subject to the important qualification that if the reason for the higher pay is past discrimination, the defence will not apply. In *Snoxell v Vauxhall Motors* (1977) the company had had separate pay scales for men and women doing the same job before the Equal Pay Act. The scales were integrated before the Act came into force and the woman's rate was fixed as the rate for the job. Thereafter all new men doing the job got the same as the women, but the men who had previously been paid on the higher rate were red-circled. As their higher rate was attributable to sex discrimination, it was held that the defence was not available and the women were entitled to equal pay. Another relevant factor was that the company had no plans to phase out the differential in the future, which may also be relevant where regrading is the reason for red-circling. In *Home Office v Bailey* (2005), another case arising from the Prison Service litigation, male prison officers employed before 1987 were awarded enhanced amounts of pensionable service, benefits which were not extended to predom-inantly female administrative staff, or to prison officers employed after that date (when the enhancement was abolished). The EAT held that red-circling the prison officers may have been justified in 1987 but was not justified 12 years later without further evidence as to why this should continue to be the case.

Pay protection arrangements have been a central issue in the public sector pay litigation discussed above (para.7–029). In *Redcar and Cleveland BC v Bainbridge (No.2)* (2008), the appellant council finally implemented the Green Book, eradi-cating previous inequality on grounds of sex, in 2004, which resulted in levelling down many of the male jobs rather than levelling up the female jobs. However, they gave pay protection arrangements to the men who would be losing out, which cushioned their loss by phasing it over three or four years. The Court of Appeal held that this perpetuated indirect sex discrimination against the women workers who had established that their work was of equal value with these men, and that there was no objective justification for this. In consequence, the women were entitled to equivalent amounts of pay.

If, however, the pay protection arrangements do not perpetuate past dis-   **7–035**
crimination, they can constitute a valid material difference even if they are not going to be phased out and the disparity becomes greater as time passes (*Haq v Audit Commission* (2013)).

Part-time working

Is the fact that the woman is part-time and the man full-time a relevant material   **7–036**
factor? As about 90 per cent of all part-time workers are women, worse terms for part-timers have a tendency to disadvantage women disproportionately. In *Jenkins v Kingsgate* (1981) the CJEU held that worse terms for part-time workers were capable of infringing TFEU art.157 because of the disproportionate effect on women, and that objective economic reasons were required to justify the dif-ference. The CJEU put the point even more strongly in *Bilka-Kaufhaus v Weber*

von Hartz (1987). It was clear from these cases that an employer who, without objective justification, treated part-timers less favourably than full-timers would usually be at risk of an indirect discrimination claim under the equal pay legislation interpreted in accordance with EU law, although it remained the case that the adverse impact on women had to be proved: it could not simply be assumed (cf. *Staffs CC v Black* (1995): see now the Part-time Workers (Prevention of Less Favourable Treatment) Regulations 2000, above, para.3–023).

Building on this the CJEU then moved to hold that state policies discriminating against part-time workers could also be in breach of EC law, holding in *Rinner-Kühn v FWW Spezial-Gebäudereinigung GmbH* (1989) that disqualifying German part-time workers from sickness benefits was discriminatory and in *Kowalska v Freie und Hansestadt Hamburg* (1990), that a redundancy scheme which excluded part-timers was unlawful: they should have received payments on a pro rata basis.

These decisions prompted the EOC to attack the rules requiring part-timers who worked between eight and 16 hours a week to have worked for more than five years before they qualified for employment protection rights. That claim was ultimately upheld by the House of Lords in *R v Secretary of State for Employment ex p EOC* (1994), as discussed in Ch.3 (see above, para.3–022).

Other material factors

7–037 Geographical differences have been held to justify different working conditions, (e.g. *NAAFI v Varley* (1977)) and would permit employers to give "London weightings", for example. Differences in qualifications or experience may also constitute a material factor, although in *Angestelltenbetriebsrat der Wiener Gebietskrankenkasse v Wiener Gebietskrankenkasse* (1999) the CJEU held that the different qualifications and training background of graduate psychologists and medical doctors meant that they were not employed on like work. It would seem from *North Yorks CC v Ratcliffe* (1996) that compulsory competitive tendering is capable of being a material factor, provided there is no taint of sex discrimination. However, in *Coventry City Council v Nicholls* (2009) the EAT held that intransigence of trade unions, alleged by the employer to be the reason for its failure to implement a job evaluation scheme, would not be a material factor.

A final area of difficulty is whether radical differences in the job packages of the employees can count as a material factor. In *Leverton v Clwyd CC* (1988) a nursery nurse employed by the Council claimed equal pay with clerical staff. Her annual salary was considerably less than theirs, but on the other hand, she worked a 32½ hour week to their 37 hours and had 70 days' holiday a year to their 20 days. Taking these things into account, their hourly rates for the times they actually worked were in fact very similar. Although there was no evidence to show that the packages had been constructed so that more and less favourable terms in one were set off against the other, the House of Lords held that there was a material difference between the two cases. However, it is difficult to reconcile this with their earlier decision in *Hayward v Cammell Laird* (1988) and the CJEU decision in *Barber v Guardian Royal Exchange* (1990), discussed next.

Remedies

If an equal pay claim succeeds, the woman's contract is deemed to include a   **7–038**
sex equality clause which has the effect that any term of the contract which is
less favourable is modified to become as favourable as the man's and any term
which is missing from her contract is added (EqA 2010 s.66).

In *Hayward v Cammell Laird* (1988), a canteen cook claimed that her work was
of equal value to that of three men employed by the same employer: a painter,
a thermal insulation engineer and a joiner. While they were training they had
all received the same rate of pay. Yet, on completion, her pay was raised to £92
per week, while they got £117 per week. They also got a higher overtime rate. In
1984 an employment tribunal decided in her favour. The employers then tried
to argue the material factor defence on the basis that although her pay rate was
less than theirs, other terms and conditions were more favourable to her than to
them. She received free meals and a paid meal break: they did not. She had two
more days of paid holiday than them. Sickness arrangements were more beneficial for her than for them. Indeed, according to the employer's calculations,
far from being £25 a week worse off than them, if you compared the whole job
package she was actually £11 better off!

The House of Lords rejected the employer's contention that overall job packages were to be compared, holding that the Act required each separate provision
to be looked at. Thus, if the jobs are of equal value, each term must be brought
up to the best possible standard—for, of course, the men can claim parity with
her for those terms of hers which are more beneficial.

Employers were most unhappy about the "leap-frogging" that would be   **7–039**
allowed by this decision; however, the House of Lords indicated that the material
factor defence might be available in such a case, although it would be necessary
for them to show that the more favourable term was designed to compensate
for the less favourable one. In *Barber v Guardian Royal Exchange* (1990) the
CJEU made it clear that the term-by-term approach was the correct one under
European law, and it seems unlikely that they would accept this qualification.

There remains some room for manoeuvre in the process of defining what
exactly is a term of the contract. In *Degnan v Redcar & Cleveland BC* (2005)
female cleaners working for the council were rated as doing work of equal value
to male gardeners, roadworkers and refuse collectors, also employed by the
council. However, while they all received the basic hourly rate, the three categories of predominantly male workers received other benefits as well. They all got
a fixed bonus of between 33 per cent and 40 per cent of their salary. The refuse
collectors and the roadworkers also got a weekly attendance allowance of £34
and £14 respectively. It was clear that the female cleaners were entitled to an
uplift on their hourly rate and the issue was whether the basic hourly rate, fixed
bonuses and the attendance allowances should be seen as separate terms. If so,
the women could claim the best bonus rate–the gardeners' 40 per cent, and the
best attendance allowance–the refuse collectors' £34, giving them a higher wage
than any of the male groups (who would then have been able to claim equality
with them). The Court of Appeal, however, held that the hourly rate, bonus and

attendance allowance had to be seen as elements of one terms on pay and that all the payments received by each category of male worker had to be totalled up, then divided by the number of hours worked to identify the hourly rate to which the women would be entitled.

Equal pay audits

7–040   Under the Equality Act 2010 (Equal Pay Audits) Regulations 2014, if an employer loses an equal pay case, or is otherwise found to have discriminated on grounds of sex in relation to pay, the tribunal must order it to carry out an equal pay audit, containing information about the pay of men and women in the categories of worker specified by the tribunal, any differences between the sexes, any explanation for the differences and a plan to avoid equal pay breaches occurring or continuing. Micro-businesses (those with fewer than 10 employees) and new businesses are exempt from this for the first 10 years of the legislation being in force. There are exceptions if the employer has already carried out an equal pay audit in the previous three years which contains the relevant information, if the action required to prevent the breach is clear without it, if the tribunal believes that there is no reason to believe that the breach is other than a one-off, or finally, if the disadvantages of carrying out an audit would outweigh the advantages. It is difficult to envisage what sort of situation would be covered by this final exception. The employer must be given at least three months to carry out the audit; it will then be considered by the tribunal, to decide whether it is satisfactory. Ultimately, the requirement can be enforced by the tribunal imposing a penalty of up to £5,000 on any employer which fails to comply. This came into force in October 2014, so it is as yet too early to assess its effects.

Maternity equality

7–041   The EqA 2010 now makes express provision for a woman's contract to contain a maternity equality clause, the difference from a sex equality clause being that no comparator is required. Under EqA 2010 s.74 the effect of the maternity equality clause is, first, that any pay increase which the woman would have received but for being on maternity leave is (a) taken into account in calculating her entitlement to statutory and contractual maternity pay, and (b) reflected in her pay on her return to work. Secondly, any bonus or other payment to which she would have been entitled while on maternity leave must be paid to her at the date it is due, not waiting until she comes back to work. This reflects the law as established by the CJEU in a number of cases (e.g. *Alabaster v Woolwich plc* (2004) above, para.6–006).

The meaning of "pay" in TFEU art.157

7–042   While the Equal Pay Act was always clear that it applied to all terms of the contract, not just pay, it did originally contain a number of exclusions relating to death or retirement benefits, as did the SDA. It was thought that these exceptions were permitted under EU law, a view apparently shared by EU administrators, who had issued directives which would eventually lead to equalisation on such matters, but not in the immediate future.

This was to reckon without the CJEU, which in a string of epoch-making decisions largely brought about total equality through its interpretation of the word "pay" in what is now TFEU art.157 as amplified by what is now art.4 of the Recast Equal Treatment Directive (2006/54/EC), which states that pay includes "all aspects and conditions of remuneration". This has been interpreted to include: travel concessions on retirement for British Rail workers (*Garland v British Rail* (1983)); access to occupational pension schemes (*Bilka-Kaufhaus v Weber von Hartz* (1986)); sick pay (*Rinner-Kühn v FWW Spezial-Gebäudereinigung* (1989)); pension ages (*Barber v Guardian Royal Exchange* (1990)); pension benefits (*Barber*); statutory or contractual severance payments (*Barber*); paid time off for union training (*Arbeiterwohlfahrt der Stadt Berlin v Bötel* (1992)); unfair dismissal compensation (*R v Secretary of State ex p Seymour-Smith* (1999)); and non-contractual bonus payments (*Lewen v Denda* (2000)).

In *Barber v Guardian Royal Exchange* the CJEU stated that its judgment would not apply retrospectively, because they recognised how disruptive this could be, but did not make it clear what this meant in practice. It was clear that retirement ages and accrual of benefits would have to be equal from 17 May 1990 (the date on which the decision was handed down), but not whether benefits paid after that date but referring to service before it should be equalised, nor whether retirement ages could be equalised upwards, to the detriment of women with retiring ages lower than men's. Most of the issues were clarified following a series of references to the CJEU in subsequent years.

In *Ten Oever* (1993) it was made clear that equal occupational pension benefits were payable only in respect of employment subsequent to 17 May 1990. This was the narrowest possible interpretation of *Barber*; however, it accorded with the agreement made by EU Member States and recorded as the second Protocol to the Treaty of Maastricht. The decision also made it clear that survivors' benefits are within the principle of equality. With regard to retirement ages, in *Smith v Avdel* (1994) and *Van den Akker v Stichting Shell* (1994) the CJEU held that retirement ages could be equalised upwards without infringing TFEU art.157; however, they could not be levelled up retrospectively and in the period between 17 May 1990 and the implementation of a common retirement age, both sexes were entitled to the best conditions for either. Emphasising the nature of the equality principle as a fundamental right, the CJEU also held that transitional provisions which would inevitably perpetuate discrimination, albeit for a limited period, could not be condoned.

7–043

The final raft of issues concerned the rights of part-timers in relation to pension schemes. It had already been decided in *Bilka-Kaufhaus v Weber von Hartz* (1986) that not allowing part-timers to join an occupational pension scheme was capable of constituting a breach of TFEU art.157. In *Vroege v NCIV Instituut voor Volkshuisvesting* (1994) and *Fisscher v Voorhuis Hengelo* (1994) the CJEU further decided that this applied to all part-timers, regardless of how many hours they worked and that there was no reason for the decision not to be applied retrospectively to 1976—the date when it was held in *Defrenne v Sabena* (1976) that

TFEU art.157 had direct effect. Unlike the situation in *Barber*, the CJEU considered that there were no grounds for employers reasonably to have thought that the position was otherwise. However, employees wishing to claim had to be prepared to pay the relevant employee contributions (*Preston v Wolverhampton Healthcare NHS Trust* (2000)).

Time limits

7–044   The extension of rights resulting from the *Barber* litigation caused some 60,000 retrospective claims to be lodged at tribunals by part-timers claiming that their employers had refused them access to occupational pension schemes, often in respect of periods of service which had finished many years earlier. The claimants faced two problems: first, the legislation provided that claims for equal pay had to be lodged within six months of the claim arising. Thus, while the refusal to deny membership could be regarded as ongoing throughout the employment relationship, the claimant would have to present any claim within six months of the employment being terminated. Secondly, the Equal Pay Act s.2(5) stated that claims for equal pay could only be backdated to two years before the claim was made. The compatibility of these limitations with EU law was referred to the CJEU in the *"Preston* litigation", involving 22 test cases coordinated by the TUC to thrash out the various preliminary issues surrounding the part-timers' claims. In *Preston v Wolverhampton Healthcare Trust* (2000) the CJEU held, in relation to the first point, that the six-month limitation period did not make the exercise of rights under EU law too difficult and was therefore compatible with EU law. There was some mitigation of this for one group of claimants: part-time teachers and lecturers employed on a series of short-term contracts for the same employer. If the six-month limitation period had been applied to them in its full rigour, they would have had to have claimed within six months of the end of each of these contracts. However, the CJEU held that provided that such employees could demonstrate that they had a "stable employment relationship" with the employer, whether or not a contract of employment was in existence for the whole period, their claims should be allowed as long as they were brought within six months of the termination of that relationship (see *Slack v Cumbria County Council* (2009) for a more recent application of this principle). As to the second point, the CJEU held that the two-year limit on backdating claims was in breach of the EU law requirement for effective remedies. This was in line with the CJEU's earlier decision in *Levez v Jennings* (1999). When that case returned to the national court (*Levez v Jennings (No.2)* (1999)) the EAT held that the limit should be six years, as for other claims for breach of contract.

As a result of the CJEU's decision, the law was amended and the current position is set out in tabular form in EqA 2010 s.129. For standard cases (which means cases not falling into the other categories) the limit is six months. In cases where there has been a stable employment relationship, even if not continuous employment, because of breaks between short-term contracts, the limitation period is six months from the date the relationship finally ended. If an employer has deliberately concealed information about inequality from the employee (e.g. details of other people's earnings) the time-limit is extended to six months from the date on which the employee could reasonably be expected to have become aware of the relevant information. If the employee was incapacitated during the six-month period, the six-month limit runs from the day on which the incapacity ceased.

In terms of backdating claims, the EqA 2010 adopts the position in *Levez v Jennings (No.2)* (1999) for backdated claims, which can now go back up to six years before the claim, or six years before the concealment or incapacity in one of those cases. The Supreme Court held in *Abdulla v Birmingham City Council* (2013) that claims which were out of time for an employment tribunal (because beyond the six-month limit) should be permitted to go ahead in the High Court.

Sick Pay

Under ERA s.1(4)(d), details of any terms or conditions of employment relating to sickness or injury, including sick pay, should be given in the written statement of particulars of employment. Therefore, there should always be an express term of the contract covering this, although this does not mean that the employer is bound to pay sick pay. However, there may still be situations where no express term covers the case, as where no written statement is given to the employee or where the employee wishes to argue that the statement is inaccurate. In such a case the court may have to decide whether there is an implied term of the contract that the employee should receive pay while off sick.

In older cases it was held that, in the absence of an express term, there was an implied term that sick pay should be paid. If the employer did not wish to pay, the remedy was either to put in an express term to that effect, or simply to dismiss the employee. Since the introduction of claims for redundancy and unfair dismissal, this reasoning is harder to justify. In any case, any presumption in favour of sick pay was cut down considerably in the leading decision of the Court of Appeal in *Mears v Safecar Security* (1982). Here there was no express term about sick pay, but it was well known that the employer's practice was not to provide it. The employee knew this—significantly, he made no attempt to claim sick pay until some time after he had left the employment altogether. It was held that the issue could not be solved simply by the application of a presumption. The tribunal or court should look at all the facts of the case and determine the correct inference in the light of all the circumstances (thus here nothing was payable). The presumption in favour of sick pay would only have effect if there was absolutely no other evidence to go on—which must be a very rare case.

Employees who are off work sick are usually entitled to state benefits—this is one of the things for which National Insurance is paid. Most employers took this entitlement into account when deciding on their own sick pay schemes. The most common provision is that the employer will top up the state benefit to the worker's usual level of wages. In 1983 the Government introduced the Statutory Sick Pay Scheme (now governed by the Social Security Contributions and Benefits Act 1992). The effect of the scheme was to shift the administrative burden of paying sickness benefits from the state to the employer. Instead of the employee putting in a claim to a government agency, the employee is now paid Statutory Sick Pay (SSP) by the employer, who, under the original scheme, deducted that amount from the National Insurance contributions it would normally have forwarded to the state. As employers pointed out, they received no allowance for the extra administrative burden of this scheme, but otherwise there was no cost to them.

7–046   The rationale behind this was that if the employer paid sick pay on a topping-up scheme, then the employer already had the administrative burden of making wage adjustments; also most employees are off work for a relatively short period of time. If the employer was already making adjustments, then it was a needless reduplication of effort for a government department to do the same thing. It also had the effect of making such benefits taxable in the hands of employees (because it is paid by the employer), whereas state benefits were not!

When introduced, the employer's obligation was relatively short term: the employer was responsible for paying SSP in respect of any individual employee for eight weeks in any one year. However, this was significantly extended by the Social Security Act 1985: the employer is now responsible for up to 28 weeks in any three-year period. To the fury of employers, the Statutory Sick Pay Act 1991 then reduced to 80 per cent the amount that they could set off against National Insurance contributions, except for small employers. This was estimated to cost industry over £250 million in its first year of operation. Not entirely unexpectedly, the Statutory Sick Pay Act 1994 removed the right to any reimbursement for employers, except small employers. Subsequently the distinction between small and large employers was removed. Any employer is now entitled to recover any amount by which their SSP payments exceed 13 per cent of their liability for National Insurance contributions in the same month (Statutory Sick Pay Percentage Threshold Order 1995 (SI 1995/12)). Thus most of the time the entire burden of SSP falls on the employer, unless or until the employee qualifies for long-term incapacity benefit.

The fact that the employer is now responsible for paying state sickness benefit has no effect on the contractual position. If an employer does not have a contractual obligation to pay sick pay, this remains the case, even though the employer must pay SSP. If under the contract the employer is bound to pay wages while the employee is off sick, then the necessary amount to top up SSP to that level must be paid.

7–047   Some employers have insurance against employees being off sick for extended periods and guarantee to continue paying wages even up to retirement if the employee continues to be unable to work. Where such permanent health insurance schemes exist, courts are generally unwilling to allow employers to defeat employee expectations by moving the goalposts. In *Aspden v Webbs Poultry* (1996) it was held that the employer was not entitled to terminate the employee's employment so as to deprive him of benefits under a generous permanent health insurance scheme once he had qualified for them. Although there was an express term of the contract permitting termination on three months' notice, the High Court held that this was subject to an implied term prohibiting termination in these circumstances, except for good cause (see also *Adin v Sedco Forex* (1997); *Villella v MFI Furniture Centres Ltd* (1999)). However, termination for good cause unrelated to the employee's illness will be allowed (*Hill v General Accident* (1998); *Briscoe v Lubrizol Ltd* (2002)).

Deductions from Wages

In the nineteenth century it was common for employers to abuse their dominant position by paying workers in kind instead of in cash (a "truck" or barter system), or by giving them vouchers which were only exchangeable in shops belonging to the employer ("tommy-shops"). The abuse lay in the fact that the goods given were not of the claimed value and the prices in the tommy-shops were artificially inflated. Protection against this exploitation began with the first Truck Act in 1831, which stipulated that workers must be paid in coin of the realm. In 1896 another Truck Act gave protection against another commonly abused power of an employer: the power to make deductions from wages as a disciplinary measure or for bad work. Such deductions had to be agreed in writing, and to be fair and reasonable.   **7–048**

The Truck Acts did not apply to all employees, but only to manual workers. In the post-War period the requirement to pay wages in coin of the realm became more onerous to employers, understandably concerned about security when large amounts of cash were needed, often on a weekly basis. The Payment of Wages Act 1960 allowed manual workers to be paid by cheque or by transfer to a bank account if they requested it in writing, but they could not be compelled to do so. The desire to facilitate the move towards "cashless pay" was the mainspring behind the reform of the Truck Acts by the Wages Act 1986 which repealed the Truck Acts 1831–1940, thus permitting employers to pay all employees by cheque or money transfer rather than by cash.

The replacement of the Truck Acts by the Wages Act 1986 (now ERA Pt II) led to significant reforms in the law relating to the employer's right to make deductions from wages. The scope of the protection is considerably greater, in that it applies to all workers, defined as including not only employees but anyone rendering personal service under a contract other than as a professional or someone carrying on a business (ERA s.230(3); see above, para.3–010). However, the protection given is narrower, in that there is no requirement that deductions must be fair and reasonable. Claims under ERA Pt II are now within the jurisdiction of employment tribunals (ERA s.23)—a point of some significance, as will be seen.

When are deductions allowed?

A deduction is unlawful unless it is authorised in one of three ways (ERA s.13(1)). First, it may be authorised by statute. Clearly there is nothing wrong with deducting PAYE contributions and the like. Secondly, it may be authorised by a term of the contract, provided that either the contract is in writing or the term is notified in writing to the worker before the deduction is made (ERA s.13(2)). Finally, it   **7–049** may be authorised by specific consent of the worker, signified in writing (ERA s.13(1)(b)). To ensure fairness to the employee, the Act gives no effect to a "consent" or to an "agreement" to a term allowing the deduction given after the events leading to it. But, provided the consent or agreement is given before the event, it is valid even if the notification in writing is given later, provided it is notified before the deduction is made (*York City & District Travel v Smith* (1990)). In *Peninsula Business Services v Sweeney* (2004) the EAT held that the employee will be bound by a signed consent whether or not he fully understood its effect.

All of this is subject to basic contractual principles. If an employer wishes to introduce a power to make deductions, this variation will require agreement from existing employees before it will become effective. In *Kerr v Sweater Shop* (1996) the EAT in Scotland held that displaying a notice in the factory was not sufficient notification to employees of a proposed variation which would reduce the employer's obligation to pay accrued holiday pay on termination.

While ERA s.13(1) states when an employer will be allowed to make deductions, ERA s.14 stipulates exceptional situations where the deduction will not infringe the Act if it is otherwise lawful. These are deductions made: for overpayment of wages or expenses; in consequence of disciplinary proceedings held by virtue of a statutory provision; because of a statutory requirement; where the worker has agreed in writing to a deduction being made in favour of a third party (e.g. union subscriptions); where the worker has taken part in industrial action; and finally where the worker has agreed for a court or tribunal order obtained against her by the employer to be satisfied in this way.

7–050 In *Home Office v Ayres* (1992) the EAT held that overpayments could only be deducted where there was power to do so at common law, thus requiring the tribunal to decide on matters of contract law. However, considering a deduction in relation to industrial action in *Sunderland Polytechnic v Evans* (1993) a different EAT concluded that the earlier decision was wrong: if a deduction comes under ERA s.14, the tribunal has no jurisdiction under the Act at all and cannot therefore consider whether it is lawful or not. This was applied by the EAT in relation to overpayments in *SIP (Industrial Products) Ltd v Swinn* (1994). However, in both of these cases there was no dispute as to the relevant facts (i.e. that the claimant had participated in industrial action in *Sunderland Polytechnic v Evans* and that there had been an overpayment in *SIP (Industrial Products) Ltd v Swinn*). In the joined cases *Gill v Ford Motor Co Ltd* (2004) and *Wong v BAE Systems Operations Ltd* (2004) the employees disputed whether, in *Gill*, they had been participating in industrial action and in *Wong*, whether there had been an overpayment. The EAT held that in such situations the tribunal had to make the relevant findings of fact on these issues to decide whether or not it had jurisdiction to hear their claims, even though that might come close to deciding the question of whether or not the deductions were lawful.

A tribunal only has jurisdiction under ERA Pt II if there has been a "deduction" and the deduction is out of "wages". The definition of both terms gave rise to a lot of case law after 1986 because the extension of protection from deductions to all kinds of employees seemed to offer a back door way of getting some contractual disputes in front of employment tribunals. Before contractual jurisdiction was conferred on employment tribunals in 1994, this was important. Suppose that an employee claiming unfair dismissal also wanted to claim that she had not received outstanding holiday pay or notice money: her entitlement to the latter depended on the contract and she could find herself needing to take county court proceedings as well as making an employment tribunal claim. Hence it became common for employees to claim that failure to pay things like notice money were really deductions from wages and within the protection of wages jurisdiction of tribunals and, from forming 1.5 per cent of all claims in 1987–88, Pt II of ERA claims formed 24 per cent by 1995. Now that tribunals can hear most contractual claims arising out of termination of employment, the problem is partly solved; however, it remains an issue where there is no termination, as in *Sunderland Polytechnic v Evans* (1993). There are also two other major attractions in bringing a contractual claim under ERA Pt II—first, there is no limit to the amount which can be claimed, and secondly, the employer cannot bring a counter-claim as it would be able to do if an employee was claiming pay in county court proceedings. For these reasons in particular, claims under ERA Pt II have continued to constitute around 20 per cent of all tribunal claims.

The question of what would count as a deduction was definitively analysed by the House of Lords in *Delaney v Staples* (1992). The claimant was summarily dismissed but was given a cheque for £82 as payment in lieu of notice. The cheque was later stopped. She also claimed to be entitled to commission and holiday pay amounting to £55.50. She claimed at an employment tribunal that these were unlawful deductions from wages contrary to the protection of wages legislation. The employer's central argument here was that no payment at all was not a deduction from payment, that there was a distinction between a deduction from a payment recognised to be due and a total non-payment resulting from a denial of liability to pay. The House of Lords rejected this argument, holding that any deficiency counts as a deduction and that the Wages Act does not distinguish between non-payment, refusal to pay and deduction.

The employer also argued that a payment in lieu of notice could not be regarded as "wages", defined in ERA s.27 as: **7–051**

"... any sums payable to the worker by his employer in connection with his employment, including—(a) any fee, bonus, commission, holiday pay or other emolument referable to his employment, whether payable under his contract or otherwise."

The House of Lords held that "wages" therefore had to be referable to work actually performed or due to be performed under the contract. Lord Browne-Wilkinson noted that "payment in lieu of notice" is commonly used in four separate situations. The first situation is where the employer lawfully terminates the contract with notice but does not require the employee to work during the notice period and pays the wages as a lump sum. This would be a payment referable to work due to be performed and thus would constitute "wages" within the meaning of ERA s.27. The second and third situations are where the employer terminates the contract summarily and pays the employee a lump sum and either the contract permits termination in this manner or the employee agrees to it. In each of these cases the employer would not be acting in breach of contract. The fourth and most common situation of payment in lieu is where the employer terminates the contract summarily without the employee's agreement and offers payment in lieu of notice. Here the employer may be in breach of contract and the payment in lieu operates as a set-off, or usually an extinction, of the employee's right to claim damages. However, in none of these three situations could the payment be said to be referable to work, as the contract would already have terminated, and so they would not count as "wages" for the purposes of ERA Pt II.

Since the final words of the definition of wages in ERA s.27 include sums which may not be contractual, it follows that bonuses which are technically discretionary but in practice paid regularly could be claimed under this section—although only if they are quantifiable (*Coors Brewers Ltd v Adcock* (2007)). It is ironic that a law which originated in a desire to prevent exploitation of the lowest-paid workers has transformed itself into a law which is very beneficial to some very highly paid workers. A striking example is *Mouradian v Tradition Securities and Futures SA* (2009), where a stockbroker successfully claimed an unlawful deduction when his bonus was reduced from £1.4 million to £1.3 million.

That employment tribunals should find themselves dealing with complex contractual disputes over such vast sums of money rather undermines any argument that suggests they should not be trusted with contractual jurisdiction more generally. The present position, where some workers are enabled to take such contractual disputes to the tribunal and others are not, is haphazard, and arguably unjust to employers, who cannot claim any right of set-off in a deduction from wages claim. It is submitted that it would make sense for the contractual jurisdiction of employment tribunals to be extended further.

Retail workers

7–052   Special provision is made under ERA ss.17–22 for retail workers who are sometimes subject to onerous contract terms requiring them to make good cash shortages or stock deficiencies out of their wages. Those involved in the supply of services (including financial services) as well as in the supply of goods are covered (ERA s.17(2)). Any deduction from wages to cover shortages (or as a disciplinary fine) would in any case have to be lawful according to the rules already considered, but for retail workers the Act limits the amount that can be recovered on any one occasion to not more than 10 per cent of the gross wage. This is to stop the worker's entire wage or a substantial part of it from being wiped out by a claw-back, as had occurred in some notorious cases. It is also necessary for the deduction to be made within 12 months of the deficiency being discovered.

This protection has been criticised as inadequate in two main respects: first, the 10 per cent limit does not apply to a final payment, so the last pay packet the worker receives could still be empty; secondly, and more fundamentally, the Act does not control the substance of such clauses, which may therefore operate when the employee is in no way at fault.

The National Minimum Wage

The best protection for employees is combination in trade unions. Collective   **7–053**
power, if not unduly limited by law, should ensure that workers' interests are
reasonably protected. However, there have always been industries where
organisation has been very difficult, and in these areas legislative protection
is needed. Among the various strategies which can be used to this end is the
minimum wage. Originally the strategy adopted in the United Kingdom was to
provide for minimum terms and conditions only in certain industries where the
problem of low wages was considered to be acute.

The genesis of this system was the Trade Boards Act 1909 which established
boards which fixed minimum wages in the "sweated trades"—those where the
exploitation of workers was most acute. They were replaced by wages councils. A wages council was composed of equal numbers of representatives from
both sides of the industry together with an uneven number of independent
members whose vote could break any deadlock. Originally wages councils could
set a minimum hourly wage and terms about holidays. In 1975 the Employment
Protection Act significantly extended their powers by allowing them to make
orders about all terms and conditions of employment and to make these orders
by their own authority rather than submitting them first to the Secretary of
State. The reforms of 1975 (consolidated with earlier legislation in the Wages
Councils Act 1979) were the high point for wages councils. The Conservative
Government of the 1980s, firmly committed to a policy of deregulation of industry, was ideologically opposed to this kind of system; however, it remained the
case that the United Kingdom was a signatory to the ILO Convention No.26,
which requires the maintenance of minimum wage fixing machinery.

In June 1985 the Government gave notice to denounce (withdraw from) the
ILO Convention, and the Wages Act 1986 repealed the Wages Councils Act 1979.
Existing wages councils (26 of them) were retained in existence, but their powers
were drastically curtailed. The final stage was reached when TURERA abolished
the remaining wages councils in 1993. During the early 1990s the Labour Party
committed itself to universal minimum wage legislation as the appropriate strategy to combat the problems of low pay. Following its return to power in May
1997, consultation on a national minimum wage was one of its first tasks. The
framework for the system was set up by the National Minimum Wage Act 1998
and implemented by the National Minimum Wage Regulations 1999.

Who is covered?

In keeping with its general policy of inclusive employment protection rights,   **7–054**
entitlement to the minimum wage is extended to "workers", defined in the
National Minimum Wage Act (NMWA) s.54 in parallel terms to s.230(3) of ERA
(see above, para.3–010), thus including at least some workers on contracts for
services. Agency workers are expressly covered by NMWA s.34 and the problem
of identifying who is the employer is solved by providing that the employer for
purposes of the NWMA is the one who is responsible for paying the worker,

or who actually pays him or her. Following the practice of the wages councils legislation, homeworkers are also included even if they sometimes get others to perform some of the work (NMWA s.35). Furthermore, the Secretary of State has power under NMWA s.41 to extend the legislation to "any individual of a prescribed description" who would not otherwise count as a worker.

The National Minimum Wage is usually reviewed annually in accordance with the recommendations of the Low Pay Commission. It is £6.70 an hour from October 2015. There are important differences for young workers, apprentices and trainees. The rates for younger workers have been criticised both on grounds of their complexity and because, in principle, it is argued not to be fair for one worker to be paid less than another where they are doing the same work. That said, however, we have seen with equal pay that experience can be a factor justifying different pay for the same work and employers have traditionally been reluctant to take on young workers on exactly the same terms as older workers. Workers aged 16 and 17 were originally not entitled to the National Minimum Wage, but evidence of exploitation led to a minimum rate of £3.00 per hour being set for the first time in 2004; they now get the apprentice rate. Those aged between 18 and 21 are entitled to a minimum "development rate" which is £5.30 per hour from October 2015. Apprentices aged under 19 used not to qualify for the national minimum wage at all and those over 19 were not entitled to it during the first 12 months of their apprenticeship; however, in October 2010 an "apprentice rate" was introduced which is £3.30 from October 2015. Since they can be paid half the amount that other workers of their age would receive, there could hardly be a greater incentive for employers to create apprenticeships for younger workers. In *Edmonds v Lawson* (2000) the Court of Appeal held that a pupil barrister aged over 26 was not entitled to the minimum wage, since although she was properly to be regarded as having a contract with the members of her chambers, this was neither a contract of employment nor of apprenticeship.

Unions have campaigned for many years for employers to pay a "living wage"—a rate which is calculated to be the minimum on which someone could realistically survive. The phrase was adopted by the Conservative Government, but in reality what they proposed was a higher minimum wage than previously. Thus, from April 2016, a new "national living wage" comes into force for workers aged 25 or over, set at £7.20 per hour in the first instance.

Calculating pay

7–055　In order to check whether there has been compliance with the obligation to pay the National Minimum Wage there has to be a mechanism for reducing all forms of payment to a notional hourly rate. This further requires rules as to which elements of a remuneration package will and will not count in this assessment and as to the period of time over which the measurement will take place. The last of these is the most straightforward element. The "pay reference period" cannot be longer than one month (reg.10). If the worker is paid at shorter intervals (e.g. weekly or daily), the period is reduced accordingly.

Which payments count towards the National Minimum Wage?

Calculations are based on gross pay less: loans from the employer; any advance   **7–056**
on wages; pension payments; a lump sum paid on retirement; redundancy
payments; an overtime premium; and any expenses paid, allowances given or
amounts deducted for expenditure required by the employer. The essential idea
is that the employer should not be able to pass itself off as paying the minimum
wage by including sums payable for other reasons or sums which are essentially
for the employer's benefit. If, for example, a shop assistant in a clothes shop
were to be given an allowance to buy clothes from the shop to wear as a kind
of uniform and advertisement for the shop's products, this allowance would
not count in assessing her hourly rate, since it is not money which she is free to
spend as she wishes but must be spent for the employer's benefit. An overtime
premium is the amount by which the overtime rate exceeds the usual hourly
rate, and the reason for excluding it is the principle that the worker should not
have to work overtime in order to reach the level of the National Minimum
Wage. However, subject to the requirements of the Working Time Regulations
(see above, para.6–043), there is nothing to stop an employer requiring workers
to do a certain amount of overtime and consolidating the amount equivalent to
the overtime premium into the basic hourly rate. Accommodation is the only
benefit in kind which can be counted towards discharging the employer's obligation to provide the National Minimum Wage, but only to a maximum £5.35 per
day (in 2015).

Elements which do count towards the minimum wage include incentive payments; performance-related pay; bonuses; and tips, gratuities or
service charges paid through the employer (cf. *Nerva v United Kingdom*
(2002)).

The hourly rate

Having established the amount of pay which the worker received in the rel-   **7–057**
evant pay reference period, the next stage is to calculate the number of hours
worked during that period. The Regulations identify four kinds of work. The
first is time work, which is work paid according to the time the worker works
and which is not salaried hours work (NMWR reg.3). The hours need not be
regular and it should be noted that this category includes piecework in situations where the worker is contracted to work for a set number of hours. To
find out if time workers are being paid the National Minimum Wage, the hours
worked in the pay reference period are simply divided by the pay received
during that period. The second kind is salaried hours work, which is work paid
for by an annual salary referable to a fixed number of basic hours per year,
divided into weekly or monthly instalments (NMWR reg.4). Variations in hours
worked in any week or month do not result in alteration to the weekly or
monthly salary. To find out whether salaried hours workers are receiving the
National Minimum Wage, their annual hours are divided by 12 or 52 (according
to the length of the pay reference period) and the amount of pay received in
the pay reference period is divided by the resulting number of hours to get the
hourly rate.

There are no great difficulties in establishing an hourly rate where hours are stipulated in this way. More problematic are the last two kinds of work. Output work is work which, but for the Act, would be paid for entirely by results—e.g. piecework where the worker has no set hours, or is paid entirely by commission (NMWR reg.5). There are two options for converting pay for output work to an hourly rate. The first is to divide the worker's pay by the actual number of hours she works in the reference period. The second is to work out a "fair piece rate" for the task or output. This is done by working out the "mean hourly output rate", which is the number of pieces (or tasks) which an average worker can produce in an hour. This can be measured either by testing all the workers or a representative sample and taking the average (NMWR regs 26, 26A). The "fair piece rate" is then set at 120 per cent of the amount which would be needed to ensure that the average worker was getting the equivalent of the National Minimum Wage for the piece or task. Setting the rate at 120 per cent rather than 100 per cent allows for some leeway so that someone who is slightly slower than average still stands a reasonable chance of earning the equivalent of the National Minimum Wage.

The final category is unmeasured work, which is anything which does not fall within one of the preceding three categories (NMWR reg.6). Again, there are two options for dealing with this: either the National Minimum Wage is paid for every hour actually worked, or it is paid in accordance with a "daily average" agreement. A daily average agreement must be in writing, agreed with the worker before the start of the reference period and set out a realistic daily average number of hours.

7–058   The importance of the difference between timed work and unmeasured work is illustrated by *Walton v Independent Living Organisation* (2003), concerning a care worker whose job required her to live in for three days a week with a client who needed someone on hand at all times in case she suffered an epileptic fit. The Court of Appeal upheld a tribunal's decision that this fell into the unmeasured time category rather than the timed work category. The significance of this was that she was then only entitled to the National Minimum Wage for the estimated seven hours per day which her duties actually required rather than 24 hours a day as she claimed (contrast *MacCartney v Oversley House Management* (2006)). It will be clear from this that the definition of working time for the purposes of the National Minimum Wage Regulations 1999 is different from that under the Working Time Regulations 1998 (see above, para.6–043).

Enforcement

7–059   Employers must keep adequate records for establishing that they are complying with the requirements to pay the National Minimum Wage. Failure to do so, or falsifying records, is a criminal offence. These records are not only for the benefit of the Inland Revenue, which is the government body responsible for enforcement of this legislation, but also for workers themselves, who have a right to inspect their own records, accompanied by someone of their choice if they wish, and to take copies of them. This is part of the policy of trying to ensure that the national minimum wage legislation is largely self-enforcing. Workers can submit a claim to an employment tribunal where they believe that they have not been paid the National Minimum Wage. In these circumstances, the normal burden of proof is reversed: the employer must prove that the claim is not well-founded. Workers may also take tribunal proceedings (under the ERA, as amended) where the employer dismisses them or subjects them to a detriment for asserting their rights to the National Minimum Wage, or because they are, or will become, eligible for it. Failure to pay wages in accordance with the National Minimum Wage Act is also a criminal offence which is punishable with a fine of half the underpaid amount, but subject to an overall cap which was £5,000 until recently. The Government raised the overall cap to £20,000 in February 2014 and expressed its intention to raise the limit to £20,000 per unpaid worker (which would require primary legislation) in order to act as a deterrent.

Critics of the minimum wage legislation argued that it would lead to higher unemployment as employers would not be able to afford to pay these rates. The contrary argument is that employers paying very low wages should not be effectively subsidised by the state through the social security system. The annual reports of the Low Pay Commission have not found evidence of an adverse impact on the availability of work and, overall, this legislation appears to be having the desired effects.

Further Reading

On equal pay see:
- ❏ A. McColgan (1997), *Just Wages for Women,* Clarendon Press
- ❏ S. Fredman (1996), "The Poverty of Equality: Pensions and the ECJ", 25 ILJ 91
- ❏ S. Fredman (2008), "Reforming Equal Pay Laws", 37 ILJ 193
- ❏ A. Lester and D. Rose (1991), "Equal Value Claims and Sex Bias in Collective Bargaining", 20 ILJ 163
- ❏ C. McCrudden (1996), "Third Time Lucky? The Pensions Act 1995 and Equal Treatment in Occupational Pensions", 25 ILJ 28

On protection for low-paid workers, see:
- ❏ S. Deakin and F. Wilkinson (1989), *Labour Law, Social Security and Economic Inequality,* Institute of Employment Rights
- ❏ C. Pond (1988), *The Great Pay Robbery,* Low Pay Unit
- ❏ G. Davidov (2009), "A Purposive Interpretation of the National Minimum Wage Act", 72 MLR 581
- ❏ S Deakin and F. Wilkinson (1994), "Rights v Efficiency? The Economic Case for Transnational Labour Standards", 23 ILJ 289
- ❏ T. Goriely (1983), "Arbitrary Deductions from Pay and the Proposed Repeal of the Truck Acts", 12 ILJ 236
- ❏ S. Keevash (1985), "Wages Councils: An Examination of Trade Union and Conservative Government Misconceptions about the Effect of Statutory Wage-Fixing", 14 ILJ 217

- C.McLaughlin (2014), "Equal Pay, Litigation and Reflexive Regulation: The Case of the UK Local Authority Sector", 43(1) ILJ 1
- D. Rowbottom (2010), "Justifying Service-related Pay in the Context of Sex Discrimination Law", 39 ILJ 382
- B. Simpson (2004), "The National Minimum Wage Five Years On", 33 ILJ 22

8. Discipline and Dismissal

Key Points

This chapter:
- Explains the concept of wrongful dismissal at common law
- Discusses developments in claims for damages for wrongful dismissal
- Looks at mechanisms whereby employees may be able to prevent dismissals in breach of contract from taking place
- Introduces the statutory concept of unfair dismissal and who can claim it
- Explains rights under disciplinary processes to be accompanied and the concept of "protected conversations"
- Discusses the meaning of dismissal in the context of unfair dismissal
- Considers when dismissals are fair or unfair
- Looks at automatic unfairness in relation to health and safety and asserting statutory rights
- Outlines the remedies for unfair dismissal

***

In a contract of indefinite duration, such as contracts of employment usually are, it is almost inevitable that disagreement will arise because one or other party is dissatisfied with some aspect of the other's performance. When the common law was all that regulated the employment relationship, virtually the only recourse for a dissatisfied party was to terminate the relationship. Clearly, this was an easier option for an employer than for an employee. Provided that the contract was terminated lawfully, usually by giving notice of a certain length, no further remedies were available. It was also open to an employer to provide for disciplinary powers short of dismissal by express term (e.g. to make deductions from wages, see above, para.7–048 and *Sagar v Ridehalgh* (1931), above, para.4–016). The weak bargaining position of the employee meant that there was no corresponding way of holding the employer to what was agreed.

8–001

The common law left employees extremely exposed since there was no fetter on the employer's ultimate disciplinary power of dismissal and workers could be lawfully deprived of their means of livelihood for no good reason. The only time the employee would have a remedy was if the dismissal was in breach of contract, in which case it was possible to sue for wrongful dismissal, although the remedy, as we shall see, was limited.

This changed with the introduction of the statutory claims for redundancy in 1965 and for unfair dismissal in 1972. These did not affect the common law position, but they did give employees an alternative, statutory claim in specified circumstances. Unfair dismissal law soon began to have an impact on employers' disciplinary practices, because employers were likely to be found to have acted unfairly if they had not followed norms of good industrial practice, especially those set out in the Acas Code of Practice (No.1) on Disciplinary Practices and Procedures in Employment, originally issued in 1977, but revised several times since then. The current Acas Code of Practice on Disciplinary and Grievance Procedures came into force in March 2015 and is much shorter than previous incarnations. More extensive guidance is given in the 2015 Acas Guide on Discipline and Grievances at Work.

8–002   In the meantime, the common law relating to termination of the contract has continued to develop, both in relation to the extent of the claim for damages and in relation to the possible enforcement of the contract. The relationship between the statutory regime and the common law has given rise to difficult issues, which are increasingly being heard in employment tribunals, as tribunals were given jurisdiction over most claims for breach of contract arising on termination of the contract of employment in 1994 (see above, para.1–017).

This chapter will first consider the common law in relation to termination of the contract of employment, principally the claim for wrongful dismissal. It will then deal with the law of unfair dismissal, including procedural issues. The claim for a redundancy payment, the third possible course of action which may be available to an employee on dismissal, will be examined in Ch.9.

Termination at Common Law

Wrongful dismissal

8–003   Wrongful dismissal is basically an action for breach of contract, where the employee is arguing that the employer has acted in fundamental breach by terminating the contract of employment. Like other claims for breach of contract, it may be brought in the county court or High Court, although employment tribunals now have jurisdiction as well in many cases. There are two conditions to be fulfilled for the employee to be able to bring a successful action for wrongful dismissal: first, that the employer terminated the contract without notice or with inadequate notice, and secondly, that the employer was not justified in doing so.

Notice

As noted already, contracts of employment are usually drawn up to last indefi- **8–004** nitely. But people cannot be tied to each other forever, and at common law the rule grew up that either party could lawfully terminate the contract of employ- ment provided that reasonable notice was given. It is interesting to contrast this with the United States, where instead the doctrine of employment-at-will devel- oped, meaning that employment continues only so long as both parties want it to, and that either party can terminate the contract without notice. American employers frequently do just that, which makes for an entirely different perspec- tive on the employer-worker relationship.

At common law it is still true that if reasonable notice to terminate is given, then the contract is terminated lawfully, and it follows that the employee has no claim for wrongful dismissal. It does not matter that the employer has termi- nated for a bad or arbitrary reason, or indeed no reason at all; nor does it matter for how long the employee has been employed, nor his record. Provided that the employer has given adequate notice, or pay in lieu of notice, the employee has no claim. This is seen as the major defect of the common law position. It seems unjust that an employee can be thrown out of work without compensation when there is no good reason for the dismissal.

Since 1963 employers have been required to give employees a written state- ment of the notice they must give, and be given, for the contract to be termi- nated (see now Employment Rights Act 1996 (ERA) s.1(4)(e)). Thus today in all cases this is something which should be covered by an express term of the con- tract. Furthermore, under ERA s.86 there are certain minimum periods of notice: an employee with between one month and two years of continuous employ- ment must be given at least one week's notice; an employee with between two and 12 years of continuous employment must have one week for every complete year of employment (thus 10 years' employment equals 10 weeks' notice), and employees who have served for over 12 years are entitled to a minimum of 12 weeks' notice.

The minimum notice which the employee must give is only one week. The **8–005** lack of symmetry may seem surprising at first sight, but in fact is a sensible rec- ognition of two facts: first, that it is usually easier for an employer to replace an employee than for an employee to get another job, hence the employee should be given more warning; secondly, that it is easier for an employer to stipulate a longer period expressly than it is for an employee. In practice most employers require employees to give the same amount of notice as they are entitled to receive.

Where the contract specifies an entitlement to notice which is greater than the minimum statutory period, the employee is entitled to rely on the more beneficial provision, and can claim for wrongful dismissal if given less notice than stated in the contract even if the notice given satisfies the statutory require- ment. It has further been held, at least once, that "reasonable notice" is capable of being longer than either the statutory or contractual period (*Hill v Parsons* (1972)). However, the facts of the case were unusual. Hill had been employed by the company as a chartered engineer for 35 years and was two years short of retirement. The employer was faced with strike action unless he was dismissed, because of his refusal to join the trade union. Reluctantly, the company dismissed him with a month's notice. Under statute, he should have had three months. However, the Court of Appeal held that reasonable notice in his case would be at least six months, and perhaps even 12. Despite this, two things should be noted: the employer here retained confidence in the employee and had no desire to dismiss him and, even more importantly, by extending his period of employment in this way, the Court of Appeal ensured that the termination would only take effect after the new law of unfair dismissal had come into force—under which Hill would have far more extensive remedies.

Contracts of apprenticeship are an exception to the rule that a contract of employment can be terminated by giving reasonable notice. They should endure for the fixed term of the training period and can only be terminated for good cause, usually defined in the contract in terms of the apprentice's conduct or capabilities and not including redundancy (*Wallace v CA Roofing Services Ltd* (1996)). The concept of apprenticeship in present employment conditions was extended by the Court of Appeal in *Flett v Matheson* (2006) (see above, para.3–021).

Justified summary dismissal

8–006 Even if the employer terminates the contract with no notice or with inadequate notice, the employee will not be able to claim wrongful dismissal if the employer is justified in thus summarily dismissing him or her. When is summary dismissal justified? Essentially, in the same circumstances in which an innocent party would be entitled to terminate any other contract: that is, when the other party has committed a fundamental breach. Translated into the language of employment law, an employer is entitled to dismiss an employee summarily if the employee has committed an act of gross misconduct. The test is whether the employee has disregarded a fundamental term of the contract (cf. *Laws v London Chronicle* (1959), above para.4–028). In that case, the employee had been faced with conflicting orders by two superiors, and should not have been dismissed for obeying the wrong one.

Generally speaking, things like disobedience, dishonesty and violence are regarded as gross misconduct, although it seems that the employer may stipulate offences as very serious which would not usually be so regarded, to take account of the employer's particular circumstances. The EAT held that an employee who deliberately gained unauthorised access to the company's computer system was guilty of gross misconduct, although they also recommended that employers should make their rules abundantly clear and have them available for reference near computer terminals (*Denco Ltd v Joinson* (1991); see also the Acas Guide to Discipline and Grievances at Work which recommends that disciplinary rules should cover use of the organisation's facilities). The Acas Code of Practice on Disciplinary and Grievance Procedures and the Acas Guide to Discipline and Grievances at Work are strictly relevant to unfair rather than wrongful dismissal cases, but in practice tend to be influential in all areas of dismissal law. The Code says (para.23) that:

"Disciplinary rules should give examples of acts which the employer regards as acts of gross misconduct. These may vary according to the nature of the organisation and what it does, but might include things such as theft or fraud, physical violence, gross negligence or serious insubordination."

This is more limited than the description of gross misconduct in the 2004 Code of Practice, but that more extended version is now found in the Guide (p.31), which identifies the following as examples of gross misconduct: theft or fraud; physical violence or bullying; deliberate serious damage to property; serious misuse of an organisation's property or name; serious insubordination; deliberately accessing internet sites containing pornographic, offensive or obscene material; unlawful discrimination or harassment; bringing the organisation into serious disrepute; serious incapability at work brought on by alcohol or illegal drugs; causing loss, damage or injury through serious negligence; a serious breach of health and safety rules; and a serious breach of confidence.

A congeries of minor offences may coalesce into a sufficient reason for   **8–007** summary dismissal, as in *Pepper v Webb* (1969), where a gardener with a history of inefficiency and insolence surpassed himself when his employer remonstrated with him by confiding, "I couldn't care less about your bloody greenhouse and your sodding garden" and walking off. Accepting that this was the last straw, the Court of Appeal held that he had not been wrongfully dismissed.

At common law, in stark contrast to the law of unfair dismissal, the employer may justify a dismissal by reference to facts only discovered after the contract has been terminated. This was established in *Boston Deep Sea Fishing v Ansell* (1888), where the managing director of a company was summarily dismissed on inadequate grounds, but was later found to have been taking bribes: a breach of his duty of good faith and thus a fundamental breach of the contract. A particularly striking example of this is *Williams v Leeds United Football Club* (2015) where the claimant was one of a number of senior staff on large salaries with long notice periods who were on notice of redundancy in a restructuring exercise. To avoid having to pay out very sizeable compensation, the employer instituted an investigation into their conduct to see if there were any grounds to justify summary dismissal. In the case of Williams, they struck lucky: five years earlier he had forwarded a pornographic email to three other people. It was held that this was a fundamental breach of contract (in this case, a breach of mutual trust and confidence by the employee) which justified his dismissal without notice. The facts that it was a long time ago and that the employer had gone looking for evidence in order to save money were irrelevant.

Boston Deep Sea Fishing v Ansell was distinguished in *Cavenagh v William Evans Ltd* (2012) where the employer lawfully dismissed the employee without notice but with pay in lieu of notice, in accordance with a term of the contract which expressly permitted such termination (known as a PILON—pay in lieu of notice—clause). Before this money was handed over, the employer discovered that the employee, who was actually the managing director of the company, had been guilty of gross misconduct by making unauthorised payments from the company into his own pension fund. The Court of Appeal held that in this situation, the notice money was now due as a debt to which the employee was unconditionally entitled, despite this misconduct. Unlike *Boston Deep Sea Fishing v Ansell*, this was not a case of the employee suing the employer for wrongful dismissal, in which case his misconduct could have been used as a defence.

Suspension

8–008   Suspending an employee with or without pay is something an employer may wish to do either as a disciplinary measure or where there is not enough work to occupy everyone. Suspension with pay is frequently used where serious allegations of misconduct need to be investigated; suspension without pay is sometimes used as a punishment in circumstances where dismissal is thought to be too severe. It is important to note that unless the contract of employment permits it, suspension without pay will be a fundamental breach of contract by the employer and thus will found an action for wrongful dismissal. A good example is *Hanley v Pease* (1915) where the employee was absent one day without permission; when he turned up the next day, the employer suspended him without pay for the day as a punishment. There was no power in the contract to do this, and so the employee was entitled to sue for his day's wages—and this was despite the fact that his absence was a breach which would have justified the employer in dismissing him. But the employer had waived the right to do that and had instead committed a fundamental breach by suspending him without pay (see also *Four Seasons Healthcare Ltd v Maughan* (2005)).

The right to suspend without pay may be useful to an employer not only as a disciplinary measure, but also where there is a fall in demand. In cases where suspension is used because of a shortage of work, employees are protected to some extent by being able to claim a redundancy payment if the lay-off is for a lengthy period (see below, para.9–019). It is possible for there to be an implied term allowing suspension, for example that it is customary in the trade (cf. *Marshall v English Electric* (1945)), but it is clearly safer to have an express term. From the point of view of employees also, it may be to their advantage for the employer to have the power to impose sanctions short of dismissal, since it may result in a job being retained following misconduct where an employer without such a power would have dismissed rather than let it go at a warning.

Suspension on full pay is not usually a breach of contract by an employer and is commonly used where there needs to be an investigation of alleged misconduct. In *Gogay v Herts CC* (2000) the employer was held to be in breach of the implied obligation to maintain mutual trust and confidence by suspending an employee without reasonable grounds to do so (see also *Yapp v Foreign and Commonwealth Office* (2014)). Suspension with pay may also constitute a breach of contract if the employee is able to establish that she has a "right to work" (see above, para.4–021).

Damages for wrongful dismissal

Since the general common law position is that dismissal can take place lawfully **8–009** at any time and for any reason, provided that adequate notice is given, it follows that employees can only complain of wrongful dismissal where they get no notice, or short notice, and no pay in lieu of notice. As a result, the basic principle of law is that the employee's damages are limited to the equivalent of net wages during the notice period. Since they could have been lawfully dismissed had proper notice been given, all they have lost by the wrongful dismissal is wages for the notice period. Considering that many manual workers only get the minimum statutory period of notice, and that even professional workers are unlikely to be entitled to more than six months' notice, wrongful dismissal is not a very expensive option for the employer, and, until employment tribunals had jurisdiction over these matters, claiming damages was rarely worth the bother for the employee.

Despite many assaults on the citadel, the courts refused to extend the damages claim, because of the principle established by the House of Lords in *Addis v Gramophone Co Ltd* (1909) that damages could not be claimed for injured feelings, loss of reputation or the fact that dismissal was likely to make it more difficult for an employee to find another job. This was relied on in *Bliss v South East Thames RHA* (1987) to prevent a claim in respect of illness said to have been brought on by the dismissal.

The principle in *Addis v Gramophone Co Ltd* is now subject to an important qualification as a result of the House of Lords' decision in *Malik v BCCI* (1997). The Bank of Credit and Commerce International collapsed in a blaze of publicity in 1991, owing US $6 billion. It had been insolvent for five years, but this was concealed through the fraudulent dealings of about 30 very senior officers of the bank, including its president and chief executive. All 1,400 UK employees lost their jobs. The two claimants, who had been employed as branch managers in London, claimed damages for breach of contract resulting from their dismissal. Essentially, this was a claim for what came to be called "stigma" damages, on the grounds that their association with a bank which had been guilty of wrongdoing would be very harmful to their career prospects in the financial services industry.

The case went to the House of Lords on the issue of whether such a claim **8–010** disclosed a cause of action, if the facts alleged were proved. The House of Lords held that their claim for damages for breach of contract should be allowed—not on the basis that they had suffered a loss arising from the circumstances of the dismissal, but because of the employer's breach of its implied obligation to maintain mutual trust and confidence (see above, para.4–026). The House of Lords held that this decision did not conflict with the rule in *Addis* because the employees' claim was not based on the manner of dismissal but on the breach of a different term of the contract. This was an issue that had not arisen in *Addis*, not least because the implied term of mutual trust and confidence was not developed until some 70 years later.

Nonetheless, the decision in *Malik v BCCI* (1997) revealed a potential route for extra damages to be claimed in wrongful dismissal cases because the employee could almost always argue that the wrongful dismissal also breached the implied duty to maintain mutual trust and confidence. In the immediate aftermath of a major common law development there is usually a period of backtracking as the courts try to contain what they fear may be a flood of litigation, followed by a gradual move forward as the new approach is assimilated. This is the pattern which followed *Malik v BCCI*, most significantly with the House of Lords' decision in *Johnson v Unisys Ltd* (2001). The claimant sought damages for mental breakdown and consequent loss of earnings alleged to have been caused by the manner of his dismissal. The House of Lords held that damages were not available for a breach of mutual trust and confidence consisting of the manner of dismissal because the term did not survive the termination of the contract and also because it would be wrong to circumvent the statutory protection for unfair dismissal (under which compensation is subject to a limit) by providing a common law remedy instead. The first reason is an argument of principle; the second, one of policy, and arguably easier to defend. The problem with the first reason in *Johnson v Unisys Ltd* is that it left it unclear as to when damages for a breach of mutual trust and confidence will be available. In *Gogay v Herts CC* (2000), where the employee was unjustifiably suspended, the Court of Appeal awarded damages for breach of mutual trust and confidence, and this decision was not disapproved by the House of Lords in *Johnson v Unisys Ltd*. This led some courts to think that the distinction was to be drawn between cases where the contract had not been terminated (like *Gogay*), where damages for breach of mutual trust and confidence could be claimed, and cases where the contract had been terminated (like *Johnson*), where the only remedy would be the statutory claim for unfair dismissal.

Further clarification was provided by the House of Lords in the joined appeals in *Eastwood v Magnox Electric plc* (2004) and *McCabe v Cornwall CC* (2004). Both cases involved employees who were dismissed after lengthy and stressful disciplinary proceedings which were found to have serious flaws. They were successful in their unfair dismissal claims, but subsequently commenced civil actions for psychiatric injury brought about by the manner of the dismissal. Again, the issue in the House of Lords was whether or not they had a valid cause of action if the alleged facts were true. The House of Lords held that the "*Johnson* exclusion area", as they termed it, applies to the dismissal itself, because in this situation only the statutory unfair dismissal regime can apply. However, the obligation to maintain mutual trust and confidence applies to the events and processes leading up to the dismissal, and if an employee acquires a cause of action for breach of contract *before* dismissal, then he may pursue it separately from an unfair dismissal claim. Thus the issue is not whether the employee is dismissed or not, but whether the breach of the implied term of trust and confidence relied upon is based on things happening before the actual dismissal. In both *Eastwood* and *McCabe* the claims were based on events before the dismissal and so the House of Lords held that the claimants had a good cause of action.

8–011   While stating this boundary line is fairly straightforward, applying it is bound to cause odd and inconsistent results, as the House of Lords frankly acknowledged in *Eastwood* and *McCabe*. First of all, it means that what is probably a continuous course of events, namely the disciplinary process culminating in dismissal, "may have to be chopped artificially into separate pieces" (*per* Lord Nicholls), raising difficult questions of causation. Secondly, in order to make sure that the employee does not recover twice over for the same heads of loss in unfair dismissal proceedings and breach of contract proceedings, it means that the tribunal and the courts will be going over the same ground, an unfortunate duplication of effort at least. Thirdly, and most strikingly, it means that an employer could escape liability for damages for breach of the implied term by the simple expedient of sacking the employee! This would have absolved the employer from liability in *Gogay v Herts CC* (2000). The employee may be able to get an injunction to prevent such a dismissal (*see* below, para.8–014)—but only if she can act quickly enough.

In *Edwards v Chesterfield Royal Hospital NHS Foundation Trust* (2012) the question was raised as to whether damages were available when the alleged breach was failure to follow the terms of a contractual disciplinary procedure, leading to the claimant's dismissal. A consultant surgeon who was dismissed for personal and professional misconduct alleged not only that the disciplinary proceedings had been in breach of the procedure laid down in his contract of employment, but also that if they had been conducted properly, he would not have been dismissed. He claimed damages of £4.3 million, of which £3.8 million was for loss of earnings on the basis that, but for the breach, he would have remained employed until he was 65. The case went to the Supreme Court, effectively on the preliminary issue of whether, if the facts alleged could be proved, his claim disclosed a cause of action as a matter of law. By a 4-3 majority, the Supreme Court held that it did not, the main reason being that the disciplinary procedure was inextricably linked with the dismissal, and thus fell inside the "*Johnson* exclusion area". The minority would have held that this was a breach of contract separate from the dismissal and thus damages could be awarded, as in *Eastwood* and *McCabe*. The view of the minority seems more in accordance with general principles of contract law although the result can be seen as reinforcing the policy approach of *Johnson v Unisys*. Even if the claimant had won, it is unlikely that he would have recovered the vast sums claimed, since it must be remembered that it was dealt with on the basis that all the claimant's allegations could be proved. Should it have ever gone to trial, it is likely that there would have been a lot of argument on whether the breach of procedure actually caused the loss and whether the claimant would have really been likely to stay in the same employment until he was 65.

While the discussion above shows some mitigation of the general rule that damages for wrongful dismissal are usually equivalent to pay in lieu of notice, it must be remembered that, in the majority of cases, the general rule still applies. This, coupled with the generally held view that a claim for damages was the only possible remedy for wrongful dismissal, explains why the common law was traditionally thought to be so inadequate a protection for employees. The only kind of worker for whom it offers much scope is the highly paid employee whose employment package also includes valuable contractual benefits such as share options, health and life insurance, private medical care, company car, travel and expenses allowances, company apartment and so on, especially if he (usually he) is also taken on for a lengthy fixed term which cannot be overridden by notice. Investment fund managers, company directors and the managers of football teams are the usual beneficiaries of these kinds of terms. In *Horkulak v Cantor Fitzgerald International* (2004) a senior director dealing in interest rate swaps was wrongfully dismissed only nine months after starting a three-year fixed-term contract. As was common in the industry, an important part of his salary package was a bonus related to performance. His contract provided for a guaranteed bonus of £100,000 over and above his salary provided that he remained employed at the end of the financial year and an annual discretionary bonus to be agreed between the employee, the chief executive and the company president. The trial judge considered that if he had remained he would have been awarded a discretionary bonus of £180,000 in the first financial year and £450,000 in the second. It was argued for the employer that the employee could not be awarded damages for this as the bonus was discretionary and not a contractual entitlement. This was in line with earlier Court of Appeal authority in *Lavarack v Woods* (1967). However, the Court of Appeal in this case distinguished *Lavarack v Woods* by construing the contract as conferring on the claimant the right to have a bona fide and rational exercise of the discretion as to whether or not to pay him a bonus, pointing out that in this kind of employment the payment of discretionary bonuses was part of the regular remuneration structure and that the clause in the contract could not be taken as simply stating the employer's power to make discretionary payments—which would not require any contractual authority in any case (see also *Clark v BET plc* (1997) and *Clark v Nomura International plc* (2000)). He was thus entitled to damages of around £900,000.

8–012   The decision in *Horkulak* confirms a trend towards some softening of the previous line on discretionary benefits and also illustrates the importance of the wrongful dismissal action for highly-paid executives. But for the average worker, the basic common law position that the most they can claim is their notice money is inadequate protection. Hence the growing interest in recent years in trying to find methods of actually enforcing the contract.

Enforcing the contract of employment

8–013   While the major drawback of the action for wrongful dismissal was that damages were limited to the notice period, which led to the introduction of the claim for unfair dismissal, in the 1980s there was also increasing disenchantment with the law of unfair dismissal. Awards of compensation were running at very low levels and only about 40 per cent of all unfair dismissal claims before tribunals were succeeding. In 1994 employment tribunals were given jurisdiction to deal with breach of contract claims related to compensation up to the value of £25,000 and this also gave a fresh impetus to the common law claim. All of these factors led to a revival of interest in the action at common law. True, damages might be limited, but what if it were possible to get an order enforcing the terms of the contract? That is, an order preventing the employer from dismissing in breach and keeping the contract alive on the terms agreed: this might be an order worth having.

The orthodox view of employment law has seen two major obstacles in the way of such developments. First, orders for specific performance or injunctions are not available to enforce contracts of personal service. Secondly, it was thought that a termination by the employer must be effective even if in breach of contract and not accepted by the employee. The strength of these objections must now be examined.

Specific performance and injunctions

As forcing someone to work for another without consent is tantamount to slavery or forced labour, it has been a general principle that specific performance of contracts of employment should not be ordered. This is one reason why the law has never reacted to strikes by ordering employees to go back to work. Also, since the contract is a contract for personal service, it has been thought similarly objectionable to compel employers to continue to employ someone they do not wish to employ. This common law position is reinforced now by the Trade Union and Labour Relations (Consolidation) Act 1992 (TULRCA) s.236, which forbids orders for specific performance or injunction to compel anyone to work.

8–014

However, this basic position has never been entirely absolute. In *Lumley v Wagner* (1852) an opera singer was tempted into breaking her contract to sing exclusively in Lumley's theatre when offered more money by another impresario. Lumley was able to get an injunction to stop her working for the rival theatre. This did not force her to work for him, but merely stopped her entering another contract in breach of the first. (Incidentally, Lumley was also able to sue the other impresario for inducing her to break her contract: *Lumley v Gye* (1853), see below, para.12–027.) The process was taken a step further in *Warner Bros v Nelson* (1937), where the film star Bette Davis was proposing to break her eight-year contract with Warner Bros. The court granted an injunction to stop her making films for any other company in breach of contract. Did this not force her to work for Warner Bros, by closing off all other activity? The court held it did not: she could make her living in some other way, at least in theory.

These cases both involved employers seeking injunctions to prevent a breach of contract. The fact that such orders are practically equivalent to forcing the employee back to the original employer suggests that the objection to forced labour in the sense of economically forced labour is not actually as strong as it seemed at first sight. What about employees getting injunctions against employers? Since 1975 employment tribunals have had the power to order employers to take back employees who have been unfairly dismissed. While it is true that in the end such an order will not be enforced against the obdurate employer (who will end up having to pay enhanced compensation, but need not take back the employee), this development nonetheless is another indication that traditional objections may have lost their strength. As a result, in more recent years there have been cases where the courts have accepted that an injunction may properly be granted against an employer to prevent a dismissal in breach of contract. One of the first was *Hill v Parsons* (1972), where an injunction was granted to prevent the employer dismissing the employee with inadequate notice. As noted above (para.8–005), the circumstances of the case were rather special in that the employer did not really want to get rid of the employee, and the effect of the temporary injunction was to keep him in employment until the Industrial Relations Act came into force.

8–015   The real game changer came a few years later in *Gunton v Richmond LBC* (1980), where a college proposed to dismiss its registrar on disciplinary grounds without following the disciplinary procedure. The Court of Appeal (by a majority, and with some reluctance) granted him a declaration that this was a breach of contract; on the facts he could not get an injunction because it was found that he had accepted the termination before the trial, but he got damages to represent his salary for the time it would have taken to operate the disciplinary procedure as well as his notice money (see also *Boyo v Lambeth LBC* (1994)).

In the same year, in *Jones v Lee* (1980), a differently constituted Court of Appeal granted an interim injunction to prevent the dismissal of a head teacher in breach of the contractual disciplinary procedure, and since then such injunctions have been granted in numerous cases (e.g. *Irani v Southampton & South West Hampshire AHA* (1985); *Dietmann v Brent LBC* (1988); *Robb v Hammersmith & Fulham LBC* (1991); *Gryf-Lowczowski v Hinchingbrooke Healthcare NHS Trust* (2006)). In *Irani v Southampton & South West Hampshire AHA* (1985), the fact that the employer retained confidence in the employee was seen as crucial to this sort of order. However, in *Gryf-Lowczowski v Hinchingbrooke Healthcare NHS Trust* (2006) an interim injunction was granted to prevent dismissal in breach of the contractual disciplinary procedure even though it was admitted that mutual trust and confidence between the parties had completely broken down. The court noted that mutual trust and confidence was not essential to enable the disciplinary procedure to be carried out and also expressed concern that employers should not be able to "snap their fingers" at employees' rights under the contract.

An indication of how much things have changed is provided by the Supreme Court's decision in *West London Mental Health Trust v Chhabra* (2014). The claimant, a consultant psychiatrist, faced disciplinary proceedings for breaching patient confidentiality by discussing patients on the telephone, dictating medical reports and reading reports on which patients' names were visible, all while travelling by train. An investigation into the allegations was set up and the claimant was given an undertaking that the Trust's human resources director would not be involved in the investigatory process. In fact, this director was involved, even to the extent of making suggestions that the draft investigation report should be "beefed up" in various ways to strengthen the case against Dr Chhabra. The Supreme Court first granted an injunction preventing the Trust from treating her conduct as gross misconduct (as opposed to serious misconduct), apparently feeling no compunction about substituting its view for that of the employer on the matter. Furthermore, it treated this as an irregularity in the disciplinary process, along with the involvement of the human resources director in the investigation. In the light of these and other procedural discrepancies, the Supreme Court granted a second injunction to prevent the Trust from pursuing its concerns without completely starting afresh, with a new investigation.

8–016   It can be safely stated that the availability of injunctions to prevent employers dismissing in breach of contractual disciplinary procedures is a well-established exception to the alleged rule that orders for the enforcement of contracts of employment are not possible. In the public sector in particular, where disciplinary procedures are normally part of the contract, this can be a powerful remedy.

A second situation where the employer's power to dismiss may be limited is where there are substantive rather than procedural limitations in the contract: that is, where the contract stipulates that it may only be terminated on certain grounds. Traditionally contracts for academic staff in universities provided that they could only be dismissed for "good cause", which was seen as fundamental to the preservation of the freedom for academics to challenge received opinion. Such contractual provisions are comparatively rare, but they were recognised as limiting the power to dismiss by the House of Lords in *McClelland v NI General Health Services Board* (1957), where a declaration was granted.

Termination effective without acceptance

One of the reasons for the Court of Appeal's reluctance to grant a declaration in *Gunton v Richmond LBC* (1980) was that there was some support at that time for the view that the employee could not keep the contract alive if the employer was determined to terminate it, even if acting in breach.   8–017

Usually, if one party to a contract commits a fundamental breach, the innocent party may elect whether to accept it as a termination of the contract or to waive it and keep the contract alive. At one time it was argued that contracts of employment were an exception to this rule, so that if an employer dismissed an employee, albeit in fundamental breach, then that dismissal brought the contract to an end without the need for acceptance by the employee—the "automatic theory of termination". One of several cases expressing this view is *Vine v National Dock Labour Board* (1957), where Lord Kilmuir said, "if the master wrongfully dismisses the servant . . . the employment is effectively terminated, albeit in breach of contract". However, at that time there was a lot of support for the view that any contract could be terminated by fundamental breach without acceptance, a view finally and firmly scotched by the House of Lords' decision in *Photo Production Ltd v Securicor Transport Ltd* (1980). That case decisively stated the rule that, for contracts in general, the "elective theory of termination" prevailed—namely, that the contract only ends when the innocent party elects to accept the repudiatory breach as terminating the contract.

Some of the difficulties reconciling the view that contracts of employment were different from other contracts in this regard were pointed out by Megarry VC in *Thomas Marshall (Exports) Ltd v Guinle* (1978), where he noted that no one had ever doubted the correctness of the decisions in *Lumley v Wagner* (1852) and *Warner Bros v Nelson* (1937), yet if contracts of employment really were an exception to the general rule then the employers of these delinquent employees would have had no choice but to accept the breach and be relegated to a claim in damages. Megarry's admirable arguments were not given the attention they deserved when this issue was canvassed in front of employment tribunals in a number of cases where employers argued that by some particularly egregious misconduct the employee had "dismissed himself"—the employee's fundamental breach terminating the contract without any acceptance (that is, dismissal) by the employer.

8–018   In unfair dismissal cases, this particular argument was finally rejected by the Court of Appeal in *LTE v Clarke* (1981) (see below, para.8–030), but even then it was argued in some quarters that this applied to unfair dismissal cases only.

The point went to the Supreme Court in *Société Générale v Geys* (2013), an everyday story of City of London folk. The claimant was managing director of one of the bank's divisions in London until the day in November 2007 when he was summarily dismissed and escorted from the building, never to return. He claimed damages of €12.5 million, but the bank insisted that he was merely entitled to €7.9 million. It was accepted that the dismissal was a fundamental breach of contract by the employer. The issue was whether it thereby terminated his contract immediately in November, or whether the contract terminated only when the employer got round to exercising its contractual right to dismiss him the following January. On this depended his right to €650,000 bonus, payable only if he was employed up to the end of the calendar year. The Supreme Court held that contracts of employment should not be treated differently from other contracts in this regard and that the elective theory should apply. As Lord Hope pointed out, if the contract were to terminate automatically on fundamental breach, it would allow the wrongdoer the advantage of choosing when the contract would end, thus benefiting from his own wrong.

The resolution of this point in favour of treating contracts of employment like other contracts is to be welcomed as a matter of legal coherence as well as being in the interests of justice.

Judicial review

8–019   A quite different avenue tried by some employees in public employment has been the claim for judicial review. If a public body acts outside its powers, in breach of procedure, or wholly unreasonably, it is possible to seek public law remedies to quash the decision (what used to be known as an order for certiorari), or sometimes to compel the body to behave in accordance with the rules. Thus an employee of a public body might seek judicial review of a decision to dismiss him in order to get the decision declared a nullity. However, it is clear that opportunities to claim judicial review are limited, in that if the essence of the dispute is a private contractual matter, judicial review will not be permitted, even though there is some "public" element to the claimant's employment. In *R v BBC ex p Lavelle* (1983) the BBC dismissed an employee when BBC property was discovered at her flat. The disciplinary procedure in her contract was not followed, and she sought a quashing order. Woolf J held that public law remedies such as an application for judicial review were inappropriate to deal with the relationship of employer and employee, which was a private law matter. A similar view was adopted by the Court of Appeal in *R v East Berks AHA ex p Walsh* (1984). Here the terms of the employee's contract as a senior nursing officer were subject to statutory regulation, but the court held that the enforcement of those terms was purely a private law matter for which public law remedies were not available.

Subsequent case-law has confirmed that for the time being judicial review is likely to be limited in scope to a fairly small category of public employees and, even then, not for all aspects of their contracts of employment. One example where it was successful was *R (Shoesmith) v OFSTED* (2011), where the claimant, who held the statutory office of Director of Children's Services in Haringey, was summarily dismissed basically on the directions of a Government minister over failings leading to the death of a toddler ("Baby P"). It was held that the case was amenable to judicial review, since she held a public office and since employment tribunal proceedings would be less effective as a remedy. The employer had acted unlawfully in its decision to dismiss and a quashing order was granted.

Unfair Dismissal

The proximate reason for the introduction of the law on unfair dismissal was the recommendation of the Donovan Commission in its 1968 Report (Ch.IX), but a consensus on the need for legislation had already developed, fuelled by similar reforms in other European countries and reflected in the United Kingdom's acceptance in 1964 of the ILO's Recommendation No.119 on Termination of Employment. This advised that contracts should be terminated only if there was a valid reason related to the conduct or capacity of the worker or the operational requirements of the business. This, broadly speaking, is the principle underlying the law of unfair dismissal, although its implementation is by no means so simple. The Donovan Commission was mainly concerned with industrial relations, but it recommended changes to the law on dismissal precisely because a number of industrial disputes were caused by dismissals—if the workforce felt that someone had been sacked unfairly, they were apt to stage a lightning strike. It was thought that if there were some other channel of complaint, disputes of this kind would be lessened. **8–020**

The Labour Government which set up the Donovan Commission gave way to the Conservative administration led by Edward Heath in 1970. That administration passed its own reforms of industrial action in the ill-fated Industrial Relations Act 1971, but that Act did include a new statutory right to claim unfair dismissal. When the Industrial Relations Act 1971 was repealed in 1974 by the Trade Union and Labour Relations Act (TULRA), the Labour Government decided to retain the law of unfair dismissal with very little alteration. There have been amendments over the years, but the basic structure has not changed fundamentally. The law on unfair dismissal is now to be found in the Employment Rights Act 1996 Pt X (as subsequently amended). As noted already, it is a claim brought exclusively in employment tribunals.

Entitlement to claim

Qualifying period of employment

8–021　The ILO Recommendation accepted that certain categories of worker could legitimately be excluded from protection against unfair dismissal, such as those taken on for a specific period rather than indefinitely, those on probation and those employed on a casual or temporary basis. Under the ERA, only employees have the right to claim unfair dismissal (see above, para.3–003), and they must have completed a minimum qualifying period of continuous employment which was increased from one year to two years in April 2012 (ERA s.108(1); see above, para.3–029). Trade unions have long argued that all employment protection rights, including the right to claim unfair dismissal, should be available from the first day of employment. The arguments in favour of a qualifying period are essentially pragmatic: first, that it is reasonable to have some sort of probation period during which the employer can decide whether or not an employee suits without having a decision to dismiss scrutinised too closely; secondly, that tribunals would be completely overwhelmed with claims if there were no qualifying period. Over the years the length of the qualifying period has fluctuated. It was two years when first introduced, then reduced to six months, then increased to one year, then (in 1985) back to two. It was reduced to one year in 1999 as a compromise between the aspirations of unions and the wishes of employers. The Coalition Government increased the qualifying period to two years again, on the basis that this would give businesses "more confidence when they consider taking on people" (*Resolving Workplace Disputes*, BIS, January 2011), although it is hard to see why the ability to treat more people unfairly should increase business confidence. By the Government's own estimate, this removed some 2.9 million workers from unfair dismissal protection.

The 1990s witnessed a huge extension of the categories of dismissal which are automatically unfair (see below, para.8–079) for which there is no qualifying period of employment. It seems that employees dismissed with less than two years' service are increasingly trying to frame their claims to fall within one of these categories or else as unlawful discrimination, where again no qualifying periods apply (see above, Ch.2). Incidentally, there is nothing to stop an employer having a longer probation period. However, after one year a decision not to confirm the employee in post will at least be reviewable by an employment tribunal.

Retirement and age discrimination

8–022　Until the introduction of the law against age discrimination in 2006 employees who continued to work past retiring age were generally excluded from the right to claim unfair dismissal, although the rationale for their exclusion was far from obvious. If no special provision had been made, making employees retire on account of their age would obviously have been direct age discrimination (see above, para.2–026). Thus the Employment Equality (Age) Regulations 2006 provided that retirement at or above the age of 65 would not be unlawful age discrimination, nor unfair dismissal, provided that the employer followed a particular procedure of giving employees at least six months' notice of their expected retirement date and then giving consideration (but not necessarily acceding) to any request by the employee to stay on.

The retirement exceptions were abolished in April 2011. This means that compelling someone to retire on grounds of age will be prima facie age discrimination unless it can be justified (see above, para.2–054) and it will also be unfair dismissal.

Excluded categories

Certain categories of employee are disqualified from unfair dismissal claims: these are share fishermen, the police, and Crown employees where the relevant minister has issued an excepting certificate on grounds of national security, as was done in the GCHQ trade union membership dispute (see below, Ch.10) (ERA ss.199, 200, 193). TURERA introduced ERA s.192 permitting members of the armed forces to claim unfair dismissal, but not under ERA s.100 (health and safety grounds). At one time employees working abroad were excluded, but this exclusion was repealed in 1999, leaving open the question of whether all employees working abroad for British companies could claim unfair dismissal. In *Lawson v Serco Ltd* (2006) the House of Lords heard three joined appeals on this issue, involving a security officer working for a British company at a Royal Air Force base on Ascension Island, a youth worker employed by the Ministry of Defence at British Army establishments in Germany and an air crew member based in the United Kingdom but employed by a company resident in Hong Kong. In all three cases the House of Lords held that the employees were entitled to claim unfair dismissal. While firmly of the view that the right to claim unfair dismissal should generally be confined to employees working in Great Britain, the House of Lords considered that there could be exceptional cases where employees working abroad could be covered. In the case of peripatetic employees such as the air crew member, the question should be where he was based, in terms of how the contract actually operated, rather than what might have been stated when the contract was first made. Employees based abroad would only come within the protection of unfair dismissal law if their work had strong connections with Great Britain, meaning not only that the employer was based in Great Britain but that there was some additional factor, such as the fact that the worker was posted abroad by the employer for the purposes of the British business and could be either brought back to the United Kingdom or posted elsewhere. Working in what was effectively a British enclave abroad, as was the case for the security officer and the youth worker, was within this principle.

8–023

In general, any attempt to contract out of the unfair dismissal protection is void; however, there are two exceptions. Under ERA s.110, a dismissals procedure voluntarily agreed between employers and independent trade unions can be designated by the Secretary of State to apply instead of the statutory regime. Such designation will be granted only if it is at least as beneficial to employees as the statutory protection. This provision was a result of the feeling among some members of the Donovan Commission that voluntary self-regulation was better than imposed regulation and could develop better systems. In fact only one such agreement was ever made and it was terminated in 2001. The other exception is where the parties opt for arbitration, discussed above, para.1–008.

Where there is any dispute as to whether a worker is entitled to claim unfair dismissal, the burden of proof is on the employee to establish his or her right to claim.

The meaning of dismissal

8–024   Another hurdle to getting an unfair dismissal claim started is that the employee must have been dismissed: that is, the contract must have been terminated in such a way that it falls within the threefold definition of dismissal to be found in ERA s.95. Any other form of termination will not suffice. Again, this is for the employee to prove if it is in dispute.

Termination with or without notice

8–025   The most straightforward case of dismissal is under ERA s.95(1)(a), where the contract is terminated by the employer with or without notice. Whereas the giving of notice of the right length is crucial to a wrongful dismissal claim, it is pretty well irrelevant to unfair dismissal, one of the differences between the statutory and the contract claim.

The only problem likely to arise in this connection is whether or not the precise form of words used meant that the employee was dismissed. Few of us would find, "You're fired!" ambiguous, and we would probably understand what was meant if we were told to get our cards and go. "On your bike" enjoyed a brief vogue in the 1980s, but is not so obvious; and being told to "go down the road" means you are dismissed in Yorkshire, but might be meaningless elsewhere. The difference between mere abuse and dismissal has caused a surprising number of problems: in *Futty v Brekkes* (1974) "Fuck off!" was taken to mean "Go away for the rest of the day and come back tomorrow", but clearly there are occasions when it could constitute termination (apart from possibly giving rise to a constructive dismissal claim, below). The test appears to be, what did the employer intend by the words used, and what would a reasonable employee have understood from what was said (*Tanner v Kean* (1978))? Where words are spoken in the heat of the moment, they should not always be taken at face value: however, it should also be noted that, once given, a notice of dismissal cannot be unilaterally revoked (although see *Roberts v West Coast Trains Ltd* (2004), below, para.8–035).

Expiry of a limited-term contract without renewal

8–026   The position of workers on fixed-term contracts is discussed in Ch.3 (see above, para.3–026). At common law, at the end of the defined term, a fixed-term contract would terminate automatically. However, under ERA s.95, for the purposes of unfair dismissal claims this situation is designated as a dismissal, because otherwise employers could indirectly evade the operation of unfair dismissal legislation, in the following way. The employer could put all staff on fixed-term contracts of, say, six months or one year's duration, renewable. At the end of every fixed period, the employer could review the situation and decide whether or not she wished to retain the employee. If she decided against renewal, the employee would have no redress, because there would have been no dismissal. It is true that if the employer dismissed the employee during the currency of the fixed term, the employee would have the usual right to claim. Yet, provided that the fixed term was not for too long a period, it would not be much of a hardship for the employer to wait until the end of the period and then let the employee go.

It was to prevent such abuses that the definition of dismissal was framed so as to include the expiry of a fixed-term contract without renewal. The fact that the employee has the right to claim does not, of course, mean that he will succeed. Thus the employer who genuinely needed someone for a specific period only should have had no fear of an adverse claim, in theory at least. However, many employers did not think that this was satisfactory: they could be faced with unmeritorious claims, and would still spend time and money defending them, which would probably not be recouped even if they won. To take account of this, then, an exception was included which allowed the employee to waive the right to claim unfair dismissal on expiry of a fixed-term contract. Unfortunately, this opened the way for precisely the abuse which the original provision was intended to prevent. There was no mechanism for ensuring that employers only used this exception when they had a genuine short-term need, and so it was possible for employers to have a pool of second-class employees on fixed-term contracts whose dismissal did not expose the employer to any kind of financial liability. The Employment Relations Act 1999 dealt with this abuse by abolishing the possibility of waivers of unfair dismissal rights in fixed-term contracts.

One issue that arose early on was whether expiry of a fixed-term contract which contained provision for termination before the end of the fixed term by either party giving notice should be regarded as a fixed-term contract for the purposes of ERA s.95(1)(b). The argument that a term entitling parties to terminate before the end of the agreed period was inconsistent with the nature of a fixed-term contract was accepted by the Court of Appeal in *BBC v Ioannou* (1975), but it was quickly realised that this decision handed employers a simple way of avoiding the legislation: they could simply ensure that provision for termination by notice was included in the contract and the employee would then have no recourse when the contract expired. The Court of Appeal admitted its mistake and held that expiry of such a contract would count as dismissal in *Dixon v BBC* (1979) (see also *Allen v National Australia Group Europe Ltd* (2004)).

The Fixed-term Employees (Prevention of Less Favourable Treatment) **8–027** Regulations 2002 introduced a wider concept than hitherto, to include contracts terminating on the completion of a particular task or on the happening (or non-happening) of a specific event, as well as those terminating on a certain date (see above, para.3–026). This entailed a new terminology: expiry of a fixed-term contract was replaced by expiry of a limited-term contract. A limited-term contract is defined by ERA ss.235(2A) and (2B) as a contract which is not intended to be permanent and which is to terminate on the happening of a "limiting event"—defined as expiry of a fixed-term contract, completion of the task in contracts terminating on the completion of a particular task and the happening (or non-happening) of a specific event in contracts providing for termination in that way. ERA s.95(1)(b) provides that where a limited-term contract comes to an end without renewal, it will constitute a dismissal for the purposes of unfair dismissal.

In relation to automatic termination on the happening of a specific event (which, at common law, would mean that neither party had terminated the contract) even before the Fixed-term Employees Regulations 2002, courts had shown themselves astute to the abuse which could arise if an employer was allowed to stipulate that the contract would terminate automatically on the happening of a certain event. The employer could, for example, stipulate that the contract would terminate automatically if the employee were to be off ill for more than two weeks or if the employee were to be late three times within a two-month period. Instead of being able to try a claim for unfair dismissal, the employee might find that he fell at the first hurdle because of the form of the termination. In *Igbo v Johnson Matthey* (1986) the Court of Appeal held that the effect of automatic termination clauses was to permit avoidance of the require-ments of the ERA, which is prohibited by ERA s.203. Thus it was held that such provisions would be void and the termination would be by the employer, and thus dismissal.

Constructive dismissal

8–028   The third situation which counts as dismissal is where:

> "the employee terminates the contract . . . (with or without notice) in circum-stances in which he is entitled to terminate it without notice by reason of the employer's conduct" (ERA s.95(1)(c)).

Thus, in this situation, resignation by the employee is construed as dismissal. In *Western Excavating v Sharp* (1978) the Court of Appeal adopted a strictly contractual approach to the interpretation of this phrase and held that the only circumstances where the employee would be entitled to terminate the contract without notice would be where the employer was in fundamental breach of con-tract. The most obvious example of such a breach would be where the employer attempts unilaterally to change the terms of the contract, perhaps by increasing hours, or reducing pay without agreement, or changing job duties in breach of contract (cf. *Land Securities Trillium Ltd v Thornley* (2005)).

Although the Court of Appeal made it clear in *Western Excavating v Sharp* that unreasonable conduct by the employer causing an employee to leave would be insufficient for constructive dismissal if it fell short of a breach of contract, to some extent notions of unreasonableness have returned by the back door through the development of the reciprocal duty of employer and employee to maintain mutual trust and confidence as a fundamental term of the contract (see above, para.4–026). Thus if an employer is so unreasonable that the work relationship becomes impossible, the employee may resign and claim to have been constructively dismissed on the basis that the employer has destroyed the mutual trust and confidence which should subsist between them.

An unreasonable accusation of theft against an employee of good character and many years standing (*Robinson v Crompton Parkinson* (1978)), arbitrary or capricious refusal of a pay rise to one employee when everyone else got one (*Gardner v Beresford* (1978)), swearing at the employee (*Palmanor v Cedron* (1978)) and giving her a dressing down in front of other employees (*Hilton International v Protopapa* (1990)) have all been held to be acts which destroy mutual trust and confidence in the context of constructive dismissal.

In *Stanley Cole (Wainfleet) Ltd v Sheridan* (2003) the EAT considered that the disproportionate response of an employer in giving the employee a final warning for relatively minor misconduct was capable of founding a constructive dismissal claim. This illustrates how the standards of acceptable behaviour have risen over the years, so that there is more likelihood of bad behaviour being held to destroy mutual trust and confidence. For example, bullying behaviour amounting to sexual harassment may lead to constructive dismissal as well as a possible sex discrimination claim (*Reed v Stedman* (1999)). Bullying and harassment are increasingly recognised also as being potential breaches of another important implied term in the contract: the employer's duty to take reasonable care for the health and safety of employees at work. In *Waltons & Morse v Dorrington* (1997) failure to treat seriously an employee's complaints about being exposed to a smoky atmosphere through proximity to a heavy-smoking colleague was held to breach a related implied duty on the employer to provide a reasonably suitable working environment, enabling the employee to claim that she had been constructively dismissed.

These are all decisions of the EAT, but the concept that a breach by the **8–029** employer of the duty to maintain mutual trust and confidence would constitute constructive dismissal was accepted by the House of Lords in *Malik v BCCI* (1997), where it was made clear also that the test is objective: the question is whether the employer's conduct was likely to have the effect of destroying or seriously damaging the employment relationship (see also *Omilaju v London Borough of Waltham Forest* (2005)). However, since it is often highly unreasonable conduct of the employer which has this effect, it is not surprising that employers have sought to argue that whether their conduct should be seen as having this effect should be judged by a "band of reasonable responses" test, such as is used in judging the fairness of a dismissal (see below, para.8–047). This argument had some success in the EAT, but was firmly rejected by the Court of Appeal in *Buckland v Bournemouth University* (2010). In this case, the university had committed a breach of the mutual trust and confidence term by changing the marks which a professor had awarded to students' examination scripts without telling him. The university subsequently tried to make amends by holding an inquiry into what had happened, which vindicated the professor and found that the re-marking should not have occurred. The university's case was that this was a reasonable response to the situation in which it found itself as an employer, and therefore it should not be considered as in breach of the trust and confidence term. The Court of Appeal rejected this because, first, the test of whether there has been a breach of contract is judged objectively, not by a reasonableness standard, and secondly, once the breach had occurred, the claimant was entitled to treat it as constructive dismissal. A contract-breaker can offer amends, but the innocent party does not have to accept and can treat the contract as at an end.

In *Lewis v Motorworld* (1986) an employee was demoted and his salary package reduced. The employee did not resign but remained in employment, thus waiving the breach and affirming the contract. However, the employer persistently and unfairly criticised the employee, threatening him with dismissal, until eventually he resigned. The Court of Appeal held that a series of minor incidents taken together could destroy mutual trust and confidence and thus amount to a fundamental breach even though the final event was not itself a breach of contract; furthermore, the employee was entitled to rely also on the unilateral demotion as evidence of the employer's breach of the implied term, even though he had waived his right to treat it as a repudiatory breach. In *Omilaju v London Borough of Waltham Forest* (2005) the Court of Appeal clarified that the "last straw" might not even be unreasonable or blameworthy conduct by the employer (although that would be unusual), as long as it contributed to the breach of the implied term and could be regarded as the last of a series of acts having that effect.

Resignation and termination by mutual agreement

8–030   A resignation other than in response to a fundamental breach by the employer will not constitute dismissal. Tribunals in general show awareness that they should not too easily find that the contract was terminated by voluntary resignation or by mutual agreement, since if there is no dismissal the tribunal has no jurisdiction to inquire into the merits of the case. Thus it has been held since the earliest cases that where an employee is faced with the choice of resigning or being dismissed and chooses to resign (because it may make trying to find another job easier) then this will usually operate in fact as a dismissal (*East Sussex CC v Walker* (1972); see also *Jones v Mid-Glamorgan CC* (1997)). In *Martin v MBS Fastenings* (1983) an employee who crashed the company minibus (which he was allowed to use in his own time) after drinking seven pints of beer was told that disciplinary proceedings were likely to result in his dismissal and it would be in his interests to resign. He did so, but later claimed he had been unfairly dismissed. It was held that his resignation was genuine: he had done it in order to pre-empt the disciplinary proceedings. Again, in *Sheffield v Oxford Controls* (1979), the director of a small private company fell out with the owner and threatened to leave. The owner asked him how much he wanted to go; they agreed on £10,000 and the director resigned. He later claimed that he had been forced to resign because he would otherwise have been dismissed. However, it was held to be a genuine resignation: it was the offer of satisfactory compensation which induced his resignation, not fear of dismissal. This can be contrasted with *Sandhu v Jan de Rijk Transport Ltd* (2007), where the operations manager of the company was called to a meeting at head office and told on arrival that he was being dismissed with more or less immediate effect. The employee managed to negotiate a three-month notice period, that he should keep his company car for a month and (most important of all) that he should retain his mobile phone. When he claimed unfair dismissal the employer argued that he had resigned, an argument accepted by the employment tribunal and EAT. The

Court of Appeal, however, held that the lower tribunals were in error and that this situation could not properly be seen as anything other than a dismissal by the employer.

Where the employer needs to declare redundancies, volunteers are often sought—a course of action preferred by trade unions and employees. But if the employees volunteer, does this mean that the contract terminates by mutual agreement rather than by dismissal? In one sense, yes. However, for a redundancy claim as with an unfair dismissal claim, it is necessary that the employee should have been dismissed. Hence the analysis usually adopted in this situation is that the employee has simply volunteered to be dismissed and that there is still a termination by the employer. It seems that employees and their advisers should be careful of this point: in *Birch v University of Liverpool* (1985) academic staff who volunteered for early retirement under what was in effect a redundancy scheme were held to have terminated their contracts by mutual agreement with the employer and not to have been dismissed (see also *AGCO Ltd v Massey Ferguson Pension Trust Ltd* (2003)). The circumstances of *Birch v University of Liverpool* were slightly unusual in that the redundancy scheme provided compensation considerably in excess of a statutory payment on the understanding that the statutory payment was not payable as well, so the employees' claims were not meritorious. But this is not meant to be the point. It is interesting further to note that the Court of Appeal treated this as a question of law and overturned the employment tribunal's decision, despite its earlier decision in *Martin v MBS Fastenings* (1983) that such issues are questions of fact.

As with termination by the employer, a resignation should not automatically be taken at face value where words are spoken in anger (*Sovereign House Security v Savage* (1989)), although again it will depend on what a reasonable employer would have understood in the circumstances. Unlike termination by the employer, it would appear that there is no room for a concept of "constructive resignation", where the employer terminates but is entitled to do so because of the employee's fundamental breach. Ingenious arguments to the contrary were finally laid to rest by the Court of Appeal in *London Transport Executive v Clarke* (1981). In general in contract law, where one party commits a fundamental breach, the contract is not terminated unless and until the innocent party accepts it as a repudiation of the contract. It is, therefore, the innocent party who terminates the contract. In *LTE v Clarke* the Court of Appeal held that contracts of employment were no exception to this rule. This, indeed, is why it is necessary to have statutory provision for an employee's resignation in the face of the employer's breach to count as dismissal, for at common law it would undoubtedly be a termination by the employee.

Frustration

As with other sorts of contract, the contract of employment may be terminated   **8–031** if it becomes impossible to perform without the fault of either party. If so, the contract is frustrated, and there is no dismissal in law. This was recognised at common law as long ago as *Poussard v Spiers & Pond* (1876), where an opera singer caught a cold and was unable to take part in a week of rehearsals and the first few performances of the opera in which she was contracted to appear. The management hired a replacement, who was only prepared to step in if she was given a month's contract. Poussard sued the management for breach of contract in not letting her return to the part once she had recovered. The court held that the illness which had prevented her from performing went to the root of the contract and discharged the defendants from further obligation to her. The circumstances were unusual, in that an absence for a matter of days would not be so crucial in most jobs; also it would have been different if the management had been able to get a temporary substitute just for the first few performances. That was not the case on the facts. Thus the contract had been frustrated.

In practice, the incapacity of the employee through illness or accident, as in *Poussard v Spiers*, is one of the main situations where frustration is likely to be argued. Incapacity of the employer is more rare: first, the personal presence of the employer is rarely essential to the performance of the contract, and secondly, if the employer is an individual who dies, or a company which is wound up, special rules apply (see below, para.8–033). Guidance on when the employee's incapacity will be taken to frustrate the contract was given in *Egg Stores v Leibovici* (1977), where the EAT said that the basic question was, "has the time arrived when the employer can no longer reasonably be expected to keep the absent employee's post open for him?" The following considerations are relevant: the length of previous employment (greater efforts should be made for a long-serving employee); how long the employment had been expected to continue (usually, but not always, indefinitely); the nature of the job; the nature, length and effect of the disabling event (will the employee make a full recovery? Is the period of absence relatively clear-cut?); the need for the work to be done by a replacement (rather than getting other workers to cover it); the risk of acquiring unfair dismissal or redundancy obligations to a replacement; whether wages have continued to be paid (if so, it is more burdensome to hold the job open, but it indicates a belief in the contract's continuance); the acts and statements of the employer (whether there has been a dismissal or not); and whether, in all the circumstances, a reasonable employer could be expected to wait any longer before replacing the employee on a permanent basis.

This guidance, with its emphasis on reasonableness, bears a striking resemblance to the criteria which would be applied if a tribunal were deciding whether an employee had been unfairly dismissed on grounds of incapability to do the job; but if the contract is frustrated, there is no dismissal, and a tribunal will not get to consider the merits. For this reason, in *Harman v Flexible Lamps* (1980), Bristow J, giving the judgment of the EAT, said that the doctrine of frustration should hardly ever be invoked in relation to ordinary contracts of employment which are, after all, terminable on notice. If the employee is absent for a long period, the contract is not really impossible to perform, since the employer is able under its terms to issue a valid notice of termination. This would, of course, constitute dismissal, and could found an action for unfair dismissal, but it is submitted that this would be desirable given the general policy underpinning the law. However, the Court of Appeal expressly disapproved this in *Notcutt v Universal Equipment* (1986), saying that although a contract might be terminable on short notice, the parties probably intended it to be long lasting, and that that intention could be frustrated by the employee's incapacity. The court adopted the approach in *Egg Stores v Leibovici*, holding that a contract of employment could be terminated both by a dramatic, shattering event, and by an uncertain event such as illness or accident where a long process would be involved before it was possible to say that there had been frustration.

Nevertheless, decisions in more recent cases show courts and tribunals **8–032** reluctant to find that contracts of employment have been frustrated and more ready to find that the circumstances were provided for in the contract. In the case of illness, it is necessary to consider any provisions in the contract for sick pay, permanent health insurance and ill-health early retirement. In *Villella v MFI* (1999) the Court of Appeal made the point that where the employee was contractually entitled to permanent health insurance benefits which were designed to last until death or retirement age, his incapacity for three years could not be regarded as frustrating the contract, as it had made provision for this very situation. In *Four Seasons Healthcare Ltd v Maughan* (2005), where the bail conditions of a nurse accused of assaulting a patient forbade him to enter the premises of the care home where he had been employed, the EAT refused to find that the contract had been frustrated by his inability to work through a 10-month period since the employer could have dismissed him following his arrest rather than awaiting the outcome of the criminal trial. In *Gryf-Lowczowski v Hinchingbrooke Healthcare NHS Trust* (2006), where a hospital had been deprived of the services of one of only two consultant surgeons specialising in a particular field for two years while doubts about his competence were investigated, the High Court held that the contract was not frustrated, taking into account his relatively long service, the catastrophic effects for him if his contract was terminated in this way and the realistic possibility that he would be able to return to work following retraining.

Apart from illness or accident, the other common situation where frustration is alleged is where the employee is sentenced to a term of imprisonment. Yet is this really a situation of impossibility without the fault of either party? It is in one sense the employee's fault, for committing the offence in the first place. But on the other hand, the employee presumably did not commit the offence with the intention of breaking the contract, and indeed, the offence might have resulted in a different punishment, like a fine. This point was recognised early on by Lord Denning, who commented; "If a prima donna thoughtlessly sits in a draught and loses her voice, the contract may be frustrated by her illness, even though it may be said to be 'self-induced'" (*Hare v Murphy Brothers* (1974)). It may be noted that some employers do attempt to distinguish between avoidable illnesses or injuries (such as sporting injuries) and the rest, declining to top up SSP in the former case.

A further complication in the imprisonment situation is that it is the employee who will be trying to argue that he or she was at fault and that it is a self-induced breach rather than frustration. For if it is frustration, the tribunal will have no jurisdiction to hear the case, whereas if the contract is terminated by the employer, it will. This is in contrast to the usual contractual disputes over frustration where the claimant is claiming that the defendant was at fault and the defendant tries to defend herself by claiming she was not at fault and that the contract is frustrated. When this situation came before the Court of Appeal in *Shepherd v Jerrom* (1986), they held that it was contrary to the general principle that no one should profit from his own wrong to allow the employee to rely on his own wrongdoing to improve his position. Thus, it was held that a prison sentence of between six months and two years was capable of frustrating an apprenticeship contract which had been due to last for four years.

Death or dissolution of the employer

8–033   At common law the death of an individual employer or the compulsory liqui- dation of a company would probably have resulted in the frustration of the contract. Since the introduction of the law of redundancy, the matter has been dealt with by statute, which provides that in these circumstances (and in cases of voluntary liquidation or the dissolution of a partnership), the employee will be treated as having been dismissed and entitled to a redundancy payment if the business is not continued under new ownership, or if the employee's contract is not continued.

The effective date of termination

8–034   The exact date on which a contract comes to an end is vitally important for two reasons. First, the employee must institute any claim within a comparatively short limitation period—three months for unfair dismissal and six months for a redundancy payment—and hence it is necessary to know from what date time begins to run. Secondly, the existence of employment protection rights and the calculation of unfair dismissal compensation and redundancy payments depend on the amount of continuous employment that the employee has, and thus it is necessary to know exactly when the contract ended in order to compute the overall period of continuous employment. Unfortunately the statutory provi- sions are less than straightforward, and complexity is compounded by the fact that the effective date can be different according to which of these two ques- tions is being answered. In *Fitzgerald v University of Kent at Canterbury* (2004) the Court of Appeal made it clear that the effective date of termination is to be judged objectively from the facts and that it is not open to the parties to decide it by agreement.

So far as limitation periods are concerned, the effective date of termination is the date on which notice expires (where the dismissal is with notice) or the date on which termination takes effect (if the dismissal is without notice) (ERA s.97). In general, this means that it is the last day on which the employee attends for work, and an employee who is dismissed with inadequate notice cannot treat the date as deferred until after the date on which she would have been dismissed if she had received the notice to which she was entitled. In the light of *Société Générale v Geys* (2013) it might be open to an employee to argue that if the termination without notice was in fundamental breach of contract, the contract does not terminate for limitation purposes until he has accepted the breach: no doubt this will arise for consideration in due course.

Difficulty arises in the very common case where the employer dismisses the employee with wages in lieu of notice. This could be interpreted as a termination at once, with a sum equivalent to damages for breach of contract, or dismissal on notice, except that the employee is not required to work for the period of notice. In the second case, the effective date would be later, thus extending the limitation period. Tribunals and courts generally prefer the first view, and therefore the limitation period runs against the employee from the last day that he was at work. However, it has been held (e.g. *Leech v Preston BC* (1985)) that sometimes the true construction may be that the employee is not being required to work his notice. One would probably advise an employee given wages in lieu of notice to claim within three months of the last day worked, but if he is already too late, it might be worth arguing for the other construction, although without much hope of success unless there is other supporting evidence. Tribunals do have discretion, under ERA s.111(2)(b), to extend the limitation period where they consider that it was not "reasonably practicable" for the employee to present the claim within three months, but in practice this discretion is exercised very sparingly.

What if the employee makes an unsuccessful internal appeal against dismissal? Is the date of the original dismissal the effective date of termination, or is it the date when the appeal is turned down? This depends on whether, on a proper construction of the contract, the situation is one where the dismissal takes effect, but there is a possibility of reinstatement, in which case the effective date of termination is the date of the original dismissal (e.g. *Sainsbury v Savage* (1981)), or whether the employee is suspended (although the contract continues) until the appeal is heard, in which case the later date is the effective date of termination (e.g. *Drage v Governors of Greenford School* (2000)). The position may be even more complicated than this. In *Roberts v West Coast Trains Ltd* (2004) the employee was dismissed following a disciplinary hearing. He appealed, but lodged an unfair dismissal claim one day within the three-month limit following the original dismissal. Two days later his employer informed him that his appeal had been successful and that the penalty of dismissal had been reduced to demotion and a period of suspension without pay (both penalties allowed under the contract). The Court of Appeal construed the contract to mean that, in this case, the contract was revived with retrospective effect, meaning that at the time he made his tribunal claim he had not been dismissed. Of course, if he had waited for the outcome of his appeal and it had not been successful, the original dismissal date would have stood and he could have found himself out of time for making a tribunal application. This was taken a step further in *McMaster v Antrim Borough Council* (2011). The employee, who had been dismissed for gross misconduct and had lost an internal appeal, had a contractual right of appeal to an external body. It ultimately upheld his appeal against dismissal—but this was six months after it had taken place and his employer refused to accept the appeal outcome. The Northern Ireland Court of Appeal held, his contract was revived by the successful appeal, so he had three months from when he was notified of it in which to make his application for unfair dismissal.

8–035

Decisions to dismiss are often communicated to the employee in person, but if sent by letter, the Supreme Court has held that the effective date of termination is not necessarily the date on which it is delivered but the date on which the employee could reasonably be expected to have read it (*GISDA Cyf v Barratt* (2010)).

For a fixed-term contract, the effective date of termination is the date on which it expires without renewal; constructive dismissal is not dealt with expressly by the statute, but usually the effective date is the date on which the employee leaves.

8–036   In assessing the date of termination of the contract for the purpose of computing the employee's period of continuous employment, the effective date is usually the same as discussed above, but with one important qualification. If the employer dismisses the employee with less notice than that to which he was entitled by statute, the balance of the statutory period of notice is added on. This may be crucial in getting the employee over the two years' continuous employment hurdle or in improving his compensation rights. Note that the balance of a contractual period of notice, if longer than the statutory minimum, may not be added in.

Procedural requirements before dismissal

8–037   One of the effects of unfair dismissal law is that it has not just provided employees with a remedy, but it has also provided employers with standards of how to treat employees. In particular, it has promoted some elements of procedural justice, rather similar to (but not the same as) the principles of natural justice. A good example is the principle that everyone should get a fair hearing: if an employer dismisses an employee for misconduct without hearing first what the employee has to say in their own defence, the dismissal is very likely to be unfair. The concept of procedural justice in relation to unfair dismissal has developed quite a lot over the last 45 years, assisted by successive Acas Codes of Practice on Disciplinary and Grievance Procedures. Some aspects of procedure have been enshrined in legislation and they are dealt with before considering fairness and unfairness more generally.

The right to be accompanied

8–038   The right to be accompanied during disciplinary and grievance hearings was introduced by Employment Relations Act (ERelA) 1999 ss.10–13 as amended by ERelA 2004. It is available to the wider category of "workers" rather than just employees and is a right to be accompanied by a fellow worker or a trade union official (who may be an official not employed by the employer). Some guidance on exercise of the right is given in the Acas Code of Practice on Disciplinary and Grievance Procedures (2015). The companion need not act unless she is willing to do so, but if she agrees, she will be entitled to paid time off to prepare for the hearing and to attend it. According to ERelA 1999 s.10(2B), (2C), the companion has a right to address the hearing on the worker's behalf, including putting the case, summing it up and responding to any views expressed, but she cannot answer questions on the worker's behalf. The limitation of the representative to co-workers or union officials excludes legal representatives or family members, for example, but it is worth noting that in *Stevens v University of Birmingham* (2015) it was held that to deny a clinician the right to be accompanied by a member of the Medical Protection Society, an organisation providing professional support services for doctors, but a company limited by guarantee rather than a trade union, was a breach of the duty of mutual trust and confidence. This might open the door for commercial organisations providing disciplinary representation services which have not managed to secure trade union status (see below, para.10–035). The employee has to make a reasonable request for representation: the 2009 version of the Acas Code suggested that this meant that the choice of the colleague who should be the representative must be reasonable, but this was disapproved by the EAT in *Toal v GB Oil* (2013). This led to the Acas Code being amended in 2015, to drop this stipulation.

The main issue which arises in relation to the right to be accompanied is identifying which hearings it applies to. In the past employers may not have distinguished clearly between the stages of investigating misconduct, say, and then disciplining the worker for it. The Act means that these stages must be distinguished and the Code makes clear that while investigations, informal interviews and counselling sessions are not within the scope of the right, any meeting which may result in the administration or confirmation of a warning, or any other disciplinary action, attracts it. Thus the possible outcome of the meeting seems to be the critical issue. In *London Underground Ltd v Ferenc-Batchelor* (2003) the claimant was denied a companion because the result of the meeting was what the employer called an "informal oral warning". This warning was going to be recorded in writing on the employee's file and would be taken into account in any later disciplinary proceedings. In these circumstances the EAT held that this was a disciplinary hearing and the employee had been wrongly denied her right to be accompanied. Contrast *Skiggs v South West Trains Ltd* (2005), where the EAT held that an employee was not entitled to be accompanied at a meeting to investigate a grievance lodged by another employee against him, notwithstanding that the outcome might mean that he would be subjected to disciplinary proceedings. In *Heathmill Multimedia Asp Ltd v Jones* (2003) the EAT held that a meeting to tell employees that they were being dismissed by reason of redundancy was not a disciplinary hearing within the meaning of ERelA 1999 s.10, and so did not attract the right to be accompanied.

As grievance proceedings are instigated by employees and may cover all sorts of issues from the trivial to the extremely serious, the Act limits the right to be accompanied to grievance hearings which concern a "duty by an employer in relation to a worker" (ERelA 1999 s.13(5)). This may be a statutory duty or a contractual duty, but would not cover, for example, a request for a pay rise or a complaint about car parking facilities. Where an employer fails to allow a worker to be accompanied, the worker may apply to a tribunal for up to two weeks' compensation. However, in practice, a stronger sanction may be the increased likelihood of a dismissal being found to have been procedurally unfair where this right has been denied to an employee.

8–039   Apart from the statutory right to be accompanied, employees may also have a right to representation in disciplinary proceedings under their contracts of employment. These usually limit representation to a fellow-employee or union official and frequently expressly exclude legal representation. Recently the refusal to allow legal representation has been attacked as a breach of ECHR art.6—the right to a fair trial. In *R (G) v Governors of X School* (2011) the Supreme Court accepted that legal representation should be permitted when the outcome of disciplinary proceedings would not just be loss of a job but possible complete exclusion from the employee's profession, but denied that it was a breach of ECHR art.6 to refuse legal representation in ordinary disciplinary proceedings. The case concerned a teaching assistant accused of an improper relationship with a pupil, whose central argument was that the outcome of the internal disciplinary proceedings were likely to have a strong influence on the Independent Safeguarding Authority (ISA) which would determine whether he should be permitted to work with children in the future. The Supreme Court held that the ISA had a duty to make its own independent judgment, the claimant could have legal representation in making his case to them, and the purpose of ISA proceedings was different from the purpose of the internal disciplinary hearing which led to his dismissal. In these circumstances, they held that his art.6 right was not infringed by denying him legal representation at the internal hearing.

An example of a hearing which was considered as involving the possible complete exclusion from the profession, and thus engaging art.6, was the decision of the General Medical Council on whether a doctor was fit to practise—*R (Bonhoeffer) v General Medical Council* (2012)—although it should be noted that this was decided before the Supreme Court's decision in *R (G) v Governors of X School*.

Statutory dispute resolution procedures

8–040   The DTI issued a consultation paper in 2001, called *Routes to Resolution*. It propounded the thesis that too many employment disputes were going to tribunals because of failures in employers' internal procedures and that if parties were compelled to follow basic procedural steps, cases could be dealt with without the need for tribunal hearings. There is no doubt that this initiative was aimed as much as anything at trying to reduce the numbers of cases going to employment tribunals. The framework for statutory procedures was established by the Employment Act 2002 and fleshed out in regulations in 2004. In October 2004, two separate statutory dispute resolution procedures came into force, one for discipline and dismissals and another for grievances. The general idea of the statutory dismissal and disciplinary procedure was that an employer wanting to discipline or dismiss an employee would have to state the problem in writing and then have a meeting with the employee to discuss it before going further, and that if disciplinary penalties or dismissal were decided on, the employee had to be given a right of appeal. The consequences for an employer of failing to follow the statutory procedure in relation to a dismissal were severe: any dismissal in breach of the procedure was automatically unfair and the employee was awarded a minimum of four weeks' pay.

Mirroring this, the statutory grievance procedure required the employee to make a complaint in writing to the employer, after which the employer had to have at least one meeting with the employee to discuss the matter. The employer would then communicate its decision and inform the employee of her right of appeal. An employee who had not gone through this process was actually barred from bringing a claim for constructive dismissal (or anything else) until the procedure had been completed.

It quickly became clear that the statutory dispute resolution procedures were a trap for the unwary and, instead of reducing claims to tribunals, were capable of giving rise to a lot of litigation in their own right. Far from encouraging local resolution, the need to be able to demonstrate compliance with the statute led to employment disputes becoming formalised from the outset, which entrenched rather than solved the disagreement. The statutory dispute resolution procedures were almost unique in being generally loathed by employers, unions, employees and practitioners. Towards the end of 2006 the Secretary of State commissioned a review of options for improving dispute resolution and the resulting report, in March 2007, recommended the radical remedy of abolishing the procedures altogether and replacing them with a more general discretion for employment tribunals to make adjustments to awards where either employer or employee had failed to follow the procedural recommendations of a statutory code of practice. This report was welcomed on all sides and implemented by the Employment Act 2008 s.1, which repealed the statutory procedures in their entirety from April 2009. Instead, s.3 of the Employment Act 2008 introduced new TULRCA s.207A, which provides that a tribunal can increase any award to an employee by up to 25 per cent where the employer has unreasonably failed to comply with a statutory code of practice. TULRCA s.207A equally entitles the tribunal to decrease any award to an employee by up to 25 per cent if the employee has failed unreasonably to comply with a statutory code of practice.

8–041 Tribunals have always been required to take the Acas Code of Practice on Discipline and Grievance Procedures into account when deciding whether a dismissal is fair or unfair (TULRCA s.207). No doubt it is because of the extra weight given to compliance with the Code by TULRCA s.207A that the 2009 revised version of the Acas Code of Practice on Discipline and Grievance Procedures went for a minimalist approach, reduced to the bare bones, with the additional (and more helpful) guidance given in the (non-statutory) Acas Guide to Discipline and Grievance Procedures. Both were revised in 2015, but in a very small way. It remains the case that compliance with good employment practice in relation to dispute resolution is very important, as we will see when we consider the substantive law of unfair dismissal.

Protected conversations

8–042 The latest initiative in the ongoing campaign to reduce the number of tribunal claims is the idea of the protected conversation. Many claims to tribunals are settled before a hearing, and the usual process is for the settlement to be recorded in what used to be called a compromise agreement (now renamed a settlement agreement by virtue of the Enterprise and Regulatory Reform Act

(ERRA) 2013). Provided that this is in writing, and the claimant has received independent legal advice, such an agreement is legally binding (ERA s.203) and precludes the claimant from subsequently pursuing a claim detailed in the agreement. Where an employment dispute is in existence, it is possible for negotiations with a view to such a settlement to be conducted on a "without prejudice" basis, meaning that the substance of the discussions cannot be later used by either party as evidence in tribunal proceedings.

The aim of the "protected conversation" is to extend this concept to discussions about termination of an employee's employment even where there is no dispute in existence. Thus, for example, an employer concerned about aspects of an employee's performance could call him in and offer him a sum of money to leave, without facing the prospect that the surprised and humiliated employee might later point to this event as evidence of a settled intention on the employer's part to get rid of him, regardless of procedural niceties, to say nothing of being strong evidence of destruction of mutual trust and confidence by the employer. Critics of this proposal argued that it would simply tend to encourage poor management or could be used as a subtle weapon to undermine an employee. Nonetheless, ERRA 2013 implemented the proposal by introducing a new ERA s.111A, which provides that offers made (by employee or by employer) or discussions held about termination of the contract of employment will usually be inadmissible in subsequent tribunal proceedings. A new Acas Code of Practice No.4 on Settlement Agreements (2013) provides further guidance and should be taken into account by tribunals where relevant; it is supplemented by a non-legally binding Acas Guide on Settlement Agreements.

It should be noted that the new regime only applies to normal claims for unfair dismissal: if the claim is for automatically unfair dismissal or discrimination, or also involves a claim of wrongful dismissal, the confidentiality provisions do not apply. Nor will they apply if either party is guilty of improper behaviour during the discussions: the Acas Code lists bullying, physical intimidation, harassment, discrimination and undue pressure (which could be the employer imposing unreasonable time constraints, or the employee threatening to go public on damaging allegations) as examples of what could constitute improper behaviour. In situations where there is an ongoing dispute between the parties, the common law concept of "without prejudice" negotiations will continue to apply, so confidentiality will only be defeated if one party is guilty of fraud, undue influence or some other unambiguous impropriety—a somewhat narrower concept than improper behaviour.

8–043 It remains to be seen whether this new provision will result in more negotiations and more settlements, or whether—as a number of commentators have predicted—it will result in yet more satellite litigation about the parameters of the confidentiality requirements.

The fair reasons for dismissal

Once the employee has established that she is qualified to claim and that there has **8–044** been a dismissal, the burden of proof shifts to the employer to show, first, what was the reason for the dismissal, and secondly, that it falls under one of the categories of fair reason laid out in ERA s.98. Neither task should cause the employer too much problem, for the categories are wide. Potentially fair reasons are:

(a) reasons relating to capability or qualifications;
(b) reasons relating to conduct;
(c) redundancy;
(d) that continued employment would be in breach of statute; and
(e) "some other substantial reason of a kind to justify dismissal".

The existence of the final category in particular means that an employer will hardly ever be unable to show that the reason for the dismissal was potentially fair, although *ASLEF v Brady* (2006) is a rare example of this phenomenon. The claimant was elected General Secretary of the union in 2003, but his election was not supported by the union's senior officials. A period of tension and worsening relations culminated in the claimant getting into a fight with the union's president at a social occasion. While an internal inquiry was critical of both men, the claimant was dismissed for misconduct while no action was taken against the president. The employment tribunal concluded that the claimant had not really been dismissed for misconduct but because of politically motivated hostility towards him. This could not fall under any of the categories above and therefore the dismissal was unfair. The EAT upheld this, stating that if an employer acts from mixed motives, the principal motive is to be taken as the reason in deciding whether a potentially fair reason had been proved.

Under ERA s.92 an employee is entitled to ask for the reasons for dismissal to be stated in writing. If the employer refuses to comply (and a persistent failure to reply may be held to amount to a refusal) the employee will be awarded two weeks' pay. Such a statement may be of use to the employee in that the employer will then lack credibility if attempting to put forward some additional or alternative reason at a tribunal hearing.

It is not uncommon for employees to dispute whether the reason put forward **8–045** by the employer is the true one. This may particularly be the case where the employee has not been employed long enough to claim unfair dismissal under the usual principles and is seeking to establish automatic unfair dismissal (below, para.8–079) for which there is no qualifying period of employment. Guidance on the burden of proof in such situations was given by the Court of Appeal in *Kuzel v Roche Products Ltd* (2008), where the claimant had argued that she had been dismissed for making a protected disclosure and the employer claimed it was for a breakdown in relationships—"some other substantial reason". The Court of Appeal confirmed that the burden of proof for showing the reason is always on the employer. If the employee contests that, she must produce some evidence to show a different reason, but does not have to discharge the burden of proving that the dismissal was for this other reason, even where she is claiming that she was dismissed for an inadmissible reason. It is then up to the tribunal to decide what was the reason, or principal reason, for the dismissal, bearing in mind that the burden of proof is on the employer for this purpose. However, if the tribunal rejects the employer's reason, it is not compelled therefore to accept the employee's reason. It is possible for the tribunal to conclude, as it did in this case, that the real reason was something different from what was claimed by either of the parties.

Employers are not compelled to classify their reason for dismissal under just one of the fair categories. In cases of under-performance, for example, it may not be clear if the reason is that the employee simply cannot do any better (a reason relating to capability) or that he does not take the trouble to work well (a reason relating to conduct), so both reasons may be given in the employer's notice of appearance. Similarly, where an employee is dismissed in the course of a reorganisation, the reason may not be within the technical definition of redundancy, so "some other substantial reason" may be relied on as well. Indeed, if in doubt, it is probably wise for the employer to plead alternatives. In *Devonshire v Trico-Folberth* (1989) the employee was dismissed for poor attendance, which the employer categorised as incapability. It was held that the employer had not acted as a reasonable employer would in dismissing on this ground—although it would have been reasonable if the dismissal had been for misconduct.

Once the decision to take action against an employee has been made, there is a temptation for the employer to gild the lily and dredge up all sorts of short-comings in order to justify the dismissal. There are dangers in this approach, as indicated by *Smith v City of Glasgow DC* (1987). Here, the employers alleged that the employee had been dismissed for incapability, evidenced by three specific allegations of incompetence. The employment tribunal considered that one of these allegations could not be substantiated. In these circumstances, the House of Lords held that the dismissal was unfair: the employers had not shown that the unsubstantiated allegation did not form a main part of their reason for dismissal, and it could not be reasonable to dismiss an employee for a reason which could not be supported.

8–046   Generally, establishing a potentially fair reason for dismissal is easy, and is rarely at issue between the parties. However, there is a further requirement and it is this that, in practice, is the focus of just about every unfair dismissal case. It is that the employer should have acted reasonably in treating the reason as a sufficient reason for dismissal. Originally the employer bore the burden of proving that the decision to dismiss was reasonable; however, since 1980 the burden of proof has been neutral. Under ERA s.98(4) it is for the employment tribunal to decide whether the employer acted reasonably or unreasonably, having regard to the circumstances including the size and administrative resources of the employer's undertaking, although in practice the employer will lead evidence about the reasonableness of the decision at the same time as evidence to show the reason for the dismissal. This means that if it is admitted that the employee has been dismissed and is otherwise qualified to claim, it will be for the employers to put their case first.

The standard of review

"We consider that the authorities establish that in law the correct approach   **8–047**
for the employment tribunal to adopt in answering the question posed by [ERA
s.98(4)] is as follows: (1) the starting point should always be the words of [s.98(4)]
themselves; (2) in applying the section an employment tribunal must consider
the reasonableness of the employer's conduct, not simply whether they (the
members of the employment tribunal) consider the dismissal to be fair; (3) in
judging the reasonableness of the employer's conduct an employment tribunal
must not substitute its decision as to what was the right course to adopt for that
of the employer; (4) in many, though not all, cases there is a band of reasonable
responses to the employee's conduct within which one employer might reasonably take one view, another quite reasonably take another; (5) the function of
the employment tribunal, as an industrial jury, is to determine whether in the
particular circumstances of each case the decision to dismiss the employee fell
within the band of reasonable responses which a reasonable employer might
have adopted" (Browne-Wilkinson J in *Iceland Frozen Foods v Jones* (1983)).

For years this passage has been taken to summarise the duties of tribunals
in deciding whether or not an employer acted reasonably in dismissing the
employee. The first point is obviously uncontroversial. The second is also clearly
supportable, because otherwise the tribunal would only be substituting its subjective view for that of the employer; it also indicates that the tribunal must
focus on judging the employer's conduct, not necessarily on whether or not the
employee was justly dismissed. Furthermore, the employer's conduct must be
judged according to the facts known to the employer at the time of the decision
to dismiss, not what was discovered later (*Devis v Atkins* (1977)). The last three
points have been controversial, especially the "band of reasonable responses"
test:

"It must be remembered that in all these cases, there is a band of reasonableness, within which one employer might reasonably take one view: another
quite reasonably take a different view. One would quite reasonably dismiss
the man. The other would quite reasonably keep him on. Both views might be
quite reasonable" (per Lord Denning MR, *British Leyland v Swift* (1981)).

This may be so, but it tends to limit the scope for a tribunal to find that a dismissal was unfair because even if a tribunal is sure that many other employers
would have dealt with a case by some penalty other than dismissal, it may not be
able to say that the employer's action is outside the band or range of reasonable
responses. This is exacerbated by the fact that the so-called reasonable employer
does not always act reasonably. In *Saunders v Scottish National Camps* (1981) it
was held fair to dismiss a homosexual employee because of a quite unfounded
concern about his coming into contact with children on the grounds that many
other employers would have reacted similarly. Thus the reasonable employer is
rather the average employer, with the prejudices of the general populace.

Although it has been denied that the band of reasonable responses approach   **8–048**
requires "that such a high degree of unreasonableness be shown . . . that nothing

short of a perverse decision to dismiss" can be unfair (*Rentokil v Mackin* (1989)), it comes pretty close to it. This led to an outspoken attack by the outgoing president of the EAT, Morison J, in *Haddon v Van den Bergh Foods* (1999), where he argued that the "band of reasonable responses" test was apt to lead tribunals to find dismissals unfair only if the decision to dismiss was perverse in the light of the facts known to the employer and implied that it should not be used. For good measure, he suggested that the fear of being found to have substituted their opinion for that of the employer was also likely to lead to tribunals failing properly to examine the employer's decision. The furore caused by *Haddon* swiftly resulted in a statement from the incoming president of the EAT, Lindsay J, in *Midland Bank v Madden* (2000) that the EAT was not at liberty to abandon the "band of reasonable responses" test, hallowed as it was by repeated approval in the Court of Appeal. The uncertainty caused by these decisions led the Court of Appeal to expedite the appeal in *Madden* and to restate firmly the *Iceland* approach (*HSBC v Madden* (2000)). It is probably not surprising that the Court of Appeal came down on the side of the orthodoxy which had prevailed for nearly 20 years, but it is unfortunate that the merits of the arguments in *Haddon* could not be explored. The result is that *Haddon* may be regarded as a minor, short-lived heresy and the "band of reasonable responses" test is more securely entrenched than before. In *Sainsbury's Supermarkets Ltd v Hitt* (2003) it was held that it applied also to the issue of whether an employer's investigation into alleged misconduct was reasonable or not.

In *Newbound v Thames Water Utilities Ltd* (2015) the Court of Appeal warned that the band of reasonable responses "is not infinitely wide" and drew attention to the fact that the words of the statute say that reasonableness is to be judged "according to equity and the substantial merits of the case"—indicating that the enquiry involves more than simply asking whether the employer followed all the necessary procedural steps. A tribunal should be entitled to find that an employer's decision was outside the band without being accused of substituting its view for that of the employer. This decision may be seen as a welcome corrective to the view that tribunals can only rarely question an employer's decision—but it is noticeable that the employment tribunal in this case actually said that no reasonable employer would have dismissed the claimant, bearing out the idea that only a perverse decision by an employer will be outside the band.

In *Turner v East Midland Trains Ltd* (2013) the Court of Appeal was asked whether the band of reasonable responses test was compatible with the claimant's right to privacy under ECHR art.8. The claimant, a senior train conductor, was dismissed for dishonesty and argued that the resulting damage to her reputation engaged ECHR art.8. The Court agreed that it did, but denied that the proportionality test used in judging whether the right to privacy had been infringed entailed different standards from the band of reasonable responses test. Specifically, they held that where the employer's investigation of the facts was regarded as reasonable for the purposes of that test, art.8 did not impose some higher standard. It was pointed out that the band of reasonable responses test has a degree of flexibility, so that reasonableness may require more of an employer where the potential consequences for the employee are particularly grave.

This rigorous standard used for reviewing the decision of the employer is directly analogous to the standard to be used by the EAT and higher courts in reviewing the decision of an employment tribunal on appeal. Appeals lie to the EAT only on questions of law, and a decision as to whether a dismissal is unfair or not has been firmly categorised as a question of fact. It is true that tribunals hearing unfair dismissal cases day in, day out develop a wealth of experience, and that because they see the witnesses, they are in the best position to judge the merits of the case. However, it is clear that the major reason for strictly limiting appeals is one of policy: a fear that the EAT, and in turn the Court of Appeal, would be swamped by the appeals which might otherwise be thrown up by several thousand employment tribunal decisions a year.

8–049

In *Piggott Bros v Jackson* (1991) the Court of Appeal summarised the situations in which the EAT would be entitled to interfere as falling into three categories. They are first, if there was a misdirection on the law; secondly, if there was no evidence to support a finding of fact; and thirdly, if the tribunal's decision was perverse. The problem with perversity is that it tends to be in the eye of the beholder. The much-quoted dictum of May LJ in *Neale v Hereford & Worcester CC* (1986) to the effect that a perverse decision can be recognised when "one can say in effect, 'My goodness, that was certainly wrong'" was thought by the court in *Piggott Bros v Jackson* (1991) to carry the danger that it might encourage the EAT to think it was entitled to intervene in any case where it strongly felt that its own decision would be different from that of the employment tribunal. "Furthermore the more dogmatic the temperament of the judges concerned, the more likely they are to take this view", as Lord Donaldson MR put it. The fact that the EAT would have come to a different decision from the employment tribunal is most emphatically not regarded as a sufficient reason for it to intervene. This led Lord Donaldson MR in *Piggott Bros v Jackson* to define perversity very restrictively, implying that it would rarely be found unless there was a misdirection on the law or a finding unsupported by the evidence. But this, of course, would be tantamount to ruling out perversity as a ground for interference as it would be subsumed in the other two categories. The EAT struck back in *East Berkshire HA v Matadeen* (1992), reasserting that perversity was a separate and distinct ground for intervention and pointing out that there would be little justification for an EAT constituted with lay representation if the only grounds for interference were misdirection or unsupported findings. Of course, since 2012, the EAT rarely sits with lay representatives.

It is submitted that the power to review tribunal decisions is already too limited, which helps to account for the fact that a browse through the reports will disclose a number of decisions which can strike the reader as distinctly odd. Cases with similar facts are therefore of limited value as precedents in this area. The lack of uniformity inevitably resulting from this approach is apparently seen as a risk worth taking to secure the benefit of a sensible workload at the appellate level but it would be regrettable if appeals were limited yet further.

Procedural fairness

8–050 In the latter part of the 1970s, when unfair dismissal law was relatively new, the EAT saw its role very much as providing assistance to employers on what was good employment relations practice, and in a series of decisions it laid down guidelines on the procedures to be followed in handling various types of dismissals. These guidelines were treated almost as statutory requirements by some employment tribunals, provoking a backlash from the Court of Appeal against putting a gloss on the words of the statute (cf. *Hollister v National Farmers' Union* (1979)). Nonetheless, the guidance given in many of the cases remained relevant and was regularly cited, as well as providing valuable assistance to managers as to what was expected of them. In relation to conduct and capability, since 1977 Acas has issued successive codes of practice and while the 2015 Acas Code of Practice on Disciplinary and Grievance Procedures is limited to minimum requirements, for reasons explained above (para.8–041), the 2009 Acas Guide to Disciplinary and Grievance Procedures explicitly aims to provide practical guidance on what constitutes reasonable behaviour. It should be noted that the Acas Code of Practice continues to recommend the key steps that were previously contained in the statutory dismissal and disciplinary procedure, namely: (1) that any disciplinary or poor performance issue should be notified to the employee in writing with sufficient detail for her to be able to prepare for a disciplinary meeting; (2) that a meeting (at which the employee has a right to be accompanied) should be held before any disciplinary decision is made; and (3) that the employee should be given an opportunity to appeal, which the Code implies, should involve a further hearing (see paras 9–28).

As noted already, TULRCA s.207 states that failure to comply with the Code does not of itself render an employer liable, but that the Code must be taken into account by tribunals in any proceedings to which it is relevant.

How far does a failure to follow norms of good procedure affect the decision as to whether a dismissal is fair or unfair? If no repercussions follow from a failure to carry out a fair procedure, then there is little incentive for an employer to follow one. This may be damaging to employment relations as well as not being consonant with the ideas of mutual respect and dignity at work which have developed in the modern era. On the other hand, it would be galling for an employer to find that a wholly undeserving employee was treated as unfairly dismissed because of some slip-up in handling the disciplinary process.

8–051 At first, the interests of employers prevailed, as happens so frequently. The EAT developed the "no-difference rule", also known as "the rule in *British Labour Pump v Byrne*" after the case in 1979 where it was articulated. According to this, if the tribunal could conclude from the evidence that it would have made no difference to the outcome if the correct procedure had been followed, because the employer could still have reasonably decided to dismiss the employee, the dismissal would be fair. The no-difference rule held sway for a decade until the House of Lords' landmark decision in *Polkey v Dayton Services* (1988). This involved an employee made redundant at a moment's notice with no prior warning or consultation. It was probable that he would have been made redundant even if a fair procedure had been implemented. However, the House of Lords held that the principle in *British Labour Pump v Byrne* (1979) was inconsistent with its own earlier decision in *Devis v Atkins* (1977) that the fairness of a dismissal was to be judged in the light of the facts known to the employer at the moment of dismissal. The no-difference rule encouraged tribunals to look at things happening after this time to judge whether, with hindsight, the dismissal was fair despite the procedural failure.

In *Polkey* the House of Lords reaffirmed the rule in *Devis v Atkins* that the reasonableness of the employer's decision to dismiss should be judged according to what the employer knew or ought to have known at the moment of making that decision. If the procedural failure affected the state of the employer's knowledge, for example, where the employer had not investigated properly, or had not given the employee an opportunity to explain, then almost certainly the employer's decision to dismiss would be unreasonable, because a proper investigation might have revealed that the employee was not to blame, or the employee might have had a valid explanation. The House of Lords accepted that there might be a few—a very few—cases where such procedural failures would not render the dismissal unfair. But this would only be if the employer, at the moment of making the decision to dismiss and acting reasonably, could say to herself, "if I investigated, or heard the employee, it could not possibly make a difference to what I am going to do". This would hardly ever be the case.

What if further investigation would have revealed that the employee certainly did commit the offence, or that he would have had no word of explanation? Was it not grossly unjust to the employer to hold the dismissal unfair? The House of Lords in *Devis v Atkins* (1977) said it was not. In these circumstances the dismissal would be technically unfair and the justice or otherwise of this should be taken into account at the next stage, consideration of the remedy. The employee could be refused re-employment and awarded no compensation. Reductions on this ground are known as "*Polkey* deductions".

8–052 Business continued to lobby the Government on this issue and their arguments were eventually accepted. The Employment Act 2002 inserted ERA s.98A(2) which provided that: "failure by an employer to follow a procedure in relation to the dismissal of an employee shall not be regarded . . . as by itself making the employer's action unreasonable if he shows that he would have decided to dismiss the employee if he had followed the procedure"—a statutory reversal of the House of Lords' decision on this point in *Polkey*. With the abolition of the statutory dispute resolution procedures by the Employment Act 2008 it became necessary to review this position. The Government's 2007 consultation on this found that the majority of respondents—including substantial numbers of employers—were in favour of a return to the previous position, i.e. the effect of procedural failure should be as stated by the House of Lords in *Polkey v Dayton Services* (1988), not least because it was clear and well understood by employers, employees and their advisers and representatives. This is what was done: the Employment Act 2008 s.2 repealed ERA s.98A completely.

Capability or qualifications

8–053   Under ERA s.98(2)(a) dismissal may be fair if it is for a reason relating to the employee's capability or qualifications for the job. These terms are defined in ERA s.98(3): capability "means . . . capability assessed by reference to skill, aptitude, health or any other physical or mental quality" and qualifications "means any degree, diploma or other academic, technical or professional qualification relevant to the position which he held". There are thus in effect two sub-categories comprised in this: dismissals for incompetence and dismissals for sickness.

In deciding whether an employer was reasonable in dismissing for incompetence, it may be relevant to know whether appropriate training was given. For example, in *Davison v Kent Meters* (1975) a woman was dismissed for assembling 471 out of 500 components incorrectly. She claimed that this was the way she had been shown to assemble them by the chargehand. The chargehand denied ever having shown her how to do it. Either way the employer was damned, for either she had been trained wrongly, or else she had never been trained. However, if an employee is recruited on the understanding that he has a particular skill or qualification, the employer would not be expected to train him in things he should already know. The question of adequate training may be particularly apposite where the nature of jobs changes substantially because of new technology. It may be fair to dismiss employees who cannot adapt, but only if they have had proper opportunities to learn. Again, depending on such things as the length of service of the employee, it might be reasonable to expect that the employer will try to find some other work for someone who cannot adapt.

Another relevant factor might be whether or not the employee was warned that her performance was not satisfactory: "in the case of incapacity, the employer will normally not act reasonably unless he gives the employee fair warning and an opportunity to mend his ways and show that he can do the job" as Lord Bridge put it in *Polkey v Dayton Services* (1988). While no amount of warning will increase someone's competence, the employee may genuinely not realise that her work is not up to scratch. Also, it is difficult to be sure whether poor performance is because of innate inability or because of lack of effort: "many do not know they are capable of jumping the five-barred gate until the bull is close behind them", as Donaldson J pointed out (*Winterhalter Gastronom v Webb* (1973)). Yet this is not a hard-and-fast rule: in *Dunning v Jacomb* (1973) a contracts manager was dismissed without a warning and time to improve because of his inability to get on with clients, many of whom had complained about him. It was held fair: in his responsible position he must have been aware that this lack of cooperation placed his job in jeopardy, and it seemed likely that he could not have changed even if he had wanted to.

8–054   Usually a continuous record of unsatisfactory performance will be relied on to justify dismissal for incompetence, but a single error may warrant dismissal if it is serious enough. In *Alidair v Taylor* (1978) a pilot was dismissed for landing his plane badly in fair weather conditions, causing damage to the plane, though no injuries to passengers. His dismissal was fair, for the employer not unreasonably had lost confidence in his ability to do the job.

In cases like these there is a clear overlap with misconduct dismissals and many employers treat incapability as something to be dealt with under the disciplinary procedure which they use for misconduct dismissals regardless of whether the employee is deliberately at fault or doing her incompetent best. This has now assumed some importance as a result of the new right in ERelA 1999 s.10 for workers to be accompanied by a trade union official or a co-worker at any disciplinary or grievance hearing. It would seem strange if a worker's right to a companion should depend on whether or not the employer has separate capability and conduct procedures. The 2015 Acas Code of Practice on Disciplinary and Grievance Procedures (para.1) states that disciplinary situations include poor performance issues and recommends that if employers have separate capability procedures they should nonetheless ensure that the basic principles of fairness in the Code are followed, adapted if necessary. It is clear that the right to be accompanied will apply to a worker in any situation where the outcome could be a formal warning or other sanction, and so will apply to formal action taken on the basis of unsatisfactory performance.

Different considerations are relevant in judging the reasonableness of a dismissal on grounds of ill-health, and the matters to be taken into account are similar to those outlined in judging whether the contract is frustrated on this ground (see *Egg Stores v Leibovici* (1977) above, para.8–031). It is first necessary for the employer to gain an informed view of the position, which will best be done by consultation with the employee (*East Lindsey DC v Daubney* (1977)). The value of consultation is not merely so that the employer is fully briefed on the medical situation, but also to keep the employee informed about the employer's thinking. If the employee knows that the employer is contemplating dismissal, she may be able to suggest some alternative herself—a sideways move, perhaps, or early retirement.

The employer may well wish to have a doctor's report on the employee's 8–055 medical condition. However, the employee's doctor will not talk to the employer without the employee's permission, and the employee has a right to see any report prepared by his doctor and can veto its transmission to the employer (Access to Medical Reports Act 1988). Furthermore, an employer does not have an implied right to require employees to undergo a medical examination by a company doctor, or an independent doctor (*Bliss v South East Thames RHA* (1987)), so this is dependent to a large extent on the employee's cooperation. However, if the employee refuses to provide information to the employer, the employer is entitled to make a decision on the evidence which is available and may be held to have acted reasonably in concluding that dismissal is necessary (see Appendix 4 of the 2015 Acas Guide to Discipline and Grievances at Work).

Once the employer has as good a grasp of the medical position as possible, it is a matter of weighing in the balance the needs of the organisation for someone else to do the job, bearing in mind the probable length of the employee's absence and the likelihood of a full recovery. In general, an employer might be expected to wait longer in the case of a long-serving employee. A further consideration for employers is the effect of disability discrimination law in this area. There has always been a risk that a dismissal on grounds of ill-health incapability could be unfair if the employer has not considered redeployment. However, if the nature of the employee's incapacity is such that she may be regarded as having a disability within the meaning of EqA 2010 (discussed above, para.2–069) the employer will be under a positive duty to make reasonable adjustments to facilitate her continued employment (EqA 2010 s.20). The employer who dismisses without considering this is very likely to be liable for unjustified discrimination. In *Kent CC v Mingo* (2000) the EAT warned that a dismissal which constituted disability discrimination should not automatically be regarded as unfair, but it upheld the finding that it was in that case and there are likely to be few cases where this is not so (cf. also *Greenhof v Barnsley MBC* (2006)).

A difficulty frequently faced by management is the worker who has a record of short absences, too short to be covered by a doctor's certificate, and perhaps involving ailments which are hard to pin down—backache, migraine, gastric attack, etc. The difficulty is knowing whether this is a genuine illness or whether the employee is malingering; even if genuine, the absences may constitute an unacceptable level of unreliability. Some employers find that a policy of self-certification, where employees are required to submit a written explanation for their absences, reduces the problem, in that people are less ready to put specious reasons in a permanent form. Others automatically investigate if absences run above a certain level, which is sometimes agreed with the trade union. The danger of this approach is that some employees treat this as an addition to their holiday entitlement, and ensure that they use all their "sick leave" each year! It is important that procedures used are suitable given that this is an area where the distinction between incapability and misconduct is blurred (cf. *Devonshire v Trico-Folberth* (1989)). In *International Sports Co v Thompson* (1980) the EAT suggested that a quasi-disciplinary procedure, involving warnings and a chance to improve, was more appropriate to this kind of absence than the usual ill-health approach. They declined to find the dismissal unfair on the ground that the company doctor had not examined the employee because he felt it would serve no useful purpose given the transient nature and variety of complaints from which the employee suffered. This is similar to the guidance given in Appendix 4 of the Acas Guide to Discipline and Grievances at Work (which is devoted to dealing with absences).

8–056   In relation to dismissals for illness it may again not always be clear whether or not the employee has a statutory right to be accompanied under s.10 of the ERelA 1999. If the situation is dealt with in a quasi-disciplinary manner it is fairly clear that the right will apply, but it is not so clear for those employers who have separate ill-health procedures which might result in ill-health early retirement rather than dismissal. It would obviously be bad employment relations practice for an employer to refuse an employee the right to be accompanied, but it is not entirely obvious that the statutory right would apply in these circumstances.

Conduct

Misconduct is by far the commonest ground put forward to justify dismissal. In judging misconduct, courts and tribunals must have regard to the 2015 Acas Code of Practice on Disciplinary and Grievance Procedures. Although its guidance does not have the force of law, tribunals are bound to take account of it in reaching their decisions. Thus failure to follow the recommendations of the Code will count against an employer in judging the reasonableness of a dismissal, but will not mean that the dismissal is necessarily unfair.

8–057

The Acas Guide to Discipline and Grievances at Work recommends that disciplinary procedures should be aimed at helping employees to improve rather than simply justifying the imposition of sanctions, although this is no longer in the Code. The Code says that rules should be specific, clear, recorded in writing and readily available to every employee (para.2). Special care should be taken to ensure that workers whose first language is not English or who have a disability affecting their ability to read can understand them. The Acas Guide suggests that disciplinary rules should usually cover things such as: timekeeping; absence; health and safety; use of organisation facilities; discrimination, bullying and harassment; personal appearance; and the sort of conduct which would be regarded as gross misconduct (discussed above, para.8–006).

The Code effectively requires, although it does not use this language, that the rules of natural justice should be observed, meaning that employees should be informed in advance of any disciplinary hearing, given the opportunity of a hearing in front of someone who has not been involved in the matter, told in advance what the allegations are against them and be given the opportunity to challenge these allegations and any evidence against them before a decision is reached. In *Hussain v Elonex* (1999) a dismissal was held not to be unfair merely because the employee had not been provided with a copy of witness statements relied on by the employer, since he had been made aware of their substance and was not therefore prejudiced by this (see also *Asda Stores Ltd v Thompson* (2002)). However, in *A v B* (2003), where inconsistent statements which were relevant to the credibility of a witness were withheld, the EAT held that this was prejudicial to the employee and a factor in finding that the dismissal was unfair.

Warnings

The 2015 Acas Code of Practice on Disciplinary and Grievance Procedures still recommends that informal action should be tried first in cases of minor misconduct—"A quiet word is often all that is required" (Foreword). However, where misconduct is established, then a warning may be appropriate. Thus, where the employee is found guilty of misconduct the Code states that it is usual to give a written warning setting out the nature of the misconduct, the change in behaviour required and the consequences of failure to change (paras 19 and 21). Where there is a failure to improve—or where the original misconduct is sufficiently serious—the employee should be given a final written warning (paras 19 and 20). If the employee still does not improve, the final stage will be dismissal or some other sanction such as demotion or loss of seniority (para.20). In relation to these lesser penalties, it must be remembered that they may only be

8–058

imposed where the employer has contractual power to do so—otherwise it would be a fundamental breach by the employer, and the employee could treat herself as constructively dismissed (cf. *Hanley v Pease* above, para.8–008; it could, of course, be a fair constructive dismissal).

Warnings are not necessary in cases of gross misconduct, where summary dismissal is justified. The meaning of gross misconduct was considered in relation to wrongful dismissal (see above, para.8–006), and that discussion is applicable here also. It should be noted that summary dismissal does not mean instant dismissal: the employer will still be under an obligation to investigate in order to have a reasonable belief in the employee's guilt and this is stressed in the Code of Practice (para.23).

Should different offences be treated separately or can they be regarded as part of a pattern of misconduct? If the purpose of a warning is to improve the employee's conduct, then it could be argued that a different offence does not warrant the next stage of procedure (for the employee has improved in the sense of not repeating the first offence). On the other hand, it would be crazy to have an employee with, say, a first written warning for lateness, a final written warning for failing to follow safety procedures and then another first warning for insubordination! Such doubt as there was on this point seems to have been resolved in *Auguste Noel v Curtis* (1990). The employee was dismissed for abuse of two cheeses (*sic*); the employment tribunal considered that two previous warnings he had received, for an altercation with other employees and for failing to keep proper worksheets were irrelevant in relation to this offence. Their decision was reversed by the EAT, who thought the employer was entitled to look at the whole picture in deciding whether the employee's conduct overall was unsatisfactory.

8–059   Warnings should not remain on the employee's file indefinitely. The 2004 version of the Acas Code suggested a six-month limit: rather surprisingly, the issue is not addressed in the 2015 version of the Code, although the six-month period is mentioned by way of example in the Acas Guide to Discipline and Grievances at Work (p.29). If a period is stipulated, the employer had better stick to it. In *Diosynth Ltd v Thomson* (2006) an employee in a chemical processing plant, where following health and safety procedures was crucially important, received a written warning for failing to carry out a safety procedure. He was told it would remain on his file for 12 months. Seventeen months later there was an explosion causing a fatality and the subsequent investigation discovered that the employee had failed to carry out this procedure on three further occasions and had falsified records to conceal this. The employer stated that because of the earlier warning he was being dismissed, on the grounds that he plainly was unwilling or unable to change. The Court of Session held that the dismissal was unfair: after 12 months the warning should have been taken off his file and not taken into account any further. Rather surprisingly, this decision was distinguished by the Court of Appeal in *Airbus (UK) Ltd v Webb* (2008), where five employees were found watching television on a night shift when they should have been working. Four had good disciplinary records and were therefore given a final warning, but the claimant had had an earlier final warning, lasting 12 months, which had expired three weeks before this incident. The Court of Appeal held that this was different from *Diosynth Ltd v Thomson* where the expired warning tipped the balance in favour of dismissing the employee. In this case, all five had committed gross misconduct which would justify dismissal, but while four had mitigating circumstances—good disciplinary records—the claimant did not.

Where it is clear that a warning would make no difference to an employee's conduct, it may be fair to dismiss without a warning first. In *Retarded Children's Aid Society v Day* (1978) the house-father in a home for adults with learning disabilities punished a resident in contravention of the home's rules. At a meeting to discuss this, it became clear that he thought the policy behind the rules was wrong and that what he had done was right. In these circumstances, it was fair to dismiss him at once, without a warning and an opportunity to improve.

Proof of misconduct

For a dismissal on grounds of misconduct to be justified, it is not necessary **8–060** to show that the employee was indeed guilty of the offence. What must be established is that the employer honestly believed on reasonable grounds that the employee was guilty, at the time when the employer took the decision to dismiss (*BHS v Burchell* (1978), approved by the Court of Appeal in *Weddel v Tepper* (1980)). It follows that the two elements of honest belief and reasonable grounds for that belief depend on a third element: that the employer has "carried out as much investigation into the matter as was reasonable in all the circumstances of the case" (per Arnold J in *BHS v Burchell*). While this threefold test evolved in the context of cases where the employee was suspected of theft from the employer, it is equally apt in any case where the question of whether or not the employee actually committed the misconduct is at issue and may be applicable to other grounds such as "some other substantial reason" (*Perkin v St George's Healthcare NHS Trust* (2005)). However, it was pointed out in *Boys and Girls Welfare Society v McDonald* (1996) that the threefold test is not necessarily appropriate in misconduct cases where there is no significant dispute as to the facts, and this was reiterated by the Court of Session in *Scottish Daily Record v Laird* (1996). In *Boys and Girls Welfare Society v McDonald* the EAT also stressed that, in applying the *Burchell* test, tribunals should not be misled into placing the burden of proof on the employer to show reasonable grounds through reasonable investigation, etc. *BHS v Burchell* was decided at a time when the employer had the burden of showing not only the reason for the dismissal, but also that it was reasonable to dismiss in the circumstances, but as noted above (para.8–044), the burden of proof is now neutral. Furthermore, the Court of Appeal has made it clear that the "band of reasonable responses" test also applies to the question of whether the level of investigation is reasonable (*Sainsbury's Supermarkets Ltd v Hitt* (2003); cf. also *Turner v East Midlands Trains Ltd* (2013)).

A reasonable investigation where facts are in dispute would involve talking to any witnesses, gathering relevant documents and, crucially, putting the charges to the employee. In *Weddel v Tepper* (1980) the unfairness was held to reside principally in the fact that the employer decided to dismiss without hearing first whether the employee had any explanation for the suspicious conduct. This may be difficult if the police have been called in, for they will take over the investigation, and the employee is likely to be advised by his solicitor to say nothing at all. In *A v B* (2003) the EAT stressed the importance of making sure that any internal investigation is even-handed in such circumstances, as the employee will probably be unable to contact witnesses himself. In that case, the police investigation (which did not result in criminal proceedings) took more than a year, contributing to a delay of two-and-a-half years between allegations of criminal conduct against the employee and the disciplinary hearing at which he was dismissed. The EAT held that this again prejudiced the employee and was a factor in making the dismissal unfair.

The possibility of lengthy delay should be borne in mind by employers who decide to suspend the employee on full pay pending the outcome of police investigations or criminal proceedings. In *Four Seasons Healthcare Ltd v Maughan* (2005) the employee was convicted of a serious work-related offence some 10 months after he was suspended—but because the employer had suspended him without pay and had no contractual right to do so, he was entitled to full pay for that period. It has been held, therefore, that an employer may act reasonably in dismissing in these circumstances if, in the light of what is known at the time, it seems on the balance of probabilities that the employee is guilty (*Harris v Courage (Eastern) Ltd* (1982); *Carr v Alexander* (1979)). While it is improper for the employer effectively to wash his hands of responsibility, deciding to dismiss automatically if the employee is found guilty by a criminal court (*McLaren v NCB* (1988)), it is reasonable for the employer to treat a guilty verdict of a criminal court as proof that the offence was committed (*P v Notts CC* (1992)).

8–061   What if the employer is certain that one or other of two employees must be guilty, but is genuinely uncertain which it is? Perhaps surprisingly, in *Monie v Coral Racing* (1981) the Court of Appeal held that dismissal of them both was fair, and in *Parr v Whitbread* (1990) the EAT extended this to a situation where four employees were under suspicion and all were dismissed. It is assumed, however, that there would be a point at which wholesale sacking would not be justified in circumstances where at least one employee must have committed the offence.

Conduct outside employment

8–062   Paragraph 31 of the Acas Code of Practice on Disciplinary and Grievance Procedures recommends that conviction for a criminal offence not related to work should not automatically be treated as a reason for discipline or dismissal. "Consideration needs to be given to what effect the charge or conviction has on the employee's suitability to do the job and their relationship with their employer, work colleagues and customers". Thus a section leader at a department store was properly dismissed after being convicted of shoplifting in another store: the offence was clearly relevant to her position (*Moore v C&A Modes* (1981)); on similar grounds it has been held fair to dismiss a schoolteacher for a conviction for indecent conduct, albeit with another consenting adult (*Notts CC v Bowly* (1978); see also *X v Y* (2004)) and a school groundsman who had been convicted of indecent assault on his daughter, a pupil at the school (*P v Notts CC*

(1992)). Surprisingly, in the last case, the Court of Appeal seemed to suggest that there might be an obligation to consider alternative employment in such a case.

Trade union officials

Employees who are lay officials for trade unions, such as shop stewards or other union representatives, are subject to the same disciplinary rules as anyone else. However, because of the chance that disciplinary action against a trade union official could be perceived as an attack on the union, the Code recommends that "it is advisable to discuss the matter at an early stage with an official employed by the union, after obtaining the employee's agreement" (para.30).

8–063

After-discovered conduct and appeals

What if, after the decision to dismiss has been taken, further relevant facts come to light? The basic position was settled early on by the House of Lords in *Devis v Atkins* (1977). The employee, manager of an abattoir, was dismissed for buying animals from dealers instead of directly from farmers, in contravention of instructions given to him. These grounds for dismissal were held to be inadequate by an employment tribunal, and this was not challenged by the employer. Their point, however, was that after they dismissed him, they discovered that he had been dealing dishonestly with the stock, and they wanted this after-discovered information to be taken into account. The House of Lords pointed out that the wording of ERA s.98(4) focuses on the conduct of the employer ("whether . . . the employer acted reasonably or unreasonably . . ."), not on the justice or injustice to the employee, and that the question is whether the decision to dismiss was reasonable or unreasonable. That could be judged only in the light of what the employer knew at the time of dismissal, not on what was uncovered later on. As the House noted, this is directly opposite to the position at common law, where after-discovered conduct may be used to justify a summary dismissal initially carried out on inadequate grounds (*Boston Deep Sea Fishing v Ansell* (1888), see above, para.8–007). After-discovered conduct might be relevant to the remedy for unfair dismissal, but could not affect the finding on fairness.

8–064

This means also that if an employer dismisses an employee for misconduct and it is later conclusively proved that the employee did not commit the offence, the dismissal can still be fair. The issue is whether the employer had reasonable grounds for believing in the employee's guilt at the time of the decision to dismiss.

The next problem, however, is how this operates when the other misconduct is discovered in the course of an appeal. If a dismissed employee appeals internally and the appeal is turned down, the dismissal usually counts as having occurred on the date of the original decision to dismiss, not on the date of the appeal decision (*Sainsbury v Savage* (1981), approved in *West Midlands Co-operative Society v Tipton* (1986)). So, in one sense, everything that happens at the appeal hearing is after the dismissal. Obviously if evidence was discovered on appeal which proved that the employee had not committed the offence, it would have to be taken into account: otherwise why have the appeal? If so, why not take into account new evidence showing that the employee did commit the offence, or that he committed some other offence? The House of Lords dealt with this in *West Midlands Co-operative Society v Tipton* (1986) by holding that the appeal process was part and parcel of the dismissal process, so that if matters came to light during the appeal which were relevant to the original decision to dismiss, they could and should be taken into account. (Thus, on the facts of the case, they found that a refusal in breach of contract to allow an appeal could itself be evidence of unfairness.) What about the discovery of different and hitherto unsuspected misconduct? Here the House approved the decision in *National Heart and Chest Hospitals v Nambiar* (1981) to the effect that the employer would not be able to use the new reason to validate the original decision to dismiss. The proper course would be for the employer to allow the appeal and then dismiss, if appropriate, for the new reason.

8–065   A further result of treating the appeal process as part and parcel of the dismissal process is that if there are any defects in the initial disciplinary proceedings, it is possible for them to be "cured" on appeal. In *Taylor v OCS Group Ltd* (2006) the Court of Appeal held that the test for this should not be whether the appeal was to be regarded as merely a review of the initial decision (which would not address initial defects) or a complete rehearing (which would) but rather whether the disciplinary process as a whole could be regarded as giving the employee a fair hearing.

In *Christou v Haringey LBC* (2013) two social workers had been disciplined, but not dismissed, for failures which had led in part to the death of a child at the hands of his mother and her partner, a case which caused a national scandal (the Baby P case). The disciplinary process was re-opened by new management, and as a result they were dismissed. Their argument that this was unfair, because the matter had already been adjudicated (albeit only by an internal disciplinary tribunal) was rejected by the Court of Appeal. The decision is perhaps understandable in the very special and unusual circumstances of the case, but in general, it is rare that such a course of action would be found to be fair.

Redundancy

8–066   It is usually fair to dismiss an employee for redundancy because in such a case the employee will be compensated by receiving a redundancy payment (see below, Ch.9). However, awards of compensation for unfair dismissal are higher than redundancy payments, so it is not surprising that employees will often seek to claim that the dismissal is unfair. There are three main grounds on which redundancy may be held to be unfair: where an unfair selection process is used; where there is no prior warning or consultation with the employees; and where redeployment is not considered.

Unfair selection process

8–067   Trade unions have traditionally preferred employers to carry out redundancies first by seeking volunteers, and then by using LIFO (last in, first out): that is, selecting employees on the basis of length of service and keeping the more senior people. Length of service has the advantage of being an objective and demonstrable fact, and one generally recognised as giving an employee a moral claim on the employer. However, it is a criterion which obviously favours older employees and is thus potentially indirectly discriminatory on grounds of age and would have to be justified as a proportionate means of achieving a legitimate aim, which may make it less attractive to employers. Length of service was held to be so justified as a "tie-breaker" in a redundancy selection process in *Rolls Royce plc v Unite the Union* (2009), but it was there used as one criterion among several. Furthermore, it may disproportionately disadvantage women, who are more likely than men to have a record of broken service because of child-rearing responsibilities. It was held in *Brook v Haringey LBC* (1992) that, even if discriminatory, LIFO could be justified, although selecting part-timers before full-timers was held to be indirect sex discrimination in *Clarke v Eley (IMI) Kynoch Ltd* (1983) and would now contravene the Part-time Workers (Prevention of Less Favourable Treatment) Regulations 2000 unless justified (see above, para.3–022). Employers may also be reluctant simply to accept volunteers. Volunteers may not come from the right parts of the business, and may be the very people you do not want to lose. For these reasons, then, the employer may well want a selection process that takes more account of a range of criteria reflecting the managerial interest.

It is recognised that choice of criteria for selection is a matter for management, and, subject to the points about to be made, in general management has a wide discretion as to what sort of selection procedure should be used. Where there are more than 20 redundancies, representatives of the workforce must be consulted over the selection criteria, but the procedure does not have to be agreed with them (see below, para.9–041). The main danger for employers is that if they wish to keep the "best" workers, they may use over-subjective methods of deciding who the best workers are. In the leading case, *Williams v Compair Maxam* (1982), managers were told to pick those to be made redundant by listing those who needed to remain in order to keep the company viable. The EAT described this as an entirely subjective criterion, subjectively applied, which allowed scope for decisions to be made on the basis of personal likes and dislikes. The selection procedure was held to be unreasonable. Managers should have objective standards against which to test who are the best workers (e.g. productivity, attendance, conduct and appraisal records) and there should be some mechanism for ensuring that the criteria are fairly applied. Where there is a recognised trade union, the EAT in *Williams v Compair Maxam* recommended that the employer should seek to get the union's agreement to the selection criteria and, after selection, should consider with the union whether the criteria had been properly applied. Now that consultation must take place with employee representatives even where there is no recognised union, it will no doubt be recognised as good practice to involve them in the same sort of way. It should be noted, however, that consultation with trade union or other representatives does not necessarily suffice. In *King v Eaton Ltd* (1996) the Court of Session said that the test must always be whether there has been fair and proper consultation, and this will sometimes mean consultation with individuals.

In order to claim unfair dismissal on grounds of unfair application of selection criteria, it seems necessary that employees should be able to see how they have been assessed against the employer's criteria and, in order to make comparisons, that they should be able to see the assessments of comparators. But this would raise problems of confidentiality as well as potentially oppressive requests for discovery of documents and drastic increases in the length of proceedings. To keep a lid on this, the Court of Appeal held in *British Aerospace v Green* (1995) that documents relating to other employees would not be relevant in anything other than exceptional circumstances and the claimant would need to be able to make a good case for such disclosure.

Automatically unfair redundancy

8–068   Under ERA s.105 selection for redundancy will be automatically unfair where the reason for selection is one for which dismissal would be automatically unfair. These are discussed below, para.8–079. It used to be the case that selection in contravention of an agreed procedure or customary arrangement was automatically unfair, unless there were special circumstances justifying the departure. This was removed by the Deregulation and Contracting Out Act 1994. However, selection in contravention of recognised procedures could well render the dismissal unfair under the general rubric of ERA s.98(4).

Failure to warn or consult

8–069   The Industrial Relations Code of Practice 1972, which was repealed in 1991, recommended giving employees as much warning as possible of impending redundancies and consulting with them over how best to handle the situation. This has become entrenched as good practice and thus survives despite the repeal. In the case of multiple redundancies, it is enforced by statute (see below, para.9–043) and in *Williams v Compair Maxam* (1982), where the EAT laid down some guidelines on how a reasonable employer should handle redundancies, the need for maximum warning and consultation were the first points made. While the caution against putting a gloss on the words of the statute may here be reiterated, the relevance of warning and consultation to fairness was emphasised by the House of Lords in *Polkey v Dayton Services Ltd* (1988). The company had four van drivers. It planned to replace them with two van salesmen and a sales representative. Having decided that three of the van drivers would not be able to cope with the sales duties as well as the driving, it was decided to make them redundant. The first Polkey knew of this was when he was called into the office out of the blue and dismissed. As a mark of consideration, the employers arranged for another driver to take Polkey home; that driver was himself made redundant on his return!

The issue which reached the House of Lords was whether the failure to give prior warning or consult with the employee could make the dismissal unfair where the employer argued that even had this been done it would have made no difference to the ultimate decision to dismiss. As noted already, the House of Lords held that this should not be taken into account because the employer's reasonableness had to be judged in the light of the facts known to the employer at the time of the decision to dismiss. The House of Lords held that the manner of dismissal could be relevant to this, and Lord Bridge said:

"... in the case of redundancy, the employer will normally not act reasonably unless he warns and consults any employees affected or their representative, adopts a fair basis on which to select for redundancy and takes such steps as may be reasonable to avoid or minimise redundancy by redeployment within his own organisation."

Failure to consider redeployment

The final procedural step recommended by Lord Bridge in *Polkey* is that the employer should consider redeployment; this is also one of the recommendations of the guidelines in *Williams v Compair Maxam* (1982). Obviously this will depend on the kind of work done by the employee and the size of the organisation. A very small company will not have much scope for offering alternative work. However, in *Vokes v Bear* (1974), where the works manager of the company, a middle-aged man with a company car and a company house, was made redundant, it was pointed out that the employing company was part of a group of 300 companies, at least one of which was seeking senior managers at that time. As no thought at all had been given to whether he could be placed in another position within the group, his dismissal was held to be unfair.

8–070

Statutory prohibition

Where the continued employment of the employee in her particular job would be in breach of statute or statutory regulation, her dismissal on this account may be fair. This provision, no doubt included for the sake of completeness, is rarely relied on in practice. It is worth noting that, to rely on this ground, the employer must establish that the continued employment of the employee would actually be in breach of statute: it is not enough for the employer reasonably to believe that this is the case. Having said that, if the reason for the dismissal was the employer's reasonable, but erroneous, belief that continued employment would be in breach of statute, this might constitute some other substantial reason of a kind to justify dismissal (*Bouchaala v Trusthouse Forte Hotels Ltd* (1980)).

8–071

The most obvious example where the statutory prohibition might apply is where someone employed as a driver is banned from driving. Even here, it does not necessarily follow that the employer would act reasonably in dismissing. The employer should consider the length of the ban, whether the employee could be redeployed for the duration, and so on.

Since 1997 it has been a criminal offence for employers to employ anyone who is not entitled to work in the United Kingdom, giving employers a powerful incentive to dismiss an employee if they have any doubt on the point. However, as British immigration law is so complex, it is not unusual for the employer to be in error. *Kelly v University of Southampton* (2008) is an example, where the employer wrongly thought that continued employment of an American lecturer was a criminal offence and dismissed her while her application for a permanent right to remain in the country was outstanding. The EAT held that the employer could not rely on the statutory prohibition reason, since there was no prohibition on her employment, but that even if they could, it would not have been reasonable to dismiss her when it seemed the position could easily be regularised (she got permanent permission to remain two weeks after the dismissal).

A point raised in *Kelly v University of Southampton* was whether her contract ceased by operation of law rather than by dismissal when her continued

8–072

employment became unlawful. As it was not unlawful, the point was not explored further. However, in *Four Seasons Healthcare Ltd v Maughan* (2005) the contract of employment of a registered mental nurse was held to be frustrated when he was convicted of offences against patients, since this meant he could no longer be lawfully employed in a care home. Thus, in some cases, the statutory prohibition reason might be unnecessary, because there would be no dismissal.

Some other substantial reason

8–073   In addition to the four reasons specified in ERA s.98(2), s.98(1)(b) states that a dismissal may be justified if it is for "some other substantial reason of a kind such as to justify the dismissal of an employee holding the position which that employee held". This formulation has been greatly criticised, in that its circularity and vagueness means that almost any reason could qualify, subject only to the qualification that it must be "substantial"—a quality which may be in the eye of the beholder. Indeed, cases over the years have shown a bewildering variety of reasons which have been held to justify dismissal on this ground, giving extra impetus to the point that it is really very easy for an employer to establish a potentially fair reason for dismissal. Bearing in mind that nearly anything can be "some other substantial reason", two of the commonest and most striking categories of cases to emerge under this heading will be examined.

The needs of the business

8–074   Where the employee is dismissed because of a reorganisation of the business with which he cannot or will not fit in, his dismissal may be fair. Surprisingly, such a dismissal may be justified even if what is required is a breach of the employee's contract. Thus in *RS Components v Irwin* (1973) the employer found it was losing business because its sales staff were moving to work for its competitors. The employer therefore sought to impose a unilateral variation of employees' contracts by inserting a restraint of trade clause which would prevent them working for competitors for a certain period after leaving. The dismissal of an employee who refused to agree was held to be fair. Similarly, in *Hollister v National Farmers' Union* (1979) the union reorganised its insurance business with the result that the terms of the group secretaries who sold it would be changed. One objected, not least because the new pension arrangements would not be so good. His dismissal was held to be fair: the Court of Appeal held that the tribunal should ask only, "whether the reorganisation was such that the only sensible thing to do was to terminate the employee's contract unless he would agree to a new arrangement" (*per* Lord Denning). In both of these cases the employer had negotiated with employees to try and get agreement to the change. However, in *Willow Oak Developments Ltd v Silverwood* (2006), which also involved an employer unilaterally forcing restrictive covenants on employees, the Court of Appeal upheld a tribunal's finding that the dismissal was unfair, because the employer had not engaged in consultation nor warned employees that failure to agree would result in dismissal.

How far can an employer go in changing employees' conditions for the worse and still get away with justifying it under "some other substantial reason"? A long way, it seems. In *St John of God (Care Services) Ltd v Brook* (1992) a charity-run hospital, faced with possible closure for financial reasons, offered totally new contracts of employment on inferior terms to the workforce. Thirty out of 170 employees refused to accept and were dismissed. An employment tribunal found that the reorganisation was a substantial reason for the dismissals, but that they were unfair because it was unreasonable of the employer to expect the workers to bear such cuts. The EAT reversed this decision and remitted the case, considering that dismissals even in these extreme circumstances were capable of being fair. Note that if they were held to be fair, the employees would get nothing at all. If the hospital had ceased trading because of its financial problems, they would at least have been entitled to redundancy payments. The position should also be compared with what would happen in similar circumstances but in the context of the transfer of an undertaking (see below, para.9–039).

While tribunals pay lip service to the need for reasonableness on the part of the employer (e.g. by insisting on consultation beforehand), the primacy of the managerial prerogative in this area is striking. It can be difficult to try to explain to an employee why it is that she is bound by the contract of employment, but it is not necessarily unfair when she is dismissed because of her employer's refusal to adhere to it.   **8–075**

Pressure from third parties

Where customers or other employees provide the pressure for the employer to dismiss, even though the employee has not done anything to warrant dismissal under one of the other headings, the dismissal may be for a substantial reason, and fair. Thus in *Treganowan v Knee* (1974) a woman who upset the other office staff by boasting about her affair with a much younger man (before this became fashionable) was fairly dismissed on that account. She was dismissed without notice, and as she had committed no fundamental breach of contract, it would have been wrongful dismissal at common law. However, this illustrates the point that whether notice is given or not is largely irrelevant to unfair dismissal cases.   **8–076**

A different kind of personality clash is illustrated by *Perkin v St George's Healthcare NHS Trust* (2005), where there was no doubt about the competence of the Trust's Director of Finance, but his abrasive manner and management style caused problems to those who worked with him and for him. During the internal disciplinary hearing he made serious allegations impugning the honesty of other witnesses, including his colleagues on the Executive Board of the Trust. The Court of Appeal held that personality could not in itself be a substantial reason for dismissal, but where it manifested itself in behaviour which caused such a breakdown in confidence between colleagues that it became impossible to work together, this could be a substantial reason of a kind to justify dismissal.

It should be noted that if pressure from other employees to dismiss the claimant takes the form of a threat to take industrial action, a tribunal should take no account of it in deciding whether or not the dismissal is fair (ERA s.107). A concerted refusal to work with a colleague would constitute such a threat (although this seems to have been overlooked in *Buck v Letchworth Palace* (1986), where a film projectionist who was homosexual was dismissed because his two colleagues refused to work with him because of an irrational fear of contracting AIDS).

8–077   The problem about allowing third party pressure to justify a dismissal is that the third party's reason for wanting the dismissal might be one that would be unfair if it were relied on directly by the employer. It seems unjust that a reason inadequate on its own can suffice when used at one remove. For example, in *Dobie v Burns International Security Services* (1984) the company provided the security service at Liverpool Airport, and the claimant was employed as a security officer there. Following a couple of incidents which the Court of Appeal were prepared to assume were not his fault, the airport authority refused to have him working there. The only alternative work that the employers could offer him was at a lower rate of pay, and he refused it. In these circumstances, the Court of Appeal held that his dismissal was capable of being fair, although the case was remitted on the facts. Yet it is fairly clear that if the employer had relied on the incidents as justifying dismissal, it would have been unfair. While appreciating the employer's dilemma in such cases, it does not seem unreasonable to expect the same standard of the employer as if the reason behind the customer's objection were the reason for dismissal.

Other cases

8–078   In *Terry v East Sussex CC* (1976) it was held that the expiry of a fixed-term contract without renewal was capable of being a dismissal for some other substantial reason. However, the onus will be on the employer to show the reason for the non-renewal to convince the tribunal that it was substantial and that the employer acted reasonably in the circumstances.

Under the Transfer of Undertakings (Protection of Employment) Regulations 2006, dismissal in connection with a transfer which is justified as being for an economic, technical or organisational reason may constitute redundancy (where appropriate) or "some other substantial reason" for dismissal (reg.7(3)(b)). It will therefore be subjected to the scrutiny of the tribunal to judge whether or not it was reasonable in the circumstances (see below, para.9–040).

Automatically unfair dismissals

8–079   Certain reasons for dismissal are categorised as automatically unfair. The range of reasons falling in this category has waxed and waned in line with government policy. They have little in common except that there is no requirement for two years' continuous employment before the employee is protected from dismissal for these reasons.

Some of these categories of automatically unfair dismissal are dealt with elsewhere in this book: dismissal on grounds of family rights (see above, paras 6–018, 6–021 and 6–025) dismissal for refusal to do shop work or betting work on a Sunday (ERA s.101, above, para.6–052); dismissal in connection with the Working Time Regulations 1998 (ERA s.101A, above, para.6–047); dismissal of an employee trustee of an occupational pension scheme (ERA s.102); dismissal of an employee representative for consultation (ERA s.103, below, para.9–041); dismissal for making a protected disclosure (ERA s.103A, above, para.4–039); dismissal contrary to the National Minimum Wage Act 1998 or the Tax Credits Act 1999 (ERA ss.104A, 104B, above, para.7–059); dismissal for taking part in protected industrial action (TULRCA s.238A, below, para.12–015); and dismissal for union membership reasons (TULRCA s.152, below, para.10–006). There remain two other categories of automatically unfair dismissal, both introduced by TURERA 1993.

Dismissal on health and safety grounds

Protection for employees against retaliation for complaints about health and safety matters was introduced as a result of the EU Framework Directive on Health and Safety (89/391/EEC). The relevant health and safety grounds, defined in ERA s.100 are sixfold: carrying out health and safety activities as an employer-designated representative; carrying out health and safety activities as a designated workers' representative; acting as a representative for consultation purposes; drawing what is reasonably believed to be a health or safety risk to the employer's attention; leaving or refusing to return to the place of work because of what is reasonably believed to be a serious and imminent danger (cf. *Piggott Bros v Jackson* (1991)); and taking appropriate steps to protect oneself or others in circumstances of serious and imminent danger. Not only is dismissal on any of these grounds automatically unfair, but also the employee must not be subjected to any detriment during employment for any of these reasons (ERA s.44). **8–080**

The scope of these grounds has received a fairly liberal interpretation. Thus in *Harvest Press v McCaffrey* (1999) the EAT held that the source of the danger could include a fellow employee, not just dangers arising from the workplace itself, so that an employee who refused to work because he was frightened of being attacked by another employee was protected. In *Goodwin v Cabletel UK Ltd* (1997) a tribunal held that an over-enthusiastic safety representative who had been heavy-handed in dealing with one of his employer's sub-contractors, causing a dispute, had been dismissed for the way he carried out his duties rather than because of his duties. The EAT held that the manner of carrying out duties could be within the protection of ERA s.100 and remitted the case to a fresh tribunal. In *Masiak v City Restaurants (UK) Ltd* (1999) the EAT held that the reference in ERA s.100(1)(e) to protecting "other persons" from danger could include members of the public as well as other employees, so that a chef dismissed for refusing to cook chicken which he thought was a health risk was covered. Finally, in *Balfour Kilpatrick Ltd v Acheson* (2003) the EAT held that the protection for employees bringing a safety risk to the employer's attention should not be limited to situations where there was no safety representative or safety committee (ERA s.100(1)(c)).

It is specifically provided that refusing to work, etc in these circumstances will not constitute participation in industrial action (as it could otherwise do if there were concerted action by a group of employees) (TULRCA ss.237 and 238). In *Balfour Kilpatrick Ltd v Acheson* (2003) the employees had walked off the job where there was no serious and imminent danger, but the employment tribunal thought that this could be regarded as bringing a risk to the employer's attention and so protected under that heading. However, the EAT reversed this, stating clearly that instituting industrial action could never be a reasonable means of communicating a risk to the employer.

8–081 There is no upper limit on compensation for dismissals held to be unfair under ERA s.100.

Dismissal for asserting a statutory right

8–082 Under ERA s.104 it is automatically unfair to dismiss an employee if the reason or principal reason is either that the employee brought proceedings to enforce a statutory right or that the employee asserted that the employer had infringed a statutory right. Provided that the employee acts in good faith, it is irrelevant that she is not in fact entitled to the right in question or that it has not been infringed (*Mennell v Newell & Wright* (1997)). The statutory rights to which this applies are, broadly, individual rights under the ERA and rights in connection with trade union membership or activities or subscriptions under TULRCA.

This new right was introduced on the back of the health and safety grounds described above and is a welcome innovation. However, comparison with the non-victimisation provisions in the EqA 2010 reveals a glaring omission, which is that there is no protection as such for assisting another employee in asserting her statutory right.

Dismissal for political opinions

8–083 A curious hybrid ground for dismissal was introduced by ERRA 2013 s.13 in response to the European Court of Human Rights' decision in *Redfearn v United Kingdom* (2012). In this case, the European Court held that the claimant's right to freedom of association under ECHR art.11 had been infringed when he was dismissed for standing for election as a local councillor as a member of the British National Party. The European Court did not hold that such a dismissal could never be justified, but the fact that the claimant had no way of testing this in front of a tribunal constituted an unwarranted interference with his right to be a member of a lawful political party, as he had not been employed long enough to claim unfair dismissal. The Government responded with ERRA 2013 s.13, which introduced new ERA s.108(4), providing that the two-year qualifying period for unfair dismissal does not apply where the reason or principal reason for the dismissal "is, or relates to, the employee's political opinions or affiliation". Note that this does not mean such a dismissal is automatically unfair, but only that no continuity of employment need be proved. The employer may be able to show that the dismissal was within the band of reasonable responses, depending on the circumstances.

Remedies for unfair dismissal

Reinstatement and re-engagement

8–084 Under ERA s.112 a tribunal which has found that an employee was unfairly dismissed must first explain the remedies of reinstatement and re-engagement and see whether the employee wishes to be re-employed. The clear intention of the legislation is that, if at all possible, the best remedy for unfair dismissal is for the employee to get his job back. Reinstatement in essence means that the employee is returned to her former job as if she had never been away. She is entitled to net back pay, any other benefits which would have been received (e.g. a Christmas bonus or annual increment) and her continuity and seniority rights are preserved intact (ERA s.114). Re-engagement should usually be as favourable as reinstatement, but differs in that it may mean that the employee is taken back in a different (though suitable) job, or the same job but in a different place, or by a new company which is in the same group as her former employer. Generally the employee should again receive back pay and other benefits (ERA s.115).

The tribunal has discretion as to whether to make an order for re-employment. The wishes of the employee are paramount in the sense that re-employment will never be ordered against the employee's wishes. However, if the employer offers reinstatement and the employee unreasonably turns it down, compensation may be reduced (ERA s.122(1)). The wishes of the employer are not taken into account, which is just as well since there would otherwise be no orders for re-employment. Employers almost invariably are unwilling to take back the employee, because they fear losing face, or that it will undermine their authority. The tribunal must consider whether it is practicable for the employer to take the employee back. The fact that a replacement has been taken on does not render re-employment impracticable; but if, for example, there have been redundancies in the meantime, or if the other workers are reluctant to have the employee back, this could be a ground of impracticability. Finally, the tribunal must also consider whether it is just to make such an order where the employee was to some extent to blame for the dismissal. This could lead to the tribunal deciding to order re-engagement rather than reinstatement, in that re-engagement need not be ordered with full back pay in these circumstances.

Although reinstatement or re-engagement have always been possible remedies for unfair dismissal, until 1975 the tribunal could only recommend them. They may now be ordered, but it remains the case that if the employer flouts the order, the only sanction is to make an additional award of compensation to the employee. In *Port of London Authority v Payne* (1994) the Court of Appeal held that the issue of practicability of re-employment should be judged afresh if the employer fails to comply with an order of reinstatement or re-engagement, meaning that the appropriateness of the original order can in effect be attacked. Furthermore, the court stressed that impracticability can be proved by a lot less than proof of impossibility and, most worrying of all, that the commercial judgment of the employer (which, you may be sure, will always argue the impracticability of re-employment) is a factor which should be taken into account. It is, perhaps, hardly surprising that despite their status as the primary remedies for unfair dismissal, reinstatement and re-engagement are still only awarded in less than 1 per cent of successful unfair dismissal cases heard by tribunals. This can partly be put down to employee reluctance to return, usually because they fear that the employer will look for the first opportunity to dismiss them, or victimise them in other ways. However, in times of high unemployment when alternative jobs are hard to find, it is difficult to believe that this is the whole explanation, and it may be that tribunals do not take seriously enough their duty to promote these orders.

Compensation

8–085   The other, and more usual, remedy is compensation. Compensation for unfair dismissal is generally made up of two elements: a basic award and a compensatory award. In some circumstances, an additional award may be payable as well. Under the ERelA 1999 s.34, compensation limits are linked to the Retail Prices Index (RPI) as it stands in September each year and used to be altered accordingly the following February. In its January 2011 consultation, *Resolving Workplace Disputes*, the Coalition Government indicated that the present formula was producing increases which were too large and proposed changing the formula. In particular, it queried whether an annual exercise was necessary and proposed a link to the Consumer Prices Index rather than the RPI (which would certainly produce lower increases). In the event, the link to the RPI remains, but the uprating now happens on 6 April each year instead of 1 February: this is in line with the policy of bringing new employment legislation into force on just two dates a year, 6 April and 6 October.

The basic award

8–086   The basic award is calculated according to a strict arithmetical formula in almost exactly the same way as a redundancy payment. The amount of a week's gross pay is multiplied by the number of years' service and then by a multiplier of ½, or 1, or 1½ according to the employee's age (ERA s.1 and 19). A week's pay is subject to a maximum limit which stood at £475 per week in 2015. Years of service refers to complete years of service and is subject to a maximum of 20. Finally, this figure is multiplied by 1½ for all years when the employee was aged over 41, by 1 for all years between the ages of 22 and 41 and by ½ for all years under the age of 22. It follows that the maximum (in 2015) is £14,250, which would be the basic award for an employee aged 61 or more with at least 20 years' service and earning at least £475 gross per week.

The basic award may be reduced by a percentage if the employee unreasonably refuses an offer of reinstatement from the employer, or if it would be just and equitable to do so on account of any conduct of the employee before the dismissal (ERA s.122(2)). This not only allows a reduction where the employee was partly to blame for the dismissal, but also in cases like *Devis v Atkins* (1977) where the misconduct is only discovered after the dismissal. It is not wholly uncommon for 100 per cent reductions to be made. However, it is not possible to reduce the basic award on account of the employee's conduct after dismissal, as the EAT held in *Soros v Davison* (1994), where the dismissed couple, butler and housekeeper to a well-known financier, sold their story to a national newspaper.

Where the employee successfully argues that his dismissal for redundancy is unfair, then the redundancy payment is set off against the basic award to prevent double compensation. If the employee was dismissed for a reason relating to trade union membership (that she was, or was not, a union member) then the basic award cannot be less than £5,807 (in 2015). This was originally part of a special regime of compensation for dismissal for union membership reasons which was punitive in nature and designed in effect to deter dismissals on these grounds. It has since been extended to certain dismissals on health and safety grounds, in working time cases or for acting as an employee representative (ERA s.120).

The compensatory award

The amount of the compensatory award is to be: 8–087

"such amount as the tribunal considers just and equitable in all the circumstances having regard to the loss sustained by the complainant . . . in so far as that loss is attributable to action taken by the employer" (ERA s.123(1)).

It will include expenses incurred as a result of the dismissal and benefits the employee would have expected to receive but for the dismissal, but is subject to the general rule that the employee has a duty to mitigate his loss. The compensatory award is subject to an overall limit, which was widely criticised as much too low (£11,300 until October 1999). In the White Paper, *Fairness at Work* (Cmnd.3968, 1998) the Government originally proposed to scrap the limit on the compensatory award altogether. It was persuaded that this might make cases more difficult to settle (since it might be harder to quantify the value of a claim) and instead it lifted the limit very substantially to £50,000. It had been raised to £78,355 by 2015.

The Coalition Government considered that the limit was too generous, and as a result ERRA s.15 gave the Secretary of State power to alter the maximum compensatory award, which was done with effect from July 2013. The maximum compensatory award is now either £78,355 (the statutory maximum) or one year's gross pay for that employee, if lower.

While the statutory formulation seems to give tribunals a wide discretion, general principles as to the heads of recoverable loss were established early on in *Norton Tool Co v Tewson* (1973). First is the immediate loss up to the time of the tribunal hearing. This will include net wages which would have been received, including such things as overtime if it is likely that the employee would have worked overtime, any benefits in kind and tips. Private health insurance, the use of a company car and any other employment perquisites may be quantified and included. The sum will be reduced by the amount of any wages earned in new employment, and in effect by the amount of any social security benefits received (although the employer will have to pay back an equivalent amount to the state). Secondly, using similar principles, the tribunal must try to quantify the employee's future loss, if the employee is still out of work by the time of the hearing or has taken lower-paid employment. This may involve the tribunal in making difficult estimates about how long the employee is likely to be out of work, or catch up the former level of earnings. Where the employee was a member of an occupational pension scheme, loss resulting from the termination of that membership should also be taken into account; finally, a small conventional sum will be awarded for loss of employment protection rights, to reflect the fact that the employee will have to build up one year of continuous employment with a new employer before being protected against unfair dismissal and two years for redundancy, etc.

8–088   Injury to feelings and general distress at the manner of the dismissal was held not to be compensatable in *Norton Tool Co v Tewson*, but in *Johnson v Unisys Ltd* (2001) (see above, para.8–010) Lord Hoffmann expressed the obiter view that this might be wrong. Given that the emphasis of the statute is on "just and equitable" compensation he suggested that it could be appropriate to make an award for distress, humiliation, damage to reputation or to family life. Naturally, this was immediately tested and the issue went to the House of Lords in *Dunnachie v Kingston-upon-Hull City Council* (2004), where the House of Lords (including Lord Hoffmann) had second thoughts. They held that compensation for injury to feelings was not recoverable for unfair dismissal, on the grounds that if Parliament had intended this to be covered, it would have said so in the legislation—as in EqA 2010, which says expressly that there can be compensation for injury to feelings.

Like the basic award, the compensatory award may be reduced by a percentage if conduct of the employee contributed to the dismissal (ERA s.123(6)). While conduct which was only discovered after dismissal would not be within this, the overall discretion in the tribunal to award what is just and equitable permits it to take subsequently discovered misconduct into account. In practice, tribunals work out the global figure for the basic and compensatory award and then knock a percentage off that is appropriate, rather than treating them separately. It should be remembered that there can be a further enhancement or reduction by up to 25 per cent in accordance with TULRCA s.207A if either the employer or the employee has failed to comply with procedural steps recommended in a code of practice (above, para.8–040).

While the maximum possible award for general unfair dismissal is £92,605 (in 2015) in practice most claimants never see anything like this amount. In 2014–15 the median award made by tribunals was only £6,955, which suggests that for the vast majority of claimants to tribunals, the level of the maximum limit on the compensatory award may not matter very much. This is one of the reasons for dissatisfaction with the law of unfair dismissal.

The additional award

8–089   If an employer refuses to implement an order for reinstatement or re-engagement, or fails to implement it fully, the tribunal may order it to pay an additional award of compensation to the employee (ERA s.117(3)). This will be between 26 and 52 weeks' gross pay (subject to the £475 maximum), at the tribunal's discretion.

Further Reading

❏ H. Collins (1992), *Justice in Dismissal: the Law of Termination of Employment,* Clarendon Press
❏ L. Dickens, M. Jones, B. Weekes and M. Hart (1985), *Dismissed,* Basil Blackwell
❏ M. Freedland (2003), *The Personal Employment Contract,* OUP
❏ C. Barnard and L. Merrett (2013), "Winners and Losers: Edwards and the Law of Unfair Dismissal" 72(2) CLJ 313

❑ D. Brodie (1998), "Specific Performance and Employment Contracts" (note), 27 ILJ 37
❑ D. Cabrelli and R. Zahn (2013), "The Elective and Automatic Theories of Termination in the Common Law of the Contract of Employment: Conundrum Resolved?", 76(6) MLR 1106
❑ H. Collins (1992), "The Meaning of Job Security", 20 ILJ 227
❑ H. Collins (2012), "Compensation for Dismissal: In Search of Principle", 41 ILJ 208
❑ P. Elias (1981), "Fairness in Unfair Dismissal: Trends and Tensions", ILJ 201
❑ K. Ewing and A. Grubb (1987), "The Emergence of a New Labour Injunction?", 16 ILJ 145
❑ K. Ewing (1989), "Job Security and the Contract of Employment", 18 ILJ 217
❑ P. Goulding (1990), "Injunctions and Contracts of Employment: The *Evening Standard* Doctrine", 19 ILJ 98
❑ G. Pitt (1989), "Dismissal at Common Law: The Relevance in Britain of American Developments", 52 MLR 22
❑ G. Pitt (1993), "Justice in Dismissal: A Reply to Hugh Collins", 22 ILJ 251
❑ A. Sanders (2013), "Does Article 6 of the ECHR Apply to Disciplinary Procedures in the Workplace?", 33(4) OJLS 791

9. Redundancy and Transfers of Undertakings

Key Points

This chapter:
- Explains the statutory concept of redundancy
- Considers situations where redundancy payments may be withheld
- Explains what is a transfer of an undertaking under TUPE
- Explains the concept of a service provision change
- Examines the implications of transfers of undertakings for contracts of employment
- Discusses the rights of employees dismissed because of a transfer
- Explains the duties of employers to consult over redundancies and transfers

***

Businesses have to be flexible in order to survive and prosper. This means that they need to be free to reorganise, relocate, change methods of production or service delivery, move out of some products and services into different areas or even cease to carry out some kinds of business altogether. Obviously, such changes can have huge effects on workers' employment, and the task of employment law must be to strike a balance between the needs of the business for flexibility and the needs of workers for secure jobs and income. It is very common for business reorganisation and restructuring to give rise to job losses, and that is the focus of this chapter. The law of redundancy gives employees rights to some level of compensation where they have been dismissed for certain kinds of economic reasons, and the law on transfers of undertakings gives employees the right to follow their jobs in some situations where businesses or parts of businesses are sold to a new owner.

9–001

Redundancy

9–002   Compensation for redundancy was one of the first protective rights introduced for employees by statute. Following closely on the Contracts of Employment Act 1963 (which gave employees the right to minimum periods of notice and a written statement of terms and conditions), the Redundancy Payments Act was passed in 1965.

Apart from amendments in 1975, the law on redundancy has remained in substantially the same form since its original enactment, although it is now to be found consolidated in Pt XI of the Employment Rights Act 1996. It could be argued that redundancy law should have been reformed in the light of the introduction of unfair dismissal law and the law on transfers of undertakings, to promote greater coherence over all. Certainly, the law of unfair dismissal had a great impact on how redundancy cases are conducted, mainly because levels of compensation for unfair dismissal are higher than for redundancy. The redundancy payment is only the equivalent of the basic award for unfair dismissal. Thus whereas before 1972, cases involved employees arguing that they were redundant while the employer argued that they had been dismissed for some other reason, afterwards the position was reversed. Employers were more willing to make the lower redundancy payment (part of which they could claim back from the state by way of rebate), while employees sought to argue that they had been unfairly dismissed, either on grounds that the reason for their dismissal was not really redundancy, or on grounds that the redundancy had been carried out unfairly (see above, para.8–066).

While the law on unfair dismissal was at least drawn up with an eye to its relationship with the law on redundancy, this can hardly be said of the other major development in this area, the Transfer of Undertakings (Protection of Employment) Regulations 2006 (TUPE). Originally introduced in 1981 by a reluctant government to comply with the Acquired Rights Directive (77/187/EEC), the regulations apply to all transfers of undertakings, whether or not a reduction of the workforce occurs. As a result, they overlap but are not coterminous with the rules on redundancy. The relationship between the two has at times been inconsistent. An overhaul of the entire structure seems overdue.

9–003   A redundancy payment is not, and never has been, intended to be a kind of unemployment benefit, tiding the worker over until a new job is found. It is more of a recognition of past service, of the employee's stake in and contribution to the enterprise. These points are illustrated by the fact that the amount of the payment depends on length of service, and that employees who are made redundant are entitled to their redundancy payment even if they have another job to go to the next day. Nevertheless, part of the rationale behind the scheme was to ease technological and other changes: it was hoped that employees receiving compensation would more easily adjust to the loss of their jobs and even consider moving to new work.

Qualification to claim redundancy

As with unfair dismissal, the worker has the burden of establishing that he **9–004** is qualified to claim: he must be an employee, must not fall into one of the excluded categories and must have at least two years' continuous employment (see above, para.8–021). Similarly, it is for the employee to prove that he was dismissed, if this is denied. The definition of dismissal in the Employment Rights Act 1996 (ERA) s.136 is generally the same as the definition of dismissal in relation to unfair dismissal, discussed above in Ch.8, although one notable difference is if the contract would be frustrated at common law because of an event affecting the employer, this is treated as termination by the employer and thus as a dismissal (ERA s.136(5)).

A particular problem apt to arise in redundancy situations is shown by *Morton Sundour Fabrics v Shaw* (1966). The employer told the employee that they would be closing his department some time that year, but did not indicate exactly when. They helped the employee to find another job, so he gave notice and left. As he was not actually under notice of dismissal at the time he left, it was held that he did not qualify for a redundancy payment (see also *Doble v Firestone* (1981)). The problem with this is that it is likely to encourage an employee to stay until the bitter end rather than to try and find another position as quickly as possible, quite the opposite of what was intended. Some palliation is provided by ERA s.142, which allows an employee to leave early without jeopardising his entitlement, provided that during his statutory notice period he serves the employer with a counter-notice stating his intention to leave early. If accepted, the employee remains entitled to his redundancy payment. If the employer does not accept, she must serve a written counter-notice to the employee's counter-notice saying that he is required up to the last day. If the employee then leaves early, an employment tribunal must decide whether it is just and equitable for him to get all or part of his redundancy payment. However, ERA s.142 would not help an employee in the circumstances of *Morton Sundour Fabrics v Shaw* because he was not on notice at the time he left.

Once it is established that the employee has been dismissed, ERA s.163(2) raises a presumption that the dismissal is by reason of redundancy, which means that the burden is on the employer to disprove it. While few cases turn on the burden of proof, the presumption proved vital in *Willcox v Hastings* (1987). W and L were employed by a small business owned by W's father. He sold it to a married couple, who both intended to work in the business and who therefore only needed one extra employee. Thus prima facie either W or L was redundant. However, the new owners planned that the third employee should be their son; so both W and L were dismissed, but only one of them for a redundancy reason. Not surprisingly, no one ever bothered to designate which of them was dismissed for what. It was held that both W and L were entitled to redundancy payments: the burden was on the employers to disprove redundancy in respect of each of them, and the employers could not do so.

The meaning of redundancy

9–005 Two situations are defined as redundancy under ERA s.139. Broadly, the first deals with the employer closing down the business, and the second, where the employee is surplus to requirements.

Cessation of business

9–006 Under ERA s.139(1)(a) an employee is dismissed for redundancy if the dismissal is wholly or mainly attributable to:

"the fact that his employer has ceased, or intends to cease—
(i) to carry on the business for the purposes of which the employee was employed by him; or
(ii) to carry on that business in the place where the employee was so employed . . ."

In general, redundancy on the ground of cessation of business is fairly straightforward as it involves a simple investigation of an objective fact—has the business ceased or not? The tribunal may not go behind the decision to inquire whether it was actually necessary to close down. In *Moon v Homeworthy Furniture* (1977) employees made redundant when a factory closed claimed that it had not been closed for economic reasons but as a retaliatory measure by the employer because it had a bad industrial relations record. Following the general principle adopted in company law, that it is for management to run the business, not the courts (*Re Smith & Fawcett* (1942)), the EAT declined to be drawn into a consideration of the reasons behind the company's decision. In *UK Coal Mining Ltd v NUM (Northumberland Area)* (2008) the EAT held that the statutory requirement for an employer to consult the workforce ahead of redundancies (see below, para.9–041) included a requirement to consult about the reason for the closure of a business. However, if the business ultimately closes, whether for the claimed reason or not, the dismissals of the employees are still bound to be for redundancy.

One reason for shutdown may be that the employer is going out of business. If this is because the business is insolvent and is being wound up, it is often the case that the assets are insufficient to meet the claims for redundancy and pay in lieu of notice of employees. In this situation the payments will be met from state funds (ERA s.166). Alternatively, when an employer ceases to trade the business may be sold to someone else. In these circumstances it is important to know whether there has been a transfer of an undertaking (in which case TUPE will apply). These issues will be considered below (para.9–023).

The main area of difficulty which has arisen under the first limb of the definition of redundancy is where the business does not cease altogether but there is a shutdown at one particular place. For example, if a company with factories in Leeds and Sheffield shuts down its Leeds factory but has jobs available at its Sheffield premises, are the Leeds workers redundant or can they be required to relocate to Sheffield? The issue here is whether the test for deciding what is the place at which the employee is employed for the purposes of ERA s.139(1)(a)(ii) should be *factual* (i.e. where has the employee actually been working?) or *contractual* (i.e. place of work means wherever the employee can be required to work according to her contract of employment). In the first case to reach the Court of Appeal on redundancy, *O'Brien v Associated Fire Alarms* (1968), it seemed that a contractual test was to be used. The employees were electricians whose work was directed from the Liverpool office. They were told that they would have to work in the Barrow area (some 120 miles away) when the Liverpool office closed for lack of work. While the Barrow area was within the region directed from the Liverpool office, they had always worked within the vicinity of Liverpool. As their work involved them travelling to jobs, the court was prepared to accept that it was an implied term of their contracts that they should travel, but that it could only be implied that they would work at places within reasonable daily travelling distance of their homes. Since the employer had no right to require them to move to Barrow, the Court of Appeal held that they were dismissed on grounds of redundancy.

The contractual test has been criticised on the grounds that when the legislation was passed it was envisaged that relocation in these circumstances would constitute a redundancy situation. But in the more recent Court of Appeal decision, *High Table Ltd v Horst* (1997), the point was made that in *O'Brien v Associated Fire Alarms* the employer had purported to dismiss the employees for breach of contract and thus it was inevitable that the focus of the decision was on whether their refusal to move was a breach of contract or not. Once the employer's ground for dismissal was held not to operate, the statutory presumption of redundancy applied.   **9–007**

This explanation of *O'Brien v Associated Fire Alarms* (1968) enabled the court in *High Table Ltd v Horst* (1997) to use the factual approach without contravening the doctrine of precedent. The employer in this case provided catering services to firms in the City of London, and the employees had worked for a number of years as waitresses at Hill Samuel before being dismissed on grounds of redundancy following a reduction in the catering service required by Hill Samuel. They argued that they were not redundant because there was an express mobility clause in their contracts, so they could have been deployed elsewhere. In deciding what was the "place where the employee was so employed" the Court of Appeal was clear that a factual test should be used, saying that if an employee had always worked in one place it would be contrary to common sense to suggest that the place of work included other places because of a mobility clause. If, however, during the period of employment the nature of the work required the employee to go from place to place, then the contract might be of assistance in deciding what the place of work was. Here, the employees had always worked in the same place so they were redundant when work there ceased.

This case was the converse of *O'Brien v Associated Fire Alarms*, in that in *High Table Ltd v Horst* the employees wanted to move but the employer did not want to redeploy them elsewhere. It would seem, however, that if the employer had told them to move and they had refused, in this case they would have been in breach of contract because of the express mobility clause. It therefore seems likely that such a dismissal would not be for redundancy. Reinforcement for this view can be found in *Home Office v Evans* (2008), where immigration officers who were employed in a "mobile grade" in the Civil Service, meaning that they could be transferred anywhere in the United Kingdom or abroad, resigned rather than accept a transfer from Waterloo International Terminal to Heathrow when the Waterloo International Terminal closed. They argued that once it was clear that the Terminal was due to close, a redundancy situation arose and the employer's redundancy procedure should have been applied to them. The Court of Appeal, however, held that the employer was perfectly entitled to invoke the mobility clause in the contract instead and their resignations could not therefore be categorised as constructive dismissal.

9–008   The result of all this is a somewhat one-sided situation, with all the flexibility on the side of the employer. Note also that even if the employer does not have a contractual right to move the employee, she may still be denied a redundancy payment if the offer of employment elsewhere is seen as an offer of suitable alternative employment which she has unreasonably refused (see below, para.9–013).

Surplus labour

9–009   The second situation where a dismissal will amount to a redundancy is where it is wholly or mainly attributable to:

> "the fact that the requirements of that business—
> (i)   for employees to carry out work of a particular kind . . . have ceased or diminished or are expected to cease or diminish" (ERA s.139(1)(b)).

This definition causes considerable problems in practice, since from the point of view of the employee, "work" is the job that she does: the whole package of the tasks performed and the terms and conditions under which they are performed. However, the statutory definition emphasises only the tasks performed, and it is unclear how far the "work of a particular kind" is linked to the employees who carry it out. While it is apt to cover the paradigm of a business whose work has fallen off so that it needs fewer people, many situations where labour is shed do not fit that pattern.

First, one situation which is increasingly common is where the amount of work remains the same, or may even have increased, but the employer decides that survival requires a cut in the salary bill—more must be done with less. In *Delanair v Mead* (1976) the company was in desperate straits and decided to cut the workforce by 10 per cent. The manager of Mead's department was told to cut his staff by one and selected Mead. The EAT remitted the case to the tribunal to consider whether the employer's true reason was that, having reappraised their needs, they did not need him (which would be redundancy) or whether they had merely decided to cut one salary—which would be a dismissal on grounds of economy, not redundancy. The decision has been criticised, for if management decides that it must make do with fewer people, for whatever reason, it must be the case that the requirements of the business have diminished. The wording of the Act does not empower the tribunal to go behind the decision to reduce the workforce and consider the motives for so doing.

This was recognised by a different EAT in *AUT v University of Newcastle* (1987) where a lecturer was dismissed when the funding for his course ceased and the tribunal considered that this was not a redundancy dismissal because the work still remained to be done, although the university could not afford to pay someone to do it. The EAT held that the requirements of the business are defined exclusively by the employer, and here it had been decided that the lecturer was not required. This was redundancy. However, *Delanair* was distinguished rather than not followed, on the grounds that there was no operational review in that case, as there had been here. It is submitted that in most cases where the employer decides that fewer employees must do the same amount of work, those dismissed are redundant as surplus to requirements. This is consistent with the House of Lords' approach in *Murray v Foyle Meats* (1999) (see below, para.9–012).

A second area of difficulty related to this is where there is a reorganisation   **9–010** of tasks among employees with the end result that someone's job disappears. In these circumstances, the employee may feel that he is not redundant but unfairly dismissed: his job is still there, but has been carved up among other people; there has been no diminution in the work. However, once more it seems clear that if such a reorganisation leads to management deciding that it needs fewer people, this is properly to be regarded as redundancy. An example is *Robinson v BI Airways* (1978). The employee had been employed as the flights operations manager, responsible to the general manager, operations and traffic. In the interests of economy and efficiency, tasks were reorganised and both these posts disappeared. A new post of operations manager was created and Robinson was dismissed. He claimed unfair dismissal, arguing that the new job was really his old job with a few added extras. It was held that the new job was sufficiently distinct from both the previous jobs that it could properly be said that his job had disappeared and that he was redundant. In these circumstances an employee may be able to claim unfair dismissal if not redeployed to the new position, but on the facts this was not the case here.

This is an illustration of the Act's emphasis on the tasks to be done rather than the employee as the holder of a job involving a package of tasks and terms and conditions. Another consequence of this is that if tasks are reorganised and the employee cannot cope with the new allocation, she may be held to be dismissed for incapability rather than because the "requirements . . . for employees to carry out work of a particular kind . . . have ceased or diminished". This in turn leads to difficult questions as to how different the package of tasks must be before it can be said that it is work of a different kind.

In *North Riding Garages v Butterwick* (1967) the respondent was the manager in charge of the repairs workshop and had been employed at the garage for 30 years. He had always been involved in doing a lot of repair work himself, but new owners of the garage put more emphasis on the managerial side. His job changed and the work was increased so that he spent less time on practical work and more on paperwork—which he did not do very well. Eight months later he was dismissed, and it was held that the reason was incompetence rather than redundancy. His argument was essentially that the employers now needed a different kind of employee and their need for employees to carry out work of the particular kind that he had done had diminished. Yet in effect it was more a reallocation of tasks, which the court felt did not actually make it a different kind of work. If new methods alter the way work is done, rather than altering the nature of the work itself, the employee can be expected to adapt, and the court evidently thought that this situation fell into the former category (see also *Hindle v Percival Boats* (1969)).

9–011   A comparatively rare example of a situation where a change in tasks was held to amount to a change in the nature of the work is provided by *Murphy v Epsom College* (1985) where a school employed two plumbers, including the claimant, who worked mostly on the heating system. The school upgraded its heating system, introducing an electronic control system. Murphy was made redundant on the grounds that what was now needed was a heating technician—someone who could deal with the electrical as well as the plumbing work—rather than a general plumber like him. The Court of Appeal upheld the tribunal's decision that this was a change in the nature of the work, and thus a genuine redundancy. In assessing this decision, it must be borne in mind that whether there has been a change in the nature of the work is again a question of fact for tribunals, and so it is entirely possible that seemingly inconsistent decisions may be upheld on appeal; it is also relevant that the "hidden agenda" in this case was that Murphy was in dispute with the school over his hours and the scope of his duties, and it seems that he was reluctant to do the new work without some improvement. The governors responded by taking the view that if he said it was outside his duties, they needed a different kind of employee. His claim was for unfair dismissal, but the employer's contention that it was redundancy was accepted—a rather different situation from *North Riding Garages v Butterwick*.

In *North Riding Garages v Butterwick* (1967) the court referred to the fact that on his dismissal a new workshop manager had been employed as an indicator that he was not redundant. While this will not invariably prove that the reason was not redundancy (see, e.g. *Murphy v Epsom College*, above), where there is no reduction in the number of employees, often there will be no redundancy. Thus in *Johnson v Nottinghamshire Combined Police Authority* (1974) two civilian clerks had been employed for more than 20 years in normal office hours from Mondays to Fridays. Outside those times, essential clerical work was carried out by police officers. In order to release officers from this work, the police authority wished the clerks to work shifts (08.00 to 13.00 and 13.00 to 20.00) over a six-day week. They refused because of their domestic duties, and were dismissed. Replacements were taken on. It was held that they were not redundant. The work remained the same, there was just as much work to be done, and the fact that it was at different hours did not change its nature. Although such a change was a breach of contract, Lord Denning said:

> "It is settled . . . that an employer is entitled to reorganise his business so as to improve its efficiency and, in so doing, to propose to his staff a change in the terms and conditions of their employment: and to dispense with their services if they do not agree. Such a change does not automatically give the staff a right to redundancy payments."

In *Macfisheries v Findlay* (1985) a change from night-shift to day-shift was held to constitute a change in the nature of the work done, the difference between day and night work being considered as of a different order of magnitude to the differences in daytime hours in *Johnson v Nottinghamshire Combined Police Authority* (1974). The clerks in that case did not claim unfair dismissal, but would probably have lost if they had, as the reorganisation would almost certainly have constituted "some other substantial reason" for dismissal.

Similarly, in *Lesney Products v Nolan* (1977) machine setters had habitually worked a long day shift and a lot of overtime in the evenings. The employers reorganised to replace this with a double day shift to cut overtime costs. The employees could not claim to be redundant. In this case, the new arrangements meant that their weekly pay was reduced from £70 to £56–a very substantial proportionate loss. This underlines again the fact that the definition of redundancy concentrates on the needs of the business and the functions performed, not the package of terms and conditions which constitute the employee's job (see also *Chapman v Goonvean & Rostowrack China* (1973)).

In these cases, there was no diminution in the amount of work, but a change **9–012** in the way employees were expected to work to deliver it, and a continuing need for the same number of employees. In *Packman v Fauchon* (2012) it was argued for an employee that there could be no redundancy if there was no diminution in the number of employees, but this was rejected by the EAT. The claimant worked as a bookkeeper for the employer, a consultant. He asked her to reduce her hours because, first, his business had been hit by the recession and he could no longer afford to employ her full time, and secondly, he had a new software package which could perform some of the jobs she did. She was dismissed when she refused to accept the reduction and the employer argued that she was not redundant. The EAT held that this was a dismissal for redundancy, since it was a reduction in the amount of work that had caused her dismissal, albeit that the employer would need to replace her.

As noted already, today employees are more likely to claim that they are not redundant and that, rather, their dismissal is unfair. If there is a flexibility clause in the contract, giving the employer the option of moving the employee to other work, can the employee argue that he is not redundant just because the usual job has disappeared? This is analogous to the argument about place of work, discussed above, and was the subject of conflicting authority until settled by the House of Lords' decision in *Murray v Foyle Meats Ltd* (1999). Lord Irvine (who gave the main opinion) stated firmly that a tribunal considering redundancy only had to answer two simple questions of fact. First, did the requirements of the business for employees diminish, meaning that the employer needed fewer employees, for whatever reason? Secondly, did that cause the dismissal of this employee? If so, the employee is redundant.

In reaching this decision the House of Lords expressly endorsed the reasoning of the EAT in *Safeway v Burrell* (1997) and so it seems that it also deals with the problem of "bumping". This is the situation where, rather than dismiss a particular redundant worker, the employer decides to redeploy her to another post and make the holder of that post redundant. Is the person so "bumped out" redundant? While it is true that his job remains, it would seem that the dismissal of the bumped employee is wholly or mainly due to a reduction in the requirements of the business for employees, which is all that the statutory definition requires, and this was the view expressed by the EAT in *Safeway v Burrell*. It may be that the victim of the bumping may be able to claim it is also unfair dismissal: this will depend on the reason for the employer choosing to keep the one rather than the other (see above, para.8–067).

Offer of suitable alternative employment

9–013   If the employer makes the employee an offer of a new contract of employment before the ending of his old contract, and the new contract is either the same work or suitable alternative employment, the employee will be disentitled to a redundancy payment if he unreasonably refuses it (ERA s.141). While it is no longer necessary that the employer's offer should be in writing, it must be made before the ending of the old contract and sufficient details must be given to enable the employee to make an informed choice. If the new contract does not start immediately on the finishing of the old one, it must begin within four weeks thereafter.

Whether an offered contract is "suitable" and whether the refusal is "reasonable" would seem to involve two separate questions about different issues. Suitability seems naturally to refer to the objective characteristics of the job itself, while judging the reasonableness of the refusal seems to allow for subjective considerations relating to the employee's personal circumstances to be taken into account. That said, some factors may be relevant to both questions: if the new job involves extra travelling time, that may be relevant both to suitability and to whether it is reasonable to turn it down, for example. Perhaps, for this reason, the Court of Appeal in *Spencer and Griffin v Gloucestershire CC* (1985) deprecated attempts to draw a rigid distinction between the two aspects. However, it is submitted that considering them separately is an aid to clarity of thought, and the wording of the Act suggests that they are separate and consecutive considerations.

As the question of whether an offer of suitable employment has been unreasonably turned down is a question of fact for a tribunal to consider, few cases are of much value as precedents. In general, anecdotal evidence seems to suggest that tribunals are reluctant to deprive employees who are prima facie redundant of their redundancy payments, and so may resolve doubtful situations in the employee's favour. Pay is a major factor to be considered, and it would be unusual for a contract on less pay to be regarded as suitable. Having said that, the fact that pay remains the same does not mean that the offer is suitable. In *Taylor v Kent CC* (1969) a redundant headmaster was offered alternative employment as one of a pool of mobile teachers, sent out to schools as required, with his pay maintained at its previous level. The drop in status and responsibility made it an unsuitable alternative.

9–014   The opportunity to exercise and maintain a level of skill may be relevant, although it should be borne in mind that an offer of an entirely different kind of work for which the employee would require retraining may be suitable. What would be relevant is whether the employee is likely to be able to complete the retraining successfully. An offer of less skilled assembly work was considered unsuitable for a skilled card wirer in *Standard Telephones & Cables v Yates* (1981).

Travelling time and cost is another major factor. Where the employer is prepared to pay travel expenses and for time spent travelling, this may help to indicate that the offer is suitable. However, for employees with domestic responsibilities in particular, it may be reasonable to refuse a job which will mean a greater time away from home. Analogously, a job which requires an employee to relocate to a different part of the country is more likely to be considered suitable if the employer is prepared to help financially and otherwise with the move; yet an employee with an employed spouse who cannot easily move, and/or children at a critical stage of schooling may reasonably refuse a generous relocation package.

A final example indicating some other factors which could be relevant to reasonable refusal is *Paton, Calvert & Co v Westerside* (1979). The company, in severe financial difficulties, sent redundancy notices to all staff. Before the notices expired, the company got a Temporary Employment Subsidy from the government, so it wrote to all employees offering them their jobs back. Once given, of course, a notice of dismissal cannot be rescinded unilaterally, so technically this was a dismissal and an offer of alternative employment. Since the new jobs were the same as the old jobs, there was no suggestion that they were unsuitable. However, Westerside, who was aged 61, had already found a new permanent job. It was held reasonable for him to reject the offer: the company's financial prospects were still uncertain, and for someone of his age, within a few years of retirement and in an age group that usually has the greatest difficulty in finding new employment, permanence was extremely important.

Trial periods

If the alternative employment offered is very different from the employee's previous job, he is taking a bit of a shot in the dark by accepting. What if it does not work out? Until 1975, the employee had to take the risk. If he decided that he did not like the new job and left, he would have forfeited his right to a redundancy payment. For this reason the Employment Protection Act 1975 introduced the concept of a trial period, during which time neither side would be finally committed. It is now to be found in ERA s.138.

9–015

Under s.138, if the terms of the new contract differ wholly or in part from the old contract, there will be a trial period of four weeks, or such longer period as the parties agree where retraining is required. If the trial period is to be longer than the statutory four weeks, it must be specified precisely in writing. If during the trial period the contract is terminated by either party, the employee is to be treated as having been dismissed as at the end of the original contract, for the original reason (usually, redundancy). This means that if the employer dismisses him for incompetence in the new job, the employee will be treated as dismissed for the original redundancy. If the employee resigns because he does not like the new job, it will be treated as a dismissal, but his entitlement to a redundancy payment will depend on whether the new job was suitable and whether his termination during the trial period was reasonable or not. Presumably the employee may have a stronger claim to say that a refusal is reasonable where he has actually tried the new work.

It has been held that in some circumstances the employee may be able to rely on the existence of a trial period at common law—which may not be for as limited a time as the statutory trial period. It all depends on how the employer handles the redeployment of the employee to new work. If the employer formally terminates the original contract, but offers a contract for different work before the old contract expires, then the only possibility is for a statutory trial period of four weeks (*Optical Express Ltd v Williams* (2008)). But if the employer instructs or requests the employee to move to different work, then assuming that there is no right to do this under the contract, the employer's instruction is in fundamental breach of contract or the request is an offer to vary the contract. By general contract principle, the innocent party faced with a fundamental breach has a reasonable time to decide whether or not to accept the breach as a termination of the contract (by resigning) or to affirm the contract. Similarly, he has a reasonable time to decide whether to accept a variation. This reasonable time in effect constitutes a trial period in the new job at common law.

9–016   Thus in *Turvey v Cheney* (1979), four employees in the polishing department were told that it was due to close because of lack of work and were offered work in different departments. They agreed to try the new work on trial. More than four weeks later, they left. The EAT pointed out that it was already well established that merely beginning to work under a new contract does not indicate acceptance of it: the employee has a reasonable time to make up his mind (see *Shields Furniture Ltd v Goff* (1973)). The statutory trial period was meant to add to an employee's rights, not to reduce them. The EAT's interpretation of this situation therefore was that if the employer had not formally given notice to terminate the employees' contracts and offer them new ones, then the request to move to different departments was not within the contract and they had a reasonable time to decide whether or not to accept this new or varied contract. At some point, whether or not they expressed their decision, it would be possible to say that a reasonable time had expired. At that stage, said the EAT, they would in theory be able to rely on the statutory four-week trial period, since by then the employment under the previous contract would have ended.

Reduction for misconduct

9–017   Under ERA s.140(1) if the employee commits an act of misconduct which at common law would entitle the employer to terminate the contract without notice, then the employee will be disentitled to a redundancy payment, subject to the exceptions in ERA s.140(2), (3). This is not a provision for a reduction in the redundancy payment but a total disqualification; however, there are exceptions. The oddity is that the exceptions seem to cover the entire ambit of the rule, leaving no situation where there would be a total disqualification.

There are two exceptions. Under ERA s.140(2), if the employee takes part in a strike or other industrial action while on notice for redundancy and is dismissed on that account, ERA s.140(1) does not apply and the employee remains entitled to her redundancy payment. This takes account of the fact that the announcement of redundancies may well result in protest action by the workforce and it could be unfair for them to lose all compensation because of it. Also, under ERA s.143, in these circumstances the employer can serve a notice of extension on the employees, requiring them to work the number of days lost through the action on top of their notice period. If the employees refuse, they will not get their redundancy payments.

The second exception, under ERA s.140(3), refers to all cases of misconduct other than taking part in a strike or other industrial action, and provides that if the employee is dismissed for this misconduct while on notice for redundancy, the tribunal may award him such part of his redundancy payment as it considers to be just and equitable—which may be the whole sum.

The peculiarity of all this is that ERA s.140(1) only applies to dismissals for **9–018** misconduct, yet the exceptions in ERA s.140(2) and (3) seem to cover all cases of misconduct, and state that at worst in these cases the employee's payment will be reduced. However, there is a difference between the two provisions. The exceptions are qualified by the requirement that the dismissals for misconduct or industrial action must have taken place while the employee was on notice for redundancy. This is not the case for ERA s.140(1), which seems therefore to make the rather obvious point that if the employee is dismissed for misconduct she cannot get a redundancy payment. If this is all it means, then one might wonder why it was stated at all. The provision was rescued from this abyss of meaninglessness by the EAT's decision in *Simmons v Hoover* (1977). In *Simmons v Hoover* a strike of some months was causing a contraction in the employer's business. The employer therefore wrote to the employees who were on strike giving them notice that they were redundant. Simmons claimed a redundancy payment on the strength of ERA s.140(2). The EAT held that ERA s.140(2) applied only if the employees went on strike when they were already on notice for redundancy. Both exceptions in effect envisage two dismissals: an original dismissal for redundancy, which is then overtaken by a dismissal for misconduct or participation in industrial action. Here there was only one dismissal—said by the employer to be for redundancy, although it could have been for going on strike. The EAT held that where the employer dismisses for redundancy but could have dismissed at common law for misconduct, ERA s.140(1) applies and the employee is disentitled to a redundancy payment.

While the decision gives meaning to ERA s.140(1), it leaves two unanswered questions. Why should an employer who can dismiss for misconduct dismiss for redundancy instead? The answer to this may simply be ignorance of the law. So, in that case, why should there be a special statutory provision to relieve an ignorant employer of the consequences of her mistake? Such a provision must be entirely unique. So far as ERA s.140(3) is concerned, it is clear that the issue is whether the employer is entitled at common law to dismiss for the misconduct. In *Bonner v Gilbert* (1989) an employee on notice for redundancy was dismissed for suspected dishonesty. On the basis that the employer honestly believed on reasonable grounds that the employee was guilty, an employment tribunal held that ERA s.140(1) and (3) applied, and that the employee should not get any part of his redundancy payment. The EAT reversed the decision, because the question must be whether the employee was actually guilty of the dishonesty (i.e. whether there was an actual breach of contract) in order to satisfy the common law test.

Lay-off and short-time working

9–019 An employer may try to avoid or at least postpone redundancies by temporarily suspending operations, or reducing the number of hours worked. Unless the employer has the power under the contract to lay off employees without pay, or reduce their hours, it will be a fundamental breach of contract entitling the employees to leave and claim constructive dismissal (see Suspension, above, para.8–008). Even where the employer has contractual power to do this, however, it is provided that in some circumstances the employee may leave and claim redundancy.

Under ERA s.147 the employee is laid off in any week in which the employer does not provide him with work and he is therefore not entitled to remuneration. "Short time" is defined as a diminution in work leading to the employee's remuneration amounting to less than half a week's pay. If employees are laid off or put on short time for four or more consecutive weeks, or for any six weeks within a 13-week period, they may give notice of an intention to claim a redundancy payment because of it. They must give the notice in writing, and must also give the proper period of contractual notice before leaving. The employer may contest the claim on the grounds that it is reasonably expected that there will be no further lay-off or short-time working in the next 13 weeks: this defence must be indicated in a counter-notice in writing served on the employee within seven days of the notice to claim (ERA ss.149 and 152).

The provisions as to notice and counter-notice, timing and supplementary provisions, of which only an outline is given above, are enormously complicated and have been described as the despair of all those concerned with the interpretation of industrial legislation (Lord McDonald in *Kenneth MacRae v Dawson* (1984)). The chances of an employee navigating them successfully and qualifying for a redundancy payment are slight without good union or legal advice. It must be doubted whether such complexity can be justified.

Calculation of the redundancy payment

9–020 A statutory redundancy payment is calculated according to a strict arithmetical formula which, generally speaking, is the same as for the calculation of the basic award for unfair dismissal (see above, para.8–086), i.e. the amount of a week's gross pay (subject to a maximum of £475) multiplied by the number of complete years of service (subject to a maximum of 20) multiplied by ½, 1, or 1½ according to the age of the employee (ERA s.162). Until the Employment Equality (Age)

Regulations 2006, service under the age of 18 and over the age of 65 did not count, but these limits have now been removed. In 2015 the maximum possible payment was therefore £14,250. Where the employee has successfully claimed that his dismissal for redundancy was unfair, the amount of the redundancy payment is set off against the basic award to prevent double compensation (ERA s.122(4)).

Insolvency of the employer

When the redundancy payments scheme was introduced, a Redundancy Fund   **9–021** was set up to which all employers contributed via a top-slicing of their National Insurance contributions. The fund served two purposes. First, it was government policy to spread some of the costs of redundancies across industry as a whole, and this was done by making all employers contribute and then allowing those who actually made people redundant to claim back a proportion of what they paid by way of rebate. Secondly, it provided a fall-back fund from which the employees of insolvent businesses could be paid.

The rebate, fixed at 50 per cent in 1969, was reduced to 41 per cent in 1977 and then to 35 per cent and only for employers with fewer than 10 employees in 1986. After these salami tactics, the rebate was finally abolished altogether by the Employment Act 1989. This reflected not so much a change of policy as a recognition that the fund, which had been in surplus until 1979, had gone into deficit thereafter as a result of high unemployment and frequent business failures during the 1980s. The Redundancy Fund itself was wound up and merged with the general National Insurance Fund under the Employment Act 1990.

The function of providing a back-up where the employer's business is insolvent now falls therefore on the National Insurance Fund. The employee makes a claim to the Secretary of State for Business, Innovation and Skills under ERA s.166. She must show that she was entitled to a payment and that she has taken reasonable steps to obtain payment from the employer. In practice the provisions work quite well and employees usually obtain their payments without difficulty. If the employee's claim is disputed, she will have to claim before an employment tribunal, where the Secretary of State will have locus standi to challenge her entitlement.

Time off to look for work

Under ERA s.52 an employee who is given notice of dismissal for redundancy is   **9–022** entitled to reasonable time off work to look for new employment or to make arrangements for retraining. This applies only to employees with two or more years of continuous employment. If the employer unreasonably refuses to permit this, the employee may bring a claim to an employment tribunal, which can order the employer to pay compensation equal to the pay the employee would have got if allowed the time off—but subject to a maximum of two-fifths of a week's pay (usually therefore two days' pay). This does not mean that reasonable time off is limited to two days, only that the remedy is so limited.

It may be questioned whether this amounts to much more than a bit of window-dressing, given that increasingly employers do not require redundant employees to work out their notice, and the lack of an effective sanction for breach.

Transfers of Undertakings

9–023 It is now necessary to consider what happens to the employees when a business is sold. Can this count as a cessation of business (by the original owners) which entitles the employees to redundancy payments? The first thing to know is how the business has been sold. In this country the vast majority of business operations are conducted through the medium of a company registered under the Companies Acts. A registered company is recognised in law as a legal person with pretty well the same capacities as a human person, but it is owned by human persons, the shareholders. If a company is being sold, the normal way of doing it is for a majority of the shares to be transferred from seller to buyer. So far as employees of the company are concerned, this kind of deal has no legal implications for their employment. The company itself is their employer, and the identity of their employer does not change merely because the share ownership changes. In practical terms, the change in the identity of the controllers may have very important effects on employees: the new owners of the company may have radically different policies from the old. For this reason, some commentators criticise the fact that it is not treated as a change of employer. Under the Employment Relations Act (ERelA) 1999 s.38, the Secretary of State has power to make regulations to extend protection under TUPE to situations not presently covered, but when the Regulations were revised in 2006 the Government specifically decided not to extend them to share sales and it was hardly surprising that the Coalition Government did not even consider the possibility in its 2013 review.

Assuming that there is a genuine change of employer, what are the implications for employees? At common law a contract of employment is personal, so a change in employer would amount to a termination of the first contract and the entering of a new one. Such a change could not be forced on an employee against her will (*Nokes v Doncaster Amalgamated Collieries* (1940)) because it would offend the general principle we have already referred to against forced labour. At first sight, then, this would suggest that the employees would be dismissed by reason of cessation of business and would thus be redundant. Redundancy law used to deal with this situation by providing that the employee would not be entitled to a redundancy payment if the new employer was prepared to keep her on. Thus, although the employee did not have to agree to a change in employer, there was a financial incentive for her to do so. The new owner of the business had a choice about whether to take on the employees; if they were not taken on, they could claim a redundancy payment from their former employer. However, this position was radically altered by the Transfer of Undertakings (Protection of Employment) Regulations (TUPE), originally passed in 1981 in order to implement the original Acquired Rights Directive (77/187/EEC). The idea behind the Acquired Rights Directive is that workers ought to be treated as having a right to their jobs. Therefore, if the business is transferred from one owner to another, workers should have the right to follow their jobs to the new owner. The Directive effected this by stating that, in these circumstances, the workers' employment should transfer automatically from the old owner of the business (the transferor) to the new owner (the transferee) (see now the Acquired Rights Directive 2001 art.3(1)).

Some of the key concepts in the original Directive (such as what was meant by a transfer of an undertaking) were not defined, leading to a fair degree of uncertainty and a lot of litigation in front of the CJEU. The Acquired Rights Directive was revised in 1998 and a consolidated version produced in 2001 (the Acquired Rights Directive (2001/23/EC)). Although the first consultation on reforming national law on transfers to take account of this was issued in 2001, it was not until 2006 that the new TUPE Regulations were passed. These completely replaced the 1981 Regulations and apply to all transfers since April 2006, although older case-law remains relevant to the interpretation of some parts of TUPE 2006. In 2013, the Coalition Government consulted on amending TUPE, specifically to get rid of any protection which went further than the minimum required by the Acquired Rights Directive. The final position, embodied in the Collective Redundancies and Transfer of Undertakings (Protection of Employment) (Amendment) Regulations 2014, amending TUPE 2006, did not in the end prove quite so radical, as will be seen.

What is a transfer of an undertaking?

The TUPE 2006 Regulations apply to two situations: a transfer of an undertaking or part of an undertaking (a "standard transfer") and a service provision change (TUPE 2006 reg.3). These will be considered in turn.   **9–024**

Standard transfers

The first situation covered by TUPE 2006 is "a transfer of an undertaking, business or part of an undertaking or business which is situated immediately before the transfer in the United Kingdom" (TUPE 2006 reg.3(1)(a)). Both in domestic courts and the CJEU the scope of the terms "transfer" and "undertaking" have given rise to numerous cases. In TUPE 2006 a transfer of an undertaking is defined as being the "transfer of an economic entity which retains its identity" and reg.3(2) explains that an "economic entity" means "an organised grouping of resources which has the objective of pursuing an economic activity, whether or not that activity is central or ancillary". This follows exactly the wording of art.1(1)(b) of the Acquired Rights Directive 2001, which itself broadly codified the relevant case-law of the CJEU (e.g. *Spijkers v Gebroeders Benedik Abattoir* (1986); *Süzen v Zehnacker* (1997); *Sánchez Hidalgo v Aser* (1999)—cases which remain relevant in considering these issues). From these cases it is clear that an organised grouping of resources need not necessarily involve significant physical resources as well as human resources. In labour-intensive industries such as cleaning or security services, it may be that the main resource used is human   **9–025** labour and any other assets used are of low value or trivial. In *Rygaard v Strø Mølle* (1996) the CJEU held that an undertaking must be a stable economic entity, implying some capacity for permanence or continuity, rather than being (as in that case) a short contract to finish some building work which was already ongoing. The requirement of stability is not expressly stated in the Directive nor in TUPE 2006, but as the case-law of the CJEU continues to be relevant, it is likely that this requirement remains.

In relation to retention of identity, the aim of the Directive is to ensure continuity of employment relationships within a business, so what is looked for is the business (or part of a business) being continued in other hands. In *Spijkers v Gebroeders Benedik Abattoir* (1986) the CJEU identified these factors as being relevant on that issue: the type of undertaking or business; whether or not the tangible assets of the business were transferred; the value of intangible assets at time of transfer; whether or not the majority of employees were taken over; whether or not customers were transferred; the degree of similarity between the activities carried on before and after the transfer; and the period, if any, for which those activities were suspended. This will be a question of fact in each case, meaning that provided tribunals apply the correct legal tests, their decisions will not normally be changed on appeal. In *Klarenberg v Ferrotron Technologies GmbH* (2009) the CJEU pointed out that no one factor would be decisive, and, in relation to retention of identity, the fact that the part of the undertaking concerned had been absorbed into the transferee's structure in such a way that it no longer had organisational autonomy did not necessarily mean that the Directive was not applicable.

By way of example, in *Law Society for England and Wales v Secretary of State for Justice* (2010) the Legal Complaints Service, which was an identifiable entity within the Law Society dealing with consumer complaints against solicitors, was replaced by a new Office for Legal Complaints set up under the Legal Services Act 2007. This would deal with complaints against barristers as well as solicitors— although 90 per cent of the work was likely still to concern solicitors. However, it was intended to symbolise a fresh start, particularly because complaints would now be handled by a body independent of the professions themselves. It was held that this was not a transfer of an undertaking, as the function of the Legal Complaints Service would not retain its identity in the new Office, and it was also relevant that the new Office was intended as a break with the past.

9–026 Regulation 3(4)(a) of TUPE 2006 states that "public and private undertakings engaged in economic activities whether or not they are operating for gain" come within the scope of the Regulations (cf. *Dr Sophie Redmond Stichting v Bartol* (1992)). The original version of TUPE excluded non-commercial ventures and there was originally some doubt as to whether the activities of central and local government departments were covered. This regulation makes it clear that non-commercial ventures and public sector employment are subject to the Regulations. However, reg.3(5) states that: "An administrative reorganisation of public or administrative authorities or the transfer of administrative functions between public administrative authorities is not a relevant transfer" (cf. Acquired Rights Directive 2001 art.1(1)(c)). Thus for inter-governmental restructuring the issue will be whether an entity engaged in an economic activity has transferred (in which case TUPE 2006 will apply) or whether it is merely the transfer of an administrative function (in which case, TUPE 2006 will not apply).

Service provision changes

In *Daddy's Dance Hall* (1988) the CJEU held that the Acquired Rights Directive could apply even if there was no direct contractual link between transferor and transferee. This set the stage for the next major development: the application of the Directive to the contracting out of services or parts of a business. The landmark case in this connection was *Rask v ISS Kantineservice* (1993). A company, Phillips, had a staff canteen at its factory in Denmark. Instead of running it themselves, through their own employees, they decided to contract it out to ISS, who were paid a fixed fee and were bound by conditions laid down by Phillips (e.g. as to price levels). ISS argued that this was not covered by the Directive because Phillips remained owner of the premises and ISS did not have the normal freedom of a typical business owner to fix prices freely to make profits; furthermore, it was not part of the core business of the company. They argued that it was in effect only a transfer of the management of an internal service. Nonetheless, the CJEU held that the Directive applied because there had been a transfer of responsibility for running a part of the business; and that was enough.

The contracting-out decisions of the CJEU, coupled with the lifting of the unauthorised "commercial venture" restriction, caused consternation to the Conservative Government of the early 1990s because of its potential to scupper its controversial policy of insisting on "market-testing" of public services. Under the Local Government Act 1988, local authorities were obliged to identify some services which would be put out to tender to see if private organisations could do them more cheaply than the authority itself. This was known as "compulsory competitive tendering" or CCT. Of course, the principal reason that private organisations could perform the services more cheaply was because they paid their employees a lot less; it is also the case that the services put up for tender usually involved low-paid occupations anyway, also that they frequently involved large numbers of women workers, but that should not come as any real surprise.

If what was transferred following a CCT exercise was an identifiable unit, which was often the case, then it was fairly clear by the early 1990s that it came within the Directive and that TUPE should be interpreted so far as possible to give effect to this. And here was the rub: if it was a relevant transfer then the new provider automatically inherited all the existing employees on their existing terms and conditions of employment. Thus it became unlikely that the new provider could perform the service more cheaply.

Over the next decade or so decisions of the CJEU and domestic courts as to the kinds of contracting out (or change of service provision) arrangements which would attract the operation of the Directive and of TUPE ebbed and flowed. No change was made to the Acquired Rights Directive on this point when it was amended in 1998, but in TUPE 2006 the government took the major step of going beyond the requirements of the Directive by applying

9–027

9–028

the TUPE Regulations to a "service provision change" as well as to the transfer of an undertaking. A service provision change is defined in TUPE 2006 reg.3(3) as existing where, immediately before the changeover, the transferor has an organised grouping of employees whose principal purpose is carrying out activities on behalf of a client and after the changeover those service activities will be carried on by a new person (the transferee) other than for a specific event or short-term task. Regulation 3(1)(b) makes it clear that a service provision change can include original outsourcing from a client to a contractor (often referred to as a first generation transfer); subsequent transfers between contractors (e.g. after a re-tendering exercise) (called a second generation transfer) and bringing a service back in-house (from contractor to client). The only real limitation on this is that the principal purpose must be the provision of a service, not merely the supply of goods from one party to another. Thus if a car manufacturer always gets components from one supplier and switches to a new supplier, this will not constitute a service provision change.

What if a health authority contracts with a firm of solicitors to provide all its legal services for a certain period and at the end of that period decides to switch to a different firm of solicitors? At one point in the development of the new regulations the government intended to have a specific exception excluding professional services, but the move foundered on the difficulty of defining what exactly professional services were. Thus, in such a case, it would seem that the change could be caught by TUPE 2006 and the crucial issue might be whether or not the service was in fact provided by an organised grouping of employees who had this as their principal purpose (cf. *Ward Hadaway v Love* (2010)).

The inclusion of service provision changes as defined in TUPE 2006 brought much greater certainty to this difficult area, as CJEU case-law was (and continues to be) complex and arguably inconsistent. In *Metropolitan Resources Ltd v Churchill Dulwich Ltd* (2009) the EAT confirmed that the regulation on change of service provision had created an entirely new statutory concept of transfer and that the multi-factor test used for other transfers would not apply to it. The question is simply whether the facts fall under one of the three situations in TUPE reg.3(1)(b) and (3). This meant, however, the definition of a change in service provision under TUPE 2006 was quite a lot wider than the Acquired Rights Directive. This was one of the reasons for the Coalition Government's 2013 consultation on reform of TUPE: dedicated to a policy that there should be no "gold-plating" of EU protections, they proposed repealing this definition. Possibly to their surprise, the consultation showed a strong consensus in favour of retaining the wider statutory definition, among employers as well as trade unions. The advantage of certainty were seen to outweigh other considerations, since if contractors are sure that TUPE applies, they can take this into account in pricing bids to provide services. In the event, the only change which took effect under the amendment is to clarify that the activities being transferred should be "fundamentally or essentially the same" as the activities being carried out beforehand—thus codifying what was stated in *Metropolitan Resources Ltd v Churchill Dulwich Ltd* (2009).

In *Enterprise Management Services Ltd v Connect-Up Ltd* (2012) the EAT held **9–029** that this test was not satisfied when 15 per cent of the activities carried out by the old contractor were not being carried out by the new contractor. Another factor was that a number of contractors were carrying out the new service, and this fragmentation also meant that the situation could not be regarded as a service provision change. It has also been held that it is essential that the service as continued should be provided to the same client as before (*Hunter v McCarrick* (2013)).

Who transfers?

Under TUPE 2006 reg.4, employees transferred are those who are assigned to **9–030** the relevant grouping of resources or employees being transferred, and who are employed up to the time of the transfer. The original version of TUPE provided for the transfer of employees who were employed "immediately before the transfer". This opened up the possibility of subverting the basic protection which was meant to be afforded by an automatic transfer of contracts. Suppose that the transferee company did not want to take on the new workforce. It could simply make it a condition of the purchase that the transferor company got rid of the workforce before the transfer, so that they were not employed "immediately before" the transfer. That way their contracts would not be transferred. True, the transferor would be liable for unfair dismissal: but if the transferor company was insolvent, which is a very common reason for selling the business, that would not matter very much.

In *Secretary of State v Spence* (1986) employees were dismissed for redundancy by the receivers of the business at 11.00, and three hours later the business was sold. The next day, the transferee re-engaged the workforce, who nonetheless claimed redundancy payments from their former (insolvent) employer. By way of defence, it was argued that their contracts were automatically transferred to the new employer by virtue of TUPE. The Court of Appeal held that they were not. That regulation applied only to those employed "immediately before" the transfer, which they held must mean the split second before the transfer took place. The employees were therefore entitled to redundancy payments from their former employer; since that company was insolvent, the Secretary of State was liable.

This issue came before the House of Lords in *Litster v Forth Dry Dock* (1989) in a different context. FDD was in receivership. A new company, Forth Estuary Engineering (FEE) was formed to take over the business. FEE had no wish to take on the employees of FDD because it planned to take on redundant workers from another shipyard who were willing to work for lower wages. The two companies therefore arranged that FDD's employees should be dismissed before the transfer. They were duly dismissed an hour before the transfer took place, and they sued for unfair dismissal. FEE argued that because they were not employed immediately before the transfer, their contracts were not transferred and they could only claim against FDD. As this company was in receivership, the claim would have been worthless to a large extent.

9–031 The House of Lords upheld the Court of Appeal's interpretation in *Secretary of State v Spence* of the words "immediately before the transfer". However, they noted that the CJEU in *P Bork International v Foreningen* (1989) made it clear that the Acquired Rights Directive was meant to prevent dismissals before the transfer. The House therefore adopted a purposive interpretation of the Regulations and held that the transferee was liable not only where employees were employed immediately before the transfer, but also where they would have been but for being unfairly dismissed. FEE was therefore liable to the employees for unfair dismissal. This is now embodied in TUPE 2006 reg.4(3), which states that employees transferred are those "employed immediately before the transfer, or who would have been so employed if he had not been dismissed" contrary to TUPE reg.7 (which deals with unfair dismissal: see below, para.9–038).

Where only part of an undertaking or business is transferred, difficult questions may arise as to whether a particular employee is assigned to that part or not. In *Botzen v Rotterdamsche Droogdok Maatschappij BV* (1986) the CJEU held that the test was whether the employee was assigned to the part of the business being transferred, rather than whether he or she worked exclusively in that part. This is essentially a question of fact for the employment tribunal. The difficulty of applying this test is well illustrated by *CPL Distribution Ltd v Todd* (2003). The company had a contract to distribute coal on behalf of British Coal and the claimant was the personal assistant to the manager of this business. This manager also had responsibility for managing business acquisitions, but most of the claimant's work was on the coal distribution business. British Coal assigned the distribution contract to another company under a TUPE transfer, but the claimant was not among the staff who were transferred to the new contractor. The manager for whom she worked stayed with the original company working on his other duties, but no longer needed a personal assistant. The claimant argued that since most of her work was on the coal distribution business, she was assigned to that part of the undertaking and should have been transferred to the new contractor. However, the Court of Appeal upheld the tribunal's finding that she was really assigned to the manager she worked for, and as he was not regarded as assigned to the coal business, it was a strong indication that she was not either.

Objecting to a transfer

9–032 What if an employee does not wish to be transferred? TUPE 2006 reg.4 provides that, on transfer, the contracts of employment of employees of the transferor are automatically transferred to the transferee. Originally this meant that the employee was deprived of her common law right not to be transferred from one employer to another without her agreement (cf. *Nokes v Doncaster Amalgamated Collieries* (1940)), but this was thought to be an inevitable side-effect of the Acquired Rights Directive. Following the CJEU decision in *Katsikas v Konstantinidis* (1993) it became clear that there had been a misunderstanding of what the Directive actually required and that it was not intended that employees should be transferred against their will. Thus TUPE 2006 reg.4(7) provides that there will be no automatic transfer where the employee informs either transferor or transferee that she objects to it. However, in these circumstances reg.4(8) provides that the transfer will terminate the employee's contract without there being a dismissal in law. This means that the employee will not even be entitled to a redundancy payment, so it is unlikely that many employees will avail themselves of this option. There are two exceptions to this position. The first is where the transfer involves a substantial change in working conditions to the material detriment of the employee. Even if this change does not involve a fundamental breach of contract, the employee may treat herself as dismissed in these circumstances and so may be able successfully to claim compensation for unfair dismissal or redundancy (TUPE 2006 reg.4(9)). The second exception is contained in TUPE 2006 reg.4(11), which expressly preserves an employee's right to leave and claim constructive dismissal in circumstances where the employer's actions amount to a repudiatory breach of contract.

In *Nationwide Building Society v Benn* (2010) a number of employees who had been employed by the Portman Building Society resigned when it was taken over by Nationwide, on the grounds that their terms had been altered detrimentally. They complained in particular of a downgrading of their roles, and that the bonus scheme would be less beneficial. The EAT upheld the tribunal's decision that this was both constructive dismissal, because the change was a fundamental breach of contract, as well as an alteration to their detriment in the terms of reg.4(9) (although ultimately holding that the dismissal was not unfair—see below, para.9–040).

What transfers?

The central provision of TUPE 2006 is reg.4, which provides that, after a transfer, the employee's contract of employment has effect as if originally made with the transferee, and that the transferee takes over all the rights, powers, duties and liabilities under the contract except any provisions relating to an occupational pension scheme (reg.10).   **9–033**

It is necessary to consider in a little more detail exactly what is meant by the statement in TUPE 2006 reg.4(1) that the employee's contract "shall have effect after the transfer as if originally made between the person so named and the transferee". In *Morris Angel & Sons Ltd v Hollande* (1993) the employee, managing director of a theatrical costumier, was contractually bound to a restrictive covenant which prevented him soliciting his former employer's customers on leaving employment. His original employer transferred the business to the claimant company and the employee's contract was terminated. The issue was the meaning of the restrictive covenant: did it now apply to the customers of the transferee or did it still cover the customers of the transferor? The Court of Appeal held that it must still apply to the transferor's customers (who were the only ones the employee really knew). Otherwise, in a transfer situation, an employee could find herself subject to a much wider obligation than she originally agreed to, which would be contrary to the spirit of the Directive.

Regulation 4(2) goes on to state that "all the transferor's rights, powers, duties and liabilities" in connection with the contract are transferred to the transferee. In *DJM International v Nicholas* (1996) it was held that this included liability for sex discrimination by the transferor in forcing the employee to retire earlier than a man would have had to. As discrimination claims can result in unlimited compensation, this could be a significant risk for a transferee. On similar reasoning the Court of Appeal held in *Bernadone v Pall Mall Services* (2000) that the transferor's liability in negligence or for breach of statutory duty for an employee's accident at work also transferred to the new employer. The good news for the transferee in this case was that the court also held that it was entitled to the benefit of the transferor's indemnity under its employers' liability insurance. There were conflicting EAT decisions on whether liability transferred for failure to consult about the transfer, but TUPE 2006 reg.15(9) provides that the transferor and transferee are jointly and severally liable for such a failure. As potential risks for unforeseen, expensive claims emerge after a transfer has gone through, it became common for transfer contracts to require full disclosure by the transferor of any possible claims against it and indemnity against such liabilities. This will no doubt continue but it is now buttressed by a requirement in TUPE 2006 reg.11 that the transferor should provide the transferee with "employee liability information" about each employee who is the subject of the transfer. This information includes the identity and age of the employee, their written particulars, information about any invocation of the disciplinary or grievance procedure in respect of the employee in the previous two years, information about any case brought by the employee against the transferor in the previous two years, or any proceedings which the transferor reasonably believes the employee might take arising from her employment, and details of any collective agreement which may be transferred.

9–034   TUPE reg.5 states that, on transfer, any collective agreements affecting the employment are transferred as if the transferee had made them. This was very relevant in the increasingly common situation or privatisation of parts of the public sector, since it meant that public sector employees could continue to get the benefit of public sector collective bargaining. In *Whent v Cartledge Ltd* (1997) the EAT adopted a dynamic interpretation and held that where employees had contracts which incorporated the collective agreement in force for the time being, they could continue to get pay increases negotiated in the public sector collective bargaining process even though they were now employed by a private sector employer which was not represented in that bargaining process and which did not recognise the trade union. The only way that the employer could avoid this would be by agreeing a variation of the contract with the employees. This stood for over a decade, but was then put in doubt by the CJEU's decision in *Werhof v Freeway Traffic Systems GmbH* (2006) that a German law providing that only existing rights under collective agreements transferred, not future benefits (a static interpretation) did not infringe the Acquired Rights Directive. The Supreme Court referred to the CJEU the question of whether this meant that the British position, that a dynamic interpretation was possible, was still permissible. In *Parkwood Leisure Ltd v Alemo-Herron* (2013), the CJEU held that it was not: where the transferee was not able to participate in the bargaining process, it would upset the fair balance between the interests of the transferee and the interests of the employees if the transferee was forced to accept terms it had no ability to affect. This would infringe the transferee employer's right to conduct a business, guaranteed by the Charter of Fundamental Rights art.16. As a result, TUPE 2006 was amended to include a new reg.4A to codify this, with effect from January 2014.

According to TUPE 2006 reg.10 occupational pension rights relating to old age, invalidity or survivors' benefits are not transferred. This is an enormously significant exception which potentially produces a large gap in TUPE protection for employees, but it is permitted by the Acquired Rights Directive (2001/23/EC) art.3(4)(a). The scope of this exception was narrowed by the CJEU's important ruling in *Beckmann v Dynamco Whicheloe Macfarlane Ltd* (2002), concerning a former NHS employee who was made redundant after being transferred to the private sector. As she was over 50, had she remained employed by the NHS she would have been entitled to very generous benefits: an immediate pension, early payment of a retirement lump sum, a compensatory annual allowance and a compensatory lump sum. She claimed equivalent benefits from the transferee and the High Court referred to the CJEU the question of whether these were old age, invalidity or survivors' benefits and thus within the scope of the exception in art.3(4)(a). In a decision echoing its equal pay decisions (see above, para.7–042) the CJEU held that these were payments in connection with a form of dismissal and therefore liability did transfer to the new employer (see also *Martin v South Bank University* (2004)). The CJEU stated that only benefits paid from the time when an employee reached the end of her normal working life could be classified as within the exception, even though the payments to the claimant were calculated in accordance with rules for pension benefits.

From 1999 the Cabinet Office issued guidelines which essentially required that transferees in the private sector should offer transferred employees benefits which were broadly comparable to those which they would have enjoyed had they remained in the public sector. This has been changed by the Fair Deal for Staff Pensions, issued by the Treasury in 2013, which instead states that employees transferred from the public sector to the private sector should retain access to their existing public sector pension scheme, as long as they remain employed in the same function. This applies to any transfers from April 2015.

A more general amelioration of the rights of transferred employees was carried out by the Transfer of Employment (Pension Protection) Regulations 2005, made under the Pensions Act 2004. Broadly, these provide that if the transferor had an occupational pension scheme for the kind of employee transferred, to which the transferor made contributions, the transferee must offer the employee the option of belonging to an occupational pension scheme or a stakeholder pension scheme to which the transferee must make some contribution. These schemes must meet certain prescribed standards. While this falls short of requiring the transferee to offer equivalent pension rights to those offered by the transferor, it is a great deal better than the position which pertained until 2005. **9–035**

Variation of contracts

Apart from pension rights, however, employees are transferred on their former terms and conditions. This is the key element in the employees' protection, but **9–036** it can pose a problem for the transferee, who may wish to alter terms and conditions in the interests of efficiency or economy, or simply to harmonise contracts with those of the existing workforce. If the new employer either dismisses them and re-engages them on new terms, or else tries to insist on their accepting new terms with the result that they resign, there will be an actual or constructive dismissal of the transferred employees. Under TUPE 2006 reg.7 such a dismissal is automatically unfair unless the employer has an economic, technical or organisational reason for it (see further, para.9–039). But what happens if the transferee gets the new employees to agree to a change in their terms and conditions? Will such an agreement be valid?

In *Daddy's Dance Hall* (1988) the CJEU held that the Directive prohibited any change in terms and conditions of employment by reason of the transfer of an undertaking, even if the employees agreed to it and even if, overall, their terms and conditions were no worse once the changes had taken place. However, this sits oddly with the Acquired Rights Directive 2001 art.4(1), which allows dismissals for economic, technical or organisational reasons entailing changes in the workforce. The issue came before the House of Lords' appeals in *Wilson v St Helens BC* (1998) where employees were made redundant by the transferor and then re-engaged on worse terms and conditions by the transferee. They tried to argue that their dismissals were void because they were in connection with the transfer and that they were entitled to the benefit of their previous terms and conditions of employment. If the dismissals were void, this raised the question of whether or not their agreement (however reluctant) to the change in their terms and conditions was valid.

In the event, the House of Lords held that the dismissals were not void, so that their only claim would have been for unfair dismissal within three months of the original termination (it was 18 months later that they actually claimed). This meant that it was not necessary for the House of Lords to decide the burning question of whether an agreement to vary because of the transfer would have been valid. Lord Slynn, giving the opinion of the House, did express the obiter view that a variation in terms and conditions could be regarded as being for an economic, technical or organisational reason rather than being because of the transfer even if it took place at the same time. Conversely, a variation some time after the transfer could yet be regarded as being connected with it and capable of giving rise to a constructive dismissal which would be unfair under what is now reg.7.

9–037   This, in effect, was what was legislated in TUPE 2006; but it has now been taken further as a result of amendment by the Collective Redundancies and Transfer of Undertakings (Protection of Employment) (Amendment) Regulations 2014. The starting point under TUPE 2005 reg.4 is that a variation of employees' contracts of employment is void if the reason for the variation is the transfer (reg.4(4)). However, under reg.4(5), variation is permitted in three situations. First, where the reason for the variation is an economic, technical or organisational reason entailing changes in the workforce. As we will see, even dismissal can be justified on this ground. A new reg.4(5A) provides that changes in the workforce includes changes to the place where the employee is employed, reversing case-law on this point. Secondly, even if the reason for the variation is the transfer, it will be allowed if the contract itself permits variation. This is a new provision, and has scope to undermine employees' protection considerably. As noted above (para.4–015) employers are increasingly likely to put variation clauses in contracts of employment, and this provides a further incentive for them to do so. Finally, while reg.4(5) no longer expressly states that variation is permissible if it is for a reason unconnected with the transfer, this is implicit in the new wording of reg.4(4), which states that a variation is only void where the reason for it is the transfer.

Another new provision, in TUPE reg.4(5B), further reduces employees' protection by providing that terms derived from collective agreements can be varied one year after the transfer provided that, overall, the employee's contract is not less favourable afterwards than it was before. This takes advantage of a derogation permitted by art.3(3) of the Acquired Rights Directive which had not previously been used. In summary, the changes to reg.4 in relation to variation of contracts following a transfer combine to decrease the safeguards previously provided for employees. There may be some doubt as to whether this is entirely compatible with the Acquired Rights Directive.

Dismissal because of the transfer

The protection afforded by TUPE 2006 reg.4 would be of little use if the transferee could simply dismiss the employees it did not want. Hence the importance of the associated provision in reg.7 which states (following amendment in 2014) that dismissal of an employee either before or after a transfer will be automatically unfair if the sole or principal reason for the dismissal is the transfer, *unless* there is an economic, technical or organisational reason entailing changes in the workforce. If the reason for the dismissal is an economic, technical or organisational reason entailing changes in the workforce it will not be automatically unfair, but will count either as redundancy (where appropriate) or else as "some other substantial reason"—which will mean that the dismissal is fair if the requirement of reasonableness is satisfied. Again, protection has been lessened by the 2014 amendment: previously, dismissals for a reason connected with a transfer, even if not the transfer itself, could be automatically unfair.

9–038

The "ETO" defence

The employer has a defence if she can show that the dismissal was for an "economic, technical or organisational reason entailing changes in the workforce" (TUPE 2006 reg.7(3)). The phrase is copied directly from the Directive, which was plainly not drafted originally in English. None of these expressions had previously been used in British employment legislation and they have never been defined in the Regulations. All that can safely be said about their interpretation is that they are potentially wide.

9–039

In the leading case of *Berriman v Delabole Slate* (1985) the employee left when the transferee reduced his pay in order to bring him into line with other employees in the transferee's business. The Court of Appeal held that it was not enough to show an economic, technical or organisational reason: it must also be shown that the reason entailed a change in the workforce as an objective rather than simply as a consequence of it. Furthermore, a change in terms and conditions of employment did not amount to a change in the workforce: this required either a change in numbers, or "possibly changes in the job descriptions of the constituent elements of the workforce which, though involving no overall reduction in number involves a change in the individual employees which together make up the workforce" (Browne-Wilkinson LJ). This makes the test considerably more stringent than it would be if it were enough just to show a reason which could be classified as economic, technical or organisational. It has, however, been watered down by the amendment in reg.7(3A) that a change in location is included in the concept of a change in the workforce.

In *Wheeler v Patel* (1987) the transferor tried to argue that the fact that the transferee had made dismissal of the employee a condition of going through with the sale was an economic reason. This was rightly rejected, since it would have made a mockery of the protection. However, in *Whitehouse v Blatchford* (1999) the Court of Appeal held that the ETO defence could be used where the client who was switching a contract from one sub-contractor to another made it a condition that the transferee should cut costs by reducing the number of employees. The court denied that this was effectively the same as sacking people in order to achieve a better price for the business, holding that on the facts it was open to the tribunal to find that the client would have insisted on the reduction anyway, even if the contract had not been transferred.

9–040   This kind of problem is particularly likely to occur when an insolvent business is put into administration and the administrators embark on dismissals in order to reduce the wage bill. The distinction which has been drawn in the case-law is between the situation where this is done basically in order to make it more attractive to a potential purchaser—which is not an ETO reason—and where it is in order to preserve the business as a going concern in the short term, even if the ultimate aim is its sale—which can be an ETO reason. *Spaceright Europe Ltd v Baillavoine* (2012) is an example of the first situation: administrators dismissed the managing director of the company, thus saving his substantial salary, on the basis that any purchaser of the business would be certain to put in their own top person. The Court of Appeal held that this was not an ETO reason, since there was no intention to continue the business, nor were there changes in the workforce, since the managing director's role would continue in the future. In contrast, in *Kavanagh v Crystal Palace FC Ltd* (2014), the administrator of a football club in dire financial straits dismissed all non-essential staff at the end of the season in order to keep the club afloat as a going concern. The longer-term aim was certainly to sell it, but the reason at the time of dismissal was to reduce the wage bill and avoid liquidation—which was held by the Court of Appeal to be a valid ETO reason.

An example of an organisational reason which was held to be sufficient for the avoidance of automatic unfair dismissal is supplied by *Nationwide Building Society v Benn* (2010). Employees of the Portman Building Society, which had been taken over by Nationwide, argued that the bonuses which they earned for getting customers to sign up to particular financial products would be much reduced. This was because the range of products offered by Nationwide did not offer the opportunity to earn equivalent amounts of commission. The EAT held that this was an organisational reason so that the dismissals were not automatically unfair.

If the employer succeeds in showing that there is an economic, technical or organisational reason for the dismissal, this does not mean that it is automatically fair. The original TUPE Regulations provided that, in these circumstances, it would count as "some other substantial reason" for dismissal, and thus could be fair or unfair according to whether it was reasonable. This was anomalous, as it did not make provision for the reason also to be redundancy, which is, after all, a common reason for dismissal connected with a transfer. The anomaly was corrected by TUPE 2006 reg.7(3), which provides that an ETO dismissal may be either redundancy (in which case the employee will at least get a redundancy payment) or some other substantial reason. In either case, it may be fair or unfair depending on the circumstances. Because of TUPE 2006 reg.4 and *Litster*, it will normally be the transferee who is liable to pay, however.

Consultation over Redundancies and Transfers

There are statutory obligations on employers to consult with workers over 9–041 redundancies and transfers of undertakings. In situations where there is a transfer which will involve redundancies, both obligations arise. The obligation to consult over redundancies was introduced as a result of the EU Directive on Collective Dismissals (75/129/EEC) (amended and replaced by the Collective Dismissals Directive (98/59/EC)) and is now contained in the Trade Union and Labour Relations (Consolidation) Act 1992 (TULRCA) ss.188–198. For transfers of undertakings, the duty is found in art.7 of the Acquired Rights Directive (200 1/23/EC) and is implemented through TUPE 2006 regs 13–16.

As originally formulated, these duties to inform and consult applied only where the employer recognised a trade union—something which used to be entirely at the employer's option. This limitation of consultation to recognised trade unions was clearly out of line with both directives, which require consultation with workers or their representatives. It was therefore no surprise when the CJEU upheld the Commission's complaint against the government in this respect in *EC Commission v United Kingdom* (1994) in 1994. Remedial action was taken via the Collective Redundancies and Transfer of Undertakings (Protection of Employment) (Amendment) Regulations 1995, which amended TULRCA s.188 and TUPE 2006, so that employers had a duty to inform and consult "appropriate representatives", who could either be employee representatives elected by affected employees or trade union representatives, where there was a recognised trade union. The 1995 Regulations were criticised on three main grounds. First, it was open to an employer to bypass a recognised union and to consult with employee representatives instead. Secondly, in stark contrast to rules on trade union ballots, no framework for the election of employee representatives was stipulated. Thirdly, provided that the employer invited the workforce to elect representatives, if no election took place the employer was absolved of further duties.

These points were addressed by the Collective Redundancies and Transfer of Undertakings (Protection of Employment) (Amendment) Regulations 1999, which establish that if a union is recognised, it should be the conduit for information and consultation (TULRCA s.188(1B); TUPE 2006 reg.13(3)). Broad standards for elections are stated: that the election is to be fair; in secret so far as possible; that sufficient numbers of representatives should be elected to ensure that the interests of different classes of employees are represented; and that no employee is unreasonably prevented from standing. Finally, if the employees fail to elect representatives, the employer now has a duty to provide the relevant information to each individually affected employee (TULRCA s.188(7B); TUPE 2006 reg.13(11)). Complaints can be made to an employment tribunal where the employer fails to comply with any of these requirements. Trade union representatives receive protection from dismissal or detriment while involved in trade union duties (see below, Ch.10). Non-union employee representatives are similarly provided with protection against dismissal or detriment for participating in the election process and for carrying out their duties (ERA ss.47 and 103). They are also entitled to reasonable time off to carry out their duties (ERA s.61).

Consultation over redundancies

9–042 For the purposes of consultation only, the definition of redundancy is extended to include any dismissal for a reason which is not related to the individual concerned (TULRCA s.195) and thus applies to some dismissals for "some other substantial reason". Originally, the duty to consult applied to all redundancies. However, when the Conservative Government amended TULRCA s.188 in 1995 it took advantage for the first time of a derogation allowed by the Collective Dismissals Directive whereby there need not be consultation if fewer than 20 employees at any one establishment are dismissed in a 90-day period. In *R v Secretary of State ex p Unison* (1996) it was argued that such changes required primary legislation, but this challenge was rejected by the Divisional Court.

When the retail chain, Woolworths, closed in January 2009 one month after becoming insolvent, causing 27,000 redundancies, there had been no prior consultation with the workforce. They claimed protective awards from the Secretary of State (see below, para.9–046)—but some 4,500 had been working in stores with fewer than 20 employees. Were these employees outside the consultation requirement, or should the numbers of employees across the country be counted together? What, in short, did "one establishment" mean? The question was referred by the Court of Appeal to the CJEU. It recently held that a business could comprise a number of different establishments, which it defined as the entity to which employees were assigned (*USDAW v WW Realisation 1 Ltd* (2015)). The case returns to the Court of Appeal for decision in the light of this guidance, but fairly clearly, it looks as if individual shops will count as separate establishments for the purposes of the numbers thresholds.

Under TULRCA s.188, the duty to consult only arises when the employer is "proposing to dismiss" employees for redundancy. Consultation starts with the employer giving the representatives in writing the reasons for the proposals, the numbers and descriptions of employees to be made redundant, the total number of employees in the categories from which redundancies will be made, the proposed selection method, the proposed method for carrying out the dismissals (including the timescale) and how any non-statutory severance payment will be calculated. Thus while it is clear that the employer's duty arises as soon as there are proposals to dismiss, the provisions as to the information to be given seem to suggest that the proposals must have reached a fairly advanced stage before the duty arises. In *Hough v Leyland DAF* (1991) the EAT described it as a situation where,

> "matters have reached a stage where a specific proposal has been formulated and . . . this is a later stage than the diagnosis of a problem and the appreciation that at least one way of dealing with it would be by declaring redundancies."

This seems out of line with the Collective Dismissals Directive, which refers to the obligation to consult arising as soon as the employer is contemplating redundancies. As Glidewell LJ pointed out in *R v British Coal ex p Vardy* (1993), "The verb 'proposes' in its ordinary usage relates to a state of mind which is much more certain and further along the decision-making process than 'contemplate'". It seems odd also that this did not feature either in the infraction proceedings taken by the Commission (*EC Commission v United Kingdom* (1994)). More recently the EAT explicitly recognised that TULRCA s.188 cannot be interpreted in such a way as to accord with the Directive (*MSF v Refuge Assurance plc* (2002)). Perhaps a different way into this problem is signposted by the ECJ's decision in *Junk v Kühnel* (2005) which held that "redundancy" for the purposes of the Collective Dismissals Directive (98/59/EC) meant the declaration of the employer of its intention to terminate employees' contracts rather than the actual termination itself (as the UK Government had argued). This meant that consultation should take place before employees were given notice of dismissal—otherwise the purpose of the Directive would be undermined. The issue was revisited in *UK Coal Mining Ltd v NUM (Northumberland Area)* (2008) where the EAT accepted, albeit with hesitation, the view in *ex p Vardy* and *MSF v Refuge* that "proposing" could not be read to include "contemplating". The EAT held that in relation to closure of a business, dismissals are proposed when the closure is proposed, which would be when it was "fixed as a clear, albeit provisional, intention". The issue was referred to the CJEU in *United States v Nolan* (2012), but it unfortunately decided it had no jurisdiction over the issue for technical reasons. The United States then appealed to the Supreme Court, essentially arguing that the law did not apply to a foreign state. That appeal was lost (*United States v Nolan* (2015)) so the issue will return to the Court of Appeal.

Under the original version of TULRCA s.188, consultation had to begin "at the **9–043** earliest opportunity" after the proposal to dismiss, but this was watered down in the 1995 amendments to a requirement to consult "in good time" (the wording used in art.2(1) of the Collective Dismissals Directive (98/59/EC)). While declaring that consultation must begin in good time, TULRCA s.188 also lays down some absolute minimum consultation periods for multiple redundancies. If between 20 and 99 employees are to be made redundant within a period of 30 days or less, the minimum consultation period is 30 days before the first dismissal takes effect; if 100 or more employees are to be made redundant within a period of 90 days or less, the minimum consultation period is 45 days before the first dismissal takes effect (downgraded in 2014: the previous minimum was 90 days). In the case of multiple redundancies, there is a duty to provide advance information to the Department of Business, Innovation and Skills under TULRCA s.193 which has some similarities to TULRCA s.188. The purpose of this is to give the Department early warning where there is likely to be a sudden strain on its resources.

The consultation obligation requires the employer to provide written information to the trade union or employee representatives covering reasons for the redundancies, numbers and descriptions of employees to be made redundant, selection methods and methods of calculating the redundancy payments (TULRCA s.188(4)). Since amendment by the Trade Union Reform and Employment Rights Act 1993 (TURERA), the substance of the consultation must encompass ways of avoiding the dismissals, reducing the number of employees to be dismissed and mitigating the consequences of the dismissals, and must be undertaken with a view to reaching agreement with the representatives (TULRCA s.188(2)). In *UK Coal Mining Ltd v NUM (Northumberland Area)* (2008) the employers proposed to close a mine under the North Sea. They claimed that it was for health and safety reasons, but the real reason was economic. The employers argued that they did not have to consult about the reasons for the closure, but the EAT held that consultation about avoiding redundancies inevitably involved engaging with the reasons for the dismissals and thus the reasons for closing the mine. It therefore upheld the union's claim that the employers were in breach of their statutory obligation to consult because they had not given truthful information.

Consultation over transfers

9–044 The obligation to consult under TUPE 2006 is broader in many ways than the obligation to consult over redundancies. First, under TUPE 2006 reg.13, both transferor and transferee have an obligation to give certain information to the appropriate representatives of any employees who will be affected. The representatives must receive information not only about the fact of the transfer but also about the "legal, economic and social implications" of it (reg.13(2)). Once again, this is a phrase lifted directly from the Directive whose actual meaning is unclear.

Secondly, where the transferor or transferee plan to take any measures which may affect their employees, they must actually consult with the employees' representatives about such measures, consider any representations made by them, and give reasons if rejecting their ideas. Since amendment by TURERA, the employer has an obligation to undertake this consultation "with a view to seeking their agreement" to the measures. This sounds quite useful, but is limited by the fact that each party to the transfer need only consult with its own workforce, and the most likely eventuality is that the transferee will take action affecting the transferor's workforce, with whom it has no direct duty to consult. Furthermore, if no measures are envisaged, there is no duty to consult—but the EAT held in *Cable Realisations Ltd v GMB Northern* (2010) that the duty to provide information was independent of this and must still be fulfilled in these circumstances.

Under TUPE 2006 no minimum period for consultation is specified: reg.13(2) says only that it must occur "long enough before" the transfer to enable consultation to take place. Further, the duty relates to the fact of the transfer, rather than a proposal to transfer. This suggests that the duty to consult arises rather later than it would if redundancies were proposed. As noted already, however, if what is proposed is a transfer resulting in redundancies, both sets of consultation requirements must be adhered to.

The special circumstances defence

An employer who fails to consult over redundancies has a defence if "there are special circumstances which render it not reasonably practicable for the employer to comply" (TULRCA s.188(7)), although the employer must try so far as possible to do so even if making out the defence. An exactly similar defence is found in TUPE 2006 reg.15(2), and it is generally interpreted in the same way.

9–045

In the leading decision, *Clarks of Hove Ltd v Bakers' Union* (1978), 368 of the 380 employees were summarily dismissed for redundancy on the same day that the company ceased to trade, with no prior consultation. It had been in severe financial difficulties for months, and that day the final hope of raising more capital had disappeared. The Court of Appeal held that something as common as financial difficulties and insolvency did not constitute special circumstances excusing the failure to consult; what mattered was the reason for the insolvency. If it had been some sudden disaster, such as the destruction of the plant, or a trading boycott, then the circumstances might be sufficiently out of the ordinary to be considered "special". But where, as here, it was simply the final manifestation of ongoing financial problems, there were no special circumstances.

This seems a realistic approach, especially given that part of the purpose of the consultation requirements is to allow the workforce time to prepare and to begin to look for other work. It is, as usual, a question of fact as to whether special circumstances are made out, and a contrast is afforded by *USDAW v Leancut Bacon* (1981) where the company spent the first half of 1979 attempting to negotiate its takeover by another company. In September, the suitor saw the company's half-yearly accounts and pulled out; this caused their bank to halt credit facilities and appoint a receiver. Two days later the workers were made redundant. The EAT considered that here the insolvency was the result of a sudden event—the bank's clampdown on credit and appointment of a receiver—and that the company could rely on the special circumstances defence. However, while the bank's final action may have been swift, it could hardly be described as unusual or unforeseeable!

Remedies for failure to consult

9–046   If the employer fails to consult over redundancies, the wrong is actionable in the employment tribunal only by an elected employee representative or the trade union (unless there are no representatives, in which case affected employees may complain). However, the remedy granted is an award which is payable to the employees in respect of whom the union should have been consulted (TULRCA s.189). The award will be for the "protected period"—that is, a period beginning with the date on which the first dismissal complained of took effect and lasting so long as the tribunal decides is just and equitable, subject to a maximum period of 90 days. In *Susie Radin Ltd v GMB* (2004) the Court of Appeal held that the purpose of the award was to be a sanction to deter employers from failing to comply rather than to compensate employees for loss. This is indicated by the fact that TULRCA s.189 instructs the tribunal to award such amount as is just and equitable having regard to the seriousness of the employer's default. In that case, an award for the maximum period was upheld where the employer had failed to consult at all even though the tribunal had also found that consultation would have been futile, because of the employer's fixed decision to shut down the factory.

The remedy under TUPE 2006 reg.16(3) is very similar to this. Again, it is for the trade union or employee representatives to apply to the employment tribunal, and the remedy is such award of pay to the affected employees as is considered to be just and equitable, having regard to the seriousness of the employer's default, but subject in this case to a maximum of 13 weeks' pay. In *Sweetin v Coral Racing* (2006) the EAT stated that the guidance in *Susie Radin Ltd v GMB* (2005) applied equally to TUPE claims. Until 1993, a protective award under TUPE was set off against a protective award under TULRCA but, again because this was regarded as an infringement of the Directive, the set-off was abolished by TURERA.

A further enhancement of employees' rights to protective awards occurred as a result of the EAT's decision in *Zaman v Kozee Sleep Products Ltd* (2011), which raised the question as to whether the statutory cap on a week's pay applied to protective awards under TUPE 2006. Regulation 16 cross-refers to ERA ss.222–228 for calculation of compensation but ERA s.227, which imposes the cap for awards under those sections, makes no mention of protective awards. The EAT rejected an argument that this was an oversight and interpreted the statute literally, thus holding that no cap on earnings should be applied.

Further Reading

❑ C. Grunfeld (1989), *The Law of Redundancy,* Sweet & Maxwell, 3rd edn
❑ J. McMullen (ed.) (2000), *Redundancy: The Law and Practice*, Sweet & Maxwell
❑ B. Napier (1993), *CCT, Market Testing and Employment Rights,* Institute of Employment Rights
❑ J. McMullen (2006), "An analysis of the TUPE Regulations 2006", 35 ILJ 113
❑ J. McMullen (2014), "TUPE: Ringing the (Wrong) Changes. The Collective Redundancies and Transfer of Undertakings (Protection of Employment) (Amendment) Regulations 2014", 43(2) ILJ 149
❑ M. Sargeant (2006), "TUPE—The Final Round", [2006] JBL 549
❑ C. Wynn Evans (2013), "In Defence of Service Provision Changes?", 42 ILJ 152

10. Freedom of Association

Key Points

This chapter:
- Introduces the concept of freedom of association
- Considers freedom of association in relation to the state
- Explains how freedom of association operates on the relationship of employer and employee
- Discusses what freedom of association means in relation to trade unions
- Looks at the law relating to the closed shop
- Discusses the historical evolution of trade unions and how that determines their current legal status
- Explains the concepts of listed trade unions and independent trade unions

***

The freedom to form and belong to associations, whether they be trade unions, religious organisations or political parties, is regarded as an aspect of human rights, and is found stated as a right in the principal treaties on the subject: the Universal Declaration of Human Rights 1948 (art.20), the International Covenant on Civil and Political Rights 1966 (art.22), the International Covenant on Economic, Social and Cultural Rights 1966 (art.8) and the European Convention on Human Rights (art.11). Additionally, the freedom is guaranteed by ILO Conventions Nos 87 and 98, the EU Charter of Fundamental Rights (art.28) and the Council of Europe's European Social Charter (art.5).   **10–001**

What exactly is the effect of such guarantees? There are essentially three issues. First, when these rather brief treaty statements are unpacked, what do they really mean? Secondly, is it possible to enforce them, or are they simply pious hopes? Thirdly, how far are they translated into English law? The first issue is connected with the second, since it is only really where there are enforcement procedures available that authoritative interpretation of treaty provisions is possible.

Freedom of Association and the State

International standards

10–002   If the freedom to associate is to mean anything at all, it must mean that the state should not prevent citizens from forming and joining associations. However, exceptions are recognised in the treaties themselves. Article 11 of the European Convention on Human Rights states in its first subparagraph:

> "Everyone has the right to freedom of peaceful assembly and to freedom of association with others, including the right to form and to join trade unions for the protection of his interests."

But this is qualified in the second sub-section, which allows restrictions prescribed by law where they are necessary in the interests of national security, or for the protection of public safety, prevention of crime and disorder, protection of health or morals, or for the protection of the rights and freedoms of others. It further permits states to restrict these rights for the police, armed forces, or those involved in the administration of the state which would seem to allow a fairly wide scope for interference with the "right". ILO Convention No.87 is narrower and more specific, permitting states to decide for themselves whether the police and armed forces should be given freedom to form and join trade unions.

The extent of both exemptions was examined in relation to civil servants employed at Government Communication Headquarters (GCHQ) at Cheltenham in the 1980s. GCHQ was responsible for the constant monitoring of foreign signals to provide intelligence to the government. Civil servants employed there had always belonged to the appropriate civil service unions. Between 1979 and 1981 the civil service unions, in dispute with the Conservative Government of the time, used the tactic of calling key personnel out on strike. On seven occasions this included GCHQ staff, and thus the round-the-clock monitoring operation was disrupted. As a result, in January 1984 the Secretary of State changed the contracts of employment of staff employed at GCHQ by removing their right to belong to an independent trade union.

The unions complained both to the ILO and to the European Commission on Human Rights. The ILO decided in 1984 that there was a violation of Convention 87 and urged the British Government to reach agreement with the unions. The Government took no steps in this direction, and in 1988 dismissed the remaining trade union members at GCHQ. This led the ILO Committee of Experts to look at the matter again, and to reiterate its recommendation. The case before the European Commission on Human Rights was lost on the basis that the GCHQ workers were involved in the administration of the state, and thus within the exception in art.11(2) (*Council of Civil Service Unions v United Kingdom* (1988)). One of the very first acts of the new Labour administration elected in May 1997 was to restore the rights of civil servants at GCHQ to belong to trade unions. Those employees who had been dismissed for refusing to give up their membership were reinstated. However, the saga showed an unfortunate divergence between the different international standards.

Since then, the position of the European Court of Human Rights has shifted somewhat. In *Demir and Baykara v Turkey* (2009) the claimants were members of a union of civil servants in Turkey who took legal action in the Turkish court over their employer's failure to adhere to a collective agreement. While it was legal for civil servants to form a union in Turkey, the Turkish court held that they had no right to make collective agreements nor to take part in collective action to enforce those agreements. The European Court held, first, that the right to freedom of association entailed the right to engage in collective bargaining (expressly resiling from its earlier case-law to the contrary), and secondly, that reliance on the proviso in art.11(2) had to be proportionate—and the Turkish government had not demonstrated any necessity for this restriction. The other important point about the decision was the European Court expressly referred to ILO standards and jurisprudence as influencing and informing its decision. This suggests divergence should be less likely in future, and also that ILO standards may thus indirectly become embedded in European law. **10–003**

Rights to join trade unions in the United Kingdom

In the United Kingdom, there is a general freedom to associate, with the exception of the police and the armed forces. Police officers are actually prohibited from being trade union members (Police Act 1996 s.64) although they can belong to relevant staff associations which perform some similar functions. Members of the armed forces can belong to trade unions relevant to their role, but cannot form a trade union to represent the armed forces. This may require revisiting in the light of *Matelly v France, ADEFROMIL v France* (2014) where the European Court held that a blanket ban on the armed forces forming and belonging to trade unions contravened art.11. Both of these groups can be discriminated against for forming and joining trade unions. They and some other workers are restricted in relation to taking industrial action. **10–004**

Freedom of Association and the Employer

The freedom to associate is meant to be guaranteed as a positive right as against one's employer, through a combination of statutory employment protection rights and the law of unfair dismissal. Thus the Trade Union and Labour Relations (Consolidation) Act 1992 (TULRCA) s.152 gives protection against dismissal on grounds of union membership and activities, TULRCA s.146 covers detriment during employment on these grounds and TULRCA s.137 makes refusal of employment on grounds of union membership unlawful. While this may appear to provide a complete and coherent protection for unionists, in fact the law was developed in piecemeal fashion for different reasons. Protection against dismissal on union membership grounds has existed in some form since the **10–005** introduction of unfair dismissal law in 1972. It is complemented by the protection from detriment during employment, which was introduced as one of a range of positive rights for employees under the Employment Protection Act 1975, and extended to the wider category of "workers" by the Employment Relations Act (ERelA) 2004. However, protection from discrimination at the point of entry into employment was given only in 1990, for a very different reason. In general, the protection afforded by all these provisions applies not only to those victimised for belonging to a union, but also to people in the opposite situation: those who are victimised for refusing to belong to a trade union. When the Employment Act 1990 introduced protection at the point of job entry, its explicit aim was to outlaw the pre-entry closed shop (see below, para.10–023). However, the policy of neutrality as between union members and those who are anti-union meant that the protection was given to union members also, although in a limited form. Protection for unionists at the point of entry to employment was increased by the Employment Relations Act 1999 (Blacklists) Regulations 2010 (SI 2010/493) (see below, para.10–015).

Dismissal and detriment on grounds of union membership

10–006   Sections 152 and 146 of TULRCA are in largely parallel terms but have been amended by the ERelA 1999 and 2004. Section 152 provides that dismissal is automatically unfair if the reason or principal reason for it is that the employee was, or proposed to become, a member of an independent trade union; or had taken part in, or proposed to take part in, the activities of an independent trade union at an appropriate time; or had made use of union services at an appropriate time. Section 146 provides that a worker has "a right not to be subjected to any detriment as an individual" by his employer for the sole or main purpose of preventing, deterring or penalising him for the same things.

Where employees are dismissed on this ground, the usual two-year qualifying period of employment does not apply (TULRCA s.154). The burden of proof is therefore on the employee to show that the dismissal was related to union membership or activities. Dismissal will also be automatically unfair if the employee is selected for redundancy on union membership grounds, but only if employees in a comparable position are not made redundant (TULRCA s.153). In *O'Dea v ISC Chemicals* (1995) the claimant's contract described him as a technical services operator, but as senior shop steward he spent 50 per cent of his time on union activities (with the employer's agreement) and had different working duties from the other two technical services operators to facilitate his time off. The Court of Appeal held that, in comparing him with other employees, the time he spent on union activities was not to be taken into account; however, the tribunal was entitled to look at his actual working duties (rather than the contractual terms) and to conclude accordingly that there was no one in a comparable position so that TULRCA s.153 did not apply. It is not clear why the protection should be limited in this way if it is established that the reason for selection was trade union activities.

The Employment Relations Act 1999 (Blacklists) Regulations 2010 (SI 2010/493) introduced TULRCA ss.104F and 105(7M), which provide that it is also automatically unfair to dismiss an employee or select for redundancy for any reason relating to a blacklist (see below, para.10–015). In addition, under reg.9, subjecting a worker to a detriment on such a ground is also actionable.

If successful in an action for unfair dismissal on union membership grounds, **10–007** the claimant qualifies for a special regime of remedies. The basic award of compensation cannot be lower than £5,807 (TULRCA s.156: 2015 figure) and the employee may apply for interim relief in order to preserve his job until a full hearing. Such an application must be made to the tribunal within seven days of dismissal and must be supported by a certificate from the union stating that there appear to be reasonable grounds for the complaint. As unfair dismissal is a remedy open only to employees, workers who are dismissed on union membership grounds have to claim instead that they have been subjected to a detriment contrary to TULRCA s.146.

Section 146 used to refer to "action short of dismissal" being taken against an individual rather than referring to "detriment". The wording was changed by the ERelA 1999 in order to reverse the effect of the House of Lords' decision in the joined appeals in *Associated Newspapers v Wilson* and *Associated British Ports v Palmer* (1995) to the effect that "action" in this context did not include omissions. Section 146 of TULRCA was therefore amended to make it unlawful for the employer to subject an employee to a detriment "by any act, or any deliberate failure to act". Detriment by omission is now covered, although it is possible that proof of detriment by omission may be difficult to come by and there may be problems in measuring the three-month limitation period for claims, which runs from the date of the act or deliberate failure to act (TULRCA s.147) (see *Southwark LBC v Whillier* (2001)).

In *Associated Newspapers Ltd v Wilson* the company derecognised the NUJ and entered into individualised contracts with employees. Those who entered into the new contracts got a pay increase but the others, those who wanted to retain collective bargaining, did not. Similarly, in *ABP v Palmer* employees who were prepared to enter individualised contracts got higher pay increases than those who stuck with collectively agreed terms. In both cases the Court of Appeal held that this contravened TULRCA s.146 because the employer's purpose was to end collective bargaining, which was likely to lead to the withering away of union membership, as there would be little point in membership of a body which had no representation rights. Hence the court held that this was an action taken to deter trade union membership.

The decision was appealed on two questions: whether the employer could be **10–008** said to be acting to deter union membership if this was a likely result of its actions but not its main or only purpose, and whether protection for union membership covered things incidental to membership such as representation for collective bargaining and other purposes. As the House of Lords decided the case on other grounds, as indicated already, its comments on these issues were strictly obiter. However, they indicated fairly clearly that they would have decided against the union members on both points. Meanwhile, the Conservative Government of the time inserted a new clause into TULRCA clarifying that an action which could be said to deter union membership contrary to TULRCA s.146 would not be actionable as long as it was also intended to change the employer's relationship with a class of employees.

The claimants in *Associated Newspapers v Wilson* and *Associated British Ports v Palmer* subsequently took action against the UK Government in the European Court of Human Rights, arguing that the decision of the House of Lords indicated that British law was in breach of the right to freedom of association guaranteed by art.11 of the European Convention on Human Rights. In 2002 the court ruled that

"by permitting employers to use financial incentives to induce employees to surrender important union rights, the respondent State failed in its positive obligation to secure the enjoyment of rights under art.11."

The court also stated that it was an essential part of freedom of association under art.11 that employees should be free not only to join trade unions but also to instruct or permit the union to make representations on their behalf. This would include individual and collective representation. However, the court stopped short of saying that freedom of association involved a right to collective bargaining so as to compel an employer to recognise a union for this purpose (*Wilson v United Kingdom, Palmer v United Kingdom, Doolan v United Kingdom* (2002)). In consequence, substantial amendments to TULRCA were made by the ERelA 2004, both to deal with the issues raised by the European Court of Human Rights and with other matters which the Government considered would probably also be regarded as contraventions of art.11 (such as the limitation of protection from dismissal and detriment on union grounds to employees: as noted already, this has now been extended to "workers"; see above, para.3–010).

The issue of financial inducements is now dealt with by new ss.145A–F inserted into TULRCA by ERelA 2004. Workers now have a right not to be offered an inducement with "the sole or main purpose" of getting them to give up membership or activities in an independent trade union, or not to make use of the services of an independent trade union (TULRCA s.145A). Where an independent trade union is either recognised or is seeking recognition from an employer, the worker has a right not to have an offer made to her with the sole or main purpose of bringing about the result that terms and conditions of employment will not be determined by collective bargaining (TULRCA s.145B). Workers may bring a complaint under either of these two sections to an employment tribunal within the usual three months, where the employer will have the burden of proof in showing what was its sole or main purpose in making the offer (TULRCA s.145D). The remedy, if the complaint is proved, is an award of £3,800 (in 2015), although the worker may also bring proceedings under s.146, because not conferring a benefit on a worker because he has not accepted an inducement is now defined as a detriment (TULRCA s.146(2D)), so the worker can claim additional compensation under that section.

10–009   At first sight, this seems to deal specifically with the first limb of the European Court's decision in *Wilson v United Kingdom*, etc. However, there is a problem in that the employer is only liable if an inducement to deter union membership or collective bargaining is the *sole or main purpose* of its action. It would seem, therefore, that if an employer can come up with a convincing explanation, the fact that the inducement was bound to have the effect of deterring union membership or collective bargaining will not render it unlawful. It may be doubted whether this result is in accordance with the European Court's interpretation of art.11. This is reinforced by the fact that even when TULRCA s.146 referred only to the employer having the purpose (as opposed to the sole or main purpose) of deterring, etc union membership, a narrow conception of "purpose" was used. Thus in *Department of Transport v Gallacher* (1994), the claimant had spent the whole of his time on union activities over a five-year period. He was advised that he would not get promotion to a higher managerial grade unless he returned to normal duties so that he would be able to demonstrate his ability to manage people. While this would inevitably mean at least a substantial reduction in his union activities, the fact that this was an inevitable consequence did not, in the opinion of the Court of Appeal, mean that this was the employer's purpose (although contrast *Southwark LBC v Whillier* (2001)).

The second limb of the European Court's decision considered whether the guarantee of freedom of association in art.11 covered representation by the union and to what extent. In *Associated Newspapers v Wilson* and *Associated British Ports v Palmer* (1995) the claimants argued that collective bargaining and union representation were so closely connected to the fact of membership that action to deter or penalise them amounted to a deterrent to or penalisation of membership. This was in line with the EAT decision in *Discount Tobacco v Armitage* (1990) where an employee was dismissed after seeking help from a union official in resolving a disagreement with her employer about her terms and conditions of employment. In response to the employer's argument that there was a difference between union membership and seeking assistance from a union official, the EAT denied the distinction, describing the use of the official as "the outward and visible manifestation of trade union membership" and "an incident of union membership". While not questioning the accuracy of this decision on its own facts, the House of Lords in *Wilson* and *Palmer* disagreed with this statement as a general proposition. Lord Bridge described it as "an unnecessary and imprecise gloss" on the language of the statute to suggest that union membership is to be equated with the use of its essential services, and Lord Lloyd went so far as to opine that protection under TULRCA ss.146 and 152 was limited purely to the fact of membership.

In the light of the European Court of Human Rights' decision that the right to join a trade union included the right to use it to represent them, ERelA 2004 amended TULRCA to confer such a right expressly. Sections 146 and 152 of TULRCA now contain an explicit reference to the worker's right not to suffer detriment or be dismissed for making use of trade union services at an appropriate time. "Trade union services" are defined as meaning services made available to a worker by an independent trade union by virtue of her membership of it, and use of them includes allowing the union to raise matters on her behalf. However, the right to make use of union services is not to be interpreted as giving a right to collective bargaining. In other words, it is not an actionable detriment if the employer refuses to enter negotiations with the worker's union (TULRCA s.145B(4)).

10–010   Protection against detriment for union membership and activities is further limited by the requirement that the claimant must have been subjected to detriment "as an individual". Thus, as was pointed out in *Wilson* and *Palmer*, derecognition of the union could not be regarded as action taken against an individual member even though representation in collective bargaining is the main reason for union membership. In *Farnsworth v McCoid* (1999) the Court of Appeal explained that this restriction was included in order to prevent collective disputes coming within TULRCA s.146, although that case illustrates that the boundary may sometimes be difficult to identify. In *Farnsworth v McCoid* a collective agreement allowed the employer to withdraw recognition from individual shop stewards on grounds of misconduct. The employer had followed this procedure in respect of the claimant, who argued that this was a breach of TULRCA s.146. The employer's defence was that this only affected his status as a shop steward, not as an employee, and therefore was not action against him "as an individual". The Court of Appeal held that this was not a collective dispute and the action could properly be regarded as directed at the claimant as an individual. The wording of the section did not warrant inclusion of a further requirement that it affected the individual in his capacity as an employee.

As well as membership, TULRCA ss.146 and 152 protect union activities. Union activities clearly include such things as the recruitment of members, representing members, holding union meetings and so on. In *Fitzpatrick v British Railways Board* (1992) it was held that dismissal of a union activist when it was discovered that her activities had been considered disruptive by a previous employer amounted to dismissal on grounds that she proposed to take part in union activities and came within the protection. However, in *Chant v Aquaboats* (1978) it was held that the protection did not extend to union-like activities, if not actually carried out by or on behalf of the union. The claimant was dismissed for organising a petition about an unsafe machine. Although a union member, he was not an official, nor was he acting at the union's request (see now, ERA s.100, above, para.8–080). An even more technical restriction is found in *Carrington v Therm-A-Stor* (1983), where the employer instructed chargehands to dismiss any 20 workers in retaliation for the union having sought recognition. They were held by the Court of Appeal to be victims of the union's activities, but had not been dismissed on grounds of their own union activities—and so fell outside the protection.

These cases apart, the concept of union activities which attract the protection is generally broad; the important limitation on it is that protection is only given for activities undertaken at an appropriate time. "An appropriate time" is defined as a time which is either:

> "outside working hours, or is a time within his working hours at which, in accordance with arrangements agreed with, or consent given by his employer, it is permissible for him to take part in those activities" (TULRCA s.146(2)).

10–011   In *Zucker v Astrid Jewels* (1978) the zealous claimant missed no opportunity of trying to persuade her fellow workers of the advantages of union membership.

She talked about it at break time, at lunchtime and while standing working at her machine. It was held that all these were appropriate times: even while working, if the employers allowed conversation as they did, they could hardly stipulate that this was an impermissible topic. Similarly, in *Bass Taverns v Burgess* (1995), where a member of the management team was permitted to address trainees on an induction course in his capacity as the union shop steward, the Court of Appeal held that he should not have been demoted for making remarks critical of the company in the course of his presentation. Having consented to him carrying out this union activity during working time, the employer could not say that the consent was subject to a limitation that he would not use the opportunity to say anything disparaging about the company.

It is clear that an implied consent by the employer will suffice, and equally clear that such an implication will not be easily made. In *Marley Tile Co Ltd v Shaw* (1980) it was held that no consent could be inferred where the employer was simply silent on being told that a meeting was to be called in working hours.

In order to claim under TULRCA s.146 or s.152, the employee must apply to the employment tribunal within three months of being subjected to the detriment or dismissed. If it upholds a detriment claim, the tribunal must make a declaration to that effect and may make an award of compensation. This is such amount as it considers to be just and equitable having regard both to the loss suffered by the employee and to the nature of the employer's infringement of the right (TULRCA s.149). It was held in *Cleveland Ambulance NHS Trust v Blane* (1997) that the inclusion of the latter phrase justified including in the award a sum for injury to feelings. An employee who is dismissed for trade union activities is compensated in the usual way for unfair dismissal, except that there is a minimum basic award, which stood at £5,807 in 2015.

In *Doherty v British Midland Airways* (2006) an employee failed in a claim of **10–012** constructive dismissal based on the employer's infringement of her right to participate in union activities, the EAT holding that there was no implied term of the contract covering the same ground as the statutory right. The employee could not, therefore, show that she had resigned because of a fundamental breach of contract by her employer.

Refusal of employment on grounds of union membership

In *City of Birmingham v Beyer* (1977) the appellant was a well-known union **10–013** activist who had been blacklisted on that account by the council. He got a job on a council construction site by giving a false name: within an hour he was recognised and sacked. He claimed he had been dismissed on account of his union activities, which would have been automatically unfair. The EAT held that he had been fairly dismissed because of his deceit when he applied for the job: it was true that he would have been discriminated against on grounds of his union membership and activities, but this, they pointed out, was not covered by the law.

This cut two ways: a refusal to employ a non-unionist (and thus to preserve a pre-entry closed shop) was lawful too. The Conservative Government of the 1980s was implacably opposed to the closed shop but was restrained from legislating against the pre-entry closed shop by the consideration that if non-unionists were protected from discrimination in recruitment, justice would demand that equal protection be given to unionists. However, following the promulgation of the European Social Charter, which recommended protection against discrimination on grounds of union membership and non-membership, both kinds of protection were granted by the Employment Act 1990 (now TULRCA ss.137–143).

Under TULRCA s.137 it is unlawful for an employer to refuse to employ someone on grounds of their trade union membership, or on the grounds that they are not trade union members. The pre-entry closed shop is specifically prohibited and it is further provided that employment agencies may not discriminate on these grounds either (s.138). The remedy is to apply to an employment tribunal, which has the same powers to make declarations, recommendations and compensation orders as under the Sex Discrimination Act 1975 and the Race Relations Act 1976.

10–014   The legislation has been criticised in that it applies only to direct discrimination (refusal to employ because of these grounds), not indirect, and because it extends only to a refusal to employ because of union membership, not union activities. On this basis, the claimant in *City of Birmingham v Beyer* would still be without a remedy. Yet as with the protection for dismissal and detriment on union grounds, this depends in large measure on whether TULRCA s.137 is interpreted as applying only to the bare fact of membership or whether the incidents of membership can be included. In *Harrison v Kent CC* (1995) the claimant had been employed as a social worker by the council for 14 years, during which time he had been an active shop steward and one of the leaders in a long and bitter strike. He left for another job, but within two years he applied for a job back in Kent. He was rejected because of the "confrontational and anti-management approach" he had exhibited in the past. The EAT, citing *Discount Tobacco v Armitage* (1990), held that it was open to a tribunal to find that this was contrary to TULRCA s.137 on the basis that there was no rigid distinction between membership and activities. Following the House of Lords' decision in *Associated Newspapers v Wilson* (1995) and *Associated British Ports v Palmer* (1995) the correctness of the decision in *Harrison v Kent CC* was in doubt. While some stretching of the concept of membership may be possible, it could well be argued that s.137 cannot cover union activities, especially in view of the fact that membership and activities are separately treated in ss.146 and 152. On the other hand, if s.137 is interpreted restrictively, it would seem likely that it would be a breach of art.11 of the European Convention on Human Rights, on the basis of the European Court's ruling in *Wilson v United Kingdom* (2002).

Blacklists

10–015   The ERelA 1999 s.3 gave the Secretary of State power to make regulations to outlaw the "blacklisting" of union members—that is, the circulation of lists of trade union members or activists to employers so that they could avoid recruiting such people. The Government consulted over draft regulations to this effect in 2003 but decided not to legislate at that stage as they considered that there was no evidence of the practice occurring. However, in 2008, the Information Commissioner discovered widespread abuse of blacklisting in the construction industry, as a result of which the Employment Relations Act 1999 (Blacklists) Regulations 2010 (SI 2010/493) were passed.

Regulation 3 prohibits the compilation, use, sale or supply of "prohibited lists". These are lists of people who are or have been trade union members or participants in trade union activities, where the list is compiled with a view to enabling employers or employment agencies to discriminate against them for that reason. Refusal of employment or employment agency services for a reason related to a blacklist is actionable in an employment tribunal (regs 5 and 6), where the remedy is compensation calculated according to tort principles, just like discrimination claims. As with discrimination claims, compensation is payable for injury to feelings (reg.8(2)).

As the claimant initially has the burden of proof, the crucial issue is how to show that the employer had the list with a view to discrimination. To assist, the Regulations provide that the burden of proof shifts to the employer if facts are shown from which the tribunal could conclude, in the absence of any other explanation, that the employer contravened reg.3. This applies also where the claimant's action is either for detriment or dismissal related to a prohibited list. It seems likely that proof that the employer possessed such a list would be sufficient for this purpose.

As employment tribunals do not have power to grant injunctions, there is an **10–016** unusual provision in reg.13 allowing a claimant to take county court proceedings for breach of statutory duty in addition to tribunal proceedings, in order to get an injunction preventing a breach of reg.3. However, the claimant can only claim compensation in one forum.

ERelA 1999 s.3 also permits the Secretary of State power to create new criminal offences relating to the use of blacklists, and some commentators have criticised the fact that this has not been used. Certainly, knowledge that using a blacklist would be a criminal offence would have been a powerful deterrent to employers.

Contracts between employers

For the sake of completeness it should also be mentioned that if one employer **10–017** were to insert a provision in a contract with another employer that the other should use only non-union labour in carrying out their contract, the term would be void and the employer would be liable to anyone adversely affected for the tort of breach of statutory duty. This is the effect of TULRCA s.144, and it operates as a further guarantee of freedom to associate, at least in theory. It has never been invoked so far as is known, and was actually introduced as part of the protection of the freedom not to associate, as will become clear below (para.10–023).

Freedom of Association and Trade Unions

10–018 So far we have considered protection for freedom of association against those who might wish people not to associate at all. Now we must look at a rather different problem. If you want to join an association, but they do not want to let you join, is your freedom to associate infringed? Is the freedom to associate only a freedom to associate with those who want to associate with you? The International Covenant on Economic, Social and Cultural Rights states that the right to join is subject to the rules of the organisation concerned (art.8(a)). This is echoed in ILO Convention No.87 (art.2), which goes further and insists on the right of workers' organisations to draw up their own constitutions and rules without interference from the state. While the European Convention on Human Rights is silent on this, in *Cheall v United Kingdom* (1986) the European Commission on Human Rights held that art.11 was not infringed by Cheall's expulsion from the union of his choice in order to comply with the Bridlington Principles. Thus it would seem that the right to associate is guaranteed by treaty only where the association is willing to accept the member.

Admission to trade unions

10–019 Until relatively recently, this was also the position under English law. It was informed at common law not so much by consideration of basic principles of freedom of association or the nature of trade unions as voluntary organisations but by the prosaic fact that no recognised cause of action exists where you complain that other people refuse to enter a contract with you. Attempts to mitigate this rigorous application of the principle of freedom of contract were spearheaded single-handedly by Lord Denning in the Court of Appeal. In *Nagle v Feilden* (1966), where the Jockey Club refused a trainer's licence to Mrs Nagle solely on grounds of sex, he predicated a "right to work" which would be infringed if a body having a monopoly of the activity in question (as was the case there) refused admission without good reason. While other judges were not so enthusiastic, they were in general prepared to consider the point to be arguable; however, even if this reasoning were correct, it would apply only in monopoly situations (such as where a union maintained a closed shop in an industry).

A claim for breach of contract would be possible if a union's rules were written so as to constitute an offer of membership to anyone eligible to join. This would be entirely exceptional, however. Again, it has been suggested that if a non-returnable fee is payable on application there might be a sufficient nexus between the parties to give the claimant a right of recourse to the courts, but there is no authority to this effect.

In *McInnes v Onslow Fane* (1978), considering whether reasons should have been given for refusing the claimant a licence to be a boxing manager, Megarry VC denied any general duty to give reasons for rejection; however, he did consider that the board was under a duty to reach an honest conclusion without bias and without pursuing a capricious policy. If imported into trade union law, this dictum could afford grounds for relief at common law to someone refused membership.

These issues are unlikely to be clarified at common law, since inroads on the **10–020** policy of abstention have been made by statute, and cases are now more likely to arise under statutory provisions. Originally, the main area where there was dissatisfaction with trade unions having an unfettered right to turn down would-be members was where union membership was necessary for a job—that is, where some form of closed shop was in operation. Thus if union membership was denied, the worker was also deprived of an opportunity to earn a living in a particular field. To counter these criticisms, the TUC set up its own Independent Review Committee in 1976, consisting of three members who would hear complaints from people refused admission to or expelled from unions belonging to the TUC. While this body had no legal status or powers, and of course only had jurisdiction over TUC members, in practice this covered most unions operating closed shops, and the Committee dealt successfully with a number of complaints. It was not seen as sufficient, however, by the Conservative Government which came to power in 1979, and so the Employment Act 1980 introduced a statutory right to complain to an employment tribunal on grounds of unreasonable refusal of admission or unreasonable expulsion from a trade union where there was a closed shop. By the end of the 1980s closed shop agreements had become unenforceable in all circumstances, so the protection against exclusion or expulsion in a closed shop situation had little practical relevance. However, by this time the Conservative Government had the Bridlington Principles in its sights.

The Bridlington Principles were originally drawn up in 1939 at a TUC Conference held in Bridlington. They were amended over the years, but the basic purpose remained intact: to control the proliferation of trade unions and to avoid inter-union disputes in situations where more than one union was appropriate for a class of workers and they were competing for members. It is frequently the case in this country that more than one union is appropriate, because of the relatively piecemeal development of unionism in this country: unlike, say, Germany, where since the Second World War there have been industrial unions.

The Bridlington Principles dealt with two kinds of dispute: disputes between unions about who should organise a particular group of workers, and disputes over individual members changing unions. Disputes were referred to the TUC's own Disputes Committee and the ultimate sanction for a union refusing to comply with its ruling was suspension or expulsion from the TUC. Most TUC unions adopted a model rule permitting expulsion to comply with a decision of the Disputes Committee. The model rule was challenged on public policy grounds in *Cheall v APEX* (1983) where Cheall was expelled from APEX, which he had joined in preference to ACTSS, following a Disputes Committee ruling that APEX was guilty of poaching contrary to Bridlington. The House of Lords held that the Bridlington Principles, aimed at orderliness in industrial relations, were not contrary to public policy, and that freedom of association must be mutual: "there can be no right of an individual to associate with other individuals who are not willing to associate with him", said Lord Diplock, although he indicated that the matter might have been viewed differently if there had been a closed shop so that Cheall's job was at stake. As noted above, the European Commission on Human Rights took the same view when Cheall's case was taken there.

10–021   However, this was regarded by the Conservative Government as an unacceptable restriction on freedom of choice. The Trade Union Reform and Employment Rights Act 1993 (TURERA) substituted a new TULRCA s.174 which provides that a union may only refuse admission to (or expel) someone on one of four grounds: that the applicant does not satisfy an enforceable membership requirement; that she does not come within the geographical area covered by the union; that she no longer works for the relevant employer in the case of a company-specific union; or because of misconduct. Enforceable membership requirements are those which stipulate criteria like employment in a particular trade or occupational group or having particular qualifications. Misconduct was defined so as not to include things like having resigned from another union or unjustifiable discipline within the meaning of TULRCA s.65 (discussed below, para.11–022). Post-the TURERA amendment, misconduct was expressly defined also as not to include being a member of a political party, so that unions could no longer have rules barring members of the Communist Party or the National Front.

The effect of TULRCA s.174, therefore, was virtually to abolish a trade union's right to define its own identity through its membership rules. There is just one limited respect in which it is narrower than the previous law, namely, that there is no reference to reasonableness. If a union refuses admission on the basis of an enforceable membership requirement, there can be no question of attacking its decision on the grounds that it is wholly unreasonable in the circumstances. Nonetheless, it was also clear that TULRCA s.174 constituted a breach of art.3 of the ILO Convention No.87, guaranteeing unions the right to draw up their rules "in full freedom". In 1989 the Committee of Experts expressed its view that TULRCA s.65 on unjustifiable discipline contravened art.3 and TULRCA s.174 went much further.

It may seem surprising, therefore, that there was initially no move to repeal TULRCA s.174 when the Labour Government came to power in 1997. It was not until unions produced evidence that they were being infiltrated by members of political parties with extreme views, such as the British National Party (and ASLEF lost a tribunal case for expelling someone on this ground) that some reform was made. The ERelA 2004 amended TULRCA s.174 so as to allow unions to expel people for conduct which consisted of political activities, but not for merely being, or having been, a member of a particular party. This was challenged by ASLEF in front of the European Court of Human Rights, alleging a breach of their right to freedom of association under art.11 of the European Convention on Human Rights (ECHR) (*ASLEF v United Kingdom* (2007)). The European Court agreed that there was a breach in compelling ASLEF to admit a member of the BNP, holding that an organisation espousing particular values or ideals must be allowed to choose its members so as to exclude those who do not share them. The Court noted that the excluded member did not suffer any detriment as a result of not being allowed into the union.

10–022   This decision resulted in further amendment to TULRCA s.174 by the Employment Act 2008 s.19. It is surprising, though, that the amendment is about as narrow as it possibly could be to accommodate the Court's ruling. Thus, membership of a political party, alone, will still not be a ground for excluding or expelling someone unless, first, such membership is contrary to a rule or objective of the union (the latter having to be ascertainable by potential members, whatever that means); secondly, the union has acted fairly and in accordance with its rules in making its decision to exclude or expel, and thirdly, that the individual will not lose his livelihood or suffer other exceptional hardship by being refused membership (TULRCA s.174(4C)–(4H)).

There is probably quite a lot to be said for the view that a union's decision not to admit someone should be liable to review if it will have direct consequences for their employment. Since the closed shop is no longer legally enforceable (as will be seen below), it may be thought that this will rarely be the case in future. However, where a union is recognised for bargaining purposes, employees will rarely have any other opportunity to negotiate about their terms and conditions of employment. There would thus seem to be a good argument for saying that, in these situations also, an individual should be entitled to review if a union refuses an application for membership; although in *ASLEF v United Kingdom* (2007) the union argued that this was not a strong reason, because it would represent everyone in a bargaining unit whether they were members or not. However, beyond that, there seems to be no justification for interfering with a union's right to define its own membership and it is submitted that TULRCA s.174 ought to be repealed or radically pruned.

The closed shop

So far we have looked at the positive aspect of freedom of association—how far 10–023 the rights of people to associate together are protected. We must now consider whether the right to associate logically entails the opposite proposition, that people have a right not to associate; or at least whether the existence of a right to join means that in fairness there ought also to be a right not to join. That they are, to use a well-worn cliché, opposite sides of the same coin, is frequently asserted; the symmetry is apparently thought to be self-evident. It is notable that art.20 of the Universal Declaration of Human Rights states the negative as well as the positive right, although the International Covenants on Economic, Social and Cultural Rights and on Civil and Political Rights do not; nor does the ECHR, nor ILO Convention No.87. However, in *Young, James and Webster v United Kingdom* (1981) the European Court of Human Rights held by a majority that art.11 of the ECHR was contravened by English law which permitted the closed shop at that time, because employees risked dismissal if they did not join. The majority view was that compulsion to join one union restricted freedom of association because it prevented workers from forming or joining another; a concurring minority was prepared to go so far as to say that the positive freedom necessarily implied the negative.

Kahn-Freund, the pre-eminent theorist of modern British labour law, argued strongly that a right not to join is not simply the converse of a right to join. He drew an analogy between participation in the collective bargaining process through trade union membership and participation in democratic government through the franchise. The results of collective bargaining are as important in one's working life as the results of legislation are in one's life as a citizen. We believe that the state has a duty to let us take an indirect part in government by voting for our representatives; so the state should also let us take our indirect part in collective bargaining by guaranteeing our right to form and join trade unions. In the same way that it is no function of the law to ensure that we do not have to exercise our rights as citizens, so (argued Kahn-Freund) it is no function of the law to ensure that we do not have to exercise our industrial rights. Hence freedom of association should be supported by the law, as an aspect of the worker's right and duty to participate in the bargaining process, but no similar considerations require legal support for the freedom not to associate.

Kahn-Freund's argument convincingly decouples the so-called positive and negative freedoms. It is not, nor was it claimed to be, a conclusive argument in favour of the closed shop. Kahn-Freund thought that this depended on essentially pragmatic and utilitarian considerations: do better or worse consequences flow from allowing the closed shop to exist?

Varieties of closed shop arrangement

10–024   It is necessary first to be more specific about what is being referred to when we talk about the closed shop. Essentially a closed shop is a workplace where belonging to a particular trade union (or one of a number of specified trade unions) is a condition of having a job. Access is "closed" to everyone else. While some closed shop arrangements were clear, written, and agreed by employers, others were informal arrangements, sometimes merely tolerated rather than specifically agreed to by management. There is an important distinction between pre-entry and post-entry closed shops: in a pre-entry closed shop, the worker must have joined the union before getting the job—union membership is in effect an essential qualification for job applicants. In a post-entry closed shop, the requirement is that the worker should join within a short period after getting the job. Clearly the pre-entry closed shop gives most power to the union, since it means that the union controls the pool of applicants for a post; it may thus seem surprising that this manifestation of the closed shop only became unlawful under the Employment Act 1990.

Most closed shop agreements made provision for exceptional cases such as conscientious objectors or people who were already there before the agreement came into force. Some allowed employees not to join provided that they paid a sum equivalent to union dues to the union or to a charity—an arrangement known as the "agency shop" in the United States. The agency shop goes some way to counter the average union member's biggest objection to non-joiners, which is that they are taking a free ride on the backs of those who do pay subscriptions, because they get the benefits of negotiated improvements without paying for them.

Arguments for and against the closed shop

Trade unionists asked to justify a membership requirement refer most frequently to the free-rider argument. As noted already, this can be mitigated by payment of an equivalent sum to the union or to charity. Some have doubted the validity of the argument altogether: there are other organisations which people pay to belong to whose activities benefit non-members, like the National Trust or CAMRA. Kahn-Freund thought that the strongest argument in favour was that it was necessary for maintaining an equilibrium in industrial relations—thus if the organisation of workers and maintenance of decent wage levels is difficult or impossible without a requirement of union membership (as is the case in much of the entertainment industry), then insistence on the closed shop is justified. Others have argued that employers like the closed shop too, because it means that they can be sure that the union speaks for the whole workforce, and that resulting collective agreements will largely be policed by the union.

10–025

The freedom of the individual is the argument most often appealed to against the closed shop. It is a powerful, emotive concept, but really without meaning unless we know what it is we are free from or free to do. If it is simply asserted that we should be free not to join a trade union if we do not want to, it may be answered that we are already as free to do that as we are free not to work for a company if we disapprove of its activities or free not to work at all if we do not wish: that is, we have the freedom if we can afford to exercise it. In any case, it could be argued that the freedom of the individual can be adequately safeguarded by permitting conscientious objector clauses in closed shop agreements rather than by abolishing the closed shop altogether.

Stronger are the practical arguments against the closed shop. In the 1960s the Donovan Commission found that the industries where the closed shop was strongest were also those which were most strike-prone, and many considered the phenomena to be linked. Certainly the Conservative Government of the 1980s firmly believed that the closed shop was responsible for inefficient restrictive practices which significantly impeded Britain's international competitiveness, for overmanning and for the retention of outdated working methods, and its abolition was one of the main planks in their programme of labour law reform.

Present legal regulation of the closed shop

No law regulating the closed shop existed in the United Kingdom until the introduction of the law of unfair dismissal. Employers could not be legally compelled to enter closed shop arrangements, nor to continue them. In *Reynolds v Shipping Federation* (1924) it was held that a union seeking the dismissal of a non-member was not liable for the tort of conspiracy. However, once unfair dismissal was introduced, it was thought necessary to have special rules stipulating whether the dismissal of a worker for refusing to join a union was fair or unfair. This further necessitated defining what exactly counted as a closed shop (or "union membership agreement" as it was called in TULRA). The position under TULRA was that in principle dismissal for refusal to belong to a union was automatically fair—but there were certain limited exceptional circumstances where it was

10–026

automatically unfair. The Employment Acts 1980–82 extended these exceptions considerably so that there was little left of the rule; but the complicated provisions were all rendered redundant by the Employment Act 1988 which finally made the dismissal of an employee for refusal to join or belong to a trade union automatically unfair whether or not there was a closed shop in operation (see now TULRCA s.152). Furthermore, it is not possible to insist on the employee making payments in lieu of membership: dismissal for refusing to make such payments is treated as if it were dismissal for not being a member. Where unfair dismissal on this ground is made out, the employee will be entitled to enhanced rates of compensation, basically set at a high level to deter dismissals for this reason. Under TULRCA s.146 an employee also has a right not to be subjected to a detriment on these grounds.

While the Employment Act 1988 meant that no post-entry closed shop arrangement could be enforced, it still left the possibility of a pre-entry closed shop, because it was still lawful to discriminate against a job candidate on grounds of non-membership of a union. This may seem odd, given that the pre-entry closed shop gives more power to a union than the post-entry closed shop, but the reason is soon explained. The general policy of the Conservative Government throughout the 1980s was formally to treat all "union membership reasons" in the same fashion. Thus if it was automatically unfair to dismiss someone for joining a union, it was automatically unfair to dismiss someone for not joining; if there was enhanced compensation for someone dismissed for not joining, then there was enhanced compensation for the unionist dismissed for being a member, and so on. It is the case that this formal equality was not maintained in all cases (see TULRCA s.222), and that in practice the provisions were much more effective as a protection for the non-unionist than the unionist, but that is another matter. The policy of facial even-handedness was important as a matter of public relations. Now, if the Government wished to outlaw discrimination against non-unionists at the point of job entry (in order to outlaw the closed shop), formal equality would require that discrimination against unionists should be outlawed also. Such tactics as circulating blacklists among employers so that union activists could be kept out of the workplace would no longer be allowed. This was not necessarily on the Conservative Government's agenda at all.

Just when it looked as if the policy of even-handedness might be dropped, and only discrimination against non-unionists made unlawful, the Charter of the Fundamental Social Rights of Workers ("the Social Charter") was produced by the European Union. It recommended Member States to prohibit discrimination on grounds of union membership and on grounds of non-membership. Delivered from its dilemma, the Government complied in 1990 (see now TULRCA ss.137–143, discussed above, para.10–013).

10–027   The Social Charter also got the Labour Party off the hook. It had remained committed to reintroducing the closed shop in some form, while recognising that this was something of an electoral liability. The Social Charter gave them a good reason to back down gracefully, so that reintroduction of protection for the closed shop was dropped as part of Labour Party policy by 1990.

It should be noted that the closed shop has not been rendered an unlawful institution by any of these measures. However, it has become impossible, or possible only on pain of very large compensation payments, to enforce any agreement between an employer and a union that all employees should be union members. As a result, even where they have not been officially terminated, closed shop agreements have largely fallen into disuse.

The Nature of Trade Unions

History in outline

Freedom of association may be a well-recognised principle today, but it certainly **10–028** was not at the beginning of the nineteenth century when the first unions were being formed. While guilds of craftsmen existed from the Middle Ages, it was not until the Industrial Revolution and the birth of an industrial working class that combinations of workers began to be created, both for the purpose of mutual support in case of sickness and unemployment and for the purpose of attempting to improve working conditions. The history of trade unionism cannot be dealt with in anything but the barest outline here; only some main themes will be identified in so far as they will aid understanding of the form of modern trade unionism.

At the beginning of the nineteenth century, trade unions were regarded by the law as illegal criminal organisations. Discovery was sure to lead to dismissal at the very least, so the early unions swore members to secrecy. However, the French Revolution was fresh in the minds of the ruling classes, who were therefore terrified of secret groups; the Unlawful Oaths Act 1797 imposed criminal penalties on any secret society which required its members to take an oath—the offence for which the Tolpuddle Martyrs were transported in 1834. Besides this, the Combination Acts 1799–1800 criminalised all agreements with the purpose of raising wages.

The Combination Acts 1824–25 reformed the law so that unions were not illegal in themselves, although most of their activities beyond the purely "friendly society" purposes of collecting and administering funds against misfortune were likely to be criminal. A strike was a criminal "molestation" of the employer, and if it involved a breach of the contract of employment, then that was a criminal offence on the part of the employee (although breach of contract by an employer was only a civil wrong). While no longer criminal organisations, unions were unlawful at civil law because their objects were in restraint of trade.

Following the extension of the franchise to a much wider class of working men **10–029** in 1868, the Liberal Government accepted union lobbying and in 1871 passed the Trade Union Act and the Criminal Law Amendment Act, which removed unions from the ambit of the law of criminal conspiracy and provided that trade union purposes were not to be considered as in restraint of trade—a provision still necessary today and to be found in TULRCA s.11. In 1875 the Conspiracy and Protection of Property Act defined an area of lawful industrial action. Thus unions had at last become fully recognised as lawful organisations; but the fact that they had to struggle so long without this recognition contributed to that general suspicion of the law which became deeply entrenched in British trade unionism. Also, the fact that unions had been organising themselves without the law for so long led to an antipathy to any sort of legal regulation of their internal affairs.

Despite the advances made in legislation, the courts remained hostile to trade unions. Throughout the nineteenth and twentieth centuries there was a discernible pattern: legislative protection granted to unions by statute; subsequently outflanked by case-law; followed by amending legislation to reinstate the advance; followed by more restrictive case-law—and so on. After 1875, the law of tort was extended in order to render union activities unlawful. However, this was subject to an important limitation. The law recognises two categories, and two categories only, of legal persons: natural persons (human beings) and corporations. Trade unions grew up as unincorporated associations—inevitably, given their history. That meant that in law a trade union had no existence of its own—the phrase "trade union" was simply a shorthand way of referring to all the members of the union. Legal opinion at the end of the nineteenth century considered that the technical difficulties in suing all the members in one action effectively precluded any action against the union in its own name. The practice developed of suing the principal officers of the union instead, and in general if an injunction was granted against an officer, the union accepted its terms too. However, this state of affairs meant that trade union funds were safe from damages awards.

The House of Lords' decision in *Taff Vale v Amalgamated Society of Railway Servants* in 1901, that a trade union could be sued in its own name, therefore sent shock waves through the trade union movement, for it meant that a union's funds could be wiped out by a single damages award resulting from industrial action. It was also seen as the apogee of judges' hostility to trade unions. A Liberal Government was returned at the 1906 election with Labour support, committed to restoring the previous position. However, the Trade Disputes Act 1906 did not provide, as it might have done, that unions could not be sued in their own name; rather it gave them an almost complete immunity from liability in tort. This basic model, an unincorporated association with many of the characteristics of a corporation, with immunity (albeit much less) for certain kinds of action, remains in place today.

Nature and status of trade unions

10–030   We have seen that when unions started they were in the nature of clubs—groups of people who unite for a common purpose. Like clubs, they were voluntary, unincorporated associations. Voluntary, in the sense that there was no legal or other compulsion to form unions; unincorporated, inevitably, given that for the first hundred years or so the law regarded them as illegal associations. When unions were legalised in the nineteenth century it was suggested that they should become corporate bodies like companies. It was suggested again by the Donovan Commission in 1968. On both occasions it was strongly resisted by the unions themselves. It has been argued that a corporate model would be inappropriate for trade unions because they are not "top-down" hierarchical organisations, as companies are. In a trade union, it is said, policy is decided by the members, and that drives the people at the top, who are ultimately accountable to and under the control of their members. This is only true up to a point: in most unions the officials are usually the people with the time and the information to initiate policy and, as in companies, they have the greatest control over communication with the members, and thus have considerable opportunities to persuade them to their point of view. However, a very good reason for resisting corporate status used to be that the internal affairs of companies are subject to a high degree of regulation and public scrutiny. Trade unions, as stated already, are suspicious of the law and would rather not have it meddling in their internal affairs. In the 1990s, however, a good deal of regulation was introduced (see below, para.11–019).

Trade union opposition to corporate status has been successful to date. The Industrial Relations Act 1971 forced corporate status on all unions who registered under the Act, but this was avoided by the vast majority of unions by the simple expedient of refusing to register, and the Act was repealed in 1974.

Trade unions are still defined according to their purposes and membership, and the definition of a trade union is wide. It is an:

"organisation—whether temporary or permanent—which consists wholly or mainly of workers of one or more descriptions and whose principal purposes include the regulation of relations between workers . . . and employers or employers' associations" (TULRCA s.1(a)).

An additional limb of the section widens the definition to include organisations of trade unions so that federations of unions such as the TUC or the International Transport Workers' Federation, which are made up of unions, are themselves to be regarded as trade unions. That the members must be workers led to the Law Society being held not to be a trade union (*Carter v Law Society* (1973)). The reference to a permanent or temporary organisation could be important. In *Midland Cold Storage v Turner* (1972) the company was blacked on the instructions of an ad hoc shop stewards' committee representing dockers. The committee had no official union status or powers. The Court of Appeal held that even though the committee had only come into being because of and for the duration of the dispute, it was properly to be considered a temporary organisation: it had a name, a basic structure, a convenor and a secretary. However, it was not a union because its purpose was to organise industrial action, not to regulate relations with employers. The case indicates that loose groupings, even in non-unionised workplaces, could be regarded as trade unions. As the limits of lawful industrial action became narrower, there was an incentive for more unofficial action to take place. The disruption of the London Underground in the summer of 1989 was a good example of this. In these cases it can be very difficult to identify the individuals against whom injunctive relief may be sought. The

Employment Act 1990 sought to deal with this by extending the range of people for whom the union may be held liable (see below, para.13–032); however, if the organisation could be identified, it would presumably qualify as a trade union, and the injunction could be granted against the body.

10–031   In *BAALPE v NUT* (1986) it was held that a union need not be capable of carrying out all the purposes of a trade union in order to come within the definition. Thus although the British Association of Advisers and Lecturers in Physical Education had only 402 members, its constitution stated that it was concerned with the professional interests of its members. In a dispute with the NUT over teachers' representation on a national negotiating committee, it was held to have the essential primary purpose of a union and was thus entitled to representation.

A definition in terms of purposes rather than structure is appropriate for an unincorporated association. As we have seen, before 1901, the unincorporated status of unions was thought to protect them from damages actions. In *Taff Vale v ASRS* (1901), the Law Lords had to explain how it was that an unincorporated association could be sued in its own name. Lord Halsbury said:

> "If the Legislature has created something which can own property, which can employ servants and which can inflict injury, it must be taken I think to have impliedly given the power to make it suable in a court of law for injuries purposely done by its power and procurement."

However, that is a policy reason rather than a legal reason. It demonstrates why the Law Lords were anxious to reach the decision they did. The means by which they did so are more opaque. In effect the decision hinged on the fact that the union was registered under the Trade Union Act 1871. This, they held, did not turn it into a corporation, but did bring it to a sort of halfway house between corporate and unincorporated status—and brought it far enough to be sued in its own name. The reasoning is dubious, but the effect was far-reaching. While the Trade Disputes Act 1906 limited its effect, it did not in any sense clarify or change the legal status of the union, which thus depended on their Lordships' opinions.

10–032   If a union had sufficient personality to be sued in tort, it must follow that it could also sue in its own name. This corollary was dramatically established in *NUGMW v Gillian* (1946), where the union successfully sued the General Secretary of another union for defaming it. In *Bonsor v Musicians' Union* (1956) the House of Lords decided that damages in contract (as opposed to simply an injunction) could be awarded against a union. Thus without satisfactorily explaining why, the courts had brought trade unions to a point where they were treated to all intents and purposes as if they had their own legal personality.

The Industrial Relations Act 1971 sought to formalise that position. The name "trade union" was given only to those unions which registered under the Act, and they became corporations. The Industrial Relations Act was deeply unpopular with the trade union movement, and refusal to register became the rallying point of the campaign against it. Thus unions avoided corporate status—at the cost of being regarded in law as "organisations of workers" rather than "trade unions". This had little practical effect, but was regarded as insulting.

When the Industrial Relations Act was repealed by TULRA in 1974 the opportunity was taken to regularise the status of unions. Section 10 of TULRCA now provides that a union is not, and is not to be treated as if it were, a body corporate; but it is capable of making contracts; it can own property, the title of which must be vested in trustees on its behalf; it can sue and be sued in its own name; it can be prosecuted in its own name; and judgments can be enforced against it as if it were a corporation. A union is specifically prohibited from registering as a company.

This means that unions are now confirmed as unincorporated associations, **10–033** but the technical inconveniences of that status are removed. This clarification does not merely restore the pre-1971 position. In *EETPU v Times Newspapers* (1980) the union sued for defamation over an article which had appeared in the newspaper. O'Connor J held that the law had changed since *NUGMW v Gillian* (1946) and a union could no longer maintain an action for defamation in its own name: the statutory injunction that a union is not and is not to be treated as a corporation meant that it should not be treated as having a personality capable of being damaged through defamation.

The effect of the present rules on the ownership of union property were considered in *News Group Newspapers v SOGAT '82* (1986), where the union's funds were subject to sequestration following its conviction for contempt. The union had about £5.25 million in its central general funds, but another £6 million was held by branches of the union. The sequestrators argued that since unions were unincorporated associations, and not charitable, a trust of branch funds would be void for perpetuity unless the funds were construed as belonging in reality to the central union (in which case they would be liable to sequestration). The Court of Appeal held that the property belonged to the branch, and that this did not infringe the rule against perpetuities. Drawing a distinction between branch funds and central funds in this way may be important in industrial disputes, since it effectively allows unions some leeway to arrange their property holdings so as to limit funds exposed to claims in the event of the industrial action being held to be unlawful.

Listing and Independence of Trade Unions

Listing

Many organisations regulated by law have to have their details recorded on a **10–034** register open to public inspection. Companies are the most obvious example. When the existence of trade unions was recognised by law in the Trade Union Act 1871, a system of registration, conferring some slight advantages on those unions which registered, was introduced. Registration under the Industrial Relations Act 1971, which replaced this system, was quite another matter. It turned registered unions into corporations and exposed them to detailed regulation as to their internal affairs. By the time the Industrial Relations Act was repealed by TULRA in 1974, the whole concept of registration had attracted such opprobrium that the replacement system, which was similar to the 1871 notion, was called "listing" instead of registration.

Under TULRCA s.2 the Certification Officer has responsibility for maintaining a list of trade unions. Any organisation believing itself to be within the definition of a trade union may apply to be put on the list on payment of a small fee. While there is no requirement that trade unions should be listed, there are advantages in becoming so. There are some tax advantages for listed unions; but more importantly, there are certain rights which are available to unions only if they can establish their status as independent or recognised unions, and listing is the first stage in establishing such status.

In 2011 the Certification Officer's annual report noted that a number of organisations were seeking to be listed as trade unions so that they could invoke the right under ERelA 1999 s.10 to accompany workers in disciplinary proceedings—for a fee. His refusal to register such an organisation was tested in *Akinosun (on behalf of the General and Health Workers Union) v Certification Officer* (2013). The claimant was director of a company which provided clients with representation services in employment tribunals on a commercial basis. As most of its clients worked in the health service, the company wanted to be able to represent them in internal disciplinary proceedings and hit on the idea of setting up a trade union so that ERelA 1999 s.10 would apply. The Certification Officer decided that the principal purpose of the "union" was to take advantage of ERelA 1999 s.10 in order to further the commercial interests of the company. It did not have the statutory purpose of regulating relations between employers and workers (see above, para.10–030) and so it could not be regarded as a trade union. The EAT upheld his decision.

Independent trade unions

10–035   Under TULRCA ss.6–9 the Certification Officer must decide whether a union is an independent trade union, and if so issue a certificate of independence. An appeal lies from his decision to the EAT. The reason for defining independent trade unions and giving them some legal support is to discourage "sweetheart unions"—which appear to represent the workforce but are in fact in the employer's pocket. An independent trade union is defined by TULRCA s.5 as one which:

"(a)   is not under the domination or control of an employer . . . and
(b)   is not liable to interference by an employer . . . (arising out of the provision of financial or material support or by any other means whatsoever) tending towards such control."

In *Squibb UK Staff Association v Certification Officer* (1979) the Court of Appeal held that the words, "liable to interference" meant "vulnerable to interference" rather than "likely in fact to be interfered with". Thus in that case where the union was so dependent on the employer's support that it could not have continued without it, it was held that it was not independent even though there was nothing to suggest that the employer was likely to abuse its power. The criteria used by the Certification Officer were set out in his Annual Report for 1976 and approved by the EAT in *Blue Circle Staff Association v Certification Officer* (1977), as follows:

1. *Finance*. If the union receives any direct subsidy from the employer, it is ruled out.
2. *Other assistance*. Employers may indirectly subsidise the union by providing free office and meeting accommodation, free mail and telephones, photo-copying or check-off facilities. In the *Squibb* case, the union was dependent on all these things and the Certification Officer felt that the union would not have been able to survive without them. However, this should not be unduly weighted: provision of many of these facilities is generally regarded as good industrial relations practice. The Acas Code of Practice (No.3) on Time Off for Trade Union Duties and Activities (revised 2010) states that "employers should, where practical, make available to union representa-tives the facilities necessary for them to perform their duties efficiently and communicate effectively with their members, colleague union representa-tives and full-time officers" (para.46). This could include accommodation for meetings, access to a communications and other equipment, such as telephones, email, intranet, internet, notice boards and, where the volume of the official's work justifies it, the use of dedicated office space.
3. *History*. Where the union was founded recently with the employer's assis-tance (as in the *Squibb* case), or where it is evolving from having been an employer-dominated organisation (as in the *Blue Circle* case), it may indicate that it is not yet truly independent.
4. *Rules*. In the *Blue Circle* case, the committee of the staff association had originally included management representatives, who had the right to call meetings and see the minutes. When the rules were changed in the quest for independence, management helped draft the new rules. These facts tended against a finding of independence.
5. *Membership base*. Where the potential membership of the union is restricted to one company or group of companies, it will clearly lack the strength of more open unions. In *Squibb*, membership was limited to workers in a particular grade at the company's two factories—a total of 291 people. However, the fact that it is a single company union is not an absolute bar to independence.
6. *Attitude*. Finally, the Certification Officer considers whether the relation-ship is too cosy, or whether the union has demonstrated what is delicately described as a "robust attitude in negotiation". This is not meant to suggest that a record of militancy is the best means to a certificate of independence.

The consequences of a certificate of independence alone are less than they were, although it is only the members of independent trade unions who are protected against dismissal and detriment on grounds of their union activities (TULRCA ss.146, 152). (There is no such limitation in TULRCA s.137 in relation to the recruitment of union members, nor in the Employment Relations Act 1999

(Blacklists) Regulations 2010.) However, there are a range of rights given to independent unions which are also recognised by their employer. Thus a union which has recognition will also desire a certificate of independence in order to claim these statutory rights. Recognition is discussed in Ch.5 (see above, para.5–014).

 # Further Reading

❑ P. Davies and M. Freedland (1983), *Kahn-Freund's Labour and the Law*, 3rd edn, Stevens, Ch.7 (very out of date on the law, but still worth reading for the arguments)

❑ F.Dorssemont, K.Lörcher and I. Schömann (eds) (2013), *The European Convention on Human Rights and the Employment Relation*, Hart Publishing

❑ S. Dunn and J. Gennard (1984), *The Closed Shop in British Industry,* Macmillan

❑ P. Elias and K. Ewing (1987), *Trade Union Democracy, Members' Rights and the Law,* Mansell, Chs 1, 3, 5 (very out of date on the law, but still worth reading for the arguments)

❑ K. Ewing (1994), *Britain and the ILO,* 2nd edn, Institute of Employment Rights

❑ W. McCarthy (1964), *The Closed Shop in Britain,* Basil Blackwell (this is the classic study: Dunn and Gennard present an updated survey)

❑ G. Morris and T. Archer (2000), *Collective Labour Law,* Hart Publishing

❑ H. Pelling (1987), *A History of British Trade Unionism,* 4th edn, Macmillan

❑ S. Corby (1986), "Limitations on Freedom of Association in the Civil Service and the ILO's Response", 15 ILJ 161

❑ B.Creighton (1994), "The ILO and Protection of Freedom of Association in the United Kingdom", in K. Ewing, C. Gearty and B. Hepple (eds), *Human Rights and Labour Law,* Mansell

❑ K. Ewing (2003), "The Implications of *Wilson* and *Palmer*", 32 ILJ 1

❑ K. Ewing (2007), "The Implications of the *ASLEF* Case", 36 ILJ 425

❑ K.D. Ewing and John Hendy (2010), "The Dramatic Implications of *Demir and Baykara*", 39 ILJ 2

❑ M. Forde (1982), "The Closed Shop Case", 11 ILJ 1

❑ G. Morris (1994), "Freedom of Association and the Interests of the State", in K. Ewing, C. Gearty and B. Hepple (eds), *Human Rights and Labour Law,* Mansell

❑ T. Novitz (1998), "Freedom of Association and Fairness at Work: An Assessment of the Impact and Relevance of ILO Convention No 87 on its Fiftieth Anniversary", 27 ILJ 169

❑ T. Novitz (2000), "International Promises and Domestic Pragamatism: To What Extent Will the Employment Relations Act 1999 Implement International Labour Standards Relating to Freedom of Association?", 63 MLR 37

❑ B. Simpson (1993), "Individualism Versus Collectivism", 22 ILJ 181

❑ Lord Wedderburn (1989), "Freedom of Association and Philosophies of Labour Law", 18 ILJ 1

❑ Lord Wedderburn (1991), "Freedom of Association or Right to Organise? The Common Law and International Sources", in Wedderburn, *Employment Rights in Britain and Europe,* Lawrence and Wishart

For the Conservative Governments arguments on the closed shop during the 1980s, see:

Removing Barriers to Employment, Cm.655 (1989), Ch.2
Trade Unions and Their Members, Cm.95 (1987), Ch.4
Working Paper for Consultations on Proposed Industrial Relations Legislation—Closed Shop, Department of Employment, July 1979

11. Trade Unions and their Members

Key Points

This chapter:
- Looks closely at the legal regulation of trade unions
- Considers how far unions can use funds for political purposes
- Looks at amendments made by the Trade Union Bill 2016
- Examines common law controls on unions' rights to discipline their members
- Considers the effect of the rules of natural justice
- Explains statutory controls over union rules
- Discusses the law on union elections

***

Trade unions have always claimed that, as voluntary associations, they should be left alone to run their internal affairs. In other voluntary associations, such as members' clubs, the members decide what rules they want, and how to run their affairs, and the law does not intervene. The same ought to be true of trade unions.

11–001

Against this view, it is often pointed out that a trade union is usually a much more important and powerful body than a members' club, often having power over the very livelihood of workers within its sphere of influence. A trade union is too important to be allowed to run itself in whatever way it thinks fit: the law should lay down minimum standards. This argument had particular force when closed shop arrangements were prevalent and expulsion from a union could indeed be a "sentence of industrial death" (as Younger LJ once put it). However, even though closed shop arrangements can no longer be enforced, it could still be argued that the collective bargaining process is so important that workers ought to have a right to be represented, and thus there should be sufficient control over the rules of a union to ensure that they are not excluded from membership without good reason.

If accepted, this is an argument for control over rules on admission and expulsion in trade unions, but not for wholesale legal intervention. It must be balanced against the injunction in ILO Convention No.87 that unions should be free to draw up their own rules without interference. Furthermore, it could well be argued that membership of many other apparently voluntary organisations is in fact essential, yet the law does not govern their internal affairs in anything like the same way that unions are controlled. To which a riposte might be, then these other organisations should be brought into line with trade unions rather than the controls on unions relaxed!

In this chapter we will examine the ways in which the law has increasingly assumed control of the internal affairs of unions. Using a broadly chronological approach, we will look first at the political activities of unions, then at the constraints developed at common law, and finally at the ongoing legislative inroads on union autonomy.

Expenditure for Political Purposes

Common law

11–002   In the nineteenth century it was obvious to trade unions that they needed parliamentary representation if they were to gain the sort of legislative framework that they needed in order to achieve their aspirations. The Labour Party was born out of this wish, and trade unions were giving money to support candidates and for other political purposes from the 1880s. Provided that this was not contrary to the union's constitution, it was difficult to see what was wrong with this. Any organisation is allowed to use its property in lawful ways permitted by its constitution. Due to the political dimension, this was bound to be challenged. The Labour Party received over 90 per cent of its income from trade unions until the 1980s, although this has now fallen to about 50 per cent. In the first reported case, *Steele v South Wales Miners' Federation* (1907) the union's constitution specifically included financial support for MPs among its objects. Following a ballot in favour, the union began levying one shilling a year from members for this purpose. The union's objects were upheld as lawful, Darling J saying:

> "It seems to me that one of the ways of regulating the relations between workmen and masters . . . is to get laws passed by Parliament for their regulation and that one of the first steps towards getting those laws passed would be to send a representative to Parliament to promote a Bill for that purpose."

However, this view was swiftly overtaken by the House of Lords' decision in *Amalgamated Society of Railway Servants v Osborne* (1910). Osborne, a Liberal, objected to a levy payable to the Labour Party. Interestingly, the main ground for the House of Lords' decision that such expenditure was beyond the powers of a union appears to have been because of an analogy drawn with the position of companies. Apparently, assuming that it would be ultra vires (outside the capacity of) a company to spend money on political purposes, their Lordships considered that trade unions should be similarly restricted.

The point is interesting because it is, of course, extremely common today for companies to give large amounts of money for political purposes, usually by way of direct donation to the Conservative Party. These amounts are greatly in excess of the income received by the Labour Party from trade unions (the Liberal Democrats do badly out of both sides of industry). Yet now it is hardly suggested that such payments by companies are ultra vires.

Osborne is another landmark case in trade union history, hardly less famous than *Taff Vale*. Again it was seen by many trade unionists (especially the railway workers!) to be an example of the system working against them. Again, it required legislation to restore the position as previously understood. However, the Trade Union Act 1913 did not reverse the effect of *Osborne* by giving unions *carte blanche* to spend money on political purposes. It required a union to set up a political fund, separate from its other funds, for such expenditure, and to allow every member the right to opt out of paying the political levy. These require-ments stood unchanged for 70 years, but were made more stringent following amendment by the Trade Union Act 1984 and the Trade Union Bill 2016. They are now to be found in the Trade Union and Labour Relations (Consolidation) Act 1992 (TULRCA) Ch.VI.

Statutory control

The first condition for political expenditure is that the members of the union **11–003** should be balloted to see whether they want a political fund. A simple major-ity of those voting is required. Under the Trade Union Act 1913 this was a once and for all vote, but the Trade Union Act 1984 introduced a requirement that there should be a ballot every 10 years. The justification for this was said to be union democracy: present members might have different views from their predecessors. However, it should be noted that members who do not wish to pay the political levy do not have to: it is thus not immediately apparent why there should be a ballot at all, since the result of a "no" vote is to deprive those members who do want to pay of the opportunity to do so. As most unions with political funds set them up soon after the 1913 Act, many had to hold a ballot within a year of the 1984 amendments. None lost the vote, having successfully persuaded their members that if they did not want to make political payments themselves, they should not prevent other people's freedom of choice. This pattern has continued in subsequent 10-year re-ballots.

The rules for the ballot must be approved in advance by the Certification Officer. Other than requiring that the ballot be secret and that every member should have a reasonable opportunity to vote, the 1913 Act did not lay down conditions as to the form of the ballot. The 1984 Act permitted workplace or postal ballots, but in line with the rules on the election of union officials the Employment Act 1988 tightened the rules further by requiring a fully postal ballot—i.e. the voting paper is sent out by post and returned by post in a prepaid envelope. Political fund ballots are also subject to similar provisions for independent scrutiny as ballots for the election of trade union officials (see below, para.11–025).

At first public funds were available for re-ballots (on whether to continue a political fund), but not for an initial ballot. It is also worth noting that while a ballot is mandatory for setting up a political fund, the law does not require that members be balloted on a decision by the executive officers to close down the political fund. Such asymmetries in the post-1984 law contributed to the generally held view that the purpose of the legislation was to make it harder for unions to make political contributions rather than to increase union democracy, which was the stated aim when the Trade Union Act 1984 was passed. Once it became mandatory for all ballots to be fully postal, there was no further need to offer inducements for unions to ballot in this way, so TURERA arranged for the phasing out of public funds to cover the cost by March 1996. At the same time TULRCA s.116, giving recognised unions the right to use the employer's premises for workplace ballots, ceased to have effect.

11–004 Given the cost of holding ballots and the fact that no union member can ever be compelled to pay the political levy, the Better Regulation Task Force (set up in 1997 to advise the Government on the burdens of regulation and possible alternatives) questioned whether it was necessary to retain the requirement for repeat ballots on the political fund. However, in its 2003 review of the Employment Relations Act (ERelA) 1999 the Government decided to keep the present rule.

Expenditure on political objects may only be made out of a political fund, not out of general funds. Political objects are defined by TULRCA s.72(1) as expenditure of money:

"(a) on any contribution to the funds of, or on the payment of expenses incurred directly or indirectly by, a political party;

(b) on the provision of any service or property for use by or on behalf of any political party;

(c) in connection with the registration of electors, the candidature of any person, the selection of any candidate or the holding of any ballot by the union in connection with any election to a political office;

(d) on the maintenance of any holder of a political office;

(e) on the holding of any conference or meeting by or on behalf of a political party or of any other meeting the main purpose of which is the transaction of business in connection with a political party;

(f) on the production, publication or distribution of any literature, document, film, sound recording or advertisement the main purpose of which is to persuade people to vote for a political party or candidate or to persuade them not to vote for a political party or candidate."

The revised objects are wider than the 1913 formulation, thus requiring more kinds of payment to come out of the political fund. Some of the amendments simply updated the old law—e.g. the inclusion of film among publications and the inclusion of Members of the European Parliament. Some make explicit what was probably covered already: in *Parkin v ASTMS* (1983) the EAT held that the union's investment of £42,000 in the development of the Labour Party Headquarters on commercial terms, but on a "sympathetic basis", came within the political objects, as did political donations from companies wholly owned by the union. While it has been held that paying money to MPs as salary for services rendered (e.g. as parliamentary consultants) is not within the political objects, a gift of money or in kind will be. In *Parkin v ASTMS*, allowing the political fund to run into deficit was held to be lawful provided that the interest on the overdraft was also charged to the political fund; this is now embodied in TULRCA s.83.

Most controversy centred on the amendment to sub-para.(f), which, it was thought, could mean that any union literature critical of the Government would have to be paid for from a political fund, despite the limitation contained in the words "the main purpose". The fear was found to be justified to some extent in *Paul v NALGO* (1987) where a member complained about the "Make People Matter" campaign of the union representing local government officials. Leaflets and posters highlighting cuts in public services, the damage caused by privatisation, and urging readers to "use your vote" were distributed near the time of local elections. Despite the inclusion of a disclaimer saying that NALGO was not affiliated to any political party and that it was not seeking or opposing the election of any particular candidate, it was held that overall its main purpose was to dissuade people from voting for Conservative candidates. Browne-Wilkinson VC stressed that such a campaign might have been paid for out of general funds if the timing had been different, but its closeness to the election clearly had a bearing on the decision about its main purpose. While not ruling out publicity critical of the Government as a lawful expenditure from general funds, this decision clearly made it a hazardous business. The result was that a number of unions representing public sector workers (whose employment conditions are therefore closely affected by government policy) took steps to establish political funds for the first time.

11–005

The Trade Union Bill 2016 amends TULRCA to introduce a new requirement for unions to give details in their annual returns of any expenditure of more than £2,000 from their political funds. They must say how much has been spent under each of the six categories in s.72(1)(a)–(f), to whom it was paid, and what the nature of the expenditure was.

Is it justified to hedge the political expenditure of unions about with so many restrictions? The usual argument is that individual members may not support the political party to which the union donates money. Of course, they need not themselves donate money; but equally it could be said that any member who does want to give money to the Labour Party can do so by joining it, or sending periodic donations. However, bearing in mind the reasoning behind the House of Lords' decision in *ASRS v Osborne* (1910), and the reality that unions give to the Labour Party and companies mostly give to the Conservative Party, it seems difficult to justify this elaborate control over union political donations when it is contrasted with the near absence until recently of any control over political donations by companies. So far as companies are concerned, it seems accepted that political donations are in the interests of shareholders, and the only statutory control for many years was the requirement in the Companies Act 1985 (Sch.7, para.3) that any donation over £200 should be disclosed in the directors' report to the Annual General Meeting. As a result of recommendations of the Neill Committee on Standards in Public Life in 1998, the Political Parties, Elections and Referendums Act 2000 amended the Companies Act 1985 so that companies could not make donations for political expenditure unless the donations had been approved by a resolution of the shareholders specifying the maximum amount which could be spent. This was replaced—and watered down—by the Companies Act 2006 ss.362–379, which permits the company to seek the retrospective approval of shareholders for unauthorised political donations or expenditure.

Members' rights

11–006   Members currently have the right to opt out of paying the political levy. When the union adopts political objects, members must be given notice of this right and it seems that they must give written notification to the union of their intention to opt out, but that it need not be in any particular form. When the 10-year review ballot comes up, members must be given a reminder of their right to opt out; however, the Trade Union Act 1984 stopped short of changing the position to one of opting in instead. The difference between opting out and opting in is significant in practice, since the most reliable human characteristic is inertia. When people must actually do something in order not to pay, the majority will not bother to do it. Thus opting out swells the political fund, and between 1927 and 1946 when opting in was necessary, political funds consequently dwindled. This, no doubt, is the main reason for the Trade Union Bill 2016 proposing to re-introduce opting in, which will have to be done by the member giving written notice to the union (new TULRCA s.84). For good measure, the notice will only last for five years and will then lapse unless the member renews, again in writing. The member may withdraw from contributing to the political fund at any time, on giving one month's notice.

Employers may not deduct union subscriptions (whether or not including political fund contributions) from wages without specific written authorisation from the member, which authorisation may be withdrawn in writing at any time (TULRCA s.68). The Trade Union Reform and Employment Rights Act 1993 (TURERA) aimed to make the check-off system more difficult for employers to operate, no doubt with the aim of discouraging them from providing this facility, by stipulating that an initial authorisation would only be valid for three years and that any increase in the subscription during that time would require new written authorisation. Furthermore, it was the employer who had to give employees written notice of any changes and of their rights to cease payment. These rather petty complications were swept aside by the Deregulation (Deduction from Pay of Union Subscriptions) Order 1998 (SI 1998/1529) which restored the previous position. In the meantime, however, many unions had persuaded their members to pay their subscriptions by direct debit instead. This has the additional advantages that employers cannot readily identify union members and that the union will continue to get income even when members are not being paid (e.g. because they are on strike). Nonetheless, many lower-paid workers in the public sector still pay subscriptions by way of check-off, and the income of public sector trade unions will no doubt suffer a further blow from the provision in the Trade Union Bill 2016 which will prevent public sector employers, as specified in regulations, from operating the check-off system at all (new TULRCA s.116B).

Finally, by TULRCA s.82 there must be no discrimination against a member who has opted out of paying the political levy, and they must not be barred from holding any office on that account, except an office which involves the control or management of the political fund itself. In *Birch v NUR* (1950) the union's rules provided that the branch chairman should also manage the political fund. As Birch was a non-contributor, he was dismissed from his post as branch chairman, the union arguing that the post involved management of the political fund. The court held that a combination of duties in this way could have the effect of excluding non-contributors from wide areas of union activity and was therefore contrary to the Act.

Union Rules at Common Law

The rules of a trade union form a contract between the union and the member. **11–007** The rules are mostly express, and to be found in a rule-book; however, they may be derived from other sources. This was recognised by the House of Lords in *Heatons Transport v TGWU* (1972) where it was pointed out that "union rule books are not drafted by parliamentary draftsmen" and should not be interpreted as if they were. In particular, it should be recognised that the rule-book might not be complete, and rules could be implied from, for example, custom and practice. On that basis, it was held that shop stewards had customary power under the union's constitution to call industrial action, although they had no express power to do so. This approach was applied in *McVitae v Unison* (1996), where the rules of the union, which had come into existence as a result of the amalgamation of three other unions, made no provision for the continuance of disciplinary proceedings begun by one of the constituent unions before amalgamation. A term to permit proceedings to be brought under the new union's rules was implied on the "officious bystander" test. In *AB v CD* (2001) the union rules required election of officials by single transferable vote, but did not state what should happen if two candidates tied for the top place. In the past such ties had been resolved by declaring elected the candidate who had scored most votes in an earlier round and it was argued that this rule should be implied on the basis of custom and practice. However, since there was no evidence that members would be aware of this, the court held that a customary rule could not be established. A term allowing the practice was implied instead on grounds that the contract was incomplete (see *Liverpool CC v Irwin* (1977) above, para.4–018).

Since 1980 there has been increasing statutory regulation of union rules, including those governing the relationship of union and member. However, even before this, controls on the enforcement of the contract between union and member had been developed at common law, and these remain of residual importance. We shall look at this first in relation to the disciplining and expulsion of members.

Discipline and expulsion

11–008   Two points are worth noting at the outset. First, unions have no wish to reduce their membership, and so they are likely to use powers to expel sparingly. Similarly, they must be circumspect in exercising disciplinary powers short of expulsion for fear that members will become disenchanted and leave. Where there were strong closed shops so that expulsion from the union meant loss of a job, these restraints on unions did not exist, and so unions having the most comprehensive and severe disciplinary codes tended to be those where the closed shop was strongest; correspondingly, weak unions have weak disciplinary rules. Secondly, it is instructive to compare the power of a union to expel a member with the power of an employer to dismiss an employee. There are differences, most notably that expulsion from a union does not mean that one loses one's livelihood and may thus be regarded as a less serious contingency than dismissal. However, as will be seen, the law places tighter controls on the union's power to expel than on an employer's power to dismiss. The courts have evolved two main grounds for their jurisdiction over the rules of trade unions: first, that the rules are contract terms to be interpreted by the court, and secondly, that the administrative law concept of natural justice applies.

Interpretation of the rules

11–009   Disciplinary rules are usually of two kinds: those which provide for specific offences and penalties (e.g. being in arrears with subscriptions); and open-ended, subjective rules which create vague offences such as "conduct prejudicial to the interests of the union", or even "conduct which, in the opinion of the branch (or national) committee, is detrimental to the union". The court's position as final arbiter on the interpretation of these rules was classically asserted in *Lee v Showmen's Guild of Great Britain* (1952), where the union had fined a member £100 for "unfair competition" contrary to the rules. The issue had been before an internal union tribunal, which had found against the member, and it was argued that their determination should not be disturbed. The Court of Appeal, led by Lord Denning, was prepared to accept that it should be bound by the findings of fact of the internal tribunal, provided that the court was satisfied that there was sufficient evidence to support their finding. Here, the Court of Appeal held that the conduct complained of was not capable of constituting unfair competition. This seems to come perilously close to the court substituting its opinion for the opinion of the internal tribunal—a tendency frequently castigated by the Court of Appeal in the EAT's handling of unfair dismissal appeals from employment tribunals, and indeed in tribunals' handling of employers' dismissal decisions.

It might be thought that subjective rules, especially those which incorporate reference to a committee's opinion, would be proof against such judicial incursions, for they seem to require only good faith on the part of the relevant committee. However, this is not the case. In *Esterman v NALGO* (1974), for example, a member refused to take part in a strike designed to disrupt local elections. She was expelled from the union for "conduct which, in the opinion of the branch committee, renders her unfit for membership". Templeman J held that no reasonable tribunal could so have categorised her conduct: "I emphatically reject the submission that it was the duty of every member blindly to obey the orders of the national executive".

Thus where matters of discipline or expulsion are at issue, the court will intervene on behalf of a member if either the rules are not followed, or if the court considers that an internal union tribunal has not interpreted the union's rules correctly. In *McVitae v Unison* (1996) it was argued that the union could not discipline or expel a member unless it had an express power in the rules to do so. However, it was held that even such a penal power could be implied, although only in exceptional circumstances. In general, however, courts have leaned towards a construction of the rules which favours the member.

Can the court go further and strike down or treat as ineffective certain rules? **11–010** It is clear that, on general principle, a rule which attempted to exclude the jurisdiction of the courts altogether, for example by stating that there was no appeal from a union decision, would be treated as void because it was contrary to public policy. However, if the rule states that all domestic procedures must be exhausted first, the effect would be to delay, rather than to remove, a right of recourse to the courts. In *Lawlor v UPOW* (1965) the member's claim was not barred by a failure to appeal internally first, but in that case there was no express rule that this should happen. However, in *Leigh v NUR* (1970) Goff J held that, while not absolutely bound by such a rule, a court would normally require a good reason to be given for failure to exhaust internal remedies, and that it might expect a member to use internal remedies first even where there was not an express rule to that effect. One good reason for trying the court first might be the length of time that it takes to go through the union's own appeal machinery: in some unions the final right of appeal is to the annual conference, and could thus be a long way off, particularly if the disciplinary decision or expulsion is treated as effective in the meantime. Thus, TULRCA s.63 provides members with a statutory right of recourse to the court if the union itself has not dealt with an application from a member within six months (see further, below, para.11–017).

This particular situation aside, there have been suggestions from time to time that rules which are unreasonable, or contrary to public policy, will be treated as ineffective. However, clear authority for this is lacking, and given present levels of legislative control over the rule-book, there would seem to be little scope for further common law development.

Natural justice

Natural justice is a public law concept stipulating certain minimum procedural **11–011** standards for decision-making bodies having quasi-judicial functions. Its requirements cannot be regarded as absolutely fixed, but basically embody two principles: first, that a person is entitled to a fair hearing before his or her case is decided, and secondly, that any decision must be taken by an unbiased tribunal. At least since *Lee v Showmen's Guild* (1952) it has been clear that trade unions must abide by the rules of natural justice when taking decisions affecting members.

The right to be heard involves being given adequate notice of the charge against you—adequate both in terms of length, so that there is time to prepare an answer, and in terms of detail, so that you know exactly what it is you are meant to have done. In *Annamunthodo v Oilfield Workers' Union* (1961) the appellant knew that he was charged with having made serious allegations of dishonesty against the union's president, for which he could be fined, but not that this was to be treated as conduct prejudicial to the union's interests for which he could be expelled. It was held that his expulsion was a breach of natural justice because insufficient notice had been given.

Most disciplinary procedures of whatever kind usually allow representation, but it seems from *Enderby FC v Football Association* (1971) that natural justice does not go so far as to require that legal representation should be allowed. Frequently it is specifically disallowed, because the presence of lawyers is sure to extend the length of the proceedings and without doubt the expense as well. On the other hand, it may be felt that the inarticulate will not get a fair hearing without a skilled advocate to speak for them.

11–012 The rule against bias must be interpreted with common sense when applied to internal tribunals, whether of trade unions or other bodies. There is a sense in which someone who has fallen out with the union is never going to believe that a tribunal composed of union people will give him a fair hearing. However, if the rule that there should not only be no actual bias but not even the appearance of bias were taken this far, then internal tribunals would become quite impracticable. It is clear that natural justice is not infringed just because union officials are involved in making the decision, but obviously anyone who has played a part in the dispute ought not to be involved in judging it. In *Roebuck v NUM (No.2)* (1978), the union president, Arthur Scargill, had successfully sued a newspaper for libel on behalf of the union. The two claimants were members who had given evidence in that action on behalf of the newspaper; afterwards Mr Scargill reported that one had contradicted in court a statement that he had given to the union's solicitors and that the other had shown official correspondence to the newspaper's solicitors. This, he contended, was conduct detrimental to the union's interests. The area council (chaired by Mr Scargill) agreed and referred the matter to the area executive committee. The area executive committee (chaired by Mr Scargill) met four times, found the charges proved and recommended that the members be suspended from office. The decision was confirmed by the area council—chaired by Mr Scargill. Not surprisingly, this was held to be a breach of natural justice; in the words of the judge, the president had been "the complainant, the pleader, the prosecutor, the advocate and the chairman in the union proceedings".

Natural justice does not require that there be an appeal procedure, although again it is common for unions to provide internal appeal procedures. It should be noted that in *Leary v NUVB* (1971) it was held that a breach of natural justice at an initial hearing could not be cured by a proper appeal.

However, it would seem that natural justice does not apply to absolutely every case of discipline or expulsion. Often union members do not signify formally an intention to resign from the union, but simply stop paying their subscriptions. Unions thus frequently have rules which provide for a member's name being automatically removed from the register after a certain period of arrears. It would seem unnecessary, in this sort of case, to insist on the member having a right to notice first. Having said that, it should be noted that in *Edwards v SOGAT* (1971), such a rule was held to be contrary to natural justice. However, the circumstances in that case were rather special: it was the fault of a union official, not the member, that the subscriptions had not been paid, and the union, once aware of the mistake, far from apologising for their error, rather refused him re-admission on two occasions and ensured his dismissal from the printing shop where he worked on the grounds that it was a closed shop! In *Cheall v APEX* (1983), the House of Lords held that it was not a breach of natural justice for the union to expel the member without a hearing first in order to comply with a ruling of the TUC under the Bridlington Agreement.

Enforcing the rules

While it is the rules about discipline and expulsion that most directly affect the member's relationship with the union, there are plenty of other rules which a member will be interested in seeing enforced. The contract of membership confers to some extent the right to have the business of the union run in accordance with the rules, but as with the enforcement of most contracts, this right is essentially negative: it is a right to restrain action in breach of contract or to sue for breach of contract rather than a right positively to insist on the conduct provided for in the rule being carried out. This is well illustrated in *Taylor v NUM (Yorkshire Area)* (1984)—one of many cases contributing to the jurisprudence of members' rights which arose out of the miners' strike of 1984–85. The National Union of Miners was a federation of Area unions. Under the national rules, no national strike action could be called unless there had been a ballot in which 55 per cent voted in favour of action. This rule, more stringent than the simple majority required by TULRCA s.226, considerably pre-dated the statutory requirement, and was repeated also in the rules of most of the Area unions. Taylor challenged the strike on the grounds that there had been no ballot. In fact there had been a ballot in Yorkshire, where 85.6 per cent had voted in favour of action—but that was in 1981. Nicholls J held that there was certainly an arguable case that this was national strike action (and there had been no national ballot) and that the ballot in Yorkshire was too remote in time to validate the Yorkshire action. However, he refused to grant an injunction either requiring the union to run a ballot or to call off the action—the only remedy to which a member was entitled was a declaration that the action was unofficial: "The member's right under the Rule is confined to being able to insist that a national strike cannot lawfully be held without a national ballot". There was no positive right to insist that the union should hold a ballot.

11–013

As we will see, members have now been given a statutory right to restrain action without a ballot, but the point remains valid that at common law action is possible to restrain breaches of the rule, not to enforce rule-observing behaviour.

The Rule in *Foss v Harbottle*

11–014   A further constraint, at least in theory, on the ability of a member to take action where a breach of the rules is threatened is found in the rule in *Foss v Harbottle*, deriving from an 1843 company law case. In essence, the rule is that where certain non-serious breaches of the organisation's rules take place (non-serious breaches meaning those which are capable of ratification by a majority vote), then an individual member may not bring an action complaining of the irregularity. Notice that it is not essential that ratification should actually have taken place: only that the breach is capable of being ratified.

There is a theoretical and a practical justification for this rule. The theoretical justification is that a breach of the rule is really a wrong done to the organisation rather than to a particular member of it; thus it is the organisation which ought to be the claimant. If the wrong done is one which the organisation itself could put right if it wished by a majority vote, then there is no need to let an individual sue. The practical justification is to protect the organisation from costly and vexatious litigation: if the majority do not wish to take action, then it would be an unnecessary drain on the organisation's resources to allow an individual to do so.

The very formulation of the rule suggests the situations in which it will not apply. For example, in all the disciplinary and expulsion cases considered above, there is never any suggestion that a member cannot complain because of the rule in *Foss v Harbottle*: there the wrong is clearly done to the member, invading his or her personal rights, rather than to the union. Secondly, it only applies to non-serious breaches which are capable of ratification: so if what the member is complaining of is a serious breach, then an individual will have the right to take action. Unfortunately, the distinction between serious and non-serious breaches is not immediately obvious, at least in trade union cases. In *Cotter v NUS* (1929) (the case in which the rule was first applied to unions) a resolution to make an interest-free loan to the Miners' Non-Political Movement (in the wake of the General Strike) was passed at a Special General Meeting of the union against the advice of some officials. One official challenged it, claiming that the meeting had not been convened according to the union's rules, and that delegates had not been properly elected. The Court of Appeal held that even if the irregularities were proved, they were only minor breaches, capable of ratification, and the claimant was therefore barred from action by the rule in *Foss v Harbottle*.

11–015   If under the union's rules a special majority is required for a particular decision (e.g. the 55 per cent in favour of strike action required by NUM rules), then a breach of that rule is one which is not capable of ratification. For if ratification was allowed, it would effectively allow the union to do by a simple majority (in ratifying) what the rule said must be done by a special majority. This exception was established in *Edwards v Halliwell* (1950), where a delegates' meeting purported to raise subscriptions without getting the necessary two-thirds approval stipulated in the rules.

An action which is ultra vires the union (i.e. outside its objects and therefore its capacity) is clearly non-ratifiable. There can be no ratification of an ultra vires act, because this is not a situation where power has been misused, but a situation where there is no power to act in this way at all. In *Thomas v NUM (South Wales Area)* (1985) it was alleged that the conduct of the strike was bound to result in breaches of the criminal law (arising out of picketing activities) and the commission of torts, and was therefore ultra vires the union. Scott J was of the view that it would be ultra vires for the union to organise activity which was definitely criminal, but he was "not clear" what the position would be if action was organised which was bound to result in a tort being committed. However, he did not feel obliged to decide either point, since he accepted that the action here carried only the usual risk of crimes and torts being committed; they were not inevitable. As the scope of trade union immunity for action in tort has now been substantially reduced, the point could become important in the future. However, this must be seen in the context of a contemporaneous first instance decision, *Taylor v NUM (Derbyshire Area) (No.3)* (1985). The energetic Taylor, having already established that the strike in Derbyshire, was ultra vires for want of a ballot, here complained about payments from union funds to relieve hardship among strikers and their families and for pickets' expenses. He sought to stop future payments and to recover some £1.7 million paid out. Vinelott J held that the payments, in connection with an ultra vires strike, were also ultra vires, and that an injunction should be granted. However, he declined to order the officials to repay the money spent. He was clearly influenced by the facts that the officials had acted in good faith, for no personal gain and that exhausting their own assets, while ruining them, would be a drop in the ocean against the sum claimed; furthermore, there was evidence that the majority of the members supported what had been done. Strictly, of course, these are not relevant considerations; in particular, if an action is ultra vires, then it cannot be ratified even if every single member wants it to be. However, Vinelott J, while restating that ratification was impossible, held that the majority could in good faith decide not to sue, and that that decision would bind the minority. It is difficult to see the difference between ratification and a decision not to sue, since both have the same practical effect of depriving a minority member of a remedy, but if the decision is not a model of legal reasoning, it may perhaps be defended as a common-sense response in a highly charged atmosphere.

Wedderburn attacked this decision more fundamentally on the ground that the ultra vires doctrine is only applicable to corporations, which, as artificial persons, must have constitutions stating what they can and cannot do, and is inappropriate for trade unions, which are unincorporated associations. According to TULRCA s.10 a union is not, and is not to be treated as if it were, a corporation. As decided in *EEPTU v Times Newspapers* (see above, para.10–033), this marks a break from past cases, such as *Cotter v NUS* (1929), where unions were treated more like corporate bodies and thought to be subject to the ultra vires doctrine. If this view is correct, it would mean that members would not be able to restrain action on grounds of its being outside the union's power to do it.

11–016   As *Taylor v NUM (Derbyshire Area) (No.3)* (1985) is a first instance decision, it is open to another court to take this view. However, by parity of reasoning, it might be considered that the rule in *Foss v Harbottle* is also a company law doctrine and inappropriate to unincorporated associations (although this was denied in *Cotter v NUS*), which would widen the possibilities for the union to be sued. The issue was not raised at all in the most recent case invoking the rule in *Foss v Harbottle, Wise v USDAW* (1996). The claimant, then president of the union, challenged decisions of the executive council in relation to the election of union officials, which, although they did not affect her personally, she argued were in breach of the rules. Chadwick J held that the rule in *Foss v Harbottle* did not preclude her claim, essentially on the grounds that any member had a personal right to enforce adherence to the contract set out in the rule-book. This is a very broad concept of personal rights, since it does not require the member to show that her interests are particularly affected by the breach of the rules. If correct, it means that it is difficult to envisage any situation where the rule in *Foss v Harbottle* will stop a member bringing an action. Elias and Ewing, writing in 1987, pointed out that the rule in *Foss v Harbottle* had been relied on successfully in only five cases against trade unions by that date, of which the most recent was as long ago as 1966 (*McNamee v Cooper*). Thus, even if still applicable in theory, it seems less and less likely in practice that it will inhibit a member who wishes to sue the union for a breach of its rules. In any case, common law rights have in many circumstances been overtaken by statutory controls over the union's rules.

Procedure

11–017   The usual route for an action for breach of contract, including the membership contract, would be the High Court. However, an important, if not widely publicised reform in the Employment Relations Act 1999 extended a parallel jurisdiction to the Certification Officer for certain kinds of breach of union rules, by inserting new ss.108A–108C into TULRCA.

Under s.108A a member may complain to the Certification Officer instead of the High Court where she or he alleges a breach or threatened breach of union rules in relation to one of the following: appointment or election to a union office; discipline or expulsion of members (but not union employees); ballots (except industrial action ballots); constitution or proceedings of any executive committee or decision-making meeting; and anything else specified by order of the Secretary of State. The member has the choice of going to the Certification Officer or the court, but cannot apply to both. The advantages of proceedings in front of the Certification Officer are speed and cost: any claim is meant to be determined within six months. It should be noted that application to the Certification Officer is not available for every breach of union rules: only those which are listed in s.108A. While including disciplinary proceedings, this does not include grievance proceedings (*Irving v GMB* (2008)).

To encourage local resolution of disputes as far as possible, the Certification Officer may refuse to entertain an application if the member has not taken all reasonable steps to use the union's internal complaints procedure first (TULRCA s.108B). However, in such circumstances the member must keep a careful eye on limitation periods: application must normally be made to the Certification Officer within six months of the alleged breach. Where internal procedures have been invoked the limitation period becomes six months from the date of the conclusion of the internal proceedings or one year from the date of their commencement, whichever is earlier.

The Certification Officer may make or refuse a declaration that there has been **11–018** a breach of the rules. If making such a declaration, he may also make an enforcement order. Declaration and enforcement orders made by the Certification Officer are enforceable as if made by a court. Appeals from the Certification Officer's decisions lie on a question of law only to the Employment Appeal Tribunal (TULRCA s.108C).

Statutory Regulation of the Rule-book

Certain basic standards of efficient organisation are an unobjectionable require- **11–019** ment, and so there is little criticism of the provisions contained in TULRCA that a member should always have the right to resign on giving reasonable notice (s.69) and that unions should keep proper accounts, to be filed annually with the Certification Officer and open to public inspection (ss.28–30). The former is in the nature of a tidying-up provision, as some unions did not have a procedure for resignation, and instead just inferred it from non-payment of subscriptions. The latter is a basic requirement for all kinds of organisation recognised by the law. However, since 1980, numerous other less neutral requirements have been introduced, many of which are fiercely resented by unions.

Financial affairs

In *Taylor v NUM (Derbyshire Area) (No.2)* (1985), the member sought to inspect **11–020** the union's accounts accompanied by an accountant. The court held that where, as here, the rules gave members the right to inspect the accounts, it impliedly gave them the right to do so with a professional agent. As a result the NUM altered its rules specifically to exclude the right to professional advice. This, coupled with the fact that in the miners' strike and certain other industrial disputes in the 1980s the whereabouts of union funds were difficult to discover, led to an amendment in 1988 to give members the right to inspect the accounts accompanied by an accountant and to oblige the union to supply them with copies if requested (TULRCA s.30). Members may only see accounts relating to their own period of membership, and may be asked to pay a reasonable administrative charge, but they can see the records of any branch or section. The accountant, but not the member, may be required to give a reasonable undertaking of confidentiality. A member may apply to the Certification Officer or to the court for an order where inspection is refused, and a deliberate failure to maintain the relevant accounts is a criminal offence.

Controls on unions' financial affairs were taken further by TURERA. The Government based its case for further intervention yet again on events surrounding the miners' strike. Following allegations in the media in the spring of 1990, Gavin Lightman QC was appointed by the NUM to investigate alleged irregularities in the conduct of union funds. The Lightman Report was critical of a number of matters, especially unauthorised dealings by senior officials of the union. The Report was commissioned by the union in response to the pressure of a media campaign: it had no obligation to look into the matter on behalf of members. Subsequently criminal proceedings were brought by the Certification Officer under what is now TULRCA s.45 on grounds that the union had failed to keep proper accounting records and to submit true and fair accounts; however, the Lightman Report was judged to be inadmissible and the charges were ultimately dropped.

The TURERA reforms tackled this in three ways: first, by increasing the powers of the Certification Officer; secondly, by extending the range of criminal offences relating to the financial affairs of trade unions; and thirdly, by providing for increased disclosure to members to encourage them to challenge the union. Under TULRCA s.37A the Certification Officer has power to require a union to produce any documents and to provide an explanation for them if he thinks that he has a good reason to do so. He is specifically enjoined to consider whether to exercise his new powers when a member complains of fraud or misconduct, or the auditor's report is critical of the accounts. In addition, TULRCA s.37B gives the Certification Officer a power to appoint an inspector to investigate the financial affairs of the union whenever there are circumstances suggesting fraud, misfeasance or misconduct: it is specifically provided that any resulting report will be admissible in criminal proceedings (TULRCA s.37C(8)).

11–021 These powers are similar to those afforded to the Serious Fraud Office in relation to the financial dealings of companies and provide expressly that refusal to make a statement is not justified on the grounds that it might incriminate the maker. However, in *Saunders v United Kingdom* (1994) (an attack on convictions resulting from the Guinness takeover scandal) the European Court of Human Rights criticised the use of information gained in this manner in subsequent criminal proceedings, suggesting that there may be a need to reform these powers.

In addition to the existing offences in TULRCA s.45 of failure to keep proper accounts and failure in relation to audit arrangements or the annual return, TURERA introduced new offences: failure to produce documents to the Certification Officer; falsification or destruction of documents; and knowingly or recklessly making false statements. The sanction for most of these offences is imprisonment for up to six months and/or a fine at level 5; furthermore, under TULRCA s.45B anyone convicted of such an offence will be banned from holding a position as a senior union officer for five or 10 years, depending on the seriousness of the offence.

The amended form of TULRCA s.32 requires that the union's annual return to the Certification Officer must include details of the remuneration package payable to the president, general secretary and members of the executive committee of the union, and under s.32A every member of the union must be provided with a financial statement containing this information. This is clearly intended to encourage union members to complain about the conduct of the union's finances and gives union members rather more information than shareholders are entitled to about the directors of their companies.

Discipline and expulsion

In Ch.10, dealing with admission to trade unions, reference was made to TULRCA s.174 which prohibits exclusion or expulsion except on the grounds there specified. One of these is conduct; hence it remains possible to expel members for misconduct. However, this is subject to major qualification by virtue of TULRCA s.64 which gives a member a right not to be unjustifiably disciplined.

11–022

Before this right was introduced by the Employment Act 1988 union members only received statutory protection against exclusion or expulsion where there was a closed shop in operation, on the grounds that in such situations the decision of the union actually affected a person's ability to work in a particular field. It seems justifiable to require adequate reasons in such situations, although it does not necessarily follow that a statutory procedure is necessary. The TUC attempted to deal with the issue by setting up its own Independent Review Committee, but this was not considered sufficient by the Government. Of course, the Independent Review Committee only dealt with unions which were members of the TUC.

Justification for such intervention might therefore be regarded as having disappeared when, with the Employment Act 1990, it became impossible for an employer to treat union membership as a prerequisite or a condition for employment. However, in the meantime the Employment Act 1988 had increased the limits on unions' powers in relation to discipline and expulsion, and this reform was fuelled by rather different considerations.

During the miners' strike attempts were made to expel members who crossed picket lines. In *Taylor v NUM (Derbyshire Area) (No.1)* (1984), it was held that this expulsion was invalid because the strike itself had not been called in accordance with the rules. Further, when the National Union attempted to add an expulsion power, the rule change was declared void as being in contempt of an earlier court order (*Clarke v Chadburn (No.2)* (1984)). Many unions have traditionally had a power to expel for strike-breaking, which is seen as one of the most serious offences that a union member can commit, since it undermines the solidarity which is fundamental to successful action and thus successful unionism. In *Esterman v NALGO* (1974) (see above, para.11–009) we saw another example of a court's reluctance to uphold an expulsion on this ground. In the aftermath of the strikes of the 1980s, a number of unions exercised their lawful powers to discipline or expel members who had disobeyed strike calls. This led the Government to introduce the right not to be unjustifiably disciplined now found in TULRCA ss.64–67. Any kind of disciplinary action is covered, and it is "unjustifiable" if the reason for it falls within the categories laid down in s.65: failure to take part in industrial action, or expressing opposition or lack of

11–023

support for it; failure to break one's contract of employment in connection with any industrial action; claiming (in good faith) that the union has broken the law, or its own rules; encouraging anyone else to act similarly; seeking assistance from the Certification Officer; failing to comply with a union ruling that is itself a contravention of s.64 and proposing to do any of the above. To these, TURERA added refusal to participate in check-off arrangements for deduction of union subscriptions and a number of acts amounting to failing to behave in accordance with the Bridlington Agreement.

In *Unison v Kelly* (2012) the compatibility of TULRCA ss.64–65 with ECHR art.11 was challenged by the union, which had been found liable for unjustifiably disciplining members. The EAT noted that the ILO Committee of Experts had stated for several years that this legislation was in breach of ILO Convention No.87 art.3 (see above, para.10–018) and that the European Committee of Social Rights had similarly concluded that TULRCA s.174 was in breach of art.5 of the European Social Charter. However, the EAT felt that the different grounds under TULRCA s.65 should be considered separately. It might be true that the prohibition on disciplining members who refuse to take part in industrial action would be in breach of ECHR art.11—insofar as freedom of association could be taken as guaranteeing a right to strike. However, this would not be the case for s.65(2)(c)— alleging that the union had broken its own rules—which was the reason that the members had been disciplined in this case.

While the list of reasons which are unjustifiable is long, it does not mean that unions can never take disciplinary action. In *Knowles v Fire Brigades Union* (1996) the union was absolutely opposed to full-time firefighters having "retained" contracts for standby duties in their free time. The claimant firefighter was expelled for accepting a retained contract in contravention of union policy. He argued that he had been expelled for refusing to take part in industrial action, contrary to TULRCA s.64, but as the Court of Appeal pointed out, although the union's policy was opposed to the wishes of the employers, the opposition had not in any sense taken the form of industrial action.

11–024   There is now such a large area of overlap between TULRCA ss.64 and 174 that it is difficult to see why two provisions have been retained. It made some sense when s.174 applied only to exclusions and expulsions in a closed shop situation, but now that it has been extended to all exclusions and expulsions except on the grounds there specified, which in substance cover the same issues as those in s.64, the duplication seems inelegant and unnecessary. There are differences, of course: most notably that s.174 only covers exclusion or expulsion; s.64 does not cover exclusion but it does cover all kinds of disciplinary action, including expulsion. In *NACODS v Gluchowski* (1996) it was held that suspension from membership did not amount to an exclusion or expulsion actionable under s.174 and the EAT also doubted that there could be a concept of "constructive expulsion" through the union committing a fundamental breach of its own rules. This would therefore be actionable only under s.64. Both sections provide that if an action is started under one of them, it cannot afterwards form the basis of a claim under the other; note, however, that any possible common law remedies are additional.

Remedies for breach of TULRCA ss.64 and 174 are also similar. If a tribunal upholds the claimant's claim, it makes a declaration to that effect, after which the union has a period of grace in which to put matters right. Any subsequent claim for compensation goes to the employment tribunal. If the union has acted on the tribunal's declaration, the tribunal can award such amount as is just and equitable subject to a maximum equivalent to the maximum of the basic and compensatory award for unfair dismissal (£98,585 in 2015). If the union has failed to act on the declaration, compensation is awarded on the same basis but subject to a minimum award (£8,868 in 2015). In *Bradley v NALGO* (1991), eight claimants who had been expelled for refusing to take part in a strike claimed compensation. The union did not contest the making of a declaration, nor did it revoke the expulsions. The EAT awarded each of them the minimum award only: there was no evidence that their job prospects would be in the least affected by their non-membership, nor that they were likely to be prejudiced if they applied to join another union. The EAT declined to import any kind of punitive element into the award, and limited itself purely to issues of compensation. The decision is interesting in a number of respects. The claimants had been subjected to an unpleasant bullying campaign after their expulsions but the EAT took the view that their injury to feelings arising from this was not an injury arising from the actual expulsions and was not therefore due to be compensated. Thus the decision is evidence of an apparent concern by the EAT to construe s.64 fairly narrowly; further, the interest in having at least an indirect say in collective bargaining which has been put forward as a justification for intervention in these matters was not argued nor raised of its own motion by the EAT. It will be interesting to see whether this point will ever be taken up, and if so how far it will be seen as of importance.

Election of trade union officials

Another plank in the policy of the Trade Union Act 1984 of increasing democracy **11–025** in trade unions was to require that certain officials should have to offer themselves periodically for re-election by the whole membership of the union. Before 1984, practice varied considerably, with at least some of the large unions (such as the NUM) providing that the president, once elected, had tenure until retirement. It was also very common for officials to be elected not directly by a ballot of all the members, but indirectly by a ballot among the representatives of the members. As union activists tend to be more radical than the membership as a whole, it is fairly clear that the Conservative Government of the 1980s believed that indirect elections led to candidates who were more left wing being elected, who would tend to favour confrontational tactics such as industrial action, and that this was an important element in making this reform.

The officials required by the Trade Union Act 1984 to offer themselves for re-election every five years were all the voting members of the principal executive committee of the union (whether called the National Executive, the National Council or whatever: the principal executive committee is that committee which is responsible for the day-to-day policy and management of the union). The requirement was restricted to voting members not just because the ones with the vote are the ones with the power, but to take account of the fact that most unions have a senior full-time official (usually designated as "General Secretary") who is an employee of the union and whose regular job is the general administration of the union; these career trade unionists, it was felt, should not have to put their jobs on the line every five years.

If the Trade Union Act 1984 was intended to make officials such as Arthur Scargill, at that time the life president of the NUM, offer themselves for re-election, it failed. For it could easily be circumvented if the official in question was prepared to give up his vote (as Mr Scargill did) and it may be doubted if this was much of a sacrifice, since decisions rarely turn on a single vote. Hence the Employment Act 1988 (in the so-called "Scargill clause") amended the Trade Union Act 1984 so that the president, general secretary, every member of the principal executive committee and even anyone entitled to attend and speak at executive committee meetings must offer themselves for re-election every five years (see now, TULRCA s.46). The selection of the five-year period was probably by analogy with the directors of public companies, who at that time were also limited to a five-year period of office. In *GMB v Corrigan* (2008) the EAT held that there was no infringement of TULRCA s.46 where an official was appointed Acting General Secretary of the union and held that office for more than a year before an election for General Secretary was held. The union had good reason for delaying the election (it was investigating electoral malpractices and overhauling its rules) and the appointment was not a sham. The EAT made the important point that s.46 does not require a union to hold an election as soon as there is a vacancy—only that anyone holding one of the designated offices should have been elected to it within the previous five years.

11–026   In the calmer employment relations atmosphere prevailing today, the Better Regulation Task Force questioned whether it was necessary for union presidents to be separately elected by a postal ballot of the membership (at considerable cost) when they were almost certain to be elected members of the union's national executive. The Government agreed and the ERelA 2004 removed this requirement for presidents who have been directly elected as members of the principal executive committee or as General Secretary within five years of their subsequent election as president. Under ERelA 2004 s.54, power is also given to the Secretary of State to change voting procedures to allow more flexibility, which could include introduction of internet voting.

In principle every member should be entitled to vote in the election, but two qualifications are allowed: some elections may be restricted to particular classes of members (e.g. by reference to a geographical or trade group), and some classes of member (e.g. unemployed members, new members) may be excluded. The mere fact that some members did not get a voting paper will not of itself invalidate the election, since the standard is reasonable practicability but unions now have a statutory obligation to maintain accurate membership lists (TULRCA s.24), so errors should not occur on a grand scale. As with political fund ballots, the original legislation permitted workplace ballots, but was changed by the Employment Act 1988 so that the ballot should be fully postal. The member must be sent the ballot paper by post with a prepaid envelope for its return.

One advantage of the old indirect system of elections was that the candidates were usually known to the voters (although some regarded this as one of the disadvantages of the old system, arguing that it perpetuated an oligarchy and gave an outsider little chance of election). Under TULRCA s.48, however, candidates may require the union to circulate an election address to all the members. The union is allowed to set a limit on this, but at least 100 words must be granted.

Since 1988, ballots for the election of officials and in relation to the political fund have been subject to independent scrutiny by a solicitor, accountant or a body such as the Electoral Reform Society. In January 1990 there were allegations of ballot-rigging in the elections for the Executive of the TGWU, which led to the ballot being re-run. *The Independent on Sunday* then revealed that the independent scrutineer, a solicitor, was a left-wing councillor, causing some furore, as the identity of the scrutineer was not widely known, and people had generally assumed that it was the Electoral Reform Society. This prompted an amendment in 1990 to the effect that the name of the scrutineer must now be notified in advance to the electorate (TULRCA s.51). TURERA greatly extended the remit of the independent scrutineer. She is now required to inspect the membership register when appropriate but especially when requested to do so by a member in the run-up to an election, and her findings as to its accuracy should be included in her report on the election. In addition, TULRCA s.51A requires that the election must actually be conducted, as opposed merely to being supervised, by an independent person, who will normally be the scrutineer. Similar scrutiny provisions apply also to political fund and industrial action ballots. The requirement to delegate the conduct of a ballot to an independent person has had some side-effects which were probably not intended. For example, in *Veness v NUPE* (1992) members complained, inter alia, that only 100 out of 1,150 members at one branch and only 11 out of 2,200 at another had received ballot papers. But as the union had delegated the conduct of the ballot to the Electoral Reform Society, it was held that they had no claim against the union. Furthermore, in *Douglas v Graphical Paper and Media Union* (1995) it was doubted whether the union could cancel an election result (because of possible prejudice to one candidate) once the scrutineer had reported that the election had been conducted satisfactorily.

11–027

Candidates for union office

Until 1984, the only restrictions on union rules about who could run for office in the union were that they should not discriminate against non-contributors to the political fund (Trade Union Act 1913), and, more recently, that they should not discriminate in a way contrary to the Equality Act 2010 s.57. Since 1984, no one may be unreasonably excluded from being a candidate, although the union is still permitted to exclude certain classes from standing (e.g. those who have not been members for a minimum period) (TULRCA s.47). The major restriction on this is that no candidate can be required directly or indirectly to be a member of a political party (s.47(2)). Thus rules which exclude members of the Communist Party from being candidates (which are fairly common) are valid; but the other common rule requiring a candidate to be a member of the Labour Party (or to be qualified to attend the Labour Party Conference, which indirectly requires

11–028

membership) is invalid. Section 47(3) provides that where a class of members is excluded from standing, that class may not be defined as those "whom the union chooses to exclude". This was held to have been infringed in *Ecclestone v NUJ* (1999) where the national executive committee refused to accept the claimant's candidature for Deputy General Secretary of the union, a post which he had previously held for 17 years but from which he had been dismissed following a serious dispute with the national executive committee. The committee's reason for refusing to accept him as a candidate was that it had lost confidence in him and therefore he was not qualified to stand for the office. The court held that this was tantamount to saying that those who the national executive committee did not want could not stand and therefore was in breach of s.47(3). It was also held to be an unreasonable exclusion in contravention of s.47(1) and a breach of the union's own rules. Similarly, in *Unison v Staunton* (2009), it was a breach of s.47 to exclude a member who was suspended pending an investigation into misconduct at the time of an election from standing as a candidate. The rules made no provision for exclusion of such members as a class and it was unreasonable to exclude him automatically just because he was suspended. As the EAT pointed out, someone suspended might be cleared (although not in this particular case) and it would be a substantial infringement of his democratic right to stand for office if he could be excluded before being found guilty of any disciplinary offence.

Many unions in effect ensure continuity and executive experience among their senior lay officials by having a tiered system at the top: the Junior Vice-President automatically becomes the Senior Vice-President and in due course President and Immediate Past President. In *Paul v NALGO* (1987) the Certification Officer held that keeping the Immediate Past President on the executive committee without a further election did not infringe the rules; however, there was an infringement in not opening the office of Junior Vice-President to all the members. The case illustrates another interesting point: only members of the principal executive committee need to stand for election; here, the members of the important national committee on conditions of service were not subject to election. It was held that this did not contravene the law.

While the legislation requires a degree of even-handedness on the part of the union towards candidates, it falls short of requiring completely equal treatment. It does not prevent the practice of designating some candidates as those having the support of the union's annual conference or of the national executive. Furthermore, in *Paul v NALGO* (1987) a practice of sending members a list of the branches expressing support for each candidate along with their voting papers was held by the Certification Officer not to constitute interference with the ballot.

11–029 TULRCA does not require unions to change their rules, nor does it invalidate anything done by officials appointed other than in accordance with its provisions. However, where there is non-compliance, any member has a right to complain either to the Certification Officer or to the High Court as outlined above (para.11–017).

Further Reading

❑ J. Bowers and S. Auerbach (1988), *The Employment Act 1988,* Blackstone Press, Chs 3, 4, 6, 7.
❑ P. Elias and K. Ewing (1987), *Trade Union Democracy, Members' Rights and the Law,* Mansell, Chs 2, 4, 8.
❑ K. Ewing (1982), *Trade Unions, the Labour Party and the Law,* Edinburgh University Press (but note that this is before the 1984 amendments)
❑ K. Ewing (1985), "The Strike, the Courts and the Rule-Books", 14 ILJ 1
❑ R. Kidner (1984), "Trade Union Democracy: Election of Trade Unions Officers", 13 ILJ 193
❑ Lord Wedderburn (1985), "Ultra Vires Out?", 14 ILJ 127

The thinking of the Conservative Government over the 1980s on this area may be followed through its Green Papers preceding trade union law reform:

Democracy in Trade Unions, Cmnd.8778 (1983)
Industrial Relations in the 1990s, Cm.1602 (1991) Chs 1, 2, 5, 6, 7
Removing Barriers to Employment, Cm.655 (1989)
Trade Unions and Their Members, Cm.95 (1987)

12. Industrial Action I

Key Points

This chapter:
- Considers how far individuals have a right to strike
- Outlines different forms of industrial action and their effect on contracts of employment
- Looks at how unfair dismissal law applies in the context of strikes and industrial action
- Explains the concept of official and unofficial industrial action
- Considers how far unions have immunity from actions in tort for organising industrial action
- Explains the torts of inducing breach of contract, causing loss by unlawful means and conspiracy
- Outlines torts relevant to industrial action which are not covered by the statutory immunity

***

The law regulating industrial action is the most politically contentious area of employment law, largely because of the propensity of industrial action to affect people who are not parties to the dispute. Where a strike affects the general public, there is likely to be a feeling that workers should not have total freedom to take industrial action because of its disruptive effect on the community. Many would argue that it is in any case a primitive method of dealing with disagreements, and would question whether a right to strike is really necessary in a modern state.

12–001

However, a number of reasons can be put forward in favour of a right to strike. The major one is related to the need to have trade unions in the first place—the equilibrium argument. That is, that workers need to be able to combine so that their aggregate power balances out the economic power of the employer. On this view, the possibility of strike action is a necessary weapon for the workers to have in their armoury, because it is only by the threat of collectively withdrawing their labour, or actually doing so, that they have any power. Can they not rely simply on the employer dealing with them fairly? In 1966 Grunfeld wrote:

". . . if one set of human beings is placed in a position of unchecked industrial authority over another set, to expect the former to keep the interests of the latter constantly in mind and, for example, to increase the latter's earnings as soon as the surplus income is available . . . is to place on human nature a strain it was never designed to bear" (C. Grunfeld, *Modern Trade Union Law*, Sweet & Maxwell, London, 1966).

Human nature has not changed much since 1966. So, according to the equilibrium argument, strikes or other forms of industrial action are an essential part of the collective bargaining process—the final stage if a negotiated agreement cannot be reached. However, while this argument supports a right of resort to industrial action, it does not presuppose an unlimited right: it would not be inconsistent with the equilibrium argument to insist on restraints, such as no action to be taken until all stages of the bargaining process have been completed and ended in deadlock, or until a specified "cooling-off" period has been exhausted. Some systems (e.g. the United States) embody such restraints, and some version of them has either been tried or suggested in this country at different times.

Related to the equilibrium argument is what Kahn-Freund called the autonomy argument, based on that unusual feature of British labour law, the absence of the law from the collective bargaining process. Collective bargaining in Britain was traditionally a voluntary process—"voluntary" here meaning that it is not compelled by law, although it might have been practically compelled by other means and so be not truly voluntary. While collective bargaining was not compelled or regulated by law but by the autonomous arrangements agreed between employers and unions, then it was argued that sanctions in the collective bargaining process—including industrial action on the union's side—should also be none of the law's business. As long ago as 1942 Lord Wright said, ". . . the right of workmen to strike is an essential element in the principle of collective bargaining" (*Crofter Hand Woven Harris Tweed v Veitch* (1942)) and this view is also supported by jurisprudence both of the ILO and the European Court of Human Rights (*Unison v United Kingdom* (2002)). This argument could support a free-for-all in employment relations which would not be to the taste of many; it also loses force where the assistance of the law is enlisted to compel recognition and to support collective bargaining, at least where such measures are effective (on which see above, para.5–016) or as employment protection laws establish minimum standards which would normally have had to be bargained for.

12–002   A different justification for industrial action was offered by nineteenth-century liberals such as Jeremy Bentham. Most people would support the notion that each of us should be free to dispose of our labour as we wish: the idea of "forced labour" is abhorrent in a free society. In that case, it is not possible to stop strikes, because that would be tantamount to forcing one person to work for another: a kind of slavery which cannot be tolerated in a society which places a high value on freedom. This is a strong argument, and probably contributes to the fact that the right to strike is also seen as an aspect of human rights: it is enshrined in the International Covenant on Economic, Social and Cultural Rights 1966 (art.8), in the Council of Europe's 1961 Social Charter (art.6) and the EU Charter of Fundamental Rights, art.28. The same reasoning is behind the rule that an order to enforce a contract of employment will not be made against an employee, established at common law in the nineteenth century and now expressed in the Trade Union and Labour Relations (Consolidation) Act 1992 (TULRCA) s.236. Only national security is seen as sufficiently important to override this right, hence the fact that the armed forces and the police may not strike.

While the liberal freedom argument is generally accepted, it will be noted that it only prohibits forcing people to return to work: rendering it economically desirable or effectively necessary for them to do so has not been seen as a contravention of this principle, even though for those at the sharp end there may seem to be little difference. Thus the argument is not terribly strong as a protection of the right to strike. It does, however, help to account for the shape of British law on industrial action, which never attempts directly to control those who are actually withdrawing their labour, but instead is aimed at those who organise the action. The freedom argument does not preclude ordering a union to call off industrial action, or imposing financial penalties if it declines to do so. While there is no guarantee that the strikers will obey the union's instructions, it can be expected that they will usually do so; for one thing, if union support is withdrawn, the facilities for organising the strike will be missing, so that in practical terms it becomes very difficult to continue. Thus we shall see that the way in which strikes and industrial action are regulated by the law is generally by the threat of unpleasant consequences for the organisers if the legal requirements are not complied with.

So far the term "right to strike" has been used rather loosely. What exactly is meant by this term? It is important to distinguish between a liberty to take strike action, and a right to do so. If you have a right to do something, not only are you legally able to do it, but others are under a duty not to interfere with your action. If you have only a liberty to do something, then all it means is that you are not under a duty to refrain from such action. It does not mean that other people are necessarily wrong in attempting to stop you: they have no duty to let you behave in this way. Thus a liberty is more precarious than a right would be. In the United Kingdom, the freedoms that are generally referred to as human rights, such as freedom of speech and freedom of association, are really only liberties. As we will see, this is the case also for the freedom to take industrial action.

Industrial Action and Individual Rights

Strikes and the contract of employment

Since being ready and willing to work is the main consideration given by the employee under the contract, it would seem axiomatic that refusal to work is a   **12–003** fundamental breach of contract. Alternatively, it will be recollected that obedience to reasonable orders is a fundamental duty of employees (*Laws v London Chronicle* (1959), above, para.4–028), so refusal to obey a reasonable order to work is also pretty clearly a fundamental breach. Hence the orthodox view has long been that a strike must be a fundamental breach of contract.

But it is comparatively unusual for employers to react to strikes by sacking the workforce. First, that action would obviously escalate the dispute, and the employer's prime objective is to get it settled; secondly, handing out dismissal notices is a tactic which the employer may wish to hold in reserve in case the dispute cannot be settled quickly. Most importantly, both sides expect the strike to be a temporary disruption of their relationship, and each has their own reasons for wanting to revert to the status quo in the future.

In an attempt to accommodate the realities of the situation, some judges began to reach towards a concept of suspension rather than termination of the contract during a strike. Foremost is the judgment of Lord Denning in *Morgan v Fry* (1968), where he held that provided notice of the strike were given, of equal length to that required for a lawful resignation, then this could be interpreted as notice to suspend the contract for the duration of the strike. The Donovan Commission considered this concept, but felt that it was fraught with difficulties: what if the strike were not settled? At what point could the contract be said to have ended? Would the concept of suspension apply to all industrial action or just to official strikes? What if the employee committed some other breach of contract while on strike?

12–004 It is submitted that none of these difficulties was insuperable; however, the Donovan Commission did not recommend any change to the existing law along these lines. When the matter was considered by the EAT in *Simmons v Hoover* (1977), Lord Denning's approach was not followed and orthodoxy prevailed. More recently, in *Sehmi v Gate Gourmet Ltd* (2009), one of the claimants contended that *Simmons v Hoover* should be reconsidered in the light of the incorporation of ECHR art.11 into English law by the Human Rights Act 1998, but the argument was decisively rejected. The EAT restated that *Simmons v Hoover* remained good law and was not affected by any case-law of the European Court of Human Rights or the Court of Justice of the European Union. The claimant's absence from work for two days in support of the industrial action was regarded as obviously a fundamental breach of contract.

However, even on the orthodox view, it must be the case that if employees collectively give adequate notice, not to suspend the contract, but to resign, then there would be no breach of contract. The fact that it is action undertaken collectively to put pressure on the employer could not turn it into a breach of contract. Thus it would be a completely lawful tactic. This was canvassed in *Boxfoldia v NGA* (1988). Here, the union gave two weeks' notice of a strike by its members, which happened to be the same as the notice period specified in their contracts. As there had been no ballot, the employer sued. The union argued that the strike notice was in fact notice of termination of employment by the workers, which it was handing on as agent for its members. Sadly, this ingenious interpretation of the events bore no relation to reality; however, if the members had invested the union with authority to give notice on their behalf, it seems that it would have been a successful argument—and a way for the union to avoid liability for inducing breach of contract. Interesting as this is to lawyers, it seems unlikely that it will catch on as a tactic, because although workers already risk losing their jobs without any compensation if they take industrial action, that is probably less of a risk than tendering one's resignation.

Treating a strike as only a suspension of the contract could presumably be negotiated as an express term of workers' contracts of employment, although it is never done. In this case, again, a strike would not be a breach of contract. Care would have to be taken in drafting such a term, to take account of the difficulties identified by the Donovan Commission, above.

Other forms of industrial action

So far, only indefinite strike action has been considered. Some commentators **12–005** suggest that a one-day strike would be different: it might be a breach of contract, but not a fundamental breach, looking at the time lost in proportion to the length of the whole contract. If one looks at this argument from the point of view of the duty to be ready and willing to work, it has some strength: a one-day strike could be a fairly minor breach of this duty. But looked at from the angle of the duty to obey reasonable orders, it fails: one refusal is a fundamental breach, (and see *Sehmi v Gate Gourmet Ltd* (2009, above). Some workers have occasionally tried to subvert this by "throwing a sickie" instead: that is, they all call in to say that they are unable to attend work because of illness on the same day. This tactic is frequently seen as an appropriate response to management failure to deal with health and safety concerns. Of course, a worker who calls in sick when she is not really ill does commit a breach of contract, but the workers hope that the employer will be unwilling to invest the resources necessary for discovering who was and who was not genuinely ill. However, if the employer were to respond by docking the absent workers' pay for the time they were claiming to be sick, the onus would be on them to sue for an unlawful deduction from pay, in which case they would presumably have to prove that they were not taking part in industrial action, which might be difficult.

A go-slow, where workers deliberately work at less than their usual rate, would seem to be a fundamental breach of contract on similar reasoning (*General Engineering Services v Kingston & St Andrew Corp* (1989)). Blacking, where workers refuse to perform some part of their duties, or refuse to handle particular goods, equally involves refusal to obey reasonable orders. It would be possible to negotiate a term whereby, for example, workers are not bound to handle goods where the supply has been officially blacked by the union. Terms of this kind are called "hot cargo" clauses in the United States. In this case, the blacking would not be a breach of contracts of employment, though it would probably put the employer in breach of the supply contract.

A lesser version of blacking, appropriately called "greylisting", has appeared in recent years. It involves boycotting an employer in dispute, insofar as this is possible without being in breach of contract. In the university sector, this would include not applying for posts or accepting honorary appointments at a university in dispute, not giving invited lectures there, not attending conferences there, not writing for journals edited from that university and not taking up new contracts as external examiners (refusing to carry out existing duties as an external examiner would, of course, be a breach of contract). The tactic has been used with some success by higher education unions, but might not be as effective in other sectors.

12–006   Breach of the implied term requiring obedience to reasonable orders would also render a sit-in or work-in at the workplace a breach of contract. The additional tort of trespass would be committed by those who were on the employer's premises without permission. In the case of a work-in (sometimes used as a tactic to oppose closure of a factory), where the workers continue to perform their normal duties although the employer does not want them to, they may also commit the tort of conversion by using the employer's materials.

The work-to-rule presents more difficulty. The leading case is the Court of Appeal decision in *Secretary of State v ASLEF (No.2)* (1972) where a work-to-rule by railway workers predictably brought chaos to the rail service. The union argued that the workers were simply carrying out the terms of their contract and so could not be faulted. The Court of Appeal found against them, but for a variety of reasons which are not all equally convincing. The first reason was that the rule-book which they followed did not actually contain the terms of the contract but only the employer's standing orders as to how they should carry out their duties (see above, para.4–012). The significance of this was that standing orders, unlike contract terms, were susceptible to unilateral change by the employer. A second reason was that they were in breach of an implied term of the contract, variously claimed as an aspect of the duty of faithful service, or a duty not to interpret instructions in an unreasonable manner (see above, para.4–029). Thirdly, it was said that by a course of dealing, one particular interpretation of the rules had been accepted, and they could not vary this unilaterally; but this seems inconsistent with the first reason. Fourthly, on the facts it seemed that the workers were in any case in breach of one rule, which required them to "prevent any avoidable delay". Finally, Lord Denning suggested that even if they were acting purely in accordance with the rules, their intention to disrupt could turn them into contract-breakers. This seems quite inconsistent with general contractual principle but, nonetheless, the theme was developed by a later Court of Appeal. In *Ticehurst v British Telecom* (1992) the Society of Telecom Executives instructed its members to withdraw goodwill in the course of a pay dispute, meaning that they should do nothing outside the terms of their contracts. They were also encouraged to swamp the administration with requests for written details about pension entitlements, applications for any jobs which they might possibly be qualified to do, and requests for training courses. None of these acts would normally constitute a breach of contract. The claimant's pay was stopped when she refused to give an undertaking not to take part in the action in future.

The claimant was employed as a supervisor, and this seems to have been an important factor in the Court of Appeal's decision that her actions placed her in breach of the implied duty to give faithful service outlined by Buckley LJ in *Secretary of State v ASLEF (No.2)* (1972). Having the intention to disrupt her employer's business was held to be enough for the breach to have occurred: there was no need for proof of actual disruption. Thus being in a state of dissent was in effect held to be a fundamental breach of the duty of good faith (although it was not a breach to refuse to sign the undertaking not to take part in action in future).

This decision has the potential to render every kind of industrial action a **12–007** fundamental breach of employees' contracts, since in every case the employee must intend some kind of disruption to the employer's business. Hitherto the test for a breach of a contract has been objective, judging the act or omission against the terms rather than the motive of the actor. Also, it would undermine the assumption which has always informed the law that not all industrial action is a breach of contract (e.g. the definition of industrial action in the Industrial Relations Act 1971 stipulated that it must involve a breach of contract, implying that some kinds did not, and the "health warning" which has to appear on ballot papers states only that industrial action *may* involve a breach of contract).

To hold that all kinds of industrial action entail a breach of the duty to give faithful service would also lead to absurd results. Take an overtime ban, for example. Whether or not a ban on overtime is a breach of contract depends on the terms of the contract itself. Only if it is obligatory under the contract for the employee to work overtime when required can it be a breach, as it was in *National Coal Board v Galley* (1958), for example. If the employee genuinely has an option as to whether to accept overtime or not, then surely refusal to work overtime cannot be a breach of contract, whatever the motivation.

This more rational view of the matter was adopted by the Privy Council in *Burgess v Stevedoring Services Ltd* (2002) where it was alleged that an overtime ban involved a breach of employees' contracts of employment. In fact the collective agreement between the employer and the union made it the union's responsibility to make up gangs for overtime and since the union refused to do so, the Privy Council held that the employees were not in breach of contract. Giving the advice of the Privy Council, Lord Hoffmann denied that motive alone would make otherwise lawful conduct unlawful. He suggested that Lord Denning's statement in *Secretary of State v ASLEF (No.2)* was limited to situations where employees would be justified in acting in a way which did not suit the employer if they had a bona fide reason for doing so, but would be in breach of contract if they so acted with the intention of disrupting the employer's business.

Remedies

The main importance of establishing whether industrial action is a breach of **12–008** contract is in relation to the tortious liability of the organisers. However, it is of course true that the employer could, if so wishing, pursue the usual contractual remedies against the employees. Traditionally employers have not done this: they have been content either to dismiss striking workers or to let bygones be bygones once the dispute is over. From a managerial point of view, it will clearly not help to re-establish good employment relations if the employer were to sue the workers for breach of contract after the strike was over. Another good reason for not suing is that very little may be recoverable by way of damages. In *National Coal Board v Galley* (1958), pit deputies refused to work overtime on Saturday mornings in breach of contract. As they were essential workers, it meant the whole shift output was lost, at a cost of £545, and the employer sued each worker for a share of the lost profit. It was held that the employer was only entitled to the cost of replacing each worker on the shift—that is, their wage of £3 18s 2d. Each worker was responsible only for the breach of his own contract—not the extra loss occasioned by the fact that they had acted in combination. It may be relevant that they were supervisory, not production workers: in one old case (*Ebbw Vale v Tew* (1935)) those actually engaged on production were held responsible for the loss of profit on what they would have produced.

In a number of disputes in the 1980s white collar workers adopted the tactic of refusing to do part of their duties as a way of pressurising their employers. The teachers' dispute in 1985–86 was a prime example of this, where teachers refused to cover for absent colleagues, to supervise children during breaks, to attend meetings or run clubs and sports outside hours. This is really an attempt to have it all ways: to take industrial action, yet to remain entitled to one's pay, for the usual amount of time is worked albeit not all duties covered. Some employers retaliated by withholding a part of the worker's pay to represent the unperformed duties. The legality of this was considered by the House of Lords in *Miles v Wakefield DC* (1987), where registrars of births, deaths and marriages refused to perform weddings on Saturday mornings. The Council deducted 3/37 of the registrar's pay, claiming that for three hours in his 37-hour week he was not working normally. The House of Lords held that an employee was entitled to pay only if he was ready and willing to work according to the terms of the contract. The employer was not bound to accept such a partial performance as was proffered here, and could refuse to accept it without terminating the contract. If, as here, the employer did accept the partial performance, then it was entitled to withhold an amount representing the work left undone. Presumably the employee could claim that the employer's quantification was wrong, but since the employer has the opportunity to withhold payment, and the employee would have to take expensive proceedings to challenge this, in practice it may not be a very attractive course of action. There is no recourse in these circumstances to an employment tribunal under the protection of wages provisions in the Employment Rights Act 1996 (ERA) Pt II (*Sunderland Polytechnic v Evans* (1993)), nor under the tribunals' contractual jurisdiction, since that is limited to termination of employment. However, in one test case, considering how a day's pay should be calculated when the employer was making a deduction from wages for a one-day strike, the High Court held that the deduction should not be more than the equivalent of the worker's wages for the day—it could not include anything to represent any extra loss to the employer from the combined action (*Cooper v Isle of Wight College* (2008)). Thus one day's pay was the annual salary divided by 260 (subtracting weekends and paid holidays from the 365 days in a year) (see also *Hartley v King Edward VI College* (2015)).

The implications of the decision in *Miles v Wakefield DC* were dramatically illustrated in *Wiluszynski v Tower Hamlets* (1989). Here local government officers refused to answer queries from councillors as part of an industrial action campaign which lasted over a month. This was not a very time-consuming part of their duties—at the end of the campaign, the claimant answered in about three hours all the queries that had built up for him. At the outset the council stated that it would not accept partial performance. The officers were not physically prevented from entering the buildings where they worked, but each day they were told to leave unless they were prepared to work normally, and warned that if they refused to do so, any work they did would be treated as having been done on a purely voluntary basis. The employees came to regard this as a bit of a farce; they entered and worked as normal but for their refusal to answer councillors' queries. The Court of Appeal, applying *Miles*, held that they were not entitled to any pay at all for the duration of the action. The employer had made it clear that partial performance was not acceptable, and was not to be taken to have accepted it just because the employees were allowed to work. It would seem that this tactic is therefore unlikely to be very popular among unions in the future.

Strikes and unfair dismissal

When the action for unfair dismissal was introduced by the Industrial Relations Act 1971 it was obviously necessary to decide what stance to take where employees had been dismissed for taking part in industrial action. The general principle adopted at that time was that, in the face of industrial action, the law's position should be neutral. It was felt that it would be disastrous if employment tribunals got drawn into adjudicating on the rights and wrongs of an industrial dispute.   **12–009**

The principle of neutrality may seem sensible; the way in which it was implemented was rather surprising. Provided that everyone who took part in the industrial action was dismissed, then none of them could claim unfair dismissal! The employment tribunal would have jurisdiction only if the employer dismissed some strikers but not others. Thus neutrality meant that, in most cases, employees could not bring unfair dismissal actions—a state of affairs that hardly looked like neutrality from a worker's point of view. Nevertheless, this remained until recently the basic position, although there was considerable amendment over the years. The Conservative administration of 1979–97 revised the law to limit even further the situations where unfair dismissal could be claimed. But in the Employment Relations Act (ERelA) 1999, the new Labour Government introduced a novel category of dismissals in relation to industrial action which would be automatically unfair.

What activities are covered?

The rules on unfair dismissal and industrial action are now to be found in TULRCA ss.237, 238 and 238A (as amended by ERelA 2004). They apply to dismissals in three situations: strikes, other industrial action and lock-outs. A "strike" is defined in TULRCA s.246 as "any concerted stoppage of work". This definition was imported from the Trade Union Act 1984, where it was used only in relation to industrial action ballots. Although TULRCA was meant to be a purely consolidating measure, the draftsman extended this definition to the whole   **12–010** of TULRCA Pt V, meaning that it applies to all statutory regulation of industrial action. However, it came too late to prevent the bizarre decision in *Lewis v Mason* (1994) that there could be industrial action with just one worker taking part. In that case, an employee was dismissed when he was steadfast in his refusal to take an unheated lorry on an overnight trip from Wales to Scotland in December (his employer having refused to pay him £5 for bed and breakfast accommodation). Other employees threatened not to work unless he was reinstated, so they were dismissed too. An employment tribunal held that they were all taking part in industrial action at the time of their dismissals, even the original driver, although at the time of his dismissal he was acting alone. The EAT upheld the tribunal saying, amazingly, that the decision could not be described as perverse. Fortunately, in *Norris v London Fire and Emergency Planning Authority* (2013) a different EAT revisited this point and held that an element of concerted action was necessary. Underhill P pointed out that *Lewis v Mason* was inconsistent with an earlier, unreported decision of the EAT, and faced with a choice, he had no doubt that the earlier decision was correct.

It has generally been thought that a strike means action involving a complete cessation of work, but in *Connex South Eastern Ltd v RMT* (1999) the Court of Appeal held, rather surprisingly, that a ban on overtime and rest day working could be regarded as "strike action". However, as TULRCA ss.237–238A cover "other industrial action" as well as strikes, the point is unlikely to be of any practical importance in the context of unfair dismissal, at any rate.

In *Power Packing Casemakers v Faust* (1983) three employees were dismissed for refusing to work overtime. Their contracts did not require them to work overtime, so this was not a breach on their part. However, the reason for their refusal was a dispute over a wage claim. In these circumstances, it was held that they were taking part in "other industrial action" at the time of their dismissal, and that therefore the tribunal had no jurisdiction to entertain their claims for unfair dismissal. It is clear from this that motive plays a part in defining the activity as industrial action or not for the purposes of the statutory definition. To hold that there can be industrial action without a breach of contract can have some strange results. Presumably, if Faust had acted alone and refused overtime because of a private dissatisfaction with wage levels, it would not have been industrial action because there would have been no element of combination. If he had been dismissed, he would have had a better than evens chance of winning an unfair dismissal claim. Why should the law be different because there were three workers involved? It is submitted that requiring proof of a breach of contract should be a minimum limitation on holding that an activity counts as industrial action, especially if it is going to be left as a question of fact for employment tribunals, as the next case shows.

12–011   *Norris v London Fire and Emergency Planning Authority* (2013) endorsed the approach in *Faust*. In this case, the claimant was in dispute with the employer about the extent of his contractual obligations before industrial action started which took the form of a work-to-rule. The employer responded by docking 20 per cent of the pay of those involved, including Norris, who had started to refuse the extra duties when the action started. When the action finished,

Norris continued to refuse the extra duties and the employer continued to dock 20 per cent of his pay. He brought a claim for unlawful deduction from wages, contrary to ERA s.13, but the employer relied on ERA s.14(5), which prevents a claim where the deduction is for taking part in industrial action, and this was upheld by an employment tribunal. As there was ample evidence that the claimant's grievance preceded the action and persisted afterwards, the EAT held that its decision was in error. Norris could not be regarded as still taking part in industrial action. He was not acting in concert with others to put pressure on the employer, even though there were other employees similarly refusing extra duties, for different reasons.

It may be surprising to find that the special regime for unfair dismissal and industrial action also applies to self-help actions by employers in industrial disputes—i.e. to lock-outs. A lock-out is where the employer responds to an industrial dispute by refusing to let the employees work—they are "locked out". This means that employees can be precluded from claiming not only when they have instigated industrial action, but also where it is the employer's initiative. It is not apparent why this should be the case: if the employer precipitates a dispute through insisting that workers accept some change to their contracts, why should this give the employer an immunity if it dismisses workers who will not agree? It actually makes it advantageous for an employer to be confrontational in introducing change.

There is no definition of the term "lock-out" in TULRCA, although there is a definition in ERA s.235(4), which deals with continuity of employment:

". . . 'lock-out' means—
  (a)   the closing of a place of employment,
  (b)   the suspension of work, or
  (c)   the refusal by an employer to continue to employ any number of persons employed by him in consequence of a dispute,

done with a view to compelling persons employed by the employer . . . to accept terms and conditions of or affecting employment."

In *Express & Star v Bunday* (1988) the Court of Appeal confirmed the widely held view that this definition was not applicable to other parts of the legislation, although it could be used for guidance, as could dictionary definitions. The issue in *Express & Star v Bunday* was whether there could be a lock-out where the employer was not acting in breach of contract. The Court of Appeal held that it was not necessary that the employer's action should be a breach of contract, although it might be a relevant consideration. Their conclusion was reached by parity of reasoning with the line that had already been taken in interpreting the phrase "industrial action" in *Power Packing Casemakers v Faust* (1983).

There can be difficulties in distinguishing industrial action from trade union **12–012** activities which, as we saw in Ch.10, receive special protection provided that they are carried out at an appropriate time. While it is clear from *Power Packing Casemakers v Faust* (1983) and *Express & Star v Bunday* (1988) that there can be industrial action or a lock-out without a breach of contract, in *Rasool v Hepworth Pipe Co* (1980), action in breach of contract was held to be a protected union activity! In this case there was a history of work at the factory being interrupted by unauthorised mass meetings of the workforce. The union convenor called a meeting although permission to do so had been refused. When the employees turned up, management representatives stood at the doors to tell them it was unauthorised. About half of the workers attended anyway, and they were all dismissed. In this case they were almost certainly acting in breach of contract yet the EAT held that it fell short of industrial action, saying rather that it was a union activity, for which time off was available under TULRCA s.170. Thus the tribunal had jurisdiction to hear their claims, although it was ultimately held that they had been fairly dismissed because they had not been taking part in union activities "at an appropriate time" (see above, para.10–010).

Finally, it should be noted that dismissals which are automatically unfair under ERA ss.98B, 99, 100, 101A(d), 103, 103A, 104C, 104D, 104E (dismissal in jury service, family, health and safety, working time, employee representative, protected disclosure, flexible working, pension scheme membership and study and training cases) are not to be taken as industrial action dismissals (TULRCA s.237(1A)). This is particularly relevant for health and safety dismissals (ERA s.100) where there might otherwise be a real risk that employees who refused to work in a dangerous situation could be regarded as taking industrial action (cf. *Lewis v Mason* (1994); *Balfour Kilpatrick Ltd v Acheson* (2003)).

Official and unofficial action

12–013 In its original meaning, official industrial action meant action which was called in accordance with the trade union's own rule-book. The rule-book would normally lay down who had authority to call strikes and other industrial action and whether any formalities had to be followed first. According to the House of Lords, the rule-book may be supplemented by custom and practice: in *Heatons Transport (St Helens) Ltd v TGWU* (1972) there was a docks dispute over containerisation. Shop stewards at Liverpool and Hull formed unofficial committees which blacked firms who acted contrary to the union's policy on this. The issue was whether the union was liable. The union argued that the stewards were acting on their own initiative and did not have authority under the union's rule-book to organise this action. The House of Lords held that the rule-book had to be interpreted in the light of custom and practice in the union. According to long-standing practice, shop stewards had implied authority to act on behalf of their members with quite a high degree of discretion. In these circumstances, given that the shop stewards were acting in accordance with union policy, the House of Lords held that the union was liable for the stewards' actions, which were within the scope of their implied authority.

Whether or not industrial action was official or unofficial used to be irrelevant to the position of individual employees taking action. They were no better off if the action had been properly called by union officers in accordance with all the requirements of the law than if it was a wildcat strike provoked for wholly inadequate reasons. However, this changed in 1982, when the Conservative Government decided to make unions liable in their own name for unlawful industrial action. That meant that it was necessary to decide for whose actions the union would be liable, and a statutory definition was devised which is somewhat wider than the common law (TULRCA s.20). Importantly, it also applies in relation to the law of unfair dismissal and industrial action, in that the law treats as "unofficial" any action which has not been authorised or endorsed by an official as defined by s.20 (regardless of what may be the position under the union's own rules).

Under TULRCA s.237 an employee who is dismissed while taking part in unofficial industrial action in this sense has no right to claim unfair dismissal even if dismissed selectively. An example of the harshness of this is provided by the Gate Gourmet dispute in 2005. The company, which had over 1,000 employees, prepared food for airlines at Heathrow airport. The workforce were concerned about the over-use of seasonal labour, and their discontent resulted in them leaving work and gathering in the canteen to discuss the issue on one particular day. All those in the canteen were dismissed, as was everyone else who failed to attend for work over the next few days—some 600 people altogether. As the action was unofficial at that stage, none of those participating could bring unfair dismissal claims. The company later took back most, but by no means all, of the workers it had dismissed—but the grounds for its selection could not be subject to investigation by an employment tribunal (*Sehmi v Gate Gourmet Ltd* (2009)).

It is therefore very important to know whether the industrial action has been authorised or endorsed by a relevant officer or organ of the union. The categories stipulated in TULRCA s.20 are: a person authorised by the union's rules for this purpose; the principal executive committee of the union; the president or general secretary of the union; any other committee of the union; and any other union official (whether or not employed by the union). In the case of the last two categories ("any other committee" and "any other official") the union may repudiate the authorisation or endorsement, provided that it acts in accordance with the procedure laid down in TULRCA s.21 (see further below, para.13–032). The employees have one day's grace before the action is then treated as unofficial.

12–014

While most industrial action is organised by trade unions and involves union members, it is possible for non-unionised workers to go on strike, or for non-members to join in action with unionists. If no one taking part in the industrial action is a union member then TULRCA s.237 has no application. However, if there is unofficial action involving non-members and members, it is treated as unofficial in relation to them all. This may seem unfair on the non-members, but is to stop members trying to avoid the impact of s.237 by suddenly resigning their membership.

Protected official action

Assuming that employees are taking part in official action in the sense discussed above, it now becomes necessary to consider whether it is protected under TULRCA s.238A, which was introduced by ERelA 1999 and amended in important ways by ERelA 2004. The basic idea behind TULRCA s.238A is that employees should be protected from dismissal if they are taking part in official, lawfully organised industrial action which has not been unduly protracted. The employer

12–015

cannot actually be prevented from dismissing the employees, but if the conditions in s.238A are met, such dismissals will be automatically unfair.

There are two conditions for TULRCA s.238A to apply. The first is that the employee should be taking part in "protected industrial action", meaning that the action is official and has been lawfully organised so that it will have immunity within the meaning of TULRCA s.219 (considered below, para.13–002) (TULRCA s.238A(1)). The second condition is that the reason or principal reason for the dismissal is that the employee took part in the industrial action (TULRCA s.238A(2)). This is a departure from TULRCA ss.237 and 238 which concentrate on the timing of the dismissal rather than the reason for it. Those sections apply only where the employee is dismissed *while* taking part in industrial action, and this wording was chosen so that tribunals would only have to establish an objective fact rather than the employer's subjective state of mind. Presumably the burden of proving the reason for the dismissal under s.238A will be on the employee, which may cause difficulties, although tribunals will probably be willing to draw appropriate inferences from the known facts about the industrial action.

Once these two conditions have been met, TULRCA s.238A sets out three situations where the dismissal will be automatically unfair. The first is where the dismissal occurs within "the protected period" (s.238A(3)), defined as "the basic period" plus any "extension period" (s.238A(7A)–(7D)). The protected period was originally set at eight weeks from the start of the industrial action, but was extended by ERelA 2004 to 12 weeks ("the basic period"), and made exclusive of any period of lock-out, so that if the employer locks out workers, an "extension period" equivalent to the length of the lock-out is added to the basic 12-week period. The second situation is where the dismissal occurs after the protected period, but the employee had stopped taking action within the protected period (s.238A(4)). The third situation is where the dismissal occurs after the protected period and the employee was still participating in the action but the employer has not "taken such procedural steps as would have been reasonable for the purposes of resolving the dispute" (s.238A(5)). The sorts of procedural steps to which tribunals should have regard are set out in s.238A(6): whether relevant collective agreements have been complied with; whether either side has offered to take part in negotiations; and whether either side has unreasonably refused a request from the other to make use of conciliation or mediation services. The substantive merits of the dispute are not to be taken into account (s.238A(7)).

12–016   Section 238A of TULRCA marks an important step forward in employees' rights. It is astonishing to think that until this provision was passed an employee could always be dismissed without redress even if provoked into industrial action by the employer's intransigence and even if acting entirely lawfully. Indeed, workers found it particularly illogical that the organisation of industrial action was hedged about with detailed rules, but that compliance with them was of no benefit to individuals. The Government's hope was that the new section would provide an incentive for employers and unions to settle disputes within a short period of starting, but there was a risk it could backfire and encourage employers to sit out the protected period and then dismiss striking workers. By the time of the Government's review of the ERA 1999 in 2003 only one case had reached a tribunal under the new law, concerning a two-year dispute at a car parts manufacturer in Wales (Friction Dynamics), which led the TUC to argue that TULRCA s.237A should be extended to provide indefinite protection for workers where the action was lawfully called. The Government stated at that time that it proposed no change to the eight-week period, noting that statistics for the previous three years indicated that 90 per cent of disputes settled within this timeframe. However, arguments for a slightly longer period ultimately prevailed, together with some attention to the lock-out anomaly. Another amendment arising from the Friction Dynamics dispute attempts to address the problem of the employer who merely goes through the motions in any kind of concili-ation or mediation process, in order to tick the "procedural steps" box where dismissing workers outside the protected period. Thus ERelA 2004 inserted new TULRCA s.237B which attempts, in nine subsections, to specify the behaviour which would constitute engaging in good faith in the conciliation or mediation process, and instructs tribunals to take account of these matters also in deciding whether reasonable procedural steps have been taken. Whether one's admira-tion for the heroic attempt at drafting should outweigh one's sympathy for the tribunal which has to apply TULRCA s.237B is a difficult call.

There remains an anomaly in that workers taking part even in protected offi-cial industrial action do not receive protection from detriment short of dismissal. During 2009–10 British Airways became engaged in a bitter dispute over the company's decision to reduce the number of cabin crew members on long-haul flights, leading to two short strikes. The company responded by removing their access to travel concessions for themselves and their families which had always been "perks" of the job. As these were non-contractual benefits, it seemed unlikely that legal action could be taken to get these restored. An attempt to test the compatibility of this position with ECHR art.11 was taken to the European Court of Human Rights, but failed because it was lodged out of time.

Other dismissals

Where employees are dismissed for industrial action which is not "unofficial", so that TULRCA s.237 does not apply, the next question must be whether s.238A applies. If it does not, perhaps because the industrial action is not protected within the meaning of TULRCA s.219 or because it has lasted for longer than the protected period and the proviso in s.238A(5) does not apply, then TULRCA s.238 comes into play. This section retains the basic concept that employers will not be liable for unfair dismissal unless they have selectively dismissed or re-engaged employees taking part in the same action. It applies to an employee who, at the date of the dismissal, was taking part in a strike or other industrial action, or was "locked out" by the employer. Such an employee may only claim for unfair dismissal if other relevant employees have not been dismissed or, if they were dismissed, have later been re-engaged.

Who are relevant employees?

Essentially the purpose of TULRCA s.238 is to allow the fairness of the dismissal to be reviewed if those taking part in the action are not treated in the same

12–017

12–018

way. Thus "relevant employees" originally meant those employed by the same employer who had taken part in the industrial action. However, in the first case to reach the House of Lords, an anomaly was discovered.

In *Stock v Frank Jones (Tipton) Ltd* (1978) about 35 employees came out on strike. Two returned to work after two weeks, but the others remained out. Three months later all those still on strike were dismissed. Of course, the employer had not dismissed the two who had gone back. It was held that they were "relevant employees" because they had originally taken part in the action. Thus all the rest had the right to claim unfair dismissal.

As a result the law was amended so that in relation to strikes and other industrial action, "relevant employees" must still be taking part in the action at the time of the complainant's dismissal. This enables an employer to act on an ultimatum, by dismissing everyone not returning to work by a certain date, without facing unfair dismissal claims from those who do not return. In turn this provides a good reason for an employer not to react to industrial action by immediately dismissing all those taking part.

12–019   In relation to a lock-out the definition of relevant employees is wider: it includes all employees "directly interested" in the dispute. It is for this reason that it may be very important to know whether the action is a strike or a lock-out. In *Campey v Bellwood* (1987) the company was trying to insist on new working conditions. Faced with the threat of industrial action organised by the workers' union, the company suspended its operations altogether. A week later, all those who would not accept the new terms were dismissed. If they had been taking part in industrial action, they would not have been able to claim, for it was only the ones still holding out who were dismissed. However, it was held to be a lock-out, and "relevant employees" therefore meant all those who had been suspended, including those who had accepted the new terms and had been kept on. Thus the sacked workers could claim unfair dismissal.

It may be difficult to know whether a particular worker, alleged to be a "relevant employee", was taking part in the action or not. In *Coates v Modern Methods and Materials* (1982) L refused to cross a picket line on the first day of the strike because she was frightened of abuse. The following day she fortuitously went down with back trouble which put her out of action for the duration of the strike. Those who were dismissed claimed that she was a "relevant employee" who had not been dismissed. But had she taken part in the action? The Court of Appeal held that she had, by refusing to cross the picket line. Her motives were irrelevant: the test of taking part was objective, according to the actions of the employee rather than her private thoughts. This was applied in *Wood Group Engineering v Byrne* (1993), where an employee who originally joined a strike and sit-in on an offshore oil platform telephoned his employer and said he wanted to cease and come ashore. The employers instructed him to stay and act as an informant about what was going on aboard the platform. Ultimately the other employees taking part were dismissed. They lodged unfair dismissal claims alleging that the informant was a relevant employee who had not been dismissed. Using the objective test, that the employee's actions, not his private intentions, are to be considered, the EAT held that the informant was a "relevant employee" (see also *Sehmi v Gate Gourmet Ltd* (2009) and *Norris v London Fire and Emergency Planning Authority* (2013)).

In *McCormick v Horsepower* (1981) an employee who had initially refused to cross a picket line was claimed as a comparator by those strikers who had been dismissed. However, before the hearing he had been made redundant. The Court of Appeal held that because he had been dismissed too, there was no jurisdiction to hear the others' complaints. It did not matter that he had been dismissed for redundancy rather than for taking part in the action. This decision led to another anomaly in the legislation, so far unaltered. In *P&O Ferries v Byrne* (1989) about 1,000 seafarers dismissed by the company following an extensive and bitter dispute claimed unfair dismissal. Although the company argued that it had dismissed everyone involved in the action, the seafarers said that at least one person had been overlooked. The company asked for this person's name to be revealed to them before the hearing—a reasonable request, as it was crucial to their side of the case. The seafarers refused for fear that the company would sack the man—and thus torpedo their one thousand claims! Recognising that the employer could do that, the Court of Appeal nonetheless ordered disclosure of the relevant employee's name.

Another amendment introduced in 1982 to make it easier for employers to avoid this kind of mishap limits "relevant employees" to those employed "at the same establishment" as the complainant. So if a company has a strike at both its Leeds and Manchester plants, and decides to use the opportunity to close down the Manchester plant, those employees cannot claim unfair dismissal on the grounds that the Leeds people are still employed. Note, however, *Bigham v GKN Kwikform Ltd* (1992), where a dismissed striker later obtained a job with another branch of the company. He had not concealed or lied about the earlier dismissal. When, four weeks later, the employers realised what had happened, they dismissed him—but the fact that he had been re-engaged, however briefly, meant that the other strikers were entitled to claim. **12–020**

Where employees dismissed for taking part in industrial action are able to bring claims under TULRCA s.238, it does not follow that their dismissals are bound to be unfair. This will be judged according to all the circumstances, and thus involves the tribunal to some extent considering the merits of the dispute. In *Sehmi v Gate Gourmet Ltd* (2009) some employees were able to bring unfair dismissal claims because they had ceased to take part in industrial action at the time of their dismissal. However, the EAT regarded it as "plain beyond argument" that their dismissals were fair and within the range of reasonable responses for the employer in circumstances where a large number of employees had withdrawn labour in a manner liable to do serious damage to the employer. This was despite the fact that there had been no investigation as to why some and not others had been dismissed for participation in the same action.

Even where dismissal for industrial action is held to be unfair it may be argued that compensation should be reduced for contributory conduct. In *Tracey v Crosville Wales Ltd* (1998) the House of Lords held that mere participation in a strike would not justify a reduction in compensation: there would have to be blameworthy conduct over and above just taking part. Nor would leading the strike amount to such blameworthy conduct, if the leader acted reasonably and not in an "over-hasty and inflammatory" manner.

Time limits

12–021 The usual limitation period requiring a claim to be made within three months of dismissal has to be modified for TULRCA s.238 dismissals, to cover the possibility that the employer might dismiss all the strikers, but then take some of them back. As originally worded, if the employer ever took back someone dismissed for industrial action, this immediately triggered a right for the others to claim, even if it was months or years later. In 1982 this was amended in two ways. First, the claimant may only claim if the relevant employee was re-engaged within three months of having been dismissed, and secondly, the claimant may not in any case claim if it is more than six months since her own dismissal unless it was not reasonably practicable to do so earlier (TULRCA s.239).

Conclusion

12–022 The ILO Committee on Freedom of Association held in 1991 that UK law on dismissals in connection with industrial action contravened ILO Conventions. Since then there has been a major step forward in the protection of individuals through the introduction of TULRCA s.238A. However, it could be argued that the protection is still inadequate. Why should the individual's protection depend, for example, on whether her union has managed successfully to negotiate all the hurdles which are still necessary for industrial action to be lawful? How can she be sure whether this is the case or not? A good argument could be made for saying that individuals should be protected where they take action which they believe in good faith to have been officially organised by their trade union. Finally, the new law still has not removed the anomaly which permits an employee to be dismissed for industrial action even if she is not committing a breach of her contract of employment.

The Right to Organise Industrial Action

12–023 Since freedom of the individual precludes directly ordering strikers to return to work, direct control over industrial action has been exercised over those who organise it, by making them liable for the consequences. Strikes and other kinds of industrial action are pretty well bound to disrupt the commercial and social life of people not directly involved in the dispute. The first question about liability is therefore about remoteness—at what point do we regard the consequences as being too far away from the action to hold the organisers responsible? It has been left to the common law to answer this question. The next question is one of policy: if we are persuaded that some level of industrial action must be permitted, it is necessary to relieve the organisers of strikes from liability which they would otherwise have. How far are we prepared to go in granting that relief? Or, to put it in more familiar terms, how far should unions and their members have immunity from liability for otherwise unlawful acts because they are taking part in industrial action?

The debate about industrial action in the United Kingdom has been cast in these terms since the beginning of the twentieth century. It may be noted that it is not the only way of dealing with this issue. In other common law jurisdictions, for example, the United States, the common law of contract and tort is largely irrelevant in industrial disputes: instead there is a statutory code enforced principally through a special body—the National Labor Relations Board—which reflects the current consensus on the limits of acceptable action in industrial disputes. There is a body of opinion which believes that something similar is required here too.

The pattern of immunity granted by statute from liability which would exist at common law was fixed in England following the famous case, *Taff Vale Railway v Amalgamated Society of Railway Servants* in 1901. The facts of the case were ordinary enough: a union official was dismissed by the company, as a result of which the workforce came out on strike, and picketed the company's railway station when replacement labour was being brought in. What made this case special was that the company sued the union, not its officials. Until that time it had been thought that a union could not be sued in its own name (see above, para.10–029). Prior to *Taff Vale,* therefore, the strategy of employers faced with strike action had been to sue named officials—the top people in the union—for an injunction requiring them to call off the action. As they were being sued as individuals there was little point in pursuing a damages claim against them because they would be likely to have only limited means. This state of affairs had worked reasonably well, for if an injunction was obtained against an official, although it could theoretically be ignored by other individuals, in practice the union played ball and acted in accordance with the order.

However, in *Taff Vale* the union was sued, and the House of Lords, albeit with **12–024** less than total clarity, held that unions had a sufficient legal existence to be sued in their own right. This was a body blow to trade unions, for it meant that their funds were now exposed to damages claims from employers following a dispute, since, as already remarked, any strike action was very likely to cause breaches of contracts and other wrongs. The controversy caused by the decision ensured that it was one of the issues in the 1906 General Election. The Liberal Party came to power, with the assistance of a pact with the nascent Labour Party, committed to restoring the situation where unions could organise industrial action without risking bankruptcy each time. This could have been done by a statutory code giving unions a protected right to strike in defined circumstances: but it was not. Instead, the Trade Disputes Act 1906 gave trade unions a complete immunity from all actions in tort, and gave individuals (officials, members and others) a partial immunity from actions in tort, provided that they were acting in contemplation or furtherance of a trade dispute. While the scope of the immunity has changed considerably over the years, this remains the basic pattern of the law today except for one major modification. In 1982 the total immunity from actions in tort enjoyed by trade unions was abolished. Today they are liable on the same basis as individuals, and so from that date on we see case references containing the names of unions as defendants rather than their presidents or general secretaries.

In 1971, a new Conservative Government, elected with a commitment to reducing union power, attempted to break the mould by providing a new, entirely statutory, code to deal with trade unions and industrial action: the Industrial Relations Act 1971. This was deeply unpopular with unions and contained technical defects which made it possible for unions to circumvent its provisions without acting illegally. It is generally accepted that it tried to do too much too soon. Its failure, and the consequent industrial unrest, were important factors in the defeat of that Government and its replacement by a Labour Government, whose first action was to repeal the Industrial Relations Act, and to replace it with the Trade Union and Labour Relations Act 1974 (TULRA).

TULRA was intended to put the law back into the pre-1971 position, although it differed from the 1906 Act in significant respects. The basic immunities contained in it were heavily amended and modified by the Employment Acts 1980–90, the Trade Union Act 1984 and the Trade Union Reform and Employment Rights Act 1993 (TURERA). Having learned from the mistakes of the Industrial Relations Act, the Conservative Government of the 1980s adopted different tactics in dealing with unions: the strategy was to introduce changes a bit at a time—a major Act at two-yearly intervals, each introducing new restrictions on industrial action. This proved more successful than the attempt at overnight wholesale revolution. The changes were consolidated in the TULRCA, but almost immediately another wave of restrictive reforms was pushed through in TURERA, with the result that TULRCA was substantially amended almost before the ink was dry. The Labour Government, elected in 1997, always made it clear that it had no intention of implementing a wholesale repeal of Conservative legislation, as many trade unionists wanted. In its White Paper, *Fairness at Work*, preceding the EReIA 1999, the Government made play of the fact that even after the reforms it did propose, the United Kingdom would still have tougher laws on industrial action than any of the other Member States of the European Union. Thus the Employment Relations Acts 1999–2004 made minor rather than major modifications to the law on organising industrial action. The Coalition Government 2010–2015 focused on reducing levels of employment protection for individuals in the name of increased economic efficiency, but the Conservative administration elected in 2015 has returned once more to the tactics of the 1980s, to reduce further the scope for lawful industrial action, as we will see.

12–025   While the pattern of the law is understandable given its history, the result of this rather piecemeal development is that it is a complicated process to decide whether a particular campaign of industrial action is lawful or not. The question must be unpacked into a number of stages. First, you must ask whether or not the action involves any sort of wrong at common law. If it does, the second question is whether it is covered by the basic immunity contained in TULRCA s.219. If not, there is liability. If it is protected by s.219, the third question is whether the immunity has been lost for some other reason. There are numerous ways in which immunity can be lost: because the action involves unprotected secondary action, because there has not been a proper ballot, and so on. Balloting has assumed even greater importance in recent years in that if a ballot has not been held, union members or even unconnected third parties may be able to stop industrial action even when it does not involve common law wrongs. In what follows, each stage will be looked at in turn. We will start by looking at whether industrial action involves any common law wrongs, and if so, whether TULRCA s.219 gives immunity. The principal torts on which the employer is likely to rely are those which allege unlawful interference with contracts—and, as we will see, it will usually be necessary to show that the union has brought about breaches of contracts of employment by the workforce.

Liability in tort

The torts which are most likely to be committed in the course of an industrial dispute are usually called the "economic torts". Broadly speaking, they normally involve deliberate action designed to cause economic loss to the claimant. While economic loss has traditionally not been recoverable in tort for negligence, it is recoverable here because the action causing loss is intentional. During a campaign of industrial action it is quite possible for other torts to be committed as well as economic ones: picketing, in particular, may involve trespass and public nuisance at least, and also crimes such as obstruction of the highway. Picketing is therefore dealt with separately after the rest of the discussion of industrial action (see below, para.13–037).

12–026

In *OBG v Allan* (2008), the House of Lords engaged in a ground-breaking reconceptualisation of the economic torts, in the context of three joined cases which had nothing to do with the law of industrial action. The discussion which follows takes account of the reclassification there proposed.

Inducement of breach of contract

We have already seen that a strike is usually a breach of contract by the workforce. Knowingly to induce someone to break a contract to the detriment of the other party to that contract was recognised as a tort actionable at the suit of the third party in *Lumley v Gye* (1853). Lumley had engaged the opera singer, Johanna Wagner, to sing exclusively at his theatre in London. The defendant, Gye, offered her more money to sing at his theatre, causing her to break her contract with Lumley. Naturally, Johanna Wagner was liable to Lumley for breach of a contract for services (*Lumley v Wagner* (1852), dealing with his remedy, is discussed above at para.8–014). The point is, however, that Gye was held liable to Lumley in tort for bringing about that breach of contract.

12–027

This tort is very likely to occur in industrial disputes in this form in two main situations: first, where a union in dispute with an employer calls out the workforce, thus inducing them to break their contracts of employment with the employer. At common law, the union would be liable to the employer for this, in the same way that Gye was liable to Lumley. The second situation is where the union has a dispute with a worker (perhaps because the worker refuses to join the union) and the union persuades the employer to sack the worker in breach of contract.

Note that if the union persuades the employer to sack the worker without a breach of contract, this tort is not committed—see *Allen v Flood* (1898), although it may involve the tort of causing loss by unlawful means, discussed below. Similarly, lawfully persuading people not to make commercial contracts with the employer does not induce any breach of contract. This is illustrated by *Middlebrook Mushrooms v TGWU* (1993). Employees dismissed by the company in a dispute over a pay cut picketed supermarkets supplied by the company in order to dissuade supermarket customers from buying Middlebrook mushrooms. The company argued that this would deter the supermarkets from performing contracts with them and that the pressure amounted to inducing breach of contract. The argument was rejected by the Court of Appeal because the persuasion was clearly aimed at the customers, not the supermarkets. At most, therefore, it could only have constituted an indirect inducement, and in these circumstances it was not tortious because no unlawful means had been used.

12–028   The elements of the tort of inducing breach of contract were restated in *OBG v Allan* (2008). At this point, the facts of the three cases in the joined appeal need to be outlined. Interestingly, only one involved an employment dispute, and that was not to do with industrial action. In the first case, *OBG v Allan*, receivers were appointed to a company under a floating charge which turned out to be invalid. Before they knew this they sold company property. The company therefore sued them for conversion, and also for the tort of interference with contractual relations (the issue of interest to us). The second case was *Douglas v Hello! Ltd*, which involved *Hello!* magazine spoiling *OK!* magazine's exclusive coverage of the wedding of Michael Douglas and Catherine Zeta-Jones by printing photographs taken by an undercover photographer posing as a waiter. *OK!* claimed that this was the tort of interference with contractual relations by unlawful means. Finally, in *Mainstream Properties Ltd v Young*, two employees of the appellant company had diverted a development opportunity which should have gone to the company to a different joint venture in which they had a personal interest—in breach of their contractual duty of good faith. The defendant had provided finance for the joint venture, and was sued by the company for inducing the employees' breach of contract.

Giving the leading speech in the House of Lords, Lord Hoffmann identified three elements of the tort of inducing breach of contract. First, the defendant must know of the contract; secondly, he must intend to procure a breach of it, and thirdly, it must be shown that a breach of the contract actually occurred.

Knowledge

12–029   For this tort to be committed, clearly the defendant must be aware of the contract between the person persuaded or prevented and the claimant. For example, suppose company A interviews B and offers her a job to start the next day, but unknown to A, B already has a job and is contractually obliged to give a month's notice. If B goes to work for A in breach of her existing contract, it would be unreasonable to make A liable to the other employer. But what if A knows that B has another job, but not the terms about notice? In other words, what degree of knowledge of the broken contract will fix the defendant with liability? In *OBG v Allan* the House of Lords stated that knowing that you are inducing an act which (whether you realise it or not) constitutes a breach is not enough: you must actually appreciate that it will have this effect. However, the House of Lords also approved the Court of Appeal's statement in *Emerald Construction v Lowthian* (1966) that wilful blindness as to whether the contract can be lawfully terminated or not will suffice.

A lesser degree of knowledge was required in *Merkur Island Shipping v Laughton* (1983), where the union had blacked, and therefore effectively block-aded, a ship in Liverpool docks. The House of Lords held that the union must be deemed to know of the almost certain existence of commercial contracts which would be broken if a fully laden ship could not leave port, and that this degree of knowledge was sufficient. This was quite a significant relaxation of the requirement. It is true that anyone would expect contracts to carry the goods on board the ship to be disrupted by the blockade. But that was not the kind of contract which the union was sued for disrupting. That contract was the charter contract between the shipowners (who brought the action) and the charterers of the vessel, who had themselves sub-chartered the vessel to the firm which was actually operating it at the time of the blacking. It is by no means obvious that a union would be aware of these rather complex arrangements. The result of this decision seems to be that knowledge that some contract will be disrupted will suffice for liability, even if the defendant is wholly unaware of the particular contract whose breach is alleged to have been procured. In reality, it is very dif-ficult for unions to escape knowledge, since it is standard practice for employers to send copies of relevant contract provisions to trade unions at once.

This did not happen in *TimePlan Education Group Ltd v NUT* (1997), where the NUT asked the New Zealand teaching union to consider whether it was appro-priate to publish TimePlan's advertisements in the union journal, given that TimePlan was in dispute with the NUT over its rates of pay to supply teachers. The New Zealand union withdrew the advertisements in breach of its contract with TimePlan. The trial judge held that the NUT was liable for inducing the breach of contract as it must have realised that the advertisements were placed in pursu-ance of a contract. The Court of Appeal allowed the NUT's appeal: the union had not been expressly informed of the contract and would not necessarily have inferred that because advertisements had appeared, there was a contract in existence for future advertisements. Importantly, the Court of Appeal was not prepared to entertain an argument that the union was "put on notice" of the pos-sibility of there being a contract and therefore should have made further inquiries.

In *Mainstream Properties v Young* (2008) the defendant had honestly not **12–030** realised that what the employees were doing was a breach of their contracts of employment. The House of Lords held that the question of whether he ought reasonably to have done so was beside the point: he was therefore not liable for the tort of inducing breach of contract. This suggests that *Metropolitan Borough of Solihull v NUT* (1985) should now be regarded as wrongly decided.

Intention

In relation to intention, the House of Lords held in *OBG v Allan* that it would be **12–031** enough if the defendant knew that the contract would be broken, even if this was not an end in itself for the defendant, but simply the means of attaining some other end which the defendant desired. However, as Lord Diplock pointed out in *Merkur Island Shipping v Laughton* (1983), the breach of contract is frequently the desired and intended outcome in industrial action cases. In the cases before it, the House of Lords held on this ground that the defendant receivers in *OBG v Allan* were not liable because they had made an honest mistake. They had no intention to bring about breaches of contract, nor to injure the claimant company.

Breach of contract

12–032   It is in relation to the last requirement, that the inducement should actually bring about a breach of contract, that the decision in *OBG v Allan* (2008) represents a break with the past. Prior to that case, a body of opinion had developed to the effect that the named economic torts, including inducing breach of contract, could all be regarded as specific examples of a more general tort of interference with contractual rights. Lord Hoffmann describes this in the case as "the unified theory". However, the House of Lords in *OBG v Allan* held that the tort of inducing breach of contract is conceptually distinct from the tort of causing loss by unlawful means. In the first tort, no unlawful means are used to bring about the breach, unless the inducement itself is to be regarded as unlawful—and to rely on that as unlawful means would involve circular reasoning. Another way of putting it, also found in the speeches of the House of Lords, is to say that the tort of inducing breach of contract involves accessory liability—the defendant can only be liable for inducing a breach if the contract-breaker has primary liability for breach of contract, as Johanna Wagner did in *Lumley v Gye* (1853).

It follows from this that the apparent "extension" of the tort of inducing breach of contract to situations where there was interference with the expected performance, but without an actual breach occurring was misguided and must now be regarded as wrong. This "extension" occurred in *Torquay Hotel v Cousins* (1969). In this case the TGWU were in dispute with hotel owners who refused to recognise the union. The union informed Esso that a particular hotel was blacked and that fuel supplies to it should stop. Esso, most of whose drivers belonged to the TGWU, made no attempt to deliver oil to the hotel. There was *a force majeure* clause in their contract with the hotel, so they were not liable for this. The Court of Appeal held that it was tortious to induce a substantial interference with the contract.

Inducing interference with contract short of a breach had been recognised as a cause of action many times since *Torquay Hotel v Cousins* and it was actually interference rather than breach which was alleged in *Merkur Island Shipping v Laughton* (1983). In *OBG v Allan* the House of Lords expressly said that *Merkur Island*, although a House of Lords' decision, should not be followed in so far as it holds that inducing an actual breach of contract is not a necessary ingredient of the tort of inducing breach of contract. Thus *Torquay Hotel v Cousins* (1969) and the line of cases following it should also no longer be regarded as good law.

Justification

There is some slight authority for the view that there may be a defence to this tort if the defendant was justified in inducing the breach. Thus in *Brimelow v Casson* (1924) it was alleged that the manager of the King Wu Tut Tut Revue chorus girls paid them such low wages that they were forced to resort to prostitution. The union which induced theatres to cancel their bookings with this rogue was held to have a defence of justification to his action for inducing breach of contract. The point was not discussed in *OBG v Allan* (2008). However, the defence had not been accepted in the earlier, less exotic case, *South Wales Miners' Federation v Glamorgan Coal Co* (1905) where the union pleaded entirely disinterested motives of safeguarding its members' interests in preventing a further reduction in their wages. "Therefore it seems that if the chorus girls in *Brimelow v Casson* had not been living in immorality, but had merely been living a life of chaste starvation, no defence of justification would have been available" (J. Riddall, *The Law of Industrial Relations*, Butterworths, London, 1982). In general it would appear that the defence has no practical relevance in industrial disputes. **12–033**

The statutory immunity

Unions or individuals who organise action which induces a breach of a contract, whether a contract of employment or a commercial contract, are protected by TULRCA s.219(1)(a) provided that they act in contemplation or furtherance of a trade dispute. **12–034**

Causing loss by unlawful means

Causing loss by unlawful means was explained by the House of Lords in *OBG v Allan* (2008) as having its origins in old cases such as *Tarleton v M'Gawley* (1793), where both the claimant and defendant were slave traders dealing off Africa. When a boat from the local community set out from the shore to deal with the claimant's ship, the defendant shot at them, which had the desired effect of deterring them from doing business with that ship and encouraging them to do business with the defendant's ship instead. Note that the defendant's action was not unlawful *vis-à-vis* the claimant; it was enough that the defendant acted to the claimant's detriment because of his unlawful threat to the local traders. It was the use of unlawful means that made this tortious: not any question of an intention to harm the defendant. This was the important principle established in *Allen v Flood* (1898), that an otherwise lawful act does not become unlawful because of intention. **12–035**

The tort exemplified by *Tarleton v M'Gawley* became known as the tort of intimidation. As the name "intimidation" and the facts of *Tarleton v M'Gawley* suggest, it was generally thought that this tort was applicable in situations where one party was put in fear of violence. It was unknown in the sphere of industrial action until the House of Lords' decision in *Rookes v Barnard* (1964). R was employed by BOAC, and had resigned from his union, the AESD. The union had a closed shop at this workplace, and so it threatened BOAC with strike action if R was not dismissed. The company bowed to this pressure and dismissed R in accordance with the terms of his contract. Since BOAC committed no breach of contract by dismissing R, he could not sue the union for inducing a breach of contract. The House of Lords held that the union had, however, committed the tort of intimidation: they had threatened the employer, who had therefore acted to the claimant's detriment. What was the unlawful act? It was the threat that employees would break their contracts of employment. Lord Devlin said, "I find . . . nothing to differentiate a threat of breach of contract from a threat of physical violence . . .".

The introduction of intimidation to industrial disputes by the decision in *Rookes v Barnard* was highly significant. For unions, it was an example of the inadequacies of a system of immunities as a way of safeguarding the right to strike. A system of immunities only works if there is a settled body of liability from which one is immune. But the economic torts were here shown, not for the first time, to be far from settled. Until 1964 there had been no immunity from liability for intimidation because it was not thought to be relevant in trade disputes. That is why it was used in *Rookes v Barnard*. The result was that the following year the Trade Disputes Act 1965 was passed to provide immunity in these circumstances (an immunity now contained in TULRCA s.219(1)(b)).

12–036   However, in *OBG v Allan* (2008) Lord Hoffmann rewrote history somewhat. He considered that the tort of causing loss by unlawful means had existed at least since *Allen v Flood* (1898), albeit not always well-recognised. The use of the term "intimidation", introduced by an early edition of *Salmond on Torts*, had obscured this fact by focusing on the use of threats of violence in *Tarleton v M'Gawley*. On this reading, the decision in *Rookes v Barnard* (1964) should not have come as a surprise—although quite clearly, it did. There was no recognition in the case, nor when the Trade Disputes Act 1965 was passed, that this was just a species of causing loss by unlawful means.

Nonetheless, the law must now be taken to be settled that causing loss by unlawful means encompasses what used to be known as the tort of intimidation. The converse is also true: there is no tort of interference with contract or interference with trade or business absent the use of unlawful means.

What, then, are the necessary elements of the tort of causing loss by unlawful means? Lord Hoffmann in *OBG v Allan* (2008) considered that there were just two conditions. First, that there is a wrongful interference with the actions of a third party in which the claimant has an economic interest. Secondly, that the defendant has an intention to cause loss to the claimant by this means. Thus *Rookes v Barnard* (1964) can be explained as the union intending to cause loss to the pilot (condition 2) and doing so by threatening BOAC with breaches of contracts of employment (strike action) (which constituted the wrongful interference). The claimant pilot had an economic interest in the third party (BOAC) because it was how he derived his livelihood.

12–037   This formulation can be applied to explain the decisions in older cases which used to be analysed as indirect versions of the tort of inducement of breach of contract. Thus in *JT Stratford Ltd v Lindley* (1965) the defendants were officials of the Watermen's Union. They called on their members not to handle barges belonging to the claimant company, because of that company's refusal to engage in negotiation with the union. This was a breach of the watermen's contracts of employment with their employer, the Port of London Authority, and caused the PLA to be in breach of a commercial contract with the claimant company. Here, the PLA is the third party in which the claimant has an economic interest (the commercial contract to move the barges) and it is wrongfully interfered with by the union committing the tort of inducing breach of contract by persuading their members to take blacking action, thus fulfilling condition 1. The union's intention is to cause loss to the claimant, satisfying condition 2.

Unlawful means

The crucial question then becomes, what will count as unlawful means for the purposes of this tort? The majority of the House of Lords in *OBG v Allan* (2008) considered that it would have to be something actionable at the suit of the third party who is used as the instrument of getting at the claimant, although including in that things which would be actionable by that third party were it not for the fact that he had suffered no loss (which would frequently be the case in intimidation situations). It must be something which interferes with the freedom of the third party to deal with the claimant. In the view of the majority, an action which was wrongful *vis-à-vis* the third party but did not interfere with his freedom to deal with the claimant would not amount to unlawful means, even if intended to damage the claimant. Thus in *Douglas v Hello! Ltd* the House of Lords held that the defendant magazine was not liable because, while they may have had the intention of causing loss to *OK!* magazine, no unlawful means had been used by the defendant. It is true that the photographer who took the unauthorised pictures was a trespasser—but he was not an agent of the magazine. He had acted as an independent freelancer, who sold the photographs afterwards.

12–038

Intention

In relation to intention, the House of Lords in *OBG v Allan* applied a similar test to that used in inducing breach of contract—except that for the tort of causing loss by unlawful means, the intention would have to be to cause the loss, whereas in the first tort, the intention is to bring about the breach of contract. Thus, if there is no intention to cause loss, but that is a foreseeable consequence of using unlawful means, Lord Hoffmann considered that there would be no liability for causing loss by unlawful means. He expressed the view that Henry J was right, therefore, in *Barretts & Baird v IPCS* (1987) to reject the claim of an abattoir for losses caused to it by a civil servants' strike, because they could not get the licences they needed to conduct their business. This is probably necessary to keep tortious liability within bounds—the potential claimants damaged by strike action would otherwise be virtually limitless. If so, this further suggests that *Falconer v ASLEF* (1986), where a hero of the commuting classes successfully sued the railway unions when he was stranded overnight in London by a rail strike, was wrongly decided. It should be noted, however, that in this kind of scenario, other affected parties might be able to use the so-called "Citizens' Charter" right which enables third parties who are not the intended victims of industrial action to sue to restrain it in some circumstances (see below, para.13–014).

12–039

The statutory immunity

12–040 Unions or individuals who organise action which causes loss by unlawful means are protected by TULRCA s.219(1) provided that they act in contemplation or furtherance of a trade dispute.

Conspiracy

12–041 The source of union strength is the power to act in combination. Hence it is hardly surprising to find that conspiracy, a crime and a tort which also depends on combination, should be used against trade unions. In the early nineteenth century, trade unions were by their very existence regarded as criminal conspiracies. This criminal liability was effectively removed by the Trade Union Act 1871, which legalised trade unions. The possibility of tortious liability, however, remained. There are two forms of this tort: conspiracy to injure, and conspiracy to use unlawful means.

Conspiracy to injure

12–042 Liability for conspiracy to injure is incurred where two or more combine with the intention of harming the plaintiff, even though they use lawful means to do so. Thus an action which would be lawful if done by one person becomes unlawful because it is done by more than one. This has been described as anomalous: if an action is all right for one person, how can it be wrong just because it is done by more than one? The usual rationale is that there is strength in numbers. You may not be damaged if, say, your business is boycotted by one person; but if it is boycotted by many, you may be forced to close down.

> "But to suggest today that acts done by one street-corner grocer in concert with a second are more oppressive and dangerous to a competitor than the same acts done by a string of supermarkets under a single ownership . . . is to shut one's eyes to what has been happening in the business and industrial world since the turn of the century" (*per* Lord Diplock in *Lonrho v Shell* (1982)).

The force of numbers argument prevailed, however, in the case which established this liability, *Quinn v Leathem* (1901). The claimant butcher used non-union labour. The defendant union official told an important customer of the claimant that there would be a strike at his place of business if he continued to deal with the claimant. On the facts the threatened strikes would not have been breaches of contract, and of course the customer committed no breach of contract by refusing to enter further contracts with the claimant. Although no unlawful means were used, the House of Lords held the defendants liable in tort, given that they had no justification for their actions. However, just three years earlier, in *Allen v Flood* (1898), the House of Lords had held that a malicious motive could not turn a lawful act into an unlawful one. The only way that *Quinn v Leathem* can be reconciled with this decision is because of the element of combination present, which serves to distinguish them. (The hidden agenda seems to be that Lord Halsbury would have liked to reverse *Allen v Flood*, but that is another story.)

A conspiracy to injure is not actionable unless the defendant's predominant purpose is to injure the claimant. Rigorous pursuit of self-interest in the knowledge that the claimant is bound to suffer damage as a result does not amount to the requisite intention. This was decided by the House of Lords in *Crofter Hand Woven Harris Tweed v Veitch* (1942). On the island of Lewis were mills producing yarn and weaving Harris tweed. Cheaper yarn was produced on the mainland, so some manufacturers began to import yarn and simply have it woven on the island—thus undercutting the price at which cloth produced wholly on the island was sold. Officials of the TGWU to which the workers belonged had the incoming yarn blacked. On the facts, the dockers who did this were not in breach of their contracts, so the claimants sued instead for a conspiracy to injure. The House of Lords held that the action was basically intended to protect the livelihoods of the union members, and that this was a justifiable motive; hence the union was not liable.

The result of this decision is that most kinds of industrial action do not attract liability for conspiracy to injure even at common law, because most of the time the action is intended to further the interests of the union and its members rather than to injure the claimant.

Conspiracy to use unlawful means

Unlike conspiracy to injure, if there is a conspiracy to use unlawful means to further the defendants' purpose, it is enough if damage to the claimant is likely to result, even if that is not the defendants' predominant purpose. This distinction between conspiracy to injure and conspiracy to use unlawful means was thrown into some doubt by the decision in *Lonrho v Shell* (1982) where the House of Lords, concerned to keep what was described as the anomalous tort of conspiracy within narrow bounds, seemed to indicate that there was no liability for a conspiracy to use unlawful means (sanctions-busting) unless the predominant purpose was to injure the claimant. This is how their decision was interpreted by the Court of Appeal in *Metall und Rohstoff AG v Donaldson Lufkin & Jenrette* (1989). However, in *Lonrho v Fayed* (1991) the House of Lords reaffirmed the traditional distinction, overruling *Metall und Rohstoff* on this point. **12–043**

Conspiracy to injure is given immunity by TULRCA s.219(2) where it is in contemplation or furtherance of a trade dispute. Conspiracy to use unlawful means is not so protected, although it is important to note that actions which are the subject of immunity will not count as unlawful means.

Other actionable wrongs

We saw in the discussion of intimidation that a lot of legal creativity has gone into the search for a cause of action which would be outside the statutory immunities. For the same reason, other wrongs have been alleged in industrial disputes with more or less success. **12–044**

Inducement of breach of statutory duty

The tort of breach of statutory duty committed in the course of a trade dispute would receive no protection; however, the tort would most likely be committed by the workers taking the action rather than the organisers. Thus it has been argued that there is also a tort of inducing breach of statutory duty, for which **12–045** the union could be held liable. In *Associated British Ports v TGWU* (1989) it was alleged that by organising a dock strike the union would be inducing a breach of the National Dock Labour Scheme set out in statutory regulations. The Court of Appeal regarded the existence of the tort as established, and by a majority held that it was not necessary for the claimants to be able to show that the actual breach of the statutory duty would have been actionable in its own right. The point was not considered by the House of Lords, who reversed the decision on other grounds.

Inducement of breach of an equitable obligation

12–046   In *Prudential Assurance v Lorenz* (1971) an insurance company alleged that the union was inducing its agents to breach their equitable duty to account for money received on the company's behalf by urging them to withhold premiums as part of an industrial action campaign. Plowman J thought the point sufficiently arguable to grant an interlocutory injunction against the union. However, in *Metall und Rohstoff AG v Donaldson Lufkin & Jenrette* (1989), the Court of Appeal denied the existence of any such tort, and considered it unnecessary, since the claimant could take action directly on the breach of the obligation. That case, of course, did not involve industrial action.

Economic duress

12–047   All industrial action is an attempt to influence an employer by means of economic pressure. Where pressure amounts to duress, then in contract law a contract may be avoided and any money paid can be restored. It is recognised that economic pressure as well as physical can amount to duress. Usually this is not relevant to industrial action since unions do not usually enter contracts with employers. However, one tactic used by the International Transport Workers' Federation (ITF) in its campaign against flags of convenience has been to require employers to make financial contributions to the union's welfare fund as part of any agreement for the union to lift the blacking of a ship flying a flag of convenience. In *Universe Tankships of Monrovia v ITF* (1982) the employers claimed the money back after the blacking had been lifted. The House of Lords held that if the economic pressure was legitimated by being within the immunities, then an employer could not circumvent that protection by bringing an action for duress instead. But if it were unprotected, then an action for restitution would be an alternative to any action in tort. On these facts the House of Lords held by a majority that a dispute over welfare payments would not have been a trade dispute, and so this action was not protected. This was taken one stage further by *Dimskal Shipping v ITF* (1992), where the facts were similar, but the money was paid in Sweden, and the pressure was lawful under Swedish law. As the contract by the shipowners to pay the money was governed by English law, the House of Lords held that they could get their money back.

Breach of EU law

12–048   Global trade brings transnational trade disputes. The longest standing is the ITF's campaign against flags of convenience, which started soon after the Second World War and which led to the cases discussed in the last paragraph as well as many others. The latest twist in the saga has revealed a new and potentially devastating source of liability for trade unions in taking industrial action.

Viking Line ABP v ITF (2008) concerned the *Rosella*, a ferry plying between Finland and Estonia, owned and run by the claimant company in Finland. Once Estonia joined the European Union in 2004, the company decided to re-flag the ship as Estonian and to replace the mainly Finnish crew with Estonians, who could be paid at a lower rate and would accept less favourable terms and conditions of employment. When the ITF and the Finnish Seamen's Union threatened industrial action against Viking Line, the company sued for an injunction, alleging that their rights under what is now TFEU art.49 would be infringed by this action. Article 49 gives people and companies the right to free establishment anywhere in the European Union. The action could be brought in the English courts because the ITF has its secretariat in the United Kingdom. The Court of Appeal referred the case to the CJEU, which held that art.49 was applicable in this situation, rejecting the argument that it was excluded because of TFEU art.153(5), which excludes the European Union from having competence to legislate on the right to strike. Having taken this crucial step, it was fairly inevitable that the CJEU would then go on to find that Viking Line's right to free establishment would be interfered with by the industrial action, in breach of art.49. The issue then became whether or not the union could establish that this was justified by an overriding reason of public interest. The CJEU recognised that collective action taken for the protection of jobs could be such a justification—but only if jobs or conditions of employment were under serious threat. This was left for the decision of the national court, but the case was settled without returning to the Court of Appeal.

A week after the *Viking Line* decision, the CJEU handed down another body blow to the trade union movement in *Laval un Partneri Ltd v Svenska Byggnadsarbetareförbundet* (2008). In this case, a Latvian building company with a subsidiary in Sweden won a contract to construct a school in Sweden. The company proposed to use Latvian workers to perform the contract, at wage rates about 40 per cent lower than they would have to pay Swedish workers, and it refused to enter a collective agreement with the Swedish trade union which would have required them to pay the workers at local rates. The Swedish union embarked on industrial action (lawful under Swedish law) and Laval sued, arguing that their rights under TFEU art.56 (freedom to provide services anywhere in the European Union) was being infringed. It should be noted that the Posted Workers Directive (96/71/EC) requires EU businesses to observe minimum terms and conditions imposed by the host state when their workers are posted to another Member State, but Sweden had no national minimum wage laws. The case was referred to the CJEU, which again held that there was an infringement of the company's right under TFEU art.56, which therefore meant that it was a breach of the Treaty unless it could be justified by an overriding reason of public interest. In this case, the CJEU considered that Swedish law in effect permitted discrimination against a foreign company and that there could be no such justification in these circumstances.

Thus industrial action to combat "social dumping"—in this context, using **12–049** workers from other Member States to drive down local terms and conditions—

appears to carry serious risks of being found to be contrary to EU law. It is ironic that a Treaty which appears to go further than British law in recognising a right to strike (EU Charter of Fundamental Rights art.28) should have so damaging an effect on workers' rights in practice.

 Further Reading

- ❏ H. Carty (2001), *An Analysis of the Economic Torts*, OUP
- ❏ K. Ewing (1991), *The Right to Strike*, Clarendon Press
- ❏ T. Novitz (2003), *International and European Protection of the Right to Strike*, OUP
- ❏ G. Pitt (1995), *The Limits of Industrial Action*, Institute of Employment Rights
- ❏ R. Benedictus (1985), "The Use of the Law of Tort in the Miners' Dispute", 14 ILJ 176
- ❏ H. Carty (2007), "*OBG v Allan*: The House of Lords Shapes the Economic Torts and Explores Commercial Confidences and Image Rights", 15 *Torts Law Journal* 283
- ❏ S. Deakin and J. Randall (2009), "Rethinking the Economic Torts", 72 MLR 519
- ❏ P. Elias (1994), "The Strike and Breach of Contract: a Reassessment", in K. Ewing, C. Gearty and B. Hepple (eds), *Human Rights and Labour Law*, Mansell
- ❏ K. Miller and C. Woolfson (1994), "Timex, Industrial Relations and the Use of the Law in the 1990s", 23 ILJ 209
- ❏ B. Napier (1987), "Strikes and the Individual Worker", [1987] CLJ 287
- ❏ R. Rideout (1997), "Industrial Relations: The Empire Strikes Back", [1997] CLP 361
- ❏ B. Simpson (2007), "Economic Tort Liability in Labour Disputes: The Potential Impact of *OBG v Allan*", 36 ILJ 468
- ❏ M. Sterling (1982), "Actions for Duress, Seafarers and Industrial Disputes", 11 ILJ 156

13. Industrial Action II

Key Points

This chapter:
- Explains the "golden formula"—acting in contemplation or furtherance of a trade dispute
- Examines situations where the golden formula does not apply so that unions lose immunity
- Notes the reduction in trade union immunity by legislation in the 1980s
- Highlights reforms made by the Trade Union Bill 2016
- Explains secondary action, and how it leads to loss of immunity
- Considers the ebb and flow of requirements to hold ballots before industrial action
- Shows how failures to comply with ballot requirements lead to loss of immunity
- Explains the concept of industrial action for prohibited reasons
- Looks at employers' remedies against trade unions for industrial action
- Discusses the concept of picketing and how far it attracts civil liability
- Examines criminal liability for picketing

***

In Ch.12 we saw that where unions commit economic torts in the course of industrial action, they are usually protected by the immunity given by the Trade Union and Labour Relations (Consolidation) Act 1992 (TULRCA) s.219; although we also saw that increasingly employers seek to rely on the commission of other torts for which there is no such protection. In this chapter, we must first look more closely at the requirements for the application of TULRCA s.219, and then, assuming that there is immunity, at the remaining question, which is, when is the immunity lost?

13–001

Immunity under TULRCA s.219

13–002 Section 219 of TULRCA gives immunity from action for the torts of inducing breach of contract, causing loss by unlawful means, threatening to do either, and conspiracy. But this immunity is applicable only when the tort is committed "in contemplation or furtherance of a trade dispute". This phrase, conveniently dubbed "the golden formula" by Wedderburn, has been hallowed by long usage, appearing first in the Conspiracy and Protection of Property Act 1875. However, the definition of the term "trade dispute", presently to be found in TULRCA s.244, was subjected to extensive alterations in the 1980s, which meant that the phrase has become one of limitation rather than of explanation.

"Trade dispute" is defined in s.244(1) of TULRCA as,
". . . a dispute between workers and their employer which relates wholly or mainly to one or more of the following:
- (a) terms and conditions of employment, or the physical conditions in which any workers are required to work;
- (b) engagement or non-engagement, or termination or suspension of employment or the duties of employment, of one or more workers;
- (c) allocation of work or the duties of employment as between workers or groups of workers;
- (d) matters of discipline;
- (e) a worker's membership or non-membership of a trade union;
- (f) facilities for officials of trade unions; and
- (g) machinery for negotiation or consultation, and other procedures, relating to any of the above matters, including the recognition by employers or employers' associations of the right of a trade union to represent workers in such negotiation or consultation or in the carrying out of such procedures."

No existing dispute

13–003 Clearly there must be an actual dispute in existence before someone can be said to be acting in contemplation or furtherance of it. Thus in *Bent's Brewery v Hogan* (1945) the union had no immunity when it was sued for inducing breach of contract by asking its members for confidential information in order to frame a pay claim. If they had put in a pay claim and had it rejected, there would have been a dispute, but there was no dispute at this preliminary stage. A similar argument was used against the ITF in *Star Sea Transport v Slater* (1978), another of the cases arising from the ITF campaign against flags of convenience. The union had blacked a ship because the crew were being paid less than internationally agreed rates. However, the Indian crew members were quite happy with the pay they were receiving, which was good by their home standards. It was held that the action did not attract the immunity because there was no dispute in existence.

In *University College London Hospital NHS Trust v Unison* (1999), there was a dispute arising from the Trust's negotiations with a consortium of private companies to build and manage a new hospital using private finance. On completion of the project, some years into the future, it was envisaged that some of the Trust's employees would be transferred to private partners. The union and its members feared that, if this came to pass, the workers would end up with terms and conditions of employment much inferior to those they enjoyed as public sector employees. One of the reasons for the Court of Appeal holding that this did not come within the trade dispute immunity was that it was not a dispute about existing terms and conditions of employment but about terms and conditions which employees might have with another employer at some point in the future (cf. also, *London Underground v NUR* (1989)).

In a number of recent cases employers have argued that industrial action is not immune because either the matters in dispute have been settled, or the union has not given a fair representation of the issues to their members. Under the Trade Union Bill 2016 reforms, the ballot paper must contain "a reasonably detailed indication" of the issues in dispute (new TULRCA s.229B), which will no doubt encourage this kind of attack, as well as opening a fruitful source of litigation over what level of information counts as "reasonably detailed".

"Workers and their employer"

Since 1982 the dispute must be between workers and their employer if there is to be immunity. Before the amendments of the Employment Act 1982, the dispute could be between any workers and any employer, or even between workers and workers, allowing for the possibility of demarcation disputes between different groups of workers to be within the protection.   **13–004**

In *University College London Hospital NHS Trust v Unison* (1999) the Court of Appeal held that the main thrust of the dispute was the union's attempt to gain binding guarantees about the terms that the private employers would offer to Trust employees who were transferred to them. This would amount to a dispute about the terms and conditions of an employer other than the employer at whom the strike action was to be aimed. It was not therefore a dispute between workers and their own employer.

Unison took this to the European Court of Human Rights arguing that this restriction on industrial action was a breach of the ECHR art.11 right to "form and join trade unions for the protection of his interests" (*Unison v United Kingdom* (2002)). The Court considered that the dispute did engage art.11 because there could be some benefit, even if it was slight, to current members and so to that extent the union's proposed action could be seen as protecting the occupational interests of its members. However, the union's claim was rejected in the end on the basis that the restriction on the right to strike applied in the case was a reasonable balance between the competing rights of the parties and fell within the proviso in art.11(2).

The limitation of protection to workers and their own employer is arguably over-restrictive in the modern era, where complex corporate structures and increased use of outsourcing and sub-contracting mean that workers may effectively be at the mercy of companies which are not strictly their direct employer. The European Committee of Social Rights, which monitors compliance with the European Social Charter, stated in 2010 that the right to strike in the United Kingdom was excessively circumscribed because, inter alia, workers could not take action against their de facto employer if different from their legal employer, and the ILO Committee of Experts made a similar comment in 2009, in relation to Convention 87. Previous and current Governments have ignored these strictures.

13–005 Does the removal of immunity from disputes between workers and workers mean that there would now be no protection for a demarcation dispute, where one group of workers claims that only its members should do a particular kind of work to the exclusion of another group?

In *Dimbleby v NUJ* (1984) journalists employed by the claimant refused to send printing work to TBF Printers rather than to their own associated printing house, where the printers were on strike. This was because TBF Printers was a subsidiary of T Bailey Forman, a company with which their union, the NUJ, was in dispute. They argued that this was a trade dispute under (c): allocation of work between groups of workers. While accepting that demarcation issues would normally be trade disputes, the House of Lords limited this to demarcation disputes where both parties worked for the same employer (cf. TULRCA s.244(5)). Thus it seems that the usual kind of demarcation dispute would be within the definition of trade dispute; furthermore, if a dispute arose because an allocation of work to outside contractors was going to lead to job losses, there would surely be a trade dispute under (b) if not under (c).

One limitation on employers getting work done by someone other than their striking workforce, introduced in 2004, was the prohibition on employment agencies supplying workers to do the work of employees taking industrial action. This restriction is also abolished by the Trade Union Bill 2016.

13–006 It is worth noting that the limitation of disputes to workers and their own employer is not what rules out sympathy action. While the initial trade dispute must be between workers and their own employer, sympathy strikers would be acting in contemplation or furtherance of that dispute—and so their action would be within the golden formula. However, it will also be secondary action and now loses protection on that account (see below, para.13–011).

Subject-matter of the dispute

13–007 Section 219 of TULRCA states that immunity will only apply if the dispute is "wholly or mainly" about one of the items listed in TULRCA s.244. This again represents a narrowing of the immunity as a result of amendment by the Employment Act 1982. Originally it was sufficient if a dispute was "connected with" one of the items. This was very wide: in effect, if the union was acting from mixed motives, it was sufficient if one of them was a trade dispute motive. A good example of difference made by the post-1982 test is provided by *Mercury Communications v Scott-Garner* (1984), where the POEU instructed its members working for the

Post Office not to connect Mercury to the British Telecom network. At this time British Telecom was being privatised and also opened up to competition, with Mercury being the first competitor. The Court of Appeal considered that the union was acting partly out of concern for the job security of its members, but was also motivated to a large extent by ideological objections to privatisation. Therefore, the dispute could not be said to be "wholly or mainly" for a trade dispute motive.

Cases such as *Mercury Communications v Scott-Garner* are often presented in the media as "political disputes" rather than trade disputes, and so it is claimed that they are outside the immunity. This is an argument that has been around a long time. In the only reported case arising from the General Strike in 1926, *NSFU v Reed* (1926), Astbury J held that:

> "No trade dispute has been alleged or shown to exist in any of the unions affected, except in the miners' case, and no trade dispute can exist between the TUC on the one hand and the Government and the nation on the other."

This prompted a famous article by Goodhart, sometime Professor of Jurisprudence at Oxford, who pointed out that much industrial action was designed to put pressure on a third party and argued that a dispute should not cease to be regarded as a trade dispute just because the third party was the Government.

Today the line between a trade dispute and a political dispute can be even harder to draw, first because of increasing government intervention in the collective bargaining process by legislation or other means, and secondly, because in the public sector (which today still employs about 18 per cent of the workforce) the Government controls policy and public expenditure and is thus the real decision-maker, not the nominal employing authority. In *Associated Newspapers v Flynn* (1970) a one-day strike against the Industrial Relations Bill (under banners proclaiming, "Demonstrate against the Bosses and the Blacklegs' Charter") was held to be political, even though it was argued that the Bill, if passed, would have a damaging effect on terms and conditions of employment. But in *Sherard v AUEW* (1973) it was accepted that a one-day strike protesting against an act which imposed a statutory wage freeze was about terms and conditions rather than being just political. Now, of course, there would be the added requirement that the purpose of the dispute was wholly or mainly trade rather than political. Unions may thus find themselves in some difficulty if their publicity attempts to galvanise members by placing their dispute in a wider national context: this makes it the more likely that they will be considered to be acting for a political motive. In *Wandsworth LBC v NAS/UWT* (1993), where the union had called on its members to boycott national tests for schoolchildren, the Court of Appeal showed itself sensitive to this issue. It finally rejected the council's claim that the boycott was motivated by ideological objections to the tests, accepting the teachers' argument that the main reason was the increased workload it would mean for them, which was clearly a trade dispute motive (cf. also *University College London Hospital NHS Trust v Unison* (1999) and *Westminster City Council v Unison* (2001)). As noted above, the new requirement for ballot papers to contain "reasonably detailed" information about the matter(s) in dispute will also be relevant to this question.

13–008

BBC v Hearn (1977) suggests a possible means whereby such disputes could clearly be established as trade disputes. Here the Association of Broadcasting Staff was planning to black the televised transmission of the Cup Final to South Africa because of the policy of apartheid in that country at that time. The Court of Appeal granted an injunction because this was a political matter; however, Lord Denning at least drew attention to the fact that the staff had not asked for a term in their contracts to say that they should be allowed to act according to conscience in this matter. This carries the implication that if such a request were made and rejected, there would then be a bona fide dispute about terms and conditions of employment. Lord Cross obiter indicated disagreement with this view, saying:

"A trade union cannot turn a dispute which in reality has no connection with terms and conditions of employment into a dispute connected with terms and conditions of employment by insisting that the employer inserts appropriate terms into the contract of employment . . ." (*Universe Tankships of Monrovia v ITF* (1982)).

However, it is difficult to see why not.

Location of the dispute

13–009　An alternative argument for the BBC staff could have been that they were acting because of the bad terms and conditions of employment for black workers in South Africa. This would have been sympathy action if it could have been shown that there was a particular real dispute between those workers and their employer. This avenue would no longer be open, because the effect of TULRCA s.219(3), as amended in 1982, is that action in contemplation or furtherance of a dispute outside the United Kingdom is protected only if those taking the action are likely to be affected by it. This might be the case if, say, a car manufacturer was proposing to close a production plant in Sweden, causing an industrial dispute, and employees of the same company at an assembly plant in the United Kingdom feared that their jobs would also be lost if the closure went ahead. However, this action again could well be secondary action, and therefore unprotected.

Loss of Immunity

13–010　We now reach the third stage in deciding whether industrial action is lawful. To recap, the first question is whether or not the action is tortious at common law. If it is, then the second question is whether or not it attracts prima facie protection under TULRCA s.219. Not all torts are so protected, and even where they are covered, it is also necessary that the action was taken in contemplation or furtherance of a trade dispute. The third question, assuming that the action has immunity under s.219, is whether that immunity is to be forfeited. This is a question which divides into several parts, for there are now several grounds on which immunity can be lost, which will be considered in turn, broadly in the order in which they were introduced in the 1980s.

Secondary action

The winter of 1978–79 became known to the newspapers as the "winter of dis-   **13–011**
content" because of a number of serious industrial disputes which ultimately
contributed in large measure to the defeat of the Labour Government in the
subsequent general election. In order to increase the pressure and thus the
effectiveness of their strikes, unions adopted the tactic of spreading disputes
as widely as possible. The aim was usually to paralyse a whole branch of industry so that something had to be done to settle the dispute. Of course, a strike
can only be spread if people not directly involved are prepared to help, either
by taking strike action themselves or by refusing to cross picket lines or refusing to do the work of the strikers. In practice, in many industries, especially
those with a long history of union activity, union solidarity was such that other
members of the same union and members of other unions were prepared to
support in this manner even if it meant losing pay and risking dismissal themselves. The use of another tactic, the "flying picket" (contingents of pickets
prepared to move swiftly to different parts of the country to ensure that
effective pickets were mounted even if local unionists were not eager to do
it) helped to make sure that the spread took place. Their activities were seen
variously as part of a brilliant strategy, stiffening the resolve of the less militant
interference in other people's business, or frankly intimidatory, according to
one's point of view.

Many people took the view that this was not really fair play, even if it was
legal. The answer of many trade unionists would be that collective action and
solidarity are the very nerve and life-blood of trade unions and that no restriction on voluntary collective action is justified. It will surprise no one that judges
tended to be in the first camp. In a famous trilogy of cases arising out of the
1978–79 strikes (*NWL v Woods* (1979); *Express Newspapers v McShane* (1980);
Duport Steels v Sirs (1980)) the Court of Appeal, led by Lord Denning, attempted
to develop a concept of "remoteness" and to remove TULRCA s.219 protection
from activities which they considered to be too far removed from the primary
dispute.

One example will suffice. In *Express Newspapers v McShane* (1980) NUJ journalists working for provincial newspapers had a long-running dispute with their
employers over pay. Dismissal of 105 journalists by the *Bolton Evening News*
precipitated a national strike by provincial journalists. This did not have the
hoped-for effect of shutting down the provincial papers because they could still
pick up copy from the Press Association, an agency supplying news stories. Thus
NUJ members working for the Press Association were instructed by the union
not to supply copy to the provincial newspapers. Only about half complied;
in consequence NUJ members working for national newspapers were told to
boycott Press Association copy. Express Newspapers, owners of a national newspaper, sued the General Secretary of the NUJ. The Court of Appeal took the view
that the only trade dispute here was between the provincial papers and their
employees. They were prepared to accept that the involvement of the Press
Association journalists was in furtherance of that primary dispute, but not the
action at the national newspapers. They considered that it was so remote from

the primary dispute that it could not be said to be in furtherance of it, and it was very unlikely to have any effect on its outcome.

13–012   In this case, as in the other two, the decision of the Court of Appeal was reversed by the House of Lords, which held that acting in furtherance was to be judged subjectively: if the union officials honestly believed that they were acting in furtherance of the primary dispute, that was enough. This was clearly the correct interpretation of the law, and the House of Lords, while not enthusiastic about it, was mindful of the danger of judges appearing to act politically if they added extra requirements to those actually appearing in the legislation. However, the new Conservative Government took up the Court of Appeal's ideas, and the Employment Act 1980 introduced the concept of "secondary action".

Secondary action is now defined by TULRCA s.224 and consists in inducing breach of, or interfering with, a contract of employment, or threatening to do so, where the employer under the contract of employment is not a party to the trade dispute. Where secondary action occurs, the protection otherwise given for these torts by TULRCA s.219 is removed, except in one situation. That is where there is lawful picketing by employees who are party to the dispute. The parameters of lawful picketing are discussed below (para.13–037). Effectively this means that all sympathy action is now unprotected, as we can see if we look again at the facts of *Express Newspapers v McShane* (1980). Today, not only the blacking of Press Association copy by journalists employed by national papers but also the instruction to Press Association union members not to supply copy to the provincial newspapers would be unprotected secondary action. The union, by asking its members at the Press Association not to send copy to the provincial papers, would be asking them to break their contracts of employment. Since their employer, the Press Association, was not a party to the dispute with the provincial journalists, the action would be secondary.

You will remember that in *Express Newspapers v McShane* the Court of Appeal was prepared to countenance the action taken by Press Association journalists. It was the action by the national journalists which they considered to be too remote. As originally framed in 1980, this was also the position taken by the law. If the employer who was not a party to the dispute had a direct contractual nexus with the employer who was involved (e.g. to supply them with goods and services, or to buy something from them) then industrial action aimed at this "first supplier" or "first customer" was protected. Anything more remote, such as the action affecting the national newspapers which had no contract with the provincial papers in *Express Newspapers v McShane*, was unprotected secondary action.

13–013   Under this regime, therefore, a limited amount of sympathy action could be taken lawfully. However, the protection for limited secondary action was removed by the Employment Act 1990. Now the only type of sympathy action which retains immunity is that which occurs in the context of lawful picketing. If workers in dispute with their own employer picket the workplace, they will not only aim to discourage other employees from going to work but also to stop all deliveries in and out. If pickets induce a lorry driver who is meant to be delivering goods to turn back (and lots of workers are very reluctant to cross picket lines) they will probably have induced a breach of the driver's contract with his employer, who is not a party to the trade dispute. This, as we know, is secondary action. But it remains protected secondary action and the immunity in TULRCA s.219 will still apply.

We saw in *Dimbleby v NUJ* (1984) that Dimbleby, in dispute with their own printers, decided to move their printing work to another firm, TBF Printers. In the United States, strikers are allowed to "follow" struck work and it is legitimate for them to institute industrial action affecting the substitute employer in order to maintain the pressure caused by their original withdrawal of labour. The 1980 definition of protected secondary action also permitted this, although in a narrower form. The exception applied only if the substitute employer was a company belonging to the same group of companies as the employer in dispute. Since the Employment Act 1990, secondary action taken to follow switched production has no immunity.

In *National Union of Rail, Maritime and Transport Workers v United Kingdom* (2014) the ban on secondary action was challenged as being incompatible with ECHR art.11, the first time that the ECtHR had considered the matter. The European Court of Human Rights noted that both the ILO Committee of Experts and the European Committee of Social Rights considered secondary action to be within the protection of freedom of association and the right to strike and so held that the claim did engage art.11. However, although holding that there was a prima facie interference with freedom of association, the European Court of Human Rights held that a ban on secondary action could be regarded as justified under art.11(2) as protecting the rights and freedoms of others. It further held that because of the sensitivity surrounding this area of law, states had a wide margin of appreciation in deciding what was appropriate for their circumstances. Ironically, the fact that the restriction had stood for 20 years and had not been altered by a Labour administration when it had the opportunity was taken by the Court to support the argument that this was not an unacceptable restriction on the right to strike.

Failure to hold a ballot

Prior to 1984 some unions, but by no means all, were required by their rules to ballot their members before industrial action (see *Taylor v NUM* (1984), above, para.11–013). In the name of increased democracy within trade unions, the 1984 Trade Union Act indirectly imposed a requirement that all unions should hold a secret ballot before calling official strike action, by providing that immunity would be removed for the torts of inducing breach of contracts of employment or interfering with their performance unless a ballot in accordance with the statutory requirements had been held. Note that this only applies to official union action (in the sense described in Ch.12, above, para.12–015). Where unofficial action is taken by union members, or where non-unionists go on strike, there is no need to have a ballot to preserve immunity. However, if the union wishes to endorse unofficial action (thus protecting members' unfair dismissal rights) it needs to ballot the members first.

13–014

Since 1984 the law has been extended in three ways. First, since 1988 every union member has a right to restrain the union from calling any industrial action (not just an all-out strike) without a ballot, whether or not the action involves a breach of members' contracts of employment (TULRCA s.62). Secondly, the Employment Act 1990 extended the constituency of those to be balloted to self-employed workers working under a contract of personal service as well as employees (TULRCA s.235). The third extension, carried out by the Trade Union Reform and Employment Rights Act 1993 (TURERA), was the most significant. Introduced under the standard of the "Citizens' Charter", it is a right of a third party to get action called off whenever it is "unlawful" (TULRCA s.235A). However, "unlawful" in this context has an extended meaning: it refers not only to action which is tortious and unprotected by immunity but also to any industrial action organised by a trade union where there has not been a ballot first. The third party need only show that the likely effect of the action would be to prevent or delay the supply of goods or services to him, or to reduce their quality; he need not show that he has any contractual right to them. *P v NAS/UWT* (2003) is one of the few examples of this right being invoked, in that case by a disruptive pupil whose schoolteachers were refusing to teach him.

Thus union members and third parties can now stop the union taking action without a ballot, although it remains the case that they cannot positively force the union to hold a ballot. It is worth noting that a non-corporate employer could also avail herself of the citizen's right to restrain action, although the reference in TULRCA s.235A to an "individual" is thought to exclude companies. Otherwise, an employer would have no right to restrain action but would have to wait until the unsanctioned action has started and then sue in tort on the ground that the action has no immunity—although in *P & O Ferries v NUS* (1988) a court granted an injunction at the instance of the employer to stop the seafarers' union balloting its members on strike action where it was clear that such strike action would be unprotected secondary action and thus have no immunity.

13–015 Balloting has thus moved to centre stage and compliance with the requirements for a valid ballot is of critical importance. As we will see, the conditions which have to be fulfilled are numerous, highly technical and rigorously construed by the courts. It has become common for employers to seek to restrain industrial action on the grounds that there has been some technical failure, a tactic which has frequently been successful. The excessive technicality of the ballot requirements was the other ground on which the RMT argued that the current law on industrial action was in breach of ECHR art.11 in *RMT v United Kingdom* (2014), but in relation to this complaint, the European Court of Human Rights considered that there was not even a prima facie breach, holding that the ballot rules were merely a procedural requirement which did not affect exercise of the union's substantive rights. This view, at odds with the opinions expressed by the ILO Committee of Experts and the European Committee of Social Rights, no doubt emboldened the new Conservative Government to tighten the ballot requirements even further.

The ballot requirements, originally introduced by the Trade Union Act 1984, are now to be found in TULRCA ss.226–234—although heavily amended since.

The Employment Relations Act (ERelA) 1999 made minor amendments to deal with the worst excesses of technicality, but managed to add some problems of its own. Amendments to remedy some of these anomalies (but not to change the basic principle) were further made by the ERelA 2004. The Trade Union Bill 2016 constitutes a further step change in making lawful industrial action ballots even harder to achieve.

Requirements for a valid ballot

Who votes?

Only those who the union reasonably believes will be called on to take part in the industrial action are entitled to vote (TULRCA s.227). This restriction is fair: it would not be right for some people to vote for other people to take action. However, there is no requirement that they should all be affected directly by the matter which is in dispute (*British Telecommunications plc v Communication Workers' Union* (2004)). Failure to allow votes to those entitled to vote, or allowing voting by those not entitled to vote, will invalidate the ballot (TULRCA s.232A). In two recent cases, employers challenged the validity of a ballot on the basis that the union had not properly selected the constituency of those to be balloted. *London Underground Ltd v ASLEF* (2012) involved a dispute over pay for drivers working on Boxing Day. The union balloted 1,950 members for a strike on that day and the employer argued this was flawed since only about a quarter of them were actually scheduled to work that day. The High Court accepted the union's evidence that it also planned three further one-day strikes so that it reasonably believed that the others would be involved; however, Eder J went so far as to say that even had it been Boxing Day only, the others could have been taking part in the sense of associating themselves with the action, even if not actually rostered to work. This obiter remark seems to undermine the philosophy underpinning the section and it remains to be seen if it would be accepted at a higher level. Nonetheless, as pointed out in *United Closures and Plastics Ltd* (2012) the union has some level of discretion in deciding who should be called out in furtherance of the dispute.

13–016

Ballots must be postal and TULRCA s.230 provides that "so far as is reasonably practicable" everyone entitled to vote must be sent a ballot paper by post. Again, failure to comply invalidates the ballot (TULRCA s.232A). Following cases where ballots were challenged because some of those to be called out had not received voting papers, the ERelA 1999 introduced new ss.232A and 232B into TULRCA providing that small accidental failures to accord entitlement to vote will not invalidate the ballot when they are on such a scale as to be unlikely to affect the result and further amendment by ERelA 2004 allows the union to call on such members to take part in the action.

In *P v NAS/UWT* (2003) school governors insisted on the reinstatement of a violent and disruptive pupil who had been expelled by the head teacher. The union balloted its members at the school on whether they should take industrial action in the form of refusing to teach the boy. Using the TULRCA s.235A right for third parties, the boy sued to have the action called off on the basis that the ballot was defective because only 30 out of the 32 teachers at the school who were members of the union had been accorded their right to vote. The two left out were teachers who had only recently moved to the school and they had not informed the union of this, so it was not reasonably practicable for the union to send them ballot papers. In these circumstances the House of Lords held that they had not been denied entitlement to vote, albeit through their own fault they had not had an opportunity to vote. This could now be dealt with by the amended version of TULRCA s.232B. An attempt to rely on the small accidental failures exception failed in *RMT v Midland Mainline Ltd* (2001) where the union failed to ballot 25 members for various reasons. The action was approved by only 25 votes to 17, with 49 others failing to record a vote. In *NURMT v SERCO Ltd* (2011) the union balloted two people in error, but the High Court held that they could not rely on the "small accidental failures" defence because they could have avoided this by the use of reasonable care. The decision was reversed by the Court of Appeal, which held that this was exactly the sort of situation in which the defence was meant to apply. In this case, 80 per cent of those voting favoured a strike, on a turnout of 78 per cent. This was taken a step further in *Balfour Beatty Engineering Services Ltd v Unite the Union* (2012), where it was possible that as many as 100 members who should have been balloted might not have received their ballot papers. The judge recognised that keeping tabs on members was particularly difficult in the construction industry, where people change jobs and employers quite regularly and noted that the union had put major efforts—some 500 hours of employees' time—in trying to ensure that voting papers went to the right people and held that the union had done everything that was reasonably practicable to comply with TULRCA s.230.

13–017   In *London Underground v RMT* (1995) the union balloted its members in August over a series of one and two-day strikes. By the time that the action was actually due to take place, active recruitment by the union had resulted in another 692 new members, who were called on to participate. The employer argued that the union should not be entitled to call out these new members, as they had not been balloted. The argument was rejected by the Court of Appeal. The Act specifically requires the union to ballot only those of its members who at the time of the ballot are reasonably expected to be called upon to participate in the industrial action. Provided that this is done, the action has the support of the ballot, which is all that the law requires. As Millett LJ noted, the ballot provisions apply only to the union and its members. There is nothing to stop the union calling out non-members, and this will not affect its immunity.

One oddity thrown up by the ballot requirement was shown by *Shipping Company Uniform Inc v ITF* (1985). The ITF is a federation of affiliated trade unions, with hardly any individual members. It argued that it was therefore exempt from the ballot requirement because it had no one to ballot. The argument was rejected by the court, with the result that a union in this position became quite unable to organise industrial action within the immunity. Such unions must change their rules so that individual members of affiliated unions are also direct members of the federation.

Notice to employers

Since 1993 it has been necessary for the union to give at least seven days' notice **13–018**
of the ballot to every single employer of employees who will be called on to vote
(TULRCA s.226A) and a further seven days' notice before the industrial action
actually starts (s.234A). The Trade Union Bill 2016 increases the notice period
before action starts to 14 days. In addition to giving notice, the union must also
send a sample voting paper to the affected employers at least three days before
the ballot is due to start.

The most controversial aspect of this was that originally, in both notices,
the union had to describe the relevant employees "so that he [the employer]
can readily ascertain them". Despite a ministerial denial that this would entail
naming names, that was precisely what was held to be necessary in the first
case to reach the Court of Appeal, *Blackpool and the Fylde College v NATFHE*
(1994). ERelA 1999 tried to deal with this by amending the Act to the effect
that the union must give the employer notice with such information "as would
help the employer to make plans and bring information to the attention" of
relevant employees and it specifically stated that failure to name the relevant
employees would not mean that the notice was non-compliant. The amended
requirement was considered in yet another case involving rail workers, *London
Underground Ltd v RMT* (2001), where the union gave notice that it would be
calling out all its members who worked for the company, some 40 per cent of
London Underground's total 17,000 employees. The union stated the approxi-
mate number of members involved and said that they were to be found in every
workplace and in every category of staff. The employer argued that this did not
give it sufficient information to be able to plan for the strike and asked for a list
of names to check against its own records. The Court of Appeal held that the
union's notice was insufficient. It should have provided a matrix showing the
number of staff in each category at each workplace—no matter that this would
be more onerous than the pre-1999 Act requirement of simply supplying a list
of names.

In consequence, the notice requirement was amended again by ERelA 2004.
The present version requires the union to give information in one of two forms.
The most onerous requires the union to provide a list of the categories of
employees to be called out, together with a list of the workplaces of employees
to be called out, and total numbers of employees affected at each workplace
(TULRCA s.226A(2A), (2B); s.234A(3A), (3B)). Note that this reverses the decision
in *London Underground Ltd v RMT* (2001) that the numbers should be further
broken down by numbers in each category at each workplace. It must be accompanied by an explanation of how the figures were arrived at. Alternatively, if at
least some of the employees have their union subscriptions deducted at source
by the employer, the union can instead give the employer information which
will "enable the employer readily to deduce" the total numbers involved, their
categories and their workplaces (TULRCA s.226A(2C); s.234(3C)). In *Metrobus
Ltd v Unite the Union* (2009) the Court of Appeal held that where most of the
members had subscriptions deducted at source and only about 10 per cent
paid by other means, the union still had to give an explanation about how its

figures for that small minority had been arrived at and its notices were defective because they did not do so. Furthermore, in *EDF Energy Powerlink Ltd v RMT* (2010), the High Court granted an interim injunction on grounds that the union had not given enough information about categories of worker to be balloted even though it was accepted that the union did not keep records of information to this level of detail. These cases highlight the fact that the amended versions of TULRCA ss.226A and 234A, far from solving the problems of the previous the problems, have in fact created new avenues for employers to attack the ballot on technical grounds, especially as the exception for "small accidental failures" does not apply to these provisions. In a welcome return to common sense, the Court of Appeal in *NURMT v SERCO Ltd* (2011) held that courts should not take the draconian step of invalidating a ballot just because the language used by the union in giving an explanation of its figures to the employer was not as precise as a statutory draughtsman might use, and that the de minimis principle could be invoked in relation to a minor infringement of the s.226A.

13–019   The real question is why the notice requirement was not removed altogether by the Employment Relations Acts 1999–2004. In relation to the first notice requirement in particular, it is unclear why unions should have to give notice to employers that they intend to undertake the perfectly lawful activity of balloting their members. The opinion of the ILO Committee of Experts is that requiring two notices is excessive.

Scrutiny

13–020   The TURERA effectively extended the rules introduced in 1988 relating to the independent scrutiny of union election and political fund ballots (see above, para.11–027) to industrial action ballots as well, unless fewer than 50 members are involved (TULRCA ss.226B–C). The scrutineer, whose name must appear on the ballot paper, must be a qualified person within the meaning of the Trade Union Ballots and Elections (Independent Scrutineer Qualifications) Order 1993 as amended, i.e. solicitors, qualified trade union auditors and certain bodies like the Electoral Reform Society. The scrutineer is not charged with actually supervising the ballot, but has to report on it within four weeks stating whether or not he is satisfied that the requirements have been complied with and that there were satisfactory arrangements for the production, storage, distribution, return and counting of the ballot papers (TULRCA s.231B). The union is obliged to comply with all reasonable requests from the scrutineer and must ensure that no one interferes with him in the performance of his functions. The union must make copies of the report available to any voting member or affected employer who asks for it within a six-month period.

Separate workplaces

13–021   Different regions, different groups of workers, even different plants may have quite different attitudes to taking industrial action. If a single result is returned for all those balloted, the fact that at plant A, say, 90 per cent opposed action may be submerged in an overall majority in favour. Unions could manipulate votes by making sure that well-known militant workplaces were always included in any ballot. Fear of this (rather than any evidence that it was actually happening) led to a limited requirement (in TULRCA s.228) that there should be separate ballots and separate results returned. Unfortunately, s.228 was framed in an extremely convoluted fashion. ERelA 1999 repealed and replaced s.228 with new TULRCA ss.228 and 228A, aimed at clarifying rather than changing the law. Thus s.228 lays down a prima facie rule of separate ballots for separate workplaces. However, s.228A allows a single ballot for different workplaces in three situations: where there is at least one worker at the workplace affected by the dispute; where there is an occupational link between all the members balloted, whether or not they work at different workplaces or even have different employers; and finally situations where all the workers of one or more employers in dispute are balloted. Allowing a single ballot of employees of different employers where there is an occupational link gives statutory force to the decision in *University of Central England v NALGO* (1993), where it was held that an aggregated ballot result could be given for staff working for different universities since they all had the same terms and conditions.

ERelA 1999 also redefines "workplace" in TULRCA s.228 as being the premises with which the worker's employment has the closest connection. This is to deal with the problems which arose in *Intercity West Coast Ltd v RMT* (1996) where it was argued that train conductors, all of whom worked at Manchester Piccadilly station (belonging to Railtrack) but who had separate employers, Intercity West Coast Ltd and North West Regional Railways, had separate workplaces. Under the new definition, the question of who owns or occupies the premises is no longer relevant.

The ballot paper

Since 1984 the ballot paper has had to contain the so-called health warning: "If **13–022** you take part in a strike or other industrial action, you may be in breach of your contract of employment" (TULRCA s.229(4)). As a result of the Employment Relations Acts 1999–2004 amendments to unfair dismissal law, which mean that dismissals for taking part in lawful industrial action are automatically unfair in some circumstances, the health warning has had to be amended too, by adding:

> "However, if you are dismissed for taking part in strike or other industrial action which is called officially and is otherwise lawful, the dismissal will be unfair if it takes place fewer than twelve weeks after you started taking part in the action, and depending on the circumstances may be unfair if it takes place later."

This falls into that category of legal statements which is completely accurate and utterly unhelpful. The reformers might as well have bitten the bullet and simply abolished the requirement to include any such statement.

Section 229(4) of TULRCA also stipulates that this statement may not be commented upon or qualified by anything else on the ballot paper, although presumably it may be accompanied by literature explaining the cryptic message. In *Newham LBC v NALGO* (1993) the employees were asked whether they were prepared to take strike action "on strike pay equivalent to full take-home pay", a formulation which passed without comment.

If industrial action short of a strike is contemplated as well as (or perhaps as a first stage before) a strike, then the two questions must be put separately on the ballot paper. Workers might be prepared to take part in an overtime ban (especially if this is not a breach of contract) but not an all-out strike. In *Post Office v UCW* (1990) the union asked members if they would be "willing to take industrial action up to and including strike action . . .". The Court of Appeal held that this rolled-up question did not comply with the requirements and rendered the ballot invalid. Under the reforms introduced by the Trade Union Bill 2016, the ballot paper must now specify what form(s) industrial action short of a strike will take, and the period or periods within which the strike and/or other forms of industrial action is expected to take place (new TULRCA ss.229(2C) and (2D)).

13–023   There used to be no requirement that the union should state on the ballot paper what the dispute is about, although this was recommended by the Code of Practice on Industrial Action Ballots. Under the Trade Union Bill 2016, as already mentioned, it now becomes a requirement that the ballot paper includes a "reasonably detailed indication" of the matters in dispute. In *London Underground Ltd v NUR* (1989) the union balloted its members on four issues. The employer argued that this was invalid because three of the topics were no longer "live" issues between the parties, and that in any case the union should have asked the question separately in relation to each issue. The court held that the union was entitled to ask a single question in relation to separate issues, but only if the issues were all trade dispute issues within the meaning of TULRCA s.244. This includes the requirement that they be matters of actual dispute.

Due to fears that shop stewards might jump the gun and use a "yes" vote to call instant industrial action before senior officials had decided if this was what they wanted to do, the ballot paper must now contain a statement of who is entitled to call industrial action in the event of a majority being in favour, and the action will not receive immunity unless that person calls the action (TULRCA s.233). In the first case to reach the Court of Appeal on this provision, *Tanks & Drums Ltd v TGWU* (1991), the union had nominated its general secretary as having authority to call a strike. Negotiations with the employer had been led by the union's district organiser. Two weeks after a ballot in favour, the district official sought and obtained the general secretary's permission to implement action if a better offer was not forthcoming after a meeting with the employer the following day. As no further offer was made, the strike went ahead. The employer sued for an interim injunction claiming that the general secretary had in effect delegated his power to decide. The court held that this was not a blanket delegation, and that the permission of the general secretary was specific enough to the particular events to warrant holding that he was the person who had called the action, as required by the legislation. This seems sensible, particularly in a union as large as the TGWU, where the general secretary was unlikely to be personally involved in every dispute.

Conduct of the ballot and notification of result

13–024   As a result of TURERA, ballots on industrial action must now be fully postal, with members enabled to vote at no cost to themselves (TULRCA s.230). There is an exception for merchant seamen. Balloting can therefore be an expensive undertaking for larger unions, but proposals to allow some form of electronic voting have been rejected by the Government. Under TULRCA ss.231 and 231A the union is enjoined to take such steps as are reasonably necessary to ensure that a breakdown of the results is given not only to all those who were entitled to take part but also to all affected employers. They must be told how many ballot papers were returned, how many voted "yes" or "no" to each question, the number of spoiled papers, and—since the Trade Union Bill 2016—how many were entitled to vote and whether the requisite majorities were achieved.

These results must be communicated to members and affected employers "as soon as reasonably practicable". In *Metrobus v Unite* (2009), a delay of at most 48 hours in informing the employer was held to breach s.231A, even though there was no suggestion that the company had been in any sense disadvantaged by the delay and even though it had still received more than seven days notice of the strike itself. The Court of Appeal held that this breach alone would have justified an injunction to prevent the action and, furthermore, that the obligation to provide the information was independent and had to be complied with even if the union decided against action and thus did not need tortious immunity. In *British Airways plc v Unite* (2010) the employer had received the information due to it under s.231A but nonetheless sought an injunction on the grounds that union members (none of whom had complained!) had not received the result as stipulated by s.231. The Court of Appeal held that the company was entitled to sue under s.231—but that the union had done enough by making the information available on its website and emailing or texting it to members who had signed up for this service—a welcome injection of common sense.

The majority required

For the past 30 years it has only been necessary that there should be a majority of those voting in favour (and a bare majority on each question if there are two: *West Midlands Travel v TGWU* (1994)). However, in the most significant of its 2016 reforms, the Trade Union Bill introduces a new requirement that the ballot will only be valid if at least 50 per cent of those entitled to vote have done so. As many have pointed out, central and local government election results are valid even if the turnout is lower than this percentage. As long as this threshold is met, then there need only be a bare majority in favour. However, in the case of "important public services", there is an additional requirement that at least 40 per cent of those entitled to vote must vote in favour of the action. This means that anyone who fails to vote effectively counts as a No vote in the ballot. The important public services to which this will apply are to be specified in regulations, but may cover anyone working in any of six specified categories: health services; education of children up to the age of 17; fire services; transport services; decommissioning of nuclear waste; and border security. The Consultation Paper preceding the Bill makes it clear that this special majority will apply also to ancillary staff working in these fields if industrial action by them would have an adverse impact on the delivery of the service. It seems, therefore, as if the 40 per cent threshold could apply very widely, to private sector as well as public sector staff.

13–025

Period of validity

13–026   Union officials cannot keep a mandate for industrial action in their back pocket indefinitely. Circumstances change, and it cannot be assumed that members will remain of the same mind for too long. Hence TULRCA s.234 originally provided that action was only protected if it commenced within four weeks of the result being announced. This gave rise to difficulties if negotiations were ongoing, since the union might be forced to start action within the time limit; even greater difficulties could arise in deciding whether action which recommenced after a period of suspension was referable to the initial ballot.

In *Monsanto plc v TGWU* (1987) the employer offered to negotiate after the action started, on condition that the action was suspended, but then the talks broke down. The Court of Appeal considered that union officials should have the flexibility to be able to suspend action temporarily, and held that in these circumstances it was not necessary to re-ballot members. In that case the suspension was just under two weeks long. In *Post Office v UCW* (1990) a ballot in September 1988 was followed by industrial action which lasted until December. No action took place between January and April; in May the union decided to restart the action and a strike took place in September 1989. While the dispute was over the same issue, the Court of Appeal held that it was a new and disconnected campaign and that a fresh ballot was needed. The question was not one of strict time limits but whether in fact the action could be regarded as part of the same campaign.

Cases like these were seized upon by the Government to justify reform of TULRCA s.234 by the Trade Union Bill 2016 to take out the requirement to start action within four weeks of the ballot—but substituting a far more stringent rule, that the ballot will remain valid for only four months. If the action is to continue beyond this period, there will need to be a fresh ballot, complying once again with all the myriad requirements.

Action for prohibited reasons

13–027   The last method to be used to limit the ambit of lawful industrial action during the 1980s was the removal of immunity from disputes over particular issues—those which particularly exercised the Conservative Government at the time of their introduction. In the early part of the 1980s this was the closed shop. Later unofficial industrial action became the prime bugbear. The result of legislating on specific topics led to an odd asymmetry in the statutes, since some topics are included in the definition of trade dispute under TULRCA s.244, but no longer attract immunity because of later amendments. However, no alteration was made by the Labour administration when it had the opportunity between 1997 and 2010.

Pressure to impose union membership and union recognition requirements

13–028   At the beginning of the 1980s, as fast as the Conservative Government extended the situations in which individuals could opt out of unions despite a closed shop agreement, so Labour-controlled councils devised new ways of trying to ensure high levels of union membership among the firms they contracted with. In principle we are all free to make contracts or not with whoever we please. Many Labour-controlled councils used their freedom to decline to enter contracts with employers who did not recognise a trade union or who did not have a closed shop arrangement with a trade union. Given the enormous economic value of public contracts, they could be very influential, so action was taken in the Employment Act 1982 to stop this practice. Now TULRCA ss.144–145 and 186–187 render void any terms in a contract which require the other party to recognise a union or to maintain a closed shop among its workers. More to the point for present purposes, TULRCA ss.222(3) and 225 provide that there will be no immunity for industrial action designed to get such terms inserted into contracts between employers.

Pressure to maintain the closed shop

The process started with the above reforms in 1982 was taken a step further by the Employment Act 1988, which removed immunity from industrial action if the reason or one of the reasons for it was to pressurise the employer into discriminating against non-union members (now TULRCA s.222). Oddly, TULRCA s.244(1)(e) still states that "the membership or non-membership of a trade union on the part of a worker" can be the subject-matter of a trade dispute.   **13–029**

Reinstatement of strikers

As part of the campaign against unofficial industrial action, unfair dismissal claims by unofficial strikers were ruled out in 1990 (see above, para.12–013). Under TULRCA s.223, industrial action which is taken even partly because of the dismissal of unofficial strikers will have no immunity. This sits uneasily with the inclusion of "termination or suspension of employment" as one of the trade dispute topics in TULRCA s.244(1)(b).   **13–030**

Liability of Unions in Tort

Before *Taff Vale v Amalgamated Society of Railway Servants* (1901) union funds were effectively immune from action because the practical difficulties in suing the union were too great. After the Trade Union Act 1906, designed to restore and clarify the pre-1901 position, union funds were effectively immune because the Act bestowed an almost complete immunity from liability in tort. The Donovan Commission thought that unions should have complete immunity only when acting in contemplation or furtherance of a trade dispute, but under the Industrial Relations Act 1971 immunity was removed altogether. In 1974, TULRA repealed the Industrial Relations Act and in effect restored the 1906 position with some minor alterations. This lasted until the Employment Act 1982, which again abolished the total immunity of trade unions from actions in tort.   **13–031**

Was total immunity ever justified? The principal argument in favour is that without this immunity, a union is at risk of having its funds wiped out in just one strike. Thus, if there ought to be a freedom to strike, then the law ought to provide conditions under which the freedom can be enjoyed in practice. Against this view, much play was made of the fact that by 1974 no other body, not even the Crown, had such extensive immunity as trade unions; and the image was presented of powerful bodies able to inflict damage at will at no risk to themselves. The line adopted by the Conservative Government of the 1980s was that there was nothing wrong with expecting unions to play by the same rules as individuals, and their immunity should be similarly limited.

Accordingly, the Employment Act 1982 took away the total immunity and gave unions the same immunity as individuals (now TULRCA s.20). However, in a partial recognition of the argument in favour of total immunity, s.22 lays down limits on the amount of damages which can be awarded against a union in any one action. The maxima are related to the size of the union: £10,000 if the union has fewer than 5,000 members; £50,000 if the union has between 5,000 and 25,000 members; £125,000 if there are between 25,000 and 100,000 members; and £250,000 if it has 100,000 members or more (TULRCA s.22(2)). Political funds and provident funds (i.e. those used to pay benefits to members) are not available for satisfying awards of damages, provided that the rules of the fund preclude it being used to finance industrial action. According to *News Group Newspapers v SOGAT '82* (1986), if rules are drafted appropriately, branch funds will not belong to the union and thus will not be available for judgments against the union. However, if more than one employer sues the union in respect of the same industrial action, each will be entitled to damages up to the limit; also the limits are not applicable to fines for contempt, which swiftly became common when unions first responded to the change in the law. For example, in the *Stockport Messenger* dispute in 1984, the NGA was ordered to pay £100,000 damages, but was fined £675,000 for contempt. Thus the limits have not been especially noticeable as a protective device, which may account for the fact that it has never been felt necessary to uprate them since 1982, although the Secretary of State has power to do so.

13–032   Of course, a trade union is a legal construct and cannot actually "do" anything in reality: a trade union can only be regarded as acting when certain human agents do things in its name or on its behalf. So once the immunity was removed, the question was immediately posed: whose acts would render the union liable in tort? When this question arose under the Industrial Relations Act 1971, the courts answered it by applying the usual principles of vicarious liability. This was criticised on the grounds that trade unions are not "top-down" hierarchical organisations, with clear lines of command and control: the leaders govern by consent and follow as often as they lead. Thus in the leading case, *Heatons Transport v TGWU* (1973), the House of Lords held that the custom and practice of the union gave shop stewards a general implied authority to institute blacking by their members. This may be seen as resulting from the non-hierarchical structure of the union and the fact that its rule-book was drawn up with the members rather than with lawyers in mind, but to hold the union liable vicariously for acts so far down the line (remembering that a union like the TGWU had hundreds of shop stewards) was to make it extremely vulnerable to action in a situation where its real ability to control might be in doubt.

Nevertheless, once their immunity was again removed in 1982, *Heatons Transport v TGWU* was once more relevant authority on the vicarious liability of a union at common law. However, the position is more complicated than this. Section 20 of TULRCA lays down a statutory test of vicarious liability where the union is sued for inducing or threatening to induce breach of contract, causing or threatening to cause loss by unlawful means, conspiracy, or contempt of an order arising from such proceedings. But where any other torts are involved, common law vicarious liability will apply, and may yield different results. Under TULRCA s.20 the union is liable if the action complained of as constituting the tort was authorised or endorsed by the president or general secretary or the principal executive committee. This is entirely reasonable, for these are the people who carry out the day-to-day administration of the union. It makes sense also for the union to be liable, as it is, if the action is authorised or endorsed by someone specifically empowered by the rules to do so. In terms of those under their control, it was originally provided that the union would also be liable for any act done by an employed official, or any committee to whom that employed official reported, subject to a defence if the senior officials had repudiated the act in question. "Employed" in this context meant employed by the union. So if a union had a full-time regional official (an employee of the trade union) the union would be liable if that official called action. If, as is usually the case, the regional official reported to a regional committee, made up principally of lay union officials who were not employees of the union, a decision of that committee could still make the union liable, unless it was repudiated by the centre. But if a shop steward called out her members, the union would not usually have been liable under the law as originally framed. This is because a shop steward is not an employee of the union but a lay official, someone who has got involved with the union at their place of work and taken on union office. Also, a shop steward is not usually empowered by the union's rules to call industrial action (despite the decision in *Heatons Transport*, above).

A main aim of the Employment Act 1990 was to reduce the incidence of unofficial industrial action, especially after an outbreak of unofficial action on the London Underground in the summer of 1989. While it is a defining characteristic of unofficial action that the union does not support it, the Government was evidently of the view that not all unofficial action was as unofficial as all that, and that with a little exertion, the union could do something about it. Hence TULRCA s.20(2)(c) now provides that the union is liable for the actions of any official and of any committee of the union. Furthermore, an act is done by an official if it is done by any group of which he is a member—regardless of whether the group is recognised by the union or not. At the same time, the requirements for a valid repudiation were tightened: the union (via its president, general secretary or principal executive committee) must now give notice of its repudiation in writing as soon as reasonably practicable, not only to the delinquent officials, but also to every member of the union who is or might take part in the action, and to the employers of these members.

It goes without saying that subsequent conduct inconsistent with this statement will render the "repudiation" inoperative. In *Express & Star v NGA* (1986) the General Secretary of the union sent out three circulars stating that action **13–033** should cease; but one branch official announced at a meeting in the presence of a national official that he had received a "nod and a wink" that they need not be distributed and another promised strike pay in the presence of a regional official. The case concerned common law vicarious liability, but affords an example of the kind of conduct that would presumably be considered inconsistent with repudiation. The end result is that unions may be vicariously liable for the actions of an enormous range of people, some of whom it cannot realistically be said to control.

Remedies

13–034   It used to be said that employers were not interested in suing for damages, but in getting industrial action called off. That statement needs some qualification now. In the 1980s it became possible to sue unions instead of the individual officials, and industrial action became unlawful in many more situations. This statutory encouragement to sue for damages was taken up increasingly by employers throughout the decade. Nevertheless, it remains the case that the primary remedy sought by an employer faced with industrial action is an injunction to stop the action. However, all legal proceedings take time: it is not at all uncommon to hear of cases coming on for trial years after a writ was first issued. This is not much use to a struck company: it needs an instant remedy; and the law provides it in the form of the interim injunction. This is designed as a holding operation: it is an order to preserve the status quo until there is a full trial of the action in situations where the claimants can give sufficient evidence that if this does not happen they will not in the long run be adequately compensated by damages if they should win the final trial.

It should be noted that the employer will never be able to get an injunction to stop the employees breaking their contracts of employment, because there can be no specific performance of contracts of employment (TULRCA s.236; see above, para.12–002). What will be sought is an injunction to stop the organisation of the industrial action, which will usually have the effect that everyone will return to work.

Most reported cases on trade disputes are in fact reports of interim proceedings. This is unfortunate in some ways, because the time constraints do not permit the most thorough analysis of the law by either counsel or the court, yet full trials are so rare that reports of interim proceedings are often the only available authorities. This applies, for example, to nearly all the cases on the validity of industrial action ballots, above.

13–035   An interim injunction may even be granted on an application by one party without notice to the other, provided that the claimant can convince the court that all reasonable steps have been taken to give notice of the proceedings to the other party (TULRCA s.221(1)). Only written evidence is given and witnesses are not called for examination. While the claimant should disclose anything favourable to the other side, it is inevitable that the story the court gets is going to be rather one-sided. Thus applications without notice should only be granted in cases of extreme urgency, and then only until there can be a hearing between the parties. Even where both parties are represented, in interim proceedings they may not have had much time for preparation—the respondent usually less than the claimant. Furthermore, while the court has a power to order cross-examination on the evidence, this happens comparatively rarely and most evidence is again likely to be given in writing only.

What must the claimant prove to get an injunction? In *American Cyanamid v Ethicon* (1975), the House of Lords held that the claimant must show that the claim is not frivolous or vexatious and that there is indeed a serious case to be tried. Provided that this can be established, the court should then consider only the balance of convenience in deciding whether or not to make an order—and of course the balance of convenience is usually in favour of the status quo. This decision represented a relaxation of the law; previously the claimant had had to show at least a prima facie case which was likely to be successful at a full trial. It was feared that the new standard would work against trade unions, since the law is so complex that, in any particular case, it would be a poor lawyer who could not raise at least an arguable case that industrial action was likely to be unlawful, and the balance of convenience in a strike situation is practically bound to be on the side of the employer. An attempt to even up the odds was therefore made by TULRCA s.221(2) so that the court is required specifically to consider the likely outcome at a full hearing, including whether the union will be able to establish a defence under TULRCA s.219. Opinions differ as to whether this has redressed the balance sufficiently. The history of the litigation between the TGWU and Associated British Ports over the deregulation of the docks in 1989 affords a good example of weak claims being held sufficient for the grant of injunctions which had the desired effect of delaying action until it was futile (*Associated British Ports v TGWU* (1989)); however, see *Viking Line ABP v ITWF* (2006) for an interesting discussion by the Court of Appeal of the balance of convenience, ultimately finding in the union's favour.

Having been used to a situation where they were rarely sued successfully, trade unions did not easily come to terms with the new legal requirements in the 1980s. Thus when employers were successful in gaining injunctions, as in the *Stockport Messenger* dispute in 1984, the Wapping dispute in 1986, the seafarers' dispute in 1988 (or when members gained injunctions, as in the miners' strike of 1984–85), the reaction of some unions was to ignore the orders, or at least to hasten slowly to put them into effect. This led to several unions being held to be in contempt of court and having heavy fines levied against them. As noted already, these fines could be unlimited in amount, and some were enormous. Where there is any doubt as to whether the union can or will pay the fine, the assets of the union are liable to sequestration, as happened to the miners, seafarers and others.

Contempt proceedings and sequestration orders should not be regarded as **13–036** remedies for employers, since they are more to do with enforcing the orders of the court, and therefore to do with upholding the authority of the court. However, it seems that in the 1980s the swift and severe punishment exacted for infraction of court orders taught unions a lesson the hard way. Today most senior union officers are anxious not to bankrupt their organisations by embarking on clearly unlawful action. However, the lesson was not at first understood among the members, who regarded the failure of the senior officials to back action as at best pusillanimous and at worst as disloyal and an indication of remoteness from ordinary members. The result was the increase of unofficial action which the Employment Act 1990 was meant to address, and the discomfort of many union officials who find themselves between a rock and a hard place.

Picketing

13–037 Picketing usually involves consideration of the criminal law as well as civil, but the problems encountered in dealing with this difficult area do not stem from this cross-over. There are three main problems. First, it is unclear whether or not the simple act of picketing (unaccompanied by violence, obstruction, large numbers, etc) is unlawful or not. Secondly, there is no clear distinction between picketing and public demonstrations. Thirdly, while the law gives protection to pickets only for the purpose of "peacefully obtaining or communicating information, or peacefully persuading any person to work or abstain from working" (TULRCA s.220), it is the case that pickets usually see their object as stopping people from working—by prevention if not by persuasion.

Why picket? From the trade union point of view, picketing is necessary to ensure the effectiveness of strike action. It is not enough to call the members out on strike; an effort must be made to see that the weaker brethren comply. Also, if the strike aims to shut down the employer's operation, it will work more quickly if the employer cannot get supplies in and out, and has no possibility of using alternative labour. On this view, if you accept the need for a freedom to strike, then you should accept the need for a freedom to picket as well. On the other hand, many would argue that no one should have the right to stop others going about their lawful business. It may be noted that the law does not in fact allow this. It could also be argued that picketing is a nineteenth-century tactic which has been out of date ever since motorised transport became common, and that it is time that British unions started devising new tactics.

Probably most people would say that people should be allowed to picket to put their point of view, but not to coerce other people. As with many liberal positions, this is actually quite difficult to translate into practice. For example, I may wish to break the strike because I am not in sympathy with the aims: but I do not want to have to walk past a line of people shouting abuse, or taking my name to display on a "roll of dishonour", or staring at me sullenly, much less putting my photograph with unflattering captions on Twitter or Facebook. Assuming that there is not the slightest physical danger to me from the pickets, am I being coerced in any of these situations if I chicken out? The increased use of social media is certainly one of the main drivers for the present Government to seek further changes in the law relating to picketing, as we will see.

Civil liability for picketing

If pickets are successful in their persuasion, they are certain to induce breaches **13–038** of contracts of employment and commercial contracts. If they turn back employees of the employer in dispute, they induce breaches of their contracts of employment. If they turn back a lorry trying to make a delivery, the possibilities are greater. They will induce a breach of the lorry driver's contract of employment, and probably a breach of the commercial contract under which the supply was due. If the lorry driver is employed by a road haulage company which was contracted by the supplier to make the delivery, then the pickets will induce a breach of the contract of carriage as well as of the supply contract.

Thus, at common law, pickets could be liable for the whole panoply of economic torts. However, the individual pickets, and the union which organises their activity will receive the basic protection of TULRCA s.219 provided that they act within the terms of TULRCA s.220. As noted already, this means that they must limit themselves to peaceful persuasion, and they must be acting in contemplation or furtherance of a trade dispute. A major restriction, however, introduced by a 1980 amendment, is that pickets will only have this immunity if they are either picketing at or near their own place of work (or where they used to work, if they have been sacked) or the picket is a union official accompanying members whom she represents, who are picketing their own place of work. There is an exception for workers who do not have a single place of work (e.g. sales representatives), or who work at a place which it is not practicable to picket (e.g. an oil rig). They may picket the place from which their work is administered.

This provision suggests that there was an intention that everyone should have somewhere to picket: it has not, however, been so interpreted in practice. *News Group Newspapers v SOGAT '82* (1986) was one of the cases resulting from Rupert Murdoch's move from Fleet Street to Wapping. His company, the claimant in the action, published the *Sun*, the *News of the World*, *The Times* and the *Sunday Times*. When the unions refused to agree to the move, and began strike action, all those taking part (some 5,500 workers) were dismissed. They picketed Wapping—but of course they had been employed in central London. It would have been quite pointless for them to have picketed their former places of work, but the court held that because they were not picketing at or near their own place of work they were not protected (see also *Union Traffic v TGWU* (1989)). However, there was a welcome recognition of realities in *Rayware Ltd v TGWU* (1989). The employer's premises were situated on a small industrial estate, which was all private property. The distance from the public highway to their premises was a little over two-thirds of a mile. The pickets would have been trespassing had they gone to the plant entrance, so they picketed at the entrance to the estate instead. It was held that this was "at or near" their place of work.

As indicated above, if picketing is successful, the contracts disrupted may **13–039** well include contracts of employment with employers who are not parties to the dispute (the contracts of the supplier's or road haulier's employees)—which of course constitutes secondary action. But this is the one exceptional situation where secondary action is allowed. Under TULRCA s.224(1), secondary action continues to be immune if it occurs as a result of lawful picketing.

The Trade Union Bill 2016 introduces new restrictions to the picketing immunity, essentially by elevating a number of suggestions in the 1992 Code of Practice on Picketing to the status of legislative conditions. A new TULRCA s.220A contains the new stipulations: the union must appoint a picketing supervisor, who is either a union official or a member familiar with the requirements of the Code of Practice; the union must take reasonable steps to notify the police of where the picketing will take place, and the identity and contact details of the supervisor; the union must provide the picket supervisor with a letter confirming his or her authority, which the supervisor must produce on request from the employer or someone acting on the employer's behalf (can the picket supervisor ask to see a letter from the employer indicating the latter's authority?); the picket supervisor must wear a badge, armband or similar means of identification, and must either be present throughout the picketing, or at least readily contactable and able to attend at short notice. Failure to observe any of these conditions, which manage to be both vague and stringent at the same time, will result in loss of immunity. In case the employer should be backward in making complaints, the Certification Officer is seen as a "key regulator" who may act on his own initiative or on receiving third party complaints of breaches.

So much for the economic torts. As we saw in relation to industrial action in general, other torts may be committed in the course of the action for which no protection is given by TULRCA s.219. This is particularly so in the case of picketing. Trespass is one which has already been mentioned. Pickets must take care to stay off property belonging to the employer. This means in practice gathering on the highway outside. Is this trespass to the highway? In *Hubbard v Pitt* (1975), a leading case on picketing which, however, involved a consumer rather than an industrial picket, Lord Denning expressed the view that pickets might well be trespassing on the highway, but as a civil matter, it would be for the highway authority to take action, which is a fairly unlikely contingency. However, trespass to the highway would only occur if there were an unreasonable use of the highway, and it seems clear that it is reasonable to use the highway other than for passage and re-passage. (See also *DPP v Jones* (1999), where the House of Lords held that a peaceful assembly on the highway was not trespassory.)

13–040   The issues were examined in relation to the Wapping dispute in *News Group Newspapers v SOGAT '82* (1986). At Wapping, the union stationed six official pickets identified with armbands at the outer gate of the premises for 24 hours a day. In addition, between 50 and 200 demonstrators attended each day, usually at the times at which employees arrived for and left work. On Wednesday and Saturday nights, and sometimes at other times, from 700 to 7,000 people rallied at Tower Hill to march to Wapping, where they would be addressed in a square near the works. The rallies were organised by the union; the union denied organising the demonstrations but Stuart-Smith J considered it at least arguable that it had done so. Evidence was given that pickets shouted abuse and used obscene language. Much was directed at individuals. The registration numbers of cars entering the works were noted. Employees complained of being followed home, of cars being vandalised, and of threats. On one occasion a coffin was suspended from a lamp post outside the works. There were reports of missiles being thrown, and that demonstrators sometimes rushed the outer gate to try and prevent lorries going through. The union condemned most of this behaviour.

The employer sought an injunction on grounds of nuisance, obstruction of the highway, interference with trade and business and intimidation. Stuart-Smith J held that obstruction of the highway was capable of being a public nuisance, actionable in tort at the suit of a private claimant on proof of special damage beyond that suffered by the general public. He considered that a march or a meeting would not necessarily amount to an unreasonable obstruction, although on the facts here the activities did. Private nuisance, that is wrongful interference with enjoyment of property rights, was also established because of extra costs of transport and security and staff turnover resulting from the campaign. As to intimidation, the judge held that swearing, abuse and even general threats such as "We'll get you!" did not amount to a threat of violence, but the serious threats that had occurred here were capable of amounting to intimidation. Interference with contract was also made out, and since the picketing went beyond the bounds of TULRCA s.220 there was no immunity.

In *Thomas v NUM* (1986) Scott J had suggested that there was a tort of harassment, which would be established where there was unreasonable interference with one's right to use the highway (as could occur if followed by abusive persons). In this case it was argued that no such tort existed: Stuart-Smith J found it unnecessary to express an opinion on this. In subsequent cases not concerned with picketing there was a conflict of authority as to whether a common law tort of harassment existed and, if so, as to its ambit (*Khorasandjian v Bush* (1993), *Burris v Azadani* (1995), *Hunter v Canary Wharf* (1997)). This has largely been overtaken by the Protection from Harassment Act 1997, which created a statutory tort of harassment. The tort is committed by either pursuing a course of conduct which the defendant knows or ought to know amounts to harassment or which the defendant knows or ought to know causes fear of violence in another person. Conduct is defined so as to include speech, and a course of conduct means on more than one occasion. It seems clear that this tort could be committed in the course of picketing. In addition to compensation (which can include damages for anxiety and distress), claimants may seek injunctive relief.

News Group Newspapers v SOGAT '82 is also interesting in that the judge addressed the issue of the distinction if any between demonstrating and picketing. Having recourse to a dictionary definition as well as the terms of TULRCA s.220, he was satisfied that the demonstrators in this case were properly to be regarded as pickets. This was not the case, however, for those involved in the rallies and marches—unless they turned to picketing after the rally had dispersed. **13–041**

Of course, during the major industrial disputes of the 1980s, there were no mobile phones nor social networks to contend with. The ability to escalate all sorts of audiovisual communications to much wider audiences, producing greater, if often short-lived, effects arguably introduces a new dimension to picketing, one which certainly concerns the current Government. Its proposal is to revise the Code of Practice on Picketing to clarify the existing legal position in relation to the use of social media as well as recommending good practice.

This also raises what was the final difficult issue in the *SOGAT* case, as with similar cases arising out of the 1984–85 miners' strike: whether or not the union is properly to be held responsible for everything which happens on the picket line or in other protests. The Wapping dispute, because it was happening in central London at more social hours than the miners' dispute, attracted the attention of various political groups and wholly unaffiliated people who could hardly be said to be under the control of the union. This was recognised by the judge, who held that the union was not liable simply for organising activities in the course of which torts occurred, even if the commission of torts was entirely foreseeable (cf. also, *Gate Gourmet London Ltd v TGWU* (2005)). However, if, as here, the union continued to organise similar activities again and again, knowing the torts would be committed, and particularly if it had taken no steps to control the situation, then it would have to be taken to have authorised what happened. The judge noted that, although the print unions were well known for having some of the most severe disciplinary powers over their members, there was no evidence that pickets who had overstepped the mark had been punished or even prevented from picketing again.

13–042 In *Thomas v NUM* (1985) Scott J expressed the view that picketing outside the ambit of TULRCA s.220. was not of itself tortious; that is, torts may be committed in the course of picketing, but the mere activity of picketing is not tortious so that it requires s.220 in order to make it lawful. This seems to be a correct statement of the law, and is a welcome clarification. However, the judge expressed the view that picketing at someone's home would constitute private nuisance, regardless of the numbers involved.

Does the presence of large numbers by itself (i.e. even if they are completely peaceful) constitute a tort? There are suggestions that this is so in *Thomas v NUM*, on the basis that large numbers are very likely to obstruct and to be intimidatory. But it is submitted that this should be treated with caution. Once, in the United States, I went to a gallery opening which was picketed by former employees of the industrialist who owned the pictures. By leaflet and placard, the pickets made it clear that they were not trying to dissuade us from attending, but wanted us to be aware of the facts about their former boss and to write letters about it, or perhaps to contribute to their campaign fund by post. Surely if there were large numbers of pickets engaged on such a purpose, the fact of large numbers would not render their conduct tortious?

The issue about numbers has been muddied because of the Code of Practice on Picketing. Like other Codes, it does not impose any legal obligations, but it is to be taken into account in any relevant proceedings. The Code recommends that

> "the organisers should ensure that in general the number of pickets does not exceed six at any entrance to, or exit from, a workplace; frequently a smaller number will be appropriate" (para.51).

Many have criticised the Code for in effect legislating by the back door. **13–043**
Certainly the figure of six has come to be treated as if it were a legal requirement,
being used in court orders to unions on picketing, and being referred to by
Scott J in *Thomas v NUM* (1985) in support of his statement that a larger number
was likely to be intimidatory. Interestingly, the Trade Union Bill 2016 does not
propose imposing a limit of six pickets per entrance.

Criminal liability for picketing

When feelings run high and picket lines become violent, as happened in the **13–044**
Wapping dispute, clearly all sorts of criminal offences can be committed, ranging
from insulting behaviour to grievous bodily harm. (During the miners' strike it was
reported that police told pickets at one colliery that shouting "scabs" or "blacklegs" at working miners would be considered insulting behaviour. After negotiation, it was agreed that it would be all right for them to shout "bounders"!)

However, even if a picket line is entirely peaceful, it may still fall foul of the
criminal law. The two most common offences with which pickets have been
charged are obstruction of the highway and obstruction of a police officer in the
execution of his duty. The two frequently go together: if a police officer considers that pickets are obstructing the highway and they refuse to obey an order to
move, they will certainly be run in for obstructing the police officer. On the basis
that using the highway for passage and re-passage is lawful, in *Tynan v Balmer*
(1967) 40 men were led round in a circle in front of the factory gates. It had the
effect of obstructing the entrance and they were told to stop by the police officer
on duty. The court agreed that this was an improper use of the highway and
that they were properly convicted of obstructing the police officer by refusing
to desist.

The police are not infallible nor do they have unlimited powers. They must
have reasonable grounds for their belief that an offence is being committed
(*Piddington v Bates* (1960)). However, the courts have shown themselves very
sensitive to the fact that they are judging with hindsight a situation that required
a swift decision, and are fairly reluctant to gainsay the assessment of the acting
officer. Since the Code of Practice, the police are apt to consider more than six
pickets at an entrance as constituting obstruction.

In *Broome v DPP* (1974) a picket failed to persuade a lorry driver not to enter a **13–045**
site, so he stood in front of the lorry and refused to move when asked to do so by
a police officer. He was then arrested and charged with obstructing the highway.
There was no anger or violence and the whole incident lasted only about nine
minutes. The magistrates therefore acquitted him, saying that this was not an
unreasonable time to delay someone in exercise of the right to picket. The House
of Lords pointed out that there is no such right, only a freedom to do so, and he
should have been convicted. As noted already, there is no right to stop a person
or vehicle if they are unwilling to stop. The Labour Government had plans to
introduce a right to stop vehicles in the Employment Protection Act 1975, but
finally dropped them, not least because of the difficulties such a right might give
rise to in practice.

It should be clear from what has been said so far that relations with the police are in practice of the utmost importance. Sometimes the police will stop vehicles to allow pickets to talk to the drivers, provided the pickets agree that they will then not try to obstruct someone who still wants to enter. The question of what the police are prepared to permit in terms of obstruction of the highway is crucially important. Given the strong political and emotional overtones of some industrial action, it is worth considering whether it is right to put the police in this position, particularly since they are meant to be impartial.

Following the miners' strike and around the time of a number of bitter disputes arising from the de-recognition of unions in some parts of the newspaper printing industry, the Public Order Act 1986 was passed. The Act replaced the old common law offences of riot, rout, unlawful assembly and affray; but of most direct relevance to picketing was the introduction of new general powers to control processions and public assemblies. Under ss.11–13, the police must be given advance notice of processions and can impose conditions if they think it necessary to avoid serious public disorder, serious damage to property or serious disruption to the life of the community. If the police believe that these powers are insufficient to prevent serious public disorder, they may apply to the council for the procession to be banned altogether. Under s.14, the senior police officer can impose conditions on the holding of any public assembly on similar grounds. A public assembly is defined as an assembly of 20 or more people in a public place which is wholly or partly open to the air. These provisions have attracted criticism on the grounds that civil liberties relating to freedom of speech should not be liable to restriction because of inconvenience to the public (which, it is feared, is what "serious disruption to the life of the community" could come to mean in practice). It is true that people should be able to live and go about their business in peace, but in a society that values freedom, it is argued that restrictions on such an important freedom as the right to demonstrate should only be countenanced if there are very compelling reasons for doing so. Under the Anti-Social Behaviour, Crime and Policing Act 2014 the police have an additional dispersal power where they believe that a person's conduct is contributing to anti-social behaviour, crime or disorder.

13–046   Specific crimes relating to picketing were laid down in the Conspiracy and Protection of Property Act 1875. These are still in force (TULRCA s.241) and were used fairly extensively in the miners' strike. The offences are committed by those who try to compel someone else to do, or not to do something (like working) without legal authority by means of:

(a)   using violence towards that person, or his or her immediate family;
(b)   persistently following the person around;
(c)   hiding their tools, clothing or other property;
(d)   "watching or besetting" their home or place of business; and
(e)   following the other person in the street with two or more persons in a disorderly manner.

The most common charge under this section is "watching and besetting". In plain English, watching seems to be enough for this, and since it can be committed at a place of business, its potential for wide application to picketing is obvious. Hence it becomes important to know whether it has been done "wrongfully and without legal authority", for only then is the criminal offence made out. It now seems clear that an action must be independently tortious or criminal before it will also constitute a criminal offence under TULRCA s.241 (*Thomas v NUM* (1985)). Thus attendance that is lawful under TULRCA ss.220–220A is clearly not an offence, and attendance outside ss.220–220A would have to be shown to be tortious or criminal on other grounds before TULRCA s.241 applied. The Protection from Harassment Act 1997, discussed above, makes the two forms of harassment into criminal offences as well as torts. In addition to the penalties of fine or imprisonment, the court has power to make a restraining order under the Act.

Other criminal liability in trade disputes

Some groups of workers are subject to special rules making it a criminal offence for them to take industrial action. The police and the armed forces are obvious examples; it is true also of merchant seamen while at sea. Prison officers are the latest group for whom organising industrial action will be a criminal offence, by virtue of the Criminal Justice and Public Order Act 1994. Reflecting the privatisation of public services, the ban on industrial action applies to private sector as well as public sector prison officers. In some countries strikes in essential services are forbidden, or at least subject to stringent control, but while this has been considered from time to time in the United Kingdom, it has not happened yet. There is a provision which could potentially be used in a great many public service disputes and some private ones, but in practice it is never used, though included in the present consolidation (TULRCA s.240). It was introduced by the Conspiracy and Protection of Property Act and states that it is a criminal offence deliberately to break your contract of employment when you know or have reasonable cause to believe that the probable consequences will be to endanger human life, or cause serious bodily injury, or even to expose valuable property to injury or destruction. Clearly industrial action by hospital workers, ambulance drivers or the fire service could endanger life; and numerous strikes in all sorts of areas could expose valuable property to injury. Curiously, there are no recorded instances of its having been used. It seems that no government has been ready to risk the opprobrium of using it, or of repealing it. There are always public-spirited persons who are prepared to try and force the authorities to take action even if they have decided not to, but as a result of *Gouriet v UPOW* (1978) they cannot bring prosecutions unless they can show an interest beyond that of the general public.

13–047

Finally, in terms of criminal offences which might be committed in a trade dispute, there are those arising out of the wrongful occupation of premises. Workers sometimes use the sit-in or work-in as a tactic, especially when they are trying to oppose the closure of a workplace. If they are present without permission, they commit the tort of trespass, and if they use materials they find there, they would commit the tort of conversion. These are civil matters for which the employer would have to take action. However, if violence is used to gain entry to premises where someone is present on the premises opposing entry, then an offence is committed under the Criminal Law Act 1977 s.6, and if any trespassers have a weapon of offence, they commit an offence under s.8 of the same Act. Thus breaking into a factory at night in order to occupy it is not an offence if there is no one there, but it is if there is a caretaker in residence. It will be an offence if anyone has a weapon, regardless of whether there is someone on the premises.

Further Reading

❑ S. Auerbach (1990), *Legislating for Conflict,* Clarendon Press
❑ S. Auerbach (1988), "Injunction Procedure in the Seafarers' Dispute", 17 ILJ 227
❑ S. Auerbach (1987), "Legal Restraint of Picketing: New Trends; New Tensions", 16 ILJ 227
❑ A. Bogg and K.Ewing (2014), "The Implications of the RMT Case", 43(3) ILJ 221
❑ H. Carty (1987), "The Public Order Act 1986: Police Powers and the Picket Line", 16 ILJ 146
❑ A. Davies (2008), "One Step Forward, Two Steps Back? The Viking and Laval Cases in the ECJ", 37 ILJ 126
❑ R. Dukes (2011), "The Right to Strike Under UK Law: Something More Than a Slogan?", 40 ILJ 302
❑ K. Ewing and B. Napier (1986), "The Wapping Dispute and Labour Law", [1986] CLJ 285
❑ M. Ford and T. Novitz (2015), "An Absence of Fairness . . . Retrictions on Industrial Action and Protest in the Trade Union Bill 2015", 44(4) ILJ 522
❑ A. Goodhart (1926), "The Legality of the General Strike", 36 *Yale Law Journal* 464 (reprinted in Goodhart, *Essays in Jurisprudence and the Common Law*)
❑ G. Lightman (1987), "A Trade Union in Chains: Scargill Unbound—The Legal Constraints of Receivership and Sequestration", 40 CLP 25
❑ G. Morris (1991), "Industrial Action in Essential Services: The New Law", 20 ILJ 89
❑ G. Morris (1993), "Industrial Action: Public and Private Interests", 22 ILJ 194
❑ T. Novitz (2014), "The Internationally Recognised Right to Strike", 30 *International Journal of Comparative Labour Law and Industrial Relations* 357
❑ B. Simpson (2013), "The Labour Injunction and Industrial Action Ballots", 42 ILJ 54
❑ P. Wallington (1986), "Injunctions and the Right to Demonstrate", [1986] CLJ 86
❑ P. Wallington (1985), "Policing the Miners' Strike", 14 ILJ 145

The thinking of the Conservative Government over the 1980s on this area may be followed through its papers preceding trade union law reform:

Democracy in Trade Unions, Cmnd.8778 (1983), Ch.3
Industrial Relations in the 1990s, Cm.1602 (1991), Chs 1–4
Removing Barriers to Employment, Cm.655 (1989), Ch.3
Review of Public Order Law, Cmnd.9510 (1985)

Trade Union Immunities, Cmnd.8128 (1981)

Unofficial Action and the Law, Cm.821 (1989)

Working Paper for Consultations on Proposed Industrial Relations Legislation—Picketing (Department of Employment, July 1979)

Working Paper on Secondary Industrial Action (Department of Employment, February 1980)

The consultation papers preceding the Trade Union Bill 2016 are as follows:

Ballot Thresholds in Important Public Services, BIS/15/418 (2015)

Hiring Agency Staff during Strike Action: Reforming Regulation, BIS/15/416 (2015)

Tackling Intimidation of Non-Striking Workers, BIS/15/415 (2015)

14. Health and Safety at Work

Key Points

This chapter:
- Considers the nature of the employer's duty of care to employees
- Explains the three-fold duty to provide competent colleagues, safe equipment and a safe system of work
- Considers how far employers are liable for stress at work
- Examines the extent of an employer's vicarious liability for employees and independent contractors
- Explains the tort of breach of statutory duty
- Discusses statutory regulation under the Health and Safety at Work etc Act
- Explains enforcement via improvement and prohibition notices
- Considers the roles of safety representatives and safety committees
- Notes the increasing influence of EU law on health and safety

***

The problem of accidents at work is still acute, although there has been a down-ward trend in recent years. In 2014–15 there were 142 fatalities at work, and over 76,000 injuries, resulting in 27.3 million days lost through work-related ill-health or workplace injury. In addition to the human costs, the economic costs of this are huge.

The main aim of the law should be to contribute so far as possible to the pre-vention of accidents. This is mainly done by statutory regulation of the standards to be observed, enforced by criminal sanctions. The other aim of the law is to ensure adequate compensation for employees whose injury at work is attribut-able to the fault of the employer or someone for whom the employer is respon-sible. This is done through the employee's common law claim for damages. As an understanding of the common law is a necessary starting point for the legislation on health and safety, the common law claims will be examined first and then

14–001

the Health and Safety at Work etc Act 1974 (HSWA) and EU legislation will be considered.

Employers' Liability at Common Law

Basis for the claim

14–002 An employee's claim for damages against the employer for breach of the duty of care sounds in both contract and tort. Traditionally the employer's duty of care was a duty to take care to protect the employee from physical injury and thus an extrapolation of general principles of negligence. Indeed, many cases regularly referred to in elucidation of the law of negligence involve employees suing their employer. On the other hand, where an employee was injured abroad it was held that he could base his claim against his employer in contract in order to be able to sue in England (*Matthews v Kuwait Bechtel Corporation* (1959)). By the 1980s the Privy Council were advising against searching for liability in tort where a contractual relationship existed between the parties (*Tai Hing Cotton Mill Ltd v Liu Chong Hing Bank Ltd* (1986)). However, this was in the context of discouraging attempts to extend obligations under the contract of employment by invoking a duty of care in the law of tort. The advice was applied in *Reid v Rush & Tompkins* (1989), where the employee had been sent to work on a project in Ethiopia. While there he was injured in a road accident through the negligence of an unknown third party. As Ethiopia did not require compulsory third party insurance, it transpired that he was not insured against the accident. He claimed that his employers had been negligent in failing to insure him or at least in failing to advise him that he was not insured, or alternatively that they were in breach of an implied term in the contract to similar effect. On these facts the Court of Appeal held that there were no grounds for implying a term of the contract that the employer should have insured him or advised him to get insurance, and also that a duty of care in tort could not be imposed to enlarge the employer's contractual obligation.

Thus a claim that the employer is in breach of the duty of care owed to the employee may be treated either as an implied term of the contract of employment or as a particular application of the general duty of care that each one of us owes our neighbour under the principle of *Donoghue v Stevenson* (1932), but in either case the content of the duty is usually the same. However, given that different rules apply to actions in contract and actions in tort, this may be an oversimplification. For example, in *Scally v Southern Health and Social Services Board* (1991) doctors employed by the board claimed that it had been negligent in failing to draw to their attention an opportunity to buy extra benefits under the applicable pension scheme so that they did not find out about the opportunity until it was too late to take advantage of it. The facts were unusual in that the right to buy extra benefits was contractual, but the employees could be excused for not knowing about it because it was not a term negotiated with them individually but introduced by statutory regulation. The loss they had suffered was purely economic, and in tort pure economic loss can rarely be recovered. The House of Lords stated that the claimants would probably not succeed in tort for this reason, but that looked at from the perspective of contract the position was quite different. Given that this was a contractual opportunity which the employees could not be expected to know about, the House of Lords considered that a term could be implied into the contract that the employer should draw it to the employees' attention.

A possible disadvantage of the contract approach is that it could be possible for the employer to exclude liability for breach. In *Johnstone v Bloomsbury HA* (1991) a junior hospital doctor argued that his hours of work, sometimes as high as 100 per week, were endangering his health. The contract required him to work a 40-hour week and then to be on call for an unlimited amount of overtime, although this was not to average more than an extra 48 hours a week. A majority of the Court of Appeal held that he had a cause of action in these circumstances. One of the majority judges held that the express term had to be read as subordinate to the employer's implied duty of care, but the other majority judge accepted the view of the dissenting judge that an implied term could not override an express term in this way. However, he thought that the express right to demand overtime was limited by an implied term that it would be exercised reasonably (see above, para.4–019). All members of the Court of Appeal considered that it was arguable that the effect of the clause was to compel the employee to assume any risks associated with working these hours, and this was in substance an exclusion clause within the meaning of the Unfair Contract Terms Act 1977 (UCTA). Thus in *Johnstone v Bloomsbury HA* the Court of Appeal accepted that the employer could in theory exclude liability for breach of the duty of care, but under UCTA such an exclusion would be void in so far as it related to excluding liability for death or personal injury (UCTA s.2). The applicability of UCTA s.3 to the contract of employment was doubted by the Court of Appeal in *Commerzbank AG v Keen* (2007), on the basis that it was unrealistic to regard an employee as a "consumer", but this does not affect liability under s.2.

It would seem that the contractual basis of the employer's duty of care is **14–003** invoked mainly by the courts in order to prevent employees from using the law of tort to impose extra obligations on the employer. Nonetheless, the nature of the duty of care is clearly defined by the law of negligence.

The employee may claim against the employer at common law in two ways: either on the basis of vicarious liability, where the employee is injured through the fault of another employee for whom the employer is responsible; or on the basis of a breach of the employer's own direct duty to take reasonable care for the safety of employees. There is obviously a high degree of overlap between these two claims, the reason for which is historical. In the nineteenth century the courts evolved the "doctrine of common employment", which meant that by taking a position with an employer you were taken to consent to the risk of negligent action by other employees (compare the defence of volenti, below, para.14–029). The doctrine soon came to be thought of as unfair to employees, but was not finally abolished until the Law Reform (Personal Injuries) Act 1948. In the meantime, a way around it was devised by the development of the concept of a non-delegable duty of care owed directly by the employer to the employee. Today either route may be relied on.

Under the Employers' Liability (Compulsory Insurance) Act 1969 all employers should be insured against potential liability to employees for negligence, and failure to have current insurance is a criminal offence. Unfortunately, however, if an employer is in breach, then the employee may be left without means of redress. This is what happened in *Richardson v Pitt-Stanley* (1995). The claimant had been injured at work because of his employer's breach of statutory duty, but the company was not insured and was unable to pay the damages. It went into liquidation. He attempted instead to sue the directors of the company, who were guilty of a criminal offence under the Act for the failure to insure, but the Court of Appeal held that the Act had not been intended to create civil liability for the breach, only criminal liability.

The direct duty of care

14–004   The duty of care owed directly by the employer to the employee may be an implied term of the contract of employment, but its content can best be understood as a specialised version of the duty of care each one of us owes our neighbour (the person who may foreseeably be affected by our actions) under the principle of *Donoghue v Stevenson* (1932). The leading case on its explication is *Wilsons & Clyde Coal Co v English* (1938), where Lord Wright described it as a threefold duty: to provide competent fellow employees, adequate plant and a safe system of work. While each case must be tested against the general question, whether the employer took reasonable care for the employee's safety, it is convenient to consider the content of the duty under these heads.

Competent fellow-employees

14–005   "Upon principle it seems to me that if, in fact, a fellow workman is not merely incompetent but, by his habitual conduct is likely to prove a source of danger to his fellow employees, a duty lies fairly and squarely on the employers to remove that source of danger" (Streatfield J, *Hudson v Ridge Manufacturing* (1957)).

The injured employee broke his wrist when wrestled to the ground by another employee engaging in horseplay. The practical joker had had a reputation for this sort of thing for four years before this incident and the employer's lack of care was in failing to maintain discipline and prevent potentially dangerous conduct. There should be no problem in establishing a fair dismissal should the employer dismiss the delinquent employee in these circumstances, provided that the employer acts reasonably in doing so. Where the employer does not know of the employee's propensity to injure others, there would be no breach of the direct duty of care; however, the employer might be vicariously liable instead for the employee's action, if it could be seen to be in the course of his employment (*Harrison v Michelin Tyre Co Ltd* (1985); contrast *Aldred v Nacanco* (1987)).

Safe plant and equipment

The employer is responsible for ensuring that the workplace is not dangerous **14–006** and that tools, machinery and other equipment used by the employees are suitable for the task and safe. The employers may not themselves have the expertise or facilities for checking equipment: in such a situation the duty will be discharged if the equipment is bought from a reputable manufacturer and then kept in good repair (*Davie v New Merton Board Mills* (1959)). However, in *Taylor v Rover* (1966) the employer was held liable when the employee was injured by a chisel splintering in use, because although the manufacturers were responsible for over-hardening the chisel, the employer knew that someone else had been injured in the same way, but failed to withdraw the chisels or to check them.

If the employer is not liable because the equipment was obtained from a reputable source and the fault lies in the manufacturing process, the employee can sue the manufacturer for negligence. This has its drawbacks, in that the employee may find it difficult to establish who is the manufacturer, or the manufacturer may have gone out of business. For this reason, the Employers' Liability (Defective Equipment) Act 1969 provides that the employer will be held liable if the defect in the equipment is attributable to the fault of a third party. The employer may, of course, join the manufacturer as a defendant to the proceedings, but the idea is that the employee should be allowed to pursue the person easiest to identify. It is not, however, strict liability. The employer will only be held liable if fault on the part of the third party can be established. Also, the Act applies only to defective equipment, and thus does not include oils, powders and other similar items which are also capable of causing injury.

In *Coltman v Bibby Tankers* (1988) the House of Lords held that the word "equipment" was wide enough to include a ship of whatever size provided by the employers for use in their business. It was there alleged that the design and construction of a bulk carrier had been defective with the result that the vessel was unseaworthy, causing it to sink with all hands. A claim under the Employer's Liability (Defective Equipment) Act 1969 was permissible.

The common law requirement to provide safe equipment is in practice largely **14–007** superseded now by the more specific obligations of the Provision and Use of Work Equipment Regulations 1998, which also stipulate a general requirement that work equipment should be suitable in relation to health and safety (reg.4). There is civil liability for breach. Under these Regulations, the concept of work equipment has also been construed broadly, so as to include a door closer that the employee was actually repairing in *Spencer-Franks v Kellogg Brown and Root Ltd* (2009), although not a ramp at a patient's home, visited by a council care worker, where the ramp was not installed or maintained by the council (*Smith v Northants CC* (2009)).

Safe system of work

It is up to the employer to ensure that the methods used to undertake the work, **14–008** the system of supervision and general organisation add up to a safe system of work. That this duty lies squarely on the employer, even where the worker is knowledgeable and experienced, was stressed by the House of Lords in *General Cleaning Contractors v Christmas* (1953). The employee, a window cleaner, was balancing on a sill cleaning a window when the sash fell on his hand, causing him to let go and fall. The employers provided safety belts, but there were no hooks on this building to attach them to. The employer argued that the employees were skilled and experienced and as well able as the employer to devise adequate precautions. Nevertheless, the employer was held liable; while it may be reasonable to leave quite a lot to the discretion of skilled employees who are sent out to different premises, this particular danger was common and it called for a system to meet it. It was the employer's responsibility to provide that system.

General Cleaning Contractors v Christmas illustrates the point that the employer's duty of care applies not only when the workers are on the employer's premises, but also on the premises of third party customers and others. The customers may also have the general liabilities of occupiers under the Occupiers' Liability Acts 1957 and 1984, although an occupier is not liable for a foreseeable risk related to the job to be done which the contractors themselves should appreciate and guard against. The case is also instructive on the relevance of trade practice. Part of the employer's defence was that this method of cleaning windows was in general use in the trade. This certainly counts in the employer's favour. As Lord Reid put it:

"A plaintiff who seeks to have condemned as unsafe a system of work which has been generally used for a long time in an important trade undertakes a heavy onus: if he is right it means that all, or practically all, the numerous employers in the trade have been substantially neglecting their duty to their men."

However, it is clear that in some circumstances it may be held that a trade practice is unsafe. Forty years on from *General Cleaning Contractors v Christmas* the Court of Appeal held that employers should simply embargo customers who do not have anchor points for a safety harness unless the window can be cleaned from the inside (*King v Smith* (1994)). In *Thompson v Smiths Shiprepairers* (1984) the claimant's was one of a selection of test cases involving 20,000 similar claims for industrial deafness. While this was regarded as simply an occupational hazard in the industry until 1963, from then on expert advice and protective devices were available which were reasonably effective against this risk. The employees claimed that they got no protection until the early 1970s. The employers argued that it was common practice to continue to ignore this risk, but it was held that they were in breach of duty in respect of injury suffered after 1963. Conversely, where it is trade practice to take a particular precaution, the employer who fails to do so is almost certain to be found to have acted negligently.

14–009   Other examples of changing standards can be seen in the recognition of new injuries caused by increasingly stressful working practices. *Pickford v ICI* (1998) was the first reported case recognising claims for repetitive strain injury (RSI). The claimant was a secretary who spent an unusual proportion of her time typing. The advent of word processors meant that typists were more likely to be typing for long spells without any break in activity, and in 1983 the Health and Safety Executive distributed an advisory booklet on avoiding health risks. In 1987 the company warned typists who spent substantially all their time typing of the need to take rest breaks before their hands and arms got tired, but this information was not passed to secretaries, because it was thought that their work was only about 50 per cent typing, interspersed with other duties. The Court of Appeal upheld the secretary's claim because the same advice had not been given to her. The House of Lords reversed, but on the grounds that in this case the Court of Appeal should not have interfered with the trial judge's findings of fact. The possibility of claims for RSI was established.

Use of safety equipment

Clearly, an important aspect of establishing a safe system of work is the provision of appropriate safety equipment: helmets, gloves, goggles, overalls, safety harnesses and guards. Is it enough if employers simply provide the equipment, or do they have an affirmative obligation to make sure that the employees actually use it? Sometimes use of particular safety equipment will be required by statutory regulation, so that both employer and employee risk criminal penalties if it is not used. But where there is no statutory requirement, the picture is less clear. **14–010**

"I deprecate any tendency to treat the relationship of employer and skilled workman as equivalent to that of a nurse and an imbecile child" declared Viscount Simonds in 1959 (*Smith v Austin Lifts*), arguing that provision of the equipment was enough. Those of us brought up in a more paternalistic society may feel that this is unduly robust. We do not always do those things that we know are good for us, especially if it is at all inconvenient to do so.

The high point of the rugged individualist view is found in *McWilliams v Arrol* (1962). A steel erector fell 70 feet to his death. At the time of the accident he was not wearing a safety belt, and indeed none was actually provided at the site. However, they had been available up to a few days before the accident and the claimant had never worn one. The court concluded that he would certainly not have worn one had they been available on the day of the accident and that therefore the employer's default had not caused his death. Yet this is dependent on seeing the default as simple non-provision of the equipment. If there were an obligation to ensure use of safety equipment, the answer would have been different. It is submitted that to require the employer to ensure use of safety equipment would not be unduly onerous, for after all the employer has supervision systems to make sure that work is being properly carried out, and this would only be one extra thing for a supervisor to check. Naturally it is impossible to guarantee that everyone will always do as they are told, but making non-use of safety equipment a disciplinary offence would be a simple step, and clearly employers who had taken such steps would not be held liable if an employee was injured while not using it.

The contrary view, expressed in *Smith v Scot Bowyers* (1986), is that such a duty would be too vague. While a duty to provide safety equipment has clear boundaries, a duty to encourage, exhort or instruct people to use safety **14–011** equipment would be indeterminate. However, there have been cases where the employer has been held to be in breach of duty where the employees have not been adequately instructed in the need for and use of such equipment, or where the equipment was awkward to use or impeded work and was not used for that reason (e.g. *Bux v Slough Metals* (1974)). In *Crouch v British Rail Engineering* (1988) a fitter injured his eye when a piece of metal flew off as he was trying to loosen a nut with a hammer and chisel. Goggles were available in the storeroom, as he knew, but that was a five-minute walk away and he would have had to get down from his scaffolding, and the task was one of seconds. In these circumstances the Court of Appeal held that the employer's duty extended to the provision of goggles—an inexpensive and common piece of equipment— into the hand of each worker who might need them. It would have been easy to make it part of his general tool kit. However, the employee was held 50 per cent to blame, since he too could easily have made sure that he had some with him.

Standard of care

14–012   The employer's duty is only to take reasonable care for the safety of employees, not to make them safe at any cost. To trade safety in a cost-benefit analysis may seem distasteful, but it is something we accept in other areas, such as road traffic regulation. In *Latimer v AEC* (1953) the factory was flooded in a storm. When the water subsided it left a greasy film over the surface. The employers had three tons of sawdust scattered over the floor to stop it being dangerously slippery, but the employee slipped on an untreated patch and was injured. The House of Lords held that the employers here had done what was reasonable: the only way to make people absolutely safe would have been to close down the factory completely until it had been properly cleaned, which would have been a very expensive course of action. While there remained a risk of injury, the employers had minimised the risk, and the kind of injury risked was not terribly serious. Slipping over is not usually life-threatening. The employers were entitled to balance the cost of a complete shutdown against the risks and keep the factory open. Where there are inherent dangers in the work, the employer may be justified in taking greater risks (e.g. *Watt v Herts CC* (1954); *King v Sussex Ambulance NHS Trust* (2002)).

On the other hand, the duty is a personal one, owed to each employee as an individual. It therefore varies according to the personal characteristics of the individual: the duty will be higher in relation to a young worker in her first job than it would be for a skilled worker with many years of experience. The best illustration of this is *Paris v Stepney BC* (1951). The employee, who was blind in one eye, was employed as a maintenance mechanic. He was rendered totally blind when a splinter of metal flew off while he was removing a bolt from a vehicle. It was not normal to provide goggles for this sort of work as the risk of such an accident was very small. However, goggles do not cost much, and the risk to him was much more serious than to an employee with normal sight, for to lose all sight is a greater disaster than to lose sight in one eye. The duty to this particular employee, therefore, was higher and he should have been provided with goggles.

It seems that the employer's obligation does not extend so far as to require dismissal of an employee, even if that is the only way that the particular employee can be made safe (*Withers v Perry Chain* (1961); *Jones v Lionite Specialities* (1961); *Hatton v Sutherland* (2002)). But in *Pape v Cumbria CC* (1991) it was held that a failure to warn employees of a danger which might not be obvious to them was a breach of the duty of care (cf. also, *Coxall v Goodyear GB Ltd* (2003)). If the employer did dismiss an employee on grounds that his health would suffer if he continued to be employed, it would seem likely that the dismissal would be fair, if properly handled. Does this lead to an unacceptable level of paternalism? In *Page v Freight Hire* (1981) a woman worked as an HGV driver, delivering chemicals. The haulage firm was informed that the chemicals could be dangerous to an unborn child and that therefore a woman of child-bearing age should not be used on this work. The claimant, aged 23 and divorced, stated that she did not intend to have children and was willing to take the risk. It was held that the employer was entitled to remove her from this work in the interests of safety, the EAT saying:

> "We accept that the individual's wishes may be a factor to be looked at, although in our judgment, where the risk is to the woman, of sterility, or to the foetus, whether actually in existence or likely to come into existence in the future, those wishes cannot be a conclusive factor."

The principle of non-delegation

It is axiomatic that the employer may not escape liability for breach of the duty **14–013** of care by showing that someone else was responsible for performance of the duty, even if that person was carefully selected and properly qualified. This is what distinguishes the direct duty of care from the principle of vicarious liability. The clearest statement of this was made in *Wilsons & Clyde Coal Co v English* (1938), where the employee was crushed when the haulage system in the mine was negligently put into operation as he was walking along a haulage road to get to the surface at the end of his shift. The employer's defence was that they had delegated operation of the haulage system to a qualified manager as they were required to do by statute. The House of Lords held that they retained a primary duty of care to the employee and were liable if it was not discharged, even if they were not themselves actually in charge at the time.

At that time the doctrine of common employment stopped the obvious claim, which would have been that the employers were vicariously liable for the actions of the manager of the haulage system. Today that would be an alternative cause of action for the employee. But the decision has two further implications: first, it means that the employer may in some circumstances be held liable for the actions of an independent contractor (compare vicarious liability, see below, para.14–019) and secondly, there may well be situations where more than one employer is liable to the employee. Both points are well illustrated by the important decision of the House of Lords in *McDermid v Nash Dredging* (1987). The claimant was employed as a deckhand by the defendant company. They lent him to an associated company, Stevin, to work on a dredging contract being carried out off Sweden. The tugmaster, an employee of Stevin, negligently set the tug at full speed while the claimant was on deck with the ropes: he became entangled, was pulled overboard, and later had to have a leg amputated. Clearly, Stevin was vicariously liable for the negligence of their employee; but there were practical difficulties in the way of suing a Dutch company (as Stevin was) in an English court in respect of an accident happening in Swedish waters. The House of Lords held that the defendant company, his permanent employer, was liable. The accident had happened because there was no safe system of work. The employer's duty to provide a safe system is non-delegable, and it was therefore liable for this failure. The theoretical basis for the employer's liability was the personal duty, not vicarious liability for the negligence of the independent contractor's employee—but the result looks very like vicarious liability for an independent contractor.

In view of the clear reaffirmation of the principle of non-delegation by the House of Lords in *McDermid v Nash Dredging* (1987) it is surprising to find it distinguished by the Court of Appeal in *Square D Ltd v Cook* (1992). In that case, an electronics engineer was sent by his employers to work on a contract in Saudi Arabia, 8,000 miles away. He was injured when he slipped into a hole in the floor made by the employees of a sub-contractor, and sued his own employer, the occupiers of the premises and the main contractor responsible for coordinating work on the premises. The Court of Appeal distinguished *McDermid* on the grounds that in that case "the hand of the employers still remained on the operation" in that they were joint contractors and it was only a small team. However, their attitude is indicated by the statement, "the suggestion that the home-based employer has any responsibility for the daily events of a site in Saudi Arabia has an air of unreality". The court seems to have been unduly impressed by the fact that in reality the employer was not in charge of what was going on. But it is clear from the decisions already looked at that this does not absolve the employer of responsibility.

Liability for psychiatric injury

14-014   In *Walker v Northumberland CC* (1995) it was held that the duty of care extends to preventing psychiatric damage as well as physical injury. In that case, a social services manager suffered two nervous breakdowns brought on by the stress caused through overload of work and the failure of his superiors to do anything to alleviate it. Colman J held that the first breakdown was not foreseeable, but the second was entirely likely unless the employer took steps to change the situation. As it had not, the council was held to be in breach of its duty to provide a safe system of work.

Walker v Northumberland CC was a landmark in that it was the first reported case of an employer being held liable for stress at work. However, the emphasis on foreseeability suggested that it might not open up the floodgates to stress claims, bearing in mind that the claimant failed to persuade the court that his original breakdown was reasonably foreseeable by his employer. Nevertheless, in the wake of *Walker v Northumberland CC*, claims for psychiatric injury based on exposure to unacceptable levels of stress became prevalent. In *Hatton v Sutherland* (2002) the Court of Appeal heard four joined appeals by employers who had been held liable for their employees' psychiatric illness caused by stress and stated no fewer than 16 "practical propositions" for dealing with such cases, while at the same time asserting that the ordinary law of negligence was applicable in this situation. The court held that an employer was entitled to assume that an employee was able to withstand the normal pressures of the job and, in most cases, to take what the employee said about her own health at face value. It was only if there were indications which would lead a reasonable employer to realise that there was a problem that a duty to take action would arise. One way in which an employer could protect itself from liability would be by offering a confidential advice service, with referral to appropriate counselling or treatment services.

In terms of whether injury to an employee was foreseeable, the court held that this did not depend on whether a person of reasonable fortitude would have been able to cope, as the employer's duty is to each employee individually. Thus the question is what was foreseeable in relation to this employee. If the employer knew or should have known that the employee had a particular vulnerability or predisposition to stress-related illness, then the employer might have a positive duty to intervene—although in these circumstances, the chance that the employee might have succumbed to such an illness in any event could be taken into account in reducing damages. In considering foreseeability, factors such as whether the workload was abnormally heavy, whether the work was particularly intellectually and emotionally demanding for this employee and the level of demands made compared with other employees would all be relevant. In judging whether the employer was in breach of the duty of care, the question of what options were available should be considered. However, if the only way of making the employee safe was to dismiss him, the Court of Appeal did not consider that the employer would be in breach of duty by letting the employee continue if she was willing to do so. Finally, the Court of Appeal emphasised the important point that the employee must show not merely that the harm was caused by occupational stress, but that it was caused by the employer's breach of duty.

The result in the four cases was that the employers' appeal succeeded in **14–015** three of them. One of the losing employees appealed and the case went to the House of Lords under the name of *Barber v Somerset CC* (2004). The House of Lords allowed the employee's appeal on the grounds that there was insufficient reason for the Court of Appeal to have set aside the decision of the trial judge. The appellant did not attack the Court of Appeal's restatement of the law, and the House of Lords approved it as useful practical guidance, while adding the almost mandatory warning against treating it as if it had statutory force. A further four joined appeals in stress cases went to the Court of Appeal in 2005 under the name of *Hartman v South Essex Mental Health and Community Care Trust* (2005), where again the applicability of general principles of negligence was emphasised, but two interesting new points emerged. In one of the cases, *Wheeldon v HSBC Bank plc* (2005), the Court of Appeal accepted that a part-time employee could have a successful stress claim, although this would be exceptional (the employee worked under job-share arrangements and was running, while at work, an extremely busy sub-branch of the bank). In another,

Melville v Home Office (2005), the Court of Appeal made the very important point that if the employer should foresee the possibility of psychiatric harm because the nature of the job itself involved exposure to traumatic incidents, it was not necessary that it should have foreseen the harm to this individual employee. The claimant in this case was a healthcare officer at a prison, and his duties included recovery of the bodies of prisoners who had committed suicide. He had dealt with eight suicides over a 17-year period and his illness was triggered by the last, but there had been nothing previously to suggest to his employers that he was likely to react in this way. Nevertheless, the employer was held liable.

The suggestion by the Court of Appeal in *Hatton v Sutherland* (2002) that an employer could protect itself by making a confidential counselling service available to employees was seized on by many, but it is clear that it should not be regarded as a fail-safe device for an employer. In *Dickins v O₂ plc* (2009) the Court of Appeal held that the advantage of such a scheme was that it might provide an outlet for employees who would otherwise admit that they were close to breakdown. But in this case, where the employee had repeatedly told her manager directly that she was not coping and was at the end of her tether, to refer her to counselling was not an adequate response (cf. also *Daw v Intel Corp (UK) Ltd* (2007)).

In *Gogay v Herts CC* (2000) the employer was held liable for psychiatric injury arising from a single event: the employee's unjustified suspension; however, in *Yapp v Foreign and Commonwealth Office* (2015) the Court of Appeal emphasised that this would be unusual. As Underhill LJ put it, it will be "exceptional that an apparently robust employee, with no history of any psychiatric ill-health, will develop a depressive illness as a result even of a very serious setback at work".

14–016   In *Frost v Chief Constable of South Yorkshire* (1999) the Court of Appeal was prepared to extend the employer's liability for psychiatric injury to the situation of police officers who suffered post-traumatic stress syndrome as a result of being on duty at the Hillsborough football stadium disaster in 1989. Their decision was reversed by the House of Lords (*White v Chief Constable of South Yorkshire* (1998)), who denied that employees were in any different position from any other secondary victim of an accident who suffers nervous shock. It is difficult to reconcile this line of authority with the developing law in relation to the duty of care and psychiatric injury.

In *Rothwell v Chemical and Insulating Co* (2007) the claimants had been exposed to asbestos dust through their employer's negligence, as a result of which they developed pleural plaques, which were not injurious in themselves, but indicated that they were at risk of developing serious asbestos-related diseases in the future. They suffered anxiety as a result of this, and one actually developed a depressive illness as a result. The House of Lords held that psychiatric illness occurring because of the possibility of an event which had not happened was not actionable.

Causation

14–017   An issue which regularly arises in the stress cases is whether the employee's psychiatric injury was caused solely by pressures at work or whether problems in their personal life were equally to blame. As in all negligence cases, the claimant must show that the defendant's breach of duty actually caused the harm complained of. However, in *Hatton v Sutherland* (2002) and *Hartman v South Essex* (2005) the Court of Appeal made it clear that it is not enough for the employer simply to raise doubts about whether the employee was subject to multiple sources of stress. Provided that the employee shows that the employer's breach of duty in relation to stressful working conditions materially contributed to the harm suffered, the onus will be on the employer to prove that other causes contributed to the injury. Only if the employer can do this will damages be reduced.

A common problem for employees is that industrial illnesses may not become manifest until many years after workers were exposed to the danger. This can make it difficult to pinpoint the employer responsible, especially if the employee has worked for a number of different employers in the industry. In *Fairchild v Glenhaven Funeral Services Ltd* (2003) the House of Lords heard three appeals in which employees had developed mesothelioma, a fatally malignant tumour, from exposure to asbestos dust. The disease may be latent for 30–40 years. The appellants had all been exposed to asbestos dust, in breach of the employer's duty of care, in more than one employment. It was not possible to attribute the onset of the disease to any one of these. In these circumstances the House of Lords took the bold step of allowing a relaxation of the usual test of causation (which is that the claimant must show that it is more likely than not, on the balance of probabilities, that the defendant's negligence caused the injury complained of), and held that the defendants were liable because their breach of duty materially contributed to the risk of the claimant getting the disease. Their justification for this was that otherwise the employers' duty of care in relation to asbestos exposure would be "empty" in that claimants would never be able to prove which exposure caused the damage.

The question of how liability would be apportioned between the defendants was not decided in that case, but it was assumed to be joint and several liability (meaning that the claimant could recover the whole amount of compensation from any defendant, who would then have to seek the appropriate contribution from the other tortfeasors). However, in *Barker v Corus Ltd* (2006), involving three more appeals in asbestos-caused mesothelioma cases, the House of Lords held that liability was several only, meaning that each defendant was responsible only for its own contribution to the claimant's injury. This meant that the claimants would bear the loss of some of the defendants having gone out of business over the lengthy period between exposure and onset of the disease, and would also face the difficult task of locating and suing all possible defendants. The Government acted swiftly to pass the Compensation Act 2006, providing that liability in these circumstances would be joint and several, with retrospective effect.

Duty to independent contractors

In contrast to the relatively high duty of care owed to employees, the employer **14–018** has no duty beyond the ordinary duty of any individual towards an independent contractor. If independent contractors come to work on the employer's premises, as an occupier the employer is entitled to expect that they will appreciate and guard against any risks relating to their work (Occupiers' Liability Act 1957 s.2(3)) and the only duty is to safeguard them from risks which are not obvious and of which they might otherwise be unaware. So far as the job itself is concerned, independent contractors are meant to take care for their own safety. This was precisely the issue in *Ferguson v Dawson* (1976) (above, para.3–007). If the worker had the status of employee he could sue the employers for his injury, but if he had really been an independent contractor, he should have taken care for his own safety. The position under the HSWA is different, as will be seen below, para.14–033.

Vicarious liability

Liability for employees

14–019   The second route by which an employee can hold the employer liable for injury suffered at work is where the employee alleges that the injury was caused by the negligence of another employee for whom the employer is responsible. Of course, not only employees but also third parties can hold the employer liable on the basis of vicarious liability. In theory, they can also claim against the actual tortfeasor; but in reality it is likely to be the employer rather than the employee who will be worth suing.

Not every action of every employee makes the employer liable. The limitation is that the employee must have been acting in the course of employment at the time of the negligent act. Discerning what is within the contract of employment and what is "a frolic of his own", in the quaint old phrase, can be difficult. One way of expressing it is to say that the employer is liable when the employee is performing her duties, even if she is performing them badly, but not when she is doing something entirely outside the scope of the contract. In the old case of *Limpus v London General Omnibus Co* (1862), bus drivers were specifically forbidden to race drivers from rival companies, but the employer was held liable when a driver engaged in a race caused an accident. He was doing what he was employed to do, but doing it badly. Similarly, in *Rose v Plenty* (1976) a milk roundsman was specifically forbidden to allow children on the float to assist in delivering milk. He nonetheless employed a 13-year-old to help, who was injured while on the float. It was held that the employer was liable. The employee was doing what he was supposed to be doing, albeit the wrong way.

However, it seems that there comes a point where an employee can be performing so badly that it can be said that she is no longer in the course of employment. In *General Engineering Services v Kingston & St Andrew Corp* (1989) firemen in Jamaica had instituted a go-slow in support of a pay claim. They made a point of not arriving at a fire until the building had substantially burned down. The Privy Council considered that this was action outside their course of employment rather than a defective performance of it.

14–020   One of the areas which has been most problematic in relation to vicarious liability has been the employee who gives someone a lift in the employer's vehicle although instructed not to, or who detours for her own purposes while on a journey on the employer's business. Some guidance was given by the House of Lords in *Smith v Stages* (1989), where Lord Goff said,

> "the fundamental principle is that an employee is acting in the course of his employment when he is doing what he is employed to do . . . or anything which is reasonably incidental to his employment . . .".

In relation to travelling, the question is whether or not the employee can be regarded as being "on duty". Travelling to and from work is not usually included, although it could be if the employee is travelling to work in transport provided by the employer. Where the job involves travel, such as delivery drivers, sales representatives or those going out to provide services at the customer's premises, the employee will be in the course of employment. Deviations or interruptions to the journey, unless purely incidental, take the employee outside the course of employment for as long as they last, and no distinction is to be drawn between outward and return journeys. What was actually at issue in the case was whether payment for travelling time indicated that the employee was in the course of employment. The employees, who installed insulation materials, had been sent on an urgent job to Wales. They were paid for 16 hours' travelling time and the cost of a rail fare but it was left to them how they travelled. They went by car. At the end they worked 24 hours to finish the job and then set off immediately to drive back home. The driver, who was uninsured, went off the road. As they were travelling from a place to which they had been sent especially and also bearing in mind that they were paid for the travelling time, the House of Lords held that they were in the course of employment.

So far as giving lifts is concerned, in *Rose v Plenty* (1976) the Court of Appeal accepted that if this was contrary to instructions it would be outside the course of employment. However, in that case they held that the milkman having the child on the float to assist him was rather a situation of the employee doing wrongly what he was employed to do properly, so the employer was liable. It would be different if a driver employed to make a delivery gave a lift to a hitchhiker.

It may seem surprising that the employer was held liable even though the milkman was acting in contravention of a direct instruction. But if employers were not liable in these circumstances, it would be quite easy for them to escape liability by drawing up lengthy and specific codes of conduct for their employees, thus undermining the policy that the employer should absorb losses attributable to activities of the enterprise. **14–021**

Where an employee engages in criminal activity, the employer can be held liable if the employee was entrusted with performance of a duty in the course of which she commits the crime (*Lloyd v Grace, Smith & Co* (1912)). But there is a distinction between this situation and one where the post merely affords an extra opportunity to commit a crime or tort. In *Heasmans v Clarity Cleaning* (1987) an employee of a company which provided office cleaning services ran up a telephone bill of over £14,000 telephoning the United States while ostensibly cleaning the claimant's offices. It was held that this was conduct outside his employment. His job had simply provided the opportunity for him to commit the crime by giving him access to the building. However, employers like this one usually insure against this kind of contingency, precisely because they might be expected to bear the responsibility. In *Lister v Hesley Hall* (2002) the House of Lords expressed the test in terms of whether or not the employee's tortious action had a "close connection" with what he was employed to do. On that basis, a children's home was held vicariously liable for a warden's sexual abuse of children in his care. In *Mattis v Pollock* (2003) the Court of Appeal went so far as to hold that a nightclub owner was liable for the actions of a bouncer who went home to get a knife before returning and stabbing a customer outside the club who had been part of a group which had earlier attacked the bouncer (cf. also, *Fennelly v Connex South Eastern Ltd* (2001)).

The "close connection" test resulted in a rugby club being held liable for one of its players who punched a player from a different team following an altercation in the scrum, even though the club's contract with the player specifically forbade assaulting other players (*Gravil v Redruth Rugby Football Club* (2008)). Indeed, the existence of an express clause in the contract dealing with this conduct was evidence of the "close connection" with employment. Note, however, that the mere fact that the incident happened at the workplace does not necessarily mean it will be in the course of employment (*Weddall v Barchester Healthcare Ltd; Wallbank v Wallbank Fox Designs Ltd* (2012), *Vaickuviene v J Sainsbury plc* (2013)).

14–022   In recent years large numbers of cases involving historical sex abuse of children have come to light, resulting not only in some notorious prosecutions but also claims for compensation based on vicarious liability. In *Catholic Child Welfare Society v Institute of the Brothers of the Christian Schools* (2013), the most recent to have reached the Supreme Court, the nature of the "close connection" needed for the imposition was examined and said to be based on the fact that the defendant employer was using the abuser employee to further the defendant's business or interests in such a way as to create or significantly enhance the risk that the victim would suffer the abuse which occurred.

The increasing use of outsourced or subcontracted labour for some tasks in the workplace, frequently under the directions of the client, can raise issues as to whether it is appropriate to hold the original employer liable for negligence. Construction sites, where typically several sub-contractors may have employees working under the direction of the general contractor, or perhaps another sub-contractor, are prime examples of this phenomenon. In the leading case of *Mersey Docks and Harbour Board v Coggins & Griffith* (1947) the House of Lords held that the crucial test, where an employee was lent by one employer to another, was which employer had control of the situation. If the temporary employer is directing and supervising the employee, then it rather than the general employer will be vicariously liable for the employee's negligence. However, if the employee has been supplied to the temporary employer precisely because of some expertise which the temporary employer lacks, it is likely that the general employer will remain vicariously liable for any negligent acts. As ever, it is easier to state the test than to apply it.

In *Viasystems (Tyneside) Ltd v Thermal Transfer (Northern) Ltd* (2006) the issue was which employer was responsible for the act of a fitter's mate who negligently fractured the fire sprinkler system, causing extensive flooding and damage to the claimant's factory. Three firms were engaged in fitting an air-conditioning system in the factory at the time. The fitter's mate and the fitter he was assisting both worked for the third defendant, but they were subject to the general supervision of another fitter working for the second defendant. Both fitters were present at the time of the negligent act. In these circumstances the Court of Appeal took the novel step of holding that both the second and third defendant could be held vicariously liable for the mate's negligence. Not surprisingly, this has been seized upon as a way for employers to attempt to minimise vicarious liability. Thus in *Hawley v Luminar Leisure Ltd* (2006) a company owning a nightclub had contracted the provision of doorman services to a security company. However, the doormen wore the owner company's uniform and were subject to the general direction of the nightclub's manager. When it came to the question of who was vicariously liable for a doorman's serious assault on a customer, the company owning the nightclub argued that either the security company was wholly responsible, as his direct employer, or else that they were both liable under the principle in *Viasystems*. This was rejected by the Court of Appeal. While affirming that the original employer will face a heavy burden of proof to establish that responsibility has shifted to the temporary employer, the court was convinced that here it was the temporary employer which had control over the relevant circumstances and it could not be regarded as an example of dual control as in *Viasystems*.

Some loosening of this position seems to be likely following *Catholic Child Welfare Society v Institute of the Brothers of the Christian Schools* (2013) where the Supreme Court commented that the test laid down in *Mersey Docks and Harbour Board v Coggins & Griffith* (1947) was so stringent as to be almost impossible to satisfy in practice and suggested that *Hawley v Luminar Leisure Ltd* (2006) could have been a dual liability situation. In *Catholic Child Welfare Society* the Supreme Court held that liability for abuse carried out as teachers at a school by lay brothers who were members of the Institute of the Brothers of the Christian Schools should be apportioned to the Institute, which directed their lives, as well as the managers of the school who were their employers. **14–023**

Liability for independent contractors

An employer is not usually liable for the actions of independent contractors, which is one of the main reasons for needing to distinguish them from employees (see above, para.3–001). However, there are exceptions. If the employer specifically instructs the contractor to perform the action which is tortious, she will be liable. Where there is strict liability the employer can be held responsible for things done by independent contractors. A good example is *Rylands v Fletcher* (1866) which established the rule of strict liability for damage done by things escaping from land where their accumulation was a non-natural user of the land. The landowners had employed independent contractors to build a reservoir on their land; through the contractors' negligence the water escaped and flooded a mine on neighbouring land. The landowners, as employers of the **14–024** independent contractors, were held liable. Finally, as seen in *McDermid v Nash Dredging* (1987) (see above, para.14–013), the employer will remain personally responsible where independent contractors have charge of the safety of the employer's employees, and in this way will be responsible for their negligence in this regard.

It should be noted that another important feature of the *Catholic Child Welfare Society v Institute of the Brothers of the Christian Schools* (2013) case is that the Institute was held liable for the acts of its members—lay brothers who were teachers—even though the relationship between them was not one of employer-employee. The Supreme Court held that the relationship had many of the elements of an employer-employee relationship, in particular that the Institute directed them what to do and the manner in which they should do it, and that their work was undertaken in order to further the objectives of the Institute. In these circumstances, the policy reasons which make it just and reasonable to impose vicarious liability on an employer were met. It remains to be seen whether this will lead to some blurring of the distinction between employees and others in terms of the employer's vicarious liability.

Liability for breach of statutory duty

14–025   The difficulty for the employee who wants to sue her employer for breach of the duty of care is that it is necessary to prove negligence by the employer or someone for whom the employer is responsible. However, if the employee can show that the injury was caused by an action which was in breach of statute or statutory regulation, she will have an alternative claim for the tort of breach of statutory duty. In this situation all that the employee has to show is that the breach was the cause of the injury. Thus in *Ferguson v Dawson* (1976) the worker fell off a roof which was unfenced in contravention of statutory regulation. He did not have to show that the employer was careless in failing to fence the roof: it was enough that the accident was caused by the breach. (Had Ferguson been an independent contractor as was argued (see above, para.3–007), it would have been his duty to ensure that the roof was fenced, not the employer's.)

The breach of statute or statutory regulation will normally attract some sanction under the enactment itself—usually criminal liability. Civil liability for the tort of breach of statutory duty is additional, and is not available in every case. Sometimes the statute itself will state whether or not a civil action is possible. The HSWA s.47, used to state that breach of the general duties laid down in ss.2–8 of the statute does not give rise to civil liability, but breach of any regulations made under the statute would do so, unless the regulations expressly stated otherwise. This was changed by the Enterprise and Regulatory Reform Act 2013 (ERRA) s.69, which completely reverses this position: for breaches occurring from 1 October 2013, there is only civil liability for breach of health and safety regulations where the regulations provide for this. Thus, at a stroke, a whole swathe of potential liability for employers has been removed. It is argued that this may be incompatible with the EU Directives on which many sets of these regulations are based (see below, para.14–042), and it is possible that this may be litigated in future. It was only in 2003 that the Management of Health and Safety at Work Regulations 1999 were amended to provide for civil liability, an amendment introduced at the insistence of the European Commission, who considered that the Regulations did not properly transpose the Framework Health and Safety Directive (89/391/EEC) because, as originally framed, they did not permit a civil action for their breach.

In the absence of an express provision the existence of liability for breach of statutory duty depends on the interpretation of the statute. In *Lonrho v Shell* (1982) the House of Lords stipulated that for civil liability it had to be shown either that the relevant provision was intended for the benefit or protection of a particular class of person including the claimant, or that it created a public right and this particular claimant suffered damage over and above that suffered by the general public because of its breach. Claims by employees are based on the first of these. In the landmark case, *Groves v Lord Wimborne* (1898), it was held that the precursor of the Factories Act was intended to protect workers and the employer was civilly liable for its breach.

However, not all parts of industrial safety legislation give rise to civil liability. **14–026** In the interpretation of the Factories Act 1961 a distinction was drawn between the safety provisions (where there was civil liability for breach) and the health and welfare provisions (such as the requirements for washing facilities) where there was not. As the provisions in older legislation are replaced by newer regulations, any uncertainty should diminish, as the position will be clear under new regulations. Finally, the damage suffered by the employee must be caused by the danger to which the provision was addressed. This requirement led to the curious decision in *Close v Steel Co of Wales* (1962) that the sections in the Factories Act stipulating that dangerous machinery should be fenced were aimed at keeping people out rather than at keeping materials in, and the employee injured by metal flying out did not have a cause of action for breach of statute. Similarly, the House of Lords held that an employee who suffered frostbite to his toe because of a hole in the steel toe capped boots provided by his employer could not claim that they were in breach of their duty under the Personal Protective Equipment at Work Regulations 1992 to provide him with "suitable" equipment, because the boots were provided to prevent crush injuries, not to prevent frostbite (*Fytche v Wincanton Logistics plc* (2004)).

Defences

There are two particular defences on which an employer faced with liability may **14–027** seek to rely: contributory negligence and volenti non fit iniuria.

Contributory negligence

At common law, if a claimant claiming for negligence or breach of statutory duty **14–028** was partly to blame for the accident, this was a complete defence to her claim. This severe rule was mitigated by the Law Reform (Contributory Negligence) Act 1945 which provided that in these circumstances the blame could be apportioned between the parties. Contributory negligence is thus a partial defence for the employer; the court will decide how far the claimant was also at fault and reduce damages by the percentage.

The court is not concerned solely with whether the claimant's conduct actually contributed to the accident but explicitly with how far this was the employee's fault.

"What is all important is to adapt the standard of what is (contributory) negligence to the facts, and to give due regard to the actual conditions under which men work in a factory or mine, to the long hours and the fatigue, to the slackening of attention which naturally comes from constant repetition of the same operation, to the noise and confusion in which the man works, to his preoccupation in what he is actually doing, at the cost of some inattention to his own safety" (Lord Wright in *Caswell v Powell Duffryn* (1940)).

Consent

14–029   If you willingly consent to take a risk you cannot complain if the danger materialises: this is the defence expressed in the maxim volenti non fit iniuria. It is generally a narrow defence. You do not consent to a risk just because you know about it (*Smith v Charles Baker & Sons* (1891)), and even where you consent to a risk you do not consent to its being made worse through someone's negligence. Thus, being a member of a lifeboat crew is more dangerous than being a teacher, and to that extent the crew consent to run a risk: but they would not be taken to have consented if their boat were lost because it had been negligently maintained.

In *Bowater v Rowley Regis Corporation* (1944) Goddard LJ said that the defence is one which:

"in the case of master and servant is to be applied with extreme caution. Indeed, I would say that it can hardly ever be applicable where the act to which the servant is said to be 'volens' arises out of his ordinary duty, unless the work for which he is engaged is one in which danger is necessarily involved."

However, one of the very few cases in which the defence has ever succeeded involved employees. In *ICI v Shatwell* (1965) a team of shotfirers were required by regulation only to carry out detonations from behind cover. On one occasion the wire was not long enough for them to get behind cover. One went to get more wire, but while he was away the other two decided to go ahead with the testing in the open. Both were injured in the subsequent explosion, but it was held that the employer was not liable, for with full knowledge of the danger, they had deliberately decided to run the risk.

Statutory Regulation of Health and Safety

14–030   In 1970 a Committee on Safety and Health at Work was set up chaired by Lord Robens. Amazingly, it was the first time that any committee had been charged with the task of carrying out a comprehensive investigation of occupational health and safety in the United Kingdom. Until then committees or commissions had been instituted on an ad hoc basis, often in response to a disaster arousing public outcry, resulting legislation being entirely reactive in nature.

At the time the Robens Committee was established, there was much criticism of the existing position. Prosecutions for breach of existing legislation were rare, but even when successful, the fines were low. Plants could expect inspection no more frequently than every four years, given the staffing levels in the inspectorates, and in 1969 the Chief Factory Inspector reported that there was no longer a trend for injuries at work to decrease; they seemed to have reached a plateau.

The Robens Committee reported in 1972 (*Report of the Committee on Safety and Health at Work*, Cmnd.5034) and was severely critical of the existing state of affairs in two main respects. First, the fact that the law had evolved in a piecemeal fashion on an industry-by-industry basis meant that existing legislation was badly structured. As well as the main statutes—the Factories Act 1961, the Offices, Shops and Railway Premises Act 1963, the Mines and Quarries Act 1954 and the Agriculture (Safety, Health and Welfare Provisions) Act 1956—there were another seven or eight major statutes and nearly 500 statutory instruments covering activities at work. Even so, it was estimated that a staggering 7 to 8 million workers were actually outside the statutory protection while at work. The Robens Committee concluded that the disorganised mass of legislation was counter-productive in that those faced with complying with it were liable to simply throw up the attempt in despair at ever working out exactly what they were meant to do. This led to the first main objective of the Robens Committee: that there should be a unified structure of law and enforcement systems covering everyone at work. But this would be difficult given the variety of needs in different industries. Therefore, the Robens Committee decided that what was needed was an umbrella enabling Act, by whose authority specific provision could be made by statutory regulation for particular industries. An advantage over the old system, where requirements were stipulated in Acts of Parliament, is that it is a lot easier to amend statutory instruments than to amend statutes.

The second main problem identified by Robens was apathy. They noted that **14–031** a large number of accidents each year were the result of stupid and entirely avoidable mistakes. No one was really interested—not employers, not workers, not trade unions. Everyone was conditioned to thinking of health and safety as matters which were regulated by outside agencies who laid down the rules. They did not regard it as part of their own responsibility. Thus the second major objective for the Robens Committee was to involve everyone in safety issues; to convince all parties that it was their responsibility too. One of the most controversial aspects of the Robens Committee Report was the idea that some aspects of safety could best be dealt with by voluntary codes of practice agreed with industry rather than by detailed regulation.

The result of the Robens Committee Report was the HSWA. The only way in which the Robens objective of a unified structure could be achieved was by making it a general enabling statute, with power devolved to the Secretary of State for Employment to make regulations to flesh out the detail (HSWA s.15).

This meant that existing legislation was not repealed: it remained in place unless and until it was replaced by new regulations made under the authority of the HSWA. The same technique was adopted at European Union level, with the Framework Health and Safety Directive on (89/391/EEC) followed by a series of more specific directives. In recent years the European Union has become an increasingly important driver for higher standards of health and safety.

As part of the Coalition Government's review of employment law and drive to reduce the so-called regulatory burden on business, a review of health and safety law was commissioned from a specialist in risk management. The main recommendations in *Reclaiming Health and Safety for All* (Cm.8219, 2011), better known as the Löfstedt Report, were that self-employed people whose work poses no risk of harm to others should be exempted from health and safety law; that the Health and Safety Executive (HSE) should review its 53 Approved Codes of Practice (ACoPs) to ensure that they are up to date and give clear guidance; that the Government should engage more closely with EU legislators on the format of EU health and safety legislation; that the 200 or so sets of health and safety regulations should be consolidated where possible; and that employers should have a "reasonably practicable" defence added to statutory regulations in any situations where strict liability was not essential. The recommendations were accepted with enthusiasm by the Government: indeed, as noted above (para.14–025) the last one was taken much further by eliminating civil liability altogether. A number of consultations have since been undertaken with some changes made and some to come. As ever, there are many who fear that reducing the regulatory burden is likely to result in reduced protection for people at work.

14–032   No change has been made to the main architecture of modern health and safety law. The HSWA begins with certain general duties relating to health and safety which apply not only to employers but also to workers. These establish a framework under which, as envisaged by the Robens Committee, three kinds of regulations can be drawn up: first, regulations about general matters, applicable to all kinds of employment (e.g. the Health and Safety (First-Aid) Regulations 1981); secondly, regulations about hazards which can occur in several industries (e.g. the Control of Substances Hazardous to Health Regulations 2002); and thirdly, regulations dealing with hazards encountered in a particular kind of industry or activity.

The general duties

14–033   The general duties are set out in HSWA ss.2–7 and, in so far as they relate to employers, bear a striking resemblance to the threefold common law duty of care. There is no civil liability for breach of the regulations, however (HSWA s.47(1)); the sanction is criminal prosecution only (HSWA s.33).

Under HSWA s.2 an employer is enjoined to ensure "so far as is reasonably practicable" the health, safety and welfare of all employees. This specifically includes a safe system of work, safe equipment and a safe working environment. It also includes provision of information, training and supervision so far as necessary to ensure safety. Under s.3, employers and independent contractors have duties to make sure that they conduct their undertakings to ensure the safety also of third parties (who could be employees of another employer, independent contractors or the general public). Designers, manufacturers, importers and suppliers of articles for use at work have a general duty imposed on them by s.6 to ensure that the article will be safe, and s.7 imposes on employees themselves a general duty to take reasonable care of safety—both in relation to their own safety and to that of others who may be affected by their actions. All are subject to the qualification "so far as is reasonably practicable".

While framed in a similar way to the common law duty of care, important differences should be noted between the statutory duty and the common law duty. In particular, it is clear that HSWA s.3 imposes a much more extensive duty on employers in respect of independent contractors than is the case at common law. This was clearly stated by the House of Lords in *R v Associated Octel* (1997). The company ran a large chemical plant, designated as a "major hazard site" by the HSE. The employee of an independent contractor taken on for specialist repair work was badly burned when fire broke out in a tank which he was inside repairing. He was working by the light of an electric bulb and had an open bucket full of acetone, giving off highly inflammable vapour. The light bulb broke and ignited the vapour. He could have had the acetone in a sealed container, the light unit could have been sealed and there could have been a ventilation system to prevent a build-up of vapour. The company was convicted under s.3, but appealed on the basis that the independent contractor was solely responsible for the conduct of the repair work.

The House of Lords stated that HSWA s.3 was not about common law vicarious **14–034** liability, where the question of who had control of an employee can be crucial. The issue, in their view, was purely whether the activity in question could be regarded as part of the employer's undertaking. If so, it was within the employer's responsibility under s.3. This is essentially a question of fact for the trial court, but the House of Lords pointed out that the conduct of the undertaking included not only running it, but also cleaning, repairs and maintenance, at least when on the employer's premises. Thus the company was properly convicted.

Similarly, in *R v Gateway Food Markets Ltd* (1997) the Court of Appeal held that the principle that a company should only be criminally liable for actions of someone who can be regarded as the "directing mind" of the company was not appropriate in deciding whether a company had committed an offence under HSWA s.2 or s.3. The issue was only whether there had been a failure to ensure health and safety within the undertaking, so the company could be criminally liable for the actions of its store managers. However, the company may make out a defence that it has ensured safety "so far as is reasonably practicable" if it has proper control and safety systems and does everything possible to ensure that employees act in accordance with them, even if an employee has been negligent (*R v Nelson Group Services (Maintenance) Ltd* (1998)).

In *R v HTM Ltd* (2006) the HSE argued that the effect of *R v Nelson Group* had been nullified by reg.21 of the Management of Health and Safety at Work Regulations 1999 which provides that an employer cannot rely on the act or default of an employee as a defence in criminal proceedings. This was rejected by the Court of Appeal because the qualification of the duty in HSWA by the words "so far as is reasonably practicable" could not be regarded as a defence. The company was prosecuted for breach of its duty under HSWA s.2 when employees were killed moving a mobile tower which came into contact with overhead power cables. The company wished to argue that the employees themselves were at fault and this was the cause of the accident. They also argued that they had done everything which was reasonably practicable by training the employees and that they could not guard against them failing to follow instructions. The Court of Appeal affirmed that the test of reasonable practicability allowed a cost-benefit analysis and that the foreseeability of an accident was relevant only to the extent of assessing the likelihood of a risk eventuating.

14–035   This case, taken with *R v Gateway* and *R v Nelson*, highlights defects in the standard of reasonable practicability. There have been arguments for some time that the test as laid out in HSWA s.2 is incompatible with the Framework Health and Safety Directive (89/391/EEC). Article 5(1) of the Directive states that, "The employer shall have a duty to ensure the safety and health of workers in every aspect related to the work" and the only derogation from this, permitted by art.5(4), is to exclude or limit employers' responsibility for occurrences due to unusual and unforeseeable circumstances beyond the employers' control or for exceptional events, the consequences of which could not have been avoided despite the exercise of all due care. But when this was tested in *Commission of the EC v United Kingdom* (2007) the CJEU held that there was no failure to implement the Directive correctly, dismissing the Commission's argument that art.5(1) meant that the employer should be strictly liable regardless of fault.

The Health and Safety Commission and Executive

14–036   From the seven or so inspectorates responsible for enforcing previous legislation, a single agency was created. The Health and Safety Commission (HSC) consists of a chairperson appointed by the Secretary of State and six to nine members, who include employer and worker representatives (HSWA s.10). The HSC has general duties of promoting occupational health and safety, control of explosives, dangerous substances and emissions into the atmosphere, carrying out research and training, providing an advisory service, issuing and approving codes of practice and submitting proposals for regulations.

It may institute investigations whenever it thinks it necessary or expedient and has wide powers, including powers of entry and inspection, to enable it to exercise its rights. In effect, the HSC is charged with taking a proactive role to improve safety standards throughout industry. It may set up committees in order to have specialist advice on particular matters, and has in fact set up a number of advisory committees on things like Major Hazards and Dangerous Substances.

Enforcement is in the hands of the HSE. The HSE consists of a Director appointed by the Secretary of State, and two other members appointed by the Secretary of State after consultation with the Director. It controls the now unified inspectorate and is responsible for enforcing the legislation. The inspectorates operate through a regional structure with area offices. The Employment Medical Advisory Service, established in 1972, is now part of the Executive, but in 2006 safety on railways was transferred to the Office of the Rail Regulator. Inevitably the effectiveness of enforcement depends to some extent on how likely it is that employers will get caught if they do not comply. During the 1970s and 1980s the number of inspectors dropped, until in 1982, when there were 742 inspectors, one study estimated that premises were likely to be inspected only once every seven years. Since then the number has increased substantially, and in 2006 there were 1,421 inspectors.

Improvement notices and prohibition notices

Novel enforcement powers were granted to inspectors under HSWA ss.21–24. **14–037** An inspector has the power under HSWA s.21 to issue an improvement notice where she believes that a person is contravening relevant statutory provisions or has done so and is likely to repeat the contravention. The notice must specify the violation, set out the reasons for the inspector's belief and what must be done to remedy it within a stated period.

In effect this provision formalised what was the practice of many inspectors already. While the HSE was criticised in the past for not bringing more prosecutions, one answer to that was that it takes up an awful lot of staff time which could better be spent on prevention. Further, the deterrent effect of the fear of prosecution and resulting bad publicity could be lost if every violation were prosecuted. Seeing their ultimate aim as prevention of accidents, inspectors would rather point out what is wrong and warn the employer that prosecution will follow if it is not put right. The parameters followed by the HSE in deciding whether to prosecute can be found in its Enforcement Policy Statement.

An employer served with an improvement notice has a right of appeal to an employment tribunal. The notice is suspended until the appeal has been dealt with. A more powerful weapon still is the prohibition notice (HSWA s.22). Where the inspector believes that the activity being carried on involves a risk of serious personal injury, she may issue a prohibition notice which can have the effect of stopping the activity at once. It is not actually required that there should be a breach of any statutory provision. As with the improvement notice, certain information must be provided in writing to the employer and there is a right of appeal to an employment tribunal. However, in this case, the appeal does not suspend the notice, unless the tribunal is prepared to make an order to that effect.

These enforcement powers have been regarded as successful, to the extent **14–038** that the strategy has been copied in other legislation (e.g. the Consumer Protection Act 1987 ss.13–15).

Regulations and Approved Codes of Practice (ACoPs)

The Secretary of State has power to make regulations, either on the proposal **14–039** of the Commission or after consultation with it (HSWA s.15). Relevant bodies should also be consulted before regulations are made. In recent years important sets of regulations have been made which apply to all workplaces, thus bringing a welcome uniformity in line with the basic Robens philosophy. The most important are the Control of Substances Hazardous to Health Regulations 2002 (COSHH), but other examples include the Health and Safety Information for Employees Regulations 1989 and the Noise at Work Regulations 1989. As noted already (para.14–025) there is no longer civil liability for breach of these regulations.

Under HSWA s.16 the HSC has power to issue and approve codes of practice "for the purpose of providing practical guidance" in relation to the general duties in HSWA ss.2–7 or any other matters covered by the legislation. The idea here was no doubt to try and involve employers and workers in safety issues rather than reinforce the view that safety standards are imposed from outside. The criticism that the provision attracted was that codes of practice could lead to a lowering of standards as employers would not be too demanding of themselves. Further, breach of a code would not attract criminal sanctions in the way breach of regulations would. However, HSWA s.1(2) refers to codes and regulations being prepared in order to "maintain and improve" existing standards, which seems to offer a safeguard against a reduction in standards.

Safety representatives and safety committees

14–040   As part of the battle against apathy and in pursuit of the policy of involvement, employers have a duty to prepare a written statement of health and safety policy and to revise it as necessary (HSWA s.2(3)). Another major plank in this policy was the provision of a right for employees to have their own safety representatives who could consult with the employer. However, the initial provision, which would have permitted employees to elect non-union representatives in some circumstances, was scotched by trade unions, who were concerned that the use of any conduit for representing employees other than a trade union would be the thin end of the wedge undermining the role of the union. Hence the Act was amended in 1975 so only recognised trade unions had the right to appoint safety representatives (HSWA s.2(4); Safety Representatives and Safety Committee Regulations 1977). Unfortunately, this meant that representation was denied to those employees whose need for it was arguably the greatest. In the wake of the Piper Alpha disaster in 1988, when 167 people were killed as a result of an explosion on a North Sea oil platform, special regulations for safety representatives and safety committees had to be made (Offshore Installations (Safety Representatives and Safety Committees) Regulations 1989).

Following the decision in *EC Commission v United Kingdom* (1994), where it was held that consultation with recognised trade unions was not sufficient to discharge obligations to consult with employees under the Collective Dismissals and Acquired Rights Directives (see above, para.9–041) it became clear that the limitation of the rules on safety representatives to recognised trade unions must similarly be in breach of the Framework Health and Safety Directive (89/391/EEC) and so the Health and Safety (Consultation with Employees) Regulations 1996 were passed. Unlike the equivalent rules for consultation over transfers and redundancies, these do not replace the existing law, but introduce a new regime only for those employees where the Safety Representatives and Safety Committees Regulations 1977 do not apply: i.e. where there is no recognised trade union. This is because the requirements of the Framework Directive could be satisfied by granting lesser powers to representatives than those enjoyed under the 1977 Regulations, and the then Conservative Government, like the present one, was very anxious that there should be "no gold-plating" of European Union law requirements.

Under the Safety Representatives and Safety Committees Regulations 1977, safety representatives should investigate potential hazards and dangerous occurrences at the workplace; investigate complaints from employees relating to health and safety; and make representations on these matters to the employer and to the health and safety inspectors. They are entitled to carry out inspections of the workplace at a minimum of three-monthly intervals and on some other occasions also (reg.5) and they are entitled to inspect and take copies of relevant documents. If two safety representatives so request in writing, the employer must establish a safety committee which can keep policy and practice under review. Under the Health and Safety (Consultation with Employees) Regulations 1996, employers must consult either with employees directly or else with their elected representatives over the introduction of any measure or any new technology which might affect health and safety; appointments under the Management of Health and Safety at Work Regulations 1999; information which it is required by law to provide, and health and safety training. The employer must make available to them such information as they need in order to participate fully and effectively in such consultation. The major differences from the Safety Representatives and Safety Committees Regulations 1977 are that there is no entitlement to a standing safety committee and no entitlement to carry out inspections.

Both kinds of safety representative are entitled to necessary time off with pay **14–041** for the purposes of carrying out their functions or receiving training in relation to their functions. There are two Codes of Practice—Safety Representatives and Safety Committees (1978) and Time Off for the Training of Staff Representatives (1978)—which amplify these provisions, but only in relation to representatives appointed under the 1977 Regulations. Both kinds are protected from dismissal and detriment while carrying out their duties (Employment Rights Act 1996 ss.44 and 100). The expansion of the law to all workplaces is to be welcomed, and it is hoped that the broader provisions in the 1977 Regulations will eventually be extended, although there is little prospect of this at present. Following a consultation exercise combining and extending the consultation regulations in a single code in 1999, the HSE did draft proposals for a consolidated set of regulations in 2003. However, they were not agreed by the HSC and were shelved in favour of an approach based on voluntary adoption of standards.

Influence of the European Union

As the above indicates, directives and regulations from the European Union **14–042** covering health and safety matters are increasingly important in this area. The Treaty on the Functioning of the European Union (TFEU) art.153 states that:

"the Union shall support and complement the activities of Member States in . . . improvement in particular of the working environment to protect workers' health and safety."

Directives under TFEU art.153 may be adopted according to the qualified majority voting procedure. The importance of the Framework Health and Safety Directive (89/391/EEC) and the large number of directives adopted under it should not be underestimated. Six important sets of statutory regulations (dubbed "the six-pack") came into force at the beginning of 1993, designed to implement these directives. The most wide-ranging are the Management of Health and Safety at Work Regulations 1999, implementing the substantive provisions of the Framework Health and Safety Directive. The regulations require employers to carry out an assessment of the risks to health and safety arising out of the conduct of the undertaking, including risks to non-employees as well as employees. The employer is also obliged to make effective arrangements for the oversight of health and safety matters, including where necessary the appointment of a competent person to assist and in particular encompassing procedures for dealing with serious and imminent dangers. There is a duty to provide information to employees on all these matters. In effect, the regulations lay down general principles of good health and safety practice (amplified by a code of practice) and further the Robens philosophy of involving the consumers of health and safety in the devising of appropriate rules. Originally civil liability was specifically excluded but this had to be amended in 2003 at the instigation of the European Commission on grounds of incompatibility with the Framework Health and Safety Directive. As noted above (para.14–025), this has now been reversed by ERRA s.69, and it remains to be seen whether this is compliant with EU obligations.

The Workplace (Health, Safety and Welfare) Regulations 1992 (implementing Directive 89/654/EEC), which lay down general principles about the safety, cleanliness, and maintenance of workplaces, including heating, lighting and ventilation, similarly apply across the board to all workplaces, as do the Provision and Use of Work Equipment Regulations 1998 (implementing Directive 89/655/EEC). The other sets of regulations in this group are the Manual Handling Operations Regulations 1992, the Personal Protective Equipment at Work Regulations 2002 and the Health and Safety (Display Screen Equipment) Regulations 1992—the VDU regulations. It seems likely that legislation from the European Union will continue to be a major source of developments in health and safety law in the twenty-first century.

 # Further Reading

☐ S. Dawson, P. William, A. Clinton and M. Bamford (1988), *Safety at Work: The Limits of Self-regulation,* CUP
☐ P. James (1993), *The European Community*: *A Positive Force for UK Health and Safety Law?,* Institute of Employment Rights, 1993
☐ R. Moore (1991), *The Price of Safety,* Institute of Employment Rights
☐ G. Shannon (2002), *Health and Safety*: *Law and Practice,* Round Hall

❑ B. Barrett (2003), "Harassment at Work: A Matter of Health and Safety", [2003] JBL 214

❑ B. Barrett and P. James (1988), "Safe Systems: Past, Present and Future?", 17 ILJ 26

❑ P. James and D. Walters (1997), "Non-union Rights of Involvement: The Case of Health and Safety at Work", 26 ILJ 35

❑ P. James, R. Johnstone, M. Quinlan and D. Walters (2007), "Regulating Supply Chains to Improve Health and Safety", 36 ILJ 163

❑ K. Miller (1991), "Piper Alpha and the Cullen Report", 20 ILJ 176

Index

LEGAL TAXONOMY
FROM SWEET & MAXWELL

This index has been prepared using Sweet and Maxwell's Legal Taxonomy. Main index entries conform to keywords provided by the Legal Taxonomy except where references to specific documents or non-standard terms (denoted by quotation marks) have been included. These keywords provide a means of identifying similar concepts in other Sweet & Maxwell publications and online services to which keywords from the Legal Taxonomy have been applied. Readers may find some minor differences between terms used in the text and those which appear in the index. Suggestions to: sweetandmaxwell.taxonomy@thomson.com

relevant transfer
generally, 9-024
service change provision, 9-027–9-029
standard transfer, 9-025–9-026
service change provision, 9-027
standard transfer, 9-025–9-026
terms and conditions of employment, and
generally, 9-033
variations, 9-036–9-037
Trust and confidence
see **Mutual trust and confidence**
Unfair dismissal
accompanied by representative, 8-038–8-039
after-discovered conduct, 8-064–8-065
age discrimination, 8-022
armed forces personnel, 8-023
asserting a statutory right, 8-082
automatically unfair reasons
asserting a statutory right, 8-082
generally, 8-079
health and safety grounds, 8-080–8-081
political opinions, 8-083
background, 8-020
capability, 8-053–8-056
compensation
additional award, 8-089
basic award, 8-086
compensatory award, 8-087–8-088
introduction, 8-085
conduct
after-discovered conduct, 8-064–8-065
appeals, 8-064–8-065
introduction, 8-057
outside employment, 8-062
proof of misconduct, 8-050–8-062
trade union officials, 8-063
warnings, 8-058–8-059
constructive dismissal, 8-028–8-029
Crown employees, 8-023
death of employer, 8-033
dismissal, meaning of
constructive dismissal, 8-028–8-029
death of employer, 8-033
dissolution of company, 8-033
expiry of limited-term contract without renewal, 8-026–8-027
frustration, 8-031–8-032
introduction, 8-024
resignation, 8-030
termination by mutual agreement, 8-030
termination with or without notice, 8-025
dismissal and disciplinary procedures, 8-040–8-041
dissolution of company, 8-033
effective date of termination, 8-034–8-036
entitlement to claim, 8-021
excluded categories of employee, 8-023
expiry of contract without renewal
fixed-term, 8-078
limited-term, 8-026–8-027
fair reasons
capability, 8-053–8-056
conduct, 8-057–8-065
introduction, 8-044–8-046
procedural fairness, 8-050–8-052
qualifications, 8-053–8-056
redundancy, 8-066–8-070
some other substantial reason, 8-073–8-078
standard of review, 8-047–8-049
statutory prohibition, 8-071–8-072
fishermen, 8-023
fixed-term contracts
generally, 8-026–8-027
some other substantial reason, 8-078
foreign-based employees, 8-023
frustration, 8-031–8-032
grievance procedures, 8-040–8-041
health and safety grounds, 8-080–8-081
industrial action
action neither unofficial nor protected, 12-017–12-020
activities covered, 12-010–12-012
conclusion, 12-021
introduction, 12-009
lock-outs, 12-011
official action, 12-013–12-016
unofficial action, 12-013–12-014
introduction, 8-020
lock-outs, 12-011
mutual agreement, 8-030
needs of the business, 8-074–8-075
'no difference' rule, 8-050
official industrial action, 12-013–12-016
police, 8-023
political opinions, 8-083
Polkey deductions, 8-051
pregnancy, 6-018–6-019
pressure from third parties, 8-076–8-077
procedural fairness, 8-050–8-052
procedural requirements
introduction, 8-037
protected conversation, 8-042–8-043
right to be accompanied, 8-038–8-039
statutory dispute resolution procedures, 8-040–8-041
protected conversation, 8-042–8-043
qualifications, 8-053–8-056
qualifying period of employment, 8-021
re-engagement, 8-084
redundancy
automatically unfair, 8-068
failure to consider redeployment, 8-070
failure to warn or consult, 8-069
introduction, 8-066
unfair selection process, 8-067